AMERICAN LITERATURE

精编美国文学教程

◎ 陈　许　陈庆生　主编

ZHEJIANG UNIVERSITY PRESS
浙江大学出版社

序

　　今年夏初，杭州电子科技大学英美文学研究所所长陈许教授、外国语学院副院长高丙梁教授和英美文学教研室陈庆生副教授一行三人来河南高校学习考察，顺访我院，送来他们刚刚编写完成的《精编英国文学教程》和《精编美国文学教程》两书的书稿，恳请我在付梓之前协助审读。我早先知道该院开设的《英美文学导论》是一门广受同行赞誉、深受学生欢迎的课程，2007年被浙江省教育厅评为浙江省普通高校精品课程。因此，我想这是他们给我的一个学习的好机会，让我享受"先睹为快"的幸事，欣然同意。

　　于是，我利用暑假较仔细地翻阅了这套教材。这次阅读不仅使我重温了英美文学，同时也勾起了我对英美文学教学的种种回忆与遐想。

　　英美文学教学，特别是英国文学教学在我国有着悠久的历史。根据史料记载，鸦片战争之后，"洋务运动"的兴起和清廷外交事务的加重，迫切需要培养外语人才，从而大大推动了我国外语教育事业的发展。外语开始作为一门独立的学科列入各级学校的教学计划。专门培训外语人才的学校相继成立。1862年创立的京师同文馆首先设立英文馆，尔后又开设法文馆、俄文馆、日文馆等。上海、广州也分别于1883年和1884年成立了类似的外语学校。1898年我国第一所国立的综合性大学——京师大学堂成立，也就是北京大学的前身。1901年同文馆并入该校，改名为京师大学堂译学馆，相当于今日综合性大学中的外语院系，揭开了我国高校外语教育新的一页。英语是该馆的主要语种。

　　1911年孙中山先生领导的辛亥革命推翻了封建帝制，宣告了中华民国的诞生，至1949年国民党政府退出中国大陆，民国时期也就此结束。在这个时期我国高等教育和外语教学都有一定的发展，据不完全统计，新中国成立前夕，我国共有205所高等学校，其中41所设有英语系或英语专业，专业教学都偏重文学，开设的课程多为英美小说、诗歌、散文、戏剧等，没有开设听、说、读、写、译等训练语言技能的课程，主要通过大量阅读文学作品和写作来提高外语水平和文化修养，深受当时英美高等学校英语系教学思想和方法的影响。

中华人民共和国成立初期,由于受当时国内外形势与国家政策的影响,俄语教学大发展,而英语和其他语种的教学任务大为压缩,教学力量严重削弱。1953年经过院系调整,我国高校仅剩下9个英语教学点,学生人数锐减,大批英语教师改行教授俄文或其他专业,甚至转业做其他工作。就以我当时在读的北京大学西语系为例,英语专业本科四个年级学生人数仅一百多人,而师资力量十分雄厚,可谓群英荟萃,拥有像李赋宁、俞大絪、杨周翰、赵萝蕤、吴兴华、朱光潜等等一大批高水平的知名教授和学者,却苦于没有多少学生可教,没有多少课可开设,造成宝贵的人才资源的极大浪费。

　　1956年开始中央发觉了这种情况,出台了一系列政策纠正原先政策上的偏颇,英语及其他一些语种得到了较大的发展。到1957年年底全国高校设有英语专业的学校增至23所,招生数量也倍增,教学也逐步走入正规。可惜好景不长。全国范围内开展的"反右运动"、"大跃进运动"、"反右倾运动"、"四清运动"等连绵不绝的政治运动,"左"倾思潮泛滥,严重地阻碍了教学工作的健康发展。所谓批判资产阶级教育路线,批判"西方资本主义腐朽文化",批判"文学路线"等使英语教学,特别是英美文学教学再次受到严重打击。1966年开始的"文化大革命",极"左"路线发展到了登峰造极的地步,教育战线和其他战线一样,受到重创。外语教育首当其冲,灾难深重,教学工作基本处于瘫痪状态。这种状况持续了整整十年之久,直至"四人帮"被打倒,"文化大革命"宣告结束,外语教育重获新生。

　　党的十一届三中全会给高校外语教育带来了复苏的春风。1978年教育部根据当年邓小平同志主持召开的全国科学大会和全国教育工作会议的精神,举行了全国外语教育座谈会。会议对如何恢复和发展外语教育提出了明确的方针和具体的措施。从此开创了我国外语教育的新局面,正如原国务院副总理李岚清在为上海外语教育出版社2008年出版的《改革开放30年中国外语教育发展丛书》写的"序"中说的那样,"……可以说,改革开放30年,是中国外语教育事业大发展的30年。"外语教育的面貌同全国其他战线一样"发生了历史性的变化"。高校英语专业发展的势头更是迅猛。据不完全统计,目前我国英语教学点已经超过1000个,与1953年时硕果仅剩的9个相比,增长了百倍以上,其发展速度真可谓"史无前例","世界第一"。英语专业在校学生近60万。2004年英语专业招收新生102388人,排在所有专业的第一位。

　　在这里我想特别要提出的是,在各类高校英语专业的发展中,理工科院校的英语专业是发展最为迅速的。据我了解在目前1000多个英语专业本科教学点中,有三分之一设在理工类院校。他们利用本校学科的优势,在教学改革和提高教学质量方面都创造了许多佳绩。杭州电子科技大学的外国语学院就是这样的一个范例。他们的办学历史和教学经验虽然不如一些"老牌"的学校悠久和丰富，但是通过他们的辛勤工作，创造出了令人钦佩的业绩。摆在我面前的这套英美文学教材就是一个明证。

由陈许和陈庆生两位教授主持编写的《精编英国文学教程》和《精编美国文学教程》是该院精品课程的有机组成部分，也是颇有特色的大学本科英语专业的文学教材。诚如他们在书的"前言"中总结归纳的那样，这套教材具有内容全面，脉络清晰；结构合理，重点突出；浅显易懂，易于自学；图文并茂，增添兴趣等鲜明特点。

这里我想强调指出的是，众所周知，英国文学具有较悠久的历史，产生了很多著名的作家，他们的作品浩如烟海，要从中选出最重要的、最具有代表性的作家和作品，又要适合我国高校，特别是理工类院校英语专业学生的实际水平和需要实是一件很不容易做好的工作。但是，这本教材的编写者们做了大量的准备工作，精心设计，精挑细拣，选择了50多位作家，90多篇作品，个个有特色，篇篇是珠玑。他们为这些作家和作品写的介绍、评析和注释也是精心安排，精益求精，正如本书的书名《精编美国文学教程》表明的那样，"精"字当头，名副其实。

我相信这套教材的出版和使用，不仅会给浙江省高校的英美文学的教学有很大的帮助，而且对其他地区的各类院校的英美文学教学也会有所裨益。在此我也向广大爱好英美文学的读者推荐本书。

我在上面用了较多篇幅简要地回忆我国外语教育发展的历史，为的是要告诉人们我们当前外语教学的大好形势来之不易，应十分珍惜。杭州电子科技大学外国语学院的同仁们做的工作正是为保持和发展这种局面作出的很好努力，也是对建国60周年的最好献礼，可喜可贺！可敬可佩！

是为序。

解放军外国语学院英语教授、博导　姚乃强
2009年8月于洛阳

3

前　言

　　21 世纪的特点是政治多极化、经济全球化、文化多元化和信息社会化。在这个瞬息万变、飞速发展的新世纪里，我国的高等教育事业在前十年里加速腾飞，由此带来了英语专业的迅猛发展，使得英语语言文学专业的本科生和硕士生人数每年递增。作为英语专业教学的重要组成部分，英美文学教学所受到的关注程度还不尽如人意。我们编写这本《精编美国文学教程》，希望能够在提高学生的美国文学学习兴趣和鉴赏能力方面尽绵薄之力，给予一定的帮助。

　　美国文学是世界文学不可忽视的组成部分。美国文学的特点在于它的"新"。从 17 世纪初叶北美拓殖开始至今也不过约四个世纪的时间。美国人一向自诩为新世界的新人。他们不愿受传统的羁束，决意走出一条新路。这种求"新"的心理状态和精神境界明显地体现在美国文学机体的质地中。各个时期的美国作家都不满足于先辈留给自己的遗产，而是努力以其独特的方式在文学园地内作出探索与尝试，竭尽全力以新成就和新发现丰富和改进它。于是，殖民时代作家，民族主义和浪漫主义作家，现实主义和自然主义作家，现代主义和后现代主义作家在不到三百年的时间里，使文学创作代代除旧布新，涌现出许多内容丰富、风格多样、具有旺盛生命力的作品。这些作品不仅为美国人民提供着精神力量，而且被世界人民传诵和喜爱。

　　《精编美国文学教程》是杭州电子科技大学"英美文学导论"校级与省级精品课程建设的重要组成部分。在多年的课程建设中，课程组所有成员认真备课，精心制作出内容丰富、生动形象的教学课件，搜集了大量的教学资料，如美国文学经典影片、文化背景等视频图像，并不断总结、积累和交流教学经验，这些都为本教材的编写打下了良好的基础。它的编写原则充分体现了本学科先进的教学思想，编写过程中紧紧围绕英语人才培训的目标和思路，力求层次分明、条理清晰、章节安排合理，既突出重点、难点，又强调对本课程基础知识的全面理解和掌握。与当前市场上已有的各种版本的教材相比，本教材具有以下主要特色：

　　1. 内容全面，脉络清晰。全书按照美国文学发展的五个阶段分为五个部分，即：殖民时期与早期美国文学、民族主义与浪漫主义年代、现实主义与自然主义年代、现代主义的诞生、现代主义与后现代主义年代。本书涉及了 31 位作家及其代表作品 37 篇。其中关注当代少数族裔作家及其作品。学生通过课堂学习和课外 自学可以对美国文学有一个比较清晰的认识和理解。

2. 结构合理，重点突出。本书每章由三个部分组成：第一部分内容介绍不同时期的历史、重大事件等相关背景知识；第二部分内容主要包括文学综述、文学史实、文学流派、重要作家简介等知识；第三部分内容为主要作家（附照片）的生平和主要作品介绍、作品简介和赏析、作品选读、作品注释和思考题。各部分侧重点不同，但相互关联、相互补充，从不同角度帮助学生，使他们对美国文学有一个全面而深刻地了解和把握。

3. 浅显易懂，易于自学。我们针对中国学生英语水平的状况，以及他们的需求和学习特点，在编写本书时力求文字简洁易懂、语言浅显流畅、论述深入浅出。并在每篇作品后附有较为详细的注释，以便降低学生的学习难度，提高他们的阅读速度和学习效率。

4. 图文并茂，增添兴趣。我国以前出版的美国文学教材，大多数没有提供图片资料，实为美中不足。针对青年学生的兴趣特点，我们为每一位作家配备了相关的图片，并附以文字说明，使得教材生动鲜活，有吸引力，也有助于学生更好地了解作家，理解作品的内涵。

5. 资料详实，观点新颖。本书在编写过程中力求观点客观全面，同时注意吸收多年来国内外有关美国文学的研究成果，努力做到资料详实、评价客观、分析深刻、观点新颖，使之更好地服务于我国高等院校英语专业的教师和学生，以及勤奋好学的英语爱好者。

参加本教材编写工作的有陈许、陈庆生、王祖友、陈怡、许焕荣、敬南菲、周小娉、钟京霞、陈圣、张婷婷和田智文等，他们在选材、录入、注释、校对、搜集图片等方面做了大量的工作。全书的构思设计和选材安排都由主编负责。

在这本《精编美国文学教程》即将付梓之际，我们要衷心感谢解放军外国语学院资深望重的姚乃强教授，他对我们编辑本教材给予了充分的肯定，并在百忙之中为本教材作序；我们还要衷心感谢浙江省教育厅、杭州电子科技大学及其教务处和外国语学院领导对本教材编写的大力支持和资助；我们也要衷心感谢浙江大学出版社的编辑，他们为本教材的出版做了大量辛勤的工作。

最后，由于水平所限和成书仓促，疏漏和谬误之处在所难免，敬请专家、学者和读者匡正，以便今后改进。

陈庆生　陈　许

2009 年 8 月于杭州电子科技大学

Contents

Part One Colonial Period and Early American

Literature (1582—1789)

Introduction

I. Historical Background

America has always been a land of beginnings. After Europeans "discovered" America in the fifteenth century, the mysterious New World became for many people a genuine hope of a new life, an escape from poverty and persecution, and a chance to start again. We can say that, as a nation, America begins with that hope. When, however, does American literature begin?

American literature begins with American experience. The first literature inspired by the newfound land was strictly utilitarian: what did the country look like, who lived there, what treasures were there, and what were the prospects for trade and settlement? Published in Europe, these travel chronicles in the form of letters, journals, and narratives served as guides for the colonists who followed. In the fifty years after Columbus' initial voyage in 1492, the Spanish had ringed the Gulf of Mexico, pushed into the Southwest, and advanced to the Pacific Coast. The French established a sphere of influence in the north and along the inland waterways to the west. In the early seventeenth century, the English began colonizing along the eastern coastal plain bordered to the west by the Alleghenies.

The first permanent colony at Jamestown in Virginia in 1607 was founded for profit. Raw materials and crops, particularly tobacco, were exchanged for manufactured goods in England. This mercantile policy fostered the growth in the southern colonies of a plantation system under which a small number of privileged landowners depended upon slave labor. Anglican, agrarian, and royalist, the southern colonists differed markedly from those who settled in New England. The Pilgrims who established their colony at Plymouth in 1620 were a nonconformist, separatist Protestant sect fleeing religious persecution in England and determined to create a better society in America. Theirs would be the first American settlement based on a social contract, outlined in the Mayflower Compact, establishing a community of believers committed to their mutual welfare. The Puritans, who wanted to reform rather than separate from the Church of England, followed in 1630, absorbing the initial Plymouth settlement into the Massachusetts Bay Company, centered in Boston, the city they founded.

As the word itself hints, Puritans wanted to make pure their religious beliefs and practices. The Puritan was a "would-be purifier". The word was coined by the opponents of the group and was applied to them in scorn; it was intended to ridicule them as persons who thought themselves holier or better than others.

The Puritans wished to restore simplicity to church services and the authority of the Bible to theology. They felt that the Church of England was too close to the Church of Rome in doctrine, form of worship, and organization of authority. Another point of controversy was that the Church of England was the established church, that is, the official church of the state. The most extreme Puritans, among them the Plymouth Plantation group, felt the influences of politics and the court had led to corruption within the church. These Puritans were "Separatists"—that is, they wished to break free from the Church of England. The Massachusetts Bay group, on the other hand, wished to reform the church but remain a part of it. Yet once they were settled in this land, they too moved gradually toward complete separation.

The Puritan definition of good writing was that which brought home a full awareness of the importance of worshipping God and of the spiritual dangers that the soul faced on Earth. Puritan style varied enormously—from complex metaphysical poetry to homely journals and crushingly pedantic religious history. Whatever the style or genre, certain themes remained constant. Life was seen as a test; failure led to eternal damnation and hellfire, and success to heavenly bliss. This world was an arena of constant battle between the forces of God and the forces of Satan, a formidable enemy with many disguises. Many Puritans excitedly awaited the millennium, when Jesus would return to earth, end human misery, and inaugurate 1,000 years of peace and prosperity.

Scholars have long pointed out the link between Puritanism and capitalism: both rest on ambition, hard work, and an intense striving for success. Although individual Puritans could not know, in strict theological terms, whether they were "saved" and among the elect who would go to heaven, Puritans tended to feel that earthly success was a sign of election. Wealth and status were sought not only for themselves, but also as welcome reassurances of spiritual health and promises of eternal life.

Moreover, the concept of stewardship encouraged success. The Puritans interpreted all things and events as symbols with deep spiritual meaning, and felt that in advancing their own profit and their community's well being, they were also furthering God's plans. They did not draw lines of distinction between the secular and religious spheres: All of life was an expression of the divine will—a belief that later resurfaces in Transcendentalism.

II. Literary Review

Given the practical difficulties of surviving in a wilderness, the early American colonists had little time to produce works of literature or to encourage their creation. What was written and published in the seventeenth century was almost exclusively religious or utilitarian in nature, with little distinction between the two. Poetry in America began with Anne Bradstreet's domestic and devotional verses collected without her approval by her brother-in-law and published in London as *The Tenth Muse Lately Sprung Up in America* (1650). This was one of the first books of poetry ever published by a woman in English. The greatest seventeenth-century poet, however, was the Westfield, Massachusetts, clergyman Edward Taylor, whose intense and metaphysical verse written as part of his private devotions remained in manuscript until they were discovered in the Yale Library and published in 1939. Today Taylor is generally regarded as the greatest American poet before the nineteenth century.

By 1700 there were half a million European Americans in all the colonies. Boston was the largest city, with a population of seven thousand. The first half of the century would begin to show the loosening of the religious grip by the Puritans on New England and the emergence of Yankee secular society. Although Puritan control and influence were clearly waning, the period still produced some of Puritanism's greatest literary achievements, most notably Cotton Mather's epic ecclesiastical history of New England, *Magnalia Christi Americana* (1702), and the works of the last great Puritan theologian, Jonathan Edwards. His "Sinners in the Hands of an Angry God" (1741) is arguably the most famous sermon ever written by an American, and his theological work *A Careful and Strict Enquiry into the Prevailing Notions of Freedom of Will* (1754) is one of the foundational documents of American philosophy, anticipating some of the main tenets of Transcendentalism. Yet the Puritans' spiritual interpretation of the world was challenged, as the century progressed, by a rational, scientific worldview advanced by Enlightenment thinkers such as John Locke, Jean Jacques Rousseau, and Voltaire. This conflict between idealism and pragmatism is a dominant theme in American thought. The exemplar of the evolving American character was unquestionably Benjamin Franklin. As the printer, Franklin played a key role in creating and producing the literature that captured the spirit of the times and moved the country toward independence. He produced the most popular almanac in America, *Poor Richard's Almanack* (1733—1758), and the first successful American magazine (the *General Magazine* in 1741). Self-educated, a scientist and inventor, Franklin perhaps more than anyone else during the period typified many of the adages he coined for his almanac: that with persistence and application virtually anything could be accomplished. Increasingly, he was asked to apply his many talents to nation building.

Beginning in the 1750s momentum began to bind the loose assembly of colonies into a confederation. Resentment over British trade and taxation policies gradually drove the colonists toward union and independence. The Stamp Act of 1764, the Boston Massacre of 1770, the Boston Tea Party of 1773, and the first shots fired at Lexington and Concord were the milestones leading to revolution. Letters, essays, pamphlets, and editorials framed the question whether Britain had the right to tax colonists without their consent. Independence, which for many was once inconceivable, began to sound inevitable, particularly as urged by Tom Paine in *Common Sense* (1776), Thomas Jefferson soon distilled this best-selling statement of the case for separation into one of the greatest political documents ever created, the Declaration of Independence.

Even before the Revolution, writers and particularly poets began to express what made American culture distinct. The first secular verses began to appear, celebrating American scenes, such as Richard Lewis' "A Journey from Petapsco to Annapolis, April 4, 1730," and American themes, such as Ebenezer Cook's satirical *The Sot Weed Factor* (1708). During the Revolution, poets contributed to the war effort in works such as Francis Hopkinson's "The Battle of the Keg" (1778) and John Trumbull's mock-epic attack on American Loyalists, *M'Fingal* (1775—1776 and 1782). Other poets commemorated American achievements and destiny in works such as Timothy Dwight's *Conquest of Canaan* (1785) and Joel Barlow's *The Vision of Columbus* (1787), his first version of an attempted American epic that would be expanded into *The Columbiad* in 1807. Philip Freneau was unquestionably the most accomplished poet of the Revolutionary period.

The author of the visionary *The Rising Glory of America* (1772), the bitingly satirical *General Gage's Confession* (1775), and the powerful *The British Prison Ship* (1781), based on his incarceration by the British, Freneau was an important transitional figure between the neoclassical style of most eighteenth-century verse written in America and what would follow: a uniquely American version of Romanticism.

As George Washington took the oath of office as the first president of the United States in 1789, Americans had won their independence, but the greater challenges of governing lay ahead. Similarly, American literature in its first two centuries had produced its initial, distinctive responses to phenomenon of America, but it had yet to achieve greatness.

John Smith (1580—1631)

Life and Major Works

Captain John Smith entered the arena of North American exploration at a time when the romantic age of buccaneers and sea dogs was giving way to the new, financially cautious policies of seventeenth-century colonization. Born into a moderately prosperous Lincolnshire family, Smith received a solid English grammar school education and, after a brief apprenticeship to a prominent merchant, enlisted at the age of fifteen to fight in the Netherlands. For ten years Smith pursued

John Smith

an adventurous military career that took him to Hungary, France, Germany, Spain, Austria, Rumania, Transylvania, Turkey, and North Africa. Toward the end of his life he wrote about these experiences in a brief autobiography, *The True Travels, Adventures, and Observations of Captain John Smith* (1630).

Upon his return to England, Smith—always eager for new adventures—joined the expedition that founded the Jamestown colony in 1607. An iron-willed disciplinarian, he tried almost single-handedly to keep a quarrelsome, inept, and frequently dissatisfied party intact. In his reports to his superiors Smith deplored the lack of skilled labor, complaining that too many of the colonists were "gentlemen" who found "not English cities, nor such fair houses, nor at their own wishes any of their accustomed dainties, with feather beds and down pillows, taverns and alehouses in every breathing place… For the country was to them a misery, a ruin, a death, a hell."

While at Jamestown, Smith conducted several short exploratory trips into the interior. During one of these journeys he was captured by Chesapeake Indians, who brought him to their king, Powhatan. As Smith many years later recounted the incident, he was condemned to death and then saved at the last minute by the timely intercession of Powhatan's favorite daughter, Pocahontas. Smith's failure to mention this dramatic episode in his first account of the Virginia expedition led a number of historians (beginning with Henry Adams) to consider the Pocahontas incident as mere fabricated afterthought. Yet, given Smith's promotional purposes at the time, it is quite possible that he wanted to omit any material that might scare off potential colonists. Whether true report or tall tale, Captain Smith's brief captivity and his hairbreadth escape has become one of the best-known passages in the literature of North American exploration.

Smith stayed on at Jamestown until the fall of 1609, when it was becoming clear that his efforts to bring effective management to the colony were futile. In 1614 he made another trip to North America, this time mapping out the coast of New England, a region he not only named but also fell so in love with that he ardently promoted its colonization in two important books, *A Description of New England* (1614) and *Advertisements for the Unexperienced Planters of New England, or Anywhere* (1631). The *Advertisements*, a list of "experienced memorandums" offering practical advice and theoretical suggestions on colonization, was addressed to the Puritan leaders who founded the Massachusetts Bay Colony in 1630. It was Smith's last work, and given the way he had been neglected during his final years, he would not have been surprised to find that most of his admonitions went unheeded.

Brief Introduction and Appreciation

Filled with themes, myths, images, scenes, characters, and events, Smith's *Description of New England* describes the fishing, soils, inhabitants, fauna, flora, and climate of the coastal region from Cape Cod to Penobscot. This work is the first to apply the term "New England" to that portion of the North America from Long Island Sound to Newfoundland. At that time it held a few trading and fishing stations, and French traders from the north and Dutch from the south carried on commerce in furs with the natives. There was a prosperous fishery to the north, where cod were taken by ships from Portugal, Holland, and Spain. To Smith, these were evidence of the richness of commodities to be had, and signs of the strategic importance to England of securing permanent settlements in the region. Smith had departed Virginia in 1609 under a cloud of accusations and had quarreled with the leaders of the privately-held Virginia

Company. Seeking a new arena for colonial opportunities in the new world, Smith saw New England as a place where English life could be transplanted to America, and this work is an extended advertisement and prospectus for investors and settlers, with Smith to provide the expertise and leadership.

Selected Reading

A Description of New England

I have not been so ill bred, but I have tasted of plenty and pleasure, as well as want and misery; nor does necessity yet, or occasion of discontent, force me to these endeavors; nor am I ignorant what small thanks I shall have for my pains, or that many would have the world imagine them to be of great judgement, that can but blemish these my designs[1] by their witty objections and detractions. Yet (I hope) my reasons with my deeds, will so prevail with some, that I shall not want employment in these affairs, to make the most blind see his own senselessness and incredulity, hoping that gain will make them affect that which religion, charity and the common good cannot. It were but a poor device in me to deceive myself, much more the King and State, my friends and country, with these inducements: which, seeing His Majesty hath given permission, I wish all sorts of worthy, honest, industrious spirits would understand, and if they desire any further satisfaction, I will do my best to give it, not to persuade them to go only, but go with them; not leave them there, but live with them there.

I will not say, but by ill providing and undue managing, such courses may be taken [that] may make us miserable enough. But if I may have the execution of what I have projected; if they want to eat, let them eat or never digest[2] me. If I perform what I say, I desire but that reward out of the gains [which] may suit my pains, quality and condition. And if I abuse you with my tongue, take my head for satisfaction. If any dislike at the year's end, defraying their charge, by my consent they should freely return. I fear not want of company sufficient, were it but known what I know of those countries; and by the proof of what wealth I hope yearly to return, if God please to bless me from such accidents as are beyond my power in reason to prevent. For I am not so simple to think that ever any other motive than wealth will ever erect there a commonwealth or draw company from their ease and humors[3] at home to stay in New England to effect my purposes.

And lest any should think the toil might be insupportable, though these things may be had by labor and diligence, I assure myself there are those who delight extremely in vain pleasure, that take much more pains in England to enjoy it than I should do here [in

New England] to gain wealth sufficient. And yet I think they should not have half such sweet content for our pleasure here is still gains; in England charges and loss. Here nature and liberty afford us that freely which in England we want, or it costs us dearly. What pleasure can be more than (being tired with any occasion ashore, in planting vines, fruits, or herbs, in contriving their own grounds, to the pleasure of their own minds, their fields, gardens, orchards, buildings, ships, and other works, etc.) to recreate themselves before their own doors, in their own boats upon the sea, where man, woman, and child, with a small hook and line, by angling may take divers sorts of excellent fish at their pleasures? And is it not pretty sport to pull up two pence, six pence, and twelve pence as fast as you can haul and veer[4] a line? He is a very bad fisher [that] cannot kill in one day, with his hook and line, one, two, or three hundred cods, which dressed and dried, if they be sold there for ten shilling the hundred [pounds], though in England they will give more than twenty, may not both the servant, the master, and merchant be well content with this gain? If a man works but three days in seven he may get more than he can spend, unless he will be excessive. Now that carpenter, mason, gardener, tailor, smith, sailor, forgers[5] or what other, may they not make this a pretty recreation, though they fish but an hour in the day, to take more than they eat in a week? Or if they will not eat it, because there is so much better choice, yet [they may] sell it or change it with the fishermen or merchants for anything they want. And what sport does yield a more pleasing content and less hurt or charge than angling with a hook and crossing the sweet air from isle to isle, over the silent streams of a calm sea? Wherein the most curious may find pleasure, profit, and content.

Thus, though all men be not fishers, yet all men, whatsoever, may in other matters do as well. For necessity does in these cases so rule a commonwealth, and each in their several functions, as their labors in their qualities, may be as profitable because there is a necessary mutual use of all.

For gentlemen, what exercise should more delight them than ranging daily those unknown parts, using fowling and fishing, for hunting and hawking? And yet you shall see the wild hawks give you some pleasure, in seeing them stoop[6] (six or seven after one another) an hour or two together at the schools offish in the fair harbors, as those ashore [do] at a fowl, and never trouble nor torment yourselves with watching, mewing[7] feeding, and attending them, nor kill a horse and man with running and crying, "See you not a hawk?" For hunting also, the woods, lakes and rivers afford not only chase sufficient for any that delight in that kind of toil or pleasure but such beast to hunt that besides the delicacy of their bodies for food, their skins are so rich as may well recompense thy daily labor with a Captain's pay.

For laborers, if those [in England] that sow hemp, rape[7], turnips, parsnips, carrots, cabbage, and such like, give twenty, thirty, forty, fifty shilling yearly for an acre of ground, and meat, drink, and wages to use it and yet grow rich, when better or at least as good ground may be had [in New England] and cost nothing but labor, it seems strange to me any such should there grow poor.

My purpose is not to persuade children from their parents, men from their wives, nor servants from their masters; only such as with free consent may be spared. But that each parish or village, in city or country, that will but apparel[9] their fatherless children of thirteen or fourteen years of age, or young married people that have small wealth to live on, here by their labor may live exceedingly well. Provided always that first there be a sufficient power to command them, houses to receive them, means to defend them, and meet[10] provisions for them; for any place may be overlain[11], and it is most necessary to have a fortress (ere this grow to practice) and sufficient masters (as carpenters, masons, fishers, fowlers, gardeners, husbandmen[12], sawyers[13], smiths, spinners, tailors, weavers, and such like) to take ten, twelve, or twenty, or as there is occasion, for apprentices. The masters by this may quickly grow rich; these [apprentices] may learn their trades themselves to do the like, to a general and an incredible benefit for king and country, master and servant.

Notes:

1. designs: i.e., his plans to colonize New England
2. digest: tolerate
3. humors: whims
4. veer: let out
5. forgers: metal workers
6. stoop: swoop
7. mewing: keeping in cages
8. rape: herb grown as a forage crop for hogs and sheep
9. apparel: prepare
10. meet: suitable
11. overlain: overthrown
12. husbandmen: farmers
13. sawyers: those who saw timber

Questions for Study and Discussion:

1. What did John Smith say was the main purpose of his mission?

2. How did Smith describe the geographical orientation of New England?

3. What seven qualities did Smith list as necessary for truly exploring and knowing a new land? Why do you think these qualities are necessary?

4. What was the main commodity of New England? How was it used, other than for consumption?

5. What seems to be Smith's purpose in writing? How does he seek to achieve his objective? Would you accept his invitation? Why or why not?

Anne Bradstreet (1612—1672)

Life and major works

Anne Bradstreet was born Anne Dudley in 1612 in England. She married Simon Bradstreet when she was 16 and they both sailed with her family to America in 1630. The difficult, cold voyage to America took 3 months to complete. John Winthrop was also a passenger on the trip. The voyage landed in Boston and the passengers joined the Massachusetts Bay Colony.

Anne Bradstreet

The men in Anne Bradstreet's family were managers and politicians. Both her father and her husband became Massachusetts governors. Her husband, Simon, often traveled for weeks throughout the colony as its administrator. Anne Bradstreet's poem, "To My Dear and Loving Husband," was written as a response to her husband's absence.

Very little is known about Anne Bradstreet's life in Massachusetts. There are no portraits of her, and she does not even have a grave marker. She and her family moved several times, each time further away from Boston into the frontier. Anne and Simon had 8 children during a 10-year period, and all of the children survived healthy and safe, a remarkable accomplishment considering the health risks and the security hazards of the period.

Anne Bradstreet was highly intelligent and largely self-educated. She took herself seriously as an intellectual and a poet, reading widely in history, science, art, and literature. Her library, before the house burned in 1666, numbered about 800 volumes. However, as a good Puritan woman, Bradstreet did not make her accomplishments public.

Bradstreet wrote poetry for herself, family, and friends, never meaning to publish them. Consider that her friend, Anne Hutchinson was intellectual, educated and led women's prayer meetings where alternative religious beliefs were discussed. She was labeled a heretic and banished from the colony. Hutchinson eventually died in an Indian attack. Is it any wonder that Anne Bradstreet was hesitant to publish her poetry and call attention to herself?

Anne Bradstreet's early poems were secretly taken by her brother-in-law to England and published in a small volume when she was 38. The volume sold well in England, but the poems were not nearly as accomplished as her later works.

Bradstreet's later works were not published during her lifetime. Her poems about her love for her husband were private and personal, meant to be shared only with her family and friends.

Though her health was frequently a concern, especially during childbirth, Anne Bradstreet lived until 60 years of age.

Brief Introduction and Appreciation

"To My Dear and Loving Husband" was written between 1641 and 1643 by Anne Bradstreet, America's first published poet. The poem, a touching display of love and affection, offers modern readers insights into Puritan attitudes toward love, marriage, and God. The idea of the poem is quite straightforward. Bradstreet uses comparisons to physical things to describe her passion, and ends the short poem with a charge to her husband to pray that God will bless him for his amazing love, as she cannot ever repay it. She urges her husband to continue to live in love with her, so that their love can live on, even when they themselves are no more; she wishes to be immortalized through love.

Mechanically, this piece is relatively unremarkable in that it has several standard poetic features. One is the two line rhyme scheme. The rhyme scheme appears to be standard rhyming couplets, the aabbcc scheme. There is a slight assonance of the long "A" vowel sound: "Thy love is such I can no way repay/The heavens reward thee manifold, I pray," (lines 9-10). Another is the anaphora, the repetition of a phrase, in the first three lines. Moreover, there is the alliteration of line 11's "While we live," and line 12's "When we live," that ends the piece on an audibly pleasing note. The popular iambic pentameter is a third feature the poem exhibits. Iambic pentameter is characterized by an unrhymed line with five feet or accents. Each foot contains an unaccented syllable and an accented syllable, as in "da Dah, da Dah, da Dah, da Dah, da Dah."

The subject of Anne Bradstreet's love poem is her professed love for her husband. She praises him and asks the heavens to reward him for his love. The poem is a touching display of love and affection, extraordinarily uncommon for the Puritan era of the Massachusetts Bay Colony in which Anne Bradstreet lived.

Bradstreet uses many figurative devices in order to convey her message. She uses the repetition of the word "ever" throughout the poem to say that never has there been love comparable to the magnitude of that between herself and her spouse. Interestingly, Anne Bradstreet's three comparisons all have the tangible aspects capitalized: the Mines in line 5, the East in line 6, and the Rivers in line 7. Lines 6-7, "I prize thy love more than Mines of gold/Or all the riches that the East doth hold." is a reference to the Orient and the Far East; during the time when Anne Bradstreet lived, these 'exotic' places were thought to be wonderful, filled with riches, and mysterious. The author believes that her relationship with her husband Simon is likewise priceless, and even "All the riches" in the East cannot equal it. "My love is such that Rivers cannot quench," (line 7) in an allusion to *Song of Solomon*, Chapter 8 in the Bible, which tells that "many waters cannot quench love, neither can the floods drown it." It is also through this Biblical reference that the poem relates to love, and surreptitiously, *death*. The tie-in with love is readily apparent, but death's correlation is harder to ascertain. With Biblical poetry, such as King Solomon's *Song of Solomon* also known as *Song of Songs*, "waters" or "rivers" generally were synonymous with "death."

Selected Reading

To My Dear and Loving Husband

If ever two were one, then surely we.
If ever man were loved by wife, then thee;
If ever wife was happy in a man,
Compare with me, ye women, if you can.
I prize thy love more than whole mines of gold
Or all the riches that the East doth hold.
My love is such that rivers cannot quench,
Nor ought but love from thee, give recompense[1].
Thy love is such I can no way repay,
The heavens reward thee manifold[2], I pray.
Then while we live, in love let's so persevere
That when we live no more, we may live ever.

Notes:

1.Nor ought but love from thee, give recompense: My love is so strong that rivers cannot relieve its thirst; only your love will satisfy me
2. manifold: In many ways
Manifold:

Questions for Study and Discussion:

1. This poem uses rhyming couplets to steadily emphasize the speaker's love for her husband. But what if he feels exactly the opposite? Write a poem in this style about a husband who hates his wife. Try to use the same iambic pentameter rhythm.
2. Study Puritan life in America during the 1600s. Not much is written about personal relationships, but find out what you can and make some assumptions. Based on the available evidence, explain whether you think Bradstreet's relationship with her husband was typical for a Puritan of her time.
3. Over the years, the power has been lost from familiar associations like "mines of gold," "riches of the East," and love that "rivers cannot quench." What fresh, new expressions could be used in their place to make readers realize how deep the speaker's love is?

Benjamin Franklin (1706—1790)

Life and Major Works

Like other leaders of the American Revolution, Benjamin Franklin lived in a time of tumultuous changes. Born into a traditional Puritan society, he grew up with the morals and ideas of America's first European settlers. In the early eighteenth century, America was still a collection of scarcely populated colonies, its people spread out over a vast area with only a few ramshackle cities. The colonies had distinctly different identities: Massachusetts was orderly and Puritan, Pennsylvania was

Benjamin Frankin

Quaker, New York was largely Dutch, Virginia was aristocratic. The colonies had little in common aside from their ties to Britain. In 1706, the year of Franklin's birth, few would have predicted that by 1790, the year of Franklin's death, the American colonies would be independent from Britain and united as a single, massive country.

Though America's eventual independence was not inevitable, in retrospect it is not surprising. America was growing rapidly, and with more people, agriculture and trade burgeoned. By 1706, the colonies were already an integral part of the British economy; by the 1750s they were Britain's most important possession. Yet Britain never seemed capable of keeping the colonists happy. Americans constantly complained of delays and inefficiencies resulting from a government located an ocean away. They resented British restrictions on trade and felt that the British government did not do enough to keep the frontier safe. Most of all, Americans hated paying taxes–and especially hated paying taxes they had no hand in creating.

In political and economic terms, America was outgrowing its status as a colony. Its intellectual climate was changing dramatically as well, as new ideas of equality, liberty, and the perfectibility of human nature circulated among intellectuals and the common people alike. Old beliefs seemed less certain and new dreams seemed suddenly possible. Most of all, the vibrant growth of the colonies made it seem as though anyone—with enough work and dedication—could prosper.

Franklin lived this dream. Born into a large, poor family, and mostly self- educated, he went on to be a master politician, inventor, scientist, military leader, and diplomat–to name just a few of his arenas. In all of these roles Franklin had accomplishments that literally changed the world. Well before his death, he was one of the most famous men in the world—famous for embodying the very essence of Americanness. His wit, humble appearance, liberal ideals, and plainspoken style distinguished him from other, more aristocratic leaders of his age. His particular mixture of idealism and pragmatism, ambition and morality, optimism and energy make him seem, in retrospect, like the quintessential American. Franklin was perhaps the original self-made man.

This image of Franklin as the first American is part of what makes him so fascinating. The image is especially fascinating because Franklin influenced so many aspects of American life in his long career, and because Franklin himself created this image. Not only was he a leader in public and intellectual life, he was the first and best public relations man, spin doctor, and self-help guru. He worked nonstop to create his image, never letting anyone see the "real" Franklin. Historians have since tried and generally failed to pin him down. Every modern American public figure, from the President to Hollywood movie stars, creates and manages a public image. Franklin was the first and best at this game. His *Autobiography* is still considered by many to be the best book to read for advice on how to win friends and influence people.

Franklin's carefully constructed image, along with his incredibly energetic mind and broad interests, makes it difficult for us to feel we really know him. He keeps a certain distance from us, just as he kept from his contemporaries. No biography of him is ever complete—he will keep historians busy for centuries to come. Franklin once wrote, in the voice of his humble character Poor Richard: "If you would not be forgotten/As soon as you are dead and rotten/Either write things worth reading/Or do things worth the writing." Franklin did both, with an energy and a passion that few have matched and perhaps none have surpassed.

Brief Introduction and Appreciation

Franklin's *Autobiography* has received widespread praise, not only its historical value as a record of an important early American but for its literary style. It is often recognized as the first American book to be taken seriously by Europeans as literature.

It is without any doubt that the *Autobiography of Benjamin Franklin* is riddled with faults. It is very muddled, particularly towards the end. It was not written in a continuous stretch, but rather pasted together out of separate fragments that were written years apart from one another. The author even often failed to remember what he had written in the previous sections. The *Autobiography* often takes an arrogant, condescending tone, but it worships the virtue of humility. And perhaps the most egregious of all, the part of Ben's life with the most historical significance—the American Revolution—is entirely omitted from the work. Moreover, there is no real mention of events after 1760, 15 years before the outbreak of war. At that year the *Autobiography* simply stops.

Then why are we still reading this tangled and sometimes difficult work over 200 years after it was written? There are several reasons. First, the work establishes in literary form the first example of the fulfillment of the American Dream. Franklin demonstrates the possibilities of life in the New World through his own rise from the lower middle class as a youth to one of the most admired men in the world as an adult. Furthermore, he asserts that he achieved his success through a solid work ethic. He proved that even undistinguished persons in Boston can, through hard work, become great figures of importance in America. When we think of the American Dream today—the ability to rise from rags to riches through industry—we are usually thinking of the model set forth by Franklin in this autobiography.

Historical reasons could also explain why the *Autobiography* remains a classic. The work was one of the premier autobiographies in the English language. While they abound today in Barnes and Nobles all over the world, the autobiography as a literary form had not emerged at the time Franklin lived, at least not in non-religious format. His autobiography defined a secular literary tradition. The autobiography is a work not only meant to tell about a person's own life but to educate the reader in ways to better live life. Although this format has been modified throughout American history, it is safe to trace the style and format of such classics as Frederick Douglass' *Narrative* and Henry Adams' *The Education of Henry Adams* to the tradition established by Franklin. Part Two of the *Autobiography,* complete with its list of virtues and ways in which one can achieve them, has influenced millions of readers over the last two centuries. It also helped spawn the genre of the mainstream self-help book.

The *Autobiography* also depicts what life was like in 18th century America. The story is told from the perspective of only one person; however, in an age when literacy was low and writing not widespread, any surviving documents are of value to historians who wish to learn how people lived from day to day. Specifics of life in colonial America abound in the book, providing invaluable information to anyone wishing to learn more about that time period. Of course, one must always keep in mind that life for Franklin was not like life for everyone else; he represents only one person out of many thousands.

Also, Franklin's *Autobiography* reflects 18th century idealism. Often called the Age of Reason, the 18th century was the age of men such as John Locke and Isaac Newton. Intellectualism flourished along with scientific inventions and advances in political thought. Many people held the optimistic belief that man could be perfected through scientific and political progress. Franklin ascribes to these beliefs partially, and Part Two of the *Autobiography* shows him trying to live them out.

Perhaps the *Autobiography* has most endured because, despite its muddled nature, it is the preeminent work that mythologizes a hero of the American Revolution. Franklin is often introduced to elementary school children as a Renaissance man, someone who seemed to master all fields of knowledge—he was, among other things, scientist, inventor, statesman and writer. The *Autobiography* is the only enduring token that enshrines all the facets of his diverse nature; it presents Americans today with a great hero from the past who helped establish the tradition of the American Dream. Numerous critics have often called Franklin the "first American" and his autobiography provides a good example of why.

When he was sixty-five, Franklin, already internationally famous, began writing his autobiography. An autobiography is the story of a person's life told by the person who lived it; Franklin told his story in the form of a letter to his son. Franklin never completed his autobiography, never reaching his account of the Declaration of

Independence. Yet Franklin was able to make clear that he enjoyed creating in himself "The American, the new man."

Selected Reading

The Autobiography

My brother had, in 1720 or 1721, begun to print a newspaper. It was the second that appeared in America, and was called the *New England Courant*. The only one before it was the *Boston News-Letter*. I remember his being dissuaded by some of his friends from the undertaking, as not likely to succeed, one newspaper being, in their judgment, enough for America. At this time (1771) there are not less than five-and-twenty. He went on, however, with the undertaking, and after having worked in composing the types and printing off the sheets, I was employed to carry the papers through the Streets to the Customers. He had some ingenious men among his friends, who amused themselves by writing little pieces for this paper, which gained it credit and made it more in demand, and these gentlemen often visited us. Hearing their conversations, and their accounts of the approbation their papers were received with, I was excited to try my hand among them; but, being still a boy, and suspecting that my brother would object to printing anything of mine in his paper if he knew it to be mine, I contrived to disguise my hand, and, writing an anonymous paper, I put it in at night under the door of the printing-house. It was found in the morning, and communicated to his writing friends when they called in as usual. They read it, commented on it in my hearing, and I had the exquisite pleasure of finding it met with their approbation, and that, in their different guesses at the author, none were named but men of some character among us for learning and ingenuity. I suppose now that I was rather lucky in my judges, and that perhaps they were not really so very good ones as I then esteemed them. Encouraged, however, by this, I wrote and conveyed in the same way to the press several more papers which were equally approved; and I kept my secret till my small fund of sense for such performances was pretty well exhausted and then I discovered it, when I began to be considered a little more by my brother's acquaintance, and in a manner that did not quite please him, as he thought, probably with reason, that it tended to make me too vain. And, perhaps, this might be one occasion of the differences that we began to have about this time. Though a brother, he considered himself as my master, and me as his apprentice, and accordingly, expected the same services from me as he would from another, while I thought he demean'd me too much in some he requir'd of me, who from a brother expected more indulgence. Our disputes were often brought before our father, and I fancy I was either generally in the right, or else a better pleader, because the judgment was generally in my favor. But my brother was passionate, and had often beaten me, which I took extremely amiss; and, thinking my apprenticeship very tedious, I was continually wishing for some opportunity of shortening it, which at length offered in a manner unexpected.*

One of the pieces in our newspaper on some political point, which I have now forgotten, gave offense to the Assembly. He was taken up, censured, and imprisoned for a month, by the speaker's warrant, I suppose, because he would not discover his author. I too was taken up and examined before the council; but, though I did not give them any satisfaction, they contented themselves with admonishing me, and dismissed me, considering me, perhaps, as an apprentice, who was bound to keep his master's secrets. During my brother's confinement, which I resented a good deal, notwithstanding our private differences, I had the management of the paper; and I made bold to give our rulers some rubs in it, which my brother took very kindly, while others began to consider me in an unfavorable light, as a young genius that had a turn for libeling and satyr. My brother's discharge was accompanied with an order of the House (a very odd one), that "James Franklin should no longer print the paper called the *New England Courant*." There was a consultation held in our printing-house among his friends, what he should do in this case. Some proposed to evade the order by changing the name of the paper; but my brother, seeing inconveniences in that, it was finally concluded on as a better way, to let it be printed for the future under the name of BENJAMIN FRANKLIN; and to avoid the censure of the Assembly, that might fall on him as still printing it by his apprentice, the contrivance was that my old indenture should be returned to me, with a full discharge on the back of it, to be shown on occasion, but to secure to him the benefit of my service, I was to sign new indentures for the remainder of the term, which were to be kept private. A very flimsy scheme it was; however, it was immediately executed, and the paper went on accordingly, under my name for several months. At length, a fresh difference arising between my brother and me, I took upon me to assert my freedom, presuming that he would not venture to produce the new indentures. It was not fair in me to take this advantage, and this I therefore reckon one of the first errata of my life; but the unfairness of it weighed little with me, when under the impressions of resentment for the blows his passion too often urged him to bestow upon me, though he was otherwise not an ill-natured man: perhaps I was too saucy and provoking.

---

* I fancy his harsh and tyrannical treatment of me might be a means of impressing me with that aversion to arbitrary power that has stuck to me through my whole life.

When he found I would leave him, he took care to prevent my getting employment in any other printing-house of the town, by going round and speaking to every master, who accordingly refused to give me work. I then thought of going to New York, as the nearest place where there was a printer; and I was rather inclined to leave Boston when I reflected that I had already made myself a little obnoxious to the governing party, and, from the arbitrary proceedings of the Assembly in my brother's case, it was likely I might, if I stayed, soon bring myself into scrapes.

[Selling some of his books to raise money, Franklin journeys first to New York, and then to Philadelphia. After sailing through a storm, walking about fifty miles, and finally rowing a small boat, he arrives on a Sunday morning in October 1723.]

I was in my working dress, my best clothes being to come round by sea. I was dirty from my journey; my pockets were stuffed out with shirts and stockings, and I knew no soul nor where to look for lodging. I was fatigued with traveling, rowing, and want of rest, I was very hungry; and my whole stock of cash consisted of a Dutch Dollar, and about a shilling in copper. The latter I gave the people of the boat for my passage, who at first refused it, on account of my rowing; but I insisted on their taking it. A man being sometimes more generous when he has but a little money than when he has plenty, perhaps thro' fear of being thought to have but little. Thus refreshed, I walked again up the street, which by this time had many clean-dressed people in it, who were all walking the same way. I joined them, and thereby was led into the great meeting-house of the Quakers near the market. I sat down among them, and, after looking round awhile and hearing nothing said, being very drowsy through labor and want of rest the preceding night, I fell fast asleep, and continued so till the meeting broke up. When one was kind enough to rouse me. This was, therefore, the first house I was in, or slept in, in Philadelphia...

[During the next several years Franklin becomes a successful printer and businessman. In the following section of his Autobiography, he tells how he put his practical instincts to work to achieve spiritual "success" as well.]

It was about this time I conceived the bold and arduous[1] project of arriving at moral perfection. I wished to live without committing any fault at any time, and to conquer all that either natural inclination, custom, or company might lead me into. As I knew, or thought I knew, what was right and wrong, I did not see why I might not always do the one and avoid the other. But I soon found I had undertaken a task of more difficulty than I had imagined. While my attention was taken up, and care employed, guarding against one fault, I was often surprised by another; habit took the advantage of inattention;

inclination was sometimes too strong for reason. I concluded at length, that the mere speculative conviction, that it was our interest to be completely virtuous, was not sufficient to prevent our slipping; and that the contrary habits must be broken, and good ones acquired and established, before we can have any dependence on a steady, uniform rectitude[2] of conduct. For this purpose I therefore contrived the following method.

In the various enumerations of the moral *virtues* I had met with in my reading, I found the catalogue more or less numerous, as different writers included more or fewer ideas under the same name. *Temperance*, for example, was by some confined to eating and drinking; while by others it was extended to mean the moderating every other pleasure, appetite, inclination, or passion, bodily or mental, even to our avarice and ambition. I proposed to myself, for the sake of clearness, to use rather more names, with fewer ideas annexed to each, than a few names with more ideas; and I included under thirteen names of virtues, all that at that time occurred to me as necessary or desirable; and annexed to each a short precept, which fully expressed the extent I gave to its meaning.

These names of virtues, with their precepts, were:

1. TEMPERANCE. — Eat not to dullness; drink not to elevation.
2. SILENCE. — Speak not but what may benefit others or yourself; avoid trifling conversation.
3. ORDER. — Let all your things have their places; let each part of your business have its time.
4. RESOLUTION. — Resolve to perform what you ought; perform without fail what you resolve.
5. FRUGALITY[3]. — Make no expense but to do good to others or yourself; that is, waste nothing.
6. INDUSTRY. — Lose no time; be always employed in something useful; cut off all unnecessary actions.
7. SINCERITY. — Use no hurtful deceit; think innocently and justly; and, if you speak, speak accordingly.
8. JUSTICE. — Wrong none by doing injuries, or omitting the benefits that are your duty.
9. MODERATION. — Avoid extremes; forbear resenting injuries so much as you think they deserve.
10. CLEANLINESS. — Tolerate no uncleanliness in body, clothes, or habitation.
11. TRANQUIILITY. — Be not disturbed at trifles, or at accidents common or unavoidable.
12. CHASTITY. — Rarely use venery but for health or offspring, never to dullness,

weakness, or the injury of your own or another's peace or reputation.

13. HUMILITY. — Imitate Jesus and Socrates.

My intention being to acquire the *habitude* of all these virtues, I judged it would be well not to distract my attention by attempting the whole at once, but to fix it on one of them at a time, and, when I should be master of that, then to proceed to another, and so on, till I should have gone through the thirteen; and, as the previous acquisition of some might facilitate the acquisition of certain others, I arranged them with that view, as they stand above. Temperance first, as it tends to procure that coolness and clearness of head which is so necessary where constant vigilance was to be kept up, and guard maintained against the unremitting attraction of ancient habits and the force of perpetual temptations. This being acquired and established, Silence would be more easy; and my desire being to gain knowledge at the same time that I improved in virtue, and considering that in conversation it was obtained rather by the use of the ears than of the tongue, and therefore wishing to break a habit I was getting into prattling, punning, and joking, which only made me acceptable to trifling company, I gave *Silence* the second place. This and the next, *Order*, I expected would allow me more time for attending to my project and my studies. *Resolution*, once because habitual, would keep me firm in my endeavors to obtain all the subsequent virtues; *Frugality* and *Industry*, freeing me from my remaining debt, and producing affluence and independence, would make more easy the practice of Sincerity and Justice, etc., Conceiving, then, that, agreeably to the advice of Pythagoras in his Garden Verses, daily examination would be necessary, I contrived the following method for conducting that examination.

I made a little book, in which I allotted a page for each of the virtues. I ruled each page with red ink, so as to have seven columns, one for each day of the week, marking each column with a letter for the day. I crossed these columns with thirteen red lines, marking the beginning of each line with the first letter of one of the virtues, on which line, and in its proper column, I might mark, by a little black spot, every fault I found upon examination to have been committed respecting that virtue, upon that day.

	S	M	T	W	T	F	S
T							
S	● ●	●		●		●	
O		●	●		●	●	●
R			●		●		
F		●		●			
I			●				
S							
J							
M							
Cl							
T							
Ch							
H							

I determined to give a week's strict attention to each of the virtues successively. Thus, in the first week, my great guard was to avoid every the least offence against *Temperance*, leaving the other virtues to their ordinary chance, only marking every evening the faults of the day. Thus, if in the first week I could keep my first line marked T, clear of spots, I supposed the habit of that virtue so much strengthened, and its opposite weakened, that I might venture extending my attention to include the next, and for the following week keep both lines clear of spots. Proceeding thus to the last, I could get through a course complete in thirteen weeks, and four courses in a year. And like him who, having a garden to weed, does not attempt to eradicate all the bad herbs at once, which would exceed his reach and his strength, but works on one of the beds at a time, and, having accomplished the first, proceeds to a second, so I should have, I hoped, the encouraging pleasure of seeing on my pages the progress I made in virtue by clearing successively my lines of their spots, till in the end, by a number of courses, I should be happy in viewing a clean book after a thirteen weeks' daily examination....

The precept of *Order* requiring that *every part of my business should have its allotted time*, one page in my little book contained the following scheme of employment for the twenty-four hours of a natural day.

The Morning Question, What good Shall I do this Day?	5	Rise, wash, and address *Powerful Goodness;* Contrive day's good shall I do this Business, and take the resolution of the day; prosecute the present Study: and breakfast?—
	6	
	7	
	8	Work
	9	
	10	
	11	
	12	Read, or overlook my Accounts, and dine.
	1	
	2	Work
	3	
	4	
	5	
	6	Put Things in their Places, Supper, Music, or Diversion, or Conversation, Examination of the Day.
	7	
Evening Question, What Good have I done to-day?	8	
	9	
	10	Sleep.
	11	
	12	
	1	
	2	
	3	
	4	

I entered upon the execution of this plan for self-examination, and continued it with occasional intermissions for some time. I was surprised to find myself so much fuller of faults than I had imagined; but I had the satisfaction of seeing them diminish. To avoid the trouble of renewing now and then my little book, which, by scraping out the marks on the paper of old faults, to make room for new ones in a new course, became full of holes, I transferred my tables and precepts to the ivory leaves of a memorandum book, on which the lines were drawn with red ink, that made a durable stain; and on those lines I marked my faults with a black-lead pencil, which marks I could easily wipe out with a wet sponge. After awhile I went through one course only in a year, and afterwards only one in several years, till at length I omitted them entirely, being employed in voyages and business abroad, with a multiplicity of affairs that interfered; but I always carried my little book with me.

My scheme of *Order* gave me the most trouble: and I found that, though it might be practicable where a man's business was such as to leave him the disposition of his time, that of a journeyman printer for instance, it was not possible to be exactly observed by a master, who must mix with the world, and often receive people of business at their own hours. *Order*, too, with regard to places for things, papers, etc., I found extremely difficult to acquire. I had not been early accustomed to it, and, having an exceedingly good memory, I was not so sensible[4] of the inconvenience attending want of method. This article, therefore, cost me much painful attention, and my faults in it vexed me...

In truth, I found myself incorrigible with respect to *Order*; and now I am grown old, and my memory bad, I feel very sensibly the want of it. But on the whole, though I never arrived at the perfection I had been so ambitious of obtaining, but fell far short of it, yet I was, by the endeavor, a better and a happier man than I otherwise should have been, if I had not attempted it. ...

Notes:

1. arduous: difficult
2. rectitude: the state of being correct or proper
3. frugality: efficient use of resources
4. sensible: aware
5. incorrigible: incapable of being corrected; uncontrollable

Questions for Study and Discussion:

1. How would you describe Franklin's writing style?

2. What does the *Autobiography* tell us about the 18th century?

3. What is the purpose of the *Autobiography*, and how does that purpose change throughout the work?

4. How does Franklin employ humor in the *Autobiography*? Pick several instances and comment on them.

5. What are some of the major flaws in the *Autobiography*? What problems does it face and how do those problems come about?

Thomas Jefferson (1743—1826)

Life and Major Works

In the thick of party conflict in 1800, Thomas Jefferson wrote in a private letter, "I have sworn upon the altar of God eternal hostility against every form of tyranny over the mind of man."

This powerful advocate of liberty was born in 1743 in Albemarle County, Virginia, inheriting from his father, a planter and surveyor, some 5,000 acres of land, and from his mother, a Randolph, high social standing. He studied at the College of William and Mary, then read law. In 1772 he married Martha

Thomas Jefferson

Wayles Skelton, a widow, and took her to live in his partly constructed mountaintop home, Monticello.

Freckled and sandy-haired, rather tall and awkward, Jefferson was eloquent as a correspondent, but he was no public speaker. In the Virginia House of Burgesses and the Continental Congress, he contributed his pen rather than his voice to the patriot cause. As the "silent member" of the Congress, Jefferson, at 33, drafted the Declaration of Independence. In years following he labored to make its words a reality in Virginia. Most notably, he wrote a bill establishing religious freedom, enacted in 1786.

Jefferson succeeded Benjamin Franklin as minister to France in 1785. His sympathy for the French Revolution led him into conflict with Alexander Hamilton when Jefferson was Secretary of State in President Washington's Cabinet. He resigned in 1793.

Sharp political conflict developed, and two separate parties, the Federalists and the Democratic-Republicans, began to form. Jefferson gradually assumed leadership of the Republicans, who sympathized with the revolutionary cause in France. Attacking Federalist policies, he opposed a strong centralized Government and championed the rights of states.

As a reluctant candidate for President in 1796, Jefferson came within three votes of election. Through a flaw in the Constitution, he became Vice President, although an opponent of President Adams. In 1800 the defect caused a more serious problem. Republican electors, attempting to name both a President and a Vice President from their own party, cast a tie vote between Jefferson and Aaron Burr. The House of Representatives settled the tie. Hamilton, disliking both Jefferson and Burr, nevertheless urged Jefferson's election.

When Jefferson assumed the Presidency, the crisis in France had passed. He slashed Army and Navy expenditures, cut the budget, eliminated the tax on whiskey so unpopular in the West, yet reduced the national debt by a third. He also sent a naval squadron to fight the Barbary pirates, who were harassing American commerce in the Mediterranean. Further, although the Constitution made no provision for the acquisition of new land, Jefferson suppressed his qualms over constitutionality when he had the opportunity to acquire the Louisiana Territory from Napoleon in 1803.

During Jefferson's second term, he was increasingly preoccupied with keeping the Nation from involvement in the Napoleonic wars, though both England and France interfered with the neutral rights of American merchantmen. Jefferson's attempted solution, an embargo upon American shipping, worked badly and was unpopular.

Jefferson retired to Monticello to ponder such projects as his grand designs for the University of Virginia. A French nobleman observed that he had placed his house and his mind "on an elevated situation, from which he might contemplate the universe."

Jefferson's first important political treatise, *A Summary View of the Rights of British America*, presented his concept of natural rights—that people have certain inalienable rights superior to civil law. Jefferson denied that the British Parliament held any political authority over the colonists, and demanded free trade and an end to British taxation. The essay's considerable influence during pre-revolutionary debates brought Jefferson wide attention and contributed to his selection by the Second Continental Congress to write the *Declaration of Independence*. Although he was one of the five committee members so chosen, most historians agree that it was Jefferson who wrote the original draft, and that he submitted it to John Adams and Benjamin Franklin, who suggested minor changes before sending it to Congress. The delegates debated its text line by line for two and a half days and adopted it July 4, 1776. Despite changes made by members of Congress, Jefferson is generally credited with authorship of the *Declaration*. He intended it to be less an original statement than an expression of beliefs held in common by most Americans: that all men are created equal and that they possess certain inalienable rights. The *Declaration* is considered the foremost literary work of the American Revolution and the single most important political document in American history.

During his tenure as governor of Virginia, Jefferson wrote *An Act for Establishing Religious Freedom, Passed in the Assembly of Virginia in the Beginning of the Year 1786*. Like the *Declaration of Independence*, this bill is based on the concept of natural rights, the assumption that each individual's conscience, rather than any secular institution, should dictate religious matters, and the contention that civil liberties should be independent from religious beliefs. While Jefferson's bill was originally intended only for Virginia, it is now considered the central document of the American experiment in the separation of church and state.

While being a governor, he produced his only full-length book, *Notes on the State of Virginia* (1785). The work covers the geography, flora, and fauna of Virginia, as well as a description of its social, economic, and political structure. Using statistics to support his patriotic intent, Jefferson disputed the beliefs of Georges Louis Leclerc de Buffon, a French naturalist and philosopher who contended that America's intellectual standards and animal life were inferior to those of Europe. Although *Notes on the State of Virginia* established Jefferson's reputation as a scholar and a scientist, the work also engendered controversy because it contains Jefferson's disparaging views regarding Native Americans and African-Americans.

Jefferson died on July 4, 1826.

Brief Introduction and Appreciation

The *Declaration of Independence*, written by Thomas Jefferson and adopted by the Second Continental Congress, states the reasons the British colonies of North America sought independence in July of 1776.

The *Declaration of Independence* is arguably one of the most influential documents in American History. It is essentially a partisan document, a justification of the American Revolution presented to the world; but its unique combination of general principles and an abstract theory of government with a detailed enumeration of specific grievances and injustices has given it enduring power as one of the great political documents of the West. Other countries and organizations have adopted its tone and manner in their own documents and declarations. For example, France wrote its "Declaration of the Rights of Man" and the Women's Rights movement wrote its "Declaration of Sentiments". However, the *Declaration of Independence* was actually not technically necessary in proclaiming independence from Great Britain.

A resolution of independence passed the Philadelphia Convention on July 2. This was all that was needed to break away from Britain. The colonists had been fighting Great Britain for 14 months while proclaiming their allegiance to the crown. Now they were breaking away. Obviously, they wanted to make clear exactly why they decided to take this action. Hence, they presented the world with the *Declaration of Independence* drafted by thirty-three years old Thomas Jefferson.

The text of the Declaration has been compared to a "Lawyer's Brief". After stating its purpose, the opening paragraphs assert the fundamental American ideal of government, based on the theory of natural rights, which had been held by, among others, John Locke, Emerich de Vattel, and Jean Jacques Rousseau.

"We hold these truths to be self-evident, that all men are created equal, that they are endowed by their Creator with certain unalienable Rights, that among these are Life, Liberty and the pursuit of Happiness. —That to secure these rights, Governments are instituted among Men, deriving their just powers from the consent of the governed, —That whenever any Form of Government becomes destructive of these ends, it is the Right of the People to alter or to abolish it, and to institute new Government, laying its foundation on such principles and organizing its powers in such form, as to them shall seem most likely to effect their Safety and Happiness. Prudence, indeed, will dictate that Governments long established should not be changed for light and transient causes; and accordingly all experience hath shewn, that mankind are more disposed to suffer, while evils are sufferable, than to right themselves by abolishing the forms to which they are accustomed. But when a long train of abuses and usurpations, pursuing invariably the same Object evinces a design to reduce them under absolute Despotism, it is their right, it is their duty, to throw off such Government, and to provide new Guards for their future security."

Then follows an indictment of George III for willfully infringing those rights in order to establish an "absolute Tyranny" over the colonies. The *Declaration of Independence* presents a long list of grievances against King George III including such items as taxation without representation, maintaining a standing army in peacetime, dissolving houses of representatives, and hiring "large armies of foreign mercenaries." The analogy is that Jefferson is an attorney presenting his case before the world court. Not everything that Jefferson wrote was exactly correct. However, it is important to remember that he was writing a persuasive essay, not a historical text. The formal break from Great Britain was complete with the adoption of this document on July 4, 1776.

The stirring closing paragraph is the formal pronouncement of independence and is borrowed from the resolution of July 2.

"We, therefore, the Representatives of the united States of America, in General Congress, Assembled, appealing to the Supreme Judge of the world for the rectitude of our intentions, do, in the Name, and by Authority of the good People of these Colonies, solemnly publish and declare, That these United Colonies are, and of Right ought to be Free and Independent States; that they are Absolved from all Allegiance to the British Crown, and that all political connection between them and the state of Great Britain, is and ought to be totally dissolved; and that as Free and Independent States, they have full Power to levy War, conclude Peace, contract Alliances, establish Commerce, and to do all other Acts and Things which Independent States may of right do.—And for the support of this Declaration, with a firm reliance on the protection of divine Providence, we mutually pledge to each other our Lives, our fortunes and our sacred Honor."

Selected Reading

Declaration of Independence (1776)[1]
IN CONGRESS, JULY 4, 1776

The unanimous Declaration of the thirteen united States of America. When in the Course of human events it becomes necessary for one people to dissolve the political bands which have connected them with another and to assume among the powers of the earth, the separate and equal station to which the Laws of Nature and of Nature's God entitle them, a decent respect to the opinions of mankind requires that they should declare the causes which impel them to the separation.

We hold these truths to be self-evident, that all men are created equal, that they are endowed by their Creator with certain unalienable Rights, that among these are Life, Liberty and the pursuit of Happiness. — That to secure these rights, Governments are instituted among Men, deriving their just powers from the consent of the governed, — That whenever any Form of Government becomes destructive of these ends, it is the Right of the People to alter or to abolish it, and to institute new Government, laying its foundation on such principles and organizing its powers in such form, as to them shall seem most likely to effect their Safety and Happiness. Prudence, indeed, will dictate that Governments long established should not be changed for light and transient causes; and accordingly all experience hath shewn[2] that mankind are more disposed to suffer, while evils are sufferable than to right themselves by abolishing the forms to which they are accustomed. But when a long train of abuses and usurpations, pursuing invariably the same Object evinces a design to reduce them under absolute Despotism, it is their right, it is their duty, to throw off such Government, and to provide new Guards for their future security. — Such has been the patient sufferance of these Colonies; and such is now the necessity which constrains them to alter their former Systems of Government. The history of the present King of Great Britain is a history of repeated injuries and usurpations, all having in direct object the establishment of an absolute Tyranny over these States. To prove this, let Facts be submitted to a candid world.[3]

He has refused his Assent to Laws, the most wholesome and necessary for the public good.

He has forbidden his Governors to pass Laws of immediate and pressing importance, unless suspended in their operation till his Assent should be obtained; and when so suspended, he has utterly neglected to attend to them.

He has refused to pass other Laws for the accommodation of large districts of people, unless those people would relinquish the right of Representation in the Legislature, a right inestimable to them and formidable to tyrants only.

He has called together legislative bodies at places unusual, uncomfortable, and distant from the depository of their Public Records, for the sole purpose of fatiguing them into compliance with his measures.

He has dissolved Representative Houses repeatedly, for opposing with manly firmness his invasions on the rights of the people.

He has refused for a long time, after such dissolutions, to cause others to be elected, whereby the Legislative Powers, incapable of Annihilation, have returned to the People at large for their exercise; the State remaining in the mean time exposed to all the dangers of invasion from without, and convulsions within.

He has endeavoured to prevent the population of these States; for that purpose obstructing the Laws for Naturalization of Foreigners; refusing to pass others to encourage their migrations hither, and raising the conditions of new Appropriations of Lands.

He has obstructed the Administration of Justice by refusing his Assent to Laws for establishing Judiciary Powers.

He has made Judges dependent on his Will alone for the tenure of their offices, and the amount and payment of their salaries.

He has erected a multitude of New Offices, and sent hither swarms of Officers to harass our people and eat out their substance.

He has kept among us, in times of peace, Standing Armies without the Consent of our legislatures.

He has affected to render the Military independent of and superior to the Civil Power.

He has combined with others to subject us to a jurisdiction foreign to our constitution, and unacknowledged by our laws; giving his Assent to their Acts of pretended Legislation:

For quartering large bodies of armed troops among us:

For protecting them, by a mock Trial from punishment for any Murders which they should commit on the Inhabitants of these States:

For cutting off our Trade with all parts of the world:

For imposing Taxes on us without our Consent:

For depriving us in many cases, of the benefit of Trial by Jury:

For transporting us beyond Seas to be tried for pretended offences:

For abolishing the free System of English Laws in a neighbouring Province, establishing therein an Arbitrary government, and enlarging its Boundaries so as to render it at once an example and fit instrument for introducing the same absolute rule into these Colonies:

For taking away our Charters, abolishing our most valuable Laws and altering fundamentally the Forms of our Governments:

For suspending our own Legislatures, and declaring themselves invested with power to legislate for us in all cases whatsoever.

He has abdicated Government here, by declaring us out of his Protection and waging War against us.

He has plundered our seas, ravaged our coasts, burnt our towns, and destroyed the lives of our people.

He is at this time transporting large Armies of foreign Mercenaries to compleat the works of death, desolation, and tyranny, already begun with circumstances of Cruelty & Perfidy scarcely paralleled in the most barbarous ages, and totally unworthy the Head of a civilized nation.

He has constrained our fellow Citizens taken Captive on the high Seas to bear Arms against their Country, to become the executioners of their friends and Brethren, or to fall themselves by their Hands.

He has excited domestic insurrections amongst us, and has endeavoured to bring on the inhabitants of our frontiers, the merciless Indian Savages whose known rule of warfare, is an undistinguished destruction of all ages, sexes and conditions.[4]

In every stage of these Oppressions We have Petitioned for Redress in the most humble terms: Our repeated Petitions have been answered only by repeated injury. A Prince, whose character is thus marked by every act which may define a Tyrant, is unfit to be the ruler of a free people.

Nor have We been wanting in attentions to our British brethren. We have warned them from time to time of attempts by their legislature to extend an unwarrantable jurisdiction over us. We have reminded them of the circumstances of our emigration and settlement here. We have appealed to their native justice and magnanimity, and we have conjured them by the ties of our common kindred to disavow these usurpations, which would inevitably interrupt our connections and correspondence. They too have been deaf to the voice of justice and of consanguinity. We must, therefore, acquiesce in the necessity, which denounces our Separation, and hold them, as we hold the rest of mankind, Enemies in War, in Peace Friends.

We, therefore, the Representatives of the united States of America, in General Congress, Assembled, appealing to the Supreme Judge of the world for the rectitude of our intentions, do, in the Name, and by Authority of the good People of these Colonies, solemnly publish and declare, That these united Colonies are, and of Right ought to be Free and Independent States, that they are Absolved from all Allegiance to the British Crown, and that all political connection between them and the State of Great Britain, is and ought to be totally dissolved; and that as Free and Independent States, they have full Power to levy War, conclude Peace, contract Alliances, establish Commerce, and to do all other Acts and Things which Independent States may of right do. — And for the support of this Declaration, with a firm reliance on the protection of Divine Providence, we mutually pledge to each other our Lives, our Fortunes, and our sacred Honor.[5]

Notes:

1. The delegates of the United Colonies of New Hampshire; Massachusetts Bay; Rhode Island and Providence Plantations; Connecticut; New York; New Jersey; Pennsylvania; New Castle, Kent, and Sussex, in Delaware; Maryland; Virginia; North Carolina, and South Carolina, In Congress assembled at Philadelphia, *Resolved* on the 10th of May, 1776, to recommend to the respective assemblies and conventions of the United Colonies, where no government sufficient to the exigencies of their affairs had been established, to adopt such a government as should, in the opinion of the representatives of the people, best conduce to the happiness and safety of their constituents in particular, and of America in general. A preamble to this resolution,

agreed to on the 15th of May, stated the intention to be totally to suppress the exercise of every kind of authority under the British crown. On the 7th of June, certain resolutions respecting independency were moved and seconded. On the 10th of June it was resolved, that a committee should be appointed to prepare a declaration to the following effect: "That the United Colonies are, and of right ought to be, free and independent States; that they are absolved from all allegiance to the British crown; and that all political connection between them and the State of Great Britain is, and ought to be, totally dissolved." On the preceding day it was determined that the committee for preparing the declaration should consist of five, and they were chosen accordingly, in the following order: Mr. Jefferson, Mr. J. Adams, Mr. Franklin, Mr. Sherman, Mr. R. R. Livingston. On the 11th of June a resolution was passed to appoint a committee to prepare and digest the form of a confederation to be entered into between the colonies, and another committee to prepare a plan of treaties to be proposed to foreign powers. On the 12th of June, it was resolved, that a committee of Congress should be appointed by the name of a board of war and ordnance, to consist of five members. On the 25th of June, a declaration of the deputies of Pennsylvania, met in provincial conference, expressing their willingness to concur in a vote declaring the United Colonies free and independent States, was laid before Congress and read. On the 28th of June, the committee appointed to prepare a declaration of independence brought in a draught, which was read, and ordered to lie on the table. On the 1st of July, a resolution of the convention of Maryland, passed the 28th of June, authorizing the deputies of that colony to concur in declaring the United Colonies free and independent States, was laid before Congress and read. On the same day Congress resolved itself into a committee of the whole, to take into consideration the resolution respecting independency. On the 2nd of July, a resolution declaring the colonies free and independent States, was adopted. A declaration to that effect was, on the same and the following days, taken into further consideration. Finally, on the 4th of July, the Declaration of Independence was agreed to, engrossed on paper, signed by John Hancock as president, and directed to be sent to the several assemblies, conventions, and committees, or councils of safety, and to the several commanding officers of the continental troops, and to be proclaimed in each of the United States, and at the head of the Army. It was also ordered to be entered upon the Journals of Congress, and on the 2nd of August, a copy engrossed on parchment was signed by all but one of the fifty six signers whose names are appended to it. That one was Matthew Thornton, of New Hampshire, who on taking his seat in November asked and obtained the privilege of signing it. Several who signed it on the 2nd of August were absent when it was adopted on the 4th of July, but, approving of it, they thus signified their approbation.

2. shewn: shown

3. This part is the Preamble of the Declaration, which runs from Jefferson's opening of the Declaration to the words, "To prove this, let Facts be submitted to a candid world." A preamble is a preliminary statement, especially the introduction to a formal document that serves to explain its purpose. In this instance, Jefferson used the preamble to discuss the basic rights of man. It has since become the most famous part of the document.

Note: Jefferson derived many of his ideas for the preamble from the Virginia Declaration of Rights written by his friend George Mason as well as from his own draft preamble to the Virginia Constitution, which in turn were based upon Locke but much more "radical".

4. A list of grievances against King George III: A grievance is:

a. An actual or supposed circumstance regarded as just cause for complaint

b. A complaint or protestation based on such a circumstance

The list of grievances runs from "He has refused his Assent to Laws, the most wholesome and necessary for the public good." to "He has excited domestic insurrections amongst us, and has endeavoured to bring on the inhabitants of our frontiers, the merciless Indian Savages, whose known rule of warfare, is an undistinguished destruction of all ages, sexes and conditions."

Note: In the *Declaration of Independence*, Thomas Jefferson listed several complaints against King George, in which he hoped to lay the foundation for the case supporting independence.

5. This part is a formal declaration of war, in which the colonists pledged their "lives, fortunes, and sacred honor."

Questions for Study and Discussion:

1. Jefferson chose to begin the Declaration with the words "The unanimous Declaration of the thirteen united States of America." Do you feel this was necessary? Why or why not?

2. Is the *Declaration of Independence* a radical document? Explain.

3. What issues did the *Declaration of Independence* fail to resolve regarding equality? Regarding the newly established national government?

4. According to Jefferson, what was the purpose of government? What does Jefferson

suggest should happen whenever government becomes "destructive of the ends for which it was created?" According to Jefferson, how do governments derive their powers?

5. What overall impact has the *Declaration of Independence* had on the United States? On the nations of the world?

Part Two   The Age of Nationalism and

Romanticism (1790—1860)

Introduction

I. Historical Background

The development of the American society nurtured "the literature of a great nation." In 1837 Ralph Waldo Emerson delivered to Harvard's Phi Beta Kappa Society the speech "The American Scholar," which Oliver Wendell Holms called "an intellectual Declaration of Independence." In it Emerson stated that "Perhaps the time is already come... when the sluggard intellect of this continent will look from under its iron lids, and fill the postponed expectation of the world with something better than the exertions of mechanical skill. Our day of dependence, or long apprenticeship to the learning of other lands, draws to a close. The millions that around us are rushing into life, cannot always be fed on the sere remains of foreign harvests. Who can doubt, that poetry will revive and lead in a new age." Emerson urged his audience to participate in the creation of a distinctive American literary tradition, and the first seventy years in the national literature of the United States show both the causes that prompted Emerson's critique and the responses that were America's first great literary achievements.

If the Revolutionary period had defined what Americans were not—subjects of England—the overriding challenge during these decisive years was to articulate what in fact America and Americans were, during a period of unprecedented territorial expansion, population growth, and technological change. Between 1790 and 1860 the American population grew from 3.9 million to 31 million. The thirteen original colonies had grown to thirty-three states by 1860. By 1830 almost half of the U.S. population of 11 million had pushed west of the Alleghenies, the western border of the American colonies. Twelve percent were recent immigrant, part of a steady flow of Europeans to work the new farmlands in the West and to supply labor for the new steam-driven factories in the Northeast, which already were beginning to transform a rural, agrarian country into a modern, urbanized industrial nation. The steamboat, railroad, and telegraph shrank the nation even as its boundaries expanded and stretched across the continent to the Pacific. Vast western territories were acquired in the Louisiana Purchase; Florida was gained from Spain; and Texas, the Southwest, and California were wrested from Mexico. Throughout the period, writers struggled to comprehend the new America that was evolving beyond the boundaries, culture, and traditions of its founding while also trying to reconcile the nation's new realities with its professed ideals. As the wilderness receded westward, the environment that had shaped American values changed. Just as important, the unresolved contradiction between the principles of liberty and the fact of institutionalized slavery drove Americans apart.

Many besides Emerson urged American writers to play a prominent role in chronicling and celebrating the ongoing national drama. Many felt the need for a literature to match the uniqueness of the country and its aspirations. However, if the nation had won its independence from Britain, its literature was still mainly subservient to English models and depreciated as secondhand and second rate. In 1820 the British critic Sydney Smith declared, with some justification: "In the four quarters of the globe, who reads an American book? Or goes to an American play? Or looks at an American picture of statue?"

II. Literary Review

Indeed, in the first two decades of America's national history there was little to challenge Smith's view. In poetry, Americans mainly imitated English neoclassical models or the more recent works of the English Romantics, such as William Wordsworth, Samuel Taylor Coleridge, and Lord Byron, as well as Sir Walter Scott. The most gifted of the American poets of this period was William Cullen Bryant, whose "Thanatopsis" was written when he was seventeen and whose first collection in 1821 showed the influence of the poets he most admired, including

Wordsworth, Scott, Alexander Pope, Thomas Gray, and Robert Burns.

The economic conditions of American book publishing contributed significantly to the struggles of American writers as they attempted to emerge from the long shadow cast by the British. Although a national copyright law was enacted in 1790, international copyright protection was not established until 1891, leaving American printers free to pirate the latest works of popular British writers such as Walter Scott and Charles Dickens. Because American readers could read the best of British writers in cheap reprints, there was scant economic incentive for publishers to support American writers who expected to be paid. Most American writers consequently found it difficult to survive by their writing; only those who produced works of exceptional distinction and popularity were rewarded.

The first significant challenges to the domination of British authors came from two New Yorkers, Washington Irving and James Fenimore Cooper. By 1800 New York City, with its population of sixty thousand, had become the largest city in the United States and its literary capital. Washington Irving, part of the city's sophisticated cultural elite, achieved his initial success with a witty and satirical look back at New York's Dutch past in *The History of New York* (1809) and went on to become the first American writer to achieve international renown with *The Sketch Book of Geoffrey Crayon* (1819—1820). Included among its depictions of English scenes are two tales set in rural New York—*Rip Van Winkle* and *The Legend of Sleepy Hollow*—that first demonstrate the imaginative possibilities of American writing, while his subsequent histories, travel books, and biographies, along with his themes, its past and its setting. Irving's popular success spawned a host of imitators of a market for American sketches and tales, helped establish and legitimize a distinctive American literary voice and subject matter.

Like Irving, James Fenimore Cooper achieved his initial success by re-creating America's past. Capitalizing on the popularity of Walter Scott's historical novels, *The Spy* (1821), the first historical romance treating the American Revolution. *The Pioneers* (1823) initiated Cooper's greatest achievement, the series of five Leather stocking Tales chronicling the career of the prototypical American frontiersman, Natty Bumppo, and his Indian companion, Chingachgook, against a background of American history of the mid-eighteenth century. More than any other writer of the period, Cooper tapped into the mythic reservoir of the American landscape and the archetypal American conflicts between the red man and the white, the individual and the community, nature and civilization.

If Irving and Cooper by their success showed that an American writer could compete with the best of Europe by exploring the thematic and poetic possibilities of America, a third figure, Edgar Allan Poe, helped raise the standard for artistry while formulating distinctive new imaginative forms. Essayist, editor, reviewer, poet, and fiction writer, Poe was America's first literary theorist as well as practitioner. While inventing detective fiction and science fiction, Poe refined an expressive symbolic theory of poetry. He was one of the first to recognize the genius of Nathaniel Hawthorne, and his review of Hawthorne's *Twice-Told Tales* (1842) helped codify the aesthetic of the prose tale or sketch, which he applied to his own works, establishing a uniquely American contribution to narrative fiction, the short story.

Although Irving, Cooper, and Poe represented an initial testing of the American imagination against dominant European modes of expression, the first breakthrough for American literature came from New England. There the particularly American strain of Romanticism known as Transcendentalism emerged. Influenced by British writers such as Wordsworth, Coleridge, and Thomas Carlyle, as well as German idealistic philosophers such as Immanuel Kant, the Transcendentalists rejected a narrow materialistic, rationalistic conception of the world in favor of a secular spirituality emphasizing the primacy of the individual in a direct relationship with the forces of Nature. Ralph Waldo Emerson's first book, *Nature* (1836), contains the first significant statements of Transcendentalism, He refined his views in *Essays* (1841) and *Essays: Second Series* (1844), solidifying his reputation as America's leading philosopher and cultural critic. Transcendentalism was less a coherent or consistent philosophical system than a call of creative self-expression and a liberation of personal authority. Because it rejected dogma and promoted intellectual and artistic risk taking, Transcendentalism embodied American notions of individualism, self-reliance, and equality. Whitman observed that it was Emerson who had brought him to a boil, and the creative energies released by Emerson and the Transcendentalists helped produce arguably the greatest creative decade in American literary history.

The artistic achievement of the 1850s began with Nathaniel Hawthorne's *The Scarlet Letter* (1850), which combines elements of the historical and gothic romance with a philosophical exploration of the nature of sin, guilt, and redemption, derived from the Puritan past. There had never been anything quite like Hawthorne's metaphysical drama in American fiction before—a rich evocation of internal states cast in a historical setting that is both sharply imagined and symbolically suggestive. Hawthorne's achievement prompted Herman Melville to call him the "American Shakespeare." Indeed, Hawthorne's influence on Melville is evident in *Moby Dick* (1852), an unprecedented experimental novel blending narrative, metaphysical, dramatic, and documentary elements into what one contemporary reviewer called a "salmagundi of fact, fiction, and philosophy." In its own way, Henry David Thoreau's *Walden* (1854) is no less a daring hybrid, combining the author's account of his stay at Walden Pond in Concord from 1845 to 1847 with social commentary and philosophical speculation. Most daring of all is Walt Whitman's *Leaves of Grass* (1855), the first installment of his ongoing American epic. In it Whitman broke all the rules of poetic form and content, abandoning traditional meter for a rhythmical free verse, as flexible as the spoken voice with a perspective wide enough to comprehend the "aggregated, inseparable, unprecedented, vast, composite, electric *Democratic Nationality*."

As America expanded westward, the opening up of each new territory threatened the delicate balance between free and slave states, exacerbating animosity between North and South and pushing the nation closer to conflict. Abolitionists in Britain and America helped publish dozens of slave narratives documenting the abuses of slavery, the most popular of which was the *Narrative of the Life of Frederick Douglass* (1845). During the 1850s, the first novel written by an African American, William Wells Brown's *Clotel; or, the President's Daughter* (1853), depicting the slave daughter of Thomas Jefferson, was published in London. Harriet Beecher Stowe's *Uncle Tom's Cabin* (1852), the biggest-selling American novel in the nineteenth century and the most controversial book published in the United States up to that time, did more than any other literary work to engage the nation in the debate over slavery. The impact is summed up in a commonly quoted statement apocryphally attributed to Abraham Lincoln. When he met Stowe, it is claimed that he said, "So you're the little woman who wrote the book that made this great war!"

Like the nation itself, American literature between 1790 and 1860 came of age, discovering distinctive voices and subjects, drawing on both what united and divided Americans. While the inauguration of the great Revolutionary War hero George Washington united the new nation, the election of Abraham Lincoln precipitated its division. Lincoln had earlier stated that "a house divided against itself cannot stand." He and the nation would shortly face the sobering reality of that assertion.

Washington Irving (1783—1859)

Life and Major Works

Largely credited as the first professional American writer of imaginative literature and historical works, Washington Irving (1783—1859) achieved international fame and earned the respect from such preeminent men of letters as Coleridge, Byron, Scott and Dickens. Born of an age when the United States began to develop an artistic culture of its own, Irving became a model of his followers in several aspects. As a prolific writer, he channeled his creative power and serious thinking into diverse literary genres, such as essays, plays, poems,

Washington Irving

sketches, historical and biographical accounts and travel books. The most successful and the best known is the short story. It probably began with Irving's *The Sketch Book* (1819—1820), which marked the beginning of American Romanticism. As a messenger sent from the new world to the old world, he spent much of his lifetime travelling, through the frontier of upper state New York and eastern part of Canada and across many countries in Europe, where he developed a strong sense of a new country and a new destiny and renovated the rich European cultural heritage in American settings. With such a patriotic conviction, he interpreted the local and European legends and folklores in his own manner. His best short stories in this respect are *The Legend of Sleepy Hollow* and *Rip Van Winkle*, both of which are included in *The Sketch Book*. The former tells of a poor schoolmaster's encounter with a headless horseman and the latter is concerned with a man who falls asleep for 20 years and awakens to find everything changed. Interestingly, Irving tried his hands at law, business, diplomacy, architecture and landscape design but none could exceed his literary reputation. His humorous stories and satirical essays remain to enjoy wide readership among American society.

Irving's early life helps a lot with his writings. The youngest of 11 children, he was born in a wealthy New York merchant family (near present-day Wall Street) at the end of the Revolutionary War on April 3, 1783. His parents, Scottish-English immigrants, admired General George Washington so much that they named their newly-born son in honor of this hero of the revolution. From childhood, he started to read over a wide range of topics, especially adventure tales like *Robinson Crusoe*, *Sinbad the Sailor* and *The World Displayed*. Those books not only provided him with some knowledge about the strange and exciting experiences but also nurtured his passion to explore new places and observe peculiar characters and manners. This is proved by an autographical account at the beginning of *The Sketch Book*: "My holiday afternoons were spent in rambles about the surrounding country. I made myself familiar with all its places famous in history or fable. I knew every spot where a murder or robbery had been committed, or a ghost seen. I visited the neighboring villages, and added greatly to my stock of knowledge, by noting their habits and customs, and conversing with their sages and great men. I even journeyed one long summer's day to the summit of the most distant hill, whence I stretched my eye over many a mile of terra incognita, and was astonished to find how vast a globe I inhabited. " It is a definite statement of Irving's extensive range of observations, which anticipated his later masterpieces. One day he set out a trip to a nearby town of Sleepy Hollow and was captured by its quaint Dutch customs and local ghost stories. Another time he trudged through the Catskill mountain region, the setting for *Rip Van Winkle*. "[O]f all the scenery of the Hudson", Irving wrote later, "the Catskill Mountains had the most witching effect on my boyish imagination."

Irving's literary career could be seen from two phases. The first starts from his debut publication in 1809 to 1832, dominated by English and other European subjects. The second refers to the remaining years of his life when he worked mainly on American materials. From his teens, Irving wrote letters under the pseudonym Jonathan Oldstyle for *Morning Chronicle*, a New York City newspaper owned by his brother Peter. The letters poured ridicule on theater, fashion, early feminism, and youth in New York society. While he became known among New Yorkers, Irving did not pursue his college degree but apprenticed himself in private law offices. Due to his poor health, he had to head towards Europe for medical treatment. Upon his return from his three-year-tour of France and Italy financed by his older brothers, he preferred to acquire more knowledge in cultural affairs and in literature and began actively socializing with a group of like-minded and well-read young bachelors. The result of such dynamic intellectual exchanges is the publication of *Salmagundi or The Whim-Whams and Opinions of Launcelot Langstaff, Esq. and Others* (1807—1808), a series of essays in collaboration with his brother William and his brother-in-law J. K. Paulding. The highly popular collection of short pieces again poked fun at the political, social, and cultural life in Irving's own time. The instant success of *Salmagundi* prompted Irving to quit his job as a law clerk and concentrate on literature. In 1809 he penned his first book *A History of New York*, a comical and purposefully inaccurate account of New York's Dutch colonization. The book was narrated by another pseudonym Diedrich Knickerbocker, an imaginary eccentric Dutch-American scholar. Its significance is several-fold. As a tender satire on self-important local history and contemporary politics, it won Irving financial success and worldwide popularity but offended some Dutch descendants. Knickerbocker grew to be the best known character in Irving's works and the word was later used to recognize the first American school of writers, the Knickerbocker Group, of which Irving was a leading figure. In addition, the Knickerbocker tales are now a beloved part of New York folklore from which any New Yorker could trace his family to the original Dutch settlers. Between 1815 and 1832, Irving started off his second trip to Europe where he reached the peak of his achievements in humorous writing and found himself America's first international literary celebrity. After the bankruptcy of his family business in England, Irving turned definitely to literature with the encouragement of Walter Scot. His second success came with *The Sketch Book of Geroffery Crayon, Gent.* (1819—1820). It consist of thirty parts, namely, half English sketches, four general travel pieces, six literary essays, two descriptions of the American Indian, three essentially unclassifiable pieces, and three short stories. The varied material in *The Sketch Book* appealed to a broad range of readers and earned respect of European critics. The stories were written under evident European influence. As far as the subject matter is concerned, *The Legend of Sleepy Hollow* and *Rip Van Winkle* were based on the German folktales, a sign of a lack of originality and power that Irving had shown. And the narrators in these works sound much more polite and refined than those in his earlier writings. After 1824 Irving increasingly shifted his attention from fiction and descriptive writing toward history and biography. In 1826 he became a U.S. diplomat in Spain and began to study and write about Spanish themes. His works during this period include *History of the Life and Voyages of Christopher Columbus* (1828), *The Conquest of Granada* (1829), and *The Alhambra* (1832). In 1832 when he was fifty Irving returned to Tarrytown, New York and spent the rest of his life in leisure and comfort, except for a period of four years (1842—1846) when he was appointed Minister to Spain. From 1848 to 1859 he was President of Astor Library, later New York Public Library. Among the notable works of Irving's later years was his five-volume *The Life of George Washington* (1732—1799), which he worked on with great resolution from the early 1850s till a few months before his death in 1859.

The most striking feature of all Irving's works is his literary style famous for his refined humor, his vivid characterization, his kindly irony, his finished and musical language and the definiteness of America. It is partly due to his aim of writing. His short stories were written without an obligation to moralize and the general truths about human nature and social issues were not didactically stated. Irving simply writes to entertain rather to enlighten, which makes his style quite profound and different from that of his contemporaries. For instance, with a humorous or sometimes satirical tone, he conveys serious message about human values in a tolerant way. However, Irving's weaknesses are recognized by some critics, including Edgar Allan Poe. He felt that while Irving should be given credit for being an innovator, the writing itself was often unsophisticated. "Irving is much over-rated", Poe wrote in 1838, "and a nice distinction might be drawn between his just and his surreptitious and adventitious reputation—between what is due to the pioneer solely, and what to the writer." What makes Irving's creations unsophisticated is a lack of intellectual depths. No sustained wisdom could be found concerning "the movement of thought behind the events" of the War with Mexico and of Waterloo. No penetrating insights could be offered into Anglo-American relations or American Imperialist expansion. After all, Irving's style and choice of subjects should be applauded. His imaginative treatment of historical themes and his use of folklore, together with other elements of romanticism, push the Romantic Movement on American literary scene.

Brief Introduction and Appreciation

Since the first day it was published, *Rip Van Winkle* by the famous 19th-century American writer Washington Irving has remained a focus in a country of continual and dynamic changes. Originated from a German folklore, this mythic and allegorical short story succeeds as a manifestation of the truth of American history and the rising Romantic Movement. As a part of the American cultural tradition, it has aroused national consciousness in ordinary Americans and inspired them to reflect on the past memories before and after Revolutionary War and ponder over how their ancestors struggled to gain physical and mental independence and managed to find a truly American identity. The greatest legacy of this masterpiece is its introduction of short story as a new literary genre. With vivid characterization, appropriate humor and satire as well as unique narrative system, *Rip Van Winkle* is worthy of international acclaim. British critics, especially, were surprised and delighted to see that an American writer was capable of creating good prose. In an 1820 review for *the Edinburgh Review*, Francis Jeffrey spoke highly of the book's "great purity and beauty of diction," and called the book "the first American work ... to which we could give this praise."

In *Rip Van Winkle*, Irving's romantic strain is characterized by a reverence for nature. When Rip is fed up with his wife Dame Van Winkle's endless complain and clamor, he has no choice but to leave the village inn and stroll away into luxuriant woods and rugged mountains with his gun and his dog "Wolf". Nature in the story is described with as much attention to imagination as to accurate detail: the "fairy mountains" surrounding Rip's village reach a "noble height" with their "magical hues and shapes." The opening in the cliffs opens and closes with "no traces." Nature in Rip's mind brings him peace, quietness and freedom. Nature in Irving's eyes tends to be mysterious where the central character is likely to undergo a life-changing experience. The significance of nature is magnified if we further investigate it in contrast to the civilized and stressful world. The latter is well embodied by Mrs. Winkle who pours out requirements for her husband to "improve himself," to make a profit from his farm and to raise her and the children's standard of living. The tension between the two worlds, a peaceful natural world and a civilized real world is at the heart of *Rip Van Winkle* because it was at the heart of the development of America in Irving's time. The moment Rip wakes up from a long enchanted sleep and returns home with long and white beard in twenty years, our attention is shifted to the differences in Rips' home village prior to Revolution and that of Washington era.

Considering the specific times, the conflict between the past and the present, the old and the new is what many Americans, mostly the early colonists, have faced up to and successfully gone through. Born of Dutch origin, Rip was a good-natured man well liked by the good wives of the village except his own. He was ready to help his neighbors with all kinds of chores but simply had no skill in any "profitable labor", leaving his farm the worst in the area. He was a friend of the children in the village but his two children, without his care, "were as ragged and wild as if they belonged to nobody". Rip enjoyed a pastoral idyll of fishing and squirrel-hunting in the Catskill village but seemed to evade domestic obligation and responsibility. He could not be considered lazy or unproductive because the neighborhood stood with him and it was only at the new American quest for profit and self-improvement that Rip failed. Rip's liquor-induced dream, however, made him miss out the entire era of American Revolution and the overnight changes bewildered this old-world man. Irving at this point provided adequate details to remind readers of the psychological difficulty Americans at the time felt in understanding their own national history. Upon his return, although the landscape remained unchanged, Rip's village became "busy, bustling, and disputatious" and the residents showed more concern about congress election and rights of citizens, political issues which were not that popular twenty years ago. Many of his friends were dead. Also gone was his hen-pecking wife. The image of King George III over the tavern had been replaced by one of General Washington. As a result of these changes, Rip lost his connection with the present world and wondered who he was. To get rid of self doubts, he made friends with the rising generation and settled into a life as one of the patriarchs of the village. Some critics have pointed to this as evidence that Rip Van Winkle is a symbol of America, baffled by rapid political changes, but freed at last from tyranny. His new useful position in society was found by becoming a story teller of his own story and stories of the past. In other words, the villager's belief in the old myth saved Rip and gave him a new social status. Rip's role as a storyteller not only bridges the gap between the past and the present but also implies another feature of *Rip Van Winkle*—the narrative system.

As informed by the subtitle, we readers get to know the whole story was from a posthumous writing of Diedrich Knickerbocker, an imaginary Dutch scholar whose tales were characteristic of scrupulous accuracy. Together with the introduction and the postscript about *Rip Van Winkle*, a balanced narrative frame of the story is created in order to help Irving openly comment on the changes in Rip's life and make the tale more believable. In the story since Rip slept through the transition from British colony to independence, he was able to investigate the new social order from the perspective of the old. This legend totally changes Rip's life. He could be a part of the legend and a reliable witness of it and it gives him an identity in which Rip can achieve his duty. It is how the personal tale of Rip Van Winkle and the national history of America are connected. Through the chain of the changes could Rip, representative of all Americans, create his own story and establish his identity.

Selected Reading

Rip Van Winkle

A POSTHUMOUS WRITING OF DIEDRICH KNICKERBOCKER.

By Woden[1], God of Saxons,

From whence comes Wensday, that is Wodensday,

Truth is a thing that ever I will keep

Unto thylke[2] day in which I creep into

My sepulchre—

CARTWRIGHT[3]

WHOEVER has made a voyage up the Hudson must remember the Kaatskill mountains[4]. They are a dismembered branch of the great Appalachian family, and are seen away to the west of the river, swelling up to a noble height, and lording it over the surrounding country. Every change of season, every change of weather, indeed every hour of the day, produces some change in the magical hues and shapes of these mountains, and they are regarded by all the good wives, far and near, as perfect barometers. When the weather is fair and settled, they are clothed in blue and purple, and print their bold outlines on the clear evening sky; but sometimes, when the rest of the landscape is cloudless, they will gather a hood of gray vapors   about their summits, which, in the last rays of the setting sun, will glow and light up like a crown of glory.

At the foot of these fairy mountains, the voyager may have descried the light smoke curling up from a village, whose shingle-roofs gleam among the trees, just where the blue tints of the upland melt away into the fresh green of the nearer landscape. It is a little village, of great antiquity, having been founded by some of the Dutch colonists, in the early times of the province, just about the beginning of the government of the good Peter Stuyvesant[5], (may he rest in peace!) and there were some of the houses of the original settlers standing within a few years, built of small yellow bricks brought from Holland, having latticed windows and gable fronts, surmounted with weathercocks.

In that same village, and in one of these very houses (which, to tell the precise truth, was sadly time-worn and weather-beaten), there lived many years since, while the country was yet a province of Great Britain, a simple good-natured fellow, of the name of Rip Van Winkle. He was a descendant of the Van Winkles who figured so gallantly in the chivalrous days of Peter Stuyvesant, and accompanied him to the siege of Fort Christina. He inherited, however, but little of the martial character of his ancestors. I have observed that he was a simple good-natured man; he was, moreover, a kind neighbor, and an obedient hen-pecked[6] husband. Indeed, to the latter circumstance might be owing that meekness of spirit which gained him such universal popularity; for those men are most apt to be obsequious and conciliating abroad, who are under the discipline of shrews at home. Their tempers, doubtless, are rendered pliant and malleable in the fiery furnace of domestic tribulation, and a curtain lecture is worth all the sermons in the world for teaching the virtues of patience and long-suffering. A termagant wife may, therefore, in some respects, be considered a tolerable blessing; and if so, Rip Van Winkle was thrice blessed.

Certain it is, that he was a great favorite among all the good wives of the village, who, as usual with the amiable sex, took his part in all family squabbles; and never failed, whenever they talked those matters over in their evening gossipings, to lay all the blame on Dame Van Winkle. The children of the village, too, would shout with joy whenever he approached. He assisted at their sports, made their playthings, taught them to fly kites and shoot marbles, and told them long stories of ghosts, witches, and Indians. Whenever he went dodging about the village, he was surrounded by a troop of them, hanging on his skirts, clambering on his back, and playing a thousand tricks on him with impunity; and not a dog would bark at him throughout the neighborhood.

The great error in Rip's composition was an insuperable aversion to all kinds of profitable labor. It could not be from the want of assiduity or perseverance; for he would sit on a wet rock, with a rod as long and heavy as a Tartar's lance, and fish all day without a murmur, even though he should not be encouraged by a single nibble. He would carry a fowling-piece on his shoulder for hours together, trudging through woods and swamps, and up hill and down dale, to shoot a few squirrels or wild pigeons. He would never refuse to assist a neighbor even in the roughest toil, and was a foremost man at all country frolics for husking Indian corn, or building stone-fences; the women of the village, too, used to employ him to run their errands, and to do such little odd jobs as their less obliging husbands would not do for them. In a word, Rip was ready to attend to anybody's business but his own; but as to doing family duty, and keeping his farm in order, he found it impossible.

In fact, he declared it was of no use to work on his farm; it was the most pestilent little piece of ground in the whole country; every thing about it went wrong, and would go wrong, in spite of him. His fences were continually falling to pieces; his cow would either go astray, or get among he cabbages; weeds were sure to grow quicker in his fields than anywhere else; the rain always made a point of setting in just as he had some outdoor work to do; so that though his patrimonial estate had dwindled away under his management, acre by acre, until there was little more left than a mere patch of Indian corn and potatoes, yet it was the worst-conditioned farm in the neighborhood.

His children, too, were as ragged and wild as if they belonged to nobody. His son Rip, an urchin begotten in his own likeness, promised to inherit the habits, with the old clothes of his father. He was generally seen trooping like a colt at his mother's heels, equipped in a pair of his father's cast-off galligaskins[7], which he had much ado to hold up with one hand, as a fine lady does her train in bad weather.

Rip Van Winkle, however, was one of those happy mortals, of foolish, well-oiled dispositions, who take the world easy, eat white bread or brown, whichever can be got with least thought or trouble, and would rather starve on a penny than work for a pound. If left to himself, he would have whistled life away in perfect contentment; but his wife kept continually dinning in his ears about his idleness, his carelessness, and the ruin he was bringing on his family. Morning, noon, and night, her tongue was incessantly going, and every thing he said or did was sure to produce a torrent of household eloquence. Rip had but one way of replying to all lectures of the kind, and that, by frequent use, had grown into a habit. He shrugged his shoulders, shook his head, cast up his eyes, but said nothing. This, however, always provoked a fresh volley from his wife; so that he was fain to draw off his forces, and take to the outside of the house—the only side which, in truth, belongs to a hen-pecked husband.

Rip's sole domestic adherent was his dog Wolf, who was as much henpecked as his master; for Dame Van Winkle regarded them as companions in idleness, and even looked upon Wolf with an evil eye, as the cause of his master's going so often astray. True it is, in all points of spirit befitting an honorable dog, he was as courageous an animal as ever scoured the woods—but what courage can withstand the ever-during and all-besetting terrors of a woman's tongue? The moment Wolf entered the house his crest fell, his tail drooped to the ground or curled between his legs, he sneaked about with a gallows air, casting many a sidelong glance at Dame Van Winkle, and at the least flourish of a broomstick or ladle, he would fly to the door with yelping precipitation.

Times grew worse and worse with Rip Van Winkle as years of matrimony rolled on; a tart temper never mellows with age, and a sharp tongue is the only edged tool that grows keener with constant use. For a long while he used to console himself, when driven from home, by frequenting a kind of perpetual club of the sages[8], philosophers, and other idle personages of the village; which held its sessions on a bench before a small inn, designated by a rubicund portrait of His Majesty George the Third. Here they used to sit in the shade through a long, lazy summer's day, talking listlessly over village gossip, or telling endless sleepy stories about nothing. But it would have been worth any statesman's money to have heard the profound discussions that sometimes took place when by chance an old newspaper fell into their hands from some passing traveller. How solemnly they would listen to the contents, as drawled out by Derrick Van Bummel, the schoolmaster, a dapper, learned little man, who was not to be daunted by the most gigantic word in the dictionary; and how sagely they would deliberate upon public events some months after they had taken place.

The opinions of this junto were completely controlled by Nicholas Vedder, a patriarch of the village, and landlord of the inn, at the door of which he took his seat from morning till night, just moving sufficiently to avoid the sun and keep in the shade of a large tree; so that the neighbors could tell the hour by his movements as accurately as by a sun dial. It is true, he was rarely heard to speak, but smoked his pipe incessantly. His adherents, however, (for every great man has his adherents), perfectly understood him, and knew how to gather his opinions. When any thing that was read or related displeased him, he was observed to smoke his pipe[9] vehemently, and to send forth short, frequent, and angry puffs; but when pleased, he would inhale the smoke slowly and tranquilly, and emit it in light and placid clouds; and sometimes, taking the pipe from his mouth, and letting the fragrant vapor curl about his nose, would gravely nod his head in token of perfect approbation.

From even this stronghold the unlucky Rip was at length routed by his termagant wife, who would suddenly break in upon the tranquility of the assemblage, and call the members all to naught; nor was that august personage,

Nicholas Vedder himself, sacred from the daring tongue of this terrible virago, who charged him outright with encouraging her husband in habits of idleness.

Poor Rip was at last reduced almost to despair; and his only alternative, to escape from the labor of the farm and the clamor of his wife, was to take gun in hand and stroll away into the woods. Here he would sometimes seat himself at the foot of a tree, and share the contents of his wallet with Wolf, with whom he sympathized as a fellow-sufferer in persecution. "Poor Wolf," he would say, "thy mistress leads thee a dog's life of it; but never mind, my lad, whilst I live thou shalt never want a friend to stand by thee!" Wolf would wag his tail, look wistfully in his master's face, and if dogs can feel pity I verily believe he reciprocated the sentiment with all his heart.

In a long ramble of the kind on a fine autumnal day, Rip had unconsciously scrambled to one of the highest parts of the Kaatskill mountains. He was after his favorite sport of squirrel shooting, and the still solitudes had echoed and re-echoed with the reports of his gun. Panting and fatigued, he threw himself, late in the afternoon, on a green knoll, covered with mountain herbage, that crowned the brow of a precipice. From an opening between the trees he could overlook all the lower country for many a mile of rich woodland. He saw at a distance the lordly Hudson, far, far below him, moving on its silent but majestic course, with the reflection of a purple cloud, or the sail of a lagging bark, here and there sleeping on its glassy bosom, and at last losing itself in the blue highlands.

On the other side he looked down into a deep mountain glen, wild, lonely, and shagged, the bottom filled with fragments from the impending cliffs, and scarcely lighted by the reflected rays of the setting sun. For some time Rip lay musing on this scene; evening was gradually advancing; the mountains began to throw their long blue shadows over the valleys; he saw that it would be dark long before he could reach the village, and he heaved a heavy sigh when he thought of encountering the terrors of Dame Van Winkle.

As he was about to descend, he heard a voice from a distance hallooing, "Rip Van Winkle! Rip Van Winkle!" He looked round, but could see nothing but a crow winging its solitary flight across the mountain. He thought his fancy must have deceived him, and turned again to descend, when he heard the same cry ring through the still evening air: "Rip Van Winkle! Rip Van Winkle!"—at the same time Wolf bristled up his back, and giving a low growl, skulked to his master's side, looking fearfully down into the glen. Rip now felt a vague apprehension stealing over him; he looked anxiously in the same direction, and perceived a strange figure slowly toiling up the rocks, and bending under the weight of something he carried on his back. He was surprised to see any human being in this lonely and unfrequented place, but supposing it to be some one of the neighborhood in need of his assistance, he hastened down to yield it.

On nearer approach, he was still more surprised at the singularity of the stranger's appearance. He was a short, square-built old fellow, with thick bushy hair, and a grizzled beard. His dress was of the antique Dutch fashion—a cloth jerkin[10] strapped round the waist—several pairs of breeches, the outer one of ample volume, decorated with rows of buttons down the sides and bunches at the knees. He bore on his shoulder a stout keg, that seemed full of liquor, and made signs for Rip to approach and assist him with the load. Though rather shy and distrustful of his new acquaintance, Rip complied with his usual alacrity; and mutually relieving one another, they clambered up a narrow gully, apparently the dry bed of a mountain torrent. As they ascended, Rip every now and then heard long rolling peals, like distant thunder, that seemed to issue out of a deep ravine, or rather cleft, between lofty rocks, toward which their rugged path conducted. He paused for an instant, but supposing it to be the muttering of one of those transient thunder-showers which often take place in the mountain heights, he proceeded. Passing through the ravine, they came to a hollow like a small amphitheatre, surrounded by perpendicular precipices, over the brinks of which impending trees shot their branches, so that you only caught glimpses of the azure sky, and the bright evening cloud. During the whole time, Rip and his companion had labored on in silence; for though the former marvelled greatly what could be the object of carrying a keg of liquor up this wild mountain, yet there was something strange and incomprehensible about the unknown, that inspired awe and checked familiarity.

On entering the amphitheatre, new objects of wonder presented themselves. On a level spot in the centre was a company of odd-looking personages playing at nine-pins. They were dressed in quaint outlandish fashion; some wore short doublets[11], others jerkins, with long knives in their belts, and most of them had enormous breeches, of similar style with that of the guide's. Their visages, too, were peculiar; one had a large beard, broad face, and small piggish eyes; the face of another seemed to consist entirely of nose, and was surmounted by a white sugar-loaf hat, set off with a little red cock's tail. They all had beards, of various shapes and colors. There was one who seemed to be the commander. He was a stout old gentleman, with a weather-beaten countenance; he wore a laced doublet, broad belt and hanger[12], high-crowned hat and feather, red stockings, and high-heeled shoes, with roses in them. The whole group reminded Rip of the figures in an old Flemish painting, in the parlor of Dominie Van Schaick, the village parson[13], and which had been brought over from Holland at the time of the settlement.

What seemed particularly odd to Rip was, that though these folks were evidently amusing themselves, yet they maintained the gravest face, the most mysterious silence, and were, withal, the most melancholy party of pleasure he had ever witnessed. Nothing interrupted the stillness of the scene but the noise of the balls, which, whenever they were rolled, echoed along the mountains like rumbling peals of thunder.

As Rip and his companion approached them, they suddenly desisted from their play, and stared at him with such fixed, statue-like gaze, and such strange uncouth, lacklustre countenances, that his heart turned within him, and his knees smote together. His companion now emptied the contents of the keg into large flagons, and made signs to him to wait upon the company. He obeyed with fear and trembling; they quaffed the liquor in profound silence, and then returned to their game.

By degrees Rip's awe and apprehension subsided. He even ventured, when no eye was fixed upon him, to taste the beverage, which he found had much of the flavor of excellent hollands. He was naturally a thirsty soul, and was soon tempted to repeat the draught. One taste provoked another; and he reiterated his visits to the flagon so often that at length his senses were overpowered, his eyes swam in his head, his head gradually declined, and he fell into a deep sleep.

On waking, he found himself on the green knoll whence he had first seen the old man of the glen. He rubbed his eyes—it was a bright sunny morning. The birds were hopping and twittering among the bushes, and the eagle was wheeling aloft, and breasting the pure mountain breeze. "Surely," thought Rip, "I have not slept here all night." He recalled the occurrences before he fell asleep. The strange man with a keg of liquor—the mountain ravine—the wild retreat among the rocks—the woebegone party at nine-pins—the flagon—"ah! That flagon! That wicked flagon!" thought Rip—"what excuse shall I make to Dame Van Winkle?"

He looked round for his gun, but in place of the clean, well-oiled fowling-piece, he found an old firelock lying by him, the barrel incrusted with rust, the lock falling off, and the stock worm-eaten. He now suspected that the grave roysters of the mountain had put a trick upon him, and having dosed him with liquor, had robbed him of his gun. Wolf, too, had disappeared, but he might have strayed away after a squirrel or partridge. He whistled after him and shouted his name, but all in vain; the echoes repeated his whistle and shout, but no dog was to be seen.

He determined to revisit the scene of the last evening's gambol, and if he met with any of the party, to demand his dog and gun. As he rose to walk, he found himself stiff in the joints, and wanting in his usual activity. "These mountain beds do not agree with me," thought Rip, "and if this frolic should lay me up with a fit of the rheumatism, I shall have a blessed time with Dame Van Winkle." With some difficulty he got down into the glen: he found the gully up which he and his companion had ascended the preceding evening; but to his astonishment a mountain stream was now foaming down it, leaping from rock to rock, and filling the glen with babbling murmurs. He, however, made shift to scramble up its sides, working his toilsome way through thickets of birch, sassafras, and witch hazel, and sometimes tripped up or entangled by the wild grape-vines that twisted their coils or tendrils from tree to tree, and spread a kind of network in his path.

At length he reached to where the ravine had opened through the cliffs to the amphitheatre; but no traces of such opening remained. The rocks presented a high impenetrable wall, over which the torrent came tumbling in a sheet of feathery foam, and fell into a broad deep basin, black from the shadows of the surrounding forest. Here, then, poor Rip was brought to a stand. He again called and whistled after his dog; he was only answered by the cawing of a flock of idle crows, sporting high in the air about a dry tree that overhung a sunny precipice; and who, secure in their elevation, seemed to look down and scoff at the poor man's perplexities.

What was to be done? The morning was passing away, and Rip felt famished for want of his breakfast. He grieved to give up his dog and gun; he dreaded to meet his wife; but it would not do to starve among the mountains. He shook his head, shouldered the rusty firelock, and, with a heart full of trouble and anxiety, turned his steps homeward.

As he approached the village he met a number of people, but none whom he knew, which somewhat surprised him, for he had thought himself acquainted with every one in the country round. Their dress, too, was of a different fashion from that to which he was accustomed. They all stared at him with equal marks of surprise, and whenever they cast their eyes upon him, invariably stroked their chins. The constant recurrence of this gesture induced Rip, involuntarily, to do the same, when, to his astonishment, he found his beard had grown a foot long!

He had now entered the skirts of the village. A troop of strange children ran at his heels, hooting after him, and pointing at his gray beard. The dogs, too, not one of which he recognized for an old acquaintance, barked at him as he passed. The very village was altered; it was larger and more populous. There were rows of houses which he had never seen before, and those which had been his familiar haunts had disappeared. Strange names were over the doors—strange faces at the windows—every thing was strange. His mind now misgave him; he began to doubt whether both he and the world around him were not bewitched. Surely this was his native village, which he had left but the day before. There stood the Kaatskill mountains—there ran the silver Hudson at a distance—there was every hill and dale precisely as it had always been—Rip was sorely perplexed—"That flagon last night," thought he, "has addled my poor head sadly!" It was with some difficulty that he found the way to his own house, which he approached with silent awe, expecting every moment to hear the shrill voice of Dame Van Winkle. He found the house gone to decay—the roof fallen in, the windows shattered, and the doors off the hinges. A half-starved dog that looked like Wolf was skulking about it. Rip called him by name, but the cur snarled, showed his teeth, and passed on. This was an unkind cut indeed—"My very dog," sighed poor Rip, "has forgotten me!"

He entered the house, which, to tell the truth, Dame Van Winkle had always kept in neat order. It was empty, forlorn, and apparently abandoned. This desolateness overcame all his connubial fears—he called loudly for his wife and children—the lonely chambers rang for a moment with his voice, and then all again was silence.

He now hurried forth, and hastened to his old resort, the village inn—but it too was gone. A large rickety wooden building stood in its place, with great gaping windows, some of them broken and mended with old hats and petticoats, and over the door was painted, "The Union Hotel, by Jonathan Doolittle." Instead of the great tree that used to shelter the quiet little Dutch inn of yore[14], there now was reared a tall, naked pole, with something on the top that looked like a red night-cap[15], and from it was fluttering a flag, on which was a singular assemblage of stars and stripes—all this was strange and incomprehensible. He recognized on the sign, however, the ruby face of King George, under which he had smoked so many a peaceful pipe; but even this was singularly metamorphosed. The red coat was changed for one of blue and buff[16], a sword was held in the hand instead of a sceptre, the head was decorated with a cocked hat, and underneath was painted in large characters, GENERAL WASHINGTON.

There was, as usual, a crowd of folk about the door, but none that Rip recollected. The very character of the people seemed changed. There was a busy, bustling, disputatious tone about it, instead of the accustomed phlegm and drowsy tranquility. He looked in vain for the sage Nicholas Vedder, with his broad face, double chin, and fair long pipe, uttering clouds of tobacco smoke, instead of idle speeches; or Van Bummel, the schoolmaster, doling forth the contents of an ancient newspaper. In place of these, a lean, bilious-looking fellow, with his pockets full of handbills, was haranguing vehemently about rights of citizens—elections—members of Congress—liberty—Bunker's hill—heroes of seventy-six—and other words, which were a perfect Babylonish jargon[17] to the bewildered Van Winkle.

The appearance of Rip, with his long grizzled beard, his rusty fowling-piece[18], his uncouth dress, and an army of women and children at his heels soon attracted the attention of the tavern politicians. They crowded round him, eying him from head to foot with great curiosity. The orator bustled up to him, and, drawing him partly aside, inquired, "On which side he voted?" Rip stared in vacant stupidity. Another short but busy little fellow pulled him by the arm, and, rising on tiptoe, inquired in his ear, "Whether he was Federal or Democrat[19]?" Rip was equally at a loss to comprehend the question; when a knowing, self-important old gentleman in a sharp cocked hat, made his way through the crowd, putting them to the right and left with his elbows as he passed, and planting himself before Van Winkle, with one arm akimbo, the other resting on his cane, his keen eyes and sharp hat penetrating, as it were, into his very soul, demanded, in an austere tone, "What brought him to the election with a gun on his shoulder, and a mob at his heels, and whether he meant to breed a riot in the village?" "Alas! Gentlemen," cried Rip, somewhat dismayed, "I am a poor quiet man, a native of the place, and a loyal subject of the king, God bless him!"

Here a general shout burst from the bystanders—"A tory! a tory! a spy! a Refugee! hustle him! away with him!" It was with great difficulty that the self-important man in the cocked hat restored order; and, having assumed a tenfold austerity of brow, demanded again of the unknown culprit, what he came there for, and whom he was seeking? The poor man humbly assured him that he meant no harm, but merely came there in search of some of his neighbors, who used to keep about the tavern.

"Well, who are they? Name them."

Rip bethought himself a moment, and inquired, "Where's Nicholas Vedder?"

There was a silence for a little while, when an old man replied, in a thin, piping voice, "Nicholas Vedder! why, he is dead and gone these eighteen years! There was a wooden tombstone in the churchyard that used to tell all about him, but that's rotten and gone too."

"Where's Brom Dutcher?" "Oh, he went off to the army in the beginning of the war; some say he was killed at the storming of Stony Point—others say he was drowned in a squall at the foot of Antony's Nose. I don't know—he never came back again."

"Where's Van Bummel, the schoolmaster?"

"He went off to the wars, too, was a great militia general, and is now in Congress."

Rip's heart died away at hearing of these sad changes in his home and friends, and finding himself thus alone in the world. Every answer puzzled him too, by treating of such enormous lapses of time, and of matters which he could not understand—war—Congress—Stony Point—he had no courage to ask after any more friends, but cried out in despair, "Does nobody here know Rip Van Winkle?"

"Oh, Rip Van Winkle!" exclaimed two or three, "Oh, to be sure! — that's Rip Van Winkle yonder, leaning against the tree."

Rip looked, and beheld a precise counterpart of himself, as he went up the mountain: apparently as lazy, and certainly as ragged. The poor fellow was now completely confounded. He doubted his own identity, and whether he was himself or another man. In the midst of his bewilderment, the man in the cocked hat demanded who he was, and what was his name?

"God knows," exclaimed he, at his wit's end; "I'm not myself—I'm somebody else—that's me yonder—no—that's somebody else got into my shoes—I was myself last night, but I fell asleep on the mountain, and they've changed my gun, and every thing's changed, and I'm changed, and I can't tell what's my name, or who I am!"

The bystanders began now to look at each other, nod, wink significantly, and tap their fingers against their foreheads. There was a whisper, also, about securing the gun, and keeping the old fellow from doing mischief, at the very suggestion of which the self-important man in the cocked hat retired with some precipitation. At this critical moment a fresh, comely woman pressed through the throng to get a peep at the graybearded man. She had a chubby child in her arms, which, frightened at his looks, began to cry. "Hush, Rip," cried she, "hush, you little fool; the old man won't hurt you." The name of the child, the air of the mother, the tone of her voice, all awakened a train of recollections in his mind. "What is your name, my good woman?" asked he.

"Judith Gardenier."

"And your father's name?"

"Ah! poor man, Rip Van Winkle was his name, but it's twenty years since he went away from home with his gun, and never has been heard of since—his dog came home without him; but whether he shot himself, or was carried away by the Indians, nobody can tell. I was then but a little girl."

Rip had but one question more to ask; but he put it with a faltering voice—

"Where's your mother?"

"Oh, she too had died but a short time since; she broke a blood-vessel in a fit of passion at a New England peddler."

There was a drop of comfort, at least, in this intelligence. The honest man could contain himself no longer. He caught his daughter and her child in his arms. "I am your father!" cried he—"Young Rip Van Winkle once—old Rip Van Winkle now! Does nobody know poor Rip Van Winkle?"

All stood amazed, until an old woman, tottering out from among the crowd, put her hand to her brow, and peering under it in his face for a moment, exclaimed, "Sure enough! It is Rip Van Winkle—it is himself! Welcome home again, old neighbor. Why, where have you been these twenty long years?"

Rip's story was soon told, for the whole twenty long years had been to him but as one night. The neighbors stared when they heard it; some were seen to wink at each other, and put their tongues in their cheeks: and the self-important man in the cocked hat, who, when the alarm was over, had returned to the field, screwed down the corners of his mouth, and shook his head—upon which there was a general shaking of the head throughout the assemblage.

It was determined, however, to take the opinion of old Peter Vanderdonk, who was seen slowly advancing up the road. He was a descendant of the historian of that name, who wrote one of the earliest accounts of the province. Peter was the most ancient inhabitant of the village, and well versed in all the wonderful events and traditions of the neighborhood. He recollected Rip at once, and corroborated his story in the most satisfactory manner. He assured the company that it was a fact, handed down from his ancestor the historian, that the Kaatskill mountains had always been haunted by strange beings. That it was affirmed that the great Hendrick Hudson, the first discoverer of the river and country, kept a kind of vigil there every twenty years, with his crew of the Half-moon; being permitted in this way to revisit the scenes of his enterprise, and keep a guardian eye upon the river, and the great city called by his name. That his father had once seen them in their old Dutch dresses playing at nine pins in a hollow of the mountain; and that he himself had heard, one summer afternoon, the sound of their balls, like distant peals of thunder.

To make a long story short, the company broke up, and returned to the more important concerns of the election. Rip's daughter took him home to live with her; she had a snug, well-furnished house, and a stout, cheery farmer for a husband, whom Rip recollected for one of the urchins that used to climb upon his back. As to Rip's son and heir, who was the ditto of himself, seen leaning against the tree, he was employed to work on the farm; but evinced a hereditary disposition to attend to any thing else but his business.

Rip now resumed his old walks and habits; he soon found many of his former cronies, though all rather the worse for the wear and tear of time; and preferred making friends among the rising generation, with whom he soon grew into great favor. Having nothing to do at home, and being arrived at that happy age when a man can be idle with impunity, he took his place once more on the bench at the inn door, and was reverenced as one of the patriarchs of the village, and a chronicle of the old times "before the war." It was some time before he could get into the regular track of gossip, or could be made to comprehend the strange events that had taken place during his torpor. How that there had been a revolutionary war—that the country had thrown off the yoke of old England—and that, instead of being a subject to his Majesty George the Third, he was now a free citizen of the United States. Rip, in fact, was no politician; the changes of states and empires made but little impression on him; but there was one species of despotism under which he had long groaned, and that was—petticoat government. Happily that was at an end; he had got his neck out of the yoke of matrimony, and could go in and out whenever he pleased, without dreading the tyranny of Dame Van Winkle. Whenever her name was mentioned, however, he shook his head, shrugged his shoulders, and cast up his eyes; which might pass either for an expression of resignation to his fate, or joy at his deliverance.

He used to tell his story to every stranger that arrived at Mr. Doolittle's hotel. He was observed, at first, to vary on some points every time he told it, which was, doubtless, owing to his having so recently awaked. It at last settled down precisely to the tale I have related, and not a man, woman, or child in the neighborhood, but knew it by heart. Some always pretended to doubt the reality of it, and insisted that Rip had been out of his head, and that this was one point on which he always remained flighty. The old Dutch inhabitants, however, almost universally gave it full credit. Even to this day they never hear a thunder-storm of a summer afternoon about the Kaatskill, but they say Hendrick Hudson and his crew are at their game of nine pins; and it is a common wish of all hen-pecked husbands in the neighborhood, when life hangs heavy on their hands, that they might have a quieting draught out of Rip Van Winkle's flagon.

NOTE

The foregoing Tale, one would suspect, had been suggested to Mr. Knickerbocker by a little German superstition about the Emperor Frederick der Rothbart, and the Kyppha ser mountain: the subjoined note, however, which he had appended to the tale, shows that it is an absolute fact, narrated with his usual fidelity:

"The story of Rip Van Winkle may seem incredible to many, but nevertheless I give it my full belief, for I know the vicinity of our old Dutch settlements to have been very subject to marvellous events and appearances. Indeed, I have heard many stranger stories than this, in the villages along the Hudson; all of which were too well authenticated to admit of a doubt. I have even talked with Rip Van Winkle myself, who, when I last saw him, was a very venerable old man, and so perfectly rational and consistent on every other point, that I think no conscientious person could refuse to take this into the bargain; nay, I have seen a certificate on the subject taken before a country justice and signed with cross, in the justice's own handwriting. The story, therefore, is beyond the possibility of doubt. D. K."

Notes:

1. Woden: According to Norse myth, the supreme god and creator
2. thylke: "the" or "that"

3. CARTWRIGHT: From the play *The Ordinary* (1651) (III.I.1050—1054), by William Cartwright (1611—1643), an English clergyman, poet and dramatist.

4. Kaatskill maintains: The Catskill Mountains in southeastern New York

5. Peter Stuyvesant: Stuyvesant (1592—1672) served as the last governor of New Netherlands from 1647 to 1664. In 1655 he led the Dutch forces to victory over Swedish colonists at Fort Christina, near what is now Wilmington, Delaware, as described in mock-epic terms in Knickerbocker's *History of New-York*.

6. hen-pecked: A scolding of a husband by his wife after the bed curtains have been drawn.

7. galligaskins: Loose breeches or pants.

8. club of the sages: a committee; "a club of the sages," as Irving describes these men with mild irony

9. pipe: a pouch or knapsack

10. jerkin: a jacket or short coat, generally armless

11. doublets: a close-fitting, commonly elaborate jacket

12. hanger: a short sword, originally hung from the belt

13. parsan: pastor

14. yore: (Middle English) long ago, time long past

15. pole...looked like a red night-cap: A liberty pole and liberty cap, or Phrygian cap worn by slaves freed by the Romans, symbols of the American and French Revolutions.

16. blue and buff: colors of Revolutionary Army uniforms

17. Babylonish jargan: A puzzle; in Genesis II:I—9 the "Confusion of Tongues" occurs at the Tower of Babel (Babel is apparently confused with Babylon.)

18. fowling-piece: a shotgun for killing fowl.

19. Federal or Democrat: Political parties that grew during George Washington's administration: the first conservative, the second liberal.

20. In July 1779 General Anthony Wayne (1745—1796) captured the British fort at Stony Point, on the Hudson River; Antony's Nose is a promontory on the Hudson, near West Point.

21. Adrian Van der Donck (1620?—1655), a Dutchman who wrote a history of New Netherland, published in Amsterdam in 1655 and (in an English translation) in New Netherland in 1656.

22. Henry Hudson (?—1611), an English navigator employed by the Dutch to

explore what is now called the Hudson River; Irving uses a Dutch form of the name Henry. The "great city called by his name" is Hudson, New York, on the East bank of the river.

23. The "superstition" of Frederick Barbarossa, the Holy Roam Emperor Frederick (1123? —1190), asleep at a table in the Kyppha ser Mountain of Germany: when his red beard (the translation of Barbarossa [Latin] and Rothart [German]) circles the table three times, he will awaken and lead Germany to world preeminence.

Questions for Study and Discussion:

1. If you fell asleep today and awakened 20 years from now, what questions would you ask the first person you saw?
2. Do you think the change is necessary or not? Why or why not?
3. What is Rip's attitude to the change and the modern democratic America?
4. What is Irving's attitude?
5. Even though he was a failure as a farmer, Rip Van Winkle was a success as a human being. What were the most praiseworthy qualities that he possessed?
6. Make a list of important published writings by Americans in the first quarter of the nineteenth century. In what ways are Irving's stories unusual? What do they share with other writings?
7. When Rip Van Winkle sleeps for twenty years, he sleeps through the American Revolution and awakens into an independent nation. Examine life in Rip's village before and after his long sleep, and in colonies like New York just before and just after the Revolution. How much effect on daily life did this large political upheaval have?

James Fenimore Cooper (1789—1851)

Life and Major Works

Generally acclaimed as the first major American novelist, James Fenimore Cooper (1789-1851) made enormous contribution to the emergence and development of truly national literature. Compared with his contemporary Washington Irving (1783-1859), another internationally

James Cooper

known forerunner in the era of early romanticism, Cooper won a distinction for his depiction of frontier life and pioneer adventures. His achievements in the novels, thematically and stylistically, have been a quest for the meaning of America, which helped to introduce western tradition into American literature. In his thirty-two years (1820-1851) of authorship, he wrote over thirty novels, the best of which are the Leather-stocking series. Apart from these, his bold attempt at social criticism in the form of prefaces, articles and other non-fictional works prove him a vigorous explorer of American nationhood.

Cooper's life experiences undoubtedly exert significant influence on his literary career. Examples can be shown in the creation of three major types of novels: historical novels, frontier adventures and sea tales. To well appreciate Cooper's works, it is better to trace back to what gives him such creative power of writing. On September 15, 1789, Cooper was born into a wealthy land-holding family of Burlington, New Jersey. In 1790 his family moved to Lake Otsego in upstate New York, where Cooper's father William Cooper had founded a settlement called Cooperstown. Not only the founder but also a Federalist judge there, William Cooper also served in the Congress for two terms. It was he who had instilled political and social beliefs in his son and cultivated his initial interest in democratic ideals. Young cooper grew up on the shores of beautiful Otsego Lake and spent his childhood in the wooded hills. Therefore, he developed a love of nature which later pervaded his major novels. It is safe to say that "the wilderness was his earliest and most potent teacher." Although at that time there were few backwoods settlers left and even fewer Indians, Cooper was deeply attracted by the local legends about American Indians. Those days in a frontier town provided adequate background for his first Leather-stocking tale *The Pioneers* (1823). At thirteen after boarding school in Albany, Cooper was admitted to Yale College in New Haven, Connecticut where he acquired his lifelong distaste for New Englanders. Before he read extensively about Shakespeare and other 18th century poets, he was expelled two years later due to improper behavior. In his early 20s, he began to be connected with sea. He first worked as a sailor on a merchant ship and then joined the United States Navy as midshipman. During his five-year service on the seas, Cooper used to think seriously of himself as a writer, which initiated his preference to sea tales. After the death of his father, he resigned from the Navy, went back to his land and got married to Susan Augusta De Lancey of a rich Loyalist family. With his father's vast fortune, Cooper was supposed to enjoy a life of comfort and even luxury. However, from 1811 till 1814 he failed to manage the family business and became bogged down in heavy debts. As a result of the division of his family estate, he had to settle on his wife's land. Unable to resolve financial and personal problems, Cooper shifted his life towards the pursuit of literary success.

Not until he reached 31 did Cooper start to try his hand at writing. Interestingly, an accident made him a writer. Such a critical moment took place when he finished reading a newly published English novel and exclaimed he could write a better story than that himself. With his wife's encouragement and support, Cooper persisted in his declaration and produced his first novel *Precaution* (1820) which described English morals and manners under the influence of Jane Austen. Although it was severely attacked by the critics, Cooper continued to search for what to write. As Cooper wrote in *A Letter to His Countryman* (1834), he felt "ashamed to have fallen into the tract of imitation", so he endeavored to produce a work that should be "purely American, and of which love of country should be the theme." What followed was his second novel, *The Spy: A Tale of Neutral Ground* in 1821. Based on the historical romance of Sir Walter Scott and engaged in a series of themes about the American Revolution, it proved to be an immense commercial success. The well-received novel not only established Cooper as an amazing new force in American literary circle but also made it possible to relate literature with national history, which aroused worldwide response. Along with Washington Irving's *The Sketch Book* (1820) and William Cullen Bryant's *Poems* (1821), Cooper's *The Spy* was considered as a proof that American culture had finally begun to create a "worthwhile democratic art". Inspired by Sir Walter Scott's major works, Cooper attempted to draw stereotypes of light and dark, good and evil, and dichotomize the female into the fair and pure and the dark and tainted. The result of such initial effort was his next novel *The Pioneers* (1823), first of his best known Leather-stocking tales and probably the first true romance of the frontier in American literature. The story took place in the Otsego Lake region during the decade after the Revolutionary War, where Cooper's childhood memories and love of nature found a full play. Devoted to the depiction of a mythical West that transcended the reality of early pioneer life, Cooper completed other four novels after twenty years. In the order of publication, they are *The Last of the Mohicans* (1826), *The Prairie* (1827), *The Pathfinder* (1840) and *The Deerslayer* (1841). But considering the integrity of the plot, so-called five-novel

Leather-stocking series should be read in such a sequence, that is, *The Deerslayer* (1841), *The Last of the Mohicans* (1826), *The Pathfinder* (1840), *The Pioneers* (1823) and *The Prairie* (1827). Cooper's remarkable creative energy went on to explode when his first and best sea tale *The Pilot* was issued in 1824. With the Revolutionary War as the backdrop, Cooper made up a complicated plot around love affairs, schemes and death. It best illustrated his precaution with mysterious life on the ocean. Starting from this one, he wrote eleven more sea adventures including *The Red Rover* (1827), *The Wing-and-Wing* (1842), *The Two Admirals* (1842), *Afloat and Ashore* (1844), *Miles Wallingford* (1844), and *The Sea Lions* (1849). Most of them put more stress on the details of seamanship than the mystery of the sea. Due respect was given to *The Pilot* (1824). Herman Melville (1819—1891) and Joseph Conrad (1857—1924), two great literary masters, did learn a lot from this novel where Cooper combined technical details with fiction to make a patriotic appeal. Instant success of these three types of novels, historical novels represented by *The Spy*, frontier adventures represented by *The Pioneers* and sea tales represented by *The Pilot*, cemented Cooper's position as the first genuinely American writer. His fame soon spread across the world, especially Europe.

However, it is not the same with Cooper's career as a social commentator who participated actively in the political and intellectual life of his nation. He used to work hard on the introduction of his interpretation of America to Europeans during his seven-year travel in Europe. From 1826 to 1833 when he served as the US consul at Lyons, France, his books about democracy, politics, and society were not widely applauded. Although the essay *Notions of the Americans* (1828), as an exception, fascinatingly evaluated his native land and defended it against the attacks of European travelers, Cooper adopted conservative and aristocratic perspectives, which added to strong dislike of him among readers at home and abroad. By means of critical writings and travel books, his intention to eliminate many misconceptions about America and educate Americans not to imitate from European customs went aborted even after he returned to homeland. At First, *A Letter to His Countrymen* (1834), a bitter attack on American cultural provincialism, immediately made him "a false aristocrat poisoned by European influences and a villain who sought to undermine democracy" in the eyes of local newspapers. Then controversies arose over the use of private property distanced himself from general public. For a long time, he got involved in an array of lawsuits meant to uphold his own political and social principles, which invited more negative criticism on him. This greatly weakened his reputation as a literary giant. Towards the last decades of his life, even if he diligently studied naval history and wrote the first trilogy (*Satanstoe, The Chainbearer, and The Redskins*, 1845—1846) in American fiction, he earned less income as well as less respect. Prior to his death, Cooper's hard work did not pay off, in other words, his farewell to literary career was not that perfect. With great disappointment and sadness, he passed away on September 14, 1851 at his home. He lies buried in the family plot in the Christ Episcopal Churchyard in Cooperstown.

Fairly speaking, Cooper has created many "first" on the American literary scene as mentioned above. Among them stand out the five-novel Leather-stocking series. These frontier adventures display the natural beauty of virgin lands, illustrate the profound changes of pioneer life over a span of sixty years and portray the clash that occurred "between the frontier wilderness and the encroaching civilization." Conflicts over possession of the landscape, the ideals of aristocracy and privilege and the democratic ideals of equality and natural rights involved various characters such as Native Americans, British loyalists, American patriots, roaming hunters, and forest-clearing farmers. All five tales succeeds brilliantly as thoroughly American fictions, not to say the invention of the Natty Bumppo, an essential archetypal Western hero. Wearing long deerskin leggings all the time, Natty is also called Leather-stocking, Deerslayer, Hawkeye, Long Rifle, Pathfinder and the Trapper. As an archetypal character originated from a legendary figure Daniel Boone, Natty Bumppo represents "the idea of the natural man in Rousseau's primitivism and the idealized American manhood". Typical of 18th Century frontiersman, he lives a virtuous and free life and stays "close to nature, while the settlers bring 'civilization' that destroys the wilderness". In him many human virtues could be found like innocence, simplicity, honesty, generosity and a perfect sense of good and evil and right and wrong. Through the adventures of this central character in the Leather-stocking tales, Cooper presented the good and pure wildness where there is freedom not tainted and fettered by any forms of human institutions. While there is much disagreement with respect to Cooper's artistic talents, few could find fault with his lamentations for an unspoiled wilderness.

To conclude, a great many audacious innovations throughout Cooper's writing career have evoked admiration as well as despise. He was posthumously more accomplished and respected abroad rather than at home. On one hand, European authors like William Makepeace Thackeray and D. H. Lawrence have held him in high regard. Generally, they have held a favorable view of his writing art. Thackeray ranked Cooper's heroes with those created by Walter Scott and said "the artist [Cooper] has deserved well of his country who devised them". In D. H. Lawrence's comments, the Leather-stocking series embodies "a decrescendo of reality and a crescendo of beauty". In addition, Balzac and Victor Hugo both admired him with discrimination. One the other hand, Americans novelists and critics seem to be more critical. The most memorable and vicious criticism comes from Mark Twain who wrote an amusing essay *Fenimore Cooper's Literary Offences* (1895) to ridicule Cooper's use of syntax, dialogue, plot, narrative pace and character development. His dreadful style, wooden characterization and unauthentic use of language become the targets of sardonic attack. Some even questioned whether the Native Americans in Cooper's works were realistic since the writer did not have much interaction with Indians, and those which he described were unlike any that could be found. James Russell Lowell, a contemporary critic, also severely assessed his depiction of women characters in a poetic way: "...the women he draws from one model don't vary. All sappy as maples and flat as a prairie." Although he is cited as a powerful but clumsy writer from the perspective of modern literature, Cooper's achievements, namely, the natural surroundings, his sense of American history, "an insatiable appetite for knowledge and a strong desire to share what he knew with his readers" , should be remembered as a brand new page in American culture and her literary development.

Brief Introduction and Appreciation

Of the five-novel Leather-stocking series starring Natty Bumppo, *The Deerslayer* was the last one written but the first chapter of the protagonist's life. Full of vivid depiction of the wilderness on the western frontier, an important factor in James Fenimore Cooper's writings, this novel easily arouses readers' curiosity about Natty's exciting excursions and violent adventures and keeps our interest in how the young man manages to face up to a variety of difficulties and challenges on the way and grows into an authentic frontier hero. Such a tradition is followed by many adventure novelists in later generations. Considered to be one of the satisfactory works by the author himself, it has not always been favorably reviewed by social and literary critics. As is known to all, the severest classic criticism of his style and technical skills comes from Mark Twain in the 19th century who listed a bunch of rules Cooper had violated in the novel. What's more, whether Cooper's historical romances are truthful has remained heatedly discussed among serious writers and readers up till now. As a result of all these negative interpretations of Cooper, the nation's first popular author, his leather-stocking tales used to be reduced to the status of elementary school texts by early 20th century and seem to many a relic of the past. Despite the mixed reception of the novel, some of the most distinguished American cultural analysts bring Cooper back into focus. In *Fenimore Cooper: The Critical Heritage* (1997) George Dekker's and John P. McWilliams quoted an unsigned review in *the New-York Mirror* that put forward an entirely positive view of the novel: "He [Cooper] is the most original thinker of any of our American novelists unrivalled in descriptive powers, and unapproached in the heartiness of his patriotic feelings." Robert Emmet Long also maintains that Cooper is perhaps the first novelist to "demonstrate...that native materials could inspire significant imaginative writing," which attaches great importance to the introduction of historical facts to his works. Through different ways of interaction between the white men, Natty included, and the American Indians on virgin lands, Cooper has achieved his aim to capture the mood, the milieu and the mind during the early colonization period. His deep concern with the social ethics, class division and other political and cultural issues related to national development is clearly shown by a fantastic web in *The Deerslayer* where the writer blends setting, theme, plot, and characters in his own manner.

The story of the novel is attractively simple and gracefully woven, especially to those interested in American history. It takes place almost exclusively in the area of a lake called "Glimmerglass" in the New York colonies near the Hudson River. Although the novel was completed in 1840 when the conquest of the west reached its heyday, Cooper looked back to the astonishing advance of civilization during the French and Indian wars of the 1740s prior to the Revolutionary period. While others commonly acclaimed the westward movement as the substitution of the lesser, barbarous culture with the superior civilization of the European settlers, he responded differently in *The Deerslayer*. With respect to the relationship between the two sides, he poured out his democratic conviction that all men were created equal and alike via the voice of Natty. By making a distinction of the red and white "gifts" in the excerpted chapter, he made clear the significance of racial purity and equality. Furthermore, he investigated what it meant to go against the moral principles, for example, Tom Hutter, one who desired to kill and scalp as many Native Americans, was in turn mortally wounded and scalped. In so doing, Cooper presented a seemingly ideal social order. However, inconsistencies exist if the author's social status is taken into account. As a son of an upper-class eighteenth-century landowner, Cooper accepted the stratification in society and government, a belief that everything had its "place"; and revealed his inclination towards the hereditary aristocracy. In contrast to Christianized white "gifts", red "gifts" are inherently vengeful and brutal. Another instance is that Natty's loyalty to his Mohican friend Chingachgook partly results from Delaware Indians' alliance with the British in the colonial wars. Little wonder that some observer says, "[the novel's] rich romantic, mythic, and pastoral elements notwithstanding, is, in a very substantial way, about social hierarchy and class." D.H. Lawrence, in *Studies in Classic American Literature* (1991), even explained the myth of Leather-stocking embodied the "wish fulfillment" of the white men who wanted to kill Indians. The same is with Cooper's portrayal of American Indians in the image of the noble savage. It is of great necessity to see how he fashioned into Natty Bumppo's characterization such an element, which makes the irresolvable problem of race in America melt into the background and remain obscured from our view.

In the "Preface to the Leather-stocking Tales", Cooper wrote that Natty was "too much a man proud of his origin to sink into the condition of the wild Indians, and too much a man of the woods not to imbibe as much as was at all desirable, from his friends and companion." His duality is fully developed in *The Deerslayer*. Of white extraction but born of the frontier, Natty is inexperienced and unprepared in many ways for what he encounters in his expeditions. But over the course of his adventures, he gradually feels the need to strike a balance of the morals of his civilized inheritance and a strong impulse to run away from the corrupt and greedy civilization. To the American Indians he is both their friend and foe. On one hand, he shows his sympathy of the unfair treatment of the natives. Unlike other frontiersmen and settlers such as Henry March ("Hurry Harry") and Tom Hutter who are crazy about taking scalps, Natty insists on his natural philosophy that every creature should follow their respective "gifts" and becomes a spokesman of Cooper's idea of democracy and justice. In addition, he learns a lot from the native virtues and woodsmanship, which contributes to his superhuman courage, unequaled martial skills, and abundant knowledge of the wilderness. On the other hand, he adheres to his Christian superiority with them. He helps push the Indians off their land when he protects new European settlers as they travel into the lawless frontier. In such a dilemma, Natty, though the first American hero, is left dangling between social and cultural values and principles.

It is noteworthy that another feature of Cooper's literary talent is his admirable depiction of adventures and vicissitudes "on the waters, and about the shore, of a little inland lake in the heart of the howling wilderness." The western frontier becomes a vehicle to romanticize the human conflicts and the quest of individual ideals. Historian Francis Parkman's review centers on Cooper's landscape descriptions, as a reflection of a national identity. To Parkman, the land is the source of all that is American, because "the vigorous life of the nation springs from the deep rich soil at the bottom of society." This is closely associated with Cooper's early memories of his frontier hometown. If the landscape descriptions do not add to his achievements, Cooper's writing style is surely lackluster. During the period of early romanticism, with awakening consciousness to create an independent America, Cooper lays more stress on the thematic significance than on literary craftsmanship. Literature, in his eye, is simply a medium for what one has to say. Due to his casual attitude towards style, he met with strong disapproval after his death. Mark Twain called *The Deerslayer* a "literary delirium tremens." He thought of Cooper as a bad observer, as he wrote "Cooper's eye was splendidly inaccurate. He seldom saw anything correctly. He saw nearly all things as through a glass eye, darkly. Of course a man who cannot see the commonest little every-day matters accurately is working at a disadvantage when he is constructing a situation." The dialog in the novel is "a tortuous blend of stilted literary English and wholly imaginary frontier dialect." It seems no one can successfully make Cooper's dialog sound like real speech. Even though its dialog may sometimes be unreadable, we will not be kept from the opportunity to enjoy the fine descriptions and vigorous sketches of characters in the novel and admire Cooper's penetration into human nature with genuine American feeling.

Selected Reading

The Deerslayer[1]
Chapter VII

When about a hundred yards from the shore, Deerslayer rose in the canoe, gave three or four vigorous strokes with the paddle, sufficient of themselves to impel the bark to land, and then quickly laying aside the instrument of labour, he seized that of war. He was in the very act of raising the rifle, when a sharp report was followed by the buzz of a bullet that passed so near his body, as to cause him involuntarily to start. The next instant Deerslayer staggered, and fell his whole length in the bottom of the canoe. A yell—it came from a single voice—followed, and an Indian leaped from the bushes upon the open area of the point, bounding towards the canoe. This was the moment the young man desired. He rose on the instant, and levelled his own rifle at his uncovered foe; but his finger hesitated about pulling the trigger on one whom he held at such a disadvantage. This little delay, probably, saved the life of the Indian, who bounded back into the cover as swiftly as he had broken out of it. In the meantime Deerslayer had been swiftly approaching the land, and his own canoe reached the point just as his enemy disappeared. As its movements had not been directed, it touched the shore a few yards from the other boat[2]; and though the rifle of his foe had to be loaded, there was not time to secure his prize, and to carry it beyond danger, before he would be exposed to another shot. Under the circumstances, therefore, he did not pause an instant, but dashed into the woods and sought a cover.

On the immediate point there was a small open area, partly in native grass, and partly beach, but a dense fringe of bushes lined its upper side. This narrow belt of dwarf vegetation passed, one issued immediately into the high and gloomy vaults of the forest. The land was tolerably level for a few hundred feet, and then it rose precipitously in a mountainside. The trees were tall, large, and so free from underbrush, that they resembled vast columns, irregularly scattered, up-holding a dome of leaves. Although they stood tolerably close together, for their ages and size, the eye could penetrate to considerable distances; and bodies of men, even, might have engaged beneath their cover, with concert and intelligence.

Deerslayer knew that his adversary must be employed in reloading, unless he had fled. The former proved to be the case, for the young man had no sooner placed himself behind a tree, than he caught a glimpse of the arm of the Indian, his body being concealed by an oak, in the very act of forcing the leathered bullet home. Nothing would have been easier than to spring forward, and decide the affair by a close assault on his unprepared foe; but every feeling of Deerslayer revolted at such a step, although his own life had just been attempted from a cover. He was yet unpractised in the ruthless expedients of savage warfare, of which he knew nothing except by tradition and theory, and it struck him as an unfair advantage to assail an unarmed foe. His colour had heightened, his eye frowned, his lips were compressed, and all his energies were collected and ready; but, instead of advancing to fire, he dropped his rifle to the usual position of a sportsman in readiness to catch his aim, and muttered to himself, unconscious that he was speaking—

"No, no—that may be red-skin warfare, but it's not a Christian's gifts. Let the miscreant charge, and then we'll take it out like men; for the canoe he *must* not, and *shall* not have. No, no; let him have time to load, and God will take care of the right!"

All this time the Indian had been so intent on his own movements, that he was even ignorant that his enemy was in the wood. His only apprehension was, that the canoe would be recovered and carried away, before he might be in readiness to prevent it. He had sought the cover from habit, but was within a few feet of the fringe of bushes, and could be at the margin of the forest, in readiness to fire, in a moment. The distance between him and his enemy was about fifty yards, and the trees were so arranged by nature that the line of sight was not interrupted, except by the particular trees behind which each party stood.

His rifle was no sooner loaded, than the savage glanced around him, and advanced incautiously as regarded the real, but stealthily as respected the fancied position of his enemy, until he was fairly exposed. Then Deerslayer stepped from behind his own cover, and hailed him.

"This-a-way, red-skin; this-a-way, if you're looking for me," he called out. "I'm young in war, but not so young as to stand on an open beach to be shot down like an owl, by day-light. It rests on yourself whether it's peace, or war, atween us; for my gifts are white gifts[3], and I'm not one of them that thinks it valiant to slay human mortals, singly, in the woods."

The savage was a good deal startled by this sudden discovery of the danger he ran. He had a little knowledge of English, however, and caught the drift of the other's meaning. He was also too well schooled to betray alarm, but, dropping the butt of his rifle to the earth, with an air of confidence, he made a gesture of lofty courtesy. All this was done with the ease and self-possession of one accustomed to consider no man his superior. In the midst of this consummate acting, however, the volcano that raged within caused his eyes to glare, and his nostrils to dilate, like those of some wild beast that is suddenly prevented from taking the fatal leap.

"Two canoes," he said, in the deep guttural tones of his race, holding up the number of fingers he mentioned, by way of preventing mistakes; "one for you—one for me."

"No, no, Mingo[4], that will never do. You own neither; and neither shall you have, as long as I can prevent it. I know it's war atween your people and mine, but that's no reason why human mortals should slay each other, like savage creature's that meet in the woods; go your way, then, and leave me to go mine. The world is large enough for us both; and when we meet fairly in battle, why, the Lord will order the fate of each of us."

"Good!" exclaimed the Indian; "my brother missionary —great talk; all about Manitou[5]."

"Not so—not so, warrior. I'm not good enough for the Moravians[6], and am too good for most of the other vagabonds that preach about in the woods. No, no, I'm only a hunter, as yet, though afore the peace is made, 'tis like enough there'll be occasion to strike a blow at some of your people. Still, I wish it to be done in fair fight, and not in a quarrel about the ownership of a miserable canoe."

"Good! My brother very young—but he very wise. Little warrior—great talker. Chief, sometimes, in council."

"I don't know this, nor do I say it, Indian," returned Deerslayer, coloring a little at the ill-concealed sarcasm of the other's manner; "I look forward to a life in the woods, and I only hope it may be a peaceable one. All young men must go on the war-path, when there's occasion, but war isn't needfully massacre. I've seen enough of the last, this very night, to know that Providence frowns on it; and I now invite you to go your own way, while I go mine; and hope that we may part fri'nds."

"Good! My brother has two scalp — grey hair under t'other. Old wisdom—young tongue."

Here the savage advanced with confidence, his hand extended, his face smiling, and his whole bearing denoting amity and respect. Deerslayer met his offered friendship in a proper spirit, and they shook hands cordially, each endeavoring to assure the other of his sincerity and desire to be at peace.

"All have his own," said the Indian; "my canoe, mine; your canoe, your'n. Go look; if your'n, you keep; if mine, I keep."

"That's just, red-skin; though you must be wrong in thinking the canoe your property. However, seein' is believin', and we'll go down to the shore, where you may look with your own eyes; for it's likely you'll object to trustin' altogether to mine."

The Indian uttered his favorite exclamation of "good!" and then they walked, side by side, towards the shore. There was no apparent distrust in the manner of either, the Indian moving in advance, as if he wished to show his companion that he did not fear turning his back to him. As they reached the open ground, the former pointed towards Deerslayer's boat, and said emphatically—"No mine—pale-face canoe. *This* red-man's. No want other man's canoe—want his own."

"You're wrong, red-skin, you're altogether wrong. This canoe was left in old Hutter's[7] keeping, and is his'n, according to all law, red or white, till its owner comes to claim it. Here's the seats and the stitching of the bark to speak for themselves. No man ever know'd an Indian to turn off such work."

"Good! My brother little old—big wisdom. Indian no make him. White man's work."

"I'm glad you think so, for holding out to the contrary might have made ill blood atween us; every one having a right to take possession of his own. I'll just shove the canoe out of reach of dispute at once, as the quickest way of settling difficulties."

While Deerslayer was speaking, he put a foot against the end of the light boat, and giving a vigorous shove, he sent it out into the lake a hundred feet or more, where, taking the true current, it would necessarily float past the point, and be in no further danger of coming ashore. The savage started at this ready and decided expedient, and his companion saw that he cast a hurried and fierce glance at his own canoe, or that which contained the paddles. The change of manner, however, was but momentary, and then the Iroquois resumed his air of friendliness, and a smile of satisfaction.

"Good!" he repeated, with stronger emphasis than ever. "Young head, old mind. Know how to settle quarrel. Farewell, brother. He go to house in water—muskrat house—Indian go to camp; tell chiefs no find canoe."

Deerslayer was not sorry to hear this proposal, for he felt anxious to join the females, and he took the offered hand of the Indian very willingly. The parting words were friendly; and, while the red-man walked calmly towards the wood, with the rifle in the hollow of his arm, without once looking back in uneasiness or distrust, the white man moved towards the remaining canoe, carrying his piece in the same pacific manner, it is true, but keeping his eyes fastened on the movements of the other. This distrust, however, seemed to be altogether uncalled for, and, as if ashamed to have entertained it, the young man averted his look, and stepped carelessly up to his boat. Here he began to push the canoe from the shore, and to make his other preparations for departing. He might have been thus employed a minute, when, happening to turn his face towards the land, his quick and certain eye told him, at a glance, the imminent jeopardy in which his life was placed. The black, ferocious eyes of the savage were glancing on him, like those of the crouching tiger, through a small opening in the bushes, and the muzzle of his rifle seemed already to be opening in a line with his own body.

Then, indeed, the long practice of Deerslayer, as a hunter, did him good service. Accustomed to fire with the deer on the bound, and often when the precise position of the animal's body had in a manner to be guessed at, he used the same expedients here. To cock and poise his rifle were the acts of a single moment, and a single motion; then, aiming almost without sighting, he fired into the bushes where he knew a body ought to be, in order to sustain the appalling countenance, which alone was visible. There was not time to raise the piece any higher, or to take a more deliberate aim. So rapid were his movements, that both parties discharged their pieces at the same instant, the concussions mingling in one report. The mountains, indeed, gave back but a single echo. Deerslayer dropped his piece, and stood, with head erect, steady as one of the pines in the calm of a June morning, watching the result; while the savage gave the yell that has become historical for its appalling influence, leaped through the bushes, and came bounding across the open ground, flourishing a tomahawk. Still Deerslayer moved not, but stood with his unloaded rifle fallen against his shoulders, while, with a hunter's habits, his hands were mechanically feeling for the powder-horn and charger. When about forty feet from his enemy, the savage hurled his keen weapon; but it was with an eye so vacant, and a hand so unsteady and feeble, that the young man caught it by the handle, as it was flying past him. At that instant the Indian staggered and fell his whole length on the ground.

"I know'd it—I know'd it!" exclaimed Deerslayer, who was already preparing to force a fresh bullet into his rifle; "I know'd it must come to this, as soon as I had got the range from the creatue's eyes. A man sights suddenly, and fires quick when his own life's in danger; yes, I know'd it would come to this. I was about the hundredth part of a second too quick for him, or it might have been bad for me! The riptyle's bullet has just grazed my side—but, say what you will, for or ag'in em, a red-skin is by no means as sartain with powder and ball as a white man. Their gifts don't seem to lie that a way. Even Chingachgook[8], great as he is in other matters, isn't downright deadly with the rifle."

By this time the piece was reloaded, and Deerslayer, after tossing the tomahawk into the canoe, advanced to his victim, and stood over him, leaning on his rifle, in melancholy attention. It was the first instance in which he had seen a man fall in battle—it was the first fellow-creature against whom he had ever seriously raised his own hand. The sensations were novel; and regret, with the freshness of our better feelings, mingled with his triumph. The Indian was not dead, though shot directly through the body. He lay on his back motionless, but his eyes, now full of consciousness, watched each action of his victor—as the fallen bird regards the fowler—jealous of every movement. The man probably expected the fatal blow, which was to precede the loss of his scalp; or, perhaps he anticipated that this latter act of cruelty would precede his death. Deerslayer read his thoughts; and he found a melancholy satisfaction in relieving the apprehensions of the helpless savage.

"No, no, red-skin," he said; "you've nothing more to fear from me. I am of a Christian stock, and scalping is not of my gifts. I'll just make sartain of your rifle, and then come back and do you what service I can. Though here I can't stay much longer, as the crack of three rifles will be apt to bring some of your devils down upon me."

The close of this was said in a sort of a soliloquy, as the young man went in quest of the fallen rifle. The piece was found where its owner had dropped it, and was immediately put into the canoe. Laying his own rifle at its side, Deerslayer then returned and stood over the Indian again.

"All inmity atween you and me's at an ind, red-skin," he said; "and you may set your heart at rest, on the score of the scalp, or any further injury. My gifts are white, as I've told you; and I hope my conduct will be white also!"

Could looks have conveyed all they meant, it is probable Deerslayer's innocent vanity, on the subject of colour, would have been rebuked a little; but he comprehended the gratitude that was expressed in the eyes of the dying savage, without in the least detecting the bitter sarcasm that struggled with the better feeling.

"Water!" ejaculated the thirsty and unfortunate creature; "give poor Indian water."

"Ay, water you shall have, if you drink the lake dry. I'll just carry you down to it, that you may take your fill. This is the way, they tell me, with all wounded people— water is their greatest comfort and delight."

So saying, Deerslayer raised the Indian in his arms, and carried him to the lake. Here he first helped him to take an attitude in which he could appease his burning thirst; after which he seated himself on a stone, and took the head of his wounded adversary in his own lap, and endeavored to soothe his anguish, in the best manner he could.

*   *   *

...With the high, innate courtesy that so often distinguishes the Indian warrior, before he becomes corrupted by too much intercourse with the worst class of the white men, he endeavored to express his thankfulness for the other's good intentions, and to let him understand that they were appreciated.

"Good!" he repeated, for this was an English word much used by the savages—"good—young head; young *heart*, too. *Old* heart tough; no shed tear. Hear Indian when he die, and no want to lie—what he call him?"

"Deerslayer is the name I bear now, though the Delawares[9] have said that when I get back from this war-path, I shall have a more manly title, provided I can 'arn one."

"That good name for boy—poor name for warrior. He get better quick. No fear *there*"—the savage had strength sufficient, under the strong excitement he felt, to raise a hand and tap the young man on his breast—"eye sartain—finger lightening—aim, death—great warrior, soon. No Deerslayer—Hawkeye—Hawkeye—Hawkeye. Shake hand."

Deerslayer—or Hawkeye, as the youth was then first named, for in after years he bore the appellation throughout all that region—Deerslayer took the hand of the savage, whose last breath was drawn in that attitude, gazing in admiration at the countenance of a stranger, who had shown so much readiness, skill and firmness, in a scene that was equally trying and novel....

Notes:

1. Deerslayer: Deerslayer is guiding his canoe across Lake Glimmerglass (Lake Otsego, near what is now Cooperstown, New York). Although the novel is set in the mid-1750s, Cooper manages to suggest a pristine locale, "a world by itself."
2. other boat: This "other boat" belongs to Deerslayer's acquaintance.
3. white gifts: Throughout the five Leather-Stocking novels Natty Bumppo distinguishes between red and white "gifts" or codes of ethics and of warfare. (White codes

are assumed to be Christian.) Thus, a Native American scalp a conquered foe but a white man may not.

4. Mingo: an Iroquois or Sioux brave

5. Manitou: Among various native tribes, an august power or deity that controls the forces of nature, synonymous with "God."

6. Moravians: A Protestant sect of missionaries who preached to Native Americans; Natty Bumpoo learned Christian principles upon them.

7. Old Hutter's: The houseboat of Floating Tom Hutter, a muskrat trapper who lives with his daughters, Hetty and Judith, in the middle of the lake.

8. Chingachgook: Natty Bumppo's lifelong companion, a Mohican chief; he dies at an advanced age in *The Pioneers* (1823).

9. Delawares: The Delaware Indians fought with the British in the colonial wars, the Iroquois with the French. The Mohicans were part of the large Delaware nation.

Questions for Study and Discussion:

1. Why does Cooper choose the West frontier as the setting for most of his novels?

2. How do Cooper's writings about the west reflect the romantic tradition?

3. Why is it interesting that some of his characters are Native Americans and also heroic?

4. Where do we see evidence of his intelligence and wisdom?

5. What seems to be Natty's religious affiliations or beliefs?

6. Is Deerslayer too good to be true? Cooper wrote that he had wanted to show some of Deerslayer's weaknesses so as to present "a reasonable picture of human nature, without offering a 'monster of goodness.'" Did he succeed? What weaknesses does Deerslayer exhibit, and how does he overcome them?

7. Who were the Moravians? Since Deerslayer was raised by Moravians, what would he have learned from them?

William Cullen Bryant (1794—1878)

Life and Major Works

William Cullen Bryant was a poet, editor and lawyer. He was born on November 3, 1794, in Cummington, Massachusetts. His father Peter Bryant is a doctor and later a state legislator; his mother Sarah Snell Bryant was a daughter of one of the first settlers. She was a person of high morals, and had great influence on William Bryant's outlook. Bryant exhibited extraordinary genius at a young age and was soon considered a child prodigy. He

William Bryant

published his first poem at 10, and his first book *Embargo*, a political satire against president Jefferson and his party at 13. Later, he was sent to his uncle, the Reverend Dr. Snell, for the study of Latin. In 1810 Bryant entered Williams College, but stayed there for only one year, finding the classes unhelpful for his literary development. At the age of 21, he was admitted into the Bar Association and started his practice.

Bryant's most famous poem "Thanatopsis" was published in 1817 in the *North American Review*. It is said the poem was submitted by Bryant's father without the writer's notice. As soon as the poem arrived at the editors', one of them was deeply impressed and exclaimed "that was never written on this side of the water" (Christina Goforth, cited Brown). Inspired by the publication of the poem together with several other pieces, Bryant offered to write some prose for the magazine and composed some literary criticism to attack the chauvinism among the Americans.

William Bryant married Fanny Fairchild in 1821 and soon was invited to address the Phi Beta Kappa Society of Harvard College at its commencement. His poem was well received and with the encouragement of his friends, he put the poem in print. As a result, we have the poem "The Ages", which is followed by "To a Waterfowl", "Inscription for the Entrance to a Wood", "The Yellow Violet", "Song", "Green River", to name just a few. According to Bradley, the publication of these poems "marks the birth of American poetry".

After ten years practice in law, Bryant decided to throw himself exclusively to literature. He took the position of associate editor of the *New York Evening Post* in

1826. By writing to this paper during that period, Bryant, as a writer and an editor, exercised great influence on shaping the public opinion on civic and political questions of his day. In 1831, Bryant's collection of works, entitled *Poems*, came into being. In the following year, with the help of Washington Irving, an expanded version was published in Britain, which established his fame on both sides of the ocean. In 1834, Bryant took a trip to Europe, and recorded his experiences in *Letters of a Traveler*, which was published in 1850. The publication of *Thirty Poems* in 1864 brought him no applaud except that from Emerson. The death of his wife in 1866 left him in great sorrow, but Bryant still worked hard in literature. He devoted his last decade to the translation of the *Iliad* and the *Odyssey*. Bryant died in 1878 of an accidental fall suffered after participating in a Central Park ceremony.

William Cullen Bryant was remembered as a poet. He defined the character and tone of poetry in America during the early 19th century both in his verse and criticism. Bryant was considered as the first American to sing native birds and American natural beauty rather than the skylark and the landscape of England. (Christina Goforth, cited Brown) He was sometimes called "American Wordsworth", and "looked to nature and the American landscape for evidence of the divine". As Wortham sees, "Few American poets have excelled Bryant in his description of nature". And Bryant managed to distinguish himself as a forerunner of American poetry and "the first American writer of verse" to draw international attention. His poems are "stylish and benign", and meanwhile, as is pointed out, in the want of "fire".

Brief Introduction and Appreciation

The title "Thanatposis" gives the theme explicitly that the poem is a "Meditation upon Death". Different from the conventional perception of the Death, which gives an air of fear and sadness, this poem approaches the theme with feelings of acquiescence. Bryant depicts death as a return to home, joining others and to be joined by more. Thus, it is not something to be frightened about but a journey with a peaceful mind.

At the beginning of the poem, we are presented with the omnipresent Nature, who is an omnipotent mother to human beings, which is implied in the word "she". She is omnipotent because she is capable of perceiving different states of mind and correspondingly gives "various languages": when in happy moment, Nature gives a "voice of gladness"; while in sorrow time, she comforts with "healing sympathy". The concluding moment comes and her "still voice" is to be heard from Earth, water and air. This is a call for the child to come back to Earth, "that nourished thee" and become a part of the Nature. The rock and clod are your brothers and you are to be united with oaks.

Never worry about the return, because no matter what they do, no matter how clever they are or how old they are, all share "one mighty sepulchre", to which Nature gives decoration of hills, vales, woods, rivers and so on. No sadness about the silent departure. People may be immersed in their own happiness or business and pay no attention, but it is only for the time being. Sooner or later, you will be joined by them. So why not bother yourself about it! Live the life to the fullest and when the final call comes, be "sustained and soothed" and take the road with an "unfaltering trust".

When passing the comforting tone of the poem, Bryant is careful about dictions. Sharp contrast is made between the common look on death and the one the poet tries to convey. The dread and melancholy air of Death is signaled through the concrete material for corpse: the "shroud" and "pall"; on the other hand, the poet reminds readers of magnificent "couch" where people could lie down and have "pleasant dreams". The tomb of man is actually the "bosom" of mother nature. So the cold, isolated stillness is replaced by the warm, comfortable companionship. Death, instead of an end, is just a part of another circle.

Selected Reading

Thanatopsis

To him who in the love of Nature holds
Communion with her visible forms, she speaks
A various language; for his gayer hours
She has a voice of gladness, and a smile
And eloquence of beauty, and she glides
Into his darker musings, with a mild
And healing sympathy, that steals away
Their sharpness, ere he is aware. When thoughts
Of the last bitter hour come like a blight
Over thy spirit, and sad images
Of the stern agony, and shroud, and pall,

And breathless darkness, and the narrow house,
Make thee to shudder, and grow sick at heart;—
Go forth under the open sky, and list
To Nature's teachings, while from all around—
Earth and her waters, and the depths of air, —
Comes a still voice—

Yet a few days, and thee
The all-beholding sun shall see no more
In all his course; nor yet in the cold ground,
Where thy pale form was laid, with many tears,
Nor in the embrace of ocean, shall exist
Thy image. Earth, that nourished thee, shall claim
Thy growth, to be resolved to earth again,
And, lost each human trace, surrendering up
Thine individual being, shalt thou go
To mix forever with the elements,
To be a brother to the insensible rock
And to the sluggish clod, which the rude swain
Turns with his share[1], and treads upon. The oak
Shall send his roots abroad, and pierce thy mould.

Yet not to thy eternal resting place
Shalt thou retire alone, nor couldst thou wish
Couch more magnificent. Thou shalt lie down
With patriarchs of the infant world—with kings
The powerful of the earth, the wise, the good,
Fair forms, and hoary seers of ages past,
All in one mighty sepulchre. The hills
Rock-ribbed and ancient as the sun, the vales
Stretching in pensive quietness between;
The venerable woods—rivers that move
In majesty, and the complaining brooks
That make the meadows green; and, poured round all,
Old Ocean's grey and melancholy waste, —

Are but the solemn decorations all
Of the great tomb of man. The golden sun,
The planets, all the infinite host of heaven,
Are shining on the sad abodes of death,
Through the still lapse of ages. All that tread
The globe are but a handful of the tribes
That slumber in its bosom. —Take the wings
Of morning, pierce the Barcan[2] wilderness,
Or lost thyself in the continuous woods
Where rolls the Oregan[3], and hears no sound,
Save his own dashings—yet the dead are there:
And millions in those solitudes, since first
The flight of years began, have laid them down
In their last sleep—the dead reign there alone.
So shalt thou rest, and what if thou withdraw
In silence from the living—and no friend
Take note of thy departure? All that breathe
Will share thy destiny. The gay will laugh,
When thou art gone, the solemn brood of care
Plod on, and each one as before will chase
His favourite phantom; yet all these shall leave
Their mirth and their employments, and shall come,
And make their bed with thee. As the long train
Of ages glide away, the sons of men,
The youth in life's green spring, and he who goes
In the full strength of years, matron, and maid,
The Speechless babe, and the gray-headed man—
Shall one by one be gathered to thy side,
By those, who in their turn shall follow them.

So live, that when thy summons comes to join
The innumerable caravan, that moves
To that mysterious realm, where each shall take
His chamber in the silent halls of death,
Thou go not, like the quarry-slave at night,

Scourged to his dungeon, but, sustained and soothed

By an unfaltering trust, approach thy grave,

Like one who wraps the drapery of his couch

About him, and lies down to pleasant dreams.

Notes:

1. share: Plowshare
2. the Barcan: The desert of Barca (in Libya, North Africa)
3. the Oregan: The Indian name, now the Columbia River

Questions for Study and Discussion:

1. What is the relation between "Thanatposis" and British Romantic poems?
2. What is the relation between human beings and nature? What attitude should we bear towards death?
3. What rhythms and rhymes are applied in the poem?

Edgar Allen Poe (1809—1849)

Life and Major Works

Edgar Allen Poe was born into an acting family in 1809 with the name Edgar Poe. His actor father David Poe, Jr. abandoned the family in 1810 and one year later his actress mother died from consumption. The two-year-old Edgar Poe was then taken into the home of John Allen, which served as his foster family. Edgar Allen Poe is the name given by his foster family.

Edgar Allen Poe

During his early ages, his foster father was quite nice to Poe and Poe's needs were satisfied with sufficient books and intercontinental travels, not to mention the daily necessities. In 1815, Poe travelled to England with the Allen family and attended a grammar school for a short time in Scotland. After studying in a boarding school for almost 2 years in London, Poe moved back to Richmond, Virginia with the Allens in 1820. In 1825, Poe got enrolled into the University of Virginia and studied there for 1 year, which period posed as a transitional period for the relation between the foster father and the son. The two came to be distanced and even hostile to each other: Poe claimed that John Allen didn't provide sufficient money for his study and daily expenses. But Poe was at that time struggling against his mounting gambling debts. It is said that John Allen did send his foster son additional money and other necessities, and John Allen had been suffering from financial crisis in his business, which probably made him quick-tempered. Another saying about the tough-growing relationship focuses on the specialization of Poe's study. John Allen intended to train Poe in trade to take over his business, but Poe was interested in language.

Poe dropped out of the university in 1827 and moved to Boston, trying to support himself by taking odd jobs, which turned out to be a failure. To maintain his daily life, Poe enlisted in the army by claiming to be 22 although he was actually 18. It is in this year that Poe published his first book *Tamerlane and Other Poems* (1827) with the byline "by a Bostonian". This book, with only 50 copies printed, received almost no attention. After serving in army for 2 years, Poe tried to end the five-year enlistment early, which could not be realized without John Allen's help to support his discharge from the army and enrollment into the West Point. However, Poe's stay in the West Point didn't last long, and he was discharged in 1829. In this year, his second book *Al Aaraaf, Tamerlane and Minor Poems* (1929) came into being. In 1831, with the financial supply of the cadets in West Point, Poe published his *Poems* (1831), from which comes the early version of the poem "Helen", selected in the book.

After John Allen disowned his foster son, Poe came to be more serious in his literary career and tried to make a living by writing. His attention shifted from poems to proses. In 1833, his prized short story "MS. Found in a Bottle" opened a new door for him and he was introduced to an editor of *Southern Literary Messenger*. After only a few weeks' working there as an assistant editor in 1835, Poe was discharged for being addicted to alcohol. After marrying his 13-year-old cousin Virginia Clemm, Poe and his family came back to the *Messenger* and resumed his early job promising good behaviors. It is during these years that Poe established his position as short story writer, poet and critic, and he successfully managed to enlarge the circulation of the *Messenger* from 700 to 3500. Since 1839, Poe frequently changed his jobs among various publications. In these years, he published some famous works: *Tales of the Grotesque and Arabesque* (1840), *The Raven* (1845) and *Tales* (1845). *The Raven* made him a household name. In 1847, Poe's wife Virginia passed away, which made him turn more to drinking. In 1849,

Poe was found on the street and was taken to hospital. 4 days later, he died there. Poe's works are "preoccupied with death and fatality and addicted to the modes of the Gothic and grotesque" (269), as G. R. Thompson puts it, and it is not hard for readers to find traces of "death, a predisposition to violence, perversity and madness" in his works, especially novels. He tries to "parallel the paradoxical mundane reality and the otherworldly" and "emphasizes meticulous craftsmanship and minute attention to details" (271). As for his poems, Thompson notices that Poe makes uses of "sound and rhythm" to achieve the "visionary state of 'supernal beauty'." (270) Related to Poe's life, many of his poems reflect the theme of "the compulsive desire to torture oneself" and "the reality of the world is capable of sudden disintegration" (274).

Poe has written about 70 stories in his short 40 years, and the stories can roughly be categorized into 4 groups: the Gothic which is closely related to the death theme and grotesque atmosphere; the detective story, for which Poe is considered to be the father; the science fiction for which Poe is a forerunner and the satire humor tales which liberates readers from social conformities.

Poe's literary theories can be found in his *The philosophy of Composition* (1846) and *The Poetic Principle* (1850). He emphasizes that the theme and mode should be concerned with a particular effect. For the sake of the effect, readers should be able to finish reading the story in a single sitting. Apart from that, for most of his stories, "a unified interior drama of the self", a psychological state and "supernatural elements" also signal some symbolic meaning.

Brief Introduction and Appreciation

To Helen

Poe's poem "To Helen" is inspired by Jane Stanard, the mother of his best friend. Poe bore some special feelings toward this lady and later described her as "the first, purely ideal love of my soul". But it is widely agreed that this poem is not dedicated to any particular person, but the general idea of beauty. Helen is the most beautiful woman in Greek mythology, and she is held here to represent the ideal beauty. The physical beauty doesn't constitute the whole, and the spiritual beauty is wanted. Thus, at the end of the poem comes Psyche, the sign for the spiritualized beauty and the idealized love.

The image of beauty doesn't arouse romances or wars for Poe, but serves to take him home, which is expressed at the beginning of the poem. It takes the long but comfortable sea way to his desired home. The manipulation of sound and rhythm has contributed to deliver this feeling: as is suggested by critics, the sound of Nicean gives an air of a gentle homecoming in a classical world. The alliteration of "weary, way-worn wanderer" gives the sense of the endless rocking on the sea.

The beauty not only provides the means (the Nicean barks of yore)of home coming. More importantly, it serves as a beacon to guide the poet home. This image is presented in "the brilliant window-niche" stands, "the agate lamp within thy hand!" The agate lamp in the beauty is like the ever-lasting light from Goddess to guide the poet home. So if Helen represents the physical beauty, which is materialized as a victorious boat, Psyche, the spiritualized beauty serves as compass in Poe's life.

Another question arising here is where the home of the poet is, and which place the "beauty" leads the poet to. The poem has mentioned "the native shore", "Greece", "Rome", "Holy-Land", and which one does Poe mean? Some suggest that by home, Poe refers to the classical past, which could be confirmed by the mention of Greece and Rome, the major periods in history. A series of images adopted from Greece and Rome seem to imply the nostalgia of the poet. The "Holy-Land" finally gives a hint. Normally, Israel and Palestine are often depicted as the Holy Land. But Poe here does not refer to religious places. For him, the sacred places of arts can be considered as holy places. And Greece and Rome can be explained as vehicles of long-term civilization with a variety of art works. The pursuit of art makes it acceptable to consider the art-born region as his home, and is consistent with his admiration of beauty, since beauty holds a central position in his literary creation.

Annabel Lee

Annabel Lee is the beloved woman of the narrator "I" and it is believed that this poem is dedicated to Poe's wife Virginia. The two are cousins and Virginia married Poe at the age of 13. Thus the love could be described since "I was a child and she was a child". The early death of Virginia leaves Poe in despair and the poet attributes the tragedy to the jealousy of the heaven. But however almighty the heaven is, the love between Annabel Lee and "I" is timeless and unconquerable.

The narrator "I" tell the story from their childhood to death with simple words, but pass faithful feelings. For "I", words are not sufficient and not a single word could be exact enough to describe the love between the two. Thus the repetition of "love" is adopted, and the strong feeling between them is "a love that was more than a love". The desperate situation with such simple and short words give an air that the feeling between them is nothing but a natural thing, so natural that even the seraphs or angels from the Almighty world cannot make an alter.

Biblically, Annabel Lee is from the eternal world. She suffers the damnation because "with a love that the winged seraphs of heaven coveted her and me". What kind of love it could be that could trigger the damnation of the heaven and the jealousy of the seraphs! What kind of love it could be that "her highborn kinsmen" would take and shut her up in a sepulcher. The reaction from the carefree Eden reflects the intensity of the admirable love.

After Annabel Lee died, the souls of the two are still melting into each other, and "Neither the angels in the heaven above, Nor the demons down under the sea" could ever separate them. In other words, the love is unconquerable in the whole space, every layer of the space. Meanwhile, it is also incomparable in the stream of time, as is repeated "in the kingdom by the sea". Sea is vast and considered to be the oldest. "By the sea" could refer to part of the holy region, but it is more likely to be taken as a reference to distinguish the love from any other one in the history. Thus, the genuineness and intensity of the love are delivered.

Selected Reading

To Helen[1]

Helen, thy beauty is to me
Like those Nicean[2] barks of yore,
That gently, o'er a perfumed sea,
The weary, way-worn wanderer bore
To his own native shore.

On desperate seas long wont to roam,
Thy hyacinth[3] hair, thy classic face,
Thy Naiad[4] airs have brought me home
To the glory that was Greece,
And the grandeur that was Rome.

Lo! in yon brilliant window-niche
How statue-like I see thee stand,

The agate lamp within thy hand!

Ah! Psyche⁵, from the regions which

Are Holy Land!

Notes:

1. Helen: Helen of Troy. According to Greek myth, Helen, the beautiful daughter of the chief god Zeus, was the fabled cause of the Trojan war.
2. Nicean: Victory ship. The word "Nicean" is derived from the Greek "nike", which means "victory".
3. hyacinth: Luxuriant and curling.
4. Naiad: Nymphlike; according to Greek myth, Naiads are female spirits who inhabit fountains and streams.
5. Psyche: "Soul" (Greek); according to Roman myth, psyche was a damsel so beautiful that the goddess of love, Venus, was jealous of her. It is used here as a sign for this spiritualized beauty.

Annabel Lee

It was many and many a year ago,

In a kingdom by the sea, ¹

That a maiden there lived whom you may know

By the name of Annabel Lee;

And this maiden she lived with no other thought

Than to love and be loved by me.

I was a child and *she* was a child,

In this kingdom by the sea,

But we loved with a love that was more than love —

I and my Annabel Lee;

With a love that the winged seraphs of heaven

Coveted her and me.

And this was the reason that, long ago,

In this kingdom by the sea,

A wind blew out of a cloud, chilling

My beautiful Annabel Lee;

So that her highborn kinsmen² came

And bore her away from me,
To shut her up in a sepulcher
In this kingdom by the sea.

The angels, not half so happy in heaven,
Went envying her and me —
Yes!—that was the reason (as all men know,
In this kingdom by the sea)
That the wind came out of the cloud one night,
Chilling and killing my Annabel Lee.

But our love it was stronger by far than the love
Of those who were older than we —
Of many far wiser than we —
And neither the angels in heaven above,
Nor the demons down under the sea,
Can ever dissever my soul from the soul
Of the beautiful Annabel Lee:

For the moon never beams without bringing me dreams
Of the beautiful Annabel Lee;
And the stars never rise but I feel the bright eyes
Of the beautiful Annabel Lee;
And so, all the night-tide, I lie down by the side
Of my darling—my darling—my life and my bride,
In the sepulchre there by the sea—
In her tomb by the sounding sea.

Notes:

1. In a kingdom by the sea: This is Poe's poetic designation of America.
2. Her highborn kinsmen: These were the angels, to whom "Annable Lee" was akin in sweet, gentle character.

Questions for Study and Discussion:

1. Helen is an ideal beauty. What features of the ideal beauty are mentioned in the poem?
2. What sound effects are given in the above two poems?
3. Both poems above mention "sea". Do they signal the same meaning? Why?

Ralph Waldo Emerson (1803—1882)

Life and Major Works

Ralph Waldo Emerson was an American essayist, philosopher, poet, and more importantly, the leader of the Transcendentalist movement in the early 19th century. There has been an argument about his position of being more a philosopher than a literacy man. It seems to the philosophers that his "verbal brilliance" and "feline shifts of tone and stance" help pave his way to the literary artistry. On the other hand, as Barbara Packer notices, the literary artists have often been "offended by his frank love of the didactic", his "preference of genius over works" and "his contempt for the mere craftsmanship" (382). Anyway, as a leading figure in embedding one's life and experience into ideas, Emerson has won the recognition in the world.

Ralph Waldo Emerson

    Emerson was born in Boston in 1803, his father a Unitarian minister. At the age of eight, Emerson lost his father and the death of the father left the family in desperate straits. The family had to maintain their life by running boardinghouses and taking charity. In 1817, he went to Harvard College where he began his lifelong practice of maintaining his journal. The journal rests at the centre of his literary life. Emerson often went back to his journals and took out relevant passages, which he would adopt for his lectures. He later revised his lectures for his essays and sermons. In 1821, Emerson helped his brother run a school for ladies and took charge of the school after his brother went to study divinity. He worked as a schoolmaster for the following years and then went to Harvard Divinity School. In 1829, Emerson took a position as a Unitarian minister but resigned in 1832. In taking this job, Emerson seems to be more interested in practicing the art of eloquence, which is so essential in his sermons and lectures, than performing the pastoral duties.

Emerson met and married his first wife, Ellen Louisa Tucker when she was 18. Two years later, she died from tuberculosis. The death of his wife left him in sorrow, but the estate she left him made it possible for him to pay visits to Europe, where Emerson made acquaintance with literacy giants, William Wordsworth, Samuel Taylor Coleridge, John Stuart Mill, and Thomas Carlyle. The meeting with Carlyle was most satisfying and fruitful and they developed a lifelong correspondence. In September 1836, Emerson and other intellectuals founded the Transcendental Club, a center for the transcendentalism. In the same year, Emerson published his ambitious book *Nature* (1936), which aims to present a theory of universe, its origin, present condition and final destiny. Emerson holds that nature is the opposite of Man, the alienated consciousness and Man is able to resume the power which is scattered in nature. Following the essay *Nature* comes the speech entitled *The American Scholar* (1837), which Oliver Wendell Holmes Sr. considered to be America's "Intellectual Declaration of Independence".

When invited to give a graduation address in Harvard Divinity School, Emerson gave *Divinity School Address* (1838), discounting biblical miracles. His comment outraged the protestant community and made himself labeled atheist. The 1940s saw the active performance of Emerson's literary life: the Transcendental Club started their journal *The Dial* in 1840; Emerson's great *Essays* came into being, with the first series and second one published respectively in 1841 and 1844. The many famous essays can be found in these two collections, among which are "Self-Reliance", "Compensation", "The Over-soul", "The Poet", "Experience", etc. Apart from essays, Emerson's other works include *Poems* (1847), *Representative Men* (1850), *English Traits* (1856), *The Conduct of Life* (1860), *May Day and Other Pieces* (1867), *Society and Solitude* (1870), *Letters and Social Aims* (1876). Emerson caught a cold in New England when he was 78 years old and the cold triggered pneumonia. In 1882 Ralph Waldo Emerson died at home in Concord, Massachusetts.

At the center of Emerson's philosophy, there are at least three key words: self-reliance, individualism and over-soul. In any of his great essays, we can find the call for self-reliance. For Emerson, the sparks of knowledge and ideas are fanned through the first-hand observation and action, the direct interaction with nature. His disciple Henry David Thoreau is the very example, who followed the guide of his mentor and carried out the philosophy by isolating himself and living in the woods for quite a long time.

As for the over-soul, it is believed to be omnipresent; it is above us meanwhile part of us. As is mentioned in his essay "Over-soul", "within man is the soul of the whole…act of seeing and the thing seen, the seer and the spectacle, the subject and the object, are one". Thus, human beings are part of the universe, and something of the two is actually of the same nature. By intuition and perception, we can get the very nature and meaning of the life and world.

Emerson advocates individualism because he believed that "reform was best achieved by the moral suasion of individuals rather than by the militant action of groups." In his personal life, he attempted not to join public groups or movement to maintain his independence. People can have individual ways to experience and have communication with the over-soul.

Brief Introduction and Appreciation

The American Scholar was a speech given by Ralph Waldo Emerson in 1837 to the Phi Beta Kappa Society in Cambridge, Massachusetts. By this speech, Emerson is supposed to point out a way for the young Americans to take a new look at the world. At that time, it has been 60 years since the United States announced its independence, but this country is still heavily influenced by Europe in culture. It is under that circumstance that Emerson called attention to the importance of forming the American identity, and it is considered as the "Intellectual Declaration of Independence".

In addition to being a call for literary independence from Europe and past traditions, the speech also serves as guidance for people to live in an authentic and active way. Being consistent with Emerson's philosophy, this speech talks about the influence on the education of scholar from the perspective of nature, books and action, which reflects his core ideas on the over-soul and self-reliance. Emerson believed that the way to reunite with the over-soul was the way to become "The American Scholar", which is to be realized by "observing nature", "studying the past through books", and more importantly "taking action". To pave the way to be a scholar, "humans also needed to develop self trust, espouse freedom and bravery, and value the individual over the masses" (Nancy Haines).

To be an individual thinking man, Emerson reminds the audience (and now readers) of the importance of the interconnectness of every phase in both human society and natural world. People should not be confined into a particular trade, and more importantly not to be instrumentalized or "metamorphosed into a thing". Human beings ought to maintain the subjectivity and play an active part to see "the continuity of this web of God" and see things in "one nature". Nature is an important source and influence of learning, because "Its [Nature's] beauty is the beauty of his own mind. Its laws are the laws of his own mind", and it is the "measure of his attainments"

As for the books, Emerson warned us not to worship or make false idols of books and other objects of art, which demonstrates his belief in the vital necessity for self-reliance and active, creative reading and writing. However, Emerson didn't deny the usefulness of books. He admitted that "Books are the best type of the influence of the past." What he emphasized is that although "books are the best vehicle available to the scholar for studying the ideas and accomplishments of past men and ages" (Nancy Haines), people living in a certain age need to read the life of their own and perceive their individual knowledge rather than stick to some books. Even the religious holy books, to Emerson, are of no exception.

Having admitted the importance of books, Emerson pointed out that "books are for the scholar's idle time" and "When he can read God directly, the hour is too precious to be wasted in other men's transcripts of their readings". By saying this, he demonstrated his belief that when it is possible, scholars should be seeking action and studying nature, thus making "life his dictionary".

As a whole, in *The American Scholar* Emerson encouraged men to have experiences and seek the one nature beneath various curtains, to read books but not let books take control of their individual and creative thinking. There is a fine line between study, appreciation and assimilation of books and ideas from the past and idolizing these books and ideas. We must examine, rewrite, create, learn from the old but write our own books from our own time and experience.

Selected Reading

The American Scholar

An Oration delivered before the Phi Beta Kappa Society, at Cambridge,
August 31, 1837

Mr. President and Gentlemen,

I greet you on the re-commencement of our literary year[1]. Our anniversary is one of hope, and, perhaps, not enough of labor. We do not meet for games of strength or skill, for the recitation of histories, tragedies, and odes, like the ancient Greeks; for parliaments of love and poesy, like the Troubadours[2]; nor for the advancement of science, like our contemporaries in the British and European capitals. Thus far, our holiday has been simply a friendly sign of the survival of the love of letters amongst a people too busy to give to letters any more. As such, it is precious as the sign of an indestructible instinct. Perhaps the time is already come, when it ought to be, and will be, something else; when the sluggard intellect of this continent will look from under its iron lids, and fill the postponed expectation of the world with something better than the exertions of mechanical skill. Our day of dependence, our long apprenticeship to the learning of other lands, draws to a close. The millions that around us are rushing into life, cannot always be fed on the sere remains of foreign harvests. Events, actions arise, that must be sung, that will sing themselves. Who can doubt that poetry will revive and lead in a new age, as the star in the constellation Harp[3], which now flames in our zenith, astronomers announce, shall one day be the pole-star[4] for a thousand years?

In the light of this hope, I accept the topic which not only usage, but the nature of our association, seem to prescribe to this day, —the AMERICAN SCHOLAR. Year by year, we come up hither to read one more chapter of his biography. Let us inquire what light new days and events have thrown on his character, his duties and his hopes.

It is one of those fables[5], which out of an unknown antiquity, convey an unlooked-for wisdom, that the gods, in the beginning, divided Man into men, that he might be more helpful to himself; just as the hand was divided into fingers, the better to answer its end.

The old fable covers a doctrine ever new and sublime; that there is One Man, — present to all particular men only partially, or through one faculty; and that you must take the whole society to find the whole man. Man is not a farmer, or a professor, or an engineer, but he is all. Man is priest, and scholar, and statesman, and producer, and soldier. In the *divided* or social state, these functions are parcelled out to individuals, each of whom aims to do his stint of the joint work, whilst each other performs his. The fable implies that the individual to possess himself, must sometimes return from his own labor to embrace all the other laborers. But unfortunately, this original unit, this fountain of power, has been so distributed to multitudes, has been so minutely subdivided and peddled out, that it is spilled into drops, and cannot be gathered. The state of society is one in which the members have suffered amputation from the trunk, and strut about so many walking monsters, —a good finger, a neck, a stomach, an elbow, but never a man.

Man is thus metamorphosed into a thing, into many things. The planter, who is Man sent out into the field to gather food, is seldom cheered by any idea of the true dignity of his ministry. He sees his bushel and his cart, and nothing beyond, and sinks into the farmer, instead of Man on the farm. The tradesman scarcely ever gives an ideal worth to his work, but is ridden by the routine of his craft, and the soul is subject to dollars. The priest becomes a form; the attorney, a statute-book; the mechanic, a machine; the sailor, a rope of a ship.

In this distribution of functions, the scholar is the delegated intellect. In the right state, he is, **Man Thinking**. In the degenerate state, when the victim of society, he tends to become a mere thinker, or, still worse, the parrot of other men's thinking.

In this view of him, as Man Thinking, the theory of his office[6] is contained. Him nature solicits, with all her placid, all her monitory pictures. Him the past instructs. Him the future invites. Is not, indeed, every man a student, and do not all things exist for the student's behoof? And, finally, is not the true scholar the only true master? But, as the old oracle said, "All things have two handles. Beware of the wrong one." In life, too often, the scholar errs with mankind and forfeits his privilege. Let us see him in his school, and consider him in reference to the main influences he receives.

I. The first in time and the first in importance of the influences upon the mind is that of nature. Every day, the sun; and, after sunset, night and her stars. Ever the winds blow; ever the grass grows. Every day, men and women, conversing, beholding and beholden. The scholar must needs stand wistful and admiring before this great spectacle. He must settle its value in his mind. What is nature to him? There is never a beginning, there is never an end to the inexplicable continuity of this web of God, but always circular power returning into itself. Therein it resembles his own spirit, whose beginning, whose ending, he never can find—so entire, so boundless. Far, too, as her splendors shine, system on system shooting like rays, upward, downward, without centre, without circumference,—in the mass and in the particle nature hastens to render account of herself to the mind. Classification begins. To the young mind, every thing is individual, stands by itself. By and by, it finds how to join two things, and see in them one nature; then three, then three thousand; and so, tyrannized over by its own unifying instinct, it goes on tying things together, diminishing anomalies, discovering roots running under ground, whereby contrary and remote things cohere, and flower out from one stem. It presently learns, that, since the dawn of history, there has been a constant accumulation and classifying of facts. But what is classification but the perceiving that these objects are not chaotic, and are not foreign, but have a law which is also a law of the human mind? The astronomer discovers that geometry, a pure abstraction of the human mind, is the measure of planetary motion. The chemist finds proportions and intelligible method throughout matter; and science is nothing but the finding of analogy, identity in the most remote parts. The ambitious soul sits down before each refractory fact; one after another, reduces all strange constitutions, all new powers, to their class and their law, and goes on forever to animate the last fibre of organization, the outskirts of nature, by insight.

Thus to him, to this school-boy under the bending dome of day, is suggested, that he and it proceed from one root; one is leaf and one is flower; relation, sympathy, stirring in every vein. And what is that Root? Is not that the soul of his soul? —A thought too bold—a dream too wild. Yet when this spiritual light shall have revealed the law of more earthly natures, —when he has learned to worship the soul, and to see that the natural philosophy that now is, is only the first gropings of its gigantic hand, he shall look forward to an ever expanding knowledge as to a becoming creator. He shall see that nature is the opposite of the soul, answering to it part for part. One is seal, and one is print. Its beauty is the beauty of his own mind. Its laws are the laws of his own mind. Nature then becomes to him the measure of his attainments. So much of nature as he is ignorant of, so much of his own mind does he not yet possess. And, in fine, the ancient precept, "Know thyself," and the modern precept, "Study nature," become at last one maxim.

II. The next great influence into the spirit of the scholar, is, the mind of the Past, —in whatever form, whether of literature, of art, of institutions, that mind is inscribed. Books are the best type of the influence of the past, and perhaps we shall get at the truth—learn the amount of this influence more conveniently—by considering their value alone.The theory of books is noble. The scholar of the first age received into him the world around; brooded thereon; gave it the new arrangement of his own mind, and uttered it again. It came into him—life; it went out from him—truth. It came to him—short-lived actions; it went out from him—

immortal thoughts. It came to him—business; it went from him—poetry. It was— dead fact; now, it is quick thought. It can stand, and it can go. It now endures, it now flies, it now inspires. Precisely in proportion to the depth of mind from which it issued, so high does it soar, so long does it sing.

Or, I might say, it depends on how far the process had gone, of transmuting life into truth. In proportion to the completeness of the distillation, so will the purity and imperishableness of the product be. But none is quite perfect. As no air-pump can by any means make a perfect vacuum, so neither can any artist entirely exclude the conventional, the local, the perishable from his book, or write a book of pure thought that shall be as efficient, in all respects, to a remote posterity, as to contemporaries, or rather to the second age. Each age, it is found, must write its own books; or rather, each generation for the next succeeding. The books of an older period will not fit this.

Yet hence arises a grave mischief. The sacredness which attaches to the act of creation, —the act of thought, —is instantly transferred to the record. The poet chanting, was felt to be a divine man. Henceforth the chant is divine also. The writer was a just and wise spirit. Henceforward it is settled, the book is perfect; as love of the hero corrupts into worship of his statue. Instantly, the book becomes noxious. The guide is a tyrant. We sought a brother, and lo, a governor. The sluggish and perverted mind of the multitude, always slow to open to the incursions of Reason, having once so opened, having once received this book, stands upon it, and makes an outcry, if it is disparaged. Colleges are built on it. Books are written on it by thinkers, not by Man Thinking; by men of talent, that is, who start wrong, who set out from accepted dogmas, not from their own sight of principles. Meek young men grow up in libraries, believing it their duty to accept the views, which Cicero, which Locke, which Bacon, have given, forgetful that Cicero, Locke, and Bacon were only young men in libraries, when they wrote these books.

Hence, instead of Man Thinking, we have the bookworm. Hence, the book-learned class, who value books, as such; not as related to nature and the human constitution, but as making a sort of Third Estate[7] with the world and the soul. Hence, the restorers of readings, the emendators, the bibliomaniacs[8] of all degrees.

This is bad; this is worse than it seems. Books are the best of things, well used; abused, among the worst. What is the right use? What is the one end which all means go to effect? They are for nothing but to inspire. I had better never see a book than to be warped by its attraction clean out of my own orbit, and made a satellite instead of a system. The one thing in the world of value, is, the active soul, —the soul, free, sovereign, active. This every man is entitled to; this every man contains within him, although, in almost all men, obstructed, and as yet unborn. The soul active sees absolute truth; and utters truth, or creates. In this action, it is genius; not the privilege of here and there a favorite, but the sound estate of every man. In its essence, it is progressive. The book, the college, the school of art, the institution of any kind, stop with some past utterance of genius. This is good, say they, —let us hold by this. They pin me down. They look backward and not forward. But genius always looks forward. The eyes of man are set in his forehead, not in his hindhead. Man hopes. Genius creates. To create, —to create, —is the proof of a divine presence. Whatever talents may be, if the man create not, the pure efflux[9] of the Deity is not his: —cinders and smoke, there may be, but not yet flame. There are creative manners, there are creative actions, and creative words; manners, actions, words, that is, indicative of no custom or authority, but springing spontaneous from the mind's own sense of good and fair.

On the other part, instead of being its own seer, let it receive always from another mind its truth, though it were in torrents of light, without periods of solitude, inquest, and self-recovery, and a fatal disservice is done. Genius is always sufficiently the enemy of genius by over-influence. The literature of every nation bear me witness. The English dramatic poets have Shakspearized now for two hundred years.

Undoubtedly there is a right way of reading, —so it be sternly subordinated. Man Thinking must not be subdued by his instruments. Books are for the scholar's idle times. When he can read God directly, the hour is too precious to be wasted in other men's transcripts of their readings. But when the intervals of darkness come, as come they must, —when the soul seeth not, when the sun is hid, and the stars withdraw their shining, —we repair to the lamps which were kindled by their ray to guide our steps to the East again, where the dawn is. We hear that we may speak. The Arabian proverb says, "A fig tree looking on a fig tree, becometh fruitful."

It is remarkable, the character of the pleasure we derive from the best books. They impress us with the conviction that one nature wrote and the same reads. We read the verses of one of the great English poets, of Chaucer, of Marvell, of

Dryden, with the most modern joy, —with a pleasure, I mean, which is in great part caused by the abstraction of all *time* from their verses. There is some awe mixed with the joy of our surprise, when this poet, who lived in some past world, two or three hundred years ago, says that which lies close to my own soul, that which I also had well-nigh thought and said. But for the evidence thence afforded to the philosophical doctrine of the identity of all minds, we should suppose some pre-established harmony, some foresight of souls that were to be, and some preparation of stores for their future wants, like the fact observed in insects, who lay up food before death for the young grub they shall never see.

I would not be hurried by any love of system, by any exaggeration of instincts, to underrate the Book. We all know, that, as the human body can be nourished on any food, though it were boiled grass and the broth of shoes, so the human mind can be fed by any knowledge. And great and heroic men have existed, who had almost no other information than by the printed page. I only would say, that it needs a strong head to bear that diet. One must be an inventor to read well. As the proverb says, "He that would bring home the wealth of the Indies, must carry out the wealth of the Indies." There is then creative reading as well as creative writing. When the mind is braced by labor and invention, the page of whatever book we read becomes luminous with manifold allusion. Every sentence is doubly significant, and the sense of our author is as broad as the world. We then see, what is always true, that as the seer's hour of vision is short and rare among heavy days and months, so is its record, perchance, the least part of his volume. The discerning will read in his Plato or Shakespeare, only that least part, —only the authentic utterances of the oracle, —and all the rest he rejects, were it never so many times Plato's and Shakespeare's.

Of course, there is a portion of reading quite indispensable to a wise man. History and exact science he must learn by laborious reading. Colleges, in like manner, have their indispensable office, —to teach elements. But they can only highly serve us, when they aim not to drill, but to create; when they gather from far every ray of various genius to their hospitable halls, and, by the concentrated fires, set the hearts of their youth on flame. Thought and knowledge are natures in which apparatus and pretension avail nothing. Gowns, and pecuniary foundations[10], though of towns of gold, can never countervail the least sentence or syllable of wit. Forget this, and our American colleges will recede in their public importance whilst they grow richer every year.

III. There goes in the world a notion that the scholar should be a recluse, a valetudinarian[11], —as unfit for any handiwork or public labor, as a penknife for an axe. The so-called "practical men" sneer at speculative men, as if, because they speculate or *see*, they could do nothing. I have heard it said that the clergy, —who are always more universally than any other class, the scholars of their day, —are addressed as women: that the rough, spontaneous conversation of men they do not hear, but only a mincing and diluted speech. They are often virtually disfranchised; and, indeed, there are advocates for their celibacy. As far as this is true of the studious classes, it is not just and wise. Action is with the scholar subordinate, but it is essential. Without it, he is not yet man. Without it, thought can never ripen into truth. Whilst the world hangs before the eye as a cloud of beauty, we cannot even see its beauty. Inaction is cowardice, but there can be no scholar without the heroic mind. The preamble of thought, the transition through which it passes from the unconscious to the conscious, is action. Only so much do I know, as I have lived. Instantly we know whose words are loaded with life, and whose not.

The world, —this shadow of the soul, or **other me**, lies wide around. Its attractions are the keys which unlock my thoughts and make me acquainted with myself. I run eagerly into this resounding tumult. I grasp the hands of those next me, and take my place in the ring to suffer and to work, taught by an instinct that so shall the dumb abyss be vocal with speech. I pierce its order; I dissipate its fear; I dispose of it within the circuit of my expanding life. So much only of life as I know by experience, so much of the wilderness have I vanquished and planted, or so far have I extended my being, my dominion. I do not see how any man can afford, for the sake of his nerves and his nap, to spare any action in which he can partake. It is pearls and rubies to his discourse. Drudgery, calamity, exasperation, want, are instructers in eloquence and wisdom. The true scholar grudges every opportunity of action past by, as a loss of power.

It is the raw material out of which the intellect moulds her splendid products. A strange process too, this, by which experience is converted into thought, as a mulberry leaf is converted into satin. The manufacture goes forward at all hours.

The actions and events of our childhood and youth are now matters of calmest observation. They lie like fair pictures in the air. Not so with our recent actions, —with the business which we now have in hand. On this we are quite unable to speculate. Our affections as yet circulate through it. We no more feel or know it, than we feel the feet, or the hand, or the brain of our body. The new deed is yet a part of life, —remains for a time immersed in our unconscious life. In some contemplative hour, it detaches itself from the life like a ripe fruit, to become a thought of the mind. Instantly, it is raised, transfigured; the corruptible has put on incorruption. Always now it is an object of beauty, however base its origin and neighborhood. Observe, too, the impossibility of antedating this act. In its grub state, it cannot fly, it cannot shine, —it is a dull grub. But suddenly, without observation, the selfsame thing unfurls beautiful wings, and is an angel of wisdom. So is there no fact, no event, in our private history, which shall not, sooner or later, lose its adhesive inert form, and astonish us by soaring from our body into the empyrean[12] . Cradle and infancy, school and playground, the fear of boys, and dogs, and ferules[13], the love of little maids and berries, and many another fact that once filled the whole sky, are gone already; friend and relative, profession and party, town and country, nation and world, must also soar and sing.

Of course, he who has put forth his total strength in fit actions, has the richest return of wisdom. I will not shut myself out of this globe of action and transplant an oak into a flower pot, there to hunger and pine; nor trust the revenue of some single faculty, and exhaust one vein of thought, much like those Savoyards[14], who, getting their livelihood by carving shepherds, shepherdesses, and smoking Dutchmen, for all Europe, went out one day to the mountain to find stock, and discovered that they had whittled up the last of their pine trees. Authors we have in numbers, who have written out their vein, and who, moved by a commendable prudence, sail for Greece or Palestine, follow the trapper into the prairie, or ramble round Algiers to replenish their merchantable stock.

If it were only for a vocabulary the scholar would be covetous of action. Life is our dictionary. Years are well spent in country labors; in town, —in the insight into trades and manufactures; in frank intercourse with many men and women; in science; in art; to the one end of mastering in all their facts a language, by which to illustrate and embody our perceptions. I learn immediately from any speaker how much he has already lived, through the poverty or the splendor of his speech. Life lies behind us as the quarry from whence we get tiles and copestones for the masonry of to-day. This is the way to learn grammar. Colleges and books only copy the language which the field and the work-yard made.

But the final value of action, like that of books, and better than books, is, that it is a resource. That great principle of Undulation in nature, that shows itself in the inspiring and expiring of the breath; in desire and satiety; in the ebb and flow of the sea, in day and night; in heat and cold, and as yet more deeply ingrained in every atom and every fluid, is known to us under the name of Polarity,—these "fits of easy transmission and reflection," as Newton called them, are the law of nature because they are the law of spirit.

The mind now thinks; now acts; and each fit reproduces the other. When the artist has exhausted his materials, when the fancy no longer paints, when thoughts are no longer apprehended, and books are a weariness—he has always the resource *to live*. Character is higher than intellect. Thinking is the function. Living is the functionary. The stream retreats to its source. A great soul will be strong to live, as well as strong to think. Does he lack organ or medium to impart his truths? He can still fall back on this elemental force of living them. This is a total act. Thinking is a partial act. Let the grandeur of justice shine in his affairs. Let the beauty of affection cheer his lowly roof. Those "far from fame" who dwell and act with him will feel the force of his constitution in the doings and passages of the day better than it can be measured by any public and designed display. Time shall teach him that the scholar loses no hour which the man lives. Herein he unfolds the sacred germ of his instinct, screened from influence. What is lost in seemliness is gained in strength. Not out of those on whom systems of education have exhausted their culture, comes the helpful giant to destroy the old or to build the new, but out of unhandselled savage nature, out of terrible Druids and Berserkirs[15], come at last Alfred and Shakespeare.

I hear therefore with joy whatever is beginning to be said of the dignity and necessity of labor to every citizen. There is virtue yet in the hoe and the spade, for learned as well as for unlearned hands. And labor is everywhere welcome; always we are invited to work; only be this limitation observed, that a man shall not for the sake of wider activity sacrifice any opinion to the popular judgments and modes of action.

I have now spoken of the education of the scholar by nature, by books, and by action. It remains to say somewhat of his duties.

They are such as become Man Thinking. They may all be comprised in self-trust. The office of the scholar is to cheer, to raise, and to guide men by showing them facts amidst appearances. He plies the slow, unhonored, and unpaid task of observation. Flamsteed and Herschel[16], in their glazed observatories, may catalogue the stars with the praise of all men, and, the results being splendid and useful, honor is sure. But he, in his private observatory, cataloguing obscure and

nebulous stars of the human mind, which as yet no man has thought of as such, —
watching days and months, sometimes, for a few facts; correcting still his old
records; —must relinquish display and immediate fame. In the long period of his
preparation, he must betray often an ignorance and shiftlessness in popular arts,
incurring the disdain of the able who shoulder him aside. Long he must stammer in
his speech; often forego the living for the dead. Worse yet, he must accept—how
often! poverty and solitude. For the ease and pleasure of treading the old road,
accepting the fashions, the education, the religion of society, he takes the cross of
making his own, and, of course, the self-accusation, the faint heart, the frequent
uncertainty and loss of time which are the nettles and tangling vines in the way of
the self-relying and self-directed; and the state of virtual hostility in which he
seems to stand to society, and especially to educated society. For all this loss and
scorn, what offset? He is to find consolation in exercising the highest functions of
human nature. He is one who raises himself from private considerations, and
breathes and lives on public and illustrious thoughts. He is the world's eye. He is
the world's heart. He is to resist the vulgar prosperity that retrogrades ever to
barbarism, by preserving and communicating heroic sentiments, noble biographies,
melodious verse, and the conclusions of history. Whatsoever oracles the human
heart in all emergencies, in all solemn hours has uttered as its commentary on the
world of actions, —these shall receive and impart. And whatsoever new verdict
Reason from her inviolable seat pronounces on the passing men and events of
to-day, —this he shall hear and promulgate.

These being his functions, it becomes him to feel all confidence in himself,
and to defer never to the popular cry. He and he only knows the world. The world
of any moment is the merest appearance. Some great decorum, some fetish of a
government, some ephemeral trade, or war, or man, is cried up by half mankind
and cried down by the other half, as if all depended on this particular up or down.
The odds are that the whole question is not worth the poorest thought which the
scholar has lost in listening to the controversy. Let him not quit his belief that a
popgun is a popgun, though the ancient and honorable of the earth affirm it to be
the crack of doom. In silence, in steadiness, in severe abstraction, let him hold by
himself; add observation to observation, patient of neglect, patient of reproach;
and bide his own time, —happy enough if he can satisfy himself alone that this
day he has seen something truly. Success treads on every right step. For the
instinct is sure that prompts him to tell his brother what he thinks. He then learns

that in going down into the secrets of his own mind, he has descended into the secrets of all minds. He learns that he who has mastered any law in his private thoughts, is master to that extent of all men whose language he speaks, and of all into whose language his own can be translated. The poet in utter solitude remembering his spontaneous thoughts and recording them, is found to have recorded that which men in crowded cities find true for them also. The orator distrusts at first the fitness of his frank confessions, —his want of knowledge of the persons he addresses, —until he finds that he is the complement of his hearers; —that they drink his words because he fulfils for them their own nature; the deeper he dives into his privatest secretest presentiment, —to his wonder he finds, this is the most acceptable, most public, and universally true. The people delight in it; the better part of every man feels. This is my music; this is myself.

In self-trust, all the virtues are comprehended. Free should the scholar be, — free and brave. Free even to the definition of freedom, "without any hindrance that does not arise out of his own constitution." Brave; for fear is a thing which a scholar by his very function puts behind him. Fear always springs from ignorance. It is a shame to him if his tranquillity, amid dangerous times, arise from the presumption that like children and women, his is a protected class; or if he seek a temporary peace by the diversion of his thoughts from politics or vexed questions, hiding his head like an ostrich in the flowering bushes, peeping into microscopes, and turning rhymes, as a boy whistles to keep his courage up. So is the danger a danger still: so is the fear worse. Manlike let him turn and face it. Let him look into its eye and search its nature, inspect its origin, —see the whelping of this lion, —which lies no great way back; he will then find in himself a perfect comprehension of its nature and extent; he will have made his hands meet on the other side, and can henceforth defy it, and pass on superior. The world is his who can see through its pretension. What deafness, what stone-blind custom, what overgrown error you behold, is there only by sufferance, —by your sufferance. See it to be a lie, and you have already dealt it its mortal blow.

Yes, we are the cowed, —we the trustless. It is a mischievous notion that we are come late into nature; that the world was finished a long time ago. As the world was plastic and fluid in the hands of God, so it is ever to so much of his attributes as we bring to it. To ignorance and sin, it is flint. They adapt themselves to it as they may; but in proportion as a man has anything in him divine, the firmament flows before him, and takes his signet[17] and form. Not he is great who can alter matter, but he who can alter my state of mind. They are the kings of the world who give the color of their present thought to all nature and all art, and persuade men by the cheerful serenity of their carrying the matter, that this thing which they do, is the apple which the ages have desired to pluck, now at last ripe, and inviting nations to the harvest. The great man makes the great thing. Wherever Macdonald sits, there is the head of the table. Linnaeus makes botany the most alluring of studies and wins it from the farmer and the herb-woman. Davy, chemistry: and Cuvier, fossils. The day is always his, who works in it with serenity and great aims. The unstable estimates of men crowd to him whose mind is filled with a truth, as the heaped waves of the Atlantic follow the moon.

For this self-trust, the reason is deeper than can be fathomed, —darker than can be enlightened. I might not carry with me the feeling of my audience in stating my own belief. But I have already shown the ground of my hope, in adverting to the doctrine that man is one. I believe man has been wronged: he has wronged himself. He has almost lost the light that can lead him back to his prerogatives. Men are become of no account. Men in history, men in the world of to-day are bugs, are spawn, and are called "the mass" and 'the herd." In a century, in a millennium, one or two men; that is to say, —one or two approximations to the right state of every man. All the rest behold in the hero or the poet their own green and crude being, —ripened; yes, and are content to be less, so *that* may attain to its full stature. What a testimony, —full of grandeur, full of pity, is borne to the demands of his own nature, by the poor clansman, the poor partisan, who rejoices in the glory of his chief. The poor and the low find some amends to their immense moral capacity, for their acquiescence in a political and social inferiority. They are content to be brushed like flies from the path of a great person, so that justice shall be done by him to that common nature which it is the dearest desire of all to see enlarged and glorified. They sun themselves in the great man's light, and feel it to be their own element. They cast the dignity of man from their downtrod selves upon the shoulders of a hero, and will perish to add one drop of blood to make that great heart beat, those giant sinews combat and conquer. He lives for us, and we live in him.

Men such as they are, very naturally seek money or power; and power because it is as good as money, —the "spoils," so called, "of office." And why not? for they aspire to the highest, and this, in their sleep-walking, they dream is highest.

Wake them, and they shall quit the false good and leap to the true, and leave governments to clerks and desks. This revolution is to be wrought by the gradual domestication of the idea of Culture. The main enterprise of the world for splendor, for extent, is the upbuilding of a man. Here are the materials strown along the ground. The private life of one man shall be a more illustrious monarchy, —more formidable to its enemy, more sweet and serene in its influence to its friend, than any kingdom in history. For a man, rightly viewed, comprehendeth the particular natures of all men. Each philosopher, each bard, each actor, has only done for me, as by a delegate, what one day I can do for myself. The books which once we valued more than the apple of the eye, we have quite exhausted. What is that but saying that we have come up with the point of view which the universal mind took through the eyes of one scribe; we have been that man, and have passed on. First, one; then, another; we drain all cisterns, and, waxing greater by all these supplies, we crave a better and more abundant food. The man has never lived that can feed us ever. The human mind cannot be enshrined in a person who shall set a barrier on any one side to this unbounded, unboundable empire. It is one central fire, which, flaming now out of the lips of Etna, lightens the capes of Sicily; and, now out of the throat of Vesuvius[18], illuminates the towers and vineyards of Naples. It is one light which beams out of a thousand stars. It is one soul which animates all men.

But I have dwelt perhaps tediously upon this abstraction of the Scholar. I ought not to delay longer to add what I have to say, of nearer reference to the time and to this country.

Historically, there is thought to be a difference in the ideas which predominate over successive epochs, and there are data for marking the genius of the Classic, of the Romantic, and now of the Reflective or Philosophical age. With the views I have intimated of the oneness or the identity of the mind through all individuals, I do not much dwell on these differences. In fact, I believe each individual passes through all three. The boy is a Greek; the youth, romantic; the adult, reflective. I deny not, however, that a revolution in the leading idea may be distinctly enough traced.

Our age is bewailed as the age of Introversion. Must that needs be evil? We, it seems, are critical. We are embarrassed with second thoughts. We cannot enjoy any thing for hankering to know whereof the pleasure consists. We are lined with eyes. We see with our feet. The time is infected with Hamlet's unhappiness, —

"Sicklied o'er with the pale cast of thought." [19]

Is it so bad then? Sight is the last thing to be pitied. Would we be blind? Do we fear lest we should outsee nature and God, and drink truth dry? I look upon the discontent of the literary class as a mere announcement of the fact that they find themselves not in the state of mind of their fathers, and regret the coming state as untried; as a boy dreads the water before he has learned that he can swim. If there is any period one would desire to be born in, —is it not the age of Revolution; when the old and the new stand side by side, and admit of being compared; when the energies of all men are searched by fear and by hope; when the historic glories of the old, can be compensated by the rich possibilities of the new era? This time, like all times, is a very good one, if we but know what to do with it.

I read with joy some of the auspicious signs of the coming days as they glimmer already through poetry and art, through philosophy and science, through church and state.

One of these signs is the fact that the same movement which effected the elevation of what was called the lowest class in the state, assumed in literature a very marked and as benign an aspect. Instead of the sublime and beautiful, the near, the low, the common, was explored and poetized. That which had been negligently trodden under foot by those who were harnessing and provisioning themselves for long journeys into far countries, is suddenly found to be richer than all foreign parts. The literature of the poor, the feelings of the child, the philosophy of the street, the meaning of household life, are the topics of the time. It is a great stride. It is a sign, —is it not? of new vigor, when the extremities are made active, when currents of warm life run into the hands and the feet. I ask not for the great, the remote, the romantic; what is doing in Italy or Arabia; what is Greek art, or Provencal Minstrelsy[20]; I embrace the common, I explore and sit at the feet of the familiar, the low. Give me insight into to-day, and you may have the antique and future worlds. What would we really know the meaning of? The meal in the firkin; the milk in the pan; the ballad in the street; the news of the boat; the glance of the eye; the form and the gait of the body: —show me the ultimate reason of these matters; —show me the sublime presence of the highest spiritual cause lurking, as always it does lurk, in these suburbs and extremities of nature; let me see every trifle bristling with the polarity that ranges it instantly on an eternal law; and the shop, the plough, and the le[d]ger, referred to the like cause by which light undulates and poets sing; —and the world lies no longer a dull miscellany and lumber room, but has form and order; there is no trifle; there is no puzzle; but one design unites and animates the farthest pinnacle and the lowest trench.

This idea has inspired the genius of Goldsmith, Burns, Cowper, and, in a newer time, of Goethe, Wordsworth, and Carlyle. This idea they have differently followed and with various success. In contrast with their writing, the style of Pope, of Johnson, of Gibbon, looks cold and pedantic. This writing is blood-warm. Man is surprised to find that things near are not less beautiful and wondrous than things remote. The near explains the far. The drop is a small ocean. A man is related to all nature. This perception of the worth of the vulgar, is fruitful in discoveries. Goethe, in this very thing the most modern of the moderns, has shown us, as none ever did, the genius of the ancients.

There is one man of genius who has done much for this philosophy of life, whose literary value has never yet been rightly estimated; —I mean Emanuel Swedenborg[21]. The most imaginative of men, yet writing with the precision of a mathematician, he endeavored to engraft a purely philosophical Ethics on the popular Christianity of his time. Such an attempt, of course, must have difficulty which no genius could surmount. But he saw and showed the connection between nature and the affections of the soul. He pierced the emblematic or spiritual character of the visible, audible, tangible world. Especially did his shade-loving muse hover over and interpret the lower parts of nature; he showed the mysterious bond that allies moral evil to the foul material forms, and has given in epical parables a theory of insanity, of beasts, of unclean and fearful things.

Another sign of our times, also marked by an analogous political movement is, the new importance given to the single person. Every thing that tends to insulate the individual, —to surround him with barriers of natural respect, so that each man shall feel the world is his, and man shall treat with man as a sovereign state with a sovereign state; —tends to true union as well as greatness. "I learned," said the melancholy Pestalozzi[22], "that no man in God's wide earth is either willing or able to help any other man." Help must come from the bosom alone. The scholar is that man who must take up into himself all the ability of the time, all the contributions of the past, all the hopes of the future. He must be an university of knowledges. If there be one lesson more than another which should pierce his ear, it is, The world is nothing, the man is all; in yourself is the law of all nature, and you know not yet how a globule of sap ascends; in yourself slumbers the whole of Reason; it is for you to know all, it is for you to dare all. Mr. President and

Gentlemen, this confidence in the unsearched might of man, belongs by all motives, by all prophecy, by all preparation, to the American Scholar. We have listened too long to the courtly muses of Europe. The spirit of the American freeman is already suspected to be timid, imitative, tame. Public and private avarice make the air we breathe thick and fat. The scholar is decent, indolent, complaisant[23]. See already the tragic consequence. The mind of this country, taught to aim at low objects, eats upon itself. There is no work for any but the decorous and the complaisant. Young men of the fairest promise, who begin life upon our shores, inflated by the mountain winds, shined upon by all the stars of God, find the earth below not in unison with these, —but are hindered from action by the disgust which the principles on which business is managed inspire, and turn drudges, or die of disgust, —some of them suicides. What is the remedy? They did not yet see, and thousands of young men as hopeful now crowding to the barriers for the career, do not yet see, that, if the single man plant himself indomitably on his instincts, and there abide, the huge world will come round to him. Patience, —patience; —with the shades of all the good and great for company; and for solace, the perspective of your own infinite life; and for work, the study and the communication of principles, the making those instincts prevalent, the conversion of the world. Is it not the chief disgrace in the world, not to be an unit; —not to be reckoned one character; —not to yield that peculiar fruit which each man was created to bear, but to be reckoned in the gross, in the hundred, or the thousand, of the party, the section, to which we belong; and our opinion predicted geographically, as the north, or the south. Not so, brothers and friends, —please God, ours shall not be so. We will walk on our own feet; we will work with our own hands; we will speak our own minds. The study of letters shall be no longer a name for pity, for doubt, and for sensual indulgence. The dread of man and the love of man shall be a wall of defence and a wreath of joy around all. A nation of men will for the first time exist, because each believes himself inspired by the Divine Soul which also inspires all men.

Notes:

1. literary year: the academic year, traditionally beginning in September
2. Troubadours: Eleventh- through thirteenth-century poets and musicians of southern France who celebrated courtly love.

3. Harp: Vega, the bright star in the northern constellation Lyra (shaped like a lyre or harp)

4. Pole-star: The North Star, the star closest to the North celestial pole.

5. fables: *Symposium*, by the Greek philosopher Plato, includes a version of this fable.

6. office: function, duty

7. Third Estate: The three "estates" or classes, recognized by feudal Europe as the clergy, the nobility, and the commoners. Emerson's analogy criticized those who value books as objects rather than as manifestations of the world and the spirit.

8. bibliomaniacs: Those who edit texts, and those obsessed with books

9. efflux: out flowing, emanation

10. pecuniary foundations: academic robes, and financial foundations

11. Valetudinarian: an invalid

12. empyrean: The highest heaven

13. ferules: rods or rulers for disciplining children

14. Savoyards: Inhabitants of Savoy, in the French Alps (then part of Italy)

15. Berserkirs: The savage times of ancient pagan Celtic priests (Druids) and legendary Norse warriors who bit their shields and foamed at the mouth (Berserkers) finally gave way to the achievements of Alfred, king of the West Saxons.

16. Flamsteed and Herschel: John Flamsteed is an astronomer who did pioneer work on mapping the Solar System; Sir William Herschel is an astronomer who discovered the planet Uranus in 1781 and conducted seminal research on nebulae and star clusters.

17. signet: Seal, identifying stamp

18. Vesuvius: Active Volcanoes, Etna, on the East coast of Sicily; Vesuvius, near Naples, Italy.

19. "Sicklied o'er with the pale cast of thought.": From Shakespeare's *Hamlet*

20. Provencal Minstrelsy: The musical entertainment of medieval troubadours, centered in Provence, in southeastern France.

21. Emanuel Swedenborg: Swedenborg was a Swedish theologian and mystic whose idea of correspondence between the spiritual and the natural world virtually made Creation an allegory of the divine mind—a concept that intrigued Emerson.

22. Pestalozzi: Johann Heinrich Pestalozzi, a Swiss educator

23. complaisant: Willing to please

Questions for Study and Discussion:

1. What should be considered as "authority" and how do we learn the "truth" ?
2. What thoughts of transcendentalism can be found in this essay?
3. Do you think Emerson's calling of scholar can be achieved? Why or Why not?

Nathaniel Hawthorne (1804—1864)

Life and Major Works

For someone interested in American literature, the name "Nathaniel Hawthorne" is justifiably associated with the genre of romance: "When a writer calls his work a Romance, it need hardly be observed that he wishes to claim a certain latitude...which he would not have felt himself entitled to assume, had he professed to be writing a Novel... The former—while, as a work of art, —has fairly a right to present that truth under circumstances, to a great extent, of the writer's own choosing or creation...he

Nathaniel Hawthorne

may so manage his atmospherical medium as to bring out or mellow the lights, and deepen and enrich the shadows, of the picture. (Hawthorne: Preface to *The House of the Seven Gables*, 1851) Indeed, it is *The Scarlet Letter,* his best known romance that has registered this name "Nathaniel Hawthorne" among the major writers of the United States ever since.

Born in Salem, Massachusetts in 1804, Hawthorne came from a Puritan family of declining fortunes. At the age of four, his father, a sea captain died of yellow fever in Surinam, Dutch Guiana, leaving the family dependent on relatives. Hawthorne attended Bowdoin College and graduated in 1825 the same class with Henry Wadsworth Longfellow. Determined to be a writer, he lived a relatively withdrawn life after he went home, ferociously reading New England history as well as writers such as John Milton, William Shakespeare, and John Bunyan, and published *Fanshawe* and numerous stories later collected in *Twice-Told Tales*. He lived at Brook Farm in 1841 only for several months because the tiring physical labor of this utopian community left him little time for thinking and writing. After their marriage in the summer of 1842, Hawthorne and his wife moved to the Old Manse in Concord, Massachusetts, where they met Ralph Waldo Emerson, Henry

David Thoreau, Amos Bronson Alcott, and other writers and thinkers. He published his second collection of stories, *Mosses from an Old Manse* during this time and drew some critic attention. But it was the coming out of *the Scarlet Letter* that brought him both fame and fortune. At the height of his creativity and productivity during the early 1850s, in addition to *The Scarlet Letter* and *The Blithedale Romance*, he wrote *The House of the Seven Gables* (1851); *The Snow-Image and Other Twice-Told Tales* (1852); *The Life of Franklin Pierce* (1852); and two collections of stories for children, *A Wonder Book* (1852) *and Tanglewood Tales* (1853).

Appointed US consul in Liverpool England, Hawthorne stayed there from 1853 to 1857 and didn't return to Concord until he and his family traveled around Europe for the next three years. His final completed work of fiction *The Marble Faun* got published in 1860, four years before his death.

Throughout his literary career, Hawthorne tried to explore the psychological implications of the Calvinist Doctrines. He seemed haunted by the constant tension and battle between the flesh and the spirit in the lives of the 17th Century Puritans. Reading his tales and romances, one cannot but be overwhelmed by the "black" vision which they reveal. Short stories like "My Kinsman, Major Molineux" (1832), "The Minister's Black Veil" (1836), "Young Goodman Brown" (1835), "The Maypole of Merrymount" (1836), "The Birth-Mark" (1843), "Rappaccini's Daughter" (1844), "Ethan Brand" (1850) and many more of the *Twice Told Tales*, and *Mosses from an Old Manse*, dealt with the themes of guilt and secrecy, intellectual and moral pride, and the corrosive effects of these spiritual dilemmas on the personality of Puritan New England.

Regarded as the finest literary embodiment of the New England traditions in which he was so deeply imbued, he analyzed the inner life, the working of the human heart and will. *The Scarlet Letter*, structurally compact in a tiny frame told seemingly simple story: Hester Prynne, a passionate young woman was put to stand on a pillory and sentenced to wear a scarlet "A (dulteress)" all her life as a punishment because she would never tell the name of the father of her illicit child. Her legal husband, delayed by the Indians for quite some time on his way to join his beautiful wife in New England happened to witness all this. Driven by the desire of revenge, he assumed the name Roger Chillingworth and disguised himself as a physician so that he could find out who the wife's lover was. It was not long before he realized that nobody else but the much "revered", "saintly" minister, Reverend Arthur Dimmesdale was the one. He ruthlessly tortured himself physically for his double sins of adultery and hypocrisy, and got ruthlessly tortured psychologically by Chillingworth. As time went on, both his physical health and psychological peace gave way to the secret torment over years. He finally made a public confession about everything on the pillory and got a kiss from the daughter Pearl and died in Hester's arms...Acclaimed by many literary historians as the first great American novel, *The Scarlet Letter* showed Hawthorne, the literary artist, at his best. It was the finest example of Hawthorne's unique gift to create strongly symbolic stories which touched the deepest roots of human's moral nature. It presented New England confrontation of individual and society, the nature of adultery, the personal character of religion and the trauma of psychological independence.

He writes, however, not to teach moral lessons, which are themselves his fictional materials rather than his conclusions. He had in himself nothing of the reformer, nothing of the hot spirit of the man who is roused to seek the remedy. The evil which Hawthorne saw in the world is as old as the world itself, began with the fall of man, and will cease only when human nature ceases. Hence he did not write "novels of purpose." He wrote as pure artist, setting down the facts and phenomena of sin with a sure hand, appealing to the individual conscience.

Hawthorne's art is the art of concentration; by depth below depth of character, of personality, of spiritual and psychic experience. Elevated in diction and restrained in rhetoric, Hawthorne's style is thus graceful and polished. His works combine an old-fashioned neoclassic purity of diction with a latent and hard complexity of meaning. They are broadly allegorical but infused with imaginative passion. His vocabulary was wide and well controlled. He chose his words with a sharp sense of precise meaning and a keen ear for pleasant sound. His sentences may seem long to contemporary readers, but grammatical subordination employed with sufficient logic made the writing smooth and clear. As Stockton Axson says of Hawthorne's talent: "The range is narrow, but the vein is deep; into these few characters Hawthorne probes until the utmost secrets of their inmost lives have been revealed..."

Hawthorne uses concrete objects as well as characters to serve as his symbols. He concentrated on a few main physical symbols repeated often (as the scaffold in *The Scarlet Letter,* or the pink ribbon in *Yong Goodman Brown*), or some symbols running through the whole story, as is the case with the black veil in *Minister's*

Black Veil, or the birthmark in *The Birthmark*. He used the fluidity of character development to illustrate the ways in which symbols grow and change based upon one's perception of them. In *The Scarlet Letter*, for instance, the symbolism of "A" changes from "Adultery", to "Able", and to "Angel".

Hawthorne was excellent at describing the complexities and ambiguities of human psychology. In fact, what makes the Hawthornian symbolism truly special is the presence of ambiguity. Even Hawthorne himself admitted that his allegorical style is vague and not easy to understand: "I am not quite sure that I entirely comprehend my own meaning in these blasted allegories". He leaves it to the readers to decide what is literally true. By presenting the co-existence of contradictory forces on the individual such as sensuality and repression of the sensuality, conformity and individualism, reason and emotion, he shows that humankind can never solve the mysteries and the ambiguities of a divided human psychology. In his preface to *The House of Seven Gables,* he says that "A high truth, indeed, fairly, finely, and skillfully wrought out, brightening at every step, and crowning the final development of a work of fiction, may add an artistic glory, but it is never any truer, and seldom any more evident, at the last page than at the first". Hawthorne's refusal to allow easy interpretations gave his work a richness which would otherwise have been impossible to achieve.

Hawthorne has long been recognized as a classic interpreter of the spiritual history of New England, in many of his short works as well as novels, he wrote masterpieces of romantic fiction, he was a leader in the development of the short story as a distinctive American genre. His influence has been great. He was accorded due recognition by his contemporary James and Edgar Allen Poe. William Faulkner and some Gothic novelists show their indebtedness to him. As Henry James put it: "(Hawthorne's) work will remain....Among the men of imagination he will have his niche."

Brief Introduction and Appreciation

Metaphorized as "the pale tint of flowers that blossomed in too retired a shade", "The Minister's Black Veil" (1836) stands as one of Hawthorne's best known and most contentious short stories. First published in the Token, the story is also included in Hawthorne's first collection of short stories, *Twice-Told Tales* (1837). On the basis of his efforts in such early stories as "The Minister's Black Veil", Hawthorne earns critical praise and begins to establish himself as an American author of repute.

It concerns Reverend Hooper, who appears one day wearing a black veil over his face. The congregation views this with "astonishment," a reaction one might expect. People begin to question whether it is really "our parson" behind the veil, some are not quite sure it is indeed their minister behind the sinister cloth; some believe "He has changed himself into something awful" while others simply conclude that "Our parson has gone mad!" Later in the afternoon, Hooper officiates at the funeral of a young woman whose corpse shudders upon seeing under the veil the face of the minister, according to one mourner. At a wedding which follows the funeral, Hooper's veil casts a somber tone over the normally joyous event. Hooper himself, when "catching a glimpse of his figure in the looking-glass...he spilt the untasted wine... and rushed forth into the darkness." Nothing, not the pleas of the elders, nor the nudging of Elizabeth, the fianc e, can persuade Hooper to remove the piece of black crape. In this manner, "good Mr. Hooper" lives in solitude for the rest of his life; while men and women avoid him and children flee from him, he "sadly smiled at the pale visages of the worldly throng as he passed by." Nevertheless, long shunned and suspected ("unloved and dimly feared") as a man, Hooper succeeds greatly as a preacher: "among all the bad influences, the black veil had the one desirable effect of making its wearer a very efficient clergyman." Before putting on the veil, the minister has a mild, persuasive influence on his congregation. But after putting on the veil, Hooper delivers "the most powerful effort that they had ever heard from their pastor's lips". The sermon in question concerns "secret sin, and those sad mysteries which we hide from our nearest and dearest, and would fain conceal from our own consciousness..." A "subtle power was breathed into his words". It is this power of revealing truths that convinces the congregation of some "unwonted attribute in their minister" and changes him to "a man of awful power." The story comes to an end when on his deathbed, the minister adamantly refuses to remove the veil so that as "a veiled corpse they brought him to the grave."

The intricacies of this enigmatic tale are very rich due to the fact that Hawthorne does not provide a conclusive and comprehensive explanation of Hooper's motivations and intentions. This has led the critics to engage in over a century of debate, resulting in many varied theories. The story is set in Puritan New England and focuses on the particular ideology and theology of that time period. At the heart of The Great Awakening, the Puritans were consumed with the idea of the pervasiveness of sin, believing that all humans sin continuously. Therefore, some critics believe the story of Reverend Mr. Hooper, the type figure so obsessed with sin as to cut himself from the rest of the world by putting a barrier (the veil) between himself and the others is to display the danger of the oppressive puritan society, which encloses the mind of individuals, turning them into extremists, into isolated human beings. Others argue that more than isolation, the minister's black veil symbolizes to his parishioners the secret, sinful nature of humans, who hide unappealing aspects of themselves behind a veneer of respectability. Putting on the veil makes it possible for the minster to reveal to himself and to others the deepest and most painful truths. In this sense the veil is not that it hides Hooper, but rather that it acts as a filter through which he views the world. Hooper wears a black veil in order to hide his face from the gaze of others and from himself to symbolize the fact that everyone else in the community puts on a fa ade of righteousness and innocence in order to hide his sinfulness from the knowledge of everyone else in the community and even from themselves. Some critics are interested in the blackness of the veil, believing it is of significance in this instance, because it gives a "darkened aspect" to things, shutting out the treacherous light which illuminates inherently false appearances, thus enabling him to see into men's souls and reveal to them what he sees.

Some scholars, such as Austin Warren and Leland Schubert, have focused on Hooper's motivations for donning the veil, reflecting upon the terrible sin Hooper must have committed to drive him to such an extreme action. Edgar Allan Poe has argued that Hooper had committed a sexual sin against the woman whose funeral Hooper conducted on the first day. Robert D. Crie has asserted that Hooper fears women and uses the veil as a means to shield himself from sexual encounters. Other scholars have found that the focus of the story is not on what motivates Hooper to wear the veil, but the effect the covering has on the minister and his congregation. Focusing on the tale's ecclesiastic setting and subject, many scholars have considered it in light of Biblical references. And still other scholars have proposed that ambiguity is the point of the story. Neal Frank Doubleday has stated: "Hawthorne's ambiguity is one of his ways of representing his pervasive sense of mystery, a kind of humility in him."

Despite the controversy over the story, critics have generally agreed that the story is successful, many praising it as an example of Hawthorne's finest work. As Robert E. Morsberger has declared, the power of the story is Hawthorne's transcendence of the Puritan setting to create a tale which is enduring and timeless and still relevant to today's reader.

Selected Reading

The Minister's Black Veil
A Parable

THE SEXTON[1] stood in the porch of Milford meeting-house, pulling busily at the bell-rope. The old people of the village came stooping along the street. Children, with bright faces, tripped merrily beside their parents, or mimicked a graver gait, in the conscious dignity of their Sunday clothes. Spruce bachelors looked sidelong at the pretty maidens, and fancied that the Sabbath sunshine made them prettier than on week days. When the throng had mostly streamed into the porch, the sexton began to toll the bell, keeping his eye on the Reverend Mr. Hooper's door. The first glimpse of the clergyman's figure was the signal for the bell to cease its summons.

"But what has good Parson Hooper got upon his face?" cried the sexton in astonishment.

All within hearing immediately turned about, and beheld the semblance[2] of Mr. Hooper, pacing slowly his meditative way towards the meeting-house. With one accord they started, expressing more wonder than if some strange minister were coming to dust the cushions of Mr. Hooper's pulpit.

"Are you sure it is our parson?" inquired Goodman Gray of the sexton.

"Of a certainty it is good Mr. Hooper," replied the sexton. "He was to have exchanged pulpits with Parson Shute, of Westbury; but Parson Shute sent to excuse himself yesterday, being to preach a funeral sermon."

The cause of so much amazement may appear sufficiently slight. Mr. Hooper, a gentlemanly person, of about thirty, though still a bachelor, was dressed with due clerical neatness, as if a careful wife had starched his band, and brushed the weekly dust from his Sunday's garb. There was but one thing remarkable in his appearance. Swathed about his forehead, and hanging down over his face, so low as to be shaken by his breath, Mr. Hooper had on a black veil. On a nearer view it seemed to consist of two folds of crape, which entirely concealed his features, except the mouth and chin, but probably did not intercept his sight, further than to give a darkened aspect to all living and inanimate things. With this gloomy shade before him, good Mr. Hooper walked onward, at a slow and quiet pace, stooping somewhat, and looking on the ground, as is customary with abstracted men, yet nodding kindly to those of his parishioners who still waited on the meeting-house steps. But so wonder-struck were they that his greeting hardly met with a return.

"I can't really feel as if good Mr. Hooper's face was behind that piece of crape," said the sexton.

"I don't like it," muttered an old woman, as she hobbled into the meeting-house. "He has changed himself into something awful, only by hiding his face."

"Our parson has gone mad!" cried Goodman Gray, following him across the threshold.

A rumor of some unaccountable phenomenon had preceded Mr. Hooper into the meeting-house, and set all the congregation astir. Few could refrain from twisting their heads towards the door; many stood upright, and turned directly about; while several little boys clambered upon the seats, and came down again with a terrible racket. There was a general bustle, a rustling of the women's gowns and shuffling of the men's feet, greatly at variance with that hushed repose which should attend the entrance of the minister. But Mr. Hooper appeared not to notice the perturbation[3] of his people. He entered with an almost noiseless step, bent his head mildly to the pews on each side, and bowed as he passed his oldest parishioner, a white-haired great-grandsire, who occupied an arm-chair in the centre of the aisle. It was strange to observe how slowly this venerable man became conscious of something singular in the appearance of his pastor. He seemed not fully to partake of the prevailing wonder, till Mr. Hooper had ascended the stairs, and showed himself in the pulpit, face to face with his congregation, except for the black veil. That mysterious emblem was never once withdrawn. It shook with his measured breath, as he gave out the psalm; it threw its obscurity between him and the holy page, as he read the Scriptures; and while he prayed, the veil lay heavily on his uplifted countenance. Did he seek to hide it from the dread Being whom he was addressing?

Such was the effect of this simple piece of crape, that more than one woman of delicate nerves was forced to leave the meeting-house. Yet perhaps the pale-faced congregation was almost as fearful a sight to the minister, as his black veil to them.

Mr. Hooper had the reputation of a good preacher, but not an energetic one: he strove to win his people heavenward by mild, persuasive influences, rather than to drive them thither[4] by the thunders of the Word. The sermon which he now delivered was marked by the same characteristics of style and manner as the general series of his pulpit oratory. But there was something, either in the sentiment of the discourse itself, or in the imagination of the auditors, which made it greatly the most powerful effort that they had ever heard from their pastor's lips. It was tinged, rather more darkly than usual, with the gentle gloom of Mr. Hooper's temperament. The subject had reference to secret sin, and those sad mysteries which we hide from our nearest and dearest, and would fain conceal from our own consciousness, even forgetting that the Omniscient[5] can detect them. A subtle power was breathed into his words. Each member of the congregation, the most innocent girl, and the man of hardened breast, felt as if the preacher had crept upon them, behind his awful veil, and discovered their hoarded iniquity of deed or thought. Many spread their clasped hands on their bosoms. There was nothing terrible in what Mr. Hooper said, at least, no violence; and yet, with every tremor of his melancholy voice, the hearers quaked. An unsought pathos came hand in hand with awe. So sensible were the audience of some unwonted attribute in their minister, that they longed for a breath of wind to blow aside the veil, almost believing that a stranger's visage would be discovered, though the form, gesture, and voice were those of Mr. Hooper.

At the close of the services, the people hurried out with indecorous[6] confusion, eager to communicate their pent-up amazement, and conscious of lighter spirits the moment they lost sight of the black veil. Some gathered in little circles, huddled closely together, with their mouths all whispering in the centre; some went homeward alone, wrapt in silent meditation; some talked loudly, and profaned the Sabbath day with ostentatious laughter. A few shook their sagacious[7] heads, intimating that they could penetrate the mystery; while one or two affirmed that there was no mystery at all, but only that Mr. Hooper's eyes were so weakened by the midnight lamp, as to require a shade. After a brief interval, forth came good Mr. Hooper also, in the rear of his flock. Turning his veiled face from one group to another, he paid due reverence to the hoary heads, saluted the middle aged with kind dignity as their friend and spiritual guide, greeted the young with mingled authority and love, and laid his hands on the little children's heads to bless them. Such was always his custom on the Sabbath day. Strange and bewildered looks repaid him for his courtesy. None, as on former occasions, aspired to the honor of walking by their pastor's side. Old Squire Saunders, doubtless by an accidental lapse of memory, neglected to invite Mr. Hooper to his table, where the good clergyman had been wont to bless the food, almost every Sunday since his settlement. He returned, therefore, to the parsonage, and, at the moment of closing the door, was observed to look back upon the people, all of whom had their eyes fixed upon the minister. A sad smile gleamed faintly from beneath the black veil, and flickered about his mouth, glimmering as he disappeared.

"How strange," said a lady, "that a simple black veil, such as any woman might wear on her bonnet, should become such a terrible thing on Mr. Hooper's face!"

"Something must surely be amiss with Mr. Hooper's intellects," observed her husband, the physician of the village. "But the strangest part of the affair is the effect of this vagary[8] even on a sober-minded man like myself. The black veil, though it covers only our pastor's face, throws its influence over his whole person, and makes him ghostlike from head to foot. Do you not feel it so?"

"Truly do I," replied the lady; "and I would not be alone with him for the world. I wonder he is not afraid to be alone with himself!"

"Men sometimes are so," said her husband.

The afternoon service was attended with similar circumstances. At its conclusion, the bell tolled for the funeral of a young lady. The relatives and friends were assembled in the house, and the more distant acquaintances stood about the door, speaking of the good qualities of the deceased, when their talk was interrupted by the appearance of Mr. Hooper, still covered with his black veil. It was now an appropriate emblem. The clergyman stepped into the room where the corpse was laid, and bent over the coffin, to take a last farewell of his deceased parishioner. As he stooped, the veil hung straight down from his forehead, so that, if her eyelids had not been closed forever, the dead maiden might have seen his face. Could Mr. Hooper be fearful of her glance, that he so hastily caught back the black veil? A person who watched the interview between the dead and living, scrupled not to affirm, that, at the instant when the clergyman's features were disclosed, the corpse had slightly shuddered, rustling the shroud and muslin cap, though the countenance retained the composure of death. A superstitious old woman was the only witness of this prodigy[9]. From the coffin Mr. Hooper passed into the chamber of the mourners, and thence to the head of the staircase, to make the funeral prayer. It was a tender and heart-dissolving prayer, full of sorrow, yet so imbued with celestial hopes, that the music of a heavenly harp, swept by the fingers of the dead, seemed faintly to be heard among the saddest accents of the minister. The people trembled, though they but darkly understood him when he prayed that they, and himself, and all of mortal race, might be ready, as he trusted this young maiden had been, for the dreadful hour that should snatch the veil from their faces. The bearers went heavily forth, and the mourners followed, saddening all the street, with the dead before them, and Mr. Hooper in his black veil behind.

"Why do you look back?" said one in the procession to his partner.

"I had a fancy," replied she, "that the minister and the maiden's spirit were walking hand in hand."

"And so had I, at the same moment," said the other.

That night, the handsomest couple in Milford village were to be joined in wedlock. Though reckoned a melancholy man, Mr. Hooper had a placid cheerfulness for such occasions, which often excited a sympathetic smile where livelier merriment would have been thrown away. There was no quality of his disposition which made him more beloved than this. The company at the wedding awaited his arrival with impatience, trusting that the strange awe, which had gathered over him throughout the day, would now be dispelled. But such was not the result. When Mr. Hooper came, the first thing that their eyes rested on was the same horrible black veil, which had added deeper gloom to the funeral, and could portend nothing but evil to the wedding. Such was its immediate effect on the guests that a cloud seemed to have rolled duskily from beneath the black crape, and dimmed the light of the candles. The bridal pair stood up before the minister. But the bride's cold fingers quivered in the tremulous hand of the bridegroom, and her deathlike paleness caused a whisper that the maiden who had been buried a few hours before was come from her grave to be married. If ever another wedding were so dismal, it was that famous one where they tolled the wedding knell. After performing the ceremony, Mr. Hooper raised a glass of wine to his lips, wishing happiness to the new-married couple in a strain of mild pleasantry that ought to have brightened the features of the guests, like a cheerful gleam from the hearth. At that instant, catching a glimpse of his figure in the looking-glass, the black veil involved his own spirit in the horror with which it overwhelmed all others. His frame shuddered, his lips grew white, he spilt the untasted wine upon the carpet, and rushed forth into the darkness. For the Earth, too, had on her Black Veil.

The next day, the whole village of Milford talked of little else than Parson Hooper's black veil. That, and the mystery concealed behind it, supplied a topic for discussion between acquaintances meeting in the street, and good women gossiping at their open windows. It was the first item of news that the tavern-keeper told to his guests. The children babbled of it on their way to school. One imitative little imp covered his face with an old black handkerchief, thereby so affrighting his playmates that the panic seized himself, and he well-nigh lost his wits by his own waggery.

It was remarkable that of all the busybodies and impertinent people in the parish, not one ventured to put the plain question to Mr. Hooper, wherefore[10] he did this thing. Hitherto, whenever there appeared the slightest call for such interference, he had never lacked advisers, nor shown himself adverse to be guided by their judgment. If he erred at all, it was by so painful a degree of self-distrust, that even the mildest censure would lead him to consider an indifferent action as a crime. Yet, though so well acquainted with this amiable weakness, no individual among his parishioners chose to make the black veil a subject of friendly remonstrance[11]. There was a feeling of dread, neither plainly confessed nor carefully concealed, which caused each to shift the responsibility upon another, till at length it was found expedient to send a deputation of the church, in order to deal with Mr. Hooper about the mystery, before it should grow into a scandal. Never did an embassy so ill discharge its duties. The minister received them with friendly courtesy, but became silent, after they were seated, leaving to his visitors the whole burden of introducing their important business. The topic, it might be supposed, was obvious enough. There was the black veil swathed round Mr. Hooper's forehead, and concealing every feature above his placid mouth, on which, at times, they could perceive the glimmering of a melancholy smile. But that piece of crape, to their imagination, seemed to hang down before his heart, the symbol of a fearful secret between him and them. Were the veil but cast aside, they might speak freely of it, but not till then. Thus they sat a considerable time, speechless, confused, and shrinking uneasily from Mr. Hooper's eye, which they felt to be fixed upon them with an invisible glance. Finally, the deputies returned abashed to their constituents, pronouncing the matter too weighty to be handled, except by a council of the churches, if, indeed, it might not require a general synod[12].

But there was one person in the village unappalled by the awe with which the black veil had impressed all beside herself. When the deputies returned without an explanation, or even venturing to demand one, she, with the calm energy of her character, determined to chase away the strange cloud that appeared to be settling round Mr. Hooper, every moment more darkly than before. As his plighted wife, it should be her privilege to know what the black veil concealed. At the minister's first visit, therefore, she entered upon the subject with a direct simplicity, which made the task easier both for him and her. After he had seated himself, she fixed her eyes steadfastly upon the veil, but could discern nothing of the dreadful gloom that had so overawed the multitude: it was but a double fold of crape, hanging down from his forehead to his mouth, and slightly stirring with his breath.

"No," said she aloud, and smiling, "there is nothing terrible in this piece of crape, except that it hides a face which I am always glad to look upon. Come, good sir, let the sun shine from behind the cloud. First lay aside your black veil: then tell me why you put it on."

Mr. Hooper's smile glimmered faintly.

"There is an hour to come," said he, "when all of us shall cast aside our veils. Take it not amiss, beloved friend, if I wear this piece of crape till then."

"Your words are a mystery, too," returned the young lady. "Take away the veil from them, at least."

"Elizabeth, I will," said he, "so far as my vow may suffer me. Know, then, this veil is a type and a symbol, and I am bound to wear it ever, both in light and darkness, in solitude and before the gaze of multitudes, and as with strangers, so with my familiar friends. No mortal eye will see it withdrawn. This dismal shade must separate me from the world: even you, Elizabeth, can never come behind it!"

"What grievous affliction hath befallen you," she earnestly inquired, "that you should thus darken your eyes forever?"

"If it be a sign of mourning," replied Mr. Hooper, "I, perhaps, like most other mortals, have sorrows dark enough to be typified by a black veil."

"But what if the world will not believe that it is the type of an innocent sorrow?" urged Elizabeth. "Beloved and respected as you are, there may be whispers that you hide your face under the consciousness of secret sin. For the sake of your holy office, do away this scandal!"

The color rose into her cheeks as she intimated the nature of the rumors that were already abroad in the village. But Mr. Hooper's mildness did not forsake him. He even smiled again—that same sad smile, which always appeared like a faint glimmering of light, proceeding from the obscurity beneath the veil.

"If I hide my face for sorrow, there is cause enough," he merely replied; "and if I cover it for secret sin, what mortal might not do the same?"

And with this gentle, but unconquerable obstinacy[13] did he resist all her entreaties. At length Elizabeth sat silent. For a few moments she appeared lost in thought, considering, probably, what new methods might be tried to withdraw her lover from so dark a fantasy, which, if it had no other meaning, was perhaps a symptom of mental disease. Though of a firmer character than his own, the tears rolled down her cheeks. But, in an instant, as it were, a new feeling took the place of sorrow: her eyes were fixed insensibly on the black veil, when, like a sudden twilight in the air, its terrors fell around her. She arose, and stood trembling before him.

"And do you feel it then, at last?" said he mournfully.

She made no reply, but covered her eyes with her hand, and turned to leave the room. He rushed forward and caught her arm.

"Have patience with me, Elizabeth!" cried he, passionately. "Do not desert me, though this veil must be between us here on earth. Be mine, and hereafter there shall be no veil over my face, no darkness between our souls! It is but a mortal veil—it is not for eternity! O! you know not how lonely I am, and how frightened, to be alone behind my black veil. Do not leave me in this miserable obscurity forever!"

"Lift the veil but once, and look me in the face," said she.

"Never! It cannot be!" replied Mr. Hooper.

"Then farewell!" said Elizabeth.

She withdrew her arm from his grasp, and slowly departed, pausing at the door, to give one long shuddering gaze, that seemed almost to penetrate the mystery of the black veil. But, even amid his grief, Mr. Hooper smiled to think that only a material emblem had separated him from happiness, though the horrors, which it shadowed forth, must be drawn darkly between the fondest of lovers.

From that time no attempts were made to remove Mr. Hooper's black veil, or, by a direct appeal, to discover the secret which it was supposed to hide. By persons who claimed a superiority to popular prejudice, it was reckoned merely an eccentric whim, such as often mingles with the sober actions of men otherwise rational, and tinges them all with its own semblance of insanity. But with the multitude, good Mr. Hooper was irreparably a bugbear[14]. He could not walk the street with any peace of mind, so conscious was he that the gentle and timid would turn aside to avoid him, and that others would make it a point of hardihood to throw themselves in his way. The impertinence of the latter class compelled him to give up his customary walk at sunset to the burial ground; for when he leaned pensively over the gate, there would always be faces behind the gravestones, peeping at his black veil. A fable went the rounds that the stare of the dead people drove him thence. It grieved him, to the very depth of his kind heart, to observe how the children fled from his approach, breaking up their merriest sports, while his melancholy figure was yet afar off. Their instinctive dread caused him to feel more strongly than aught[15] else, that a preternatural horror was interwoven with the threads of the black crape. In truth, his own antipathy to the veil was known to be so great, that he never willingly passed before a mirror, nor stooped to drink at a still fountain, lest, in its peaceful bosom, he should be affrighted by himself. This was what gave plausibility to the whispers, that Mr. Hooper's conscience tortured him for some great crime too horrible to be entirely concealed, or otherwise than so obscurely intimated. Thus, from beneath the black veil, there rolled a cloud into the sunshine, an ambiguity of sin or sorrow, which enveloped the poor minister, so that love or sympathy could never reach him. It was said that ghost and fiend consorted with him there. With self-shudderings and outward terrors, he walked continually in its shadow, groping darkly within his own soul, or gazing through a medium that saddened the whole world. Even the lawless wind, it was believed, respected his dreadful secret, and never blew aside the veil. But still good Mr. Hooper sadly smiled at the pale visages of the worldly throng as he passed by.

Among all its bad influences, the black veil had the one desirable effect, of making its wearer a very efficient clergyman. By the aid of his mysterious emblem—for there was no other apparent cause—he became a man of awful power over souls that were in agony for sin. His converts always regarded him with a dread peculiar to themselves, affirming, though but figuratively, that, before he brought them to celestial light, they had been with him behind the black veil. Its gloom, indeed, enabled him to sympathize with all dark affections. Dying sinners cried aloud for Mr. Hooper, and would not yield their breath till he appeared; though ever, as he stooped to whisper consolation, they shuddered at the veiled face so near their own. Such were the terrors of the black veil, even when Death had bared his visage! Strangers came long distances to attend service at his church, with the mere idle purpose of gazing at his figure, because it was forbidden them to behold his face. But many were made to quake ere they departed! Once, during Governor Belcher's administration, Mr. Hooper was appointed to preach the election sermon. Covered with his black veil, he stood before the chief magistrate, the council, and the representatives, and wrought so deep an impression that the legislative measures of that year were characterized by all the gloom and piety of our earliest ancestral sway.

In this manner Mr. Hooper spent a long life, irreproachable in outward act, yet shrouded in dismal suspicions; kind and loving, though unloved, and dimly feared; a man apart from men, shunned in their health and joy, but ever summoned to their aid in mortal anguish. As years wore on, shedding their snows above his sable veil, he acquired a name throughout the New England churches, and they called him Father Hooper. Nearly all his parishioners, who were of mature age when he was settled, had been borne away by many a funeral: he had one congregation in the church, and a more crowded one in the churchyard; and having wrought so late into the evening[16] and done his work so well, it was now good Father Hooper's turn to rest.

Several persons were visible by the shaded candle-light, in the death chamber of the old clergyman. Natural connections he had none. But there was the decorously grave[17], though unmoved physician, seeking only to mitigate the last pangs of the patient whom he could not save. There were the deacons, and other eminently pious members of his church. There, also, was the Reverend Mr. Clark, of Westbury, a young and zealous divine, who had ridden in haste to pray by the bedside of the expiring minister. There was the nurse, no hired handmaiden of death, but one whose calm affection had endured thus long in secrecy, in solitude, amid the chill of age, and would not perish, even at the dying hour. Who, but Elizabeth! And there lay the hoary head of good Father Hooper upon the death pillow, with the black veil still swathed about his brow, and reaching down over his face, so that each more difficult gasp of his faint breath caused it to stir. All through life that piece of crape had hung between him and the world: it had separated him from cheerful brotherhood and woman's love, and kept him in that saddest of all prisons, his own heart; and still it lay upon his face, as if to deepen the gloom of his darksome chamber, and shade him from the sunshine of eternity.

For some time previous, his mind had been confused, wavering doubtfully between the past and the present, and hovering forward, as it were, at intervals, into the indistinctness of the world to come. There had been feverish turns, which tossed him from side to side, and wore away what little strength he had. But in his most convulsive struggles, and in the wildest vagaries of his intellect, when no other thought retained its sober influence, he still showed an awful solicitude lest the black veil should slip aside. Even if his bewildered soul could have forgotten, there was a faithful woman at his pillow, who, with averted eyes, would have covered that aged face, which she had last beheld in the comeliness of manhood. At length the death-stricken old man lay quietly in the torpor of mental and bodily exhaustion, with an imperceptible pulse, and breath that grew fainter and fainter, except when a long, deep, and irregular inspiration seemed to prelude the flight of his spirit.

The minister of Westbury approached the bedside.

"Venerable Father Hooper," said he, "the moment of your release is at hand. Are you ready for the lifting of the veil that shuts in time from eternity?"

Father Hooper at first replied merely by a feeble motion of his head; then, apprehensive, perhaps, that his meaning might be doubtful, he exerted himself to speak.

"Yea," said he, in faint accents, "my soul hath a patient weariness until that veil be lifted."

"And is it fitting," resumed the Reverend Mr. Clark, "that a man so given to prayer, of such a blameless example, holy in deed and thought, so far as mortal judgment may pronounce; is it fitting that a father in the church should leave a shadow on his memory, that may seem to blacken a life so pure? I pray you, my venerable brother, let not this thing be! Suffer us to be gladdened by your triumphant aspect as you go to your reward. Before the veil of eternity be lifted, let me cast aside this black veil from your face!"

And thus speaking, the Reverend Mr. Clark bent forward to reveal the mystery of so many years. But, exerting a sudden energy, that made all the beholders stand aghast, Father Hooper snatched both his hands from beneath the bedclothes, and pressed them strongly on the black veil, resolute to struggle, if the minister of Westbury would contend with a dying man.

"Never!" cried the veiled clergyman. "On earth, never!"

"Dark old man!" exclaimed the affrighted minister, "with what horrible crime upon your soul are you now passing to the judgment?"

Father Hooper's breath heaved; it rattled in his throat; but, with a mighty effort, grasping forward with his hands, he caught hold of life, and held it back till he should speak. He even raised himself in bed; and there he sat, shivering with the arms of death around him, while the black veil hung down, awful at that last moment, in the gathered terrors of a lifetime. And yet the faint, sad smile, so often there, now seemed to glimmer from its obscurity, and linger on Father Hooper's lips.

"Why do you tremble at me alone?" cried he, turning his veiled face round the circle of pale spectators. "Tremble also at each other! Have men avoided me, and women shown no pity, and children screamed and fled, only for my black veil? What, but the mystery which it obscurely typifies[18] has made this piece of crape so awful? When the friend shows his inmost heart to his friend; the lover to his best beloved; when man does not vainly shrink from the eye of his Creator, loathsomely treasuring up the secret of his sin; then deem me a monster, for the symbol beneath which I have lived, and die! I look around me, and, lo! on every visage a Black Veil!"

While his auditors shrank from one another, in mutual affright, Father Hooper fell back upon his pillow, a veiled corpse, with a faint smile lingering on the lips. Still veiled, they laid him in his coffin, and a veiled corpse they bore him to the grave. The grass of many years has sprung up and withered on that grave, the burial stone is moss-grown, and good Mr. Hooper's face is dust; but awful is still the thought that it mouldered beneath the Black Veil!

NOTE. Another clergyman in New England, Mr. Joseph Moody, of York, Maine, who died about eighty years since, made himself remarkable by the same eccentricity that is here related of the Reverend Mr. Hooper. In his case, however, the symbol had a different import. In early life he had accidentally killed a beloved friend; and from that day till the hour of his own death, he hid his face from men.

Notes:

1. sexton: church employee who takes care of the building and other small jobs
2. semblance: shape or form
3. perturbation: disturbed feelings
4. thither: there
5. the Omniscient: the God, the all-knowing
6. indecorous: inappropriate
7. sagacious: wise
8. vagary: irresponsible whim
9. prodigy: unusual event
10. wherefore: why

11. remonstrate: protest, objection

12. synod: a very large group of churches

13. obstinacy: stubbornness

14. bugbear: always a problem

15. aught: anything

16. the evening: a metaphor to mean old age

17. grave: politely solemn

18. typifies: mystically represents

Questions for Study and Discussion:

1. What incidents start rumors about Mr. Hooper's reason for wearing the veil?

2. Why does Elizabeth break her engagement to Mr. Hooper?

3. As time passes, how do people treat Mr. Hooper? Consider the actions of children and of the dying. Why do you think they treat him that way?

4. Hawthorne is careful to describe Rev. Clark of Westbury as "young and zealous." What difference does Rev. Clark's age make? How might a minister closer to Mr. Hooper's age have handled the situation?

5. Why do you think Mr. Hooper will not remove the veil, even as he is dying?

Part Three The Age of Realism and Naturalism

(1861—1914)

Introduction

I. Historical Background

The Romantic idealism of American writing before 1861 gave way to a realistic perspective on what America had become under the pressure of war and expansion as well as the acceleration of the technological, economic, and social change. Those who lived through the Civil War found it increasingly hard to imagine prewar realities. Harvard professor George Ticknor observed in 1868 that the Civil War had opened a "great gulf between what happened before in our century and what has happened since, or what is likely to happen hereafter. It does not seem to me as if I were living in the country in which I was born."

The war put an end to slavery and the Southern plantation aristocracy while setting in motion forces that transformed the nation. Between 1861 and 1914 America metamorphosed from a rural, agrarian, insular nation to an industrialized, urbanized world power. At every stage in this radical transformation, citizens must have looked back on the prewar world as quaint and lost forever while indulging a nostalgia for a simpler America of small villages, stable communities, and shared cultural values. Who Americans were and what America had become were the dominant themes of literature as the first clear outlines of modern American life took shape.

In 1860 the U.S. population was less than 40 million; by 1900 it had doubled, and by 1920 it had swelled to almost 106 million. Before the Civil War the vast majority of the population lived in rural areas, with 60 percent of the work force engaged in farming; by 1900 a third of the population were city dwellers and more worked in industry than in agriculture. To win the Civil War, Northern industries were modernized and expanded—a process that made a few enormously wealthy and set in motion a scramble for power and gain that worried President Lincoln, who feared that by winning the war the American democracy might be destroyed. He predicted this with uncanny accuracy in a letter discussing the postwar period: "I see in the near future a crisis that unnerves and causes me to tremble for the safety of my country. By the result of the war, corporations have been enthroned, and an era of corruption in high places will follow, and the money power of the country will endeavor to prolong its reign by working upon the prejudices of the people, until all wealth is aggregated in a few hands and the Republic is destroyed." Mark Twain called the postwar era that Lincoln feared the "Gilded Age," others the "Great Barbecue." It was the age of the robber barons, of unchecked accumulation by a few, widespread political corruption, and a widening gap between rich and poor that threatened to turn the democracy into a plutocracy. By 1904, 1 percent of the nation's businesses controlled 40 percent of the industrial production. Cheap labor came from abroad, and by the turn of the century a million immigrants were arriving annually, most living in appalling slum conditions and working in dangerous settings. By 1914 the United States had grown into the industrial powerhouse of the world, eclipsing every other nation in its productivity and resources. Electricity was beginning to power the nation, a rail system connected all regions, horsepower was being replaced by the automobile, and the telephone made communication instantaneous.

II. Literary Review

Generally speaking, American realism and naturalism refer to the American literature between the Civil War and World War I in relation to the literary movements. No other period in American history brought more dynamic change or anxiety over what America was becoming. Writers developed a new aesthetic to come to terms with the dislocations affecting an increasingly ethnically diverse population caught in the grips of accelerating social change. In the words of literary historian Robert E. Spiller, "Regionalism and realism took the place of imagination and idealism." American literature between the Civil War and World War I broadened its perspective by incorporating the voices and scenes of its hinterlands and its new urban centers while finding innovative ways to explore contemporary American experience and its implications for the American psyche.

The initial shock to the system was of course the war itself. And yet, although unquestionably the most written-about single event in American history, the Civil War produced relatively few imaginative responses from its participants and eyewitnesses. Among the major literary figures before the war, only Herman Melville and Walt Whitman produced important poems treating the war experience. The significant postwar writers—Mark Twain, William Dean Howells, and Henry James—sat out the war in safety, respectively, in the West, in Venice, and in Newport and Cambridge. The greatest literary treatment to the Civil War, Stephen Crane's *The Red Badge of Courage*, did not appear until 1895, the work of a twenty-four-year-old writer born in 1871 who claimed that he learned about combat on the playing fields of Syracuse University.

For the most part, writers of the period immediately following the war directed their attention closer to home. For the first time in American literature, significant writing began to emerge west of the Mississippi. Mark Twain, Bret Harte, Hamlin Garland and Joaquin Miller portrayed life in California and the Far West exuberantly and idiomatically. Their stories and poems were the first in a steady stream of literature with distinctive regional characteristics from all parts of the country. Contributors to this proto-realistic movement, dubbed local colorists, include Edward Eggleston, John Hay, Sarah Orne Jewett, Mary Eleanor Wilkins Freeman, Harriet Beecher Stowe, and George Washington Cable. These writers tapped into the rich resources of local scenes, speech, and customs to revitalize American writing enervated by the war while paving the way for an increasingly realistic aesthetic, the dominant mode of American literary expression during the period.

The greatest of the regionalists was Mark Twain. In his masterpiece, *Adventures of Huckleberry Finn* (1884), Twain transformed a boy's adventure tale into what Lionel Trilling called "One of the world's great books and one of the central documents of American culture." With Huck and Jim's trip down river into the heart of America's racial conflict, Twain tapped the poetic resources of the American vernacular and the dramatic and thematic possibilities of the American landscape, earning his friend William Dean Howells's praise as "the Lincoln of our literature." Although an overstatement, Ernest Hemingway's oft-quoted claim that "All modern American literature comes from one book by Mark Twain called *Huckleberry Finn*" is not far off the mark.

Twain showed his readers what their fellow Americans outside the settled Northeast actually looked and sounded like, while poking holes in the prevailing sentimental and Romantic ethos of the literary establishment. The main theorist and influential supporter of the new realism was William Dean Howells, who as the editor of the prestigious *Atlantic Monthly* (1866-1881) and *Harper's* (1886-1892) helped legitimize the efforts of the regionalists while advocating the refinement of the American novel into a truth-telling instrument. "Let fiction cease to lie about life," he argued; "let it portray men and women as they are, actuated by the motives and passions in the measure we all know." Howells supported fiction that emphasized the commonplace over the exceptional and would apply his theories in novels such as *A Modern Instance* (1882), *The Rise of Silas Lapham* (1885), *Indian Summer* (1886) and *A Hazard of New Fortunes* (1890), which helped raise the standards of realism in American fiction and slowly pushed open the doors to subjects previously off-limits to writers.

The third crucial figure in the realistic refinement of American fiction during the period was Henry James, who, by absorbing the lessons of writers such as Honor de Balzac, Ivan Turgenev, and Gustave Flaubert, introduced the techniques and sensibilities of European novelists into American fiction. For James, American life was too unformed, without sufficient past and precedent, lacking the clear lines of European culture and hierarchy desirable for a writer interested in the intricate drama of manners. By transporting the vitality and earnestness of his Americans to Europe to be tested, James found the ideal stage for moral and psychological explorations of consciousness and social values, in works such as *The Pupil*(1891), *Daisy Miller* (1879), *The Portrait of a Lady* (1881), and his masterful trio of late novels—The *Wings of the Dove* (1902), *The Ambassadors* (1903), and *The Golden Bowl* (1904)—which anticipated the main preoccupations of modern fiction. James, perhaps more than any other writer, turned the American novel into literature while shifting its focus from the outer world to inner states of consciousness.

The realistic standards that Twain, Howells, and James established for American fiction were extended by the naturalist novelists of the 1890s and 1900s, who threatened the last vestiges of genteel discretion in their clinical treatment of modern life. If the realist insisted on the autonomy of the individual as paramount, the naturalist shifted the attention of the novel to the forces of environment and heredity that controlled destiny and the often brutal instincts needed to survive in a hostile world. Stephen Crane's *Maggie: A Girl of the Streets* (1893), Frank Norris's *Mc Teague* (1899), Theodore Dreiser's *Sister Carrie* (1900), and Upton Sinclair's *The Jungle* (1906) took their readers into a threatening urban landscape populated by victims and damaged survivors. Such works demonstrated that American fiction had come of age and had become the principal literary tool for critiquing contemporary American life.

While American fiction increasingly focused on harsh realities, the nation's poets, with a few notable exceptions, sought to reassure rather than to provoke. The dominant prewar poets—Henry W. Longfellow, James Russell Lowell, William Cullen Bryant and

John G. Whittier—remained influential, if increasingly remote from the scenes and attitudes that were transforming America. Whitman attempted to maintain his optimistic faith in American democracy while continuing his epic campaign to bring commonplace life and forbidden subjects such as human sexuality within poetic range. Opposite in every way except for her genius, Emily Dickinson wrote introspective verses, echoing the traditions of the Romantics and her Puritan ancestors and treating the drama of daily life with an existential intensity and psychological realism that greatly influenced modern American poetry. Her poetry was unknown to her contemporaries and only gradually began to appear in the 1890s. By the end of the period, both kinds of poetic realism, Whitman's unrestrained panorama and Dickinson's inner truthfulness, had set the direction for a new American poetry, led by figures such as Edwin Arlington Robinson, Carl Sandburg, Robert Frost, and Ezra Pound, whose first poems began appearing before World War I.

The period witnessed the emergence of a host of minority voices. Figures such as Paul Laurence Dunbar, Charles W. Chesnutt, Booker T. Washington, and W.E.B Du Bois reflected the African American experience. One of the first widely read works by writers of Asian heritage was Sui Sin Far's *Mrs. Spring Fragrance* (1912), and the period also saw the first major works by Jewish American writers, most notably Abraham Cahan's *Yekl, a Tale of the New York Ghetto* (1896) and Mary Antin's *The Promised Land* (1912). Two of the most daring assaults on conventional views of the identity and role of women in America were Charlotte Perkins Gilman's *The Yellow Wallpaper* (1892) and Kate Chopin's *The Awakening* (1899).

The Civil War, fought to resolve American sectional differences and determine the scope of American democracy, managed to preserve the Union, and the ambitions, originality, and drive of its citizens during the succeeding decades created a world power. In the process, the evolving American literary aesthetic shifted from entertainment to truth-telling, exploring the divisive issues of social and racial equality and justice.

Walt Whitman (1819—1892)

Life and Major Works

As Malcolm Cowley remarked that "before Walt Whitman America hardly existed", it is with Whitman that one sees the emergence of a distinctively American poetry, an imaginative response to the new continent of individual vitality, variety, and creativity. Breaking away from the metrical structures of European poetry, Whitman initiates his experimental free verse style to cover the American continent and achievement, thus blazing a new trail for later poets to follow.

On May 31, 1819, Walt Whitman was born to Walter Whitman, a house builder, and Louisa Van Velsor as the second of nine children, living in Brooklyn and Long Island in the 1820s and 1830s. While in Brooklyn, he attended the Brooklyn public schools for six years, sharing his classes with students of a variety of ages and backgrounds. Then by the age of eleven, Whitman finished his formal education, but forged his own rough and informal curriculum of literature,

Walt Whitman

theater, history, geography, music, and archeology out of the developing public resources of America's fastest growing city. At the age of twelve, young Walt began to learn the printer's trade, and fell in love with the written word and was already contributing to the newspaper and experiencing the exhilaration of getting his own words published. These early years on his own in Brooklyn and New York remained a formative influence on his writing, for it was during this time that he developed the habit of close observation of the ever-shifting panorama of the city, and a great deal of his journalism, poetry, and prose came to focus on catalogs of urban life and the history of New York City, Brooklyn, and Long Island.

This job as a printer in New York City continued for 5 years until a devastating fire in the printing district demolished the industry. So In 1836, at the age of 17, he began his career as a teacher in the one-room schoolhouses of Long Island. It was in 1841, five years later that he turned to journalism as a full-time career. The weekly newspaper, *Long-Islander,* founded by himself, devoted to covering the towns around Huntington. In the following years, he worked as an editor for a number of Brooklyn and New York papers, which gave Whitman a platform from which to comment on various issues from street lighting to politics, from banking to poetry. But Whitman claimed that what he most valued was not the ability to promote his opinions, but rather something more intimate, the "curious kind of sympathy… that arises in the mind of a newspaper conductor with the public he serves. He gets to love them."

In 1848, Whitman left the *Brooklyn Daily Eagle* to become editor of the *New Orleans Crescent.* It was in New Orleans that he experienced firsthand the viciousness of slavery in the slave markets of that city. On his return to Brooklyn in the fall, he founded a "free soil" newspaper, the *Brooklyn Freeman,* and continued to develop the unique style of poetry: that odd joining of the scriptural and the vernacular, the transcendent and the mundane, which would later so astonished Ralph Waldo Emerson.

In 1855, Whitman published the first edition of *Leaves of Grass*, the explosive book of twelve untitled poems that he wrote in the early years of the 1850s, which would eventually lead many to view him as America's greatest and most revolutionary poet. For the rest of his life, he would add, delete, fuse, separate, and rearrange poems as he issued six very distinct editions of *Leaves of Grass*.

The experimental verse of this book, cast in unrhymed long lines with no identifiable meter was an extraordinary accomplishment: it was an uncanny combination of oratory, journalism, and the Bible—haranguing, mundane, and prophetic—all in the service of identifying a new American democratic attitude, an absorptive and accepting voice that would catalog the diversity of the country and manage to hold it all in a vast, single, unified identity. This new voice spoke confidently of union at a time of incredible division and tension in the culture, and it spoke with the assurance of one for whom everything, no matter how degraded, could be celebrated as part of itself: "What is commonest and cheapest and nearest and easiest is Me." His work echoed with the lingo of the American urban working class and reached deep into the various corners of the roiling nineteenth-century culture, reverberating with the nation's stormy politics, its motley music, its new technologies, its fascination with science, and its evolving pride in an American language that was forming as a tongue distinct from British English.

At the outbreak of the Civil War, Whitman vowed to live a "purged" and "cleansed" life. He traveled to Washington, D.C. in December 1862 to care for his brother and also for other Union and Confederate soldiers. The Civil War had its effect on the writer, which is shown in his prose *Memoranda During the War* (1875) and in the poems published under the title of *Drum-Taps* in 1865. In *Sequel to Drum-Taps* (1865—1866) appeared the great elegy on President Abraham Lincoln, "When Lilacs Last in the Dooryard Bloom'd." Another famous poem published about the death of Lincoln is "O Captain! My Captain!"

In the early 1870s, Whitman settled in Camden, NJ, where he had come to visit his dying mother at his brother's house. However, after suffering a stroke, Whitman found it impossible to return to Washington. He stayed with his brother until the 1882 publication of *Leaves of Grass* gave Whitman enough money to buy a home in Camden. In the simple two-story clapboard house, Whitman spent his declining years working on additions and revisions to a new edition of the book and preparing his final volume of poems and prose, *Good-Bye, My Fancy* (1891). After his death on March 26, 1892, Whitman was buried in a tomb he designed and had built on a lot in Harleigh Cemetery.

It is with Whitman that one sees the emergence of a distinctively American poetry, an imaginative response to the new continent rather than an attempt to describe North American life using imported European forms. Such a definitive break with Europe made the way clear for the rapid and invigorating poetic evolution of America in the twentieth century.

Introduction and Appreciation of "I Hear America Singing"

No other poem can better catch the unique liveliness of the newly born United States than Whitman's " I hear America Singing", representing his literary style of singing praises of self and nature in America both in content and in technique.

In the first line of the poem, the speaker establishes his position as a keen listener of the laborers' democratic chants. The repetition of "I hear" serves to assert the significance of the poet's role is that of listening, rather than of speaking, and though the composition requires a conductor, it belongs to the common laborer, not to the captains of industry, not to political leaders, nor even to the poet. At the same time, the first line introduces the poem's controlling metaphor: "I hear America singing" when the poet envisions America as the culmination of the voices of the American people who are unique individuals.

What follows in the next several lines is the specification of this uniqueness, a chronicle of various characters, defined by occupations familiar to the American society then: "boatman", "shoemaker", "wood-cutter", "ploughboy", "the mother", "the young wife at work", "the girl sewing or washing", who are "singing what belongs to him" or "singing what belongs to her". Each figure, man and woman alike, is depicted engaged in his or her respective working duties. It must be noted that here Whitman uses opposites to show how wide the range of Americans and their work environments are: male and female, ashore and on water, preparing or finishing work. For Whitman, democracy is built not on organizations but on individual souls. He takes poetry out of the study and puts it on the workbench, which establishes his work as what William Saroyan called "the beginning of American poetry... when the unschooled took to the business."

Varied as the American singing seems, in the final lines, the readers find the working people in the day "at night" turns to "a party of fellows", sharing a lot in common: "young", and "robust", and "friendly". Their individual "carols" blend into one enormous chorus that is America. Ezra Greenspan noted in *The Cambridge Companion to Walt Whitman* that "the poem blends the individual acts of singing into a harmonious participial ensemble of America singing." In this manner the poem alludes to the democratic ideal of a nation where people insist "we stand together, alone."

Now, with this poem which is infused with prosaic language and metric variation, we finally have a complete notion of the America Whitman celebrates: a nation full of vitality, variety, and unity that are considered to be built into the distinguished American character. According to David Kresh, the reference specialist in poetry in the Humanities and Social Sciences Division of the Library of Congress, The America which Whitman heard singing was one which he imagined shared many qualities with himself: Exuberant. Expansive. Adhesive. Inclusive.

I Hear America Singing

I hear America singing, the varied carols I hear;

Those of mechanics—each one singing his, as it should be, blithe and strong;

The carpenter singing his, as he measures his plank or beam,

The mason[1] singing his, as he makes ready for work, or leaves off work;

The boatman singing what belongs to him in his boat—the deckhand singing on the steamboat deck;

The shoemaker singing as he sits on his bench—the hatter singing as he stands;

The wood-cutter's song—the ploughboy's, on his way in the morning, or at the noon intermission, or at sundown;

The delicious singing of the mother—or of the young wife at work—or of the girl sewing or washing—Each singing what belongs to her, and to none else;

The day what belongs to the day—At night, the party of young fellows, robust, friendly,

Singing, with open mouths, their strong melodious[2] songs.

Notes:

1. mason: a person whose trade is building with units of various natural or artificial mineral products, as stones, bricks, cinder blocks, or tiles, usually with the use of mortar or cement as a bonding agent.
2. melodious: of the nature of or characterized by melody; tuneful

Questions for Study and Discussion:

1. What do you notice about the people in this poem? Who are they? Do they have anything in common?

2. How would you characterize the singing in Whitman's poem "I Hear America Singing?"

3. By rhapsodizing the trades and occupations of different Americans in "I Hear America Singing," what characteristics does Whitman express?

Introduction and Appreciation of "Beat! Beat! Drums!"

"Beat! Beat! Drums!" was published in September 1861 in *Harper's Weekly* and *The New York Leader,* believed by many to allude to the battle of Bull Run, the first real major conflict of the American Civil War. The speaker, listening to the banging of war drums and shrill sounds of bugles, relates the interruption these war sounds have on the harmony of people's lives.

The three stanzas can be seen as three dimensions of the disastrous effects that war could bring to human life. The images in the first stanza symbolize how the war threatens the basic fabric of a common person's life: when the drums "burst like a ruthless force" into the "church", a symbol of spiritual resort, people can no longer keep a peaceful soul; when into the "school", the institution for education, there's nothing left to nurture the mind. When the "peaceful farmer" is disturbed, no grain can be gathered therefore the physical body of people has no way to sustain itself; when the newly married "bridegroom" and "bride", which often associates with a lively family full of sweet hopes, have no "happiness", there is every chance that they are going to suffer. With the image of all the three fundamental needs of body, mind, and soul of both individual and family are all at risk when a war approaches. The drums "burst like a ruthless force" into people's common life symbolizes the shattering power of war. Besides, the ending line of this stanza suggests the drums are only getting louder: "So fierce you whirr and pound you drums—so shrill you bugles blow," forming a sharp contrast to the quietness of the "solomn" church and the school where "scholar is studying".

The second stanza focuses on how war disturbs people from all walks of life with no remorse. The drums sweep over both the lower "bargainers", and the higher "brokers", or "speculators"; "rumble of wheels in the streets", and the voices of "bargainers", "talkers", "singers", "the lawyers" all get drowned by the bugles. Again, the speaker finishes off the second section with the drums and bugles getting louder and heavier, "then rattle quicker, heavier drums—you bugles wilder blow."

The third stanza begins by claiming "Make no parley—stop for no expostulation," implying that the war has no desire to make "parley" or truces and will keep fighting even if it is ruining everyday life. Who cares about the "timid" or the weak, who cares if people are in "prayer" to stop the war? The war will keep going and people will have to keep their lives on hold. With these lines "Mind not the old man beseeching the young man; Let not the child's voice be heard, nor the mother's entreaties;" he tries to get the point across that the drums will stop for no one and the war callously trashes the basic human emotions such as love and sympathy. The poem ends by presenting the image of the drums being so "strong" as to "shake the dead", who just "lie awaiting the hearses". Be it man or woman, young or old, rich or poor, alive or dead, there's no way whatsoever for anyone to escape from the cold terrors and horrible effects of war.

Beat! Beat! Drums!

BEAT! beat! drums!—Blow! bugles! blow!

Through the windows—through doors—burst like a ruthless force,

Into the solemn church, and scatter the congregation[1];

Into the school where the scholar is studying;

Leave not the bridegroom quiet—no happiness must he have now with his bride;

Nor the peaceful farmer any peace, plowing his field or gathering his grain;

So fierce you whirr and pound, you drums—so shrill you bugles blow.

Beat! beat! drums!—Blow! bugles! blow!

Over the traffic of cities—over the rumble of wheels in the streets:

Are beds prepared for sleepers at night in the houses? No sleepers must sleep in those beds;

No bargainers' bargains by day—no brokers or speculators—Would they continue?

Would the talkers be talking? would the singer attempt to sing?

Would the lawyer rise in the court to state his case before the judge?

Then rattle quicker, heavier drums—you bugles wilder blow.

Beat! beat! drums!—Blow! bugles! blow!

Make no parley[2]—stop for no expostulation;

Mind not the timid—mind not the weeper or prayer;

Mind not the old man beseeching[3]the young man;

Let not the child's voice be heard, nor the mother's entreaties[4];

Make even the trestles to shake the dead, where they lie awaiting the hearses,

So strong you thump, O terrible drums—so loud you bugles blow.

Notes:

1. congregation: an assembly of persons brought together for common religious worship
2. parley: an informal conference between enemies under a truce, esp. to discuss terms, conditions of surrender, etc.
3. beseeching: begging eagerly for
4. entreaty: an earnest request

Questions for Study and Discussion:

1. Poetry is meant to be read aloud. When you read the first line of each stanza, what sounds or rhythms do you hear?
2. What is the mood of the poem?
3. What effect is created by the repetition of the "b" sound in the first line of each stanza?
4. What purpose do the sounds of drums and bugles serve in the poem?
5. How does Whitman create unity in the poem?
6. Why does Whitman, in the last line, call the drums "terrible"?

Emily Dickinson (1830—1886)

Life and Major Works

One of the finest lyric poets in the English language, Emily Dickinson was born in Amherst, Massachusetts in 1830 to a politically prominent family headed by the father, Edward Dickinson, a lawyer, and a Congressman. Her strangely eventless life has long been the source of complex interpretations: She attended Mount Holyoke Female Seminary in South Hadley, but returned home after one year due to severe homesickness. Ever since then, she began to gradually withdraw from village activities and ceased to leave home except for short trips to visit relatives. Unmarried, she died in her father's house in 1886.

Emily Dickinson

Readers tried to find out correspondence between the contents of her poems and her actual life, since she was regarded as a private poetess, who wrote confessional poems without intending to publish them. While Dickinson was extremely prolific as a poet and regularly enclosed poems in letters to friends, she was not publicly recognized during her lifetime. Among the 40 hand-bound volumes of more than 800 of Dickinson's poems the family discovered upon her death, only seven of them got published. The wave of posthumous publications gave Dickinson's poetry its first real public exposure. In 1955 Thomas H. Johnson prepared for Harvard University Press a three-volume edition, chronologically arranged. Here, for the first time, the reader saw the poems as Dickinson had left them. The Johnson text of the 1,775 extant poems is now the standard one.

As a keen observer of nature and a wise interpreter of human passion, she presents the common subjects of earthly life such as love, death, and nature in depth and intensity. The chief tension in her work comes from her inability to accept the orthodox religious faith of her day and her longing for its spiritual comfort. She is keen on treating antithesis, she alternates confident statements of belief with lyrics of despairing uncertainty that were both reverent and rebellious, and she switches between seeing nature as a testament to the glory of Creation and as a symbol of transition.

If what she writes is considered both simple and deep, how she writes gets the reputation of being original and creative. Instead of presenting her thoughts and feelings directly to the reader, Dickinson conveys her subtle emotion by annulling ordinary referential correspondences between words and things. By disturbing the originality of the authoritative language, she presents the reader a different reality. Drawing from primarily musical forms such as hymns and ballads, and modifying them with her own sense of rhythm and sound, a Dickinson poem is unusual in that it both slows down and speeds up, interrupts itself, holds its breath, and sometimes trails off. The reader is led through the poem by the shape of her stanza forms, typically quatrains, her idiosyncratic vocabulary and imagery, and her unusual emphasis of words, either through capitalization or line position…

Reynolds declares that Dickinson's supposed "representativeness lies in her incomparable flexibility, her ability to be by turns coy, fierce, domestic, romantic, protofeminist, antifeminist, prudish, erotic" (Reynolds 421). Readers are required to transform their reading strategies along with her shifting elusive texts and are almost banned from reading them according to any literary or critical principles. If there is something left for the readers to form the basis of their readings, it is only her language and her texts that are there that is called Emily Dickinson.

Appreciation of "Success Is Counted Sweetest"

One aspect of Emily Dickinson's talent, among other things, is how she can catch accurately and represent originally the antithetical relationships in human life, such as death and immortality, love and loneliness, joy and sorrow, as well as success and failure. Her choice of living life internally within the confines of her home brought her world into sharp focus, rather than impinge upon her creative sensibilities. As Michael Myers points out, "Dickinson found irony, ambiguity, and paradox lurking in the simplest and commonest experiences." In the poem "Success is Counted Sweetest", Dickinson provokes as well as moves the reader to understand, however reluctantly, that life is really full of paradoxes .

In this poem "Success is Counted Sweetest", Dickinson disturbs the peace of our mind right with the opening statement: "Success is counted sweetest, by those who never succeed. To comprehend nectar, requires the sorest needs". Here, The dilemma is obvious: Those who want success most can never get it, while those who achieve success cannot understand it. In either case, the enthusiastically pursued success turns meaningless.

Then the next two stanzas visualizes the readers an image of a defeated soldier who heard the cheering of victors as he lay dying. "Distant" and "forbidden" and "agonized" as those cheers are, the soldier, more than anyone else, heard them "clear" with his lingering flicker of consciousness. One can hardly disagree that in such a case, victory is desired and valued most by the defeated, since it is they rather than the winners that have tasted the misery of failure, of being deprived of the "nectar" of victory. If so, isn't it perplexed that if one knows and wants success too much, he is doomed a failure, and at the same time, if one succeeds, he can never fully appreciate the values of winning.

Conventional as the topic of success and failure seems, Dickinson finds complex meaning latent in them. Furthermore, her unconventional interpretation of those conventional themes is conveyed via her unconventional innovative literary style: her ingenious choice of words, her verbal constructions, her deviational usage of capitalization and dash display how creative she is when trying to defy the poetic norms that stood in the way of the overflowing of her thought and her images. Her poetic language like " forbidden ear", " Purple host", "sorest need", "comprehend a nectar" deviates from the conventional form and disturbs the authoritative principle of language and saves herself from using limited languages that equate words and things.

Dickinson's supposed "representativeness lies in her incomparable flexibility, her ability to be by turns coy, fierce, domestic, romantic, protofeminist, antifeminist, prudish, erotic". Dickinson's poetry is challenging because her poems require active engagement from the reader, because she seems to leave out so much with her elliptical style and remarkable contracting metaphors. But these apparent gaps are filled with meaning if we are sensitive to her use of devices such as personification, allusion, symbolism, and startling syntax and grammar. Her poetry has an undeniable capacity to move and provoke.

Success Is Counted Sweetest

Success is counted sweetest
By those who ne'er succeed.
To comprehend a nectar[1]
Requires sorest need.

Not one of all the purple Host
Who took the Flag today
Can tell the definition
So clear, of Victory

As the defeated—dying—
On whose forbidden ear
The distant strains of triumph
Burst agonized and clear!

Notes:

1. nectar: A sweet liquid secreted by flowers of various plants, consumed by pollinators, such as hummingbirds and insects, and gathered by bees for making honey.

Questions for Study and Discussion:

1. In stanza one, why does the poet use alliteration? i.e., are the words significant? What are the associations of "nectar"? Does "nectar" pick up any word in the first line?
2. In stanza two, what does "purple" connote? Are these connotations appropriate to the poem? In a battle, what does a flag represent? Why is victory described in terms of taking the losing side's flag?
3. In stanza three, what words are connected by d sounds and by s sounds? Is there any reason for connecting or emphasizing these words?

Appreciation of "Because I Could Not Stop for Death"

Dickinson's famous poem "Because I Could Not Stop for Death" draws on the sentimental idea of death as a gentle lover escorting his love to a new and blissful home. The motif of death as a courtly lover is highlighted in the poem's first three stanzas. Death here is "kindly" and offers the narrator a smooth journey to the afterlife.

The journey is slow, not frighteningly hasty or bumpy, and death is full of chivalric "Civility." The journey includes familiar scenes as the carriage glides past the school and fields. In the first three stanzas, the spatial coordinates of the poem are clear and consistent. The carriage journeys straight away from the home and town, eventually passing "the Setting Sun." However, when the narrator suddenly adds, "Or rather—He passed Us—," the journey's progress suddenly becomes confusing. This abrupt turn in the poem flags a movement away from the sentimental idea of death as an easy spiritual journey. Instead of moving smoothly past the setting sun to the heavens, the journey ends rather abruptly and the scene becomes threatening. The poem has quickly moved from the positive image of "the Fields of Gazing Grain" to the darker image of the "Dews...quivering and chill" that threaten a vulnerable body clad with "only Gossamer" and "only Tulle." The journey ends not with the arrival at a heavenly home, but in the buried and suffocating home "in the Ground" —the physical grave. The carriage that seemed so comfortable in the first half of the poem is not a chariot that transports a soul to an afterlife but a hearse transporting a body to the cemetery. "Eternity" seems nothing more than "Centuries" of physical decay in the earth that feel shorter than "the Day" when the narrator first noticed she was on her way to death. This poem's last stanza also suggests that true eternity lies in the single day in which we recognize death and thus capitalize on the present moment, which is itself infinite.

Death, Immortality, and the Sun are all personified in the poem; they are given human qualities that make the poem come to life: Death is described as a "kind" and "civil" driver, Immortality is riding in the carriage with the woman, and the Sun passes by the carriage. The carriage ride, which can be seen as a metaphor for the cycle of life, begins when the woman enters the carriage. The imagery is very strong when they pass "the school, where Children strove/At Recess, in the Ring," the "fields of the Gazing Grain," and the "Setting Sun." The reader can picture the carriage passing each of these places and the woman silently staring out of the window. By mixing imagery with personification, Dickinson crafts a miniature story, that when closely examined holds many shades of meaning.

Through her effective use of rhythm and structure, imagery, and symbolism, Dickinson reminds the reader that death is not something to fear. She makes it clear that while death takes one away from the earthly world, there is still something to look forward to eternal Eternal life.

Because I Could Not Stop for Death

Because I could not stop for Death—

He kindly stopped for me—

The Carriage held but just Ourselves—

And Immortality.

We slowly drove—He knew no haste

And I had put away

My labor and my leisure too,

For His Civility—

We passed the School, where Children strove

At Recess—in the Ring—

We passed the Fields of Gazing Grain—

We passed the Setting Sun—

Or rather—He passed Us—

The Dews drew quivering and chill—

For only Gossamer[1] my Gown—

My Tippet[2]—only Tulle[3]—

We paused before a House that seemed

A Swelling of the Ground—

The Roof was scarcely visible—

The Cornice—in the Ground—

Since then—It is Centuries—and yet

Feels shorter than the Day

I first surmised the Horses' Heads

Were towards Eternity—

Notes:

1. gossamer: a fine, filmy cobweb seen on grass or bushes or floating in the air in calm weather, esp. in autumn
2. Tippet: a scarf, usually of fur or wool, for covering the neck, or the neck and shoulders, and usually having ends hanging down in front
3. Tulle: a thin, fine, machine-made net of acetate, nylon, rayon, or silk

Questions for Study and Discussion:
1. Is Death a kind, polite suitor?
2. Is Death actually a betrayer, and is his courtly manner an illusion to seduce her?
3. Is there irony in the contrast between her passivity and inactivity in the coach and their energetic activity?
4. The activity of stanza three contrasts with the inactivity of the speaker in stanzas four and five. They pause at the grave. What is the effect of describing it as a house?
5. Why does she have to guess? She has experienced life, but what does she specifically know about being dead?

Samuel Langhorne Clemens/Mark Twain (1835—1910)

Life and Major Works

Samuel Langhorne Clemens (November 30, 1835—April 21, 1910), better known by the pen name Mark Twain, was an American author and humorist. As his literature provides insight into the past, the events of his personal life further demonstrate his role as an eyewitness to history. During his lifetime, Sam watched a young United States evolve from a nation torn apart by internal conflicts to one of international power. He experienced the country's vast growth and change —from westward expansion to industrialization, the end of

Mark Twain

slavery, advancements in technology, big government and foreign wars. And along the way, he often had something to say about the changes happening in America.

Samuel Clemens was born on November 30, 1835 in Florida, Missouri, the sixth of seven children. At the age of four, Sam and his family moved to the small frontier town of Hannibal, Missouri on the banks of the Mississippi River. Missouri, at the time, was a fairly new state (it had gained statehood in 1821) and comprised part of the country's western border. It was also a slave state. Sam's father owned one slave and his uncle owned several. In fact, it was on his uncle's farm that Sam spent many boyhood summers playing in the slave quarters, listening to tall tales and the slave spirituals that he would enjoy throughout his life.

In 1847, when Sam was 11, his father died. Shortly thereafter he left school, having completed the fifth grade, to work as a printer's apprentice for a local newspaper. His job was to arrange the type for each of the newspaper's stories, allowing Sam to read the news of the world while completing his work.

At 18, Sam headed east to New York City and Philadelphia where he worked on several different newspapers and found some success at writing articles. By 1857, he had returned home to embark on a new career as a riverboat pilot on the Mississippi River. With the outbreak of the Civil War in 1861, however, all traffic along the river came to a halt, as did Sam's pilot career. Inspired by the times, Sam joined a volunteer Confederate unit called the Marion Rangers, but he quit after just two weeks. In search of a new career, Sam headed west in July of 1861, at the invitation of his brother, Orion, who had just been appointed Secretary of the Nevada Territory. Lured by the infectious hope of striking it rich in Nevada's silver rush, Sam traveled across the open frontier from Missouri to Nevada by stagecoach. Along the journey Sam encountered Native American tribes for the first time as well as a variety of unique characters, mishaps and disappointments. These events would find a way into his short stories and books, particularly *Roughing It.*

After failing as a silver prospector, Sam began writing for the *Territorial Enterprise,* a Virginia City, Nevada newspaper where he used, for the first time, his pen name, Mark Twain. Wanting a change by 1864, Sam headed for San Francisco where he continued to write for local papers.

In 1865, Sam's first "big break" came with the publication of his short story, "Jim Smiley and His Jumping Frog" in papers across the country. A year later, Sam was hired by the *Sacramento Union* to visit and report on the Sandwich Islands (now Hawaii). His writings were so popular that, upon his return, he embarked upon his first lecture tour, which established him as a successful stage performer.

Hired by the *Alta California* to continue his travel writing from the east, Sam arrived in New York City in 1867. He quickly signed up for a steamship tour of Europe and the Holy Land. His travel letters, full of vivid descriptions and tongue-in-cheek observations, met with such audience approval that they were later reworked into his first book, *The Innocents Abroad* in 1869. It was also on this trip that Clemens met his future brother-in-law, Charles Langdon. Langdon reportedly showed Sam a picture of his sister, Olivia, and Sam fell in love at first sight.

After courting for two years, Sam Clemens and Olivia (Livy) Langdon were married in 1870. They settled in Buffalo, New York where Sam had become a partner, editor and writer for the daily newspaper the *Buffalo Express*. While living in Buffalo, their first child, Langdon Clemens was born.

In an effort to be closer to his publisher, Sam moved his family to Hartford, Connecticut in 1871. For the first few years the Clemenses rented a house in the heart of Nook Farm, a residential area that was home to numerous writers, publishers and other prominent figures. In 1872, Sam's recollections and tall tales from his frontier adventures were published in his book, *Roughing It.* That same year the Clemenses' first daughter Susy was born, but their son, Langdon, died at the age of two from diphtheria.

In 1873, Sam's focus turned toward social criticism. He and Hartford Courant publisher Charles Dudley Warner co-wrote *The Gilded Age,* a novel that attacked political corruption, big business and the American obsession with getting rich that seemed to dominate the era. Ironically, a year after its publication, the Clemenses' elaborate, $40,000 and 19-room house on Farmington Avenue was completed.

For the next 17 years (1874-1891), Sam, Livy and their three daughters (Clara was born in 1874 and Jean in 1880) lived in the Hartford home. During those years Sam completed some of his most famous works. Novels such as *The Adventures of Tom Sawyer* (1876) and *Life on the Mississippi* (1883) captured both his Missouri memories and depictions of the American scene. Yet, his social commentary continued. *The Prince and the Pauper* (1881) explored class relations as does *A Connecticut Yankee in King Arthur's Court* (1889) which, going a step further, criticized oppression in general while examining the period's technology explosion. And, in perhaps his most famous work, *Adventures of Huckleberry Finn* (1884) Clemens satirized the institution of slavery and railed against the failures of Reconstruction and the continued poor treatment of African-Americans overall.

Huckleberry Finn was also the first book published by Sam's own publishing company, The Charles L. Webster Company. In an attempt to gain control over publication as well as to make substantial profits, Sam created the publishing company in 1884. A year later, he contracted with Ulysses S. Grant to publish Grant's memoirs; the two-volume set provided large royalties for Grant's widow and was a financial success for the publisher as well.

Although Sam enjoyed financial success during his Hartford years, he continually made bad investments in new inventions, which eventually brought him to bankruptcy. In an effort to economize and pay back his debts, Sam and Livy moved their family to Europe in 1891. When his publishing company failed in 1894, Sam was forced to set out on a worldwide lecture tour to earn money. In 1896, tragedy struck when Susy Clemens, at the age of 24, died from meningitis while on a visit to the Hartford home. Unable to return to the place of her death, the Clemenses never returned to Hartford to live.

From 1891 until 1900, Sam and his family traveled throughout the world. During those years, Sam witnessed the increasing exploitation of weaker governments by European powers, which he described in his book, *Following the Equator* (1897). The Boer War in South Africa and the Boxer Rebellion in China fueled his growing anger toward imperialistic countries and their actions. With the Spanish-American and Philippine War in 1898, Sam's wrath was redirected toward the American government. When he returned to the United States in 1900, his finances restored, Sam readily declared himself an anti-imperialist and, from 1901 until his death, served as the vice president of the Anti-Imperialist League.

In these later years, Sam's writings turned dark. They began to focus on human greed, cruelty and questioned the humanity of the human race. His public appearances followed suit and included a harshly sardonic public introduction of Winston Churchill in 1900. Even though Sam's lecture tour had managed to get him out of debt, his anti-government writings and speeches threatened his livelihood once again. Labeled by some as a traitor, several of Sam's works were never published during his lifetime either because magazines would not accept them or because of a personal fear that his marketable reputation would be ruined.

Brief Introduction and Appreciation

One of Twain's earliest literary successes and most accomplished early sketches, this 2,600-word narrative was written following a three-month stay at Jackass Hill and Angel's Camp in California's Calaveras County in late 1864 and early 1865. Twain first heard the tale of the jumping frog from Ben Coon, a fixture at the Angel's Camp Hotel bar. He liked the story, jotting down its details in a notebook, but was especially taken with Coon's masterful oral delivery of the anecdote: like other mining camp raconteurs, Coon recounted the episode with utter seriousness for dramatic and humorous effect. This particular brand of deadpan humor told in rich vernacular proved to be most influential on Twain's development as a writer and humorist.

Upon returning to San Francisco from Calaveras County, Twain received a letter from his friend and literary mentor, the writer Artemus Ward, requesting that he send a piece of writing to be included in a work Ward was editing about Nevada Territory travels. Twain thereupon began writing his own version of the frog story, but it took six months and several failed attempts to produce something to his satisfaction. In October 1865 he sent the manuscript of the sketch to New York for inclusion in the Ward collection, but it was turned down, probably because the book was about to go to press. The publisher sent the story to the *Saturday Press*, where it appeared in November, 1865 as "Jim Smiley and His Jumping Frog." The tale was an overnight sensation, and was reprinted in magazines and newspapers all over the country. In December 1865 Twain published a revised version of the story in the *Californian*, and a further revised version was used as the title story in his 1867 collection, *The Celebrated Jumping Frog of Calaveras Country, and Other Sketches*. The story has also been published under the title "The Notorious Jumping Frog of Calaveras County," and is often referred to by scholars simply as "The jumping frog story."

The tale is told using the structure of a traditional Southwestern frame story, wherein a genteel, educated narrator recounts a story he has heard from an unsophisticated teller, and gives a secondhand account of a career gambler who gets taken by a stranger passing through town. In the earliest published version of the story, Twain himself narrates the frame in the form of a letter to his friend Ward about a visit to the mining camp Noomerang where he hears the story of Jim Greeley's frog. Later versions of the story drop the epistolary structure, use an anonymous narrator, change the name "Noomerang" to "Angel's Camp," and substitute the name "Smiley" for "Greeley. "

The narrator, a mannered Easterner, describes his visit to a mining camp where, on behalf of a friend, he is searching for one Leonidas W. Smiley. He stops in an old tavern, where he meets "goodnatured, garrulous" old Simon Wheeler, who cannot recall a Leonidas Smiley, but does remember a Jim Smiley who lived in the camp around 1849 or 1850. Without prompting, Wheeler launches into an extended narrative about the gambler Smiley and his exploits. Smiley, he says, was "uncommon lucky," and had a reputation for betting on anything he could: horse races, dog fights, and even which of two birds sitting on a fence would fly first. His broken-down old nag somehow always managed to win races when Smiley bet on her. His bullpup, Andrew Jackson, also won all its fights. Smiley also owned rat terriers, chicken cocks, and tom-cats, and wagered on all of them—and won.

Smiley, Wheeler goes on, once caught a frog, which he named Dan'l Webster, and trained him to jump. And that frog was a remarkable jumper, beating out any frog brought from near and far to challenge him. One day a stranger came to the mining camp and, on seeing Smiley's frog, remarked he didn't see anything unusual about it. Smiley wagered $40 that his frog could outjump any other in Calaveras County. Since the stranger had no frog, Smiley went out to find him one. In Smiley's absence, the stranger pried open Dan'l Webster's mouth and filled it with quail-shot. When Smiley brought the new frog to challenge Dan'l, it hopped off, but Dan'l couldn't budge. The stranger took his $40 in winnings and remarked again that he really could not see any special points about Smiley's frog. When Smiley examined his frog and realized what had happened, he took off after the stranger, but never caught him.

At this point in the narrative, Wheeler is called outside. When he returns, he begins a new anecdote about Smiley's tail-less, one-eyed cow, but the narrator, sure he will not learn anything about Leonidas W. Smiley from another "interminable narrative," does not have the patience to listen to it, and departs.

With its complexity of characterization, sophisticated narrative structure, and controlled style, "Jim Smiley and His Jumping Frog" was the best work Twain had written to date, and marks a turning point in his development as an artist. While the sketch has its stylistic roots in the classical Southwestern frame story, there are touches in the tale that are purely Twain's, and which mark his later writing. Some major themes in the story that are found in other Southwestern folktales include that of shrewdness outwitted, as the wily old gambler finally meets his match in the person of the stranger; the confrontation between East and West, between the green Easterner and the slick Westerner, represented by the narrator and Wheeler; and the fantastic, as Wheeler's account of Smiley's assortment of animals and their talents becomes more and more improbable. However, as noted by several scholars, Twain overturns the traditional use of these themes as they are found in conventional Southwestern burlesques. Wheeler's innocence and self-absorbed frankness is a departure from the bragging style of the typical frontiersman. The genteel narrator's tale is not told at the expense of the yokel whose story he recounts, as is typical, but rather the joke is on himself, since his quest for the elusive Leonidas W. Smiley is in vain. Twain elevates the typical Southwestern humorous tale to new heights of sophistication with the creation of memorable characters and events and with his subtle use of shifting points of view and believably wrought narrative voices. The use of satire lurking beneath the surface of a supposedly simple, straightforward tale and the seriousness of voice betraying no recognition of the humor in the situations described are elements found in Twain's later works.

The immediate response to Twain's story was almost entirely positive, and the story was reprinted more than ten times in the decade following its appearance in the *Saturday Press.* However, Twain was at first uncomfortable with the immediate reputation as a "western humorist" that the story conferred upon him, and dismissed it in an 1866 letter to his mother as a "villainous backwoods sketch." But his estimation of the story grew when he eventually cast off the bohemian sophistication he had hoped to achieve and recognized that public acceptance of this particular brand of writing and the persona of a "wild man of the West" could be a literary asset. Ten years after its initial publication, he wrote and published an elaboration of the story, called "The Jumping Frog in English, Then in French, Then Clawed Back into Civilized Language Once More by Patient, Unremunerated Toil," in response to a poor French translation of the tale and its accompanying unflattering assessment of his place in American letters. A further indication of the importance he attributed to the story is that almost twenty years later, Twain published "The Private History of the Jumping Frog Story," in which he considers a contemporary scholar's (unbeknownst to him, erroneous) claim that the frog story had a prototype in Greek literature.

Critical analysis of the story has focused on many issues, but all recognize that the story marks a transition in Twain's development as a writer, and agree that the seeds of his later genius are clearly found in the sketch. Early discussions tended to stress the story's origins in Southwestern folklore and its relationship to the work of other Westerners writing in the same genre. The first sustained critical commentary dealing with the content of the sketch was presented in 1950 by Edgar M. Branch, who pointed out the relationship between the storytellers Mark Twain and Simon Wheeler as representations of Eastern and Western sensibilities. Modern critics have taken up this point and have examined the related contrast between the narrative methods and structures of the two men's tales, which, they consider, tell us something about their attitudes. Some scholars have pointed out that there are actually several layers of stories within the framed story, and each successive tale in turn reveals the attitudes of characters toward each other: the genteel narrator's attitude toward Wheeler, Wheeler's attitude toward Smiley, Smiley's attitude toward the stranger, etc. Other critical analyses reveal the circumstances in Twain's life that occasioned the writing of the tale; examine Twain's use of satire; discuss humorous techniques found in the story that are developed in later works; understand the story as an assertion of true American values; and show how Twain's genius unfolds in this early work.

Selected Reading

The Celebrated Jumping Frog of Calaveras County

In compliance with the request of a friend of mine, who wrote me from the East, I called on good-natured, garrulous old Simon Wheeler, and inquired after my friend's friend, Leonidas W. Smiley, as requested to do, and I hereunto append the result. I have a lurking suspicion that Leonidas W. Smiley is a myth; that my friend never knew such a personage; and that he only conjectured that, if I asked old Wheeler about him, it would remind him of his infamous Jim Smiley, and he would go to work and bore me nearly to death with some infernal[1] reminiscence of him as long and tedious as it should be useless to me. If that was the design, it certainly succeeded.

I found Simon Wheeler dozing comfortably by the bar-room stove of the old, dilapidated tavern in the ancient mining camp of Angel's[2], and I noticed that he was fat and bald-headed, and had an expression of winning gentleness and simplicity upon his tranquil countenance. He roused up and gave me good-day. I told him a friend of mine had commissioned me to make some inquiries about a cherished companion of his boyhood named Leonidas W. Smiley—Rev. Leonidas W. Smiley—a young minister of the Gospel, who he had heard was at one time a resident of Angel's Camp. I added that, if Mr. Wheeler could tell me any thing about this Rev. Leonidas W. Smiley, I would feel under many obligations to him.

Simon Wheeler backed me into a corner and blockaded me there with his chair, and then sat me down and reeled off the monotonous narrative which follows this paragraph. He never smiled, he never frowned, he never changed his voice from the gentle-flowing key to which he tuned the initial sentence, he never betrayed the slightest suspicion of enthusiasm; but all through the interminable narrative there ran a vein of impressive earnestness and sincerity, which showed me plainly that, so far from his imagining that there was any thing ridiculous or funny about his story, he regarded it as a really important matter, and admired its two heroes as men of transcendent genius in finesse.

To me, the spectacle of a man drifting serenely along through such a queer yarn without ever smiling, was exquisitely absurd. As I said before, I asked him to tell me what he knew of Rev. Leonidas W. Smiley, and he replied as follows. I let him go on in his own way, and never interrupted him once:

There was a feller here once by the name of Jim Smiley, in the winter of '49—or may be it was the spring of '50—I don't recollect exactly, somehow, though what makes me think it was one or the other is because I remember the big flume wasn't finished when he first came to the camp; but anyway, he was the curiosest man about always betting on any thing that turned up you ever see, if he could get any body to bet on the other side; and if he couldn't, he'd change sides. Any way that suited the other man would suit him—any way just so's he got a bet, he was satisfied. But still he was lucky, uncommon lucky; he most always come out winner. He was always ready and laying for a chance; there couldn't be no solit'ry thing mentioned but that feller'd offer to bet on it, and take any side you please, as I was just telling you. If there was a horse-race, you'd find him flush[3], or you'd find him busted at the end of it; if there was a dog-fight, he'd bet on it; if there was a cat-fight, he'd bet on it; if there was a chicken-fight, he'd bet on it; why, if there was two birds setting on a fence, he would bet you which one would fly first; or if there was a camp-meeting, he would be there reg'lar, to bet on Parson Walker, which he judged to be the best exhorter[4] about here, and so he was, too, and a good man. If he even seen a straddle-bug start to go anywheres, he would bet you how long it would take him to get wherever he was going to, and if you took him up, he would foller that straddle-bug to Mexico but what he would find out where he was bound for and how long he was on the road. Lots of the boys here has seen that Smiley, and can tell you about him. Why, it never made no difference to him—he would bet on any thing—the dangdest feller. Parson Walker's wife laid very sick once, for a good while, and it seemed as if they warn's going to save her; but one morning he come in, and Smiley asked how she was, and he said she was considerable better—thank the Lord for his inf'nit mercy and coming on so smart that, with the blessing of Providence, she'd get well yet; and Smiley, before he thought, says, "Well, I'll risk two-and-a-half[5] that she don't, any way."

Thish-yer[6] Smiley had a mare—the boys called her the fifteen-minute nag, but that was only in fun, you know, because, of course, she was faster than that—and he used to win money on that horse, for all she was so slow and always had the asthma, or the distemper, or the consumption[7], or something of that kind. They used to give her two or three hundred yards start, and then pass her under way; but always at the fag-end of the race she'd get excited and desperate-like, and come cavorting and straddling up, and scattering her legs around limber, sometimes in the air, and sometimes out to one side amongst the fences, and kicking up m-o-r-e dust, and raising m-o-r-e racket with her coughing and sneezing and blowing her nose—and always fetch up at the stand[8] just about a neck ahead, as near as you could cipher it down[9].

And he had a little small bull pup, that to look at him you'd think he warn't worth a cent, but to set around and look ornery, and lay for a chance to steal something. But as soon as money was up on him, he was a different dog; his underjaw'd begin to stick out like the fo'castle of a steamboat, and his teeth would uncover, and shine savage like the furnaces. And a dog might tackle him, and bully- rag him, and bite him, and throw him over his shoulder two or three times, and Andrew Jackson which was the name of the pup—Andrew Jackson would never let on but what he was satisfied, and hadn't expected nothing else—and the bets being doubled and doubled on the other side all the time, till the money was all up; and then all of a sudden he would grab that other dog jest by the j' int of his hind leg and freeze on it—not chew, you understand, but only jest grip and hang on till they throwed up the sponge[10], if it was a year. Smiley always come out winner on that pup, till he harnessed a dog once that didn't have no hind legs, because they'd been sawed off by a circular saw, and when the thing had gone along far enough, and the money was all up, and he come to make a snatch for his pet bolt, he saw in a minute how he'd been imposed on, and how the other dog had him in the door[11], so to speak, and he peered surprised, and then he looked sorter discouraged-like, and didn't try no more to win the fight, and so he got shucked out bad. He give Smiley a look, as much as to say his heart was broke, and it was his fault, for putting up a dog that hadn't no hind legs for him to take bolt of, which was his main dependence in a fight, and then he limped off a piece and laid down and died. It was a good pup, was that Andrew Jackson, and would have made a name for hisself if he'd lived, for the stuff was in him, and he had genius—I know it, because he hadn't had no opportunities to speak of, and it don't stand to reason that a dog could make such a fight as he could under them circumstances, if he hadn't no talent. It always makes me feel sorry when I think of that last fight of his'n, and the way it turned out.

Well, thish-yer Smiley had rat-terriers[12], and chicken cocks, and tomcats, and all of them kind of things, till you couldn't rest, and you couldn't fetch nothing for him to bet on but he'd match you. He ketched a frog one day, and took him home, and said he cal'klated[13] to educate him; and so he never done nothing for three months but set in his back yard and learn[14] that frog to jump. And you bet you he did learn him, too. He'd give him a little punch behind, and the next minute you'd see that frog whirling in the air like a doughnut—see him turn one summerset, or may be a couple, if he got a good start, and come down flat-footed and all right, like a cat. He got him up so in the matter of catching flies, and kept him in practice so constant, that he'd nail a fly every time as far as he could see him. Smiley said all a frog wanted was education, and he could do most any thing and I believe him. Why, I've seen him set Dan'l Webster[15] down here on this floor—Dan'l Webster was the name of the frog—and sing out, "Flies, Dan'l, flies!" and quicker'n you could wink, he'd spring straight up, and snake a fly off'n the counter there, and flop down on the floor again as solid as a gob of mud, and fall to scratching the side of his head with his hind foot as indifferent as if he hadn't no idea he'd been doin' any more'n any frog might do. You never see a frog so modest and straightforward as he was, for all he was so gifted. And when it come to fair and square jumping on a dead level, he could get over more ground at one straddle than any animal of his breed you ever see. Jumping on a dead level was his strong suit, you understand; and when it come to that, Smiley would ante up[16] money on him as long as he had a red. Smiley was monstrous proud of his frog, and well he might be, for fellers that had traveled and been everywheres, all said he laid over any frog that ever they see.

Well, Smiley kept the beast in a little lattice box, and he used to fetch him downtown sometimes and lay for a bet. One day a feller—a stranger in the camp, he was— come across him with his box, and says:

"What might it be that you've got in the box?"

And Smiley says, sorter indifferent like, "It might be a parrot, or it might be a canary, may be, but it isn't— it's only just a frog."

And the feller took it, and looked at it careful, and turned it round this way and that, and says, "H'm— so it is. Well, what's he good for?"

"Well," Smiley says, easy and careless, "He's good enough for one thing, I should judge— he can outjump any frog in Calaveras county."

The feller took the box again, and took another long, particular look, and give it back to Smiley, and says, very deliberate, "Well, I don't see no p'ints[17] about that frog that's any better'n any other frog."

"May be you don't," Smiley says. "May be you understand frogs, and may be you don't understand 'em; may be you've had experience, and may be you isn't only a amature, as it were. Anyways, I've got my opinion, and I'll risk forty dollars that he can outjump any frog in Calaveras county."

And the feller studied a minute, and then says, kinder sad like, "Well, I'm only a stranger here, and I an't got no frog; but if I had a frog, I'd bet you."

And then Smiley says, "That's all right that's all right if you'll hold my box a minute, I'll go and get you a frog." And so the feller took the box, and put up his forty dollars along with Smiley's, and set down to wait.

So he set there a good while thinking and thinking to himself, and then he got the frog out and prized his mouth open and took a tea-spoon and filled him full of quail shot[18] filled him pretty near up to his chin and set him on the floor. Smiley he went to the swamp and slopped around in the mud for a long time, and finally he ketched a frog, and fetched him in, and give him to this feller, and says:

"Now, if you're ready, set him alongside of Dan'l, with his fore-paws just even with Dan'l, and I'll give the word." Then he says, "One—two—three—jump!" and him and the feller touched up the frogs from behind, and the new frog hopped off, but Dan'l give a heave, and hysted up his shoulders—so—like a Frenchman, but it wan's no use—he couldn't budge; he was planted as solid as an anvil, and he couldn't no more stir than if he was anchored out. Smiley was a good deal surprised, and he was disgusted too, but he didn't have no idea what the matter was, of course.

The feller took the money and started away; and when he was going out at the door, he sorter jerked his thumb over his shoulders—this way—at Dan'l, and says again, very deliberate, "Well, I don't see no p'ints about that frog that's any better'n any other frog." Smiley he stood scratching his head and looking down at Dan'l a long time, and at last he says, "I do wonder what in the nation that frog throw'd off for—I wonder if there ant something the matter with him—he 'pears to look mighty baggy, somehow." And he ketched Dan'l by the nap of the neck, and lifted him up and says, "Why, blame my cats, if he don't weigh five pound!" and turned him upside down, and he belched out a double handful of shot. And then he see how it was, and he was the maddest man—he set the frog down and took out after that feller, but he never ketchd him. And—

[Here Simon Wheeler heard his name called from the front yard, and got up to see what was wanted.] And turning to me as he moved away, he said: "Just set where you are, stranger, and rest easy—I am not going to be gone a second."

But, by your leave, I did not think that a continuation of the history of the enterprising vagabond Jim Smiley would be likely to afford me much information concerning the Rev. Leonidas W. Smiley, and so I started away. At the door I met the sociable Wheeler returning, and he buttonholed[19] me and recommenced:

"Well, thish-yer Smiley had a yeller one-eyed cow that didn't have no tail, only jest a short stump like a bannanner, and—"

"Oh! hang Smiley and his afflicted cow!" I muttered, good-naturedly, and bidding the old gentleman good-day, I departed.

Notes:

1. infernal: awful or thoroughly unpleasant
2. Angel's: referring to Angel's Camp
3. flush: here implying "having a large amount of money"
4. exhorter: someone who urges by giving strong advice or warning; here, a preacher
5. risk two-and-a-half: meaning "risk, or bet, $2.50"
6. Thish-yer: dialect for "this here."
7. consumption: another name for "tuberculosis"
8. fetch up at the stand: meaning"arrive at the grandstand",which was placed at the finish line
9. cipher it down: meaning "calculate it"
10. throwed up the sponge: meaning "gave up the contest"
11. had him in the door: meaning "had him at a disadvantage or in a tight place"
12. rat-tarriers: dogs once used for catching rats
13. cal'klated: dialect for calculated, meaning "planned"
14. learn: here meaning "teach"
15. Dan'l Webster: referring to Daniel Webster (1782—1852)
16. ante up: meaning "to put into the pool" or "to bet"
17. p'ints: dialect for points, meaning "qualities"
18. quail shot: is ammunition made up of small lead pellets
19. buttonholed: meaning "detained in conversation"

Questions for Study and Discussion:

1. How does the narrator come to meet Simon Wheeler and to hear his story? How does the narrator describe Wheeler's storytelling style?
2. For what reason does Wheeler call Smiley "the curiosest man"? What evidence does Wheeler use to support his statement?
3. Summarize the methods that Smiley's mare and bull pup use to win. What eventually becomes of Smiley's dog?
4. What amazing things can Smiley's frog do? What personality traits does Wheeler attribute to the frog?
5. Summarize what happens after Smiley meets the stranger.

6. What can you infer about the narrator's attitude toward Wheeler? Support your answer using details from the story.

7. What conclusions can you draw about Smiley's character, based on the tale Wheeler tells? Use details from the story to support your ideas.

8. What do you think Wheeler tells about the mare and bull pup first, before focusing on the frog?

9. What aspects of Wheeler's description of Smiley's frog do you find particularly absurd?

10. What event or events determine the outcome of the encounter with the stranger? Explain your answer.

Bret Harte (1836—1902)

Life and Major Works

Francis Brett Harte was born in Albany, New York, from mostly English and Dutch heritage. His father was a teacher who moved from school to school almost yearly, never able to find or keep a good position. The family followed, fully aware of their own financial desperation. When his father died in 1845, his mother and the four children moved to New York City, supported by the charity of relatives. Frank, as he was called by his family, was sickly as a boy and sought pleasure in novels, which he read passionately. This home reading proved more beneficial to him than public school,

Bret Harte

which he left at age thirteen to work in a lawyer's office. His health improved as a young man, active in various office work about town. In 1850, his elder brother was drawn to California by the gold rush. His mother followed in 1853 to marry "Colonel" Andrew Williams, a college friend of his father, while Frank and his younger sister suffered a difficult sea passage early the next year to join the new couple in the dull, stagnant village of Oakland.

Before settling in San Francisco in 1860, Harte worked in the Sierra foothills as a teacher and, briefly, as a gold-miner; and in Uniontown (now Arcata) he was a tutor, apothecary clerk, typesetter, editorial assistant, and finally reporter for the weekly newspaper *The Northern Californian*. This last year-long experience helped the young author to prune his pretentious literary style and develop more concise and accurate prose. However, he resigned this position under death threats after writing an editorial condemning the slaughter of over 60 Digger Indians, mostly women and children, by white vigilantes near Eureka. This response suggested the attitude he would later develop through his fiction and poetry—sympathy for social outcasts and ironic criticism toward hypocrites who profited by frontier corruption or lawlessness.

In the city by the bay, he first began using the pen name Bret Harte, but he languished for a year as a typesetter and minor contributor to *The Colder* Era newspaper. Through the intercession of Jessie Fremont, wife of the explorer John Charles Fremont and patron to the young author, he received lucrative appointments to federal government jobs. These positions allowed him the financial stability to quit his typesetting job and to marry New Yorker Anna Griswold in 1862, and eventually they provided him a steady income and free time to work on his writing. He was fairly prolific during this period, publishing poems and fiction in both *The Golden Era* and *The Californian*, a respectable literary newspaper that also attracted the talents of Mark Twain.

By 1867, Harte was a central figure in the "local color" movement, which sought to capture the lore, folkways, and dialects of picturesque Western characters who told tall tales about con games, horse swapping, and hunting. Initially, the local color writers were journalists outside the literary mainstream who humorously criticized the values and customs of the West. But Harte tried to temper this debunking tendency when he became editor of *The Overland Monthly* in 1868. Anton Roman, the publisher, was a capitalistic booster of California's natural beauty, seeking to encourage wealthy Eastern and Midwestern families to relocate. Therefore, in Harte's Gold Rush tales, most of which he wrote while editing the magazine for three years, he balanced the satire and vernacular style of Western humor with a sentimental perspective so that these parables could both romanticize character types (such as the charitable gambler or the whore with a heart of gold) and advance a socially critical view.

Unfortunately, these characteristic works, collected in *The Luck of Roaring Camp, and Other Sketches* (1870), which brought Harte national fame, marked his literary peak, after which he merely parodied himself. There is some evidence, too, that celebrity spoiled him when he put the West behind him and returned to the East, which remained for him the locus of civilization. In New York through the 1870s, he had trouble writing, lavishly outspent his income, became estranged from his wife, and spent time away from his family on ill-prepared lecture tours, desperately trying to raise funds to pay off hounding creditors. When in 1878 President Rutherford Hayes offered Harte a position as commercial agent for the United States in Germany, he jumped at the opportunity, leaving his family behind. He subsequently served for five years as U.S. consul to Glasgow, but spent more time in London hobnobbing with British writers than at his post, which he lost in 1895 for "inattention to duty." It is doubly ironic that he was able to attain his lifelong goal of becoming a gentleman only through writing about the unrefined West, but that his cultured life was impoverished as literary material.

"The Outcasts of Poker Flat" first appeared in the January 1869 issue of *The Overland Monthly*, though the setting is 1850, just after the California gold rush began. The text is from the collection *The Luck of Roaring Camp, and Other Sketches* (New York: Regent, 1871), pages 19-36.

Brief Introduction and Appreciation

When "The Outcasts of Poker Flat" first appeared in the January 1869 issue of *The Overland Monthly*, the story was an immediate critical and popular success. Critics such as Emily S. Forman, writing for Old and New, praised Harte's use of "novel vernacular" and "vivid portraiture" to "thrill the very depths of the heart and soul." Harte's critical stature declined in subsequent years as people's tastes in literature changed. Despite this shift in tastes, "The Outcasts of Poker Flat" is continually recognized as one of Harte's best stories and is widely anthologized and read today.

As late as 1936, Arthur Hobson Quinn argued in *American Fiction: An Historical and Critical Survey* that the tale was "a masterpiece." But within seven years, Harte's reputation was seriously challenged by Cleanth Brooks and Robert Penn Warren's seminal text *Understanding Fiction*, which was published in 1943. In their analysis of Harte's "Tennessee's Partner," Brooks and Warren cited what later became standard criticisms of the author's work in general: inconclusive plots, lack of realism, and a reliance on melodrama and sentiment.

Such charges are interesting for they are essentially denouncing the traits that were responsible for Harte's initial success. In his heyday, Harte was celebrated for providing a realistic picture of the West. However, later generations possessing the advantage of historical hindsight were quick to label the author as a fraud. In 1973 Kevin Starr categorized Harte's work as "pseudo-history" complete with "comforting memories of finite human comedy and civilizing human sentiment." Given such attitudes it is not surprising that literary critics often take the position that Harte's stories lack artistic merit but are significant because of their influence on others. As an example, James K. Folsom cautioned, "In any discussion of Bret Harte one must begin by making a clear distinction between importance and quality."

Other critics argue that it is important to understand Harte in the context of nineteenth-century literature. In an article for American Literary Realism, Patrick Morrow suggested an alternate approach that sidesteps the issue of whether or not Harte's writing qualifies as great literature and focuses on its importance as a product of the culture in which it was written. Morrow points out that although Harte quickly fell from favor with critics, his work remained immensely popular with the public well into the twentieth century. Rather than denouncing him as a "hack" or "servant of the masses," scholars should recognize his stories as a major component of nineteenth-century popular culture and utilize them as a tool to help understand the past. This idea is closely related to the observations of Donald E. Glover, who argued in Western American Literature that Harte's later fiction, a body of work traditionally dismissed by literary scholars, is qualitatively similar to his early stories. Glover believed the calibre of Harte's writing did not decline; rather, the audience for his work changed and his style shifted accordingly.

In his interpretation of "The Outcasts of Poker Flat," Harold H. Kolb, Jr. suggested another explanation for the author's declining appeal. Kolb claimed that critical misunderstanding has long undermined an appreciation of Harte's work and that too much emphasis has been placed on the notion of Harte as a realist. Arguing that "Harte is not concerned with an impression of actuality, his interests lie elsewhere," Kolb pointed to Harte's reliance on juxtaposition, such as the contrast between the crudeness of his characters and the sophistication of the narrator, as a form of humor. Despite its somber ending, "The Outcasts of Poker Flat" was designed to be read as a comedy. But as Kolb explained, "the irony of his ironic style is that, for a century, he has had to be content with the enjoyment of his own fun."

Selected Reading

The Outcasts of Poker Flat

As Mr. John Oakhurst, gambler, stepped into the main street of Poker Flat on the morning of the twenty-third of November, 1850, he was conscious of a change in its moral atmosphere from the preceding night. Two or three men, conversing earnestly together, ceased as he approached, and exchanged significant glances. There was a Sabbath lull in the air, which, in a settlement unused to Sabbath influences, looked ominous.

Mr. Oakhurst's calm, handsome face betrayed small concern of these indications.

Whether he was conscious of any predisposing cause, was another question. "I reckon they're after somebody," he reflected; "likely it's me." He returned to his pocket the handkerchief with which he had been whipping away the red dust of Poker Flat from his neat boots, and quietly discharged his mind of any further conjecture.

In point of fact, Poker Flat was "after somebody." It had lately suffered the loss of several thousand dollars, two valuable horses, and a prominent citizen. It was experiencing a spasm of virtuous reaction, quite as lawless and ungovernable as any of the acts that had provoked it. A secret committee[1] had determined to rid the town of all improper persons. This was done permanently in regard of two men who were then hanging from the boughs of a sycamore in the gulch, and temporarily in the banishment of certain other objectionable characters. I regret to say that some of these were ladies. It is but due to the sex, however, to state that their impropriety was professional, and it was only in such easily established standards of evil that Poker Flat ventured to sit in judgment.

Mr. Oakhurst was right in supposing that he was included in this category. A few of the committee had urged hanging him as a possible example, and a sure method of reimbursing themselves from his pockets of the sums he had won from them. "It's agin[2] justice," said Jim Wheeler, "to let this yet young man from Roaring Camp—an entire stranger—carry away our money." But a crude sentiment of equity residing in the breasts of those who had been fortunate enough to win from Mr. Oakhurst, overruled this narrower local prejudice.

Mr. Oakhurst received his sentence with philosophic calmness, none the less coolly, that he was aware of the hesitation of his judges. He was too much of a gambler not to accept Fate. With him life was at best an uncertain game, and he recognized the usual percentage in favor of the dealer.

A body of armed men accompanied the deported wickedness of Poker Flat to the outskirts of the settlement. Besides Mr. Oakhurst, who was known to be a coolly desperate man, and for whose intimidation the armed escort was intended, the expatriated party consisted of a young woman familiarly known as "The Duchess" another, who had gained the infelicitous title of "Mother Shipton[3]," and "Uncle Billy," a suspected sluice-robber[4] and confirmed drunkard. The cavalcade provoked no comments from the spectators, nor was any word uttered by the escort. Only when the gulch which marked the uttermost limit of Poker Flat was reached, the leader spoke briefly and to the point. The exiles were forbidden to return at the peril of their lives.

As the escort disappeared, their pent-up feelings found vent in a few hysterical tears from "The Duchess," some bad language from Mother Shipton, and a Parthian[5] volley of expletives from Uncle Billy. The philosophic Oakhurst alone remained silent. He listened calmly to Mother Shipton's desire to cut somebody's heart out, to the repeated statements of "The Duchess" that she would die in the road, and to the alarming oaths that seemed to be bumped out of Uncle Billy as he rode forward. With the easy good-humor characteristic of his class, he insisted upon exchanging his own riding-horse, "Five Spot," for the sorry mule which the Duchess rode. But even this act did not draw the party into any closer sympathy. The young woman readjusted her somewhat draggled plumes with a feeble, faded coquetry; Mother Shipton eyed the possessor of "Five Spot" with malevolence, and Uncle Billy included the whole party in one sweeping anathema.

The road to Sandy Bar—a camp that not having as yet experienced the regenerating influences of Poker Flat, consequently seemed to offer some invitation to the emigrants—lay over a steep mountain range. It was distant a day's severe journey. In that advanced season, the party soon passed out of the moist, temperate regions of the foot-hills, into the dry, cold, bracing air of the Sierras[6]. The trail was narrow and difficult. At noon the Duchess, rolling out of her saddle upon the ground, declared her intention of going no further, and the party halted.The spot was singularly wild and impressive. A wooded amphitheatre, surrounded on three sides by precipitous cliffs of naked granite, sloped gently toward the crest of another precipice that overlooked the valley. It was undoubtedly the most suitable spot for a camp, had camping been advisable. But Mr. Oakhurst knew that scarcely half the journey to Sandy Bar was accomplished, and the party were not equipped or provisioned for delay. This fact he pointed out to his companions curtly, with a philosophic commentary on the folly of "throwing up their hand before the game was played out." But they were furnished with liquor, which in this emergency stood then in place of food, fuel, rest and prescience. In spite of his remonstrances, it was not long before they were more or less under its influence. Uncle Billy passed rapidly from a bellicose state into one of stupor, the Duchess became maudlin, and Mother Shipton snored. Mr. Oakhurst alone remained erect, leaning against a rock, calmly surveying them.

Mr. Oakhurst did not drink. It interfered with a profession which required coolness, impassiveness and presence of mind, and, in his own language, he "couldn't afford it." As he gazed at his recumbent fellow-exiles, the loneliness begotten of his pariah-trade[7], his habits of life, his very vices, for the first time seriously oppressed him. He bestirred himself in dusting his black clothes, washing his hands and face, and other acts characteristic of his studiously neat habits, and for a moment forgot his annoyance. The thought of deserting his weaker and more pitiable companions never perhaps occurred to him. Yet he could not help feeling the want of that excitement, which singularly enough was most conducive to that calm equanimity for which he was notorious. He looked at the gloomy walls that rose a thousand feet sheer above the circling pines around him; at the sky, ominously clouded; at the valley below, already deepening into shadow. And doing so, suddenly he heard his own name called.

A horseman slowly ascended the trail. In the fresh, open face of the newcomer, Mr. Oakhurst recognized Tom Simson, otherwise known as "The Innocent" of Sandy Bar. He had met him some months before over a "little game," and had, with perfect equanimity, won the entire fortune—amounting to some forty dollars—of that guileless youth. After the game was finished, Mr. Oakhurst drew the youthful speculator behind the door and thus addressed him: "Tommy, you're a good little man, but you can't gamble worth a cent. Don't try it over again." He then handed him his money back, pushed him gently from the room, and so made a devoted slave of Tom Simson.

There was a remembrance of this in his boyish and enthusiastic greeting of Mr. Oakhurst. He had started, he said, to go to Poker Flat to seek his fortune. "Alone?" No, not exactly alone; in fact—a giggle—he had run away with Piney Woods. Didn't Mr. Oakhurst remember Piney? She that used to wait on the table at the Temperance House? They had been engaged a long time, but old Jake Woods had objected, and so they had run away, and were going to Poker Flat to be married, and here they were. And they were tired out, and how lucky it was they had found a place to camp and company. All this The Innocent delivered rapidly, while Piney—a stout, comely damsel of fifteen—emerged from behind the pine tree, where she had been blushing unseen, and rode to the side of her lover.

Mr. Oakhurst seldom troubled himself with sentiment. Still less with propriety. But he had a vague idea that the situation was not felicitous. He retained, however, his presence of mind sufficiently to kick Uncle Billy, who was about to say something, and Uncle Billy was sober enough to recognize in Mr. Oakhurst's kick a superior power that would not bear trifling. He then endeavored to dissuade Tom Simson from delaying further, but in vain. He even pointed out the fact that there was no provision, nor means of making a camp. But, unluckily, "The Innocent" met this objection by assuring the party that he was provided with an extra mule loaded with provisions, and by the discovery of a rude attempt at a log-house near the trail. "Piney can stay with Mrs. Oakhurst, " said The Innocent, pointing to the Duchess, "and I can shift for myself."

Nothing but Mr. Oakhurst's admonishing foot saved Uncle Billy from bursting into a roar of laughter. As it was, he felt compelled to retire up the canon[8] until he could recover his gravity. There he confided the joke to the tall pine trees, with many slaps of his leg, contortions of his face, and the usual profanity. But when he returned to the party, he found them seated by a fire—for the air had grown strangely chill and the sky overcast—in apparently amicable conversation. Piney was actually talking in an impulsive, girlish fashion to the Duchess, who was listening with an interest and animation she had not shown for many days. The Innocent was holding forth, apparently with equal effect, to Mr. Oakhurst and Mother Shipton, who was actually relaxing into amiability. "Is this yer a d-d picnic?" said Uncle Billy, with inward scorn, as he surveyed the sylvan[9] group, the glancing fire-light and the tethered animals in the foreground. Suddenly an idea mingled with the alcoholic fumes that disturbed his brain. It was apparently of a jocular nature, for he felt impelled to slap his leg again and cram his fist into his mouth.

As the shadows crept slowly up the mountain, a slight breeze rocked the tops of the pine trees, and moaned through their long and gloomy aisles. The ruined cabin, patched and covered with pine boughs, was set apart for the ladies. As the lovers parted, they unaffectedly exchanged a parting kiss, so honest and sincere that it might have been heard above the swaying pines. The frail Duchess and the malevolent Mother Shipton were probably too stunned to remark upon this last evidence of simplicity, and so turned without a word to the hut. The fire was replenished, the men lay down before the door, and in a few minutes were asleep.

Mr. Oakhurst was a light sleeper. Toward morning he awoke benumbed and cold. As he stirred the dying fire, the wind, which was now blowing strongly, brought to his cheek that which caused the blood to leave it—snow!

He started to his feet with the intention of awakening the sleepers, for there was no time to lose. But turning to where Uncle Billy had been lying he found him gone. A suspicion leaped to his brain and a curse to his lips. He ran to the spot where the mules had been tethered; they were no longer there. The tracks were already rapidly disappearing in the snow.

The momentary excitement brought Mr. Oakhurst back to the fire with his usual calm. He did not waken the sleepers. The Innocent slumbered peacefully, with a smile on his good-humored, freckled face; the virgin Piney slept beside her frailer sisters as sweetly as though attended by celestial guardians, and Mr. Oakhurst, drawing his blanket over his shoulders, stroked his mustachios and waited for the dawn. It came slowly in a whirling mist of snow-flakes that dazzled and confused the eye. What could be seen of the landscape appeared magically changed. He looked over the valley, and summed up the present and future in two words—"Snowed in!"

A careful inventory of the provisions, which, fortunately for the party, had been stored within the hut, and so escaped the felonious fingers of Uncle Billy, disclosed the fact that with care and prudence they might last ten days longer. "That is," said Mr. Oakhurst, sotto voce[10] to The Innocent, "if you're willing to board us. If you aint—and perhaps you'd better not—you can wait till Uncle Billy gets back with provisions." For some occult reason, Mr. Oakhurst could not bring himself to disclose Uncle Billy's rascality, and so offered the hypothesis that he had wandered from the camp and had accidentally stampeded the animals. He dropped a warning to the Duchess and Mother Shipton, who of course knew the facts of their associate's defection. "They'll find out the truth about us all, when they find out anything," he added, significantly, "and there's no good frightening them now."

Tom Simson not only put all his worldly store at the disposal of Mr. Oakhurst, but seemed to enjoy the prospect of their enforced seclusion. "We'll have a good camp for a week, and then the snow'll melt, and we'll all go back together." The cheerful gayety of the young man and Mr. Oakhurst's calm infected the others. The Innocent, with the aid of pine boughs, extemporized a thatch for the roofless cabin, and the Duchess directed Piney in the rearrangement of the interior with a taste and tact that opened the blue eyes of that provincial maiden to their fullest extent. "I reckon now you're used to fine things at Poker Flat," said Piney. The Duchess turned away sharply to conceal something that reddened her cheeks through its professional tint, and Mother Shipton requested Piney not to "chatter." But when Mr. Oakhurst returned from a weary search for the trail, he heard the sound of happy laughter echoed from the rocks. He stopped in some alarm, and his thoughts first naturally reverted to the whiskey—which he had prudently cach d[11]. "And yet it don't somehow sound like whiskey," said the gambler. It was not until he caught sight of the blazing fire through the still blinding storm, and the group around it, that he settled to the conviction that it was "square fun."

Whether Mr. Oakhurst had cach d his cards with the whiskey as something debarred the free access of the community, I cannot say. It was certain that, in Mother Shipton's words, he "didn't say cards once" during that evening. Haply the time was beguiled by an accordeon, produced somewhat ostentatiously by Tom Simson, from his pack. Notwithstanding some difficulties attending the manipulation of this instrument, Piney Woods managed to pluck several reluctant melodies from its keys, to an accompaniment by The Innocent on a pair of bone castinets. But the crowning festivity of the evening was reached in a rude camp-meeting hymn, which the lovers, joining hands, sang with great earnestness and vociferation. I fear that a certain defiant tone and Covenanter's swing[12] to its chorus, rather than any devotional quality, caused it to speedily infect the others, who at last joined in the refrain:

> "I'm proud to live in the service of the Lord,
>   And I'm bound to die in His army[13]."

The pines rocked, the storm eddied and whirled above the miserable group, and the flames of their altar leaped heavenward, as if in token of the vow.

At midnight the storm abated, the rolling clouds parted, and the stars glittered keenly above the sleeping camp. Mr. Oakhurst, whose professional habits had enabled him to live on the smallest possible amount of sleep, in dividing the watch with Tom Simson, somehow managed to take upon himself the greater part of that duty. He excused himself to The Innocent, by saying that he had "often been a week without sleep." "Doing what?" asked Tom. "Poker!" replied Oakhurst, sententiously; "when a man gets a streak of luck—nigger-luck—he don't get tired. The luck gives in first. Luck," continued the gambler, reflectively, "is a mighty queer thing. All you know about it for certain is that it's bound to change. And it's finding out when it's going to change that makes you. We've had a streak of bad luck since we left Poker Flat—you come along and slap you get into it, too. If you can hold your cards right along you're all right. For," added the gambler, with cheerful irrelevance,

> "I'm proud to live in the service of the Lord,
>   And I'm bound to die in His army."

The third day came, and the sun, looking through the white-curtained valley, saw the outcasts divide their slowly decreasing store of provisions for the morning meal. It was one of the peculiarities of that mountain climate that its rays diffused a kindly warmth over the wintry landscape, as if in regretful commiseration of the past. But it revealed drift on drift of snow piled high around the hut; a hopeless, uncharted, trackless sea of white lying below the rocky shores to which the castaways still clung. Through the marvellously clear air, the smoke of the pastoral village of Poker Flat rose miles away. Mother Shipton saw it, and from a remote pinnacle of her rocky fastness, hurled in that direction a final malediction. It was her last vituperative attempt, and perhaps for that reason was invested with a certain degree of sublimity. It did her good, she privately informed the Duchess. "Just you go out there and cuss, and see." She then set herself to the task of amusing "the child," as she and the Duchess were pleased to call Piney. Piney was no chicken, but it was a soothing and ingenious theory of the pair to thus account for the fact that she didn't swear and wasn't improper.

When night crept up again through the gorges, the reedy notes of the accordeon rose and fell in fitful spasms and long-drawn gasps by the flickering camp-fire. But music failed to fill entirely the aching void left by insufficient food, and a new diversion was proposed by Piney—story-telling. Neither Mr. Oakhurst nor his female companions caring to relate their personal experiences, this plan would have failed, too, but for The Innocent Some months before he had chanced upon a stray copy of Mr. Pope's[14] ingenious translation of the Iliad[15]. He now proposed to narrate the principal incidents of that poem having thoroughly mastered the argument and fairly forgotten the words—in the current vernacular of Sandy Bar. And so for the rest of that night the Homeric demi-gods again walked the earth. Trojan bully and wily Greek wrestled in the winds, and the great pines in the canon seemed to bow to the wrath of the son of Peleus[16]. Mr. Oakhurst listened with quiet satisfaction. Most especially was he interested in the fate of "Ash-heels[17]," as The Innocent persisted in denominating the "swift-footed Achilles."

So with small food and much of Homer and the accordeon, a week passed over the heads of the outcasts. The sun again forsook them, and again from leaden skies the snow-flakes were sifted over the land. Day by day closer around them drew the snowy circle, until at last they looked from their prison over drifted walls of dazzling white, that towered twenty feet above their heads. It became more and more difficult to replenish their fires, even from the fallen trees beside them, now half-hidden in the drifts. And yet no one complained. The lovers turned from the dreary prospect and looked into each other's eyes, and were happy. Mr. Oakhurst settled himself coolly to the losing game before him. The Duchess, more cheerful than she had been, assumed the care of Piney. Only Mother Shipton—once the strongest of the party—seemed to sicken and fade. At midnight on the tenth day she called Oakhurst to her side. "I'm going," she said, in a voice of querulous weakness, "but don't say anything about it. Don't waken the kids. Take the bundle from under my head and open it." Mr. Oakhurst did so. It contained Mother Shipton's rations for the last week, untouched. "Give em to the child," she said, pointing to the sleeping Piney. "You've starved yourself," said the gambler. "That's what they call it," said the woman querulously, as she lay down again, and turning her face to the wall, passed quietly away.

The accordeon and the bones were put aside that day, and Homer was forgotten.

When the body of Mother Shipton had been committed to the snow, Mr. Oakhurst took The Innocent aside, and showed him a pair of snow-shoes, which he had fashioned from the old pack-saddle. "There's one chance in a hundred to save her yet," he said, pointing to Piney; "but it's there," he added, pointing toward Poker Flat. "If you can reach there in two days she's safe." "And you?" asked Tom Simson. "I'll stay here," was the curt reply.

The lovers parted with a long embrace. "You are not going, too," said the Duchess, as she saw Mr. Oakhurst apparently waiting to accompany him. "As far as the canon," he replied. He turned suddenly, and kissed the Duchess, leaving her pallid face aflame, and her trembling limbs rigid with amazement.

Night came, but not Mr. Oakhurst. It brought the storm again and the whirling snow. Then the Duchess, feeding the fire, found that some one had quietly piled beside the hut enough fuel to last a few days longer. The tears rose to her eyes, but she hid them from Piney.

The women slept but little. In the morning, looking into each other'; faces, they read their fate. Neither spoke; but Piney, accepting the position of the stronger, drew near and placed her arm around the Duchess's waist. They kept this attitude for the rest of the day. That night the storm reached its greatest fury, and rending asunder the protecting pines, invaded the very hut.

Toward morning they found themselves unable to feed the fire, which gradually died away. As the embers slowly blackened, the Duchess crept closer to Piney, and broke the silence of many hours: "Piney, can you pray?" "No, dear," said Piney, simply. The Duchess, without knowing exactly why felt relieved, and putting her head upon Piney's shoulder, spoke no more And so reclining, the younger and purer pillowing the head of her soiled sister upon her virgin breast, they fell asleep.

The wind lulled as if it feared to waken them. Feathery drifts of snow shaken from the long pine boughs flew like white-winged birds, and settled about them as they slept. The moon through the rifted clouds looked down upon what had been the camp. But all human stain, all trace of earthly travail, was hidden beneath the spotless mantle mercifully flung from above.

They slept all that day and the next, nor did they waken when voices and footsteps broke the silence of the camp. And when pitying fingers brushed the snow from their wan faces, you could scarcely have told from the equal peace that dwelt upon them, which was she that had sinned. Even the Law of Poker Flat recognized this, and turned away, leaving them still locked in each other's arms.

But at the head of the gulch, on one of the largest pine trees, they found the deuce of clubs[18] pinned to the bark with a bowie knife. It bore the following, written in pencil, in a firm hand:

BENEATH THIS TREE

LIES THE BODY

OF

JOHN OAKHURST,

WHO STRUCK A STREAK OF BAD LUCK

ON THE 23D OF NOVEMBER, 1850,

AND

HANDED IN HIS CHECKS

ON THE 7TH DECEMBER, 1850

And pulseless and cold, with a Derringer[19] by his side and a bullet in his heart though still calm as in life, beneath the snow, lay he who was at once the strongest and yet the weakest of the outcasts of Poker Flat.

Notes:

1. secret committee: vigilance committee, a group of citizens that bands together to punish criminals when usual law enforcement agencies are lacking.

2. agin: dialect variation of *against*

3. "Mother Shipton": English woman accused of witchcraft (1488—1560)

4. sluice-robber: one who steals from sluices. A sluice is a long sloping trough used for washing gold ore

5. Parthian: referring to an ancient people of southwest Asia, whose cavalry was noted for shooting at an enemy while retreating or pretending to retreat

6. Sierras: Sierra Nevada mountain range in eastern California.

7. pariah-trade: despicable occupation. A pariah is one who is despised; an outcast.

8. canon: variant of *canyon*

9. sylvan: characteristic of the woods

10. sotto voce: Italian for "under the voice"; in an undertone

11. cach d: modified French for "hidden"

12. Covenanter's swing: implying a lively rhythm. Covenanters were Scottish Presbyterians who demanded separation from the Church of England.

13. "I'm...army": The lines are from "Service of the Lord," an early American spiritual.

14. Mr. Pope's: referring to Alexander Pope (1688—1744), an English poet.

15. Iliad: Greek epic poem by Homer, describing the war between the Trojians, natives of ancient Troy, and the Greeks.

16. son of Peleus: Achilles, Greek warrior hero in the Trojan War.

17. Ash-heels: mispronunciation of Achilles, emphasizing his one vulnerable spot, his heel.

18. deuce of clubs: two of clubs, considered to have the lowest value in a deck of cards.

19. Derringer: small short-barreled pistol, named after Henry Deringer(1806—1868), an American gunsmith.

Questions for Study and Discussion:

1. As the story opens, what has the secret committee of Poker Flat decided to do? Who is directly affected by the committee's decision?

2. What is John Oakhurst's "profession"? How does he receive his "sentence", according to the fifth paragraph?

3. Why are Tom Simson and Piney Woods going to Poker Flat? What natural event puts them and the outcasts in danger?

4. What does Mother Shipton do to help Piney? Why does Tom leave the group?

5. When the rescue party arrives, what do they find?

6. Briefly describe John Oakhurst and his attitude toward life. Explain how his final actions relate to his philosophy of life.

7. What are Tom and Piney like? What effect do they have on Mother Shipton and on Oakhurst?

8. What forces do all the characters have to face? How do all of them expect Uncle Billy behave in this crisis?

9. Which elements of this story are common elements of Western fiction that you have encountered in films, TV shows, or other works about the West?

Henry James (1843—1916)

Life and Major Works

Before Henry James, there were a number of great novelists—but to James we owe the first consciousness of the novel as an art form, and the first attempts to codify a theory of the novel. If this critical awareness were all he contributed. James would be always remembered. How much greater is our debt then, for James practiced what he preached, being a consummate novelist, short-story writer, and the virtual creator of the novella in English.

Henry James

Henry James was born in New York City on April 15, 1843, son of a well known theologian of the same name, and brother of William James, the famous psychologist and philosopher. He was educated both in New York and abroad and in 1862 entered Harvard Law School. Legal studies, however, interested him little, and he soon began contributing sketches and articles to several magazines, gradually developing the determination to live by his pen. His early stories, dealing mostly with the American scene, drew unreserved praise from a number of critics, but it was not until after he had traveled abroad again, for the first time as an adult, that he felt sufficiently secure to publish his first novel, *Roderick Hudson* (1875), in which his recurring theme of American innocence confronted by European cultivation received its first exposition. Felling somehow uncomfortable and stifled in his native America, James left for Europe in 1875; in 1876 he settled in England, where he was to live out most of his life.

The American appeared in 1877, and two years later *Daisy Miller* was published. By this time he had earned a considerable international reputation, confirmed with the publication of his early masterpiece, *The Portrait of A Lady*. With this complex, superbly imagined and realized tale of the corruption of American innocence by an evil European influence, sharply depicted through the indestructible character of Isabel Archer, James' first period may be said to have come to an end.

In the latter half of the 80s, James wrote several social novels, notably *The Bostonians, the Princess Casamassima* (1886), and *The Tragic Muse*, which he felt permanently alienated his readers, and he turned to the theater in an effort to regain his audience. Actually, these novels, though limited in popularity during James' day, have endured as some of his finest works, while as a playwright he was a total failure. From 1890 to 1895 he published no long fiction, devoting most of his time to his writing for the stage; but it was during this period that he produced some of his best short stories, many of them covertly autobiographical, dealing with artists misunderstood by their public. James terminated his theatrical career following the fiasco of *Guy Domville* (1895), which was hooted from the stage in its first performance. In 1896, he moved to a house in Rye, where he began producing some of his more memorable novellas, foreshadowing the subtle psychological explorations of his later novels, and their tight, unified form. *The Spoils of Poynton* appeared in 1897; that year also saw *What Maisie Knew*; and in 1898, he published *The Turn of The Screw*. James expanded his form in *The Awkward Age* (1899) and *The Sacred Fount* (1901), followed by his last three great novels: *The Wings of the Dove* (1902*), The Ambassadors* (1903), and *The Golden Bowl* (1904). In these last works he paid such close attention to the details of psychological motivation, that he has been attacked for "writing in a social vacuum." Objects and everyday events are closely explored in a cumulative revelation of character and insight into motive that is stunning in its impact.

James was no less skilled as a critic, and is highly regarded for his *French Poets and Novelists* (1878); a biography of Hawthorne, an early and valuable appreciation (1879); *Partial Portraits* (1888); and *Notes on Novelists* (1914). His most valuable criticism perhaps, was the series of prefaces to his own works, prepared for the collected edition. They were gathered by R. P. Blackmur and printed as *The Art of The Novel* in 1949. His travel books include *A Little Tour In France* (1885) and *The American Scene* (1905).

James became a British subject in July, 1915, to show his sympathy with the English people in World War I. For some years he was engaged in writing several volumes of autobiography, publishing *A small Boy and Others* and *Notes of a Son and Brother. The Middle Years* was left uncompleted at his death, on February 28, 1916.

Brief Introduction and Appreciation

The Pupil is one of many stories by Henry James about the victimization of the young, like his *The Turn of the Screw* and several others. It was first published in *Longman's Magazine* in 1891.The theme periodically compelled James' imagination: it was another way, and a peculiarly poignant way, in which to indicate the manipulation of the vulnerable personality by the selfish and self-seeking. Nowhere does James deal with this theme to better or more moving effect than in *The Pupil*.

The pathos of Morgan Moreen's fate is twofold, that of the child and that of the genius. As a genius, Morgan is nobody's child—the great point of his curious existence is that nothing has come to him from his parents. Henry James speaks of the "mysteries of transmission" and of the "far jumps of heredity," speculating that the quality of Morgan's spirit can perhaps be traced to some unknown remote ancestor. But he really means that Morgan's quality, like all great human endowments, cannot be explained.

If the quality of Morgan's spirit does indeed amount to genius, it is not of the artistic kind. Rather, it is a genius of perception and morality—Morgan possesses the rare gift of seeing things as they really are and of judging them justly. He is thus at the opposite extreme from his family, all of whom are committed only to the appearance of things. As the boy says in one of his moments of expressed misery, "All they care about is to make an appearance and to pass for something or other." They are sunk in worldiness, hopelessly bound to the hope of acquiring social standing. Their whole view of life, we are told, is not only "rapacious and mean," but also "dim and confused and instinctive," devoid of any trace of the bright conscious intelligence that makes Morgan what he is.

In some sense Morgan is no less worldly than his family. For it is the world—the worldly world of "society," of social status and the petty scheming by which it is won—that makes the matter upon which his intelligence exercises itself. About the actualities of this world he knows far more than his family does. If we respond to him as a truly innocent person, it is not because he is ignorant of corruption, or naive about it. His innocence derives from his gift of seeing things as they are and calling them by their right names.

Our attention is attracted in the first paragraph of the story, for nothing could be more precisely indicative of the moral life of Morgan's family than the condition of Mrs. Moreen's gloves, those "soiled *gants de Suede*." Thereafter James misses no opportunity to remind us of the slovenliness of the Moreen mode of life. Mrs. Moreen's handkerchief is as soiled as her gloves; she thinks nothing of having an interview with Pemberton in his bedroom in the morning, wearing a dressing gown and sitting on the unmade bed; her daughters are not likely to be presentably dressed except when company is expected; her husband has been seen shaving in the drawing room.

The disorder and sordidness of the Moreen household are not indicative of any moral depravity, only of a deficient sense of reality. Mr. and Mrs. Moreen are very much at ease in talking about high ideals of moral sensibility. This, to be sure, suits their purposes of frand, especially in their dealings with poor Pemberton, but they are not wholly insincere, or at least they are not wholly conscious of their insincerity. In some part they are themselves taken in by what they say about delicacy of conduct. And it is just this easy self-deception that defeats them in their career of deceit. For these people have no talent whatever for the way of life they have chosen. Brother Ulick fancies himself a gambler, but it is usually he who is fleeced. Paula and Amy are never able to advance their plans for advantageous marriages. And the mother who aspires to marry one of her daughters to an English lord does not have sense enough to know that this is an enterprise that requires clean gloves and handkerchiefs.

It is only Morgan who comprehends the hopelessness of the family's undertaking and it is only he who perceives what it is that makes their failure inevitable-they lack the simple self-respect that is necessary for success even in a life of fraud. Nothing pains Morgan more than his family's deficiency of pride, which, as he sees, makes them the object of the world's contempt. And it offends his intelligence, his acute sense of reality, that because they lack pride they must scheme and cheat with no possible chance of success, that concerned as they are with appearances they do not know how they themselves appear to others.

James's condemnation of the Moreen "troupe" is open and unqualified. Yet he would have had no story if he had not given us the right to feel at least a little tenderness for Morgan's family. There would have been no story, that is, if Morgan did not love them, and he would not have loved them if they had not loved him. They do not love him enough, or wisely. But they do cherish him, or some idea of him; it was they who first perceived his "genius", which they respect without understanding. Their relation to Morgan is said to be possession rather than love, yet even possession is connection of a kind, and it is not until his parents surrender possession of him that Morgan dies.

And yet it is not the Moreens whom the story seems to hold accountable for Morgan's death. The blame falls upon Pemberton. We are naturally reluctant to observe this. For one thing, all through the story our censure has been directed to the Moreens; we have been trained, as it were, to hold them responsible for everything bad. And of course we have it well in mind how admirably Pemberton has behaved for four long years. We can grant that he is a rather passive young man who cannot think of a better way to make a living than as a private tutor and who is unable to insist on his rights; inevitably this somewhat diminishes the nobility we want to attribute to his devotion to Morgan. Yet even when these deductions are made, Pemberton still seems to stand as an example of that medieval loyalty of one person to another upon which Henry James set the highest moral value.

Pemberton's loyalty, however, turns out to be fatally flawed. James gives no explanation of the change that has occurred in Pemberton to make him think so bitterly of the proposal that he take charge of Morgan's life. The idea of Morgan's going away to live with Pemberton had not originated, we recall, either with Morgan or the Moreens but with Pemberton himself—it was he who, in the first flush of his affection for Morgan, had suggested that the two "go off and live somewhere together." It had then been only a fantasy, although not without its seriousness. But now, when Pemberton returns to the Moreens after his period in England, he has the sense that Morgan is delivering the whole of his life into his care, and he can think of the responsibility only in an ugly way.

Morgan's life presents itself to him as nothing but a "burden," and a burden which is not merely heavy but "blighting." What he had once seen as so bright and precious now figures in his mind as a "dreadful little life." Morgan, recovering from his crushing humiliation over his parents' sordid ruin, is enraptured at the prospect of going off with his friend, but the tutor, once so spontaneous in his affection, cannot meet the boy's rush of joy with anything more than the awareness that a warm response was called for. "When he [Morgan] stammered, 'My dear fellow, what do you say to that?' how could one not say something enthusiastic?" We are told that Morgan's seizure "immediately followed" Pemberton's response to Morgan's joy with nothing more than a recognition of the obligation to be enthusiastic. Mrs. Moreen's wail, "But I thought he *wanted* to go to you!" urges it upon us that Morgan's death "followed" not merely in point of time but as an effect follows a cause—the mother seems to see that the boy would not have died if he had wanted to go to Pemberton. We conclude that he no longer wanted to go because he was no longer wanted.

Throughout most of the story we have accepted Pemberton as not much more than the person through whose eyes we observe events. But as the story comes to its end, we must see him as something more, a moral agent. As such he fails. Out of his love for Morgan, he had given much, four years of his life. Yet is seems to be one of the paradoxes of love that the more one gives the more one commits oneself to give. If we pass an adverse judgment on Pemberton, it must be with the awareness of how very difficult love is, with the understanding that only a saint or a genius of morality would have met the demands of the situation in which this poor young man was placed. Still, we cannot avoid judging him adversely: there are occasions when, if a man is not a saint or a moral genius, he is nothing at all.

Selected Reading

The Pupil

I

The poor young man hesitated and procrastinated: it cost him such an effort to broach the subject of terms, to speak of money to a person who spoke only of feelings and, as it were, of the aristocracy. Yet he was unwilling to take leave, treating his engagement as settled, without some more conventional glance in that direction than he could find an opening for in the manner of the large affable lady who sat there drawing a pair of soiled *gants de Suede*[1] through a fat jewelled hand and, at once pressing and gliding, repeated over and over everything but the thing he would have liked to hear. He would have liked to hear the figure of his salary; but just as he was nervously about to sound that note the little boy came back—the little boy Mrs. Moreen had sent out of the room to fetch her fan. He came back without the fan, only with the casual observation that he couldn't find it. As he dropped this cynical confession he looked straight and hard at the candidate for the honour of taking his education in hand. This personage reflected somewhat grimly that the thing he should have to teach his little charge would be to appear to address himself to his mother when he spoke to her—especially not to make her such an improper answer as that.

When Mrs. Moreen bethought herself of this pretext for getting rid of their companion Pemberton supposed it was precisely to approach the delicate subject of his remuneration. But it had been only to say some things about her son that it was better a boy of eleven shouldn't catch. They were extravagantly to his advantage save when she lowered her voice to sigh, tapping her left side familiarly, "And all overclouded by *this*, you know; all at the mercy of a weakness—!" Pemberton gathered that the weakness was in the region of the heart. He had known the poor child was not robust: this was the basis on which he had been invited to treat, through an English lady, an Oxford acquaintance, then at Nice, who happened to know both his needs and those of the amiable American family looking out for something really superior in the way of a resident tutor.

The young man's impression of his prospective pupil, who had come into the room as if to see for himself the moment Pemberton was admitted, was not quite the soft solicitation the visitor had taken for granted. Morgan Moreen was somehow sickly without being "delicate," and that he looked intelligent—it is true Pemberton wouldn't have enjoyed his being stupid—only added to the suggestion that, as with his big mouth and big ears he really couldn't be called pretty, he might too utterly fail to please. Pemberton was modest, was even timid; and the chance that his small scholar might prove cleverer than himself had quite figured, to his anxiety, among the dangers of an untried experiment. He reflected, however, that these were risks one had to run when one accepted a position, as it was called, in a private family; when as yet one's university honours had, pecuniarily speaking, remained barren. At any rate when Mrs. Moreen got up as to intimate that, since it was understood he would enter upon his duties within the week she would let him off now, he succeeded, in spite of the presence of the child, in squeezing out a phrase about the rate of payment. It was not the fault of the conscious smile which seemed a reference to the lady's expensive identity, it was not the fault of this demonstration, which had, in a sort, both vagueness and point, if the allusion didn't sound rather vulgar. This was exactly because she became still more gracious to reply: "Oh I can assure you that all that will be quite regular."

Pemberton only wondered, while he took up his hat, what "all that" was to amount to—people had such different ideas. Mrs. Moreen's words, however, seemed to commit the family to a pledge definite enough to elicit from the child a strange little comment in the shape of the mocking foreign ejaculation "Oh la-la!"

Pemberton, in some confusion, glanced at him as he walked slowly to the window with his back turned, his hands in his pockets and the air in his elderly shoulders of a boy who didn't play. The young man wondered if he should be able to teach him to play, though his mother had said it would never do and that this was why school was impossible. Mrs. Moreen exhibited no discomfiture; she only continued blandly: "Mr. Moreen will be delighted to meet your wishes. As I told you, he has been called to London for a week. As soon as he comes back you shall have it out with him."

This was so frank and friendly that the young man could only reply, laughing as his hostess laughed: "Oh I don't imagine we shall have much of a battle."

"They'll give you anything you like," the boy remarked unexpectedly, returning from the window. "We don't mind what anything costs—we live awfully well."

"My darling, you're too quaint!" his mother exclaimed, putting out to caress him a practised but ineffectual hand. He slipped out of it, but looked with intelligent innocent eyes at Pemberton, who had already had time to notice that from one moment to the other his small satiric face seemed to change its time of life. At this moment it was infantine, yet it appeared also to be under the influence of curious intuitions and knowledges. Pemberton rather disliked precocity and was disappointed to find gleams of it in a disciple not yet in his teens. Nevertheless he divined on the spot that Morgan wouldn't prove a bore. He would prove on the contrary a source of agitation. This idea held the young man, in spite of a certain repulsion.

"You pompous little person! We're not extravagant!" Mrs. Moreen gaily protested, making another unsuccessful attempt to draw the boy to her side. "You must know what to expect," she went on to Pemberton.

"The less you expect the better!" her companion interposed. "But we *are* people of fashion."

"Only so far as *you* make us so!" Mrs. Moreen tenderly mocked. "Well then, on Friday—don't tell me you're superstitious—and mind you don't fail us. Then you'll see us all. I'm so sorry the girls are out. I guess you'll like the girls. And, you know, I've another son, quite different from this one."

"He tries to imitate me," Morgan said to their friend.

"He tries? Why he's twenty years old!" cried Mrs. Moreen.

"You're very witty," Pemberton remarked to the child—a proposition his mother echoed with enthusiasm, declaring Morgan's sallies to be the delight of the house.

The boy paid no heed to this; he only enquired abruptly of the visitor, who was surprised afterwards that he hadn't struck him as offensively forward: "Do you *want* very much to come?"

"Can you doubt it after such a description of what I shall hear?" Pemberton replied. Yet he didn't want to come at all; he was coming because he had to go somewhere, thanks to the collapse of his fortune at the end of a year abroad spent on the system of putting his scant patrimony into a single full wave of experience. He had had his full wave but couldn't pay the score at his inn. Moreover he had caught in the boy's eyes the glimpse of a far-off appeal.

"Well, I'll do the best I can for you," said Morgan; with which he turned away again. He passed out of one of the long windows; Pemberton saw him go and lean on the parapet of the terrace. He remained there while the young man took leave of his mother, who, on Pemberton's looking as if he expected a farewell from him, interposed with: "Leave him, leave him; he's so strange!" Pemberton supposed her to fear something he might say. "He's a genius—you'll love him," she added. "He's much the most interesting person in the family." And before he could invent some civility to oppose to this she wound up with: "But we're all good, you know!"

"He's a genius—you'll love him!" were words that recurred to our aspirant before the Friday, suggesting among many things that geniuses were not invariably loveable. However, it was all the better if there was an element that would make tutorship absorbing: he had perhaps taken too much for granted it would only disgust him. As he left the villa after his interview he looked up at the balcony and saw the child leaning over it. "We shall have great larks!" he called up.

Morgan hung fire a moment and then gaily returned: "By the time you come back I shall have thought of something witty!"

This made Pemberton say to himself "After all he's rather nice."

II

On the Friday he saw them all, as Mrs. Moreen had promised, for her husband had come back and the girls and the other son were at home. Mr. Moreen had a white moustache, a confiding manner and, in his buttonhole, the ribbon of a foreign order—bestowed, as Pemberton eventually learned, for services. For what services he never clearly ascertained: this was a point—one of a large number—that Mr. Moreen's manner never confided. What it emphatically did confide was that he was even more a man of the world than you might first make out. Ulick, the firstborn, was in visible training for the same profession—under the disadvantage as yet, however, of a buttonhole but feebly floral and a moustache with no pretensions to type. The girls had hair and figures and manners and small fat feet, but had never been out alone. As for Mrs. Moreen Pemberton saw on a nearer view that her elegance was intermittent and her parts didn't always match. Her husband, as she had promised, met with enthusiasm Pemberton's ideas in regard to a salary. The young man had endeavoured to keep these stammerings modest, and Mr. Moreen made it no secret that *he* found them wanting in "style." He further mentioned that he aspired to be intimate with his children, to be their best friend, and that he was always looking out for them. That was what he went off for, to London and other places—to look out; and this vigilance was the theory of life, as well as the real occupation, of the whole family. They all looked out, for they were very frank on the subject of its being necessary. They desired it to be understood that they were earnest people, and also that their fortune, though quite adequate for earnest people, required the most careful administration. Mr. Moreen, as the parent bird, sought sustenance for the nest. Ulick invoked support mainly at the club, where Pemberton guessed that it was usually served on green cloth.[2] The girls used to do up their hair and their frocks themselves, and our young man felt appealed to to be glad, in regard to Morgan's education, that, though it must naturally be of the best, it didn't cost too much. After a little he *was* glad, forgetting at times his own needs in the interest inspired by the child's character and culture and the pleasure of making easy terms for him.

During the first weeks of their acquaintance Morgan had been as puzzling as a page in an unknown language—altogether different from the obvious little Anglo-Saxons who had misrepresented childhood to Pemberton. Indeed the whole mystic volume in which the boy had been amateurishly bound demanded some practice in translation. To-day, after a considerable interval, there is something phantasmagoria, like a prismatic reflexion or a serial novel, in Pemberton's memory of the queerness of the Moreens. If it were not for a few tangible tokens—a lock of Morgan's hair cut by his own hand, and the half-dozen letters received from him when they were disjoined—the whole episode and the figures peopling it would seem too inconsequent for anything but dreamland. Their supreme quaintness was their success—as it appeared to him for a while at the time; since he had never seen a family so brilliantly equipped for failure. Wasn't it success to have kept him so hatefully long? Wasn't it success to have drawn him in that first morning at dejeuner,[3] the Friday he came—it was enough to *make* one superstitious—so that he utterly committed himself, and this not by calculation or on a signal, but from a happy instinct which made them, like a band of gipsies, work so neatly together? They amused him as much as if they had really been a band of gipsies. He was still young and had not seen much of the world—his English years had been properly arid; therefore the reversed conventions of the Moreens—for they had *their* desperate proprieties—struck him as topsy-turvy. He had encountered nothing like them at Oxford; still less had any such note been struck to his younger American ear during the four years at Yale in which he had richly supposed himself to be reacting against a Puritan strain. The reaction of the Moreens, at any rate, went ever so much further. He had thought himself very sharp that first day in hitting them all off in his mind with the "cosmopolite" label. Later it seemed feeble and colourless—confessedly helplessly provisional.

He yet when he first applied it felt a glow of joy—for an instructor he was still empirical—rise from the apprehension that living with them would really he to see life. Their sociable strangeness was an intimation of that—their chatter of tongues, their gaiety and good humour, their infinite dawdling (they were always getting themselves up, but it took forever, and Pemberton had once found Mr. Moreen shaving in the drawing-room), their French, their Italian and, cropping up in the foreign fluencies, their cold tough slices of American. They lived on macaroni and coffee—they had these articles prepared in perfection—but they knew recipes for a hundred other dishes. They overflowed with music and song, were always humming and catching each other up, and had a sort of professional acquaintance with Continental cities. They talked of "good places" as if they had been pickpockets or strolling players. They had at Nice a villa, a carriage, a piano and a banjo, and they went to official parties. They were a perfect calendar of the "days" of their friends, which Pemberton knew them, when they were indisposed, to get out of bed to go to, and which made the week larger than life when Mrs. Moreen talked of them with Paula and Amy. Their initiations gave their new inmate at first an almost dazzling sense of culture. Mrs. Moreen had translated something at some former period—an author whom it made Pemberton feel *borne*[4] never to have heard of. They could imitate Venetian and sing Neapolitan, and when they wanted to say something very particular communicated with each other in an ingenious dialect of their own, an elastic spoken cipher which Pemberton at first took for some *patois*[5] of one of their countries, but which he "caught on to" as he would not have grasped provincial development of Spanish or German.

"It's the family language—Ultramoreen," Morgan explained to him drolly enough;

but the boy rarely condescended to use it himself, though he dealt in colloquial Latin as if he had been a little prelate.

Among all the "days" with which Mrs. Moreen's memory was taxed she managed to squeeze in one of her own, which her friends sometimes forgot. But the house drew a frequented air from the number of fine people who were freely named there and from several mysterious men with foreign titles and English clothes whom Morgan called the princes and who, on sofas with the girls, talked French very loud—though sometimes with some oddity of accent—as if to show they were saying nothing improper. Pemberton wondered how the princes could ever propose in that tone and so publicly: he took for granted cynically that this was what was desired of them. Then he recognised that even for the chance of such an advantage Mrs. Moreen would never allow Paula and Amy to receive alone. These young ladies were not at all timid, but it was just the safeguards that made them so candidly free. It was a houseful of Bohemians who wanted tremendously to be Philistines.

In one respect, however, certainly they achieved no rigour—they were wonderfully amiable and ecstatic about Morgan. It was a genuine tenderness, an artless admiration, equally strong in each. They even praised his beauty, which was small, and were as afraid of him as if they felt him of finer clay. They spoke of him as a little angel and a prodigy—they touched on his want of health with long vague faces. Pemberton feared at first an extravagance that might make him hate the boy, but before this happened he had become extravagant himself. Later, when he had grown rather to hate the others, it was a bribe to patience for him that they were at any rate nice about Morgan, going on tiptoe if they fancied he was showing symptoms, and even giving up somebody's "day" to procure him a pleasure. Mixed with this too was the oddest wish to make him independent, as if they had felt themselves not good enough for him. They passed him over to the new members of their circle very much as if wishing to force some charity of adoption on so free an agent and get rid of their own charge. They were delighted when they saw Morgan take so to his kind playfellow, and could think of no higher praise for the young man. It was strange how they contrived to reconcile the appearance, and indeed the essential fact, of adoring the child with their eagerness to wash their hands of him. Did they want to get rid of him before he should find them out? Pemberton was finding them out month by month. The boy's fond family, however this might be, turned their backs with exaggerated delicacy, as if to avoid the reproach of interfering. Seeing in time how little he had in common with them—it was by *them* he first observed it; they proclaimed it with complete humility—his companion was moved to speculate on the mysteries of transmission, the far jumps of heredity. Where his detachment from most of the things they represented had come from was more than an observer could say—it certainly had burrowed under two or three generations.

As for Pemberton's own estimate of his pupil, it was a good while before he got the point of view, so little had he been prepared for it by the smug young barbarians to whom the tradition of tutorship, as hitherto revealed to him, had been adjusted. Morgan was scrappy and surprising, deficient in many properties supposed common to the *genus* and abounding in others that were the portion only of the supernaturally clever. One day his friend made a great stride: it cleared up the question to perceive that Morgan *was* supernaturally clever and that, though the formula was temporarily meagre, this would be the only assumption on which one could successfully deal with him. He had the general quality of a child for whom life had not been simplified by school, a kind of homebred sensibility which might have been as bad for himself but was charming for others, and a whole range of refinement and perception—little musical vibrations as taking as picked-up airs—begotten by wandering about Europe at the tail of his migratory tribe. This might not have been an education to recommend in advance, but its results with so special a subject were as appreciable as the marks on a piece of fine porcelain. There was at the same time in him a small strain of stoicism, doubtless the fruit of having had to begin early to bear pain, which counted for pluck and made it of less consequence that he might have been thought at school rather a polyglot little beast. Pemberton indeed quickly found himself rejoicing that school was out of the question: in any million of boys it was probably good for all but one, and Morgan was that millionth. It would have made him comparative and superior—it might have made him really require kicking. Pemberton would try to be school himself—a bigger seminary than five hundred grazing donkeys, so that, winning no prizes, the boy would remain unconscious and irresponsible and amusing—amusing, because, though life was already intense in his childish nature, freshness still made there a strong draught for jokes. It turned out that even in the still air of Morgan's various disabilities jokes flourished greatly. He was a pale lean acute undeveloped little cosmopolite, who liked intellectual gymnastics and who also, as regards the behaviour of mankind, had noticed more things than you might suppose, but who nevertheless had his proper playroom of superstitions, where he smashed a dozen toys a day.

III

At Nice once, toward evening, as the pair rested in the open air after a walk, and looked over the sea at the pink western lights, he said suddenly to his comrade: "Do you like it, you know—being with us all in this intimate way?"

"My dear fellow, why should I stay if I didn't?"

"How do I know you'll stay? I'm almost sure you won't, very long."

"I hope you don't mean to dismiss me," said Pemberton.

Morgan debated, looking at the sunset. "I think if I did right I ought to."

"Well, I know I'm supposed to instruct you in virtue; but in that case don't do right."

"You're very young—fortunately," Morgan went on, turning to him again.

"Oh yes, compared with you!"

"Therefore it won't matter so much if you do lose a lot of time."

"That's the way to look at it," said Pemberton accommodatingly.

They were silent a minute; after which the boy asked: "Do you like my father and my mother very much?"

"Dear me, yes. They're charming people."

Morgan received this with another silence; then unexpectedly, familiarly, but at the same time affectionately, he remarked: "You're a jolly old humbug!"

For a particular reason the words made our young man change colour. The boy noticed in an instant that he had turned red, whereupon he turned red himself and pupil and master exchanged a longish glance in which there was a consciousness of many more things than are usually touched upon, even tacitly, in such a relation. It produced for Pemberton an embarrassment; it raised in a shadowy form a question—this was the first glimpse of it—destined to play a singular and, as he imagined, owing to the altogether peculiar conditions, an unprecedented part in his intercourse with his little companion. Later, when he found himself talking with the youngster in a way in which few youngsters could ever have been talked with, he thought of that clumsy moment on the bench at Nice as the dawn of an understanding that had broadened. What had added to the clumsiness then was that he thought it his duty to declare to Morgan that he might abuse him, Pemberton, as much as he liked, but must never abuse his parents. To this Morgan had the easy retort that he hadn't dreamed of abusing them; which appeared to be true: it put Pemberton in the wrong.

"Then why am I a humbug for saying I think them charming?" the young man asked, conscious of a certain rashness.

"Well—they're not your parents."

"They love you better than anything in the world—never forget that," said Pemberton.

"Is that why you like them so much?"

"They're very kind to me," Pemberton replied evasively.

"You *are* a humbug!" laughed Morgan, passing an arm into his tutor's. He leaned against him looking oft at the sea again and swinging his long thin legs.

"Don't kick my shins," said Pemberton while he reflected "Hang it, I can't complain of them to the child!"

"There's another reason, too," Morgan went on, keeping his legs still.

"Another reason for what?"

"Besides their not being your parents."

"I don't understand you," said Pemberton.

"Well, you will before long. All right!"

He did understand fully before long, but he made a fight even with himself before he confessed it. He thought it the oddest thing to have a struggle with the child about. He wondered he didn't hate the hope of the Moreens for bringing the struggle on. But by the time it began any such sentiment for that scion was closed to him. Morgan was a special case, and to know him was to accept him on his own odd terms. Pemberton had spent his aversion to special cases before arriving at knowledge. When at last he did arrive his quandary was great. Against every interest he had attached himself. They would have to meet things together. Before they went home that evening at Nice the boy had said, clinging to his arm:

"Well, at any rate you'll hang on to the last."

"To the last?"

"Till you're fairly beaten."

"You ought to be fairly beaten!" cried the young man, drawing him closer.

IV

A year after he had come to live with them Mr. and Mrs. Moreen suddenly gave up the villa at Nice. Pemberton had got used to suddenness, having seen it practised on a considerable scale during two jerky little tours—one in Switzerland the first summer, and the other late in the winter, when they all ran down to Florence and then, at the end of ten days, liking it much less than they had intended, straggled back in mysterious depression. They had returned to Nice "for ever," as they said; but this didn't prevent their squeezing, one rainy muggy May night, into a second-class railway-carriage—you could never tell by which class they would travel—where Pemberton helped them to stow away a wonderful collection of bundles and bags. The explanation of this manoeuvre was that they had determined to spend the summer "in some bracing place"; but in Paris they dropped into a small furnished apartment—a fourth floor in a third-rate avenue, where there was a smell on the staircase and the *portier*[6] was hateful—and passed the next four months in blank indigence.

The better part of this baffled sojourn was for the preceptor and his pupil, who, visiting the Invalides[7] and Notre Dame, the Conciergerie[8] and all the museums, took a hundred remunerative rambles. They learned to know their Paris, which was useful, for they came back another year for a longer stay, the general character of which in Pemberton's memory to-day mixes pitiably and confusedly with that of the first. He sees Morgan's shabby knickerbockers—the everlasting pair that didn't match his blouse and that as he grew longer could only grow faded. He remembers the particular holes in his three or four pair of coloured stockings.

Morgan was dear to his mother, but he never was better dressed than was absolutely necessary—partly, no doubt, by his own fault, for he was as indifferent to his appearance as a German philosopher. "My dear fellow, you *are* coming to pieces," Pemberton would say to him in sceptical remonstrance; to which the child would reply, looking at him serenely up and down: "My dear fellow, so are you! I don't want to cast you in the shade." Pemberton could have no rejoinder for this—the assertion so closely represented the fact. If however the deficiencies of his own wardrobe were a chapter by themselves he didn't like his little charge to look too poor. Later he used to say "Well, if we're poor, why, after all, shouldn't we look it?" and he consoled himself with thinking there was something rather elderly and gentlemanly in Morgan's disrepair—it differed from the untidiness of the urchin who plays and spoils his things. He could trace perfectly the degrees by which, in proportion as her little son confined himself to his tutor for society, Mrs. Moreen shrewdly forbore to renew his garments. She did nothing that didn't show, neglected him because he escaped notice, and then, as he illustrated this clever policy, discouraged at home his public appearances. Her position was logical enough—those members of her family who did show had to be showy.

During this period and several others Pemberton was quite aware of how he and his comrade might strike people; wandering languidly through the Jardin des Plantes[9] as if they had nowhere to go, sitting on the winter days in the galleries of the Louvre, so splendidly ironical to the homeless, as if for the advantage of the *calorifere*.[10] They joked about it sometimes: it was the sort of joke that was perfectly within the boy's compass. They figured themselves as part of the vast vague hand-to-mouth multitude of the enormous city and pretended they were proud of their position in it—it showed them "such a lot of life" and made them conscious of a democratic brotherhood. If Pemberton couldn't feel a sympathy in destitution with his small companion—for after all Morgan's fond parents would never have let him really suffer—the boy would at least feel it with him, so it came to the same thing. He used sometimes to wonder what people would think they were—to fancy they were looked askance at, as if it might be a suspected case of kidnapping. Morgan wouldn't be taken for a young patrician with a preceptor—he wasn't smart enough; though he might pass for his companion's sickly little brother. Now and then he had a five-franc piece, and except once, when they bought a couple of lovely neckties, one of which he made Pemberton accept, they laid it out scientifically in old books. This was sure to be a great day, always spent on the quays, in a rummage of the dusty boxes that garnish the parapets.[11] Such occasions helped them to live, for their books ran low very soon after the beginning of their acquaintance. Pemberton had a good many in England, but he was obliged to write to a friend and ask him kindly to get some fellow to give him something for them.

If they had to relinquish that summer the advantage of the bracing climate the young man couldn't but suspect this failure of the cup when at their very lips to have been the effect of a rude jostle of his own. This had represented his first blow-out, as he called it, with his patrons; his first successful attempt—though there was little other success about it—to bring them to a consideration of his impossible position. As the ostensible eve of a costly journey the moment had struck him as favourable to an earnest protest, the presentation of an ultimatum. Ridiculous as it sounded, he had never yet been able to compass an uninterrupted private interview with the elder pair or with either of them singly. They were always flanked by their elder children, and poor Pemberton usually had his own little charge at his side. He was conscious of its being a house in which the surface of one's delicacy got rather smudged; nevertheless he had preserved the bloom of his scruple against announcing to Mr. and Mrs. Moreen with publicity that he shouldn't be able to go on longer without a little money. He was still simple enough to suppose Ulick and Paula and Amy might not know that since his arrival he had only had a hundred and forty francs; and he was magnanimous enough to wish not to compromise their parents in their eyes. Mr. Moreen now listened to him, as he listened to every one and to every thing, like a man of the world, and seemed to appeal to him—though not of course too grossly—to try and be a little more of one himself. Pemberton recognised in fact the importance of the character—from the advantage it gave Mr. Moreen. He was not even confused or embarrassed, whereas the young man in his service was more so than there was any reason for. Neither was he surprised—at least any more than a gentleman had to be who freely confessed himself a little shocked—though not perhaps strictly at Pemberton.

"We must go into this, mustn't we, dear?" he said to his wife. He assured his young friend that the matter should have his very best attention; and he melted into space as elusively as if, at the door, he were taking an inevitable but deprecatory precedence. When, the next moment, Pemberton found himself alone with Mrs. Moreen it was to hear her say "I see, I see"—stroking the roundness of her chin and looking as if she were only hesitating between a dozen easy remedies. If they didn't make their push Mr. Moreen could at least disappear for several days. During his absence his wife took up the subject again spontaneously, but her contribution to it was merely that she had thought all the while they were getting on so beautifully. Pemberton's reply to this revelation was that unless they immediately put down something on account he would leave them on the spot and for ever. He knew she would wonder how he would get away, and for a moment expected her to enquire. She didn't, for which he was almost grateful to her, so little was he in a position to tell.

"You won't, you *know* you won't—you're too interested," she said. "You *are* interested, you know you are, you dear kind man!" She laughed with almost condemnatory archness, as if it were a reproach—though she wouldn't insist; and flirted a soiled pocket-handkerchief at him.

Pemberton's mind was fully made up to take his step the following week. This would give him time to get an answer to a letter he had despatched to England. If he did in the event nothing of the sort—that is if he stayed another year and then went away only for three months—it was not merely because before the answer to his letter came (most unsatisfactory when it did arrive) Mr. Moreen generously counted out to him, and again with the sacrifice to "form" of a marked man of the world, three hundred francs in elegant ringing gold. He was irritated to find that Mrs. Moreen was right, that he couldn't at the pinch bear to leave the child. This stood out clearer for the very reason that, the night of his desperate appeal to his patrons, he had seen fully for the first time where he was. Wasn't it another proof of the success with which those patrons practised their arts that they had managed to avert for so long the illuminating flash? It descended on our friend with a breadth of effect which perhaps would have struck a spectator as comical, after he had returned to his little servile room, which looked into a close court where a bare dirty opposite wall took, with the sound of shrill clatter, the reflexion of lighted back windows. He had simply given himself away to a band of adventurers. The idea, the word itself, wore a romantic horror for him—he had always lived on such safe lines. Later it assumed a more interesting, almost a soothing, sense: it pointed a moral, and Pemberton could enjoy a moral. The Moreens were adventurers not merely because they didn't pay their debts, because they lived on society, but because their whole view of life, dim and confused and instinctive, like that of clever colour-blind animals, was speculative and rapacious and mean. Oh they were "respectable," and that only made them more *immondes*! [12]The young man's analysis, while he brooded, put it at last very simply—they were adventurers because they were toadies and snobs. That was the completest account of them—it was the law of their being. Even when this truth became vivid to their ingenious inmate he remained unconscious of how much his mind had been prepared for it by the extraordinary little boy who had now become such a complication in his life. Much less could he then calculate on the information he was still to owe the extraordinary little boy.

V

But it was during the ensuing time that the real problem came up—the problem of how far it was excusable to discuss the turpitude of parents with a child of twelve, of thirteen, of fourteen. Absolutely inexcusable and quite impossible it of course at first appeared; and indeed the question didn't press for some time after Pemberton had received his three hundred francs. They produced a temporary lull, a relief from the sharpest pressure. The young man frugally amended his wardrobe and even had a few francs in his pocket. He thought the Moreens looked at him as if he were almost too smart, as if they ought to take care not to spoil him. If Mr. Moreen hadn't been such a man of the world he would perhaps have spoken of the freedom of such neckties on the part of a subordinate. But Mr. Moreen was always enough a man of the world to let things pass—he had certainly shown that. It was singular how Pemberton guessed that Morgan, though saying nothing about it, knew something had happened. But three hundred francs, especially when one owed money, couldn't last for ever; and when the treasure was gone—the boy knew when it had failed—Morgan did break ground. The party had returned to Nice at the beginning of the winter, but not to the charming villa. They went to an hotel, where they stayed three months, and then moved to another establishment, explaining that they had left the first because, after waiting and waiting, they couldn't get the rooms they wanted. These apartments, the rooms they wanted, were generally very splendid; but fortunately they never *could* get them—fortunately, I mean, for Pemberton, who reflected always that if they had got them there would have been a still scantier educational fund. What Morgan said at last was said suddenly, irrelevantly, when the moment came, in the middle of a lesson, and consisted of the apparently unfeeling words: "You ought to *filer*, you know—you really ought."

Pemberton stared. He had learnt enough French slang from Morgan to know that to *filer* meant to cut sticks. "Ah my dear fellow, don't turn me off!"

Morgan pulled a Greek lexicon toward him—he used a Greek-German—to look out a word, instead of asking it of Pemberton. "You can't go on like this, you know."

"Like what, my boy?"

"You know they don't pay you up," said Morgan, blushing and turning his leaves.

"Don't pay me?" Pemberton stared again and feigned amazement. "What on earth put that into your head?"

"It has been there a long time," the boy replied rummaging his book.

Pemberton was silent, then he went on: "I say, what are you hunting for? They pay me beautifully."

"I'm hunting for the Greek for awful whopper," Morgan dropped.

"Find that rather for gross impertinence and disabuse your mind. What do I want of money?"

"Oh that's another question!"

Pemberton wavered—he was drawn in different ways. The severely correct thing would have been to tell the boy that such a matter was none of his business and bid him go on with his lines. But they were really too intimate for that; it was not the way he was in the habit of treating him; there had been no reason it should be. On the other hand Morgan had quite lighted on the truth—he really shouldn't be able to keep it up much longer; therefore why not let him know one's real motive for forsaking him? At the same time it wasn't decent to abuse to one's pupil the family of one's pupil; it was better to misrepresent than to do that. So in reply to his comrade's last exclamation he just declared, to dismiss the subject, that he had received several payments.

"I say—I say!" the boy ejaculated, laughing.

"That's all right," Pemberton insisted. "Give me your written rendering."

Morgan pushed a copybook across the table, and he began to read the page, but with something running in his head that made it no sense. Looking up after a minute or two he found the child's eyes fixed on him and felt in them something strange. Then Morgan said: "I'm not afraid of the stern reality."

"I haven't yet seen the thing you *are* afraid of—I'll do you that justice!"

This came out with a jump—it was perfectly true—and evidently gave Morgan pleasure. "I've thought of it a long time," he presently resumed.

"Well, don't think of it any more."

The boy appeared to comply, and they had a comfortable and even an amusing hour. They had a theory that they were very thorough, and yet they seemed always to be in the amusing part of lessons, the intervals between the dull dark tunnels, where there were waysides and jolly views. Yet the morning was brought to a violent as end by Morgan's suddenly leaning his arms on the table, burying his head in them and bursting into tears: at which Pemberton was the more startled that, as it then came over him, it was the first time he had ever seen the boy cry and that the impression was consequently quite awful.

The next day, after much thought, he took a decision and, believing it to be just, immediately acted on it. He cornered Mr. and Mrs. Moreen again and let them know that if on the spot they didn't pay him all they owed him he wouldn't only leave their house but would tell Morgan exactly what had brought him to it.

"Oh you *haven't* told him?" cried Mrs. Moreen with a pacifying hand on her well-dressed bosom.

"Without warning you? For what do you take me?" the young man returned.

Mr. and Mrs. Moreen looked at each other; he could see that they appreciated, as tending to their security, his superstition of delicacy, and yet that there was a certain alarm in their relief. "My dear fellow," Mr. Moreen demanded, "what use *can* you have, leading the quiet life we all do, for such a lot of money?"—a question to which Pemberton made no answer, occupied as he was in noting that what passed in the mind of his patrons was something like: "Oh then, if we've felt that the child, dear little angel, has judged us and how he regards us, and we haven't been betrayed, he must have guessed—and in short it's *general!*" an inference that rather stirred up Mr. and Mrs. Moreen, as Pemberton had desired it should. At the same time, if he had supposed his threat would do something towards bringing them round, he was disappointed to find them taking for granted—how vulgar their perception _had_ been!—that he had already given them away. There was a mystic uneasiness in their parental breasts, and that had been the inferior sense of it. None the less however, his threat did touch them; for if they had escaped it was only to meet a new danger. Mr. Moreen appealed to him, on every precedent, as a man of the world; but his wife had recourse, for the first time since his domestication with them, to a fine *hauteur*, reminding him that a devoted mother, with her child, had arts that protected her against gross misrepresentation.

"I should misrepresent you grossly if I accused you of common honesty!" our friend replied; but as he closed the door behind him sharply, thinking he had not done himself much good, while Mr. Moreen lighted another cigarette, he heard his hostess shout after him more touchingly:

"Oh you do, you do, put the knife to one's throat!"

The next morning, very early, she came to his room. He recognised her knock, but had no hope she brought him money; as to which he was wrong, for she had fifty francs in her hand. She squeezed forward in her dressing-gown, and he received her in his own, between his bath-tub and his bed. He had been tolerably schooled by this time to the "foreign ways" of his hosts. Mrs. Moreen was ardent, and when she was ardent she didn't care what she did; so she now sat down on his bed, his clothes being on the chairs, and, in her preoccupation, forgot, as she glanced round, to be ashamed of giving him such a horrid room. What Mrs. Moreen's ardour now bore upon was the design of persuading him that in the first place she was very good-natured to bring him fifty francs, and that in the second, if he would only see it, he was really too absurd to expect to be *paid*. Wasn't he paid enough without perpetual money—wasn't he paid by the comfortable luxurious home he enjoyed with them all, without a care, an anxiety, a solitary want? Wasn't he sure of his position, and wasn't that everything to a young man like him, quite unknown, with singularly little to show, the ground of whose exorbitant pretensions it had never been easy to discover? Wasn't he paid above all by the sweet relation he had established with Morgan—quite ideal as from master to pupil—and by the simple privilege of knowing and living with so amazingly gifted a child; than whom really (and she meant literally what she said) there was no better company in Europe? Mrs. Moreen herself took to appealing to him as a man of the world; she said "Voyons, mon cher,"[13] and "My dear man, look here now"; and urged him to be reasonable, putting it before him that it was truly a chance for him. She spoke as if, according as he *should* be reasonable, he would prove himself worthy to be her son's tutor and of the extraordinary confidence they had placed in him.

After all, Pemberton reflected, it was only a difference of theory and the theory didn't matter much. They had hitherto gone on that of remunerated, as now they would go on that of gratuitous, service; but why should they have so many words about it? Mrs. Moreen at all events continued to be convincing; sitting there with her fifty francs she talked and reiterated, as women reiterate, and bored and irritated him, while he leaned against the wall with his hands in the pockets of his wrapper, drawing it together round his legs and looking over the head of his visitor at the grey negations of his window. She wound up with saying: "You see I bring you a definite proposal."

"A definite proposal?"

"To make our relations regular, as it were—to put them on a comfortable footing."

"I see—it's a system," said Pemberton. "A kind of organised blackmail."

Mrs. Moreen bounded up, which was exactly what he wanted. "What do you mean by that?"

"You practise on one's fears—one's fears about the child if one should go away."

"And pray what would happen to him in that event?" she demanded, with majesty.

"Why he'd be alone with *you*."

"And pray with whom *should* a child be but with those whom he loves most?"

"If you think that, why don't you dismiss me?"

"Do you pretend he loves you more than he loves *us*?" cried Mrs. Moreen.

"I think he ought to. I make sacrifices for him. Though I've heard of those you make I don't see them."

Mrs. Moreen stared a moment; then with emotion she grasped her inmate's hand. "Will you make it—the sacrifice?"

He burst out laughing. "I'll see. I'll do what I can. I'll stay a little longer. Your calculation's just—I *do* hate intensely to give him up; I'm fond of him and he thoroughly interests me, in spite of the inconvenience I suffer. You know my situation perfectly. I haven't a penny in the world and, occupied as you see me with Morgan, am unable to earn money."

Mrs. Moreen tapped her undressed arm with her folded banknote. "Can't you write articles? Can't you translate as *I* do?"

"I don't know about translating; it's wretchedly paid."

"I'm glad to earn what I can," said Mrs. Moreen with prodigious virtue.

"You ought to tell me who you do it for." Pemberton paused a moment, and she said nothing; so he added: "I've tried to turn off some little sketches, but the magazines won't have them—they're declined with thanks."

"You see then you're not such a phoenix,"[14] his visitor pointedly smiled—"to pretend to abilities you're sacrificing for our sake."

"I haven't time to do things properly," he ruefully went on. Then as it came over him that he was almost abjectly good-natured to give these explanations he added: "If I stay on longer it must be on one condition—that Morgan shall know distinctly on what footing I am."

Mrs. Moreen demurred. "Surely you don't want to show off to a child?"

"To show *you* off, do you mean?"

Again she cast about, but this time it was to produce a still finer flower. "And *you* talk of blackmail!"

"You can easily prevent it," said Pemberton.

"And *you* talk of practising on fears," she bravely pushed on.

"Yes, there's no doubt I'm a great scoundrel."

His patroness met his eyes—it was clear she was in straits. Then she thrust out her money at him. "Mr. Moreen desired me to give you this on account."

"I'm much obliged to Mr. Moreen, but we *have* no account."

"You won't take it?"

"That leaves me more free," said Pemberton.

"To poison my darling's mind?" groaned Mrs. Moreen.

"Oh your darling's mind—!" the young man laughed.

She fixed him a moment, and he thought she was going to break out tormentedly, pleadingly: "For God's sake, tell me what *is* in it!" But she checked this impulse—another was stronger. She pocketed the money—the crudity of the alternative was comical—and swept out of the room with the desperate concession: "You may tell him any horror you like!"

VI

A couple of days after this, during which he had failed to profit by so free a permission, he had been for a quarter of an hour walking with his charge in silence when the boy became sociable again with the remark: "I'll tell you how I know it; I know it through Zenobie."

"Zenobie? Who in the world is *she*?"

"A nurse I used to have—ever so many years ago. A charming woman. I liked her awfully, and she liked me."

"There's no accounting for tastes. What is it you know through her?"

"Why what their idea is. She went away because they didn't fork out. She did like me awfully, and she stayed two years. She told me all about it—that at last she could never get her wages. As soon as they saw how much she liked me they stopped giving her anything. They thought she'd stay for nothing—just because, don't you know?" And Morgan had a queer little conscious lucid look. "She did stay ever so long—as long an she could. She was only a poor girl. She used to send money to her mother. At last she couldn't afford it any longer, and went away in a fearful rage one night—I mean of course in a rage against *them*. She cried over me tremendously, she hugged me nearly to death. She told me all about it," the boy repeated. "She told me it was their idea. So I guessed, ever so long ago, that they have had the same idea with you."

"Zenobie was very sharp," said Pemberton. "And she made you so."

"Oh that wasn't Zenobie; that was nature. And experience!" Morgan laughed.

"Well, Zenobie was a part of your experience."

"Certainly I was a part of hers, poor dear!" the boy wisely sighed. "And I'm part of yours."

"A very important part. But I don't see how you know that I've been treated like Zenobie."

"Do you take me for the biggest dunce you've known?" Morgan asked. "Haven't I been conscious of what we've been through together?"

"What we've been through?"

"Our privations—our dark days."

"Oh our days have been bright enough."

Morgan went on in silence for a moment. Then he said: "My dear chap, you're a hero!"

"Well, you're another!" Pemberton retorted.

"No I'm not, but I ain't a baby. I won't stand it any longer. You must get some occupation that pays. I'm ashamed, I'm ashamed!" quavered the boy with a ring of passion, like some high silver note from a small cathedral cloister, that deeply touched his friend.

"We ought to go off and live somewhere together," the young man said.

"I'll go like a shot if you'll take me."

"I'd get some work that would keep us both afloat," Pemberton continued.

"So would I. Why shouldn't I work? I ain't such a beastly little muff[15] as *that* comes to."

"The difficulty is that your parents wouldn't hear of it. They'd never part with you; they worship the ground you tread on. Don't you see the proof of it?" Pemberton developed. "They don't dislike me; they wish me no harm; they're very amiable people; but they're perfectly ready to expose me to any awkwardness in life for your sake."

The silence in which Morgan received his fond sophistry struck Pemberton somehow as expressive. After a moment the child repeated: "You *are* a hero!" Then he added: "They leave me with you altogether. You've all the responsibility. They put me off on you from morning till night. Why then should they object to my taking up with you completely? I'd help you."

"They're not particularly keen about my being helped, and they delight in thinking of you as *theirs*. They're tremendously proud of you."

"I'm not proud of _them_. But you know that," Morgan returned.

"Except for the little matter we speak of they're charming people," said Pemberton, not taking up the point made for his intelligence, but wondering greatly at the boy's own, and especially at this fresh reminder of something he had been conscious of from the first—the strangest thing in his friend's large little composition, a temper, a sensibility, even a private ideal, which made him as privately disown the stuff his people were made of. Morgan had in secret a small loftiness which made him acute about betrayed meanness; as well as a critical sense for the manners immediately surrounding him that was quite without precedent in a juvenile nature, especially when one noted that it had not made this nature "old-fashioned," as the word is of children—quaint or wizened or offensive. It was as if he had been a little gentleman and had paid the penalty by discovering that he was the only such person in his family. This comparison didn't make him vain, but it could make him melancholy and a trifle austere. While Pemberton guessed at these dim young things, shadows of shadows, he was partly drawn on and partly checked, as for a scruple, by the charm of attempting to sound the little cool shallows that were so quickly growing deeper. When he tried to figure to himself the morning twilight of childhood, so as to deal with it safely, he saw it was never fixed, never arrested, that ignorance, at the instant he touched it, was already flushing faintly into knowledge, that there was nothing that at a given moment you could say an intelligent child didn't know. It seemed to him that he himself knew too much to imagine Morgan's simplicity and too little to disembroil his tangle.

The boy paid no heed to his last remark; he only went on: "I'd have spoken to them about their idea, as I call it, long ago, if I hadn't been sure what they'd say."

"And what would they say?"

"Just what they said about what poor Zenobie told me—that it was a horrid dreadful story, that they had paid her every penny they owed her."

"Well, perhaps they had," said Pemberton.

"Perhaps they've paid you!"

"Let us pretend they have, and *n'en parlons plus*."[16]

"They accused her of lying and cheating"—Morgan stuck to historic truth. "That's why I don't want to speak to them."

"Lest they should accuse me, too?" To this Morgan made no answer, and his companion, looking down at him—the boy turned away his eyes, which had filled—saw what he couldn't have trusted himself to utter. "You're right. Don't worry them," Pemberton pursued. "Except for that, they *are* charming people."

"Except for *their* lying and their cheating?"

"I say—I say!" cried Pemberton, imitating a little tone of the lad's which was itself an imitation.

"We must be frank, at the last; we must come to an understanding," said Morgan with the importance of the small boy who lets himself think he is arranging great affairs—almost playing at shipwreck or at Indians. "I know all about everything."

"I dare say your father has his reasons," Pemberton replied, but too vaguely, as he was aware.

"For lying and cheating?"

"For saving and managing and turning his means to the best account. He has plenty to do with his money. You're an expensive family."

"Yes, I'm very expensive," Morgan concurred in a manner that made his preceptor burst out laughing.

"He's saving for *you*," said Pemberton. "They think of you in everything they do."

"He might, while he's about it, save a little—" The boy paused, and his friend waited to hear what. Then Morgan brought out oddly: "A little reputation."

"Oh there's plenty of that. That's all right!"

"Enough of it for the people they know, no doubt. The people they know are awful."

"Do you mean the princes? We mustn't abuse the princes."

"Why not? They haven't married Paula—they haven't married Amy. They only clean out Ulick."

"You *do* know everything!" Pemberton declared.

"No, I don't, after all. I don't know what they live on, or how they live, or *why* they live! What have they got and how did they get it? Are they rich, are they poor, or have they a *modeste aisance*?[17] Why are they always chiveying[18] me about—living one year like ambassadors and the next like paupers? Who are they, any way, and what are they? I've thought of all that—I've thought of a lot of things. They're so beastly worldly. That's what I hate most—oh, I've *seen* it! All they care about is to make an appearance and to pass for something or other. What the dickens do they want to pass for? What *do* they, Mr. Pemberton?"

"You pause for a reply," said Pemberton, treating the question as a joke, yet wondering too and greatly struck with his mate's intense if imperfect vision. "I haven't the least idea."

"And what good does it do? Haven't I seen the way people treat them—the 'nice' people, the ones they want to know? They'll take anything from them—they'll lie down and be trampled on. The nice ones hate that—they just sicken them. You're the only really nice person we know."

"Are you sure? They don't lie down for me!"

"Well, you shan't lie down for them. You've got to go—that's what you've got to do," said Morgan.

"And what will become of you?"

"Oh I'm growing up. I shall get off before long. I'll see you later."

"You had better let me finish you," Pemberton urged, lending himself to the child's strange superiority.

Morgan stopped in their walk, looking up at him. He had to look up much less than a couple of years before—he had grown, in his loose leanness, so long and high. "Finish me?" he echoed.

"There are such a lot of jolly things we can do together yet. I want to turn you out—I want you to do me credit."

Morgan continued to look at him. "To give you credit—do you mean?"

"My dear fellow, you're too clever to live."

"That's just what I'm afraid you think. No, no; it isn't fair—I can't endure it. We'll separate next week. The sooner it's over the sooner to sleep."

"If I hear of anything—any other chance—I promise to go," Pemberton said.

Morgan consented to consider this. "But you'll be honest," he demanded; "you won't pretend you haven't heard?"

"I'm much more likely to pretend I have."

"But what can you hear of, this way, stuck in a hole with us? You ought to be on the spot, to go to England—you ought to go to America."

"One would think you were *my* tutor!" said Pemberton.

Morgan walked on and after a little had begun again: "Well, now that you know I know and that we look at the facts and keep nothing back—it's much more comfortable, isn't it?"

"My dear boy, it's so amusing, so interesting, that it will surely be quite impossible for me to forego such hours as these."

This made Morgan stop once more. "You *do* keep something back. Oh you're not straight—*I* am!"

"How am I not straight?"

"Oh you've got your idea!"

"My idea?"

"Why that I probably shan't make old—make older—bones, and that you can stick it out till I'm removed."

"You *are* too clever to live!" Pemberton repeated.

"I call it a mean idea," Morgan pursued. "But I shall punish you by the way I hang on."

"Look out or I'll poison you!" Pemberton laughed.

"I'm stronger and better every year. Haven't you noticed that there hasn't been a doctor near me since you came?"

"I'm your doctor," said the young man, taking his arm and drawing him tenderly on again.

Morgan proceeded and after a few steps gave a sigh of mingled weariness and relief. "Ah now that we look at the facts it's all right!"

VII

They looked at the facts a good deal after this and one of the first consequences of their doing so was that Pemberton stuck it out, in his friend's parlance, for the purpose. Morgan made the facts so vivid and so droll, and at the same time so bald and so ugly, that there was fascination in talking them over with him, just as there would have been heartlessness in leaving him alone with them. Now that the pair had such perceptions in common it was useless for them to pretend they didn't judge such people; but the very judgement and the exchange of perceptions created another tie. Morgan had never been so interesting as now that he himself was made plainer by the sidelight of these confidences. What came out in it most was the small fine passion of his pride. He had plenty of that, Pemberton felt—so much that one might perhaps wisely wish for it some early bruises. He would have liked his people to have a spirit and had waked up to the sense of their perpetually eating humble- pie. His mother would consume any amount, and his father would consume even more than his mother. He had a theory that Ulick had wriggled out of an "affair" at Nice: there had once been a flurry at home, a regular panic, after which they all went to bed and took medicine, not to be accounted for on any other supposition. Morgan had a romantic imagination, led by poetry and history, and he would have liked those who "bore his name"—as he used to say to Pemberton with the humour that made his queer delicacies manly—to carry themselves with an air. But their one idea was to get in with people who didn't want them and to take snubs as it they were honourable scars. Why people didn't want them more he didn't know—that was people's own affair; after all they weren't superficially repulsive, they were a hundred times cleverer than most of the dreary grandees, the "poor swells" they rushed about Europe to catch up with. "After all they *are* amusing—they are!" he used to pronounce with the wisdom of the ages. To which Pemberton always replied: "Amusing—the great Moreen troupe? Why they're altogether delightful; and if it weren't for the hitch that you and I (feeble performers!) make in the *ensemble* they'd carry everything before them."

What the boy couldn't get over was the fact that this particular blight seemed, in a tradition of self-respect, so undeserved and so arbitrary. No doubt people had a right to take the line they liked; but why should his people have liked the line of pushing and toadying and lying and cheating? What had their forefathers—all decent folk, so far as he knew—done to them, or what had he done to them? Who had poisoned their blood with the fifth-rate social ideal, the fixed idea of making smart acquaintances and getting into the *monde chic*,[19] especially when it was foredoomed to failure and exposure? They showed so what they were after; that was what made the people they wanted not want *them*. And never a wince for dignity, never a throb of shame at looking each other in the face, never any independence or resentment or disgust. If his father or his brother would only knock some one down once or twice a year! Clever as they were they never guessed the impression they made. They were good- natured, yes—as good-natured as Jews at the doors of clothing-shops! But was that the model one wanted one's family to follow? Morgan had dim memories of an old grandfather, the maternal, in New York, whom he had been taken across the ocean at the age of five to see: a gentleman with a high neck-cloth and a good deal of pronunciation, who wore a dress-coat in the morning, which made one wonder what he wore in the evening, and had, or was supposed to have "property" and something to do with the Bible Society. It couldn't have been but that he was a good type. Pemberton himself remembered Mrs. Clancy, a widowed sister of Mr. Moreen's, who was as irritating as a moral tale and had paid a fortnight's visit to the family at Nice shortly after he came to live with them. She was "pure and refined," as Amy said over the banjo, and had the air of not knowing what they meant when they talked, and of keeping something rather important back. Pemberton judged that what she kept back was an approval of many of their ways; therefore it was to be supposed that she too was of a good type, and that Mr. and Mrs. Moreen and Ulick and Paula and Amy might easily have been of a better one if they would.

But that they wouldn't was more and more perceptible from day to day. They continued to "chivey," as Morgan called it, and in due time became aware of a variety of reasons for proceeding to Venice. They mentioned a great many of them—they were always strikingly frank and had the brightest friendly chatter, at the late foreign breakfast in especial, before the ladies had made up their faces, when they leaned their arms on the table, had something to follow the demitasse, and, in the heat of familiar discussion as to what they "really ought" to do, fell inevitably into the languages in which they could *tutoyer*.[20] Even Pemberton liked them then; he could endure even Ulick when he heard him give his little flat voice for the "sweet sea-city." That was what made him have a sneaking kindness for them—that they were so out of the workaday world and kept him so out of it. The summer had waned when, with cries of ecstasy, they all passed out on the balcony that overhung the Grand Canal.[21] The sunsets then were splendid and the Dorringtons had arrived. The Dorringtons were the only reason they hadn't talked of at breakfast; but the reasons they didn't talk of at breakfast always came out in the end. The Dorringtons on the other hand came out very little; or else when they did they stayed—as was natural—for hours, during which periods Mrs. Moreen and the girls sometimes called at their hotel (to see if they had returned) as many as three times running. The gondola was for the ladies, as in Venice too there were "days," which Mrs. Moreen knew in their order an hour after she arrived. She immediately took one herself, to which the Dorringtons never came, though on a certain occasion when Pemberton and his pupil were together at St. Mark's—where, taking the best walks they had ever had and haunting a hundred churches, they spent a great deal of time—they saw the old lord turn up with Mr. Moreen and Ulick, who showed him the dim basilica as if it belonged to them. Pemberton noted how much less, among its curiosities, Lord Dorrington carried himself as a man of the world; wondering too whether, for such services, his companions took a fee from him. The autumn at any rate waned, the Dorringtons departed, and Lord Verschoyle, the eldest son, had proposed neither for Amy nor for Paula.

One sad November day, while the wind roared round the old palace and the rain lashed the lagoon, Pemberton, for exercise and even somewhat for warmth—the Moreens were horribly frugal about fires; it was a cause of suffering to their inmate—walked up and down the big bare *sala* [22]with his pupil. The scagliola[23] floor was cold, the high battered casements shook in the storm, and the stately decay of the place was unrelieved by a particle of furniture. Pemberton's spirits were low, and it came over him that the fortune of the Moreens was now even lower. A blast of desolation, a portent of disgrace and disaster, seemed to draw through the comfortless hall. Mr. Moreen and Ulick were in the Piazza, looking out for something, strolling drearily, in mackintoshes, under the arcades; but still, in spite of mackintoshes, unmistakeable men of the world. Paula and Amy were in bed—it might have been thought they were staying there to keep warm. Pemberton looked askance at the boy at his side, to see to what extent he was conscious of these dark omens. But Morgan, luckily for him, was now mainly conscious of growing taller and stronger and indeed of being in his fifteenth year. This fact was intensely interesting to him and the basis of a private theory—which, however, he had imparted to his tutor—that in a little while he should stand on his own feet. He considered that the situation would change—that in short he should be "finished," grown up, producible in the world of affairs and ready to prove himself of sterling ability. Sharply as he was capable at times of analysing, as he called it, his life, there were happy hours when he remained, as he also called it—and as the name, really, of their right ideal—"jolly" superficial; the proof of which was his fundamental assumption that he should presently go to Oxford, to Pemberton's college, and, aided and abetted by Pemberton, do the most wonderful things. It depressed the young man to see how little in such a project he took account of ways and means: in other connexions he mostly kept to the measure. Pemberton tried to imagine the Moreens at Oxford and fortunately failed; yet unless they were to adopt it as a residence there would be no *modus vivendi*[24] for Morgan. How could he live without an allowance, and where was the allowance to come from? He, Pemberton, might live on Morgan; but how could Morgan live on *him*? What was to become of him anyhow? Somehow the fact that he was a big boy now, with better prospects of health, made the question of his future more difficult. So long as he was markedly frail the great consideration he inspired seemed enough of an answer to it. But at the bottom of Pemberton's heart was the recognition of his probably being strong enough to live and not yet strong enough to struggle or to thrive. Morgan himself at any rate was in the first flush of the rosiest consciousness of adolescence, so that the beating of the tempest seemed to him after all but the voice of life and the challenge of fate. He had on his shabby little overcoat, with the collar up, but was enjoying his walk.

It was interrupted at last by the appearance of his mother at the end of the sala. She beckoned him to come to her, and while Pemberton saw him, complaisant, pass down the long vista and over the damp false marble, he wondered what was in the air. Mrs. Moreen said a word to the boy and made him go into the room she had quitted. Then, having closed the door after him, she directed her steps swiftly to Pemberton. There was something in the air, but his wildest flight of fancy wouldn't have suggested what it proved to be. She signified that she had made a pretext to get Morgan out of the way, and then she enquired—without hesitation—if the young man could favour her with the loan of three louis. While, before bursting into a laugh, he stared at her with surprise, she declared that she was awfully pressed for the money; she was desperate for it—it would save her life.

"Dear lady, *c'est trop fort!*"[25] Pemberton laughed in the manner and with the borrowed grace of idiom that marked the best colloquial, the best anecdotic, moments of his friends themselves. "Where in the world do you suppose I should get three louis, *du train dont vous allez?*"[26]

"I thought you worked—wrote things. Don't they pay you?"

"Not a penny."

"Are you such a fool as to work for nothing?"

"You ought surely to know that."

Mrs. Moreen stared, then she coloured a little. Pemberton saw she had quite forgotten the terms—if "terms" they could be called—that he had ended by accepting from herself; they had burdened her memory as little as her conscience. "Oh yes, I see what you mean—you've been very nice about that; but why drag it in so often?" She had been perfectly urbane with him ever since the rough scene of explanation in his room the morning he made her accept *his* "terms"—the necessity of his making his case known to Morgan. She had felt no resentment after seeing there was no danger Morgan would take the matter up with her. Indeed, attributing this immunity to the good taste of his influence with the boy, she had once said to Pemberton "My dear fellow, it's an immense comfort you're a gentleman. " She repeated this in substance now. "Of course you're a gentleman—that's a bother the less!" Pemberton reminded her that he had not "dragged in" anything that wasn't already in as much as his foot was in his shoe; and she also repeated her prayer that, somewhere and somehow, he would find her sixty francs. He took the liberty of hinting that if he could find them it wouldn't be to lend them to *her*—as to which he consciously did himself injustice, knowing that if he had them he would certainly put them at her disposal. He accused himself, at bottom and not unveraciously, of a fantastic, a demoralised sympathy with her. If misery made strange bedfellows it also made strange sympathies. It was moreover a part of the abasement of living with such people that one had to make vulgar retorts, quite out of one's own tradition of good manners. "Morgan, Morgan, to what pass have I come for you?" he groaned while Mrs. Moreen floated voluminously down the sala again to liberate the boy, wailing as she went that everything was too odious.

Before their young friend was liberated there came a thump at the door communicating with the staircase, followed by the apparition of a dripping youth who poked in his head. Pemberton recognised him as the bearer of a telegram and recognised the telegram as addressed to himself. Morgan came back as, after glancing at the signature—that of a relative in London—he was reading the words: "Found a jolly job for you, engagement to coach opulent youth on own terms. Come at once." The answer happily was paid and the messenger waited. Morgan, who had drawn near, waited too and looked hard at Pemberton; and Pemberton, after a moment, having met his look, handed him the telegram. It was really by wise looks—they knew each other so well now—that, while the telegraph- boy, in his waterproof cape, made a great puddle on the floor, the thing was settled between them. Pemberton wrote the answer with a pencil against the frescoed wall, and the messenger departed. When he had gone the young man explained himself.

"I'll make a tremendous charge; I'll earn a lot of money in a short time, and we'll live on it."

"Well, I hope the opulent youth will be a dismal dunce—he probably will—" Morgan parenthesised—"and keep you a long time a-hammering of it in."

"Of course the longer he keeps me the more we shall have for our old age."

"But suppose *they* don't pay you!" Morgan awfully suggested.

"Oh there are not two such—!" But Pemberton pulled up; he had been on the point of using too invidious a term. Instead of this he said "Two such fatalities."

Morgan flushed—the tears came to his eyes. "*Dites toujours* [27]two such rascally crews!" Then in a different tone he added: "Happy opulent youth!"

"Not if he's a dismal dunce."

"Oh they're happier then. But you can't have everything, can you?" the boy smiled.

Pemberton held him fast, hands on his shoulders—he had never loved him so. "What will become of *you*, what will you do?" He thought of Mrs. Moreen, desperate for sixty francs.

"I shall become an *homme fait*." [28] And then as if he recognised all the bearings of Pemberton's allusion: "I shall get on with them better when you're not here."

"Ah don't say that—it sounds as if I set you against them!"

"You do—the sight of you. It's all right; you know what I mean. I shall be beautiful. I'll take their affairs in hand; I'll marry my sisters."

"You'll marry yourself!" joked Pemberton; as high, rather tense pleasantry would evidently be the right, or the safest, tone for their separation.

It was, however, not purely in this strain that Morgan suddenly asked: "But I say—how will you get to your jolly job? You'll have to telegraph to the opulent youth for money to come on."

Pemberton bethought himself. "They won't like that, will they?"

"Oh look out for them!"

Then Pemberton brought out his remedy. "I'll go to the American Consul; I'll borrow some money of him—just for the few days, on the strength of the telegram."

Morgan was hilarious. "Show him the telegram—then collar the money and stay!"

Pemberton entered into the joke sufficiently to reply that for Morgan he was really capable of that; but the boy, growing more serious, and to prove he hadn't meant what he said, not only hurried him off to the Consulate—since he was to start that evening, as he had wired to his friend—but made sure of their affair by going with him. They splashed through the tortuous perforations and over the humpbacked bridges, and they passed through the Piazza, where they saw Mr. Moreen and Ulick go into a jeweller's shop. The Consul proved accommodating—Pemberton said it wasn't the letter, but Morgan's grand air—and on their way back they went into Saint Mark's for a hushed ten minutes. Later they took up and kept up the fun of it to the very end; and it seemed to Pemberton a part of that fun that Mrs. Moreen, who was very angry when he had announced her his intention, should charge him, grotesquely and vulgarly and in reference to the loan she had vainly endeavoured to effect, with bolting lest they should "get something out" of him. On the other hand he had to do Mr. Moreen and Ulick the justice to recognise that when on coming in *they* heard the cruel news they took it like perfect men of the world.

VIII

When he got at work with the opulent youth, who was to be taken in hand for Balliol,[29] he found himself unable to say if this aspirant had really such poor parts or if the appearance were only begotten of his own long association with an intensely living little mind. From Morgan he heard half a dozen times: the boy wrote charming young letters, a patchwork of tongues, with indulgent postscripts in the family Volapuk[30] and, in little squares and rounds and crannies of the text, the drollest illustrations—letters that he was divided between the impulse to show his present charge as a vain, a wasted incentive, and the sense of something in them that publicity would profane. The opulent youth went up in due course and failed to pass; but it seemed to add to the presumption that brilliancy was not expected of him all at once that his parents, condoning the lapse, which they good-naturedly treated as little as possible as if it were Pemberton's, should have sounded the rally again, begged the young coach to renew the siege.

The young coach was now in a position to lend Mrs. Moreen three louis, and he sent her a post-office order even for a larger amount. In return for this favour he received a frantic scribbled line from her: "Implore you to come back instantly—Morgan dreadfully ill." They were on there rebound, once more in Paris—often as Pemberton had seen them depressed he had never seen them crushed—and communication was therefore rapid. He wrote to the boy to ascertain the state of his health, but awaited the answer in vain. He accordingly, after three days, took an abrupt leave of the opulent youth and, crossing the Channel, alighted at the small hotel, in the quarter of the Champs Elysees,[31] of which Mrs. Moreen had given him the address. A deep if dumb dissatisfaction with this lady and her companions bore him company: they couldn't be vulgarly honest, but they could live at hotels, in velvety *entresols*,[32] amid a smell of burnt pastilles, surrounded by the most expensive city in Europe. When he had left them in Venice it was with an irrepressible suspicion that something was going to happen; but the only thing that could have taken place was again their masterly retreat. "How is he? where is he?" he asked of Mrs. Moreen; but before she could speak these questions were answered by the pressure round hid neck of a pair of arms, in shrunken sleeves, which still were perfectly capable of an effusive young foreign squeeze.

"Dreadfully ill—I don't see it! the young man cried. And then to "Morgan: "Why on earth didn't you relieve me? Why didn't you answer my letter?"

Mrs. Moreen declared that when she wrote he was very bad, and Pemberton learned at the same time from the boy that he had answered every letter he had received. This led to the clear inference that Pemberton's note had been kept from him so that the game practised should not be interfered with. Mrs. Moreen was prepared to see the fact exposed, as Pemberton saw the moment he faced her that she was prepared for a good many other things. She was prepared above all to maintain that she had acted from a sense of duty, that she was enchanted she had got him over, whatever they might say, and that it was useless of him to pretend he didn't know in all his bones that his place at such a time was with Morgan. He had taken the boy away from them and now had no right to abandon him. He had created for himself the gravest responsibilities and must at least abide by what he had done.

"Taken him away from you?" Pemberton exclaimed indignantly.

"Do it—do it for pity's sake; that's just what I want. I can't stand *this*—and such scenes. They're awful frauds—poor dears!" These words broke from Morgan, who had intermitted his embrace, in a key which made Pemberton turn quickly to him and see that he had suddenly seated himself, was breathing in great pain, and was very pale.

"*Now* do you say he's not in a state, my precious pet?" shouted his mother, dropping on her knees before him with clasped hands, but touching him no more than if he had been a gilded idol. "It will pass—it's only for an instant; but don't say such dreadful things!"

"I'm all right—all right," Morgan panted to Pemberton, whom he sat looking up at with a strange smile, his hands resting on either side of the sofa.

"Now do you pretend I've been dishonest, that I've deceived?" Mrs. Moreen flashed at Pemberton as she got up.

"It isn't *he* says it, it's I!" the boy returned, apparently easier, but sinking back against the wall; while his restored friend, who had sat down beside him, took his hand and bent over him.

"Darling child, one does what one can; there are so many things to consider," urged Mrs. Moreen. "It's his *place*—his only place. You see *you* think it is now."

"Take me away—take me away," Morgan went on, smiling to Pemberton with his white face.

"Where shall I take you, and how—oh *how*, my boy?" the young man stammered, thinking of the rude way in which his friends in London held that, for his convenience, with no assurance of prompt return, he had thrown them over; of the just resentment with which they would already have called in a successor, and of the scant help to finding fresh employment that resided for him in the grossness of his having failed to pass his pupil.

"Oh we'll settle that. You used to talk about it," said Morgan. "If we can only go all the rest's a detail."

"Talk about it as much as you like, but don't think you can attempt it. Mr. Moreen would never consent—it would be so *very* hand-to-mouth," Pemberton's hostess beautifully explained to him. Then to Morgan she made it clearer: "It would destroy our peace, it would break our hearts. Now that he's back it will be all the same again. You'll have your life, your work and your freedom, and we'll all be happy as we used to be. You'll bloom and grow perfectly well, and we won't have any more silly experiments, will we? They're too absurd. It's Mr. Pemberton's place—every one in his place. You in yours, your papa in his, me in mine—*n'est-ce pas,cheri*? [33] We'll all forget how foolish we've been and have lovely times."

She continued to talk and to surge vaguely about the little draped stuffy salon while Pemberton sat with the boy, whose colour gradually came back; and she mixed up her reasons, hinting that there were going to be changes, that the other children might scatter (who knew?—Paula had her ideas) and that then it might be fancied how much the poor old parent- birds would want the little nestling. Morgan looked at Pemberton, who wouldn't let him move; and Pemberton knew exactly how he felt at hearing himself called a little nestling. He admitted that he had had one or two bad days, but he protested afresh against the wrong of his mother's having made them the ground of an appeal to poor Pemberton. Poor Pemberton could laugh now, apart from the comicality of Mrs. Moreen's mustering so much philosophy for her defence—she seemed to shake it out of her agitated petticoats, which knocked over the light gilt chairs—so little did their young companion, *marked*, unmistakeably marked at the best, strike him as qualified to repudiate any advantage.

He himself was in for it at any rate. He should have Morgan on his hands again indefinitely; though indeed he saw the lad had a private theory to produce which would be intended to smooth this down. He was obliged to him for it in advance; but the suggested amendment didn't keep his heart rather from sinking, any more than it prevented him from accepting the prospect on the spot, with some confidence moreover that he should do so even better if he could have a little supper. Mrs. Moreen threw out more hints about the changes that were to be looked for, but she was such a mixture of smiles and shudders—she confessed she was very nervous—that he couldn't tell if she were in high feather or only in hysterics. If the family was really at last going to pieces why shouldn't she recognise the necessity of pitching Morgan into some sort of lifeboat? This presumption was fostered by the fact that they were established in luxurious quarters in the capital of pleasure; that was exactly where they naturally *would* be established in view of going to pieces. Moreover didn't she mention that Mr. Moreen and the others were enjoying themselves at the opera with Mr. Granger, and wasn't *that* also precisely where one would look for them on the eve of a smash? Pemberton gathered that Mr. Granger was a rich vacant American—a big bill with a flourishy heading and no items; so that one of Paula's "ideas" was probably that this time she hadn't missed fire—by which straight shot indeed she would have shattered the general cohesion. And if the cohesion was to crumble what would become of poor Pemberton? He felt quite enough bound up with them to figure to his alarm as a dislodged block in the edifice.

It was Morgan who eventually asked if no supper had been ordered for him; sitting with him below, later, at the dim delayed meal, in the presence of a great deal of corded green plush, a plate of ornamental biscuit and an aloofness marked on the part of the waiter. Mrs. Moreen had explained that they had been obliged to secure a room for the visitor out of the house; and Morgan's consolation—he offered it while Pemberton reflected on the nastiness of lukewarm sauces—proved to be, largely, that his circumstance would facilitate their escape. He talked of their escape—recurring to it often afterwards—as if they were making up a "boy's book" together. But he likewise expressed his sense that there was something in the air, that the Moreens couldn't keep it up much longer. In point of fact, as Pemberton was to see, they kept it up for five or six months. All the while, however, Morgan's contention was designed to cheer him. Mr. Moreen and Ulick, whom he had met the day after his return, accepted that return like perfect men of the world. If Paula and Amy treated it even with less formality an allowance was to be made for them, inasmuch as Mr. Granger hadn't come to the opera after all. He had only placed his box at their service, with a bouquet for each of the party; there was even one apiece, embittering the thought of his profusion, for Mr. Moreen and Ulick. "They're all like that," was Morgan's comment; "at the very last, just when we think we've landed them they're back in the deep sea!"

Morgan's comments in these days were more and more free; they even included a large recognition of the extraordinary tenderness with which he had been treated while Pemberton was away. Oh yes, they couldn't do enough to be nice to him, to show him they had him on their mind and make up for his loss. That was just what made the whole thing so sad and caused him to rejoice after all in Pemberton's return—he had to keep thinking of their affection less, had less sense of obligation. Pemberton laughed out at this last reason, and Morgan blushed and said: "Well, dash it, you know what I mean." Pemberton knew perfectly what he meant; but there were a good many things that—dash it too!—it didn't make any clearer. This episode of his second sojourn in Paris stretched itself out wearily, with their resumed readings and wanderings and maunderings, their potterings on the quays, their hauntings of the museums, their occasional lingerings in the Palais Royal[34] when the first sharp weather came on and there was a comfort in warm emanations, before Chevet's wonderful succulent window. Morgan wanted to hear all about the opulent youth—he took an immense interest in him. Some of the details of his opulence—Pemberton could spare him none of them—evidently fed the boy's appreciation of all his friend had given up to come back to him; but in addition to the greater reciprocity established by that heroism he had always his little brooding theory, in which there was a frivolous gaiety too, that their long probation was drawing to a close. Morgan's conviction that the Moreens couldn't go on much longer kept pace with the unexpended impetus with which, from month to month, they did go on. Three weeks after Pemberton had rejoined them they went on to another hotel, a dingier one than the first; but Morgan rejoiced that his tutor had at least still not sacrificed the advantage of a room outside. He clung to the romantic utility of this when the day, or rather the night, should arrive for their escape.

For the first time, in this complicated connexion, our friend felt his collar gall him. It was, as he had said to Mrs. Moreen in Venice, trop fort—everything was *trop fort*.[35] He could neither really throw off his blighting burden nor find in it the benefit of a pacified conscience or of a rewarded affection. He had spent all the money accruing to him in England, and he saw his youth going and that he was getting nothing back for it. It was all very well of Morgan to count it for reparation that he should now settle on him permanently—there was an irritating flaw in such a view. He saw what the boy had in his mind; the conception that as his friend had had the generosity to come back he must show his gratitude by giving him his life. But the poor friend didn't desire the gift—what could he do with Morgan's dreadful little life? Of course at the same time that Pemberton was irritated he remembered the reason, which was very honourable to Morgan and which dwelt simply in his making one so forget that he was no more than a patched urchin. If one dealt with him on a different basis one's misadventures were one's own fault. So Pemberton waited in a queer confusion of yearning and alarm for the catastrophe which was held to hang over the house of Moreen, of which he certainly at moments felt the symptoms brush his cheek and as to which he wondered much in what form it would find its liveliest effect.

Perhaps it would take the form of sudden dispersal—a frightened *sauve qui peut*,[36] a scuttling into selfish corners. Certainly they were less elastic than of yore; they were evidently looking for something they didn't find. The Dorringtons hadn't re-appeared, the princes had scattered; wasn't that the beginning of the end? Mrs. Moreen had lost her reckoning of the famous "days"; her social calendar was blurred—it had turned its face to the wall. Pemberton suspected that the great, the cruel discomfiture had been the unspeakable behaviour of Mr. Granger, who seemed not to know what he wanted, or, what was much worse, what *they* wanted. He kept sending flowers, as if to bestrew the path of his retreat, which was never the path of a return. Flowers were all very well, but—Pemberton could complete the proposition. It was now positively conspicuous that in the long run the Moreens were a social failure; so that the young man was almost grateful the run had not been short. Mr. Moreen indeed was still occasionally able to get away on business and, what was more surprising, was likewise able to get back. Ulick had no club but you couldn't have discovered it from his appearance, which was as much as ever that of a person looking at life from the window of such an institution; therefore Pemberton was doubly surprised at an answer he once heard him make his mother in the desperate tone of a man familiar with the worst privations. Her question Pemberton had not quite caught; it appeared to be an appeal for a suggestion as to whom they might get to take Amy. "Let the Devil take her!" Ulick snapped; so that Pemberton could see that they had not only lost their amiability but had ceased to believe in themselves. He could also see that if Mrs. Moreen was trying to get people to take her children she might be regarded as closing the hatches for the storm. But Morgan would be the last she would part with.

One winter afternoon—it was a Sunday—he and the boy walked far together in the Bois de Boulogne.[37] The evening was so splendid, the cold lemon- coloured sunset so clear, the stream of carriages and pedestrians so amusing and the fascination of Paris so great, that they stayed out later than usual and became aware that they should have to hurry home to arrive in time for dinner. They hurried accordingly, arm-in-arm, good-humoured and hungry, agreeing that there was nothing like Paris after all and that after everything too that had come and gone they were not yet sated with innocent pleasures. When they reached the hotel they found that, though scandalously late, they were in time for all the dinner they were likely to sit down to. Confusion reigned in the apartments of the Moreens—very shabby ones this time, but the best in the house—and before the interrupted service of the table, with objects displaced almost as if there had been a scuffle and a great wine-stain from an overturned bottle, Pemberton couldn't blink the fact that there had been a scene of the last proprietary firmness. The storm had come—they were all seeking refuge. The hatches were down, Paula and Amy were invisible—they had never tried the most casual art upon Pemberton, but he felt they had enough of an eye to him not to wish to meet him as young ladies whose frocks had been confiscated—and Ulick appeared to have jumped overboard. The host and his staff, in a word, had ceased to "go on" at the pace of their guests, and the air of embarrassed detention, thanks to a pile of gaping trunks in the passage, was strangely commingled with the air of indignant withdrawal.

When Morgan took all this in—and he took it in very quickly—he coloured to the roots of his hair. He had walked from his infancy among difficulties and dangers, but he had never seen a public exposure. Pemberton noticed in a second glance at him that the tears had rushed into his eyes and that they were tears of a new and untasted bitterness. He wondered an instant, for the boy's sake, whether he might successfully pretend not to understand. Not successfully, he felt, as Mr. and Mrs. Moreen, dinnerless by their extinguished hearth, rose before him in their little dishonoured salon, casting about with glassy eyes for the nearest port in such a storm. They were not prostrate but were horribly white, and Mrs. Moreen had evidently been crying. Pemberton quickly learned however that her grief was not for the loss of her dinner, much as she usually enjoyed it, but the fruit of a blow that struck even deeper, as she made all haste to explain. He would see for himself, so far as that went, how the great change had come, the dreadful bolt had fallen, and how they would now all have to turn themselves about. Therefore cruel as it was to them to part with their darling she must look to him to carry a little further the influence he had so fortunately acquired with the boy—to induce his young charge to follow him into some modest retreat. They depended on him—that was the fact—to take their delightful child temporarily under his protection; it would leave Mr.

Moreen and herself so much more free to give the proper attention (too little, alas! had been given) to the readjustment of their affairs.

"We trust you—we feel we *can*," said Mrs. Moreen, slowly rubbing her plump white hands and looking with compunction hard at Morgan, whose chin, not to take liberties, her husband stroked with a paternal forefinger.

"Oh yes—we feel that we *can*. We trust Mr. Pemberton fully, Morgan," Mr. Moreen pursued.

Pemberton wondered again if he might pretend not to understand; but everything good gave way to the intensity of Morgan's understanding. "Do you mean he may take me to live with him for ever and ever?" cried the boy. "May take me away, away, anywhere he likes?"

"For ever and ever? *Comme vous-y-allez!*"[38] Mr. Moreen laughed indulgently. "For as long as Mr. Pemberton may be so good."

"We've struggled, we've suffered," his wife went on; "but you've made him so your own that we've already been through the worst of the sacrifice."

Morgan had turned away from his father—he stood looking at Pemberton with a light in his face. His sense of shame for their common humiliated state had dropped; the case had another side—the thing was to clutch at *that*. He had a moment of boyish joy, scarcely mitigated by the reflexion that with this unexpected consecration of his hope—too sudden and too violent; the turn taken was away from a good boy's book—the "escape" was left on their hands. The boyish joy was there an instant, and Pemberton was almost scared at the rush of gratitude and affection that broke through his first abasement. When he stammered "My dear fellow, what do you say to *that*?" how could one not say something enthusiastic? But there was more need for courage at something else that immediately followed and that made the lad sit down quietly on the nearest chair. He had turned quite livid and had raised his hand to his left side. They were all three looking at him, but Mrs. Moreen suddenly bounded forward. "Ah his darling little heart!" she broke out; and this time, on her knees before him and without respect for the idol, she caught him ardently in her arms. "You walked him too far, you hurried him too fast!" she hurled over her shoulder at Pemberton. Her son made no protest, and the next instant, still holding him, she sprang up with her face convulsed and with the terrified cry "Help, help! he's going, he's gone!" Pemberton saw with equal horror, by Morgan's own stricken face, that he was beyond their wildest recall. He pulled him half out of his mother's hands, and for a moment, while they held him together, they looked all their dismay into each other's eyes, "He couldn't stand it with his weak organ," said Pemberton—"the shock, the whole scene, the violent emotion."

"But I thought he *wanted* to go to you!", wailed Mrs. Moreen.

"I *told* you he didn't, my dear," her husband made answer. Mr. Moreen was trembling all over and was in his way as deeply affected as his wife. But after the very first he took his bereavement as a man of the world.

Notes:

1. (French)Suede gloves(literally,Swedish gloves)
2. Here it is an allusion to gambling.
3. (French)breakfast
4. (French)limited,parochial
5. (French)provincial dialect
6. (French)doorkeeper and janitor
7. The Hotel des Invalides was founded as a military hospital.It now contains the imposing tomb of Napoleon and a military museum.
8. The old prison of the Palais de Justice,chiefly notable to tourists for its use as a place of execution during the Reign of Terror.
9. A large botanical garden,containing also a museum and a small zoo
10. (French)hot-air stove
11. the booksellers' movable stalls,set up on parapets along the Seine
12. (French)impure,morally detestable
13. (French)practically the equivalent of Mrs.Moreen's following sentence in English
14. Here it is in the sense of one of unequalled excellence.
15. (Colloquial)one who is awkward or stupid
16. (French)Let's not say any more about it.
17. Here it refers to an income leaving them in moderately easy circumstances.
18. (British colloqualism)chasing,harassing
19. It refers to fashionable society.
20. French tutoyer:to address by the informal pronoun *tu*,not the formal *vous*
21. The family has now arrived in Venice,the "sweet sea-city."
22. (Italian)the reception hall
23. It refers to plasterwork imitating marble.
24. The term here has ironical force.
25. (French)It's too bad;that is,I'm sorry.
26. (French)The way you go on.

27. (French)Say what you intended to.
28. (French)a grown-up man
29. It refers to a college of Oxford University.
30. Here it refers to one of the artificially constructed international languages,combining elements from a number of tongues.
31. It refers to an expensive district in Paris.
32. They refer to mezzanine rooms.
33. (French)Isn't that right,dear?
34. It is a palace now occupied by the Council of State and the Theatre Francais,and containing shops.
35. (French)too much to stand,too painful
36. (French)everyone for himself
37. It refers to a large park,with woods and lakes.
38. (French)How you go on!

Questions for Study and Discussion:

1. What do you think of the relationship between Pemberton and Morgan?
2. Why did Morgan advise Pemberton to escape his family's baleful influence? Did Pemberton do as what Morgan had told him? Why or why not?
3. In the story the author depicts Pemberton, Morgan and Mrs. Moreen and their relationships toward each other in varying lights.What do you think of the characterization of these three characters?
4. Tone and point of view are two very important elements in fiction.How well does the author use them in the story?

Hamlin Garland (1860—1940)

Life and Major Works

In the late 1880s, when American local-color writers began to depict the brutal, dehumanizing aspects of life, the work which most effectively expressed the hardships of farmers of the northern prairies was Hamlin Garland's *Main Traveled Roads* (1891).

Garland was born near West Salem, Wis., on Sept. 14,

Hamlin Garland

1860. Garland's father was an industrious farmer who moved his family from farm to farm in Wisconsin, Iowa, and South Dakota, hoping to wrest a better living from the fertile but unreliable fields. The successive homesteads—Garland later described them as "bare as boxes, dropped on the treeless plains" —provided little in the way of literature, but what little was available young Hamlin read with enthusiasm. His parents encouraged his literary interests and helped him get as much education as the area and his necessary work on the farm would allow. In 1882 he received a diploma from Cedar Valley Seminary in Osage, Iowa, where his family was then living. He took a brief trip to New England and then returned to teach school for 2 years in Illinois.

Garland's brief visit to Boston (which still kept up its pretense of being the literary capital of America) inspired him to return, and in 1884 he went to resume his education there. The only "university" he could afford was the Boston Public Library, but it proved ideal for him: whenever possible he devoted 14 hours a day to reading.

Garland entered Moses True Brown's Boston School of Oratory, working for his tuition. But, lacking money, he soon decided to give up his studies temporarily. When Brown heard that his brilliant pupil was quitting school, he proposed to make Garland a teacher. Consequently, in 1885 Hamlin Garland, "Professor of Elocution and Literature," presented public lectures on American, French, and German authors, the admission fee being his pay.

His lectures brought Garland the attention of Boston literary people, and his reviews, articles, and stories were soon appearing in *the Transcript*, *Harper's Weekly*, and other publications. His admiring reviews of William Dean Howells eventually led to a meeting with that important novelist and critic, beginning what Garland called "the longest and most important friendship" of his life. Garland's praise of poet Walt Whitman similarly brought him the acquaintance and encouragement of that giant. Garland's appearance— he was a strikingly handsome young man with well-tended long brown hair and beard— prompted Whitman to comment, "Garland is much better mettle than his polished exterior would indicate."

However polished his exterior, Garland's stories were intentionally plain and rough. This was apparent in his first and best book, *Main Traveled Roads*. His objective was to convey the hard, unromantic truth of life on the plains, and he accomplished it effectively. His hostility toward landowners is manifest in one of the best stories in this collection, "Under the Lion's Paw." A poor man with a sick wife and hungry children rents a dilapidated farm from a greedy town merchant who turns farmers' misery to his profit. The tenant farmer has the owner's promise that he can buy the property at a reasonable price if he can make it pay, and so he and his family slave for 3 years to improve the house, barn, and fences which will one day be their own. But when they have doubled the value of "their" farm, the owner doubles the price, ensuring that both land and tillers will remain mortgaged to him forever. Garland dedicated the book to his parents "whose half-century pilgrimage on the main roads of life has brought them only toil and deprivation."

Garland's commitment to realism in literature was expressed in his stories and also in his vigorous support of the new realistic drama and of many young realistic writers, most notably Stephen Crane. Crumbling Idols (1894) states Garland's theory of "veritism": "The realist or veritist is really an optimist, a dreamer. He sees life in terms of what it might be, as well as in terms of what it is; but he writes of what is, and, at his best, suggests what is to be, by contrast." Garland seldom attained this ideal after 1891. His next novels, *Jason Edwards*, *A Member of the Third House*, and *A Spoil of Office* (all 1892), were hastily written propaganda pieces, not carefully wrought works of fiction. *Rose of Dutcher's Coolly* (1895) comes closer to fulfilling Garland's critical standard, although it is severely flawed.

In 1899 Garland married Zulime Taft, a beautiful woman with artistic training. Two daughters were born to the couple. After his marriage Garland consciously or unconsciously abandoned his bleak realism and in such books as *The Captain of the Gray-Horse Troop* (1902) achieved greater popularity at the cost of literary value. But if his fiction declined in quality, he found a new medium in which he could excel: autobiography. *A Son of the Middle Border* (1917) and *A Daughter of the Middle Border* (1921) treat his own life with honesty and understanding. The latter book received the Pulitzer Prize in 1922. Many honors came to Garland in his later years. He continued to write memoirs and accounts of psychic research until his death on March 4, 1940.

Brief Introduction and Appreciation

Henry Nash Smith, in his *Virgin Land: The American West as Symbol and Myth*, refers to Hamlin Garland as one of the pioneer Middle Western realists, one whose fiction embodies a "disillusioned view of farm life on the frontier" Garland and other realists such as E. W. Howe, Edward Eggleston, and William Dean Howells were instrumental in portraying the Western farmer in literature as a "human being" rather than as an idealized figure filtered through the guise of "literature, class prejudice, or social theory." Smith makes particular reference to Garland's short story "Under the Lion's Paw," for its effective dramatization of crucial issues of the West—land speculation and the "single tax" —and its unglamorous portrait of what it was like to try to earn a living as a frontier farmer. The Western realists used their writings to provide a counter-narrative to the "Myth of the Garden" story perpetuated by legislation such as the Homestead Act and in the notions of the "Jeffersonian" yeoman farmer and Timothy Flint's "fee-simple empire" (see Chapters XII, XIII, and XVI).

Tocqueville called the ideas of the yeoman farmer and the myth of the garden poetic. These ideas rarely were successfully converted into fiction, however, as problems of class identity inevitably complicated the portrayal of rugged farmers and wild, wooly scouts. Elsewhere in Virgin Land, Nash Smith discusses James Fenimore Cooper's calisthenic attempts to elevate his Western heroes' social status; Cooper's efforts often rang false, as he tried to have it both ways—rugged frontier physicality and refined, aristocratic sensibility. The problem of class impinged upon Cooper's desire to bestow elegance and manners to such uncultivated sorts as the farmer and the frontiersmen; such characters were unavoidably relegated to a lesser status than the urbane, aristocratic figures that populated the highbrow, sentimental novels of the 19th century. But when writers such as Garland, the "local-color realists," as they are sometimes described, rejected the aristocratic preoccupations of Cooper and wrote a more unrefined, gritty style, free of his sentimentalizing and contrived "suitable marriage" endings, they were able to make an important contribution to Americans' understanding of life in the West.

The Western farmer had at least two social strikes against him, according to Nash Smith. A "theocratic suspicion" of the farmer as a fugitive from civilized society was often accompanied by an impression that the farmer was a walking, talking rebuke to 19th century notions of human progress. These attitudes enforced the portrayal of the farmer as of low social class; by 1890, however, writers like Garland and Joseph Kirkland had presented the farmer as a sometimes unfortunate but nevertheless dignified human being. It is this shift in both social attitudes and literary conventions that makes Garland important to the argument of Virgin Land. Garland's main strength as a writer lies in his basic humanitarian sympathy for his characters, those pioneers struggling to make a living in the West. However, in "Under the Lion's Paw," Garland manages more than mere pathos; this short story includes a pointed commentary on the exploitation of single tenant farmers by land speculators.

Naturalist writers often promote a negative view of society focusing on the hardships the poor and uneducated face in everyday life. This deterministic view, used by many of the naturalist authors, disseminates a pessimistic outlook on human existence and is prevalent in the stories they write. The short story "Under the Lions Paw" written by

Hamlin Garland illustrates his cynical vision of society by telling the heart-wrenching tale of a young farmer's economic struggle against overwhelming odds. Appealing to the reader's emotions, Garland successfully propagates his deterministic view by emphasizing the inherent hardships of the independent farmer, projecting class division between the have's and the have not's, and correlating land speculation with greed.

Garland exploits the reader's emotions by accentuating the endless struggle the independent farmer faces in pursuit of "The American Dream." The story opens with a detailed description of a farmer plowing his fields in the driving snow. Yet, what farmer plows his fields in the snow? This first paragraph sets the mood for the entire story by exaggerating the futile toil of an independent farmer and his continuous struggle against the elements. Garland writes, "No slave in the Roman galleys could have toiled so frightfully and lived, for this man thought himself a freeman, and that he was working for his wife and babes". This line conveys subconsciously to the reader that the farmer is not the freeman he foolishly believes, but merely a puppet controlled by something or someone greater than he. It leaves the reader with the idea that no matter how hard and how long the farmer works, there will always be something or someone that will impede his progress, forever keeping him "Under the Lions Paw."

Garland further propagates his deterministic view by projecting a separation of class through cleverly placed descriptions that chronicle the disparity in lifestyles between the protagonist and antagonist, Mr. Haskins and Mr. Butler. In Garland's description of Mr. Butler, he writes favorably of the hard work that led Butler to his present day financial stability, but cleverly injects the thought, "at this period of his life he earned all he got". This statement suggests that Mr. Butler presently does not earn all he gets as he once did and that his current occupation of land speculation is somehow an exploitive occupation rather than actual work. He also takes the liberty to chronicle his hunting and fishing activities throughout the year, implying that he spends more time enjoying the finer things in life while his share croppers are forced to spend long hours scratching the earth to eke out a meager living, all the while enriching Mr. Butler. In one scene, Mr. Butler is found, "wearin' out his pants on some salt barrel somewears", further emphasizing the class separation between Mr. Butler and his sharecroppers. Mr. Butler is able to sit around chewing the fat with fellow friends while his poor sharecroppers are toiling at the back of a plow. Garland masterfully illustrates class division through creatively placed back-stories and descriptive caricatures further drawing in the reader and fine tuning his deterministic jargon.

Finally, Garland ensnares the reader in an emotional trap by correlating greed with land speculation. In the final scene, Mr. Butler is walking around the land he leased to Mr. Haskins on shares. Many improvements have been made and Mr. Haskins has done an incredible job of turning a run down farm into a top-notch producer. Mr. Haskins, high on emotion, with another successful season under his belt is now ready to talk seriously about setting up terms to buy the farm from Mr. Butler. Mr. Haskins is crushed when he learns the new asking price for the farm is more than double what Mr. Butler was willing to accept just three years ago. The clever way Garland tells the story makes it impossible not to feel a sense of voracity put forth by Mr. Butler. In the eyes of the reader, Mr. Butler has greedily raised the price of the farm by more than double knowing that Mr. Haskins will have little choice but to pay it or leave behind three years of hard work.

In some ways, it is easy to see why Mr. Haskins is so upset at the new price of the farm and why he feels he has been taken advantage of, but what is harder to see is the truth of the situation. The farm was available for half the amount just three years ago, but that was before Mr. Butler had equally gone into partnership with Mr. Haskins. Mr. Butler supplied him with land to raise crops and a home for his family all in the hopes of a good harvest. What if there would have been bad weather, insects had infested the crops or Mr. Haskins had been a bad farmer? The big loser would have been Mr. Butler, for it is his land and his home, and his repayment for its use squarely rests on the harvest. After three good years of harvest the farm is worth significantly more than it was just three years prior. Mr. Haskins had the opportunity to buy it three years ago but decided to do a test run on the land to see if he could make a go of it. He has gained not just a good farm and a good home for his family but the knowledge that the land he is currently using is well worth buying. All was made possible by the generosity of only one man, Mr. Butler, who took a chance on a penniless unknown farmer. Not only does Mr. Butler deserve gratitude but he also deserves a fair price on his farm.

The truth of the situation is cunningly glossed over by the artistic writing style of Hamlin Garland. As a reader, it is easy to feel all the pain and toil of Mr. Haskins and his family and relate to his feelings of betrayal. It is much harder to take a step back and look at the overall situation to gain the perspective of both men and their motivation when only one character's situation is laid out in detail. Garland wittingly engages the reader's emotional side by calling attention to the difficult challenges that the independent farmer faces, promoting class division and associating land speculation with greed. Garland uses these tools because it is much easier for one to react with emotion than to counter with perception.

Selected Reading

Under the Lion's Paw

I

It was the last of autumn and first day of winter coming together. All day long the ploughmen on their prairie farms had moved to and fro in their wide level fields through the falling snow, which melted as it fell, wetting them to the skin—all day, notwithstanding the frequent squalls of snow, the dripping, desolate clouds, and the muck of the furrows, black and tenacious as tar.

Under their dripping harness the horses swung to and fro silently with that marvellous uncomplaining patience which marks the horse. All day the wild geese, honking wildly, as they sprawled sidewise down the wind, seemed to be fleeing from an enemy behind, and with neck outthrust and wings extended, sailed down the wind, soon lost to sight.

Yet the ploughman behind his plough, though the snow lay on his ragged great-coat, and the cold clinging mud rose on his heavy boots, fettering him like gyves[1], whistled in the very beard of the gale. As day passed, the snow, ceasing to melt, lay along the ploughed land, and lodged in the depth of the stubble, till on each slow round the last furrow stood out black and shining as jet[2] between the ploughed land and the gray stubble.

When night began to fall, and the geese, flying low, began to alight invisibly in the near corn field, Stephen Council was still at work "finishing a land."[3] He rode on his sulky-plough[4] when going with the wind, but walked when facing it. Sitting bent and cold but cheery under his slouch hat, he talked encouragingly to his weary four-in-hand[5].

"Come round there, boys!—Round agin! We got t' finish this land. Come in there, Dan! Stiddy, Kate!—stiddy! None o' y'r tantrums, Kittie. It's purty tuff, but got a be did. Tchk! tchk! Step along, Pete! Don't let Kate git y'r single-tree[6] on the wheel. Once more!"

They seemed to know what he meant, and that this was the last round, for they worked with greater vigor than before.

"Once more, boys, an' sez I, oats an' a nice warm stall, an' sleep f'r all."

By the time the last furrow was turned on the land it was too dark to see the house, and the snow was changing to rain again. The tired and hungry man could see the light from the kitchen shining through the leafless hedge, and he lifted a great shout, "Supper f'r a half a dozen!"

It was nearly eight o'clock by the time he had finished his chores and started for

223

supper. He was picking his way carefully through the mud, when the tall form of a man loomed up before him with a premonitory cough.

"Waddy ye want ?" was the rather startled question of the farmer.

"Well, ye see," began the stranger, in a deprecating tone, "we'd like t' git in f'r the night. We've tried every house f'r the last two miles, but they hadn't any room f'r us. My wife's jest about sick, 'n' the children are cold and hungry—"

"Oh, y' want 'o stay all night, eh?"

"Yes, sir; it 'ud be a great accom—"

"Waal, I don't make it a practice t' turn anybuddy way hungry, not on sech nights as this. Drive right in. We ain't got much, but sech as it is—"

But the stranger had disappeared. And soon his steaming, weary team, with drooping heads and swinging single-trees, moved past the well to the block beside the path. Council stood at the side of the schooner[7] and helped the children out—two little half-sleeping children—and then a small woman with a babe in her arms.

"There ye go!" he shouted jovially, to the children. "Now we're all right! Run right along to the house there, an' tell Mam' Council you wants sumpthin' t' eat. Right this way, Mis'—keep right off t' the right there. I'll go an' git a lantern. Come," he said to the dazed and silent group at his side.

"Mother," he shouted, as he neared the fragrant and warmly lighted kitchen, "here are some wayfarers an' folks who need sumpthin' t' eat an' a place t' snooze." He ended, pushing them all in.

Mrs. Council, a large, jolly, rather coarse-looking woman, took the children in her arms. "Come right in, you little rabbits. 'Most asleep, hey? Now here's a drink o' milk f'r each o' ye. I'll have s'm' tea in a minute. Take off y'r things and set up t' the fire."

While she set the children to drinking milk, Council got out his lantern and went out to the barn to help the stranger about his team, where his loud, hearty voice could be heard as it came and went between the hay-mow and the stalls.

The woman came to light as a small, timid, and discouraged-looking woman, but still pretty, in a thin and sorrowful way.

"Land sakes! An' you've travelled all the way from Clear Lake' t'day in this mud! Waal! Waal! No wonder you're all tired out. Don't wait f'r the men, Mis'—" She hesitated, waiting for the name.

"Haskins."

"Mis' Haskins, set right up to the table an' take a good swig o' that tea, whilst I make y' s'm' toast. It's green tea, an' it's good. I tell Council as I git older I don't seem to enjoy Young Hyson n'r Gunpowder[8]. I want the reel green tea, jest as it comes off'n the vines. Seems t' have more heart in it some way. Don't s'pose it has. Council says it's all in m' eye." Going on in this easy way, she soon had the children filled with bread and milk and the woman thoroughly at home, eating some toast and sweet melon pickles, and sipping the tea.

"See the little rats!" she laughed at the children. "They're full as they can stick now, and they want to go to bed. Now, don't git up, Mis' Haskins; set right where you are an' let me look after 'em. I know all about young ones, though I am all alone now. Jane went an' married last fall. But, as I tell Council, it's lucky we keep our health. Set right there, Mis' Haskins; I won't have you stir a finger."

It was an unmeasured pleasure to sit there in the warm, homely kitchen, the jovial chatter of the housewife driving out and holding at bay the growl of the impotent, cheated wind.

The little woman's eyes filled with tears which fell down upon the sleeping baby in her arms. The world was not so desolate and cold and hopeless, after all.

"Now I hope Council won't stop out there and talk politics all night. He's the greatest man to talk politics an' read the Tribune. How old is it?"

She broke off and peered down at the face of the babe.

"Two months 'n' five days," said the mother, with a mother's exactness.

"Ye don't say! I want 'o know! The dear little pudzy-wudzy," she went on, stirring it up in the neighborhood of the ribs with her fat forefinger."Pooty tough on 'oo to go gallivant'n' 'cross lots this way—"

"Yes, that's so; a man can't lift a mountain," said Council, entering the door. "Sarah, this is Mr. Haskins, from Kansas. He's been eat up 'n' drove out by grasshoppers."

"Glad t' see yeh! Pa, empty that wash-basin, 'n' give him a chance t' wash."

Haskins was a tall man, with a thin, gloomy face. His hair was a reddish brown, like his coat, and seemed equally faded by the wind and sun. And his sallow face, though hard and set, was pathetic somehow. You would have felt that he had suffered much by the line of his mouth showing under his thin, yellow mustache.

"Hain't Ike got home yet, Sairy?"

"Hain't seen 'im."

"W-a-a-l, set right up, Mr. Haskins; wade right into what we've got; 'taint much, but we manage to live on it—least I do; she gits fat on it," laughed Council, pointing his thumb at his wife.

After supper, while the women put the children to bed, Haskins and Council talked on, seated near the huge cooking stove, the steam rising from their wet clothing. In the Western fashion Council told as much of his own life as he drew from his guest. He asked but few questions, but by-and-by the story of Haskins' struggles and defeat came out. The story was a terrible one, but he told it quietly, seated with his elbows on his knees, gazing most of the time at the hearth.

"I didn't like the looks of the country, anyhow," Haskins said, partly rising and glancing at his wife. "I was ust t' northern Ingyannie[9], where we have lots o' timber 'n' lots of rain, 'n' I didn't like the looks o' that dry prairie. What galled me the worst was goin' s' far away acrosst so much fine land layin' all through here vacant."

"And the 'hoppers eat ye four years, hand runnin', did they?"

"Eat! They wiped us out. They chawed everything that was green. They jest set around waitin' f'r us to die t' eat us, too. My God! I ust t' dream of 'em sittin' 'round on the bedpost, six feet long, workin' their jaws. They eet the fork-handles. They got worse 'n' worse till they jest rolled on one another, piled up like snow in winter. Well, it ain't no use; if I was t' talk all winter I couldn't tell nawthin'. But all the while I couldn't help thinkin' of all that land back here that nobuddy was usin', that I ought 'o had 'stead o' bein' out there in that cussed country."

"Waal, why didn't ye stop an' settle here ?" asked Ike, who had come in and was eating his supper.

"Fer the simple reason that you fellers wantid ten 'r fifteen dollars an acre fer the bare land, and I hadn't no money fer that kind o' thing."

"Yes, I do my own work," Mrs. Council was heard to say in the pause which followed. "I'm a gettin' purty heavy t' be on m'laigs all day, but we can't afford t' hire, so I keep rackin' around somehow, like a foundered horse. S'lame—I tell Council he can't tell how lame I am, f'r I'm jest as lame in one laig as t' other." And the good soul laughed at the joke on herself as she took a handful of flour and dusted the biscuit board to keep the dough from sticking.

"Well, I hain't never been very strong," said Mrs. Haskins. "Our folks was Canadians an' small-boned, and then since my last child I hain't got up again fairly. I don't like t' complain—Tim has about all he can bear now—but they was days this week when I jest wanted to lay right down an' die."

"Waal, now, I'll tell ye," said Council, from his side of the stove silencing everybody with his good-natured roar, "I'd go down and see Butler, anyway, if I was you. I guess he'd let you have his place purty cheap; the farm's all run down. He's been anxious t' let t' somebuddy next year. It 'ud be a good chance fer you. Anyhow, you go to bed, and sleep like a babe. I've got some ploughing t' do anyhow, an' we'll see if somethin' can't be done about your case. Ike, you go out an' see if the horses is all right, an' I'll show the folks t' bed."

When the tired husband and wife were lying under the generous quilts of the spare bed, Haskins listened a moment to the wind in the eaves, and then said, with a slow and solemn tone,"There are people in this world who are good enough t' be angels, an' only haff t' die to be angels."

II

Jim Butler was one of those men called in the West "land poor." [10] Early in the history of Rock River he had come into the town and started in the grocery business in a small way, occupying a small building in a mean[11] part of the town. At this period of his life he earned all he got, and was up early and late sorting beans, working over butter, and carting his goods to and from the station. But a change came over him at the end of the second year, when he sold a lot of land for four times what he paid for it. From that time forward he believed in land speculation[12] as the surest way of getting rich. Every cent he could save or spare from his trade he put into land at forced sale[13], or mortgages on land, which were "just as good as the wheat," he was accustomed to say.

Farm after farm fell into his hands, until he was recognized as one of the leading landowners of the county. His mortgages were scattered all over Cedar County, and as they slowly but surely fell in he sought usually to retain the former owner as tenant.

He was not ready to foreclose; indeed, he had the name of being one of the "easiest" men in the town. He let the debtor off again and again, extending the time whenever possible.

"I don't want y'r land," he said. "All I'm after is the int'rest on my money—that's all. Now, if y' want 'o stay on the farm, why, I'll give y' a good chance. I can't have the land layint vacant." And in many cases the owner remained as tenant.

In the meantime he had sold his store; he couldn't spend time in it—he was mainly occupied now with sitting around town on rainy days smoking and "gassin' with the boys," or in riding to and from his farms. In fishing-time he fished a good deal. Doc Grimes, Ben Ashley, and Cal Cheatham were his cronies on these fishing excursions or hunting trips in the time of chickens or partridges. In winter they went to Northern Wisconsin to shoot deer.

In spite of all these signs of easy life Butler persisted in saying he "hadn't enough money to pay taxes on his land," and was careful to convey the impression that he was poor in spite of his twenty farms. At one time he was said to be worth fifty thousand dollars, but land had been a little slow of sale of late, so that he was not worth so much.

A fine farm, known as the Higley place, had fallen into his hands in the usual way the previous year, and he had not been able to find a tenant for it. Poor Higley, after working himself nearly to death on it in the attempt to lift the mortgage, had gone off to Dakota, leaving the farm and his curse to Butler.This was the farm which Council advised Haskins to apply for; and the next day Council hitched up his team and drove down-town to see Butler.

"You jest let me do the talkin'," he said. "We'll find him wearin' out his pants on some salt barrel somew'ers; and if he thought you wanted a place, he'd sock it to you hot and heavy. You jest keep quiet; I'll fix 'im."

Butler was seated in Ben Ashley's store telling "fish yarns," when Council sauntered in casually.

"Hello, But; lyin' agin, hey?"

"Hello, Steve! How goes it?"

"Oh, so-so. Too dang much rain these days. I thought it was goin' t' freeze up f'r good last night. Tight squeak if I get m' ploughin' done. How's farmin' with you these days?"

"Bad. Ploughin' ain't half done."

"It 'ud be a religious idee f'r you t' go out an' take a hand y'rself."

"I don't haff to," said Butler, with a wink.

"Got anybody on the Higley place?"

"No. Know of anybody?"

"Waal, no; not eggsackly. I've got a relation back t' Michigan who's ben hot an' cold on the idea o' comin' West f'r some time. Might come if he could get a good lay-out. What do you talk on the farm?"

"Well, I d' know. I'll rent it on shares or I'll rent it money rent."

"Waal, how much money, say?"

"Well, say ten per cent, on the price—$250."

"Waal, that ain't bad. Wait on 'im till 'e thrashes?"[14]

Haskins listened eagerly to this important question, but Council was coolly eating a dried apple which he had speared out of a barrel with his knife. Butler studied him carefully.

"Well, knocks me out of twenty-five dollars interest."

"My relation'll need all he's got t' git his crops in," said Council, in the same, indifferent way.

"Well, all right; say wait," concluded Butler.

"All right; this is the man. Haskins, this is Mr. Butler—no relation to Ben—the hardest-working man in Cedar County."

On the way home Haskins said: "I ain't much better off. I'd like that farm; it's a good farm, but it's all run down, an' so 'm I. I could make a good farm of it if I had half a show. But I can't stock it n'r seed it."

"Waal, now, don't you worry," roared Council in his ear. "We'll pull y' through somehow till next harvest. He's agreed t' hire it ploughed, an' you can earn a hundred dollars ploughin' an' y' c'n git the seed o' me, an' pay me back when y' can."

Haskins was silent with emotion, but at last he said, "I ain't got nothin' t' live on."

"Now, don't you worry 'bout that. You jest make your headquarters at ol' Steve Council's. Mother'll take a pile o' comfort in havin' y'r wife an' children 'round. Y' see, Jane's married off lately, an' Ike's away a good 'eal, so we'll be darn glad t' have y' stop with us this winter. Nex' spring we'll see if y' can't git a start agin." And he chirruped to the team, which sprang forward with the rumbling, clattering wagon.

"Say, looky here, Council, you can't do this. I never saw—" shouted Haskins in his neighbor's ear.

Council moved about uneasily in his seat and stopped his stammering gratitude by saying: "Hold on, now; don't make such a fuss over a little thing. When I see a man down, an' things all on top of 'm, I jest like t' kick 'em off an' help 'm up. That's the kind of religion I got, an' it's about the only kind."

They rode the rest of the way home in silence. And when the red light of the lamp shone out into the darkness of the cold and windy night, and he thought of this refuge for his children and wife, Haskins could have put his arm around the neck of his burly companion and squeezed him like a lover. But he contented himself with saying, "Steve Council, you'll git y'r pay f'r this some day."

"Don't want any pay. My religion ain't run on such business principles."

The wind was growing colder, and the ground was covered with a white frost, as they turned into the gate of the Council farm, and the children came rushing out, shouting, "Papa's come!" They hardly looked like the same children who had sat at the table the night before. Their torpidity[15], under the influence of sunshine and Mother Council, had given way to a sort of spasmodic cheerfulness, as insects in winter revive when laid on the hearth.

III

Haskins worked like a fiend, and his wife, like the heroic woman that she was, bore also uncomplainingly the most terrible burdens. They rose early and toiled without intermission till the darkness fell on the plain, then tumbled into bed, every bone and muscle aching with fatigue, to rise with the sun next morning to the same round of the same ferocity of labor.

The eldest boy, now nine years old, drove a team all through the spring, ploughing and seeding, milked the cows, and did chores innumerable, in most ways taking the place of a man.

An infinitely pathetic but common figure—this boy—on the American farm, where there is no law against child labor. To see him in his coarse clothing, his huge boots, and his ragged cap, as he staggered with a pail of water from the well, or trudged in the cold and cheerless dawn out into the frosty field behind his team, gave the city-bred visitor a sharp pang of sympathetic pain. Yet Haskins loved his boy, and would have saved him from this if he could, but he could not.

By June the first year the result of such Herculean[16] toil began to show on the farm. The yard was cleaned up and sown to grass, the garden ploughed and planted, and the house mended. Council had given them four of his cows.

"Take 'em an' run 'em on shares. I don't want 'o milk s' many. Ike's away s' much now, Sat'd'ys an' Sund'ys, I can't stand the bother anyhow."

Other men, seeing the confidence of Council in the newcomer, had sold him tools on time; and as he was really an able farmer, he soon had round him many evidences of his care and thrift. At the advice of Council he had taken the farm for three years, with the privilege of re-renting or buying at the end of the term.

"It's a good bargain, an' y' want 'o nail it," said Council. "If you have any kind ov a crop, you c'n pay y'r debts, an' keep seed an' bread."

The new hope which now sprang up in the heart of Haskins and his wife grew almost as a pain by the time the wide field of wheat began to wave and rustle and swirl in the winds of July. Day after day he would snatch a few moments after supper to go and look at it.

"Have ye seen the wheat t'-day, Nettie?" he asked one night as he rose from supper.

"No, Tim, I ain't had time."

"Well, take time now. Le's go look at it."

She threw an old hat on her head—Tommy's hat—and looking almost pretty in her thin, sad way, went out with her husband to the hedge.

"Ain't it grand, Nettie? Just look at it."

It was grand. Level, russet here and there, heavy-headed, wide as a lake, and full of multitudinous whispers and gleams of health, it stretched away before the gazers like the fabled field of the cloth of gold[17].

"Oh, I think—I hope we'll have a good crop, Tim; and oh, how good the people have been to us!"

"Yes; I don't know where we'd be t'-day if it hadn't been f'r Council and his wife."

"They're the best people in the world," said the little woman, with a great sob of gratitude.

"We'll be in the field on Monday sure," said Haskins, gripping the rail on the fences as if already at the work of the harvest.

The harvest came bounteous, glorious, but the winds came and blew it into tangles, and the rain matted it here and there close to the ground, increasing the work of gathering it threefold.

Oh, how they toiled in those glorious days! Clothing dripping with sweat, arms aching, filled with briers, fingers raw and bleeding, backs broken with the weight of heavy bundles, Haskins and his man toiled on. Tommy drove the harvester, while his father and a hired man bound on the machine. In this way they cut ten acres every day, and almost every night after supper, when the hand went to bed, Haskins returned to the field shocking the bound grain in the light of the moon. Many a night he worked till he staggered with utter fatigue; worked till his anxious wife came out to call him in to rest and lunch.

At the same time she cooked for the men, took care of the children, washed and ironed, milked the cows at night, made the butter, and sometimes fed the horses and watered them while her husband kept at the shocking.

No slave in the Roman galleys[18] could have toiled so frightfully and lived, for this man thought himself a free man, and that he was working for his wife and babes.

When he sank into his bed with a deep groan of relief, too tired to change his grimy, dripping clothing, he felt that he was getting nearer and nearer to a home of his own, and pushing the wolf of want a little farther from his door.

There is no despair so deep as the despair of a homeless man or woman. To roam the roads of the country or the streets of the city, to feel there is no rood of ground on which the feet can rest, to halt weary and hungry outside lighted windows and hear laughter and song within—these are the hungers and rebellions that drive men to crime and women to shame.

It was the memory of this homelessness, and the fear of its coming again, that spurred Timothy Haskins and Nettie, his wife, to such ferocious labor during that first year.

IV

"'M, yes; 'm, yes; first-rate," said Butler, as his eye took in the neat garden, the pig-pen, and the well-filled barnyard. "You're gitt'n' quite a stock around yeh. Done well, eh?"

Haskins was showing Butler around the place. He had not seen it for a year, having spent the year in Washington and Boston with Ashley, his brother-in-law, who had been elected to Congress.

"Yes, I've laid out a good deal of money durin' the last three years. I've paid out three hundred dollars f'r fencin'."

"Um h'm! I see, I see," said Butler, while Haskins went on:

"The kitchen there cost two hundred; the barn ain't cost much in money, but I've put a lot o' time on it. I've dug a new well, and I—"

"Yes, yes, I see. You've done well. Stock worth a thousand dollars," said Butler, picking his teeth with a straw.

"About that," said Haskins, modestly. "We begin to feel's if we was gitt'n' a home f'r ourselves; but we've worked hard. I tell you we begin to feel it, Mr. Butler, and we're goin' t' begin to ease up purty soon. We've been kind o' plannin' a trip back t' her folks after the fall ploughin's done."

"Eggs-actly!" said Butler, who was evidently thinking of something else. "I suppose you've kind o' calc'lated on stayin' here three years more?"

"Well, yes. Fact is, I think I c'n buy the farm this fall, if you'll give me a reasonable show."

"Um—m! What do you call a reasonable show?"

"Well, say a quarter down and three years' time."

Butler looked at the huge stacks of wheat, which filled the yard, over which the chickens were fluttering and crawling, catching grasshoppers, and out of which the crickets were singing innumerably. He smiled in a peculiar way as he said, "Oh, I won't be hard on yeh. But what did you expect to pay f'r the place?"

"Why, about what you offered it for before, two thousand five hundred, or possibly three thousand dollars," he added quickly, as he saw the owner shake his head.

"This farm is worth five thousand and five hundred dollars," said Butler, in a careless and decided voice.

"What!" almost shrieked the astounded Haskins. "What's that? Five thousand? Why, that's double what you offered it for three years ago."

"Of course; and it's worth it. It was all run down then—now it's in good shape. You've laid out fifteen hundred dollars in improvements, according to your own story."

"But you had nothin' t' do about that. It's my work an' my money."

"You bet it was; but it's my land."

"But what's to pay me for all?"

"Ain't you had the use of 'em?" replied Butler, smiling calmly into his face.

Haskins was like a man struck on the head with a sandbag; he couldn't think; he stammered as he tried to say: "But—I never 'd git the use. You'd rob me! More'n that: you agreed—you promised that I could buy or rent at the end of three years at—"

"That's all right. But I didn't say I'd let you carry off the improvements, nor that I'd go on renting the farm at two-fifty. The land is doubled in value, it don't matter how; it don't enter into the question; an' now you can pay me five hundred dollars a year rent, or take it on your own terms at fifty-five hundred, or—git out."

He was turning away when Haskins, the sweat pouring from his face, fronted him, saying again:

"But you've done nothing to make it so. You hadn't added a cent. I put it all there myself, expectin' to buy. I worked an' sweat to improve it. I was workin' for myself an' babes."

"Well, why didn't you buy when I offered to sell? What y' kickin' about?"

"I'm kickin' about payin' you twice f'r my own things—my own fences, my own kitchen, my own garden."

Butler laughed. "You're too green t' eat, young feller. Your improvements! The law will sing another tune."

"But I trusted your word."

"Never trust anybody, my friend. Besides, I didn't promise not to do this thing. Why, man, don't look at me like that. Don't take me for a thief. It's the law. The reg'lar thing. Everybody does it."

"I don't care if they do. It's stealin' jest the same. You take three thousand dollars of my money. The work o' my hands and my wife's." He broke down at this point. He was not a strong man mentally. He could face hardship, ceaseless toil, but he could not face the cold and sneering face of Butler.

"But I don't take it," said Butler, coolly "All you've got to do is to go on jest as you've been a-doin', or give me a thousand dollars down, and a mortgage at ten per cent on the rest."

Haskins sat down blindly on a bundle of oats near by, and with staring eyes and drooping head went over the situation. He was under the lion's paw. He felt a horrible numbness in his heart and limbs. He was hid in a mist, and there was no path out.

Butler walked about, looking at the huge stacks of grain, and pulling now and again a few handfuls out, shelling the heads in his hands and blowing the chaff away. He hummed a little tune as he did so. He had an accommodating air of waiting.

Haskins was in the midst of the terrible toil of the last year. He was walking again in the rain and the mud behind his plough, he felt the dust and dirt of the threshing. The ferocious husking-time, with its cutting wind and biting, clinging snows, lay hard upon him. Then he thought of his wife, how she had cheerfully cooked and baked, without holiday and without rest.

"Well, what do you think of it?" inquired the cool, mocking, insinuating voice of Butler.

"I think you're a thief and a liar!" shouted Haskins, leaping up. "A black-hearted houn'!" Butler's smile maddened him; with a sudden leap he caught a fork in his hands, and whirled it in the air. "You'll never rob another man, damn ye!" he grated through his teeth, a look of pitiless ferocity in his accusing eyes.

Butler shrank and quivered, expecting the blow; stood, held hypnotized by the eyes of the man he had a moment before despised—a man transformed into an avenging demon. But in the deadly hush between the lift of the weapon and its fall there came a gush of faint, childish laughter and then across the range of his vision, far away and dim, he saw the sun-bright head of his baby girl, as, with the pretty, tottering run of a two-year-old, she moved across the grass of the dooryard. His hands relaxed: the fork fell to the ground; his head lowered.

"Make out y'r deed an' mor'gage, an' git off'n my land, an' don't ye never cross my line agin; if y' do, I'll kill ye."

Butler backed away from the man in wild haste, and climbing into his buggy with trembling limbs drove off down the road, leaving Haskins seated dumbly on the sunny pile of sheaves, his head sunk into his hands.

Notes:

1. gyves: shackles, chains
2. jet: velvet black, coallike mineral
3. "finishing a land": completing work on a section of a farm
4. sulky-plough: plow having wheels and a driver's seat
5. four-in-hand: team of four horses driven by one person
6. single-tree: the swinging bar to which the harness is attached
7. schooner: prairie schooner, a broad-wheeled covered wagon

8. Young Hyson n'r Gunpowder: types of Chinese green tea

9. Ingyannie: dialect form of Indiana

10. "land poor": owing land but having little money

11. mean: poor

12. land speculation: buying and selling land for a profit

13. forced sale: buying cheaply from someone who is forced to sell

14. Wait…thrashes?: Wait for rent payment until the first crop of wheat is threshed?

15. torpidity: lack of energy

16. Herculean: requiring great strength; referring to the Greek hero Hercules

17. field…gold: place in France where French King Francois I met the English King Henry VIII in 1520; a magnificent spectacle

18. Roman galleys: ancient ships propelled by slaves chained to rows of oars

Questions for Study and Discussion:

1. The first section of this story pictures two important elements of life on the Middle Border. Identify each of them.

2. What natural disaster drove the Haskins family from Kansas?

3. Why does Stephen Council take Haskins to meet Jim Butler? How does Council attempt to outsmart Butler?

4. Who helps Tim Haskins work the farm? In what ways does Stephen Council give assistance?

5. When Butler sees the improvements that the Haskins family have made on the farm, what does he do?

6. What does Haskins do when he realizes that he is "under the lion's paw"? What makes him abandon his violent impulses, and, consequently, what does he say and do?

7. Contrast the characters of Council and Butler. Discuss whether Butler should be considered a producer or a nonproducer in society.

8. To appreciate literary realism, compare this story with "The Outcasts of Poker Flat" as to plot and characterization. What special satisfaction does each type of story offer? Which type do you prefer?

Part Four   The Birth of Modernism

(1915—1949)

Introduction

I. Historical Background

Many historians have characterized the period between the two world wars as the United States' traumatic "coming of age," despite the fact that U.S. direct involvement was relatively brief (1917—1918) and its casualties were many fewer than those of its European allies and foes. The period 1915—1949 is one of the richest and most crucial in American literary history. No other period produced so many masterworks or had such a profound and durable historical, social, and cultural legacy. This thirty-five-year period shaped social and literary policies and practices for the remainder of the twentieth century. Sinclair Lewis, America's first Nobel Prize winner in literature (1930), called the era America's second "coming of age", a period of maturation when poetry, fiction, and drama broke with conventions and achieved unparalleled creative achievement. American expatriate poets such as Ezra Pound and T.S. Eliot forged new methods of modern expression. In fiction there were probably more serious contenders for the mythical title of "Great American Novel"— *The Great Gatsby, An American Tragedy, A Farewell to Arms, U.S.A, The Grapes of Wrath, Gone with the Wind, Absalom, Absalom!*—than in any other period in American history. In drama, the first great classics of the American stage were performed. Although the forces of change and innovation were apparent before World War I (1914—1918), it accelerated and intensified those energies.

World War I symbolically divided the nineteenth from the twentieth century. What was unimaginable before 1914 became the reality of the twentieth-century world. Four years of slaughter in the trenches of the Western Front purged Americans' faith in progress and the perfectibility of man and replaced it with a cynicism preoccupied with dislocation, fragmentation, and dehumanization. American participation in the war also marked a fundamental turning point in the nation's emergence as a world power, which by 1945 had been projected into every region of the globe.

II. Literary Review

"Modernism" is the name of the major artistic movement that attempted to develop a response to the sense of social breakdown occurring in the aftermath of World War I. Just as America was thrust into the center of international politics, so too its writers and artists emerged as leading intellectual and artistic voices who addressed the shattered confidence in a civilization that seemed hell-bent on self-destruction. It fell to artists and writers to interpret the meaning of total mechanized warfare and America's new role on the world's stage. The result was an explosion of literary achievement far surpassing the first great American literary renaissance of the mid-nineteenth century.

The war also opened the door for European influences. American writers increasingly absorbed, imitated, and transformed the ideas and methods of European modernist masters such as James Joyce and Marcel Proust, and their predecessors, such as Henrik Ibsen, Fyodor Dostoyevsky, Charles Baudelaire, and Joseph Conrad. Modernism originated in an erosion of faith in the social, spiritual, and psychological absolutes of the nineteenth century and a consequent drive to discover new artistic modes of representing reality, new ways of self-understanding and emotional and spiritual renewal. World War I showed conclusively that old beliefs were corrupt and must be replaced.

Pound's rallying cry, "Make It New," defined the modernist agenda: sift the fragments of an exploded culture in search of new and sustaining sources of order, coherence, and faith. New language, new artistic forms, new relations between the artist and society were needed. As Hemingway's protagonist Frederic Henry in A *Farewell to Arms* (1929) says, "I was always embarrassed by the words sacred, glorious, and sacrifice and the expression in vain...I had seen nothing sacred, and the things that were glorious had no glory and the sacrifices were like the stockyards at Chicago if nothing was done with the meat except to bury it... Abstract words such as glory, honor, courage, or hallow were obscene beside the concrete names of villages, the numbers of roads, the names of rivers, the numbers of regiments and the dates." Frederic Henry and his generation needed a new vocabulary and sources of authenticity that the literary modernist attempted to supply.

For the first time in history, Americans would lead the charge. It was an American, T. S. Eliot, who wrote what William Carlos Williams later would describe as the "atomic bomb" of modern poetry, *The Waste Land.* In 1929, William Faulkner published the first great American modernist novel, *The Sound and the Fury*, and followed it with a succession of breathtaking literary experiments that helped redefine fiction's possibilities. Hemingway's lean, muscular style revolutionized the novel and short story, and his work became one of America's most influential literary exports. During the period, America also discovered its first great playwright, Eugene O'Neill, who built upon and extended the innovations of the great European modern dramatists, such as Henrik Ibsen, George Bernard Shaw, and August Strindberg. And America's unique contribution to the world's stage, the American musical, achieved mastery. It is also during this period that African American writers pioneered the literary uses of other indigenous cultural forms, the blues and jazz.

The period between the wars saw unprecedented change brought about by urbanization, industrialization, and immigration, as well as by technological innovations such as electricity, the telephone, and the automobile. These things linked the nation and reduced regional distinctions. Formerly silent minority voices were also heard in increasing numbers. Women left the home in unprecedented numbers during the wars and won the right to vote in 1920. African American writers, in particular, voiced their concerns loudly and frankly about racism and black culture, heralding a new and important tributary to the mainstream of American culture.

With these changes came the new concept of American identity, and the new concepts of justice and success. Magazines, book clubs, radio, motion pictures, and finally television helped create for the first time an American mass culture. The gap created between highbrow and lowbrow, between an audience trained to appreciate the complexity of modernist experiments and an audience demanding to be entertained, grew more and more pronounced. Writers for the first time became stars like those in Hollywood, in a growing cult of celebrity, feted by and sacrificed to what Norman Mailer called the "bitch-goddess" fame.

Despite these overriding trends, no other literary period is more symmetrically subdivided by its constituent decades. The 1920s, 1930s, and 1940s form distinctly different eras. America emerged from the war as virtually the only great power left standing, and the 1920s became a boom time of prosperity. A remarkable explosion of creative energy captured both the new spirit of youthful rebellion and the conservative traditionalism that still held sway in the American heartland. The 1920s might have been the era of the liberated flapper and gangster, but it was also the period of legislating morality through prohibition. Writers such as F. Scott Fitzgerald, Sherwood Anderson, Theodore Dreiser, John Dos Passos, Sinclair Lewis, and others mined the rich complexity of the American scene for characters and plots that explored the contradictions between the nation's ideals and realities between its desires and its limitations. In 1929, the stock market crash marked the symbolic end of the party and the beginning of America's greatest social challenge—the Great Depression.

The modernist movement of the 1920s celebrated the artist as a detached observer who produced art for art's sake, but the financial crash and its aftermath led a large segment of the American literary community to shift to a literature of engagement. What had caused the crash? What was the solution? To many writers, the depression signaled the collapse of capitalism, exposing the system's intractable inequities. The modernist focus had been on the individual consciousness and the innovations necessary to reveal it. But in the 1930s, in masterworks such as Dos Passos's *U.S.A* and John Steinbeck's *The Grapes of Wrath*, writers began to emphasize theme over formal innovation, putting art in the service of protest and reform. Many embraced radical causes and delivered social realism in the interest of a proletarian literature, rejecting the modernist movement as too detached and too elitist, Others celebrated what they perceived as America's collective greatness and solidarity. If the underlying theme of much of the literature of the 1920s concerned personal liberation, the 1930s forced a concern with economics and politics.

Like the 1929 crash that ended the boom time of the 1920s, the outbreak of war in 1939 brought a shift that characterized the next decade. After the economic deprivation and political unrest of the 1930s, American society united again in the war effort, emerging victorious as an economic and technological powerhouse. The result was a period of unprecedented prosperity for the average American. Yet the Allied victory in 1945 secured an uneasy peace, shadowed by an ongoing cold war and its threat of thermonuclear annihilation. Writers faced a new America. The 1940s became a testing ground both for the generation of prewar writers, who tried to interpret the transformed postwar world, and for the next generation of writers, who had experienced combat or come of age during the bloodiest war in history. Established literary figures such as Hemingway, Faulkner, Dos Passos, and Steinbeck won an audience but not with the strength and power they had enjoyed before the war. A new generation of writers—John Hersey, Norman Mailer, James Jones, and John Hawkes—who focused on combat or at least the war experience—began to gain increasing attention. In poetry the decade produced important works by the great figures of the post-World War I era, such as T. S. Eliot, Ezra Pound, Robert Frost, Wallace Stevens, and William Carlos Williams, alongside new voices, such as Robert Lowell, Elizabeth Bishop, and Randall Jarrell. In drama, the 1940s saw Eugene O'Neill's final Broadway production during his lifetime, *The Iceman Cometh* (1946), as well as the failure of *A Moon for the Misbegotten* (1947) to achieve a New York production. By the decade's end, the significant figures of American drama between the wars—O'Neill, Robert Sherwood, Maxwell Anderson, Clifford Odets, Lillian Hellman, S. N. Behrman—were pushed offstage by two new playwrights of distinction: Tennessee Williams and Arthur Miller.

Intellectually and artistically, the postwar era of the 1940s did not generate the explosive creative energy released by the disillusionment that followed World War I and the synthesis of modernist ideas. Rather, it marked the beginning of an age of criticism. The dominant mode of literary analysis at the time, the New Criticism, championed the close examination of literary works without much regard for their biographical or historical influences. Yet a search for moral and social meaning in literature also ensued in response to the collapse of the political and social ideologies of the 1930s. Existentialism, derived from French writers such as Jean-Paul Sartre and Albert Camus, began to influence American writers and thinkers. Writers sifted and resifted the wreckage of traditional beliefs brought into question by the war and searched for its implications about human nature and the meaning of existence. Such preoccupations, at times verging on brooding despair, drove much postwar inquiry and artistic expression. Three titles in particular captured this tone: Saul Bellow's first novel, *Dangling Man* (1944); Ralph Ellison's *Invisible Man*, published in 1952 but mainly composed during the 1940s; and Nelson Algren's *The Man with the Golden Arm* (1949), a novel of addiction and bohemianism that blazed the path for the Beat literature of the 1950s.

By the decade's end, intellectuals and creative writers alike began to sense that the previous prewar ways of understanding the world, including the modernist faith in art and the artistic vision, were inadequate. To chart the literary course out of the 1940s—characterized by both destruction and prosperity—would require new responses and methods as distinctive and as radical as any that emerged in the aftermath of World War I.

Robert Frost (1874—1963)

Life and Major Works

Robert Frost

Though regarded as the quintessential New England poet, Robert Frost was born in San Francisco, where he spent the first eleven years of his life. Then, his father died, and the family moved to New England, where his mother supported the family by teaching school. Frost excelled in high school and graduated in 1891. Upon graduation, he was already in love with his co-valedictorian at Lawrence High School, Elinor White, to whom he was engaged and finally married. After leaving his high school, Frost entered Dartmouth College, where he stayed for only one semester because he disliked the academic attitude there. Back home, Frost worked as a bobbin boy in a Massachusetts mill. In 1896, Frost and Elinor got married and their son Elliott was born in the same year. In the next year, Frost matriculated at Harvard University and continued his study, especially in the Classics. However, due to the financial as well as emotional pressures of having a growing family, Frost's study at Harvard lasted only for three semesters. In the following years, Frost adopted a variety of jobs including teaching, editing, making shoes, and finally farming. These years are marked by the births of four children and the poverty of the family.

In 1912, Frost made a new start and moved his family to England. This transition proved to be a wise and successful one. Not only did Frost meet many of his British contemporaries, but also he befriended Ezra Pound, the American ex-patriot. Frost worked on his poetry and at last found a publisher for his first book, *A Boy's Will*. This collection of poems (including lyrics such as "Into My Own," "Revelation," "Mowing," and "Reluctance," etc.), with the characteristic flavor of New England life, appeared in 1913, and was praised by Ezra Pound. Pound recommended Frost's poems to American editors and helped Frost publish the second book, *North of Boston*, in 1914. This volume (containing poems such as "Mending Wall," "The Death of the Hired Man," "The Wood-Pile," and "Home Burial," etc.) won the author high appraisal both in America and England and the favorable reception urged Frost to go back home. The Frosts returned to New England in 1915 and Frost bought another farm in New Hampshire. Now, there was no worrying about money: the sales of his books and the teaching and lecturing in various colleges provided Frost with financial stability. In 1916, *Mountain Interval* appeared, including such brilliant poems as "The Road not Taken," "Birches," "Bond and Free," "Snow," and "An Old Man's Winter Night," etc.

In 1917, Frost began teaching at Amherst College, and then he served as Poet-in-Residence at the University of Michigan. Later he also held similar positions at Harvard University, Dartmouth College, and the Bread Loaf School of English at Middlebury College. These experiences, together with his poetry readings and talks all around the country, made Frost a second reputation as a teacher and lecturer.

Yet he never gave up his literary career. In 1923, with the publication of *New Hampshire* (including poems such as "Stopping by Woods on a Snowy Evening," "The Star-Splitter," "Fire and Ice," and "New Hampshire."), Frost received his first Pulitzer Prize. In 1928, *West-Running Brook*, a book with the same warm lyric quality that had characterized his first book, was issued. In 1930, Frost won Pulitzer Prize for the second time with the publication of *Collected Poems*. In 1936, the same honor was again conferred to Frost for his *A Further Range*. Then a new edition of *Collected Poems* (1939) was followed by *A Witness Tree* (1942), the fourth collection of poems winning Pulitzer Prize. Besides the above-mentioned, Frost also wrote two blank-verse plays, *A Masque of Reason*

(1945) and *A Masque of Mercy* (1947); and two books of later lyrics, *Steep Bush* (1947) and *In the Clearing* (1962). In 1961, at John F. Kennedy's inauguration, Frost was invited to read a poem "The Gift Outright" and this was his crowning public moment.

Frost died on January 29, 1963.

Frost's poems fall into several types: there are nature lyrics describing and commenting on a scene or event, such as "After Apple-Picking" and "Birches"; there are narrative poems about the lives of country people, such as "The Death of the Hired Man"; and there are poems of generalization such as "The Gift Outright." In the nature lyrics, the poet often compares the outer scene to the psyche. This comparison is expressed as "outer and inner weather" in one of his poems.

Frost's poems are characterized by its clear diction, colloquial rhythms, and the simple images. These elements make the poems look natural and unplanned. In the context of modernism, Frost's simplicity and ruralism might be seen as an echo to modernism's distaste for cities. However, Frost is never a modernist poet or a follower of imagism. His poems are anyway traditional and he restores the tradition of New England regionalism instead of affirming the modernist internationalism. Because Frost identifies himself as a New Englander and because his poems are so closely related to nature, Frost is often understood as an ideological descendant of the nineteenth-century American Transcendentalists. However, just like the fact that he does not belong to the school of modernism; he is neither a true follower of transcendentalism. While the transcendentalists see a benevolent creator in nature, Frost feels differently and finds "no expression, nothing to express."

It was rather late that Robert Frost established himself as a poet, at the age of forty. However, from then to his death, he was probably the nation's best-known and best-loved serious poet. As a poet, Frost favored the language used by common people, and showed in his poems the voices and visions of the New England countryside. His poems are beautiful, accessible, fresh, and timeless. Robert Graves said that "Frost was the first American poet who could honestly be reckoned a master-poet by world standards." T.S. Eliot commented that "[Frost is our] most eminent [and] most distinguished ... Anglo-American poet." And John F. Kennedy gave the following remarks: "[Frost] has bequeathed his nation a body of imperishable verse from which Americans will forever gain joy and understanding."

Brief Introduction and Appreciation

For appreciation, we choose the following four poems: "The Road Not Taken," "Fire and Ice," "Nothing Gold Can Stay," and "Stopping by Wood on a Snowy Evening."

"The Road Not Taken" is a wonderful poem which can be understood in many different ways. It consists of four stanzas of five lines and the rhyme scheme is abaab. There are four stressed syllables each line, varying on an iambic tetrameter base. The most commonly accepted understanding of this poem is the celebration of non-conformity, individuality, and self-reliance. Because the speaker in the poem chooses a road "less traveled by," and because he claims that "that has made all the difference," many readers believe he is proud of his individual choice. However, some scholars hold a completely different view. The poem is not about the celebration of independent choices, but about the difficulty of having to make choices at all. While the first viewpoint interprets the word "sigh" as a nostalgic relief, the second understands the word "sigh" as a symbol of regret: we feel sorry and helpless that we have to make a choice sometime in life and no one can experience life twice. Furthermore, the word "difference" in the last stanza can be understood either as a positive "difference," or merely a factual "difference." Interestingly, a third group of scholars hold the view that there is no definite interpretation of the poem at all. They attribute their belief to the following fact: Frost claims that he wrote this poem about his friend Edward Thomas, with whom he had walked many times through the New England countryside. While walking, they would come to different paths. Every time after choosing one, Thomas would always fret wondering what they might have missed by not taking the other path. Thus this poem might be a mocking to the indecisive character or just an inspiration from a friend's mannerism.

"Fire and Ice" is an extremely compacted little poem full of philosophical implications. It has an irregular rhyme scheme: line 1, 3, and 4 end with an –*ire*; line 2, 5, 7 and 9 end with an –*ice*; and line 6 and 8 end with an –*ate*. Each line contains either four or eight syllables and most of the lines can be read as iambic. In this poem, Frost compares two destructive forces: fire and ice. The first two lines of the poem tell us the two present ideas for the end of the world: some people say the world will end in fire, while others believe it will end in ice. In the next two lines, Frost relates fire to desire, which he has tasted in his life. Because desire is something consuming and destroying, Frost agrees with the first viewpoint that it is quite reasonable that the world will end in fire. However, in the next sentence (line 5 to line 9), Frost compares ice to hatred which implies rigidness and coldness, and concludes that it is also possible that the world will end in ice. In spite of the simple language, "Fire and Ice" proves to be a masterpiece in poetry.

"Nothing Gold Can Stay" is again a good lyric. It contains eight lines with a rhyme of aabbccdd. The theme of this poem is a sense of fleeting beauty, youth, and everything good. The tone of the poem is melancholy. The "first green" in the first line implies the beauty of spring, of bloom, and of the beginning of life. This is as precious as gold, which is often a symbol for purity. The second line discloses the cruel fact that this very "green" can not last long, and it is nature's "hardest hue to hold." In the next line, the "early leaf" replaces the "first green" in line one, meaning the same thing: beauty in its first bloom. Here, the "early leaf" is quaintly compared to "a flower," a symbol of beauty as well as delicacy. Despite the magnificence of a flower in bloom, the charm of it lasts but for a short time. The poet uses exaggeration in line four to reveal this cruelty: "But only so an hour." So, after the prime time of the "early leaf," when it can rival the beauty of a flower, it "subsides" to merely a leaf. So does the human life: from the promising new-born stage to the inevitable winter of life. Line five is the highlight of the poem, with an allusion of the Garden of Eden, where the first man and woman "sank to grief" by committing the original sin. This line is especially meaningful to the Christians because it implies the loss of perfection for all creation. The last two lines summarize the theme again: "So dawn goes down to day" and "Nothing gold can stay." There is no exception.

The last poem selected here is "Stopping by Woods on a Snowy Evening," a much anthologized piece. The poem contains 4 four-lined stanzas. The rhyme scheme of the first three stanzas is aaba, with the third line of the previous stanza setting up the rhyme for the next stanza. The last stanza is an exception in rhyme: the third line rhymes with the previous two as well as the last line. Literally, the poem tells the following episode: a traveler stops by some woods on a snowy evening and is greatly attracted to the beautiful and serene scenery. When he is lingering in the dark woods, he remembers his errands and decides to go on with his long journey. Figuratively, this poem can be read in another much complicated way. As a traveler on the voyage of life, the speaker stops for a moment and is fascinated by the scene of the dark and mysterious woods. Yet, besides this natural world, there is human society, the real world, calling for him. The owner of the woods, the traveler's little horse, and the sound of the "harness bell," all remind the man the reality and his unfulfilled responsibilities in his life. And the two lines in the last stanza "But I have promises to keep/And miles to go before I sleep" show the speaker's resolution to finish his duties in life. The refrain in the last stanza is thought-provoking: "And mile to go before I sleep/And miles to go before I sleep." You may understand the first line in its literal meaning that the traveler has a long way to go before he can get home and go to bed. And, for the second line, it might refer to the rest of time the man has before he dies.

Selected Reading

The Road Not Taken

Two roads diverged[1] in a yellow wood,
And sorry I could not travel both
And be one traveler, long I stood
And looked down one as far as I could
To where it bent in the undergrowth[2];

Then took the other, as just as fair,
And having perhaps the better claim[3],
Because it was grassy and wanted wear;
Though as for that, the passing there
Had worn them really about the same,

And both that morning equally lay
In leaves no step had trodden black.
Oh, I kept the first for another day!
Yet knowing how way leads on to way,
I doubted if I should ever come back.

I shall be telling this with a sigh
Somewhere ages and ages hence[4]:
Two roads diverged in a wood and I—
I took the one less traveled by,

And that has made all the difference.

Notes:

1. diverged: extend in a different direction
2. undergrowth: the brush (small trees and bushes and ferns etc.) growing beneath taller trees in a wood or forest
3. claim: an assertion of a right
4. hence: from this time

Fire and Ice

Some say the world will end in fire,
Some say in ice.
From what I've tasted of desire
I hold with those who favor fire.
But if it had to perish[1] twice,
I think I know enough of hate
To say that for destruction ice
Is also great
And would suffice[2].

Notes:

1. perish: pass from physical life and lose all bodily attributes and functions necessary to sustain life.
2. suffice: be sufficient; be adequate, either in quality or quantity

Nothing Gold Can Stay

Nature's first green is gold,
Her hardest hue[1] to hold.
Her early leaf's a flower; [2]
But only so an hour. [3]
Then leaf subsides[4] to leaf.
So Eden sank to grief. [5]
So dawn goes down to day.
Nothing gold can stay.

Notes:

1. hue: the quality of a color
2. Here the new and green leaf is compared to a beautiful flower.
3. implication of the fleeting beauty, youth, and everything good.
4. subsides: sink to a lower level or form a depression
5. allusion to the fall of Adam and Eve.

Stopping by Woods on a Snowy Evening

Whose woods these are I think I know.
His house is in the village, though;
He will not see me stopping here
To watch his woods fill up with snow.

My little horse must think it queer[1]
To stop without a farmhouse near
Between the woods and frozen lake
The darkest evening of the year. [2]

He gives his harness[3] bells a shake
To ask if there is some mistake.
The only other sound's the sweep
Of easy wind and downy[4] flake.

The woods are lovely, dark, and deep,
But I have promises to keep,
And miles to go before I sleep,
And miles to go before I sleep.

Notes:

1. queer: curious, odd, beyond or deviating from the usual or expected
2. This line can either be taken literally as the most lightless night, or it can be

taken as the night of the darkest emotions.

3. harness: stable gear consisting of an arrangement of leather straps fitted to a draft animal so that it can be attached to and pull a cart.

4. downy: as soft as down

Questions for Study and Discussion:

1. Is there any difference between the two roads in "The Road not Taken"? Then why did the speaker choose the second one?

2. What might the roads in "The Road not Taken" represent?

3. How do you understand the word "sigh" in "The Road not Taken"? Is it a sigh of regret that he did not choose the first road? Or is it a sigh of relief that he did choose the second one?

4. How do you think the world should end? Should it end in ice or in fire?

5. What are the similarities between "fire" and "desire"? And what are the similarities between "ice" and "hatred"?

6. What tone does the poet adopt in the poem "Fire and Ice"?

7. In the poem "Nothing Gold can Stay," what is the ultimate fate of "nature's first green," "her early leaf," "Eden," and "dawn"?

8. Give your understanding of "gold" in "Nothing Gold can Stay."

9. In the poem "Stopping by Woods on a Snowy Evening," what might the incident in the woods represent? Does this poem remind you of any of your personal occasions?

10. Describe the rhyme scheme of "Stopping by Woods on a Snowy Evening."

Eugene O' Neill (1888—1953)

Life and Major Works

Eugene O'Neill is generally considered as the foremost American dramatist. In his lifetime, he wrote more than fifty plays and won four Pulitzer Prizes. In 1936, he was awarded Nobel Prize for his great contribution to world literature, which was a precedent in the dramatic literature of America. It is said that what America owed to O'Neill is just like what England owed to Shakespeare,

Eugene O'Neill

249

Norway to Ibsen, Russia to Chekhov, and Germany to Brecht. As a dramatist who carried on the past and opened a way for future, O'Neill was greatly influenced by Strindberg, Chekhov, the Greek tragedians, to name just a few, and he also exerted profound influence on the later American playwrights such as Arthur Miller and Tennessee Williams.

The O'Neill canon consists of fifty-odd plays among which only one is a complete comedy—*Ah, Wilderness*! The rest are either one hundred percent tragedies or serious plays with solemn phenomenon such as the sea plays of the early practicing years. O'Neill's devotion to playwriting might be roughly divided into three periods: the early apprentice years (1913—1920), the middle experimental years (1920—1934), and the late mature years (1934—1943). In the first period, the young writer composed mostly one-act plays among which *Bound East for Cardiff*, *Moon of the Caribbees*, and *Ile* are comparatively popular. Then he produced his first long play *Beyond the Horizon*, which won him his first Pulitzer Prize. This play switched O'Neill's creating career to a new period that is full of experiments and surprises. Works like *All God's Chillun Got Wings*, *Desire under the Elms*, *The Great God Brown*, *Strange Interlude*, *Mourning Becomes Electra*, *Lazarus Laughed*, and *Days without End*, etc., all belong to this period. After the extremely innovative middle period, O'Neill then again returned to realism in playwriting. The third mature period includes one one-act play (*Hughie*) and three full-length plays (*The Iceman Cometh*, *Long Day's Journey into Night*, and *A Moon for the Misbegotten*). The style of this period was raw, spare, and utterly devoid of theatrical tricks and machinery. Yet the plays of this period stood the test of time.

Enjoying the longest sustained reputation in his own country as well as abroad, O'Neill is surely in addition a most legendary figure in the American theatrical field. He was born on October 16, 1888, the third child of James O'Neill, a prominent actor who made his fortune playing the lead role of *The Count of Monte Cristo*. His mother, Ella Quinlan, was the daughter of a successful Irish immigrant businessman. Ella loved her husband but hated the drifting lifestyle and later resorted to morphine. As a son of an actor, Eugene O'Neill spent most of his childhood touring with his parents around the country, acquiring an intimate knowledge of the theatre. In his youth, O'Neill had been a gold-searcher, a sailor, a derelict, an actor, a journalist, etc. He gave up his Catholic faith at the age of fifteen because God could not save his mother from morphine addiction. He entered Princeton University in 1906 and was expelled from it a year later for a reckless conduct. In 1909, he married secretly a girl whose name was Kathleen Jenkins and soon abandoned her and their newly born son. Two years later, he attempted suicide and was found and saved by his drunkard friends. It was after he was sent to a sanatorium for his tuberculosis in 1912 that he read enormously and systematically and decided to become a playwright. In 1914, the young and ambitious O'Neill enrolled in the famous playwriting course of George Pierce Baker of playwriting at Harvard, whereupon he began his career-long fumbling with tragedy. In 1918, O'Neill married Agnes Boulton, a writer of short stories and they later had a son and a daughter. Their marriage lasted for 11 years. In 1929, O'Neill married his third wife, Carlotta Monterey, a young and beautiful actress, who bore no child for him but accompanied him for the rest of his life. In the 1930s, O'Neill began to suffer from Parkinson's disease and lived in relative seclusion. By 1943, he was physically dependent upon his wife Carlotta and became increasingly depressed. His health went from bad to worse and gradually he became paralyzed. He died on November 27, 1953 in a hotel in Boston.

The uncommon experiences in his youth not only provided Eugene O'Neill with various source materials for literary creations but also led to his never-ceasing spirit of exploration. The expressions of these effects are the diversity of the subjects of his works and the innovations of his theatrical techniques. On the one side, the subjects of O'Neill's plays covered a large category, including social injustice, conflict of races, conflict of capital and labor, man versus machine, hostility of bourgeois society to art and artist, etc. On the other side, his artistic explorations were rather surprising: he used symbolism in *The Emperor Jones*, expressionism in *The Hairy Ape*, masks in *The Great God Brown*, soliloquies and stream-of-consciousness technique in *Strange Interlude*, Greek myth in *Mourning Becomes Electra*, and Biblical material in *Lazarus Laughed*. Despite the variety of his subjects and the richness of his theatrical techniques, the fundamental phenomenon of O'Neill's plays is bleak and tragic. The playwright conveyed through most of his plays his tragic vision: human beings in conflict with other human beings, with themselves, and with fate.

Brief Introduction and Appreciation

O'Neill's tremendous success as a dramatist depends to a great extent upon the fact that he had something to say about the modern social order that has been worth saying. In O'Neill's eyes, the mechanized industrial process of the materialistic America distorted man's spirit and divorced man from the qualities of humanity which gave him dignity and the sense of manhood. For a period of time, man might be content with or even proud of his position in such a materialistic society. However, the loss of normal identity as a self-sufficient human being will surely smash man's spiritual world sooner or later. *The Hairy Ape* is an extreme instance of the alienation and deformation of modern man living in a materialistic society dominated by mechanized industry.

Produced in 1922, *The Hairy Ape* belongs to the works of O'Neill's middle experimental years. The play consists of eight scenes, four in the ocean liner and four outside it, and tells the spiritual struggle and crushing of a stoker. In the first scene, we see a group of firemen sit in the forecastle of a ship drinking and talking. They are workers who shovel coal into the engine of a transatlantic ocean liner. Among them, Yank is the most massive and brutish one. He seems to be the leader of this vulgar group. He is possessed of a proud dignity that he belongs to the age of steam, power, and speed. The second scene introduces to us another key figure, the delicate and pretty Mildred Douglas, daughter of the owner of Nazareth Steel. In college, Mildred studied sociology and is on a crusade to help the poor. Now, this lavishly spoiled young lady is accompanied by her aunt to Europe where she will embark on some service projects. Miss Mildred decides to have a look at the lives of the "other half" (Yank and the firemen) in the liner. Escorted by the second engineer, Mildred goes down into the stokehole where Yank and the men are hard at work shoveling coal. In scene three, the gorilla-faced Yank encounters the pale and pretty Mildred. At the sight of Yank, the girl paralyzes with horror, terror, and her whole personality crushes. She utters "filthy beast" and whimpers for others to take her away, leaving Yank bewildered and humiliated.

The firemen have again gathered in the stokehold in scene four. They replay and rehash the Mildred scene and mock Yank, the filthy beast. Infuriated, Yank lunges toward the door to confront Mildred, but is restrained by the other firemen. After this unexpected interlude, Yank can never be at peace with himself. Finally, he decides to go out of the liner to find Mildred, the person who has insulted him and disturbed his mental world.

The next scene finds Yank and his fireman friend Long walking down Fifth Avenue in New York city. Long means to show Yank that Mildred is only one of the upper class people who are of the same ilk. To attract attention to himself,

Yank keeps bumping into people, but receives no response but "I beg your pardon" from those aloof ladies and gentlemen. At last, he is arrested because he makes a gentleman miss his bus. In scene six, Yank is in prison. He gets the knowledge from his fellow prisoners that if he wants to get even with Mildred and her father's company, he should join the Industrial Workers of the World (I.W.W.). In scene seven, Yank visits the local I.W.W. However, his radicalism and his preoccupation to destroy everything in the capitalist society arouse nothing but suspicion. The secretary of I.W.W. identifies Yank as a governmental spy and kicks him out on the street. Yank is totally lost in mind and doesn't know where to go.

Scene eight is the last scene and also the climax of the whole play. Homeless and hopeless, Yank visits the monkey house at the zoo. This lonely and wretched man attempts to befriend the gorilla in the cage. He tells the gorilla that they are of the same kind, both caged and scoffed. Yank calls the gorilla "brother" and sets it free from the cage and approaches to shake hands with it. The gorilla wraps its huge arms around Yank and gives him a murderous hug and then tosses him into the cage. Yank finally dies in the gorilla's cage. Maybe this is the very place where Yank at last belongs.

The Hairy Ape is generally considered one of the foremost achievements of expressionism of the American stage. It is also regarded as O'Neill's first existential tragedy. It won for O'Neill a second round of international acclaim in the early 1920s after the successful *Emperor Jones*. While Brutus Jones (the protagonist in *Emperor Jones*) is a racial misfit, Yank is a socioeconomic outcast. Yank's problem is not a problem of unemployment but of absence of self-identification. He is crying out against a social system which has not only exploited man's body but his spirit as well. Yank is a man bewildered by the disharmony of his primitive pride and individualism at war with the mechanistic development of society. O'Neill captures the mood of pessimism that prevailed in the 1920s following man's discovery that while the industrial world provided him with material benefits it also crushed and threatened to obliterate his humanity.

The following excerpt is the last scene of *The Hairy Ape*.

Selected Reading

The Hairy Ape

Scene VIII

SCENE: *Twilight of the next day. The monkey house at the Zoo. One spot of clear gray light falls on the front of one cage so that the interior can be seen. The other cages are vague, shrouded in shadow from which chatterings pitched in a conversational tone can be heard. On the one cage a sign from which the word "Gorilla" stands out. The gigantic animal himself is seen squatting on his haunches on a bench in much the same attitude as Rodin's "Thinker."[1] YANK enters from the left. Immediately a chorus of angry chattering and screeching breaks out. The gorilla turns his eyes but makes no sound or move.*

YANK. [*With a hard, bitter laugh*]. Welcome to your city, huh? Hail, hail, de gang's all here! [*At the sound of his voice the chattering dies away into an attentive silence. YANK walks up to the gorilla's cage and, leaning over the railing, stares in at its occupant, who stares back at him, silent and motionless. There is a pause of dead stillness. Then YANK begins to talk in a friendly confidential tone, half-mockingly, but with a deep undercurrent of sympathy.*] Say, you're some hard-looking' guy, aren't your? I seen lots of tough nuts dat de gang called gorillas, but you're de foist real one I ever seen. Some chest your got, and shoulders, and dem arms and mits! I bet you got a punch in eider fist dat'd knock 'em all silly! [*This with genuine admiration. The gorilla, as if he understood, stands upright, swelling out his chest and pounding on it with his fist. YANK grins sympathetically.*] Sure, I get you. Yuh challenge de whole woild, huh? You got what I was saying' even if you muffed de woids. [*Then bitterness creeping in.*] And why wouldn't you get me? Aren't we both members of de same club—de Hairy Apes? [2] [*They stare at each other—a pause—then YANK goes on slowly and bitterly.*] So you're what she seen when she looked at me, de white-faced tart! [3] I was you to her, get me? Onl'y outa de cage—broke out—free to moider her, see? Sure! Dat's what she tought.[4] She wasn't wise dat I was in a cage, too—worser'n yours—sure—a damn sight—'cause you got some chanct to bust loose—but me— [*He grows confused.*] Aw, hell! It's all wrong, ain't it? [*A pause.*] I s'pose yuh wanter know what I'm doin' here, huh? I been warmin' a bench down to de Battery[5]—ever since last night. Sure. I seen de sun come up. Dat was pretty, too—all red and pink and green. I was lookin' at de skyscrapers—steel—and all de ships comin' in, sailin' out, all over de oith—and dey was steel, too. De sun was warm, dey wasn't no clouds, and dere was a breeze blowin'. Sure, it was great stuff. I got it aw right—what Paddy[6] said about dat bein' de right dope—on'y I couldn't get in it, see? I couldn't belong in dat. It was over my head. And I kept tinkin'—and den I beat it up here to see what yourself was like. And I waited till dey was all gone to git you alone. Say, how d'you feel sittin' in dat pen all de time, having' to stand for 'em comin' and starin' at you—de white-faced, skinny tarts and de boobs[7] what marry 'em—makin' fun of you, laughin' at you, gittin' scared of you—damn 'em! [*He pounds on the rail with his fist. The gorilla rattles the bars of his cage and snarls. All the other monkeys set up an angry chattering in the darkness. YANK goes on excitedly.*] Sure! Dat's de way it hits me, too. On'y yuh're lucky, see? You don't belong wit 'em and yuh know it. But me, I belong wit 'em—but I don't[8], see? Dey don't belong wit me, dat's what. Get me? Tinkin' is hard— [*He passes one hand across his forehead with a painful gesture. The gorilla growls impatiently. YANK goes on gropingly.*] It's dis way, what I'm drivin' at. Youse can sit and dope dream in de past, green woods, de jungle and de rest of it. Den yuh belong and dey don't. Den you kin laugh at 'em, see? You're de champ of de woild. But me—I ain't got no past to tink in, nor nothin' dat's comin', on'y what's now—and dat don't belong. Sure, you're de best off! You can't tink, can yuh? Yuh can't talk neider. But I kin make a bluff at talkin' and tinkin'—a'most get away with it—a'most!—and dat's where de joker comes in. [*He laughs.*] I ain't on oith and I ain't in heaven[9], get me? I'm in de middle tryin' to separate 'em, takin' all de woist punches from bot' of 'em. Maybe dat's what dey call hell, huh? But you, you're at de bottom. You belong! Sure! You're de on'y one in de woild dat does, you lucky stiff! [*The gorilla growls proudly.*] And dat's why dey gotter put you in a cage, see? [*The gorilla roars angrily.*] Sure! You get me. It beats it when you try to tink it or talk it—it's way down—deep—behind—you 'n' me we feel it. Sure! Bot' members of dis club! [*He laughs—then in a savage tone.*] What de hell! T' hell wit it! A little action, dat's our meat! Dat belongs! Knock 'em down and keep bustin' 'em till dey croaks you wit a gat—wit steel! Sure! Are you game? Dey've looked at yours, ain't dey—in a cage? Wanter git even? Wanter wind up like a sport 'stead of croakin' slow in dere? [*The gorilla roars an emphatic affirmative. YANK goes on with a sort of furious exaltation.*] Sure! You're reg'lar! You'll stick to de finish! Me 'n' you, huh? —bot' members of this club! We'll put up one last star bout dat'll knock 'em offen deir seats! Dey'll have to make de cages stronger after we're trou! [*The gorilla is straining at his bars, growling, hopping from one foot to the other. YANK takes a jimmy from under his coat and forces the lock on the cage door. He throws this open.*] Pardon from de governor! Step out and shake hands. I'll take you for a walk down Fif' Avenoo[10.] We'll knock 'em offen de oith and croak wit de band playin'. Come on, Brother. [*The gorilla scrambles gingerly out of his cage. Goes to* YANK *and stands looking at him.* YANK *keeps his mocking tone—holds out his hand.*] Shake—de secret grip of our order. [*Something, the tone of mockery, perhaps, suddenly enrages the animal. With a spring he wraps his huge arms around* YANK *in a murderous hug. There is a crackling snap of crushed ribs—a gasping cry, still mocking, from* YANK.] Hey, I didn't say kiss me! [*The gorilla lets the crushed body slip to the floor; stands over it uncertainly, considering; then picks it up, throws it in the cage, shuts the door, and shuffles off menacingly into the darkness at left. A great uproar of frightened chattering and whimpering comes from the other cages. Then* YANK *moves, groaning, opening his eyes, and there is silence. He mutters painfully.*] Say—dey oughter match him—wit Zybszko[11.] He got me, aw right. I'm trou. Even him didn't think I belonged. [*Then, with sudden passionate despair.*] Christ, where do I get off at? Where do I fit in? [*Checking himself as suddenly.*] Aw, what de hell! No squawkin', see! No quittin', get me! Croak wit your boots on! [*He grabs hold of the bars of the cage and hauls himself painfully to his feet—looks around him bewilderedly—forces a mocking laugh.*] In de cage, huh? [*In the strident tones of a circus barker.*] Ladies and gents, step forward and take a slant at de one and only— [*His voice weakening.*] —one and original—Hairy Ape from de wilds of—[*He slips in a heap on the floor and dies. The monkeys set up a chattering, whimpering wail. And, perhaps, the Hairy Ape at last belongs.*]

[Curtain.]

Notes:

1. Rodin's "Thinker": The French artist Auguste Rodin (1840—1917) had a profound influence on 20th-century sculpture. "The Thinker" is one of Rodin's most famous sculptures. It is depicted as a man in sober meditation battling with a powerful internal struggle.

2. de Hairy Apes: Here Yank self-mockingly identifies himself with the gorilla in the zoo. In scene three, Mildred, a young and rich woman visits the stokehole. When she encounters Yank, she is frightened and calls him "filthy beast." Later in scene four, Paddy, one of the stokers, recollects that at the sight of Yank, Mildred reacts as if she has seen a great hairy ape escaped from the zoo. Such remarks infuriate Yank and lead to his final dramatic death in the zoo.

3. de white-faced tart: Here refers to Mildred Douglas, daughter of the owner of

Nazareth Steel.

4. Dat's what she tought: That's what she thought. When Mildred sees Yank, she is so frightened at his vulgar appearance and words that she faints. Yank is deeply hurt to be regarded as a murderous beast.

5. de Battery: a park at the southern end of Manhattan Island

6. Paddy: As one of Yank's fellow stokers, Paddy is an old Irishman who likes to drink heavily. He has experienced life on the sea that was free, where he was empowered and valued. Paddy's experiences let him have real opinions.

7. de white-faced, skinny tarts and de boobs: refer to the aloof and hypocritical ladies and gentlemen Yank meets on Fifth Avenue.

8. But me, I belong wit 'em—but I don't: Here Yank is lamenting that he has no place to belong and is intensely alone.

9. I ain't on oith and I ain't in heaven: I am not on earth and I am not in heaven. Earth and Heaven both represent states of happiness, neither of which Yank can find his way into. Yank is the victim of a society that won't "let him in" or find belonging anywhere.

10. Fif' Avenoo: Fifth Avenue is a major thoroughfare in the center of the borough of Manhattan in New York City.

11. Zybszko: Stanislaus Zybszko, a famous wrestler of the 1920s.

Questions for Study and Discussion:

1. Describe the language of Yank and comment on his disposition and social position.

2. Pay attention to O'Neill's stage directions. How are they important to one's reading of the play?

3. Why would O'Neill compare the gorilla in the cage with Rodin's "Thinker"? What effect is to be achieved?

4. In your opinion, does Yank finally find a sense of "belonging"? Is "belonging" possible?

5. Does Yank deserve sympathy? Why?

Earnest Hemingway (1899—1961)

Life and Major Works

Ernest Hemingway was born and raised in Oak Park, Illinois. His father, Dr. Clarence Edmonds Hemingway, was a successful physician who enjoyed outdoor life such as hunting and fishing. His mother, Grace Hall, was a strong and active woman who loved music and even considered a career as an opera singer before her marriage. Hemingway attended the public schools in Oak Park and practiced writing in his high school newspaper. In 1917, Hemingway graduated from high school and took his first job as a reporter for the *Kansas City Star*. Then the United States entered the World War I and the young man became eager to join the army. Due to the eye problem, Hemingway was barred from the army and

Earnest Hemingway

finally he managed to join a volunteer ambulance unit. Unfortunately, within three weeks, he suffered a severe leg wound by shrapnel on the Italy front and had to stay in the hospital for six months. Though the Italian government decorated Hemingway twice for his brave behavior in the war (when he was wounded, Hemingway had carried a comrade more badly hurt than he to safety), the impact of the cruelty of war could never be removed from the man's mind. In January 1919, Hemingway returned to the United States. Back home, the young man became increasingly estranged from his family, especially his mother, who declared one day that either he find a regular job or leave the home. Hemingway chose the latter.

In 1920, he married Hadley Richardson and went with her to Paris, where he worked as the foreign correspondent for the *Toronto Star*. In Paris, he wrote to support himself and wrote to become a writer. He began to know such literary figures as Gertrude Steine, F. Scott Fitzgerald, Sherwood Anderson, Ezra Pound, and other expatriates. Encouraged and helped by these friends, Hemingway published his first books: *Three Stories & Ten Poems* in 1923 and *In Our Time* in 1925. These early stories did not bring the author much fame, yet they had already showed the attitude of mind and technique for which he later became famous. Hemingway's first serious novel *The Sun Also Rises* appeared in 1926 and it was a great success. The novel tells the moral collapse of a group of English and American expatriates in France and Spain. The empty search for sensation of these disillusioned people is in sharp contrast to the rich tradition of peasant life in Spain. The story is narrated by an American journalist and the main characters are Lady Brett Ashley and Jake Barnes. In 1927, Hemingway divorced Hadley and married Pauline Pfeiffer, a fashion editor. In the same year, a collection of stories

Men Without Women was published. Hemingway's next successful novel was *A Farewell to Arms*, published in 1929. This novel tells a romance between an American army officer, Frederick Henry, and a British nurse, Catherine Barkley. They run away from war to look for peaceful life, yet Catherine dies in childbirth. Hemingway's affair with an American nurse during his hospital recuperation gave basis for this novel.

In 1930s, Hemingway produced the following works: *Death in the Afternoon* (1932); *Winner Take Nothing* (1933); *Green Hill of Africa* (1935); *To Have and Have Not* (1937); and *The Fifth Column and the First Forty-Nine Stories* (1938). The last book includes the most frequently anthologized short story "The Snows of Kilimanjaro."

In 1940, shortly after his second divorce, Hemingway married Martha Gellhorn, a writer and war correspondent he met in Madrid. His longest novel *For Whom the Bell Tolls* was published in the same year. It tells an incident in the Spanish Civil War and has universality in its thesis that the loss of liberty in one place means a loss everywhere. In 1945, Hemingway divorced Gellhorn, and his fourth and last wife was Mary Welsh, a correspondent for *Time* magazine. For a long time, Hemingway issued no new novel, and the publication of *Across the River and into the Trees* in 1950 was poorly received. However, his next work, *The Old Man and the Sea* (1952), a parable of man against nature, restored his fame. It tells the allegorical story of an old Cuban fisherman by the name of Santiago, who finally catches a giant marlin after weeks of disappointments. *The Old Man and the Sea* won Hemingway a Pulitzer Prize in 1953 and it was crucial in bringing him the Nobel Prize in 1954.

In his last years, Hemingway's productivity declined dramatically and he almost published nothing. Furthermore, he suffered from mental depressions and was hospitalized for several times, receiving electric shock therapy. On July 2, 1961, Hemingway committed suicide with his favorite shotgun at his home in Ketchum, Idaho. Several books have been published posthumously: *A Moveable Feast* (1964), a book of reminiscences about his life in 1920s Paris; *Islands in the Stream* (1970), a novel about literary fame and sexual ambiguity; *A Nick Adams Stories* (1972), a collection that added eight previously unpublished stories to the group. In 1981, his *Selected Letters* was issued.

Ernest Hemingway is a giant of modern literature and his work is a great contribution to modern fiction. In his individual way, he moulds the typical

Hemingway hero: a man of honor and integrity who expresses himself not with words, but with action; a man who proves his strength in an extreme crisis situation; a man that can be destroyed but not be defeated. Influenced by his early journalist career, Hemingway's writing style is terse and direct: concrete words, short sentences, and spare dialogues. The characteristic of his writing style is also expressed in his famous "ice-berg theory": If a writer of prose knows enough about what he is writing about he may omit things that will have a feeling of those things as strongly as though the writer had stated them. The dignity of movement of an iceberg is due to only one-eighth of it being above water. A good writer does not need to reveal every detail of a character or action.

Despite his achievements, Hemingway is not without his critics. Some scholars complain that his tough subject matter lacks deep insight and that his depiction of female characters lacks dimension.

Brief Introduction and Appreciation

Hemingway has won great acclaim for his crisp and almost journalistic prose style, free of the long and flowery language common to much of the precedent literature. His short stories are among those most frequently studied and anthologized, such as "The Snows of Kilimanjaro," "A Clean, Well-Lighted Place," and "In Another Country," etc. In the following selected reading, we present "In Another Country" for appreciation.

The story opens in the fall in Milan. The narrator, a wounded American soldier, is recuperating from his injury in the World War I. Every afternoon, he receives mechanical treatments at the hospital, where he meets up with a group of wounded soldiers. There are four Italian boys who are about the same age as the narrator is and an Italian major who professes no faith in machines. The doctor assures the narrator and the major of the full recovery of their limbs (the narrator has an injured leg, while the major has a withered hand), yet his prognosis seems to be dubious. The major used to be an excellent fencer, but is now an angry and bitter man. The daily meeting for medical treatments and the occasional walkings to the same caf socialize the five young men and they become friends. However, compared with the medals of the other three Italian boys, the American narrator's medals seem to be undeserved. So the narrator feels he is not truly one of them and gradually finds kinship with the fourth Italian boy who has no medal at all. Due to the fact that they all have combated with death, these former soldiers are detached to some extent. The major is an extreme example: he does not believe in bravery and is not interested in the heroic stories of the young men with medals. During the everyday rehabilitation, the major teaches the narrator Italian grammar lessons. One day, in a usual conversation with the narrator, the major suddenly becomes agitated. First, he scolds the narrator for not learning well his grammar; then he angrily negates the narrator's idea of getting married; finally he asks the attendant to turn off the machine and leaves the place. When he returns, he apologizes to the narrator and brings the news that his wife has just died from pneumonia. In great sorrow, the major breaks into tears. He then does not appear at the hospital for three days. When he turns up again, he has a black band around his sleeve. At the end of the story, the doctor puts large framed photographs around the wall, showing all sorts of wounds before and after they had been cured by the machines. While the narrator wonders the origin of these pictures, the major only looks out of the window.

The title of the story is tricky. On the surface, "In Another Country" refers to the fact that the American narrator is indeed in another country—Italy. He is wounded in the war and has to stay in a hospital in Milan. Besides this literal understanding of "another country," the title also can be explained in depth. It might refer to the realm of sickness, injury, and despair after the ruthless war. So, both the American soldier and those Italian soldiers are living in a symbolic foreign land where there is little hope for future and where they suffer from the nightmarish memory of war.

The major theme of the story is loss, failure, detachment, and the ways of confronting them. Many of the characters wrestle with a loss of physical function as well as a loss of spiritual faith. The American narrator loses the use of a leg; the Italian major loses the use of a hand; one of the Italian boys loses his nose; and the other three boys all have casualties of some sort. For these soldiers whose injury is not only physical but also spiritual, courage means not only to face the enemy fire on the front but also to take heart of grace and face the prospect of tomorrow. At the end of the story, the major says repeatedly "I am utterly unable to resign myself." On the one hand, it expresses the irresolvability of his grief in losing his wife. On the other hand, it implies his inability to forget the war; to pick up the once damaged life; and to live as if nothing has happened. The meaning of the machines in the story is also debatable: they might refer to the modern technology on which both war and medicine are so dependent; or they just imply the incapability of modern technology to cure people from their emotional wounds.

Another theme of this short story is the American response to World War I in contrast to that of the European. According to some scholars, the story shows that the long-term consequences of war are more significant for Italian soldiers because they are fighting close to their home country. To emphasize this theme, Hemingway depicts the narrator more a tourist figure than a real soldier: he has got his undeserved medals because he is an American; he has the spiritual luxury to comment on the local chestnut and the "patriotism" of the caf girls; and he learns a little Italian language but does not take a great interest in it. For the Italian soldiers, the war leaves them the damaged country and the broken domestic lives. While the American narrator can still go back to his own country and find a wife and start a new life, the Italian soldiers have nowhere to return and they have to face squarely all the ravages the war has left.

Selected Reading

In Another Country

In the fall the war[1] was always there, but we did not go to it any more. It was cold in the fall in Milan[2] and the dark came very early. Then the electric lights came on, and it was pleasant along the streets looking in the windows. There was much game hanging outside the shops, and the snow powdered in the fur of the foxes and the wind blew their tails. The deer hung stiff and heavy and empty, and small birds blew in the wind and the wind turned their feathers. It was a cold fall and the wind came down from the mountains.

We were all at the hospital every afternoon, and there were different ways of walking across the town through the dusk to the hospital. Two of the ways were alongside canals, but they were long. Always, though, you crossed a bridge across a canal to enter the hospital. There was a choice of three bridges. On one of them a woman sold roasted chestnuts. It was warm, standing in front of her charcoal fire, and the chestnuts were warm afterward in your pocket. The hospital was very old and very beautiful, and you entered a gate and walked across a courtyard and out a gate on the other side. There were usually funerals starting from the courtyard. Beyond the old hospital were the new brick pavilions, and there we met every afternoon and were all very polite and interested in what was the matter, and sat in the machines that were to make so much difference.

The doctor came up to the machine where I was sitting and said: "What did you like best to do before the war? Did you practice a sport?"

I said: "Yes, football."

"Good," he said. "You will be able to play football again better than ever."

My knee did not bend and the leg dropped straight from the knee to the ankle without a calf, and the machine was to bend the knee and make it move as riding a tricycle. But it did not bend yet, and instead the machine lurched[3] when it came to the bending part. The doctor said: "That will all pass. You are a fortunate young man. You will play football again like a champion."

In the next machine was a major who had a little hand like a baby's. He winked at me when the doctor examined his hand, which was between two leather straps that bounced up and down and flapped the stiff fingers, and said: "And will I too play football, captain-doctor?" He had been a very great fencer, and before the war the greatest fencer in Italy.

The doctor went to his office in a back room and brought a photograph which showed a hand that had been withered almost as small as the major's, before it had taken a machine course, and after was a little larger. The major held the photograph with his good hand and looked at it very carefully. "A wound?" he asked.

"An industrial accident," the doctor said.

"Very interesting, very interesting," the major said, and handed it back to the doctor.

"You have confidence?"

"No," said the major.

There were three boys who came each day who were about the same age I was. They were all three from Milan, and one of them was to be a lawyer, and one was to be a painter, and one had intended to be a soldier, and after we were finished with the machines, sometimes we walked back together to the Caf Cova, which was next door to the Scala[4]. We walked the short way through the communist quarter because we were four together. The people hated us because we were officers, and from a wine-shop someone called out, "A basso gli ufficiali!"[5] as we passed. Another boy who walked with us sometimes and made us five wore a black silk handkerchief across his face because he had no nose then and his face was to be rebuilt. He had gone out to the front from the military academy and been wounded within an hour after he had gone into the front line for the first time. They rebuilt his face, but he came from a very old family and they could never get the nose exactly right. He went to South America and worked in a bank. But this was a long time ago, and then we did not any of us know how it was going to be afterward. We only knew then that there was always the war, but that we were not going to it any more.

We all had the same medals, except the boy with the black silk bandage across his face, and he had not been at the front long enough to get any medals. The tall boy with a very pale face who was to be a lawyer had been lieutenant of Arditi[6] and had three medals of the sort we each had only one of. He had lived a very long time with death and was a little detached. We were all a little detached[7], and there was nothing that held us together except that we met every afternoon at the hospital. Although, as we walked to the Cova through the tough part of town, walking in the dark, with light and singing coming out of the wine-shops, and sometimes having to walk into the street when the men and women would crowd together on the sidewalk so that we would have had to jostle[8] them to get by, we felt held together by there being something that had happened that they, the people who disliked us, did not understand.

We ourselves all understood the Cova, where it was rich and warm and not too brightly lighted, and noisy and smoky at certain hours, and there were always girls at the tables and the illustrated papers on a rack on the wall. The girls at the Cova were very patriotic, and I found that the most patriotic people in Italy were the caf girls—and I believe they are still patriotic.

The boys at first were very polite about my medals and asked me what I had done to get them. I showed them the papers, which were written in very beautiful language and full of fratellanza and abnegazione[9], but which really said, with the adjectives removed, that I had been given the medals because I was an American. After that their manner changed a little toward me, although I was their friend against outsiders. I was a friend, but I was never really one of them after they had read the citations, because it had been different with them and they had done very different things to get their medals. I had been wounded, it was true; but we all knew that being wounded, after all, was really an accident. I was never ashamed of the ribbons, though, and sometimes, after the cocktail hour, I would imagine myself having done all the things they had done to get their medals; but walking home at night through the empty streets with the cold wind and all the shops closed, trying to keep near the street lights, I knew that I would never have done such things, and I was very much afraid to die, and often lay in bed at night by myself, afraid to die and wondering how I would be when I went back to the front again.

The three with the medals were like hunting-hawks; and I was not a hawk, although I might seem a hawk to those who had never hunted; they, the three, knew better and so we drifted apart. But I stayed good friends with the boy who had been wounded his first day at the front, because he would never know now how he would have turned out; so he could never be accepted either, and I liked him because I thought perhaps he would not have turned out to be a hawk either.

The major, who had been a great fencer, did not believe in bravery, and spent much time while we sat in the machines correcting my grammar. He had complimented me on how I spoke Italian, and we talked together very easily. One day I had said that Italian seemed such an easy language to me that I could not take a great interest in it; everything was so easy to say. "Ah, yes," the major said. "Why, then, do you not take up the use of grammar?" So we took up the use of grammar, and soon Italian was such a difficult language that I was afraid to talk to him until I had the grammar straight in my mind.

The major came very regularly to the hospital. I do not think he ever missed a day, although I am sure he did not believe in the machines. There was a time when none of us believed in the machines, and one day the major said it was all nonsense. The machines were new then and it was we who were to prove them. It was an idiotic idea, he said, "a theory, like another." I had not learned my grammar, and he said I was a stupid impossible disgrace, and he was a fool to have bothered with me. He was a small man and he sat straight up in his chair with his right hand thrust into the machine and looked straight ahead at the wall while the straps thumbed up and down with his fingers in them.

"What will you do when the war is over if it is over?" he asked me. "Speak grammatically!"

"I will go to the States."

"Are you married?"

"No, but I hope to be."

"The more of a fool you are," he said. He seemed very angry. "A man must not marry."

"Why, Signor Maggiore[10]?"

"Don't call me Signor Maggiore."

"Why must not a man marry?"

"He cannot marry. He cannot marry," he said angrily. "If he is to lose everything, he should not place himself in a position to lose that. He should not place himself in a position to lose. He should find things he cannot lose."

He spoke very angrily and bitterly, and looked straight ahead while he talked.

"But why should he necessarily lose it?"

"He'll lose it," the major said. He was looking at the wall. Then he looked down at the machine and jerked his little hand out from between the straps and slapped it hard against his thigh. "He'll lose it," he almost shouted. "Don't argue with me!" Then he called to the attendant who ran the machines. "Come and turn this damned thing off."

He went back into the other room for the light treatment and the massage. Then I heard him ask the doctor if he might use his telephone and he shut the door. When he came back into the room, I was sitting in another machine. He was wearing his cape and had his cap on, and he came directly toward my machine and put his arm on my shoulder.

"I am sorry," he said, and patted me on the shoulder with his good hand. "I would not be rude. My wife has just died. You must forgive me."

"Oh—" I said, feeling sick for him. "I am so sorry."

He stood there biting his lower lip. "It is very difficult," he said. "I cannot resign myself."

He looked straight past me and out through the window. Then he began to cry. "I am utterly unable to resign myself," he said and choked. And then crying, his head up looking at nothing, carrying himself straight and soldierly, with tears on both cheeks and biting his lips, he walked past the machines and out the door.

The doctor told me that the major's wife, who was very young and whom he had not married until he was definitely invalided out of the war, had died of pneumonia. She had been sick only a few days. No one expected her to die. The major did not come to the hospital for three days. Then he came at the usual hour, wearing a black band on the sleeve of his uniform. When he came back, there were large framed photographs around the wall, of all sorts of wounds before and after they had been cured by the machines. In front of the machine the major used were three photographs of hands like his that were completely restored. I do not know where the doctor got them. I always understood we were the first to use the machines. The photographs did not make much difference to the major because he only looked out of the window.

Notes:

1. the war: referring to World War I
2. Milan: city in northern Italy
3. lurch: move abruptly
4. the Scala: famous opera house in Milan
5. "A basso gli ufficiali!": "Down with officers!"
6. Arditi: corps of soldiers specially selected for dangerous operations.
7. a little detached: detachment and disillusionment with warfare were common among the "lost generation."
8. jostle: shove, come into rough contact with while moving
9. fratellanza and abnegazione: Italian for "brotherhood" and "self-denial."
10. Signor Maggiore: Italian for "Mr. Major." In Italy it was a sign of respect to say "Signor" before an officer's rank.

Questions for Study and Discussion:

1. What is the difference between the narrator's medals and those of the three Italian boys'? Why do the three Italian boys change their attitude toward the narrator after reading the citations?
2. Is the narrator ashamed of his medals? Why does he feel kinship with the boy who had been wounded his first day at the front?
3. Do the narrator and the major believe the power of "the machines"? What might "the machines" symbolize?
4. What happened to the major's wife? Stand in the major's shoes and explain his assertion "A man must not marry."
5. Are the wounds of the characters in the story merely physical injuries? Why?
6. Who are the "lost generation"? Is this story a good explanation of the attitude of the "lost generation"? Why?

F. S. Fitzgerald (1896—1940)

Life and Major Works

Francis Scott Fitzgerald is one of the literary giants among modern American novelists, an outstanding "chronicler" and mouthpiece of the Jazz Age, and a most representative author of "the Lost Generation". He is a very productive writer, leaving behind him five novels (the last one unfinished), 178 short stories and a lot of letters and essays. He incorporated his own life experiences into his creation to a large extent, which makes his books enchanting worldwide.

He was born on September 24, 1896 in St. Paul, Minnesota and was the only son of an aristocratic father and a provincial, working-class mother. His great grand

F.Scott Fitzgerald.

father was the author of the American national anthem "The Star-Spangled Banner", after whom he was named, showing the great pride in whom the family took. His family was never out of financial pressure, as a result, he was exceedingly conflicting toward the notion of the American dream which was vulgar and dazzlingly promising to him at the same time. The events of Fitzgerald's life can be seen as a struggle to realize the promises the American Dream implied to him. He attended St. Paul Academy in St. Paul from 1908 to 1911. His first literary effort, a detective story, was published in a school newspaper when he was 12. He attended Newman School, a prep school in Hackensack, New Jersey, from 1911 to 1912, and entered Princeton University in 1913. There he became a prominent figure in the literary circle of the university and made lifelong friendships with Edmund Wilson and John Peale Bishop who helped him a lot in improving his literary creation and establishing his literary status. However, with all his achievements in literature, Fitzgerald struggled academically and would have flunked out of Princeton University if he had not been recruited to the army in 1917 during World War I. But the war was ended before he could attend any battle.

Fitzgerald's love story is legendary. At the age of 18, he fell in love with the 16-year-old Ginevra King, the prototype of Daisy Buchanan in his masterpiece *The Great Gatsby*. Their love lasted for about two years only to end hopelessly with King's marrying a wealthy young guy because of his poverty. Then in November 1917, while stationed at Camp Sheridan (near Montgomery, Alabama), he met Zelda Sayre, the daughter of an Alabama Supreme Court judge, and the two fell deeply in love very soon. However, due to his seemingly hopeless financial circumstances, Zelda broke up their engagement.

Only when he became famous and rich with the publication of his first novel *This Side of Paradise* in the spring of 1920 did Zelda return to him and marry him, becoming his "golden girl". They became a couple of the Jazz Age—the era of the wild and the beautiful people, reminiscent of *The Great Gatsby* and the parties in *Tender Is the Night*. They also toured around America and Europe. As a result, the Fitzgeralds were constantly deep in debt disregard him being one of the best-paid writer. In 1922, Fitzgerald's second novel, *The Beautiful and Damned* was published. In 1924, the Fitzgeralds moved to France together with their daughter, where they became part of a group of wealthy American expatriates like Hemingway, Stein, Pound and others. Fitzgerald described this society in his fourth novel, *Tender Is the Night* (1934). In 1925, Fitzgerald published his masterpiece, *The Great Gatsby*, his best known novel.

In the thirties, Fitzgerald and his wife faced personal and professional decline: Fitzgerald became an alcoholic, and Zelda became mentally unstable. The novel *Tender Is the Night* gives readers some glimpse into their life at this period. Throughout the 1930s the Fitzgeralds fought an ultimately unsuccessful battle to save their marriage. Unfortunately, *Tender Is the Night* was considered technically faulty and was commercially unsuccessful. Crushed by the failure of this book and his despair over Zelda, Fitzgerald became an even heavier drinker. In 1937, he managed to acquire a job as a script-writer in Hollywood for money. There he met and fell in love with Sheilah Graham, a famous Hollywood gossip columnist. For the rest of his life, though he frequently had drunken spells in which he became bitter and violent, he lived quietly with Ms. Graham. Occasionally he went to visit Zelda or his daughter.

In October 1939, Fitzgerald began a novel about Hollywood entitled *The Last Tycoon*. The career of its hero, Monroe Stahr, is based on that of the renowned Hollywood producer Irving Thalberg. On December 21, 1940, Fitzgerald suffered a fatal heart attack, leaving the novel unfinished. Even in its half-completed state, *The Last Tycoon* is considered the equal of the rest of Fitzgerald's works for its intensity. The novel was published by Edmund Wilson in 1941.

It is Fitzgerald who coined the term "the Jazz Age" which refers to the decade after World War I and before the stock market crash in 1929, during which Americans embarked upon what he called "the gaudiest spree in history." He was both an earnest participant and "chronicler" of the age, of its morality and decadence. Compared with his involvement in the spree of the Jazz Age, his exposure of the origins of social decadence is much more important.

His writing can be divided into three stages and is parallel to his own life. His early works represented a younger generation that perceived itself as departing entirely from the tradition of the generations before it. Amory in *This Side of the Paradise* is a typical character in this period. His vanity and egotism, his flirtatious affairs with young women, his startling ideas (such as about socialism), and his vague contempt for nineteenth-century tradition all struck a chord with that generation who were fanciful, rebellious and ambitious to pursue their own way of life. They thought they understood the society, stood for the fashion, however, no matter how hard they made efforts, they just could not get rid of the fetters of the reality and the tradition. Fitzgerald's faithful and vivid description of America's post-war prosperity and the beliefs, mind and life of the younger generation placed his works among the best-selling ones despite the fact that his creation was not yet mature enough technically. In reality, his works are the mirror of the romantic and extravagant life of Fitzgerald and his newly-wed beautiful wife who are admired as "the golden couple" in the earthly heaven.

His subsequent works are about the disillusionment of the American Dream, which are considered the best of his works. With the increase of experience and deepening of observation, Fitzgerald became an acute and sharp social critic from a spokesperson for the younger generation. *The Great Gatsby* renders the final break up of a romantic and ideal dream of a noble and ardent hero, while *Tender Is the Night* presents an embarrassing situation in which a seemingly harmonious but spiritually divergent couple found themselves psychologically ill and frequently drunk. Both the heroes strived with utmost efforts for their dreams and were accomplished to a certain degree, only to find themselves having lost something precious, esp. their honor and dignity and ended in lamentable endings. By skillfully dealing with the double theme of money and love, the author applied very sober moral standards to analyze the distortion and corrosion of love by money, exposing that various evil deeds, coldness and insatiable pursuit of money were the sources of social decadence.

The themes of this period are parallel to his own life experience with his career and his marriage.

In his late works he did not give the readers a colorful and legendary world, instead, he bravely probed into and reflected on his own character and his way of life, made very serious self-criticism, which made him much nobler and re-earned himself popularity. However, alcoholism, back-breaking writing and mental pressure brought this talented writer to regrettable early death. With the revival of works, his value as a legendary literary figure has been more universally recognized throughout the world.

Brief Introduction and Appreciation

"Babylon Revisited", written when Fitzgerald was in his prime of creation, is widely considered the apex of Fitzgerald's short stories. First published in The *Saturday Evening Post* on February 21, 1931, it was re-published in his short story collection *Taps at Reveille* in 1935. It was adapted into a movie as well, entitled *The Last Time I Saw Paris*.

"Babylon Revisited" tells the story of Charlie Wales, a reformed sinner, who, after enduring the death of his wife and his own battle with alcoholism, returned to Paris, the setting of his previous dissolution. He came back to regain custody of his daughter from his sister-in-law, Marion, but failed at last for his own sake. Similar to his works in this period, Fitzgerald provided very profound insights into the decadence of the Jazz Age and its reasons. And shadows of his own life and that of the people around him can be found as usual.

The story was based on a true incident among Fitzgerald, his daughter, his wife's sister Rosalind and her husband Newman Smith, with the latter two being the models of Marion and her husband Lincoln. Rosalind and Newman were unable financially to live as well as Scott and Zelda during the 1920s, and they always regarded Scott as an irresponsible drunkard whose obsession with high living was responsible for Zelda's mental problems. When Zelda suffered a breakdown and was committed to a sanitarium in Switzerland, Rosalind felt that Scott was unfit to raise their daughter and that Rosalind and Newman should adopt her.

The whole story is an allegory of honor. In trying to regain the custody of his daughter, Charlie was not only trying to secure her guardianship, but also his own reputation. Charlie's daughter is an allegory of his honor (as her name denotes)—he lost her when he was at the lowest point in his life, a prisoner of his own dishonor. Charlie agreed to Marion's guardianship when he was in a sanitarium for alcoholism soon after his wife's death. Because of the stock market crash, he had also lost his fortune. At that time, when women were not traditionally part of the workforce, a man's honor was intertwined with his ability to provide for his family, and to be a good husband and father. After the crash, Charlie was able to regain his fortune quickly, but his status as husband and father were not so easily reclaimed. In Charlie's eyes, his daughter represented his honor, not merely his flesh and blood.

The point of view of this story is very special, i.e. from Charlie himself who recalled his own actions in the past and reflected on where he was wrong, immoral, and ridiculous, which was confirmed and strengthened by the pitiful situations of his old "friends" upon his revisiting the place of his former failure and commented by Marion and her husband. This makes the development of the plot and the revelation of comments intended by the author very convenient.

The author mainly dealt with two things that led to Charlie's sheer irresponsibility and destruction: dissipation and alcoholism. He explored how money and hedonism corrupted a person: he once believed in character, he once worked hard, but when he earned too much money from the stock market effortlessly, he developed a disillusion that he need not work any more, on the contrary, he began to squander money: awarding thousand-franc notes for a single piece of orchestral performance, tossing hundred-franc notes to the door-man for calling the cab only. When he revisited Paris, he suddenly realized the meaning of the word "dissipate"—to dissipate into thin air; to make nothing out of something. What's more serious, he developed an affair with Lorraine who was one of those helping him to "make months into days in the lavish times of three years ago". He noticed but ignored his wife Helen's unhappiness, which led to her flirtation with other men, which in turn led to his locking her out, which further resulted in the death of the latter. There is another reason accounting for his failure, i.e. alcoholism. From the fact that *Le Grand Vatel,* the restaurant in which he dined with his daughter was "the only restaurant he could think of not reminiscent of champagne dinners", it can be seen how heavy a drunkard he was. It was an equally fatal problem for Charlie. If not for it, he would not have done so many illogical things, like locking Helen out, not insisting on his daughter's guardianship, lying in the sanitarium upon Helen's death, and so on. Dissipation and alcoholism are also the two most serious problems that Fitzgerald suffered from.

Fitzgerald is an expert in using figurative language to help deliver complicated meanings and significant themes in so compact a space. The title "Babylon Revisited" is a metaphor: it is not difficult for the readers to identify Paris with Babylon which symbolizes a city of great luxury, sexuality, and often vices and corruption. And it is obvious that what Babylon was to Babylonians is what Paris to Charlie. By projecting the metaphoric meanings of Babylon onto that of Paris, the author implied that Charlie incurred destruction for his own decadent life just as Babylonians were punished by God to lose their kingdom. As Charlie reflected, he "spoiled this city" as he spoiled himself, and he left Paris symbolically after his failure.

The structure of the story is also highly metaphoric. It begins with great hope at the Ritz Bar and ends at the same place with as great frustration. This circular structure symbolizes the repetition of the same thing: self-destruction. Last time before Charlie was forced to leave Paris, he lost everything he wanted—his wife and his child in the boom; this time, he also lost the thing he wanted most—his daughter when everything turned for the better.

Two symbols are important for the full understanding of the novel. One is Honoria's doll. The doll that Charlie presented Honoria with upon his return to Paris is, in a sense, representing her, and the bond of parenthood. Since Honoria claimed it as her daughter, it helped recreate a familiar family scene of a father, mother and child—much like their life before the crash. Another symbol is snow. In the novel, it is the snow that killed Helen, and at the same time, "snow" is a kind of cocaine. So snow here represents feelings of vice, loss, emptiness and death. It is the beginning of Charlie's destruction: Helen's sister Marion blamed him for Helen's death, and swore that Charlie had ceased to exist to her after that, which caused her to harbor dislike and hate toward him and hindered him to regain his daughter's custody later.

F. Scott Fitzgerald is often cited as one of the great Modernist writers. Modernism is a literary movement that gathered force in the aftermath of World War I. Writers began experimenting with form and ideas, and rejecting traditional writing techniques and subject matter that were popular during the Victorian Era. American Modernism was exemplified by the works of a group of expatriates living in Paris during the 1920s and 1930s, including Fitzgerald, Gertrude Stein and Ernest Hemingway. Although their works was often drastically different from one another's, they had many similar themes, like a growing disillusion with society. "Babylon Revisited" epitomized many of the characteristics of typical Modernist writing. The themes of dissolution, alienation, and alcoholism seen in "Babylon Revisited" are reflective of this. Besides, Fitzgerald's use of the vernacular and informal language was surprising and experimental at the time.

Selected Reading

Babylon Revisited

I

"And where's Mr. Campbell?" Charlie asked.

"Gone to Switzerland. Mr. Campbell's a pretty sick man, Mr. Wales."

"I'm sorry to hear that. And George Hardt?" Charlie inquired.

"Back in America, gone to work."

"Where is the Snow Bird[1]?"

"He was in here last week. Anyway, his friend, Mr. Schaeffer, is in Paris."

Two familiar names from the long list of a year and a half ago. Charlie scribbled an address in his notebook and tore out the page.

"If you see Mr. Schaeffer, give him this," he said. "It's my brother-in-law's address. I haven't settled on a hotel yet."

He was not really disappointed to find Paris was so empty. But the stillness in the *Ritz* bar[2] was strange and portentous. It was not an American bar any more—he felt polite in it, and not as if he owned it. It had gone back into France. He felt the stillness from the moment he got out of the taxi and saw the doorman, usually in a frenzy of activity at this hour, gossiping with a *chasseur*[3] by the servants' entrance.

Passing through the corridor, he heard only a single, bored voice in the once-clamorous women's room. When he turned into the bar he traveled the twenty feet of green carpet with his eyes fixed straight ahead by old habit; and then, with his foot firmly on the rail, he turned and surveyed the room, encountering only a single pair of eyes that fluttered up from a newspaper in the corner. Charlie asked for the head man, Paul, who in the latter days of the bull market had come to work in his own custom-built car—disembarking, however, with due nicety at the nearest corner. But Paul was at his country house today and Alix giving him information.

"No, no more," Charlie said, "I'm going slow[4] these days."

Alix congratulated him: "You were going pretty strong a couple of years ago."

"I'll stick to it all right," Charlie assured him. "I've stuck to it for over a year and a half now."

"How do you find conditions in America?"

"I haven't been to America for months. I'm in business in Prague, representing a couple of concerns there. They don't know about me down there."

Alix smiled.

"Remember the night of George Hardt's bachelor dinner here?" said Charlie.

"By the way, what's become of Claude Fessenden?"

Alix lowered his voice confidentially: "He's in Paris, but he doesn't come here any more. Paul doesn't allow it. He ran up a bill of thirty thousand francs, charging all his drinks and his lunches, and usually his dinner, for more than a year. And when Paul finally told him he had to pay, he gave him a bad check."

Alix shook his head sadly.

"I don't understand it, such a dandy fellow. Now he's all bloated up—" He made a plump apple of his hands.

Charlie watched a group of strident queens[5] installing themselves in a corner.

"Nothing affects them," he thought. "Stocks rise and fall, people loaf or work, but they go on forever." The place oppressed him. He called for the dice and shook with Alix for the drink.

"Here for long, Mr. Wales?"

"I'm here for four or five days to see my little girl."

"Oh-h! You have a little girl?"

Outside, the fire-red, gas-blue, ghost-green signs shone smokily through the tranquil rain. It was late afternoon and the streets were in movement; the *bistros*[6] gleamed. At the corner of the *Boulevard des Capucines*[7] he took a taxi. The *Place de la Concorde*[8] moved by in pink majesty; they crossed the logical *Seine*[9], and Charlie felt the sudden provincial quality of the left bank.

Charlie directed his taxi to the *Avenue de l'Opera*[10], which was out of his way. But he wanted to see the blue hour spread over the magnificent faĉade, and imagine that the cab horns, playing endlessly the first few bars of *Le Plus que Lent*[11], were the trumpets of the Second Empire[12]. They were closing the iron grill in front of Brentano's Bookstore, and people were already at dinner behind the trim little bourgeois hedge of *Duval's*. He had never eaten at a really cheap restaurant in Paris. Five-course dinner, four francs fifty, eighteen cents, wine included. For some odd reason he wished that he had.

As they rolled on to the Left Bank and he felt its sudden provincialism, he thought, "I spoiled this city for myself, I didn't realize it, but the days came along one after another, and then two years were gone, and everything was gone, and I was gone."

He was thirty-five, and good to look at. The Irish mobility of his face was sobered by a deep wrinkle between his eyes. As he rang his brother-in-law's bell in the Rue[13] Palatine, the wrinkle deepened till it pulled down his brows; he felt a cramping sensation in his belly. From behind the maid who opened the door darted a lovely little girl of nine who shrieked "Daddy!" and flew up, struggling like a fish, into his arms. She pulled his head around by one ear and set her cheek against his.

"My old pie," he said.

"Oh, daddy, daddy, daddy, daddy, dads, dads, dads!"

She drew him into the salon, where the family waited, a boy and a girl his daughter's age, his sister-in-law and her husband. He greeted Marion with his voice pitched carefully to avoid either feigned enthusiasm or dislike, but her response was more frankly tepid, though she minimized her expression of unalterable distrust by directing her regard toward his child. The two men clasped hands in a friendly way and Lincoln Peters rested his for a moment on Charlie's shoulder.

The room was warm and comfortably American. The three children moved intimately about, playing through the yellow oblongs that led to other rooms; the cheer of six o'clock spoke in the eager smacks of the fire and the sounds of French activity in the kitchen. But Charlie did not relax; his heart sat up rigidly in his body and he drew confidence from his daughter, who from time to time came close to him, holding in her arms the doll he had brought.

"Really extremely well," he declared in answer to Lincoln's question. "There's a lot of business there that isn't moving at all, but we're doing even better than ever. In fact, damn well. I'm bringing my sister over from America next month to keep house for me. My income last year was bigger than it was when I had money. You see, the Czechs—"

His boasting was for a specific purpose; but after a moment, seeing a faint restiveness in Lincoln's eyes, he changed the subject:

"Those are fine children of yours, well brought up, good manners."

"We think Honoria's a great little girl too."

Marion Peters came back from the kitchen. She was a tall woman with worried eyes, who had once possessed a fresh American loveliness. Charlie had never been sensitive to it and was always surprised when people spoke of how pretty she had been. From the first there had been an instinctive antipathy between them.

"Well, how do you find Honoria?" she asked.

"Wonderful. I was astonished how much she's grown in ten months. All the children are looking well."

"We haven't had a doctor for a year. How do you like being back in Paris?"

"It seems very funny to see so few Americans around."

"I'm delighted," Marion said vehemently. "Now at least you can go into a store without their assuming you're a millionaire. We've suffered like everybody, but on the whole it's a good deal pleasanter."

"But it was nice while it lasted," Charlie said. "We were sort of royalty, almost infallible, with a sort of magic around us. In the bar this afternoon"—he stumbled, seeing his mistake—"there wasn't a man I knew."

She looked at him keenly. "I should think you'd have had enough of bars."

"I only stayed a minute. I take one drink every afternoon, and no more."

"Don't you want a cocktail before dinner?" Lincoln asked.

"I take only one drink every afternoon, and I've had that."

"I hope you keep to it," said Marion.

Her dislike was evident in the coldness with which she spoke, but Charlie only smiled; he had larger plans. Her very aggressiveness gave him an advantage, and he knew enough to wait. He wanted them to initiate the discussion of what they knew had brought him to Paris.

At dinner he couldn't decide whether Honoria was most like him or her mother. Fortunate if she didn't combine the traits of both that had brought them to disaster. A great wave of protectiveness went over him. He thought he knew what to do for her. He believed in character; he wanted to jump back a whole generation and trust in character again as the eternally valuable element. Everything else wore out.

He left soon after dinner, but not to go home. He was curious to see Paris by night with clearer and more judicious eyes than those of other days. He bought a *strapontin*[14] for the Casino and watched Josephine Baker go through her chocolate arabesques.

After an hour he left and strolled toward *Montmartre*[15], up the *Rue Pigalle* into the *Place Blanche*. The rain had stopped and there were a few people in evening clothes disembarking from taxis in front of cabarets, and *cocottes* prowling singly or in pairs, and many Negroes. He passed a lighted door from which issued music, and stopped with the sense of familiarity; it was *Bricktop's*, where he had parted with so many hours and so much money. A few doors farther on he found another ancient rendezvous and incautiously put his head inside. Immediately an eager orchestra burst into sound, a pair of professional dancers leaped to their feet and a *ma tre d'h tel*[16] swooped toward him, crying, "Crowd just arriving, sir!" But he withdrew quickly.

"You have to be damn drunk," he thought.

Zelli's was closed, the bleak and sinister cheap hotels surrounding it were dark; up in the *Rue Blanche* there was more light and a local, colloquial French crowd. The Poet's Cave had disappeared, but the two great mouths of the *Caf* of Heaven and the *Caf* of Hell still yawned—even devoured, as he watched, the meager contents of a tourist bus—a German, a Japanese, and an American couple who glanced at him with much frightened eyes.

So much for the effort and ingenuity of *Montmartre*. All the catering to vice and waste was on an utterly childish scale, and he suddenly realized the meaning of the word "dissipate"—to dissipate into thin air; to make nothing out of something. In the little hours of the night every move from place to place was an enormous human hump, an increase of paying for the privilege of slower and slower motion.

He remembered thousand-franc notes given to an orchestra for playing a single number, hundred-franc notes tossed to a doorman for calling a cab.

But it hadn't been given for nothing.

It had been given, even the most wildly squandered sum, as an offering to destiny that he might not remember the things most worth remembering, the things that now he would always remember—his child taken from his control, his wife escaped to a grave in Vermont.

In the glare of a *brasserie*[17] a woman spoke to him. He bought her some eggs and coffee, and then, eluding her encouraging stare, gave her a twenty-franc note and took a taxi to his hotel.

II

He woke upon a fine fall day—football weather. The depression of yesterday was gone and he liked the people on the streets. At noon he sat opposite Honoria at *Le Grand Vatel* [18], the only restaurant he could think of not reminiscent of champagne dinners and long luncheons that began at two and ended in a blurred and vague twilight.

"Now, how about vegetables? Oughtn't you to have some vegetables?"

"Well, yes."

"Here's *pinards* [19] and *chou-fleur* [20] and carrots and *haricots* [21]."

"I'd like *chou-fleur*."

"Wouldn't you like to have two vegetables?"

"I usually only have one at lunch."

The waiter was pretending to be inordinately fond of children. *"Qu'elle est mignonne la petite! Elle parle exactement comme une Fran aise."* [22]

"How about dessert? Shall we wait and see?"

The waiter disappeared. Honoria looked at her father expectantly.

"What are we going to do?"

"First, we're going to that toy store in the *Rue Saint-Honor* and buy you anything you like. And then we're going to the vaudeville at the Empire."

She hesitated. "I like it about the vaudeville, but not the toy store."

"Why not?"

"Well, you brought me this doll." She had it with her. "And I've got lots of things. And we're not rich any more, are we?"

"We never were. But today you are to have anything you want."

"All right," she agreed resignedly.

When there had been her mother and a French nurse he had been inclined to be strict; now he extended himself, reached out for a new tolerance; he must be both parents to her and not shut any of her out of communication.

"I want to get to know you," he said gravely. "First let me introduce myself. My name is Charles J. Wales, of Prague."

"Oh, daddy!" Her voice cracked with laughter.

"And who are you, please?" he persisted, and she accepted a r le[23] immediately: "Honoria Wales, *Rue Palatine*, *Paris*."

"Married or single?"

"No, not married. Single."

He indicated the doll. "But I see you have a child, madame."

Unwilling to disinherit it, she took it to her heart and thought quickly: "Yes,

I've been married, but I'm not married now. My husband is dead."

He went on quickly, "And the child's name?"

"Simone. That's after my best friend at school."

"I'm very pleased that you're doing so well at school."

"I'm third this month," she boasted. "Elsie"—that was her cousin—"is only about eighteenth, and Richard is about at the bottom."

"You like Richard and Elsie, don't you?"

"Oh, yes. I like Richard quite well and I like her all right."

Cautiously and casually he asked: "And Aunt Marion and Uncle Lincoln—which do you like best?"

"Oh, Uncle Lincoln, I guess."

He was increasingly aware of her presence. As they came in, a murmur of "...adorable" followed them, and now the people at the next table bent all their silences upon her, staring as if she were something no more conscious than a flower.

"Why don't I live with you?" she asked suddenly. "Because mamma's dead?"

"You must stay here and learn more French. It would have been hard for daddy to take care of you so well."

"I don't really need much taking care of any more. I do everything for myself."

Going out of the restaurant, a man and a woman unexpectedly hailed him.

"Well, the old Wales!"

"Hello there, Lorraine....Dunc."

Sudden ghosts out of the past: Duncan Schaeffer, a friend from college. Lorraine Quarrles, a lovely, pale blonde of thirty; one of a crowd who had helped them make months into days in the lavish times of three years ago.

"My husband couldn't come this year," she said, in answer to his question.

"We're poor as hell. So he gave me two hundred a month and told me I could do my worst on that....This is your little girl?"

"What about coming back and sitting down?" Duncan asked.

"Can't do it." He was glad for an excuse. As always, he felt Lorraine's passionate, provocative attraction, but his own rhythm was different now.

"How about dinner?" she asked.

"I'm not free. Give me your address and let me call you."

"Charlie, I believe you're sober," she said judicially. "I honestly believe he's sober, Dunc. Pinch him and see if he's sober."

Charlie indicated Honoria with his head. They both laughed.

"What's your address?" said Duncan skeptically.

He hesitated, unwilling to give the name of the hotel.

"I'm not settled yet. I'd better call you. We're going to see the vaudeville at the Empire."

"There! That's just what we'll do, Dunc."

"We've got to do an errand first," said Charlie. "Perhaps we'll see you there."

"All right, you snob....Good-bye, beautiful little girl."

"Good-bye."

Honoria bobbed politely.

Somehow, an unwelcome encounter. They liked him because he was functioning, because he was serious; they wanted to see him, because he was stronger than they were now, because they wanted to draw a certain sustenance from his strength.

At the Empire, Honoria proudly refused to sit upon her father's folded coat. She was already an individual with a code of her own, and Charlie was more and more absorbed by the desire of putting a little of himself into her before she crystallized utterly. It was hopeless to try to know her in so short a time.

Between the acts they came upon Duncan and Lorraine in the lobby where the band was playing.

"Have a drink?"

"All right, but not up at the bar. We'll take a table."

"The perfect father."

Listening abstractedly to Lorraine, Charlie watched Honoria's eyes leave their table and he followed them wistfully about the room, wondering what they saw. He met her glance and she smiled.

"I liked that lemonade," she said.

What had she said? What had he expected? Going home in a taxi afterward, he pulled her over until her head rested against his chest.

"Darling, do you ever think about your mother?"

"Yes, sometimes," she answered vaguely.

"I don't want you to forget her. Have you got a picture of her?"

"Yes, I think so. Anyhow, Aunt Marion has. Why don't you want me to forget her?"

"She loved you very much."

"I loved her too."

They were silent for a moment.

"Daddy, I want to come and live with you," she said suddenly.

His heart leaped; he had wanted to come like this.

"Aren't you perfectly happy?"

"Yes, but I love you better than anybody. And you love me better than anybody, don't you, now that mummy's dead?"

"Of course I do. But you won't always like me best, honey. You'll grow up and meet somebody your own age and go marry him and forget you ever had a daddy."

"Yes, that's true," she agreed tranquilly.

He didn't go in. he was coming back at nine o'clock and he wanted to keep himself fresh and new for the thing he must say then.

"When you're safe inside, just show yourself in that window."

"All right. Good-bye, dads, dads, dads, dads."

He waited in the dark street until she appeared, all warm and glowing, in the window above and kissed her fingers out into the night."

III

They were waiting. Marion sat behind the coffee service in a dignified black dinner dress that just faintly suggested mourning. Lincoln was walking up and down with the animation of one who had already been talking. They were as anxious as he was to get into the question. He opened it almost immediately:

"I supposed you know what I want to see you about—why I really came to Paris."

Marion played with the black stars on her necklace and frowned.

"I'm awfully anxious to have a home," he continued. "And I'm awfully anxious to have Honoria in it. I appreciate your taking in Honoria for her mother's sake, but things have changed now"—he hesitated and then continued more forcibly —"changed radically with me, and I want to ask you to reconsider the matter. It would be silly for me to deny that about three years ago I was acting badly—"

Marion looked up at him with hard eyes.

"—but all that's over. As I told you, I haven't had more than a drink a day for over a year, and I take that drink deliberately, so that the idea of alcohol won't get too big in my imagination. You see the idea?"

"No," said Marion succinctly.

"It's a sort of stunt I set myself. It keeps the matter in proportion."

"I get you," said Lincoln. "You don't want to admit it's got any attraction for you."

"Something like that. Sometimes I forget and don't take it. But I try to take it. Anyhow, I couldn't afford to drink in my position. The people I represent are more than satisfied with what I've done, and I'm bringing my sister over from Burlington to keep house for me, and I want awfully to have Honoria too. You know that even when her mother and I weren't getting along well we never let anything that happened touch Honoria. I know she's fond of me and I know I'm able to take care of her and –well, there you are. How do you feel about it?"

He knew that now he would have to take a beating. It would last an hour or two hours, and it would be difficult, but if he modulated his inevitable resentment to the chastened attitude of the reformed sinner, he might win his point in the end.

Keep your temper, he told himself. You don't want to be justified. You want Honoria.

Lincoln spoke first: "We've been talking it over ever since we got your letter last month. We're happy to have Honoria here. She's a dear little thing, and we're glad to be able to help her, but of course that isn't the question—"

Marion interrupted suddenly. "How long are you going to stay sober, Charlie?" she asked.

"Permanently, I hope."

"How can anybody count on that?"

"You know I never did drink heavily until I gave up business and came over here with nothing to do. Then Helen and I began to run around with—"

"Please leave Helen out of it. I can't bear to hear you talk about her like that."

He stared at her grimly; he had never been certain how fond of each other the sisters were in life.

"My drinking only lasted about a year and a half—from the time we came over until I—collapsed."

"It was time enough."

"It was time enough," he agreed.

"My duty is entirely to Helen," she said. "I try to think what she would have wanted me to do frankly, from the night you did that terrible thing you haven't really existed for me. I can't help that. She was my sister."

"Yes."

"When she was dying she asked me to look out for Honoria. If you hadn't been in a sanitarium then, it might have helped matters."

He had no answer.

"I'll never in my life be able to forget the morning when Helen knocked at my door, soaked to the skin and shivering and said you'd locked her out."

Charlie gripped the sides of the chair. This was more difficult than he expected; he wanted to launch out into a long expostulation and explanation, but he only said: "The night I locked her out—" and she interrupted, "I don't feel up to going over that again."

After a moment's silence Lincoln said: "We're getting off the subject. You want Marion to set aside her legal guardianship and give you Honoria. I think the main point for her is whether she has confidence in you or not."

"I don't blame Marion," Charlie said slowly, "but I think she can have entire confidence in me. I had a good record up to three years ago. Of course, it's within human possibilities I might go wrong any time. But if we wait much longer I'll lose Honoria's childhood and my chance for a home." He shook his head, "I'll simply lose her, don't you see?"

"Yes, I see," said Lincoln.

"Why didn't you think of all this before?" Marion asked.

"I suppose I did, from time to time, but Helen and I were getting along badly. When I consented to the guardianship, I was flat on my back in a sanitarium and the market had cleaned me out. I knew I'd acted badly, and I thought if it would bring any peace to Helen, I'd agree to anything. But now it's different. I'm functioning, I'm behaving damn well, so far as—"

"Please don't swear at me," Marion said.

He looked at her, startled. With each remark the force of her dislike became more and more apparent. She had built up all her fear of life into one wall and faced it toward him. This trivial reproof was possibly the result of some trouble with the cook several hours before. Charlie became increasingly alarmed at leaving Honoria in this atmosphere of hostility against himself; sooner or later it would come out, in a word here, a shake of the head there, and some of that distrust would be irrevocably implanted in Honoria. But he pulled his temper down out of his face and shut it up inside him; he had won a point for Lincoln realized the absurdity of Marion's remark and asked her lightly since when she had objected to the word "damn."

"Another thing," Charlie said: "I'm able to give her certain advantages now

I'm going to take a French governess to Prague with me. I've got a lease on a new apartment—"

He stopped, realizing he was blundering. They couldn't be expected to accept with equanimity the fact that his income was again twice as large as their own.

"I suppose you can give her more luxuries than we can," said Marion. "When you were throwing away money we were living along watching every ten francs.... I suppose you'll start doing it again."

"Oh, no," he said. "I've learned. I've worked hard for ten years, you know—until I got lucky in the market, like so many people. Terribly lucky. It didn't seem any use working any more, so I quit."

There was a long silence. All of them felt their nerves straining, and for the first time in a year Charlie wanted a drink. He was sure now that Lincoln Peters wanted him to have his child.

Marion shuddered suddenly; part of her saw that Charlie's feet were planted on the earth now, and her own maternal feeling recognized the naturalness of his desire; but she had lived for a long time with a prejudice—a prejudice founded on a curious disbelief in her sister's happiness, and which, in the shock of one terrible night, had turned to hatred for him. It had all happened at a point in her life where the discouragement of ill health and adverse circumstances made it necessary for her to believe in tangible villainy and a tangible villain.

"I can't help what I think!" she cried out suddenly. "How much you were responsible for Helen's death, I don't know. It's something you'll have to square with your own conscience."

An electric current of agony surged through him; for a moment he was almost on his feet, an unuttered sound echoing in his throat. He hung on to himself for a moment, another moment.

"Hold on there," said Lincoln uncomfortable. "I never thought you were responsible for that."

"Helen died of heart trouble," Charlie said dully.

"Yes, heart trouble." Marion spoke as if the phrase had another meaning for her.

Then, in the flatness that followed her outburst, she saw him plainly and she knew he had somehow arrived at control over the situation. Glancing at her husband, she found no help from him, and as abruptly as if it were a matter of no importance, she threw up the sponge.

"Do what you like!" she cried, springing up from her chair. "She's your child. I'm not the person to stand in your way. I think if it were my child I'd rather see her—" She managed to check herself. "You two decide it. I can't stand this. I'm sick. I'm going to bed."

She hurried from the room; after a moment Lincoln said:

"This has been a hard day for her. You know how strongly she feels—" His voice was almost apologetic: "When a woman gets an idea in her head."

"Of course."

"It's going to be all right. I think she sees now that you—can provide for the child, and so we can't very well stand in your way or Honoria's way."

"Thank you, Lincoln."

"I'd better go along and see how she is."

"I'm going."

He was still trembling when he reached the street, but a walk down the *Rue Bonaparte* to the *quais* [24] set him up, and as he crossed the Seine, fresh and new by the *quai* lamps, he felt exultant. But back in his room he couldn't sleep. The image of Helen haunted him. Helen whom he had loved so until they had senselessly begun to abuse each other's love, tear it into shreds. On that terrible February night that Marion remembered so vividly, a slow quarrel had gone on for hours. There was a scene at the Florida, and then he attempted to take her home, and then she kissed young Webb at a table; after that there was what she had hysterically said. When he arrived home alone he turned the key in the lock in wild anger. How could he know she would arrive an hour later alone, that there would be a snowstorm in which she wandered about in slippers, too confused to find a taxi? Then the aftermath, her escaping pneumonia by a miracle, and all the attendant horror. They were "reconciled," but that was the beginning of the end, and Marion, who had seen with her own eyes and who imagined it to be one of the many scenes from her sister's martyrdom, never forgot.

Going over it again brought Helen nearer, and in the white, soft light that steals upon half sleep near morning he found himself talking to her again. She said that he was perfectly right about Honoria and that she wanted Honoria to be with him. She said she was glad he was being good and doing better. She said a lot of other things—very friendly things—but she was in a swing in a white dress, and swinging faster and faster all the time, so that at the end he could not hear clearly all that she said.

IV

He woke up feeling happy. The door of the world was open again. He made plans, vistas, futures for Honoria and himself, but suddenly he grew sad, remembering all the plans he and Helen had made. She had not planned to die. The present was the thing—work to do and someone to love. But not to love too much, for he knew the injury that a father can do to a daughter or a mother to a son by attaching them too closely: afterward, out in the world, the child would seek in the marriage partner the same blind tenderness and, failing probably to find it, turn against love and life.

It was another bright, crisp day. He called Lincoln Peters at the bank where he worked and asked if he could count on taking Honoria when he left for Prague.

Lincoln agreed that there was no reason for delay. One thing—the legal guardianship. Marion wanted to retain that a while longer. She was upset by the whole matter, and it would oil things if she felt that the situation was still in her control for another year. Charlie agreed, wanting only the tangible, visible child.

Then the question of a governess. Charles sat in a gloomy agency and talked to a cross *B arnaise* and to a buxom *Breton* peasant, neither of whom he could have endured. There would be others whom he would see tomorrow. He lunched with Lincoln Peters at Griffons, trying to keep down his exultation. "There's nothing quite like your own child," Lincoln said. "But you understand how Marion feels too."

"She's forgotten how hard I worked for seven years there," Charlie said. "She just remembers one night."

There's another thing." Lincoln hesitated. "While you and Helen were tearing around Europe throwing money away, we were just getting along. I didn't touch any of the prosperity because I never got ahead enough to carry anything but my insurance. I think Marion felt there was some kind of injustice in it—you not even working toward the end, and getting richer and richer."

"It went just as quick as it came," said Charlie.

"Yes, a lot of it stayed in the hands of *chasseurs* and saxophone players and *ma tre d'h tel*—well, the big party's over now. I just said that to explain Marion's feeling about those crazy years. If you drop in about six o'clock tonight before Marion's too tired, we'll settle the details on the spot."

Back at his hotel, Charlie found a *pneumatique*[25] that had been redirected from the Ritz bar where Charlie had left his address for the purpose of finding a certain man.

DEAR CHARLIE: You were so strange when we saw you the other day that I wondered if I did something to offend you. If so, I'm not conscious of it. In fact, I have thought about you too much for the last year, and it's always been in the back of my mind that I might see you if I came over here. We did have such good times that crazy spring, like the night you and I stole the butcher's tricycle, and the time we tried to call on the president and you had the old derby rim and wire cane. Everybody seems so old lately, but I don't feel old a bit. Couldn't we get together some time today for old time's sake? I've got a vile hang-over for the moment, but will be feeling better this afternoon and will look for you about five in the sweatshop at the Ritz. "Always devotedly, LORRAINE."

His first feeling was one of awe that he had actually, in his mature years, stolen a tricycle and pedaled Lorraine all over the *toile*[26] between the small hours and dawn. In retrospect it was a nightmare. Locking out Helen didn't fit in with any other act of his life, but the tricycle incident did—it was one of many. How many weeks or months of dissipation to arrive at that condition of utter irresponsibility?

He tried to picture how Lorraine had appeared to him then—very attractive; Helen was unhappy about it, though she said nothing. Yesterday, in the restaurant, Lorraine had seemed trite, blurred, worn away. He emphatically did not want to see her, and he was glad Alix had not given away his hotel address. It was a relief to think, instead, of Honoria, to think of Sundays spent with her and of saying good morning to her and of knowing she was there in his house at night, drawing her breath in the darkness.

At five he took a taxi and bought presents for all the Peters—a piquant cloth doll, a box of Roman soldiers, flowers for Marion, big linen handkerchiefs for Lincoln.

He saw, when he arrived in the apartment, that Marion had accepted the inevitable. She greeted him now as though he were a recalcitrant member of the family, rather than a menacing outsider. Honoria had been told she was going; Charlie was glad to see that her tact made her conceal her excessive happiness. Only on his lap did she whisper her delight and the question "When?" before she slipped away with the other children.

He and Marion were alone for a minute in the room, and on an impulse he spoke out boldly:

"Family quarrels are bitter things. They don't go according to any rules.

They're not like aches or wounds; they're more like splits in the skin that won't heal because there's not enough material. I wish you and I could be on better terms."

"Some things are hard to forget," she answered. "It's a question of confidence." There was no answer to this and presently she asked, "When do you propose to take her?"

"As soon as I can get a governess. I hoped the day after tomorrow."

"That's impossible. I've got to get her things in shape. Not before Saturday."

He yielded. Coming back into the room, Lincoln offered him a drink.

"I'll take my daily whisky," he said.

It was warm here, it was a home, people together by a fire. The children felt very safe and important; the mother and father were serious, watchful. They had things to do for the children more important than his visit here. A spoonful of medicine was, after all, more important than the strained relations between Marion and himself. They were not dull people, but they were very much in the grip of life and circumstances. He wondered if he couldn't do something to get Lincoln out of his rut at the bank.

A long peal at the door-bell; the *bonne   tout faire*[27] passed through and went down the corridor. The door opened upon another long ring, and then voices, and the three in the salon looked up expectantly; Richard moved to bring the corridor within his range of vision and Marion rose. Then the maid came back along the corridor, closely followed by the voices, which developed under the light into Duncan Schaeffer and Lorraine Quarrles.

They were gay, they were hilarious, they were roaring with laughter. For a moment Charlie was astounded; unable to understand how they ferreted out the Peters' address.

"Ah-h-h!" Duncan wagged his finger roguishly at Charlie. "Ah-h-h!"

They both slid down another cascade of laughter. Anxious and at a loss, Charlie shook hands with them quickly and presented them to Lincoln and Marion. Marion nodded, scarcely speaking. She had drawn back a step toward the fire; her little girl stood beside her, and Marion put an arm about her shoulder.

With growing annoyance at the intrusion, Charlie waited for them to explain themselves. After some concentration Duncan said:

"We came to invite you out to dinner. Lorraine and I insist that all this chi-chi, cagy business 'bout your address got to stop."

Charlie came closer to them, as if to force them backward down the corridor.

"Sorry, but I can't. Tell me where you'll be and I'll phone you in half an hour." This made no impression. Lorraine sat down suddenly on the side of a chair, and focusing her eyes on Richard, cried, "Oh, what a nice little boy! Come here, little boy." Richard glanced at his mother, but did not move. With a perceptible shrug of her shoulders, Lorraine turned back to Charlie:

"Come and dine. Sure your cousins won' mine. See you so sel'om. Or solemn."

"I can't," said Charlie sharply. "You two have dinner and I'll phone you."

Her voice became suddenly unpleasant. "All right, we'll go. But I remember once when you hammered on my door at four A.M. I was enough of a good sport to give you a drink. Come on, Dunc."

Still in slow motion, with blurred, angry faces, with uncertain feet, they retired along the corridor.

"Good night," Charlie said.

"Good night!" responded Lorraine emphatically.

When he went back into the salon Marion had not moved, only now her son was standing in the circle of her other arm. Lincoln was still swinging Honoria back and forth like a pendulum from side to side.

"What an outrage!" Charlie broke out. "What an absolute outrage!"

Neither of them answered. Charlie dropped into an armchair, picked up his drink, set it down again and said:

"People I haven't seen for two years having the colossal nerve—"

He broke off. Marion had made the sound "Oh!" in one swift, furious breath, turned her body from him with a jerk and left the room.

Lincoln set down Honoria carefully.

"You children go in and start your soup," he said, and when they obeyed, he said to Charlie:

"Marion's not well and she can't stand shocks. That kind of people make her really physically sick."

"I didn't tell them to come here. They wormed your name out of somebody. They deliberately—"

"Well, it's too bad. It doesn't help matters. Excuse me a minute."

Left alone, Charlie sat tense in his chair. In the next room he could hear the children eating, talking in monosyllables, already oblivious to the scene between their elders. He heard a murmur of conversation from a farther room and then the ticking bell of a telephone receiver picked up, and in a panic he moved to the other side of the room and out of earshot.

In a minute Lincoln came back. "Look here, Charlie. I think we'd better call off dinner for tonight. Marion's in bad shape."

"Is she angry with me?"

"Sort of," he said, almost roughly. "She's not strong and..."

"You mean she's changed her mind about Honoria?"

"She's pretty bitter right now. I don't know. You phone me at the bank tomorrow."

"I wish you'd explain to her I never dreamed these people would come here. I'm just as sore as you are."

"I couldn't explain anything to her now."

Charlie got up. He took his coat and hat and started down the corridor. Then he opened the door of the dining room and said in a strange voice, "Good night, children."

Honoria rose and ran around the table to hug him.

"Good night, sweetheart," he said vaguely, and then trying to make his voice more tender, trying to conciliate something, "Good night, dear children."

V

Charlie went directly to the Ritz bar with the furious idea of finding Lorraine and Duncan, but they were not there, and he realized that in any case there was nothing he could do. He had not touched his drink at the Peters', and now he ordered a whisky-and-soda. Paul came over to say hello.

"It's a great change," he said sadly. "We do about half the business we did. So many fellows I hear about back in the States lost everything, maybe not in the first crash, but then in the second. Your friend George Hardt lost every cent, I hear. Are you back in the States?"

"No, I'm in business in Prague."

"I heard that you lost a lot in the crash."

"I did," and he added grimly, "but I lost everything I wanted in the boom."

"Selling short."

"Something like that."

Again the memory of those days swept over him like a nightmare—the people they had met traveling; then people who couldn't add a row of figures or speak a coherent sentence. The little man Helen had consented to dance with at the ship's party, who had insulted her ten feet from the table; the women and girls carried screaming with drink or drugs out of public places—The men who locked their wives out in the snow, because the snow of twenty-nine wasn't real snow. If you didn't want it to be snow, you just paid some money.

He went to the phone and called the Peters' apartment; Lincoln answered.

"I called up because this thing is on my mind. Has Marion said anything definite?"

"Marion's sick," Lincoln answered shortly. "I know this thing isn't altogether your fault, but I can't have her go to pieces about it. I'm afraid we'll have to let it slide for six months; I can't take the chance of working her up to this state again."

"I see."

"I'm sorry, Charlie."

He went back to his table. His whisky glass was empty, but he shook his head when Alix looked at it questioningly. There wasn't much he could do now except send Honoria some things; he would send her a lot of things tomorrow. He thought rather angrily that this was just money—he had given so many people money....

"No, no more," he said to another waiter. "What do I owe you?"

He would come back some day; they couldn't make him pay forever. But he wanted his child, and nothing was much good now, beside that fact. He wasn't young any more, with a lot of nice thoughts and dreams to have by himself. He was absolutely sure Helen wouldn't have wanted him to be so alone.

1931

Notes:

1. Snow bird: also slang for a cocaine ("snow") addict who also sometimes sells the drug.
2. *Ritz* bar: the bar at the Ritz Hotel in Paris, a prime gathering spot for rich Americans; Fitzgerald mentioned many well-known Parisian locales to show the bygone luxurious life of the hero.
3. *chasseur*: (French) hotel porter
4. go slow: not drink much
   go strong: drink much
5. queen: used as a disparaging term for a gay or homosexual man
6. *bistros*: pubs or small bars
7. *Boulevard des Capucines*: one of the best boulevards in Paris, famous for some of the most gorgeous buildings on its sides, including the Paris Opera.

8. *Place de la Concorde:* Place de la Concorde, in the center of Paris and on the northern bank of Seine, the most famous square in Paris, and one of the most beautiful squares in the world. "Place" in French means "square".

9. *Seine*: A river flowing through Paris generally northwest, an inlet of the English Channel, an important commercial waterway since Roman times.

10. *Avenue de l'Opera*: an avenue in Paris named after the renowned Op ra national de Paris.

11. *Le Plus que Lent*: a piece of music for a very slow and elegant dance

12. The Second Empire: the empire claimed to be established by the Prusian King William I in Versailles Palace in 1870 after the defeat of France during the Prusian-French war. This empire lasted only for 47 years, breaking up after the World War One.

13. Rue: French for "street"

14. *strapontin*: foldaway seat

15. *Montmartre*: a region of Paris

16. *ma tre d'h tel*: hotel manager

17. *brasserie:* French for restaurant

18. *Le Grand Vatel*: name of the restaurant

19. *pinards*: French for spinach.

20. *chou-fleur*: French for cauliflower

21. *haricots*: French for haricots

22. *Qu'elle est mignonne la petite! Elle parle exactement comme une Fran aise*: French for "How lovely the little girl!" "She speaks French exactly like a French!"

23. *r le*: French for role

24. *quais*: French for quays

25. *pneumatique*: French for pneumatique, a letter or package posted pheumatically

26. *toile*: the original name of Place Charles de Gaulle

27. *bonne   tout faire:* Housemaid to do all the housework

Questions for Study and Discussion:

1. How is "Babylon" important to the whole story? (Babylon was an ancient city-kingdom in Southwest Asia where the Israelites fled into exile after the destruction of the first Temple (587 B.C.); the name is synonymous with civic corruption and perverse luxury.)

2. How does the story relate to Fitzgerald and his life?

3. What does "Honoria" reveal about the theme of the story?

4. What does "snow" symbolize in the story?

5. How is the detail that Charlie left his address in the Ritz Bar important to the whole plot?

6. How does Charlie's attitude towards money change at the end of the story?

7. How to understand Charlie's reflection "I spoiled this city for myself..." when he rolled on to the Left Bank of Seine?

8. What does the author intend to criticize in the story?

William Faulkner (1897—1962)

Life and Major Works

William Faulkner was born in New Albany, Mississippi, on September 28, 1897. He was the oldest of four sons of Murray Charles Faulkner and Maud Butler Faulkner. Murray was a reclusive man who loved hunting and drinking. Maud, on the other hand, was sensitive and literary. She introduced poetry and music to her son and exerted profound influence on Faulkner as a youth. For the first few years, the family lived a happy and content life: the father enjoying his role as a railroad worker and the mother being satisfied with her role as a housewife.

William Faulkner

However, the happiness of the family was shattered in mid 1902, when Faulkner's grandfather, the owner of the railroad, decided to sell the railroad and the Faulkner family had to move to Oxford to make a new living. Leaving the railroad, the passion of his youth, Murray became devastated and silent. Maud, failing to save her husband from drinking and depression, became weary and disappointed. The family tension shadowed the childhood of Faulkner. Besides his mother, there were two figures that played important roles in the life of Faulkner: Phil Stone and Estelle Oldham. Phil Stone was the son of one of Maud's friends. He appreciated young Faulkner's talent in literature and became the latter's mentor and friend for years. Estelle Oldham was Faulkner's childhood sweetheart, who appeared repeatedly in the latter's stories and poetry. It is even believed that without the despair Estelle would cause in Faulkner, he would have followed his original desire to become a railroad engineer and never have metamorphosed into William Faulkner the writer.

In 1915, Faulkner dropped out of high school and worked briefly in his grandfather's bank. In 1918, Estelle married another man and Faulkner was in desperation. To battle with depression, Faulkner left Oxford for a while. First, he went to New Haven where his best friend Phil Stone was in the Yale law school; then he enlisted in the British Royal Flying Corps and had basic training in Canada. However, before he had a chance to see any action and practice a solo flight, the war ended. Eager to earn some respect, Faulkner wore the illegitimate uniform of an Air Force Lieutenant and claimed a feigned wound on his returning to Oxford. After the war he studied literature at the University of Mississippi, where he wrote poems and drew cartoons for the university's humor magazine. In 1920, he left the university without taking a degree. In the next a few years, Faulkner drifted from one job to another, searching for an identity: he used to be a bookstore clerk, an undutiful postmaster, and a bohemian poet.

In 1924, Faulkner published *The Marble Faun*, a volume of poetry. It did not gain success. In 1925, he went to New Orleans and mingled with literary people there. Sherwood Anderson became his mentor, who encouraged him to develop his own style and concentrate on prose. Faulkner then produced his first novel, *Soldier's Pay*, and got it published in 1926 with the help of Anderson. It is a melancholy story in the vein of the "lost generation": an injured soldier comes home to die and finds himself abandoned by his beloved and betrayed by his friend. This first full-length novel of Faulkner is always regarded as his literary manifestation of his hollowness after the loss of Estelle. Faulkner's next novel was *Mosquitoes* (1927), a satire on the artists and intellectuals in New Orleans. In 1929, Faulkner married Estelle, who had been divorced and returned to Oxford. The next year he bought a traditional southern house in Oxford, and named it Rowan Oak.

With the publication of *Sartoris* (1929), Faulkner found his own themes and setting, because it was the first of fifteen novels set in Yoknapatawpha County, a fictional region of Mississippi, and actually Lafayette County in reality. The Chickasaw Indian term means "water passes slowly through flatlands." The Yoknapatawpha saga recorded the decline of the Compson, Sartoris, Benbow, and McCaslin families, representatives of the Old South, and the rise of the Snopes family. *The Sound and the Fury* (1929), Faulkner's first masterwork, introduces the significant but decadent Compson family in a remarkably structured story. The novel won the author both literary recognition and economic reward. *As I Lay Dying* (1930) tells the illness, death, and burial of a bitter woman, Addie Bundren. The book is remarkable for its interior monologues and shifting perspectives and the characters are well developed. *Sanctuary* (1931), a book dedicated to Sherwood Anderson, is a sadistic horror story: a young woman is raped by a murderer and she finds sanctuary in a brothel. *Light in August* (1932) is again a book filled with horrors. Through the stories of Lena Grove, a pregnant woman in search of the father of her child, and Joe Christmas, a man tortured by the question of his mixed-race parentage, the book presents the contrast of positive and negative forces of life, the racial hatred in the South, and the violent and immoral relations between men and women. *Absalom, Absalom!* (1936) is generally considered Faulkner's masterpiece. It tells the tragic downfall of the dynastic desires of the planter Colonel Sutpen, with a setting in early 19th-century Jefferson. The book records a range of voices and vocabularies, trying to unknot the mysteries of Thomas Sutpen's life. The other Yoknapatawpha novels include *The Unvanquished* (1938), *The Wild Palms* (1939), *The Hamlet* (1940), etc. Many of the characters and settings of Yoknapatawpha cycle appear in stories collected in books such as *Go Down, Moses* (1942), *The Portable Faulkner* (1946), *Big Woods* (1955), etc.

To earn money and support the family, Faulkner had worked intermittently in Hollywood as a script writer since 1930s. He wrote mostly for director Howard Hawks and they cooperated in the films *To Have and Have Not* (1944), based freely on Ernest Hemingway's novel, and *The Big Sleep* (1946), based on Raymond Chandler's novel.

In 1949, Faulkner was awarded the Nobel Prize for Literature.

On July 6, 1962, Faulkner died of a coronary occlusion.

Brief Introduction and Appreciation

"A Rose for Emily" is perhaps Faulkner's most popular and most anthologized short story. It first appeared on the magazine *Saturday Evening Post* in 1930 and was later reprinted in his collection of stories *These Thirteen* in 1931, *Collected Stories* in 1950, and *Selected Short Stories* in 1961. It is a story full of gothic elements: a decaying mansion, a corpse, a murder, and a mysterious servant. Narrated through a third person's point of view, the story tells the tragic life of Miss Emily Grierson, a lonely aristocratic woman who poisons her lover and sleeps with his corpse in her bedroom for many years.

The story is divided into five sections and flashback is adopted to disclose the secret of the heroine. Section one starts off with Miss Emily's funeral: the whole town went to her funeral because she was sort of "a fallen monument" and her extremely secluded life in the past ten years aroused great curiosity to the town people, especially women. Ingeniously, the author does not continue his narration of the discovery in the funeral, which the reader expects; instead, he traces back to an interlude in Miss Emily's life to indicate the town's relation to her. In the year when Emily's father died, the mayor of the time Colonel Sartoris remitted her taxes. When the age of Colonel Sartoris was over and the mayor of a new generation asked her to pay her taxes, Miss Emily stubbornly refused. This section ends with the interesting dialogue between the deputation asking for taxes and the aloof aristocratic woman.

Section two begins with another event in Emily's life: the mysterious smell. It was two years after her father's death and shortly after the disappearance of her sweetheart that the town people began to be troubled by the terrible smell from Emily's house. However, no one could find the truth of the smell, nor could anybody persuade her to stop it, until the smell itself faded out. Leaving this suspense unsolved, the author now begins to tell us the story of Miss Emily as a young girl shadowed by a patriarchal and overwhelming father. Her father drove away all the possible suitors of Emily and made her a spinster at the age of thirty. Then the father died, leaving her nothing but the house. This section ends with the narrator's comment on Emily's natural response to the death of her father.

In the third section, we are introduced to the change of Miss Emily (she cut her hair short) and her acquaintance with Homer Barron, a "Yankee" and a foreman. It seemed that Miss Emily was fond of Homer because they spent every Sunday afternoon together. The town began to have gossip on them and some people even pitied Emily for her reckless choice. Miss Emily, however, "carried her head high enough" and paid no attention to the gossip. Again, the author stops writing the unconventional romance of Miss Emily and starts to tell another strange interlude in her life: the arsenic. About a year after she got to know Homer, Miss Emily went to the drugstore and demanded to buy some poison. Although the druggist inquired the usage of the poison again and again, Miss Emily refused to give an answer.

The fourth section describes the town's reaction to Miss Emily's relationship with Homer Barron, who declared himself "not a marrying man." People in the town now regarded the Sunday afternoon scene of Miss Emily and Homer "in the yellow-wheeled buggy" as a disgrace to the town and tried to intervene. At first, a minister was sent to Miss Emily; he returned and refused to go back. Then, the minister's wife wrote to Miss Emily's estranged relatives in Alabama and Emily's two female cousins arrived. Finally, the town was sure of the marriage of Emily and Homer. A series of events happened then: first, Homer disappeared for some time; second, the female cousins went back to Alabama; third, Homer went back to Miss Emily. And according to the narrator, that was the last time Homer appeared in the town. The rest of this section tells the lonely life of Miss Emily after her short romance and her death at the age of seventy-four.

The last section brings us back to the funeral of Miss Emily. This section involves mystery as well as discovery. The mystery is the disappearance of Miss Emily's Negro servant, who opened the door for the town and was not seen again. The discovery is a terrifying fact which may explain all suspense in the previous passages: Miss Emily intentionally killed her lover who loved freedom more than her, and had slept with his corpse for many years.

One characteristic of this work is the author's mastery of narration. Instead of telling the story chronologically, the author makes the story run in a cycle: the beginning is the ending and the ending echoes the beginning. In order to make up all the gaps and know the whole story, the reader has to pay great attention to all the details in the previous passages. Another celebrated feature of this work is symbolism. For example, the detailed description of the decayed house is an echo to the depiction of the physical and mental deterioration of Miss Emily, who in turn can also be a symbol of the Old South. The house loses its magnificence for the lack of renovation, while Miss Emily loses her beauty for the lack of love and care.

Although the author modestly described "A Rose for Emily" a "ghost story," many scholars are fascinated by the versatility of this masterpiece and various ways of appreciation are suggested: it can be read as a tragedy of a woman; a Gothic horror tale; an allegory of the relations between North and South; a study in abnormal psychology, etc.

Selected Reading

A Rose for Emily
I

When Miss Emily Grierson died, our whole town went to her funeral: the men through a sort of respectful affection for a fallen monument, the women mostly out of curiosity to see the inside of her house, which no one save an old manservant—a combined gardener and cook—had seen in at least ten years.

It was a big, squarish frame house that had once been white, decorated with cupolas and spires and scrolled balconies in the heavily lightsome style of the seventies, set on what had once been our most select street. But garages and cotton gins had encroached and obliterated even the august names of that neighborhood; only Miss Emily's house was left, lifting its stubborn and coquettish decay above the cotton wagons and the gasoline pumps—an eyesore among eyesores. And now Miss Emily had gone to join the representatives of those august names where they lay in the cedar-bemused cemetery among the ranked and anonymous graves of Union and Confederate soldiers who fell at the battle of Jefferson[1].

Alive, Miss Emily had been a tradition, a duty, and a care; a sort of hereditary obligation upon the town, dating from that day in 1894 when Colonel Sartoris[2], the mayor—he who fathered the edict that no Negro woman should appear on the streets without an apron—remitted her taxes, the dispensation dating from the death of her father on into perpetuity. Not that Miss Emily would have accepted charity. Colonel Sartoris invented an involved tale to the effect[3] that Miss Emily's father had loaned money to the town, which the town, as a matter of business, preferred this way of repaying. Only a man of Colonel Sartoris' generation and thought could have invented it, and only a woman could have believed it.

When the next generation, with its more modern ideas, became mayors and aldermen[4], this arrangement created some little dissatisfaction. On the first of the year they mailed her a tax notice. February came, and there was no reply. They wrote her a formal letter, asking her to call at the sheriff's office at her convenience. A week later the mayor wrote her himself, offering to call or to send his car for her, and received in reply a note on paper of an archaic shape, in a thin, flowing calligraphy in faded ink, to the effect that she no longer went out at all. The tax notice was also enclosed, without comment.

They called a special meeting of the Board of Aldermen. A deputation waited upon her, knocked at the door through which no visitor had passed since she ceased giving china-painting lessons eight or ten years earlier. They were admitted by the old Negro into a dim hall from which a stairway mounted into still more shadow. It smelled of dust and disuse—a close, dank smell. The Negro led them into the parlor. It was furnished in heavy, leather-covered furniture. When the Negro opened the blinds of one window, they could see that the leather was cracked; and when they sat down, a faint dust rose sluggishly about their thighs, spinning with slow motes in the single sun-ray. On a tarnished gilt easel before the fireplace stood a crayon portrait of Miss Emily's father.

They rose when she entered—a small, fat woman in black, with a thin gold chain descending to her waist and vanishing into her belt, leaning on an ebony cane with a tarnished gold head. Her skeleton was small and spare; perhaps that was why what would have been merely plumpness in another was obesity in her. She looked bloated, like a body long submerged in motionless water, and of that pallid hue. Her eyes, lost in the fatty ridges of her face, looked like two small pieces of coal pressed into a lump of dough as they moved from one face to another while the visitors stated their errand.

She did not ask them to sit. She just stood in the door and listened quietly until the spokesman came to a stumbling halt. Then they could hear the invisible watch ticking at the end of the gold chain.

Her voice was dry and cold. "I have no taxes in Jefferson. Colonel Sartoris explained it to me. Perhaps one of you can gain access to the city records and satisfy yourselves."

"But we have. We are the city authorities, Miss Emily. Didn't you get a notice from the sheriff, signed by him?"

"I received a paper, yes," Miss Emily said. "Perhaps he considers himself the sheriff ... I have no taxes in Jefferson."

"But there is nothing on the books to show that, you see. We must go by the—"

"See Colonel Sartoris. I have no taxes in Jefferson."

"But, Miss Emily—"

"See Colonel Sartoris." (Colonel Sartoris had been dead almost ten years.) "I have no taxes in Jefferson. Tobe!" The Negro appeared. "Show these gentlemen out."

I

So she vanquished them, horse and foot[5], just as she had vanquished their fathers thirty years before about the smell. That was two years after her father's death and a short time after her sweetheart—the one we believed would marry her—had deserted her. After her father's death she went out very little; after her sweetheart went away, people hardly saw her at all. A few of the ladies had the temerity to call, but were not received, and the only sign of life about the place was the Negro man—a young man then—going in and out with a market basket.

"Just as if a man—any man—could keep a kitchen properly, " the ladies said; so they were not surprised when the smell developed. It was another link between the gross, teeming world and the high and mighty Griersons.

A neighbor, a woman, complained to the mayor, Judge Stevens, eighty years old.

"But what will you have me do about it, madam?" he said.

"Why, send her word to stop it," the woman said. "Isn't there a law?"

"I'm sure that won't be necessary," Judge Stevens said. "It's probably just a snake or a rat that nigger of hers killed in the yard. I'll speak to him about it."

The next day he received two more complaints, one from a man who came in diffident deprecation. "We really must do something about it, Judge. I'd be the last one in the world to bother Miss Emily, but we've got to do something." That night the Board of Aldermen met—three graybeards and one younger man, a member of the rising generation.

"It's simple enough," he said. "Send her word to have her place cleaned up. Give her a certain time to do it in, and if she don't..."

"Dammit, sir," Judge Stevens said, "will you accuse a lady to her face of smelling bad?"

So the next night, after midnight, four men crossed Miss Emily's lawn and slunk about the house like burglars, sniffing along the base of the brickwork and at the cellar openings while one of them performed a regular sowing motion with his hand out of a sack slung from his shoulder. They broke open the cellar door and sprinkled lime there, and in all the outbuildings. As they recrossed the lawn, a window that had been dark was lighted and Miss Emily sat in it, the light behind her, and her upright torso motionless as that of an idol. They crept quietly across the lawn and into the shadow of the locusts that lined the street. After a week or two the smell went away.

That was when people had begun to feel really sorry for her. People in our town, remembering how old lady Wyatt, her great-aunt, had gone completely crazy at last, believed that the Griersons held themselves a little too high for what they really were. None of the young men were quite good enough for Miss Emily and such. We had long thought of them as a tableau, Miss Emily a slender figure in white in the background, her father a spraddled silhouette in the foreground, his back to her and clutching a horsewhip, the two of them framed by the back-flung front door. [6] So when she got to be thirty and was still single, we were not pleased exactly, but vindicated; even with insanity in the family she wouldn't have turned down all of her chances if they had really materialized.

When her father died, it got about that the house was all that was left to her; and in a way, people were glad. At last they could pity Miss Emily. Being left alone, and a pauper, she had become humanized. Now she too would know the old thrill and the old despair of a penny more or less.

The day after his death all the ladies prepared to call at the house and offer condolence and aid, as is our custom. Miss Emily met them at the door, dressed as usual and with no trace of grief on her face. She told them that her father was not dead. She did that for three days, with the ministers calling on her, and the doctors, trying to persuade her to let them dispose of the body. Just as they were about to resort to law and force, she broke down, and they buried her father quickly.

We did not say she was crazy then. We believed she had to do that. We remembered all the young men her father had driven away, and we knew that with nothing left, she would have to cling to that which had robbed her, [7] as people will.

III

She was sick for a long time. When we saw her again, her hair was cut short, making her look like a girl, with a vague resemblance to those angels in colored church windows—sort of tragic and serene.

The town had just let the contracts for paving the sidewalks, and in the summer after her father's death they began the work. The construction company came with niggers and mules and machinery, and a foreman named Homer Barron, a Yankee[8]—a big, dark, ready man, with a big voice and eyes lighter than his face. The little boys would follow in groups to hear him cuss the niggers, and the niggers singing in time to the rise and fall of picks. Pretty soon he knew everybody in town. Whenever you heard a lot of laughing anywhere about the square, Homer Barron would be in the center of the group. Presently we began to see him and Miss Emily on Sunday afternoons driving in the yellow-wheeled buggy and the matched team of bays from the livery stable.

At first we were glad that Miss Emily would have an interest, because the ladies all said, "Of course a Grierson would not think seriously of a Northerner, a day laborer." But there were still others, older people, who said that even grief could not cause a real lady to forget *noblesse oblige*[9]—without calling it *noblesse oblige*. They just said, "Poor Emily. Her kinsfolk should come to her." She had some kin in Alabama; but years ago her father had fallen out with them over the estate of old lady Wyatt, the crazy woman, and there was no communication between the two families. They had not even been represented at the funeral.

And as soon as the old people said, "Poor Emily," the whispering began. "Do you suppose it's really so?" they said to one another. "Of course it is. What else could..." This behind their hands; rustling of craned silk and satin behind jalousies closed upon the sun of Sunday afternoon as the thin, swift clop-clop-clop of the matched team passed: "Poor Emily."

She carried her head high enough—even when we believed that she was fallen. It was as if she demanded more than ever the recognition of her dignity as the last Grierson; as if it had wanted that touch of earthiness to reaffirm her imperviousness. Like when she bought the rat poison, the arsenic. That was over a year after they had begun to say "Poor Emily," and while the two female cousins were visiting her.

"I want some poison," she said to the druggist. She was over thirty then, still a slight woman, though thinner than usual, with cold, haughty black eyes in a face the flesh of which was strained across the temples and about the eyesockets as you imagine a lighthouse-keeper's face ought to look. "I want some poison," she said.

"Yes, Miss Emily. What kind? For rats and such? I'd recom—"

"I want the best you have. I don't care what kind."

The druggist named several. "They'll kill anything up to an elephant. But what you want is—"

"Arsenic," Miss Emily said. "Is that a good one?"

"Is ...arsenic? Yes, ma'am. But what you want—"

"I want arsenic."

The druggist looked down at her. She looked back at him, erect, her face like a strained flag. "Why, of course," the druggist said. "If that's what you want. But the law requires you to tell what you are going to use it for."

Miss Emily just stared at him, her head tilted back in order to look him eye for eye, until he looked away and went and got the arsenic and wrapped it up. The Negro delivery boy brought her the package; the druggist didn't come back. When she opened the package at home there was written on the box, under the skull and bones: "For rats."

IV

So the next day we all said, "She will kill herself"; and we said it would be the best thing. When she had first begun to be seen with Homer Barron, we had said, "She will marry him." Then we said, "She will persuade him yet," because Homer himself had remarked—he liked men, and it was known that he drank with the younger men in the Elks' Club—that he was not a marrying man. Later we said, "Poor Emily" behind the jalousies as they passed on Sunday afternoon in the glittering buggy, Miss Emily with her head high and Homer Barron with his hat cocked and a cigar in his teeth, reins and whip in a yellow glove.

Then some of the ladies began to say that it was a disgrace to the town and a bad example to the young people. The men did not want to interfere, but at last the ladies forced the Baptist minister[10]—Miss Emily's people were Episcopal[11]—to call upon her. He would never divulge what happened during that interview, but he refused to go back again. The next Sunday they again drove about the streets, and the following day the minister's wife wrote to Miss Emily's relations in Alabama.

So she had blood-kin under her roof again and we sat back to watch developments. At first nothing happened. Then we were sure that they were to be married. We learned that Miss Emily had been to the jeweler's and ordered a man's toilet set in silver, with the letters H. B. on each piece. Two days later we learned that she had bought a complete outfit of men's clothing, including a nightshirt, and we said, "They are married." We were really glad. We were glad because the two female cousins were even more Grierson than Miss Emily had ever been.

So we were not surprised when Homer Barron—the streets had been finished some time since—was gone. We were a little disappointed that there was not a public blowing-off, but we believed that he had gone on to prepare for Miss Emily's coming, or to give her a chance to get rid of the cousins. (By that time it was a cabal, and we were all Miss Emily's allies to help circumvent the cousins.) Sure enough, after another week they departed. And, as we had expected all along, within three days Homer Barron was back in town. A neighbor saw the Negro man admit him at the kitchen door at dusk one evening.

And that was the last we saw of Homer Barron. And of Miss Emily for some time. The Negro man went in and out with the market basket, but the front door remained closed. Now and then we would see her at a window for a moment, as the men did that night when they sprinkled the lime, but for almost six months she did not appear on the streets. Then we knew that this was to be expected too; as if that quality of her father which had thwarted her woman's life so many times had been too virulent and too furious to die.

When we next saw Miss Emily, she had grown fat and her hair was turning gray. During the next few years it grew grayer and grayer until it attained an even pepper-and-salt iron-gray, when it ceased turning. Up to the day of her death at seventy-four it was still that vigorous iron-gray, like the hair of an active man.

From that time on her front door remained closed, save for a period of six or seven years, when she was about forty, during which she gave lessons in china-painting. She fitted up a studio in one of the downstairs rooms, where the daughters and granddaughters of Colonel Sartoris' contemporaries were sent to her with the same regularity and in the same spirit that they were sent to church on Sundays with a twenty-five-cent piece for the collection plate. Meanwhile her taxes had been remitted.

Then the newer generation became the backbone and the spirit of the town, and the painting pupils grew up and fell away and did not send their children to her with boxes of color and tedious brushes and pictures cut from the ladies' magazines. The front door closed upon the last one and remained closed for good. When the town got free postal delivery, Miss Emily alone refused to let them fasten the metal numbers above her door and attach a mailbox to it. She would not listen to them.

Daily, monthly, yearly we watched the Negro grow grayer and more stooped, going in and out with the market basket. Each December we sent her a tax notice, which would be returned by the post office a week later, unclaimed. Now and then we would see her in one of the downstairs windows—she had evidently shut up the top floor of the house—like the carven torso of an idol in a niche, looking or not looking at us, we could never tell which. Thus she passed from generation to generation—dear, inescapable, impervious, tranquil, and perverse.

And so she died. Fell ill in the house filled with dust and shadows, with only a doddering Negro man to wait on her. We did not even know she was sick; we had long since given up trying to get any information from the Negro. He talked to no one, probably not even to her, for his voice had grown harsh and rusty, as if from disuse. [12]

She died in one of the downstairs rooms, in a heavy walnut bed with a curtain, her gray head propped on a pillow yellow and moldy with age and lack of sunlight.

V

The Negro met the first of the ladies at the front door and let them in, with their hushed, sibilant voices and their quick, curious glances, and then he disappeared. He walked right through the house and out the back and was not seen again.

The two female cousins came at once. They held the funeral on the second day, with the town coming to look at Miss Emily beneath a mass of bought flowers, with the crayon face of her father musing profoundly above the bier and the ladies sibilant and macabre; and the very old men—some in their brushed Confederate uniforms—on the porch and the lawn, talking of Miss Emily as if she had been a contemporary of theirs, believing that they had danced with her and courted her perhaps, confusing time with its mathematical progression, as the old do, to whom all the past is not a diminishing road but, instead, a huge meadow which no winter ever quite touches, divided from them now by the narrow bottle-neck of the most recent decade of years.

Already we knew that there was one room in that region above stairs which no one had seen in forty years, and which would have to be forced. They waited until Miss Emily was decently in the ground before they opened it.

The violence of breaking down the door seemed to fill this room with pervading dust. A thin, acrid pall as of the tomb seemed to lie everywhere upon this room decked and furnished as for a bridal: upon the valance curtains of faded rose color, upon the rose-shaded lights, upon the dressing table, upon the delicate array of crystal and the man's toilet things backed with tarnished silver, silver so tarnished that the monogram was obscured. Among them lay a collar and tie, as if they had just been removed, which, lifted, left upon the surface a pale crescent in the dust. Upon a chair hung the suit, carefully folded; beneath it the two mute shoes and the discarded socks.

The man himself lay in the bed.

For a long while we just stood there, looking down at the profound and fleshless grin. The body had apparently once lain in the attitude of an embrace, but now the long sleep that outlasts love, that conquers even the grimace of love, had cuckolded him. What was left of him, rotted beneath what was left of the nightshirt, had become inextricable from the bed in which he lay; and upon him and upon the pillow beside him lay that even coating of the patient and biding dust.

Then we noticed that in the second pillow was the indentation of a head. One of us lifted something from it, and leaning forward, that faint and invisible dust dry and acrid in the nostrils, we saw a long strand of iron-gray hair.

Notes:

1. Jefferson: the seat of Faulkner's fictional Yoknapatawpha county; Jefferson is clearly his home town of Oxford, Mississippi.
2. Colonel Sartoris: Sartoris appears as a major or minor character in many Faulkner short stories.
3. To the effect: with the meaning, or giving the information that...
4. aldermen: member of a county or borough council, next in rank below the mayor.
5. horse and foot: meaning completely, as in the defeat of an army's cavalry (horses) and infantry (foot).
6. This sentence implies the relationship between a tough and protective father and a delicate and obedient daughter.
7. When Miss Emily's father drove away all her suitors, he also robbed her of her freedom and happiness.
8. Yankee: inhabitant of any of the Northern States, esp. those of New England.
9. noblesse oblige: high birth obligates, or the obligation of honorable, generous, and responsible behavior associated with high rank of birth.
10. Baptist minister: a minister of a Protestant Church that believes in baptism by immersion at an age when a person is old enough to understand what the ceremony means.
11. Episcopal: the Episcopal Church, or the Anglican Church in the US and Scotland.
12. One explanation is that Miss Emily poisoned the Negro servant so that he could never speak out her secret murder.

Questions for Study and Discussion:
1. Does this story remind you of the Gothic traditions in horror tales? Find out the Gothic elements in the story and explain them.
2. Could the ending of the story be anticipated? Find out the important details that foreshadow the conclusion of the story.

3. Is this story told in a chronological way? Could you reconstruct the story in its normal order? Why is the story told in this way?

4. What is your understanding of the title?

5. What do you think happened when the Baptist minister called on Miss Emily?

6. What role does the narrator play in the story? What people and values does the narrator represent?

Part Five   The Age of Modernism and

Postmodernism (1950—1999)

Introduction

I. Historical Background

The last five decades of the twentieth century are the most perplexing and contradictory in American history. The United States ended the century triumphant, the last superpower left standing after a protracted ideological struggle with the Soviet Union. During the period, the standard of living, freedom, and opportunity Americans enjoyed became the envy of the world. The nation's scientific prowess put men on the moon and pioneered a computer revolution comparable in its impact to the invention of the printing press. American ideas and innovations had achieved an unrivaled dominant position in political, economic, and cultural affairs worldwide by the century's end.

Yet the period 1950—1999 is also one of the most socially disruptive eras in American history. Losing the first war in U.S. history traumatized the American psyche, as did the assassinations of John F. Kennedy, Martin Luther King Jr., and Robert Kennedy. The struggles for racial justice, gender equality, and sexual freedom fractured the nation. Despite great technological advances and apparent material plenty, America seemed increasingly a frustratingly dangerous and threatening place. If one dominant theme of the period was liberation—the redefinition of traditional concepts of gender, race, and class—a countertheme was the dissolution of long-esteemed sources of order and authority, necessitating an anxious search for sustaining values. In a society that increasingly seemed to lack coherence and consensus, the writers of the period became preoccupied with defining who Americans were. They reveled in an unprecedented freedom of expression but were as beset by the same underlying tensions, uncertainties, and paradoxes that their readers faced.

II. Literary Review

The period of postwar ushers in a new epoch in American literature and witnesses all kinds of literary forms' development on an unprecedented tell range and scale. In retrospect, the 1950s represents a benchmark of stability against which to measure the changes to come. The decade, at least as we nostalgically recall it, seemed the calm before the storm, an era of material prosperity, contentment, and conformity. The postwar economy supported a growing middle class who redefined the American Dream as owning a home, fitted with the latest labor-saving appliances, in burgeoning suburban America. Large families, stay-at-home mothers, and "Father Knows Best" were the norm for the culturally dominant white middle class. Despite a war in Korea, anxiety over nuclear annihilation, and anti-Communist hysteria fomented by Senator Joseph McCarthy and others, Americans during the 1950s were determined to enjoy their prosperity and their dominance in the world. Much of the serious writing during the decade challenged that complacency. The ruling aesthetic was still that of the pre-war literary modernists, including Ernest Hemingway, William Faulkner, T.S. Eliot, Ezra Pound, and Eugene O'Neill, whose final significant works appeared during the 1950s. New directions and divergent points of view began to appear from Southerners, such as Flannery O'Connor, who blended regional, grotesque, and spiritual elements into darkly comic existential works that helped revitalize the American short story. Jewish American writers such as Saul Bellow, Bernard Malamud, Isaac Bashevis Singer, and Philip Roth provided an alternative to the WASP norm. African American writers such as Ralph Ellison, James Baldwin, and Lorraine Hansberry produced innovative and searing woks on America's racial divide.

If these writers challenged the narrow and smug perspective of many Americans during the decade, more direct and extensive critiques of their values and limitations came from a number of provocative sociological and cultural studies. David Riesman's *The Lonely Crowd* (1950) anatomized American conformity, the subject also of Sloan Wilson's novel *The Man in the Gray Flannel Suit*(1955). C.Wright Mills's *White Collar* (1951) assessed the American middle class, while his *The Power Elite* (1956) suggested that the control of America rested in a powerful corporate, military, and political cadre. Paul Goodman's *Growing Up Absurd* (1959) analyzed the contradictions faced by the young in a materially oriented but spiritually empty society. Youthful angst and alienation in a world dominated by adult "phoniness" were the subjects of J.D. Salinger's iconic 1950s novel *The Catcher in the Rye* (1951). Rebellion and protest over accepted American values and conventional literary methods formed the agenda of the Beats, a collection of New York and San Francisco writers including Jack Kerouac, Allen Ginsberg, Lawrence Ferlinghetti, and Gary Snyder, who became the precursors of the counterculture of the 1960s. Ginsberg's *Howl* (1956) and Kerouac's *On the Road* (1957) were milestone works of dissent from accepted societal norms that also expressed an experimental aesthetic of spontaneity and personal intensity in opposition to the detached formalism of the literary modernists. By decade's end, a spirit of opposition, new viewpoints, and experimental modes of expression were coalescing to produce the cultural revolution of the 1960s.

Bounded by the presidential elections of John F. Kennedy and Richard M. Nixon, dominated by the civil rights movement, opposition to the war in Vietnam, and a youth culture that challenged social norms with drug use and sexual experimentation, the 1960s were among the most expressive and experimental years in American literary history. In 1959, Grove Press's publication of D. H. Lawrence's *Lady Chatterley's Lover* effectively ended censorship in America, a harbinger of the subsequent decade's assault on traditional values. While some novelists such as John Cheever and John Updike relied on realistic methods to survey the social and personal dislocations of the period, others pursued a more radical approach. Joseph Heller's *Catch-22* (1961) and Kurt Vonnegut's *Slaughterhouse-Five* (1969) reimagined World War II as absurdist comedy, while Ken Kesey's *One Flew over the Cuckoo's Nest* (1962) inverted accepted views of madness and sanity and celebrated the heroism of the nonconformist rebel. Others, such as John Barth, John Hawkes, Robert Coover, Thomas Pynchon, and Donald Barthelme, destabilized novelistic conventions with a self-reflective, ironic antirealism that established the basic outlines of postmodernism. Still others undermined the distinction between the novel and nonfiction, between subjective and objective representation, in works such as Truman Capote's *In Cold Blood* (1966) and Norman Mailer's *Armies of the Night* (1968).

In poetry, Robert Lowell's intensely personal *Life Studies* (1959) challenged modernist detachment and initiated a new introspective, intimately autobiographical mode of expression of the so-called confessional poets, who included W. D. Snodgrass, Anne Sexton, John Berryman, and Sylvia Plath. Other poets, such as Gwendolyn Brooks, Denise Levertov, and Adrienne Rich, emphasized public rather than private themes, confronting the major political, gender, and racial issues of the period.

In drama, Edward Albee became the most prominent of a new generation of playwrights, who created one of the most experimental periods in American theater history. Strongly influenced by European drama, particularly the theater of the absurd, Albee and playwrights such as Jack Gelber and Arthur Kopit challenged audiences with both strong social and psychological content and symbolic, nonrepresentational techniques. The creative energy of American drama shifted during the decade from Broadway to off-Broadway and off-off-Broadway venues and to experimental and regional companies that served as launch pads for the careers of playwrights such as LeRoi Jones (Amiri Baraka), Ed Bullins, Sam Shepard, and Lanford Wilson.

If the 1960s saw an explosion of creative energy released by new modes of expression and imaginative responses to the crisis and contradictions of American experience, the 1970s were years of consolidation of energies and a transition to the more socially conservative, self-centered 1980s and 1990s, as once-radical ideas joined with, but became diluted in, the main current of American thought. Increasingly, the writer as college faculty member came to dominate American literary culture. Subsidized by a teaching salary, American writers of so-called serious literature relied far less on reaching a wide popular audience. The effect was to widen the gap between highbrow and lowbrow writing, with the bestseller list dominated by less demanding formulaic entertainment. Movies and television, rather than books, increasingly became the principal means to reach a mass audience.

Among the noteworthy achievements during the 1970s were the first major imaginative assessments of the Vietnam experience and its personal and national costs, including Robert Stone's *Dog Soldiers* (1974), David Rabe's *Sticks and Bones* (1972) and *Streamers* (1976), Michael Herr's *Dispatches* (1977), Philip

Caputo's *A Rumor of War* (1977), and Tim O'Brien's *Going After Cacciato* (1978). Other fictional accomplishments of the period included Thomas Pynchon's encyclopedic rendering of World war II and its aftermath in forming modern consciousness (*Gravity's Rainbow,* 1973), E. L. Doctorow's remarkable fictional reanimation of American history at the turn of the century (*Ragtime,* 1975), and the first novels of Toni Morrison, who would become one of the few challenging literary authors to claim a wide popular audience. The major poets of the period include James Merrill and John Ashbery. In drama several important American playwrights including David Mamet, Charles Durang, and Beth Henley, achieved their initial successes.

During the 1980s and 1990s important work continued to appear from authors who remained productive throughout the entire five decades, such as Saul Bellow, Norman Mailer, Philip Roth, John Updike, and Gore Vidal. One of the most important trends was the emergence of stripped-down realism used to portray everyday American life. Labeled minimalism, it was most often associated with the short fiction of Raymond Carver. The postmodernist fabulists, such as John Barth, Thomas Pynchon, and Don DeLillo, along with the neo-realists, such as Carver, Bobbie Anne Mason, and Richard Ford, set in motion an oscillation between the centrifugal and the centripetal, between writers who tried to encompass all of the protean American experience in their works and others who sought to strip its often baffling complexities down to essentials—polarities that characterize much of the writing of the period.

American writing during the final years of the twentieth century lacked a dominating synthesizing presence of the magnitude of William Faulkner, Ernest Hemingway, or T. S. Eliot. In compensation, the diversity of ethnic and racial perspectives broadened the concept of what constitutes American experience. Toni Morrison, who in 1993 became the first American writer of color to be awarded the Nobel Prize in literature, headed the distinguished list of successful and acclaimed African American fiction writers of the period, which included Alice Walker, Ernest Gaines, John Edgar Wideman, Charles Johnson, and Terry McMillan. African American poets of note included Maya Angelou (selected to read a poem at President Bill Clinton's inauguration in 1993), Michael Harper, Audre Lord, and Rita Dove, chosen as Poet Laureate in 1993. Prominent Asian American writers included Maxine Hong Kingston, Amy Tan, David Henry Hwang, Frank Chin, Cathy Song, Garrett Hongo, and Chang-Rae Lee. Among the leading

Hispanic writers were Rolando Hinojosa, Oscar Hijuelos, Lorna Dee Cisneros, Sandra Cisneros, Julia Alvarez, and Denise Chavez. Native American writers of note included N. Scott Momaday, Leslie Marmon Silko, James Welch, and Louise Erdrich. Such writers show that their own cultural tradition have become part of the American cultural experience.

By exploring the reflexive relationship between the forms of art and the concerns of culture, by reconfiguring the relationship between margin and mainstream and among disparate groups as a two-way street, and by exploring the fluidity of experience and persistence of meaning, American writing from 1950 to 1999 bears witness to the genius and imaginative richness of these troubled times. In the chorale of narrative, no one voice or style holds absolute sway. But together they generate ever more creative ferment. Out of many differences, from the borders to the center of experience, in traditional or insurgent forms, postwar American culture is enriched by ideals of openness and the affirmative value of the individual voice. With roots of heritage extending around the world, postwar American writing flourishes as a bountiful art nourished by diversity. It joins in serving and contributing to a global ideal: the power of art to inspire recognitions and dialogues across cultures.

Bernard Malamud (1914—1986)

Life and Major Works

Bernard Malamud was born on April 26, 1914, in Brooklyn, New York, the first of Max and Bertha Fidelman Malamud's two sons. His parents, whom he described as "gentle, honest, kindly people," had come to the United States from Russia in the early 1900s and ran their own grocery store. They were not highly educated and knew very little about literature or the arts. "There were no books that I remember in the house, no records, music, pictures on the wall," Malamud said.

Bernard Malamud

Malamud liked to read and to attend a local Yiddish (the language spoken by Jews in Europe) theater. He began to try to write stories of his own.

Malamud attended high school in Brooklyn and received his bachelor's degree from the City College of New York in 1936. After graduation he worked in a factory and as a clerk at the Census Bureau in Washington, D.C. Although he wrote in his spare time, Malamud did not begin writing seriously until hearing of the horrors of the Holocaust, when the Germans, led by Adolf Hitler (1889–1945), put six million Jewish people to death during World War II (1939–45; a war in which Great Britain, France, the Soviet Union, and the United States battled Germany, Italy, and Japan). Malamud also began reading about Jewish tradition and history. In 1949 he started teaching at Oregon State University. He left this post in 1961 to teach creative writing at Bennington College in Vermont, where he remained until shortly before his death.

Malamud's first novel, *The Natural* (1952), traces the life of Roy Hobbs, an American baseball player. The book has mythic elements and explores such themes as initiation and isolation. Malamud's second novel, *The Assistant* (1957), tells the story of Morris Bober, a Jewish immigrant who owns a grocery store in Brooklyn. Although he is struggling to make ends meet, Bober hires an anti-Semitic (prejudiced against Jewish people) youth, whom he learns is homeless and on the verge of starvation. This novel shows the value of maintaining faith in the goodness of the human soul. Malamud's first collection of short stories, *The Magic Barrel* (1958), was awarded the National Book Award in 1959. Many of Malamud's best-known short stories were republished in *The Stories of Bernard Malamud* in 1983.

A New Life (1961), considered one of Malamud's most true-to-life novels, is based in part on Malamud's teaching career at Oregon State University. This work focuses on an ex-alcoholic Jew from New York City who becomes a professor at a college in the Pacific Northwest. It examines the main character's search for self-respect, while poking fun at life at a learning institution. Malamud's next novel, *The Fixer* (1966), is one of his most powerful works. The winner of both the Pulitzer Prize and the National Book Award, this book is based on the historical account of Mendel Beiliss, a Russian Jew who was accused of murdering a Christian child. With *The Tenants* (1971), Malamud returns to a New York City setting in a contrast between two writers—one Jewish and the other African American—struggling to survive in an urban ghetto (the run-down part of a city).

In *Dubin's Lives* (1979), which took Malamud over five years to write, the main character, William Dubin, attempts to create a sense of worth for himself, both as a man and as a writer. Malamud's last finished novel, *God's Grace* (1982), studies both the original Holocaust and a new, imagined Holocaust of the future. The novel is a wild, at times brilliant, at times confusing, description of a flood similar to that in the Bible story of Noah's ark.

Malamud continued to place stories in top American magazines. Mervyn Rothstein reported in the *New York Times* that Malamud said at the end of his life, "With me, it's story, story, story." In Malamud's next-to-last collection, *Rembrandt's Hat*, only one story, "The Silver Crown," deals with Jewish themes. Malamud's final, unfinished work, "The Tribe," concerns the adventures of a Russian Jewish peddler, Yozip, among the western Native American Indians. Malamud gave few interviews, but those he did grant provided the best insight into his work, as when he told Michiko Kakutani in the *New York Times*: "People say I write so much about misery, but you write about what you write best." Bernard Malamud died on March 18, 1986.

Brief Introduction and Appreciation

"The Magic Barrel" is a short story. It is a wonderful examination of one short piece of the life of a confused young Jewish Rabbi. The story was set in New York City, the story begins with an detailed and excellent description of the meager surroundings. The confused young Jewish Rabbi, named Leo, is studying to become a Rabbi. But he is in trouble finding a mate for life. So hopefully, he seeks the services of a matchmaker to assist him to find the right partner for him. The expectant service the matchmaker providing is very disappointing for Leo.

The matchmaker is a very humble and devoted fellow, named Salzman. Malamud spent a lot effort in describing the appearance, character, even very detailed slight movement of him. Although Salzman did a very good job finding an appropriate mate for Leo, yet Leo is unhappy with all of the choices. The reasons for his unsatisfaction seem to be abundant, too old, not pretty enough, or not having enough dowry. As more dates go by, Salzman's prospects turn worse. He becomes more dissatisfied with his matchmaker, and more confused of his own love-life, and even confused about himself in some ways.

To surprise us, the ending once again proved some old wisdom. No one is a better matchmaker than God. It seems that the magic barrel for each one is resting on the desk in God's office.

The story of "The Magic Barrel" is a story of an experience to learn and to grow. For Leo, he used to be certain of his life, his belief, his outlook, and his every aspect of life. He is a young man with a plan, he knows what he is doing, he knows what he wants. It is a strong belief of his traditional values instructed from his very early age. He never questions about any of them. Yet the matchmaking process disturbs his life into an upside-down condition. He is uncertain and confused of every single thing. Growth is always like this. Once one used to believe in certain philosophy, never questioned about it, thought the whole world abide by this philosophy. One day, some thing happened, and the world is no longer the one it used to be like. To see things in new perspective, and to gain more of insight into everything is what growth brings.

The story of Leo is also a reflection of the Jewish value in the American society. In such diverse culture, the Jews are no longer that traditional in thinking and behaving. Even if some of them are still acting so, sooner or later, they will encounter some things make them confuse like Leo does. With clashes of different cultures in one society, confusion, loss, hesitation, and doubt are feelings bound to be experienced. Leo is a traditional young man. Yet from the very limited description of Stella, we are certain, she is a different young lady from Leo Finkle. She seems to have forgotten all about their Jewish tradition. Both of these growths end with their affection for each other. We can foresee a come-back to the Jewish traditional culture. It may well be the purpose of Bernard Malamud, to exert an idea that a native culture is too strong to be forgotten, one way or another, the culture will have its share on you some day. It may also be the inevitable result of any kind of growth, growth is more of a journey out than a journey back. To be grown or not, one's native culture is something that can never be left behind without exerting influence on shaping your thought.

In the story, Leo planned to have a certain kind of life, yet he could not plan to meet a girl like that and to fall in love madly with her; Salzman is more organized and controlled than Leo himself. His job is to make things and certain life happen, yet he can not stop or forbid Leo from falling desperately in love with Stella; Stella, little as we know of her, may of even much less possibility to have dated and had feelings for a young man that came from her father's clients. From this, growth or return is something that few people can have control of.

Selected Reading

The Magic Barrel

Not long ago there lived in uptown New York, in a small, almost meager room, though crowded with books, Leo Finkle, a rabbinical[1] student in the Yeshivah[2] University. Finkle, after six years of study, was to be ordained in June and had been advised by an acquaintance that he might find it easier to win himself a congregation[3] if he were married. Since he had no present prospects of marriage, after two tormented days of turning it over in his mind, he called in Pinye Salzman, a marriage broker whose two-line advertisement he had read in the Forward.

The matchmaker appeared one night out of the dark fourth-floor hallway of the graystone rooming house where Finkle lived, grasping a black, strapped portfolio that had been worn thin with use. Salzman, who had been long in the business, was of slight but dignified build, wearing an old hat, and an overcoat too short and tight for him. He smelled frankly of fish, which he loved to eat, and although he was missing a few teeth, his presence was not displeasing, because of an amiable manner curiously contrasted with mournful eyes. His voice, his lips, his wisp of beard, his bony fingers were animated, but give him a moment of repose and his mild blue eyes revealed a depth of sadness, a characteristic that put Leo a little at ease although the situation, for him, was inherently tense.

He at once informed Salzman why he had asked him to come, explaining that his home was in Cleveland, and that but for his parents, who had married comparatively late in life, he was alone in the world. He had for six years devoted himself almost entirely to his studies, as a result of which, understandably, he had found himself without time for a social life and the company of young women. Therefore he thought it the better part of trial and error—of embarrassing fumbling—to call in an experienced person to advise him on these matters. He remarked in passing that the function of the marriage broker was ancient and honorable, highly approved in the Jewish community, because it made practical the necessary without hindering joy. Moreover, his own parents had been brought together by a matchmaker. They had made, if not a financially profitable marriage—since neither had possessed any worldly goods to speak of—at least a successful one in the sense of their everlasting devotion to each other. Salzman listened in embarrassed surprise, sensing a sort of apology. Later, however, he experienced a glow of pride in his work, an emotion that had left him years ago, and he heartily approved of Finkle.

The two went to their business. Leo had led Salzman to the only clear place in the room, a table near a window that overlooked the lamp-lit city. He seated himself at the matchmaker's side but facing him, attempting by an act of will to suppress the unpleasant tickle in his throat. Salzman eagerly unstrapped his portfolio and removed a loose rubber band from a thin packet of much-handled cards. As he flipped through them, a gesture and sound that physically hurt Leo, the student pretended not to see and gazed steadfastly out the window. Although it was still February, winter was on its last legs, signs of which he had for the first time in years begun to notice. He now observed the round white moon, moving high in the sky through a cloud menagerie[4], and watched with half-open mouth as it penetrated a huge hen, and dropped out of her like an egg laying itself. Salzman, though pretending through eye-glasses he had just slipped on, to be engaged in scanning the writing on the cards, stole occasional glances at the young man's distinguished face, noting with pleasure the long, severe scholar's nose, brown eyes heavy with learning, sensitive yet ascetic lips, and a certain, almost hollow quality of the dark cheeks. He gazed around at shelves upon shelves of books and let out a soft, contented sigh.

When Leo's eyes fell upon the cards, he counted six spread out in Salzman's hand.

"So few?" he asked in disappointment.

"You wouldn't believe me how much cards I got in my office," Salzman replied. "The drawers are already filled to the top, so I keep them now in a barrel, but is every girl good for a new rabbi?"

Leo blushed at this, regretting all he had revealed of himself in a curriculum vitae he had sent to Salzman. He had thought it best to acquaint him with his strict standards and specifications, but in having done so, felt he had told the marriage broker more than was absolutely necessary.

He hesitantly inquired, "Do you keep photographs of your clients on file?"

"First comes family, amount of dowry, also what kind of promises," Salzman replied, unbuttoning his tight coat and settling himself in the chair. "After comes pictures, rabbi."

"Call me Mr. Finkle. I'm not yet a rabbi."

Salzman said he would, but instead called him doctor, which he changed to rabbi when Leo was not listening too attentively.

319

Salzman adjusted his horn-rimmed spectacles, gently cleared his throat and read in an eager voice the contents of the top card:

"Sophie P. Twenty-four years. Widow one year. No children. Educated high school and two years college. Father promises eight thousand dollars. Has wonderful wholesale business. Also real estate. On the mother's side comes teachers, also one actor. Well known on Second Avenue."

Leo gazed up in surprise. "Did you say a widow?"

"A widow don't mean spoiled, rabbi. She lived with her husband maybe four months. He was a sick boy she made a mistake to marry him."

"Marrying a widow has never entered my mind."

"This is because you have no experience. A widow, especially if she is young and healthy like this girl, is a wonderful person to marry. She will be thankful to you the rest of her life. Believe me, if I was looking now for a bride, I would marry a widow."

Leo reflected, then shook his head.

Salzman hunched his shoulders in an almost imperceptible gesture of disappointment. He placed the card down on the wooden table and began to read another:

"Lily H. High school teacher. Regular. Not a substitute. Has savings and new Dodge car. Lived in Paris one year. Father is successful dentist thirty-five years. Interested in professional man. Well Americanized family. Wonderful opportunity."

"I knew her personally," said Salzman. "I wish you could see this girl. She is a doll. Also very intelligent. All day you could talk to her about books and theater and what not. She also knows current events."

"I don't believe you mentioned her age?"

"Her age?" Salzman said, raising his brows. "Her age is thirty-two years."

"Leo said after a while, "I'm afraid that seems a little too old.

Salzman let out a laugh. "So how old are you, rabbi?"

"Twenty-seven."

"So what is the difference, tell me, between twenty-seven and thirty-two? My own wife is seven years older than me. So what did I suffer? —Nothing. If Rothschild's daughter wants to marry you, would you say on account her age, no?"

"Yes," Leo said dryly.

Salzman shook off the no in the yes. "Five years don't mean a thing. I give you my word that when you will live with her for one week you will forget her age.

What does it mean five years—that she lived more and knows more than somebody who is younger? On this girl, God bless her, years are not wasted. Each one that it comes makes better the bargain."

"What subject does she teach in high school?"

"Languages. If you heard the way she speaks French, you will think it is music. I am in the business twenty-five years, and I recommend her with my whole heart. Believe me, I know what I'm talking, rabbi."

"What's on the next card?" Leo said abruptly.

Salzman reluctantly turned up the third card:

"Ruth K. Nineteen years. Honor student. Father offers thirteen thousand cash to the right bridegroom. He is a medical doctor. Stomach specialist with marvelous practice. Brother in law owns garment business. Particular people."

Salzman looked as if he had read his trump card.

"Did you say nineteen?" Leo asked with interest.

"On the dot."

"Is she attractive?" He blushed. "Pretty?"

Salzman kissed his finger tips. "A little doll. On this I give you my word. Let me call the father tonight and you will see what means pretty."

But Leo was troubled. "You're sure she's that young?"

"This I am positive. The father will show you the birth certificate."

"Are you positive there isn't something wrong with her?" Leo insisted.

"Who says there is wrong?"

"I don't understand why an American girl her age should go to a marriage broker."

A smile spread over Salzman's face.

"So for the same reason you went, she comes."

Leo flushed. "I am pressed for time."

Salzman, realizing he had been tactless, quickly explained. "The father came, not her. He wants she should have the best, so he looks around himself. When we will locate the right boy he will introduce him and encourage. This makes a better marriage than if a young girl without experience takes for herself. I don't have to tell you this."

"But don't you think this young girl believes in love?" Leo spoke uneasily.

Salzman was about to guffaw but caught himself and said soberly, "Love comes with the right person, not before."

Leo parted dry lips but did not speak. Noticing that Salzman had snatched a glance at the next card, he cleverly asked, "How is her health?"

"Perfect," Salzman said, breathing with difficulty. "Of course, she is a little lame on her right foot from an auto accident that it happened to her when she was twelve years, but nobody notices on account she is so brilliant and also beautiful."

Leo got up heavily and went to the window. He felt curiously bitter and upbraided himself for having called in the marriage broker. Finally, he shook his head.

"Why not?" Salzman persisted, the pitch of his voice rising.

"Because I detest stomach specialists."

"So what do you care what is his business? After you marry her do you need him? Who says he must come every Friday night in your house?"

Ashamed of the way the talk was going, Leo dismissed Salzman, who went home with heavy, melancholy eyes.

Though he had felt only relief at the marriage broker's departure, Leo was in low spirits the next day. He explained it as arising from Salzman's failure to produce a suitable bride for him. He did not care for his type of clientele[5]. But when Leo found himself hesitating whether to seek out another matchmaker, one more polished than Pinye, he wondered if it could be—his protestations[6] to the contrary, and although he honored his father and mother—that he did not, in essence, care for the matchmaking institution? This thought he quickly put out of mind yet found himself still upset. All day he ran around the woods—missed an important appointment, forgot to give out his laundry, walked out of a Broadway cafeteria without paying and had to run back with the ticket in his hand; had even not recognized his landlady in the street when she passed with a friend and courteously called out, "A good evening to you, Doctor Finkle." By nightfall, however, he had regained sufficient calm to sink his nose into a book and there found peace from his thoughts.

Almost at once there came a knock on the door. Before Leo could say enter, Salzman, commercial cupid, was standing in the room. His face was gray and meager, his expression hungry, and he looked as if he would expire on his feet. Yet the marriage broker managed, by some trick of the muscles, to display a broad smile.

"So good evening. I am invited?"

Leo nodded, disturbed to see him again, yet unwilling to ask the man to leave.

Beaming still, Salzman laid his portfolio on the table. "Rabbi, I got for you tonight good news."

"I've asked you not to call me rabbi. I'm still a student."

"Your worries are finished. I have for you a first-class bride."

"Leave me in peace concerning this subject." Leo pretended lack of interest.

"The world will dance at your wedding."

"Please, Mr. Salzman, no more."

"But first must come back my strength," Salzman said weakly. He fumbled with the portfolio straps[7] and took out of the leather case an oily paper bag, from which he extracted a hard, seeded roll and a small, smoked white fish. With a quick emotion of his hand he stripped the fish out of its skin and began ravenously to chew. "All day in a rush," he muttered.

Leo watched him eat.

"A sliced tomato you have maybe?" Salzman hesitantly inquired.

"No."

The marriage broker shut his eyes and ate. When he had finished he carefully cleaned up the crumbs[8] and rolled up the remains of the fish, in the paper bag. His spectacled eyes roamed the room until he discovered, amid some piles of books, a one-burner gas stove. Lifting his hat he humbly asked, "A glass of tea you got, rabbi?"

Conscience-stricken, Leo rose and brewed the tea. He served it with a chunk of lemon and two cubes of lump sugar, delighting Salzman.

After he had drunk his tea, Salzman's strength and good spirits were restored.

"So tell me rabbi," he said amiably, "you considered some more the three clients I mentioned yesterday?"

"There was no need to consider."

"Why not?"

"None of them suits me."

"What then suits you?"

Leo let it pass because he could give only a confused answer.

Without waiting for a reply, Salzman asked, "You remember this girl I talked to you—the high school teacher?"

"Age thirty-two?"

But surprisingly, Salzman's face lit in a smile. "Age twenty-nine."

Leo shot him a look. "Reduced from thirty-two?"

"A mistake," Salzman avowed. "I talked today with the dentist. He took me to his safety deposit box and showed me the birth certificate. She was twenty-nine years last August. They made her a party in the mountains where she went for her vacation. When her father spoke to me the first time I forgot to write the age and I told you thirty-two, but now I remember this was a different client, a widow."

"The same one you told me about? I thought she was twenty-four?"

"A different. Am I responsible that the world is filled with widows?"

"No, but I'm not interested in them, nor for that matter, in school teachers."

Salzman pulled his clasped hand to his breast. Looking at the ceiling he devoutly exclaimed, "Yiddishe kinder, what can I say to somebody that he is not interested in high school teachers? So what then you are interested?"

Leo flushed but controlled himself.

"In what else will you be interested," Salzman went on, "if you not interested n this fine girl that she speaks four languages and has personally in the bank ten thousand dollars? Also her father guarantees further twelve thousand. Also she has a new car, wonderful clothes, talks on all subjects, and she will give you a first-class home and children. How near do we come in our life to paradise?"

If she's so wonderful, why wasn't she married ten years ago?"

"Why?" said Salzman with a heavy laugh. "—Why? Because she is partikiler. This is why. She wants the best."

Leo was silent, amused at how he had entangled[9] himself. But Salzman had arouse his interest in Lily H., and he began seriously to consider calling on her. When the marriage broker observed how intently Leo's mind was at work on the facts he had supplied, he felt certain they would soon come to an agreement.

Late Saturday afternoon, conscious of Salzman, Leo Finkle walked with Lily Hirschorn along Riverside Drive. He walked briskly and erectly, wearing with distinction the black fedora[10] he had that morning taken with trepidation out of the dusty hat box on his closet shelf, and the heavy black Saturday coat he had thoroughly whisked clean. Leo also owned a walking stick, a present from a distant relative, but quickly put temptation aside and did not use it. Lily, petite and not unpretty, had on something signifying the approach of spring. She was au courant[11], animatedly, with all sorts of subjects, and he weighed her words and found her surprisingly sound—score another for Salzman, whom he uneasily sensed to be somewhere around, hiding perhaps high in a tree along the street, flashing the lady signals with a pocket mirror; or perhaps a cloven-hoofed Pan, piping nuptial ditties as he danced his invisible way before them, strewing wild buds on the walk and purple grapes in their path, symbolizing fruit of a union, though there was of course still none.

Lily startled Leo by remarking, "I was thinking of Mr. Salzman, a curious figure, wouldn't you say?"

Not certain what to answer, he nodded.

She bravely went on, blushing, "I for one am grateful for his introducing us. Aren't you?"

He courteously replied, "I am."

"I mean," she said with a little laugh—and it was all in good taste, to at least gave the effect of being not in bad—"do you mind that we came together so?"

He was not displeased with her honesty, recognizing that she meant to set the relationship aright, and understanding that it took a certain amount of experience in life, and courage, to want to do it quite that way. One had to have some sort of past to make that kind of beginning.

He said that he did not mind. Salzman's function was traditional and honorable —valuable for what it might achieve, which, he pointed out, was frequently nothing.

Lily agreed with a sigh. They walked on for a while and she said after a long silence, again with a nervous laugh, "Would you mind if I asked you something a little bit personal? Frankly, I find the subject fascinating." Although Leo shrugged, she went on half embarrassedly, "How was it that you came to your calling? I mean was it a sudden passionate inspiration?"

Leo, after a time, slowly replied, "I was always interested in the Law."

"You saw revealed in it the presence of the Highest?"

He nodded and changed the subject. "I understand that you spent a little time in Paris, Miss Hirschorn?"

"Oh, did Mr. Salzman tell you, Rabbi Finkle?" Leo winced but she went on, "It was ages ago and almost forgotten. I remember I had to return for my sister's wedding."

And Lily would not be put off. "When," she asked in a trembly voice, "did you become enamored of God?"

He stared at her. Then it came to him that she was talking not about Leo Finkle, but of a total stranger, some mystical figure, perhaps even passionate prophet that Salzman had dreamed up for her—no relation to the living or dead. Leo trembled with rage and weakness. The trickster had obviously sold her a bill of goods, just as he had him, who'd expected to become acquainted with a young lady of twenty-nine, only to behold, the moment he laid eyes upon her strained and anxious face, a woman past thirty-five and aging rapidly. Only his self control had kept him this long in her presence.

"I am not," he said gravely, "a talented religious person." and in seeking words to go on, found himself possessed by shame and fear. "I think," he said in a strained manner, "that I came to God not because I love Him, but because I did not."

This confession he spoke harshly because its unexpectedness shook him.

Lily wilted[12]. Leo saw a profusion of loaves of bread go flying like ducks high over his head, not unlike the winged loaves by which he had counted himself to sleep last night. Mercifully, then, it snowed, which he would not put past Salzman's machinations.

He was infuriated with the marriage broker and swore he would throw him out of the room the minute he reappeared. But Salzman did not come that night, and when Leo's anger had subsided, an unaccountable despair grew in its place. At first he thought this was caused by his disappointment in Lily, but before long it became evident that he had involved himself with Salzman without a true knowledge of his own intent. He gradually realized—with an emptiness that seized him with six hands—hat he had called in the broker to find him a bride because he was incapable of doing it himself. This terrifying insight he had derived as a result of his meeting and conversation with Lily Hirschorn. Her probing questions had somehow irritated him into revealing—to himself more than her—the true nature of his relationship to God, and from that it had come upon him, with shocking force, that apart from his parents, he had never loved anyone. Or perhaps it went the other way, that he did not love God so well as he might, because he had not loved man. It seemed to Leo that his whole life stood starkly revealed and he saw himself for the first time as he truly was—unloved and loveless. This bitter but somehow not fully unexpected revelation brought him to a point to panic, controlled only by extraordinary effort. He covered his face with his hands and cried.

The week that followed was the worst of his life. He did not eat and lost weight. His beard darkened and grew ragged. He stopped attending seminars and almost never opened a book. He seriously considered leaving the Yeshiva, although he was deeply troubled at the thought of the loss of all his years of study —saw them like pages torn from a book, strewn over the city—and at the devastating effect of this decision upon his parents. But he had lived without knowledge of himself, and never in the Five Books and all the Commentaries— mea culpa[13]—had the truth been revealed to him. He did not know where to turn, and in all this desolating loneliness there was no to whom, although he often thought of Lily but not once could bring himself to go downstairs and make the call. He became touchy and irritable, especially with his landlady, who asked him all manner of personal questions; on the other hand, sensing his own disagreeableness, he waylaid her on the stairs and apologized abjectly, until mortified, she ran from him. Out of this, however, he drew the consolation that he was a Jew and that a Jew suffered. But gradually, as the long and terrible week drew to a close, he regained his composure and some idea of purpose in life to go on as planned.

Although he was imperfect, the ideal was not. As for his quest of a bride, the thought of continuing afflicted him with anxiety and heartburn, yet perhaps with this new knowledge of himself he would be more successful than in the past. Perhaps love would now come to him and a bride to that love. And for this sanctified seeking who needed a Salzman?

The marriage broker, a skeleton with haunted eyes, returned that very night. He looked, withal, the picture of frustrated expectancy—as if he had steadfastly waited the week at Miss Lily Hirschorn's side for a telephone call that never came.

Casually coughing, Salzman came immediately to the point: "So how did you like her?"

Leo's anger rose and he could not refrain from chiding the matchmaker: "Why did you lie to me, Salzman?"

Salzman's pale face went dead white, the world had snowed on him.

"Did you not state that she was twenty-nine?' Leo insisted.

"I give you my word—"

"She was thirty-five, if a day. At least thirty-five."

"Of this don't be too sure. Her father told me—"

"Never mind. The worst of it was that you lied to her."

"How did I lie to her, tell me?"

"You told her things about me that weren't true. You made out to be more, consequently less than I am. She had in mind a totally different person, a sort of semi-mystical Wonder Rabbi."

"All I said, you was a religious man."

"I can imagine."

Salzman sighed. "This is my weakness that I have," he confessed. "My wife says to me I shouldn't be a salesman, but when I have two fine people that they would be wonderful to be married, I am so happy that I talk too much." He smiled wanly. "This is why Salzman is a poor man."

Leo's anger left him. "Well, Salzman, I'm afraid that's all."

The marriage broker fastened hungry eyes on him.

"You don't want any more a bride?"

"I do," said Leo, "but I have decided to seek her in a different way. I am no longer interested in an arranged marriage. To be frank, I now admit the necessity of premarital love. That is, I want to be in love with the one I marry."

"Love?" said Salzman, astounded. After a moment he remarked "For us, our love is our life, not for the ladies. In the ghetto they—"

"I know, I know," said Leo. "I've thought of it often. Love, I have said to myself, should be a by-product of living and worship rather than its own end. Yet for myself I find it necessary to establish the level of my need and fulfill it."

Salzman shrugged but answered, "Listen, rabbi, if you want love, this I can find for you also. I have such beautiful clients that you will love them the minute your eyes will see them."

Leo smiled unhappily. "I'm afraid you don't understand."

But Salzman hastily unstrapped his portfolio and withdrew a manila packet from it.

"Pictures," he said, quickly laying the envelope on the table.

Leo called after him to take the pictures away, but as if on the wings of the wind, Salzman had disappeared.

March came. Leo had returned to his regular routine. Although he felt not quite himself yet—lacked energy—he was making plans for a more active social life. Of course it would cost something, but he was an expert in cutting corners; and when there were no corners left he would make circles rounder. All the while Salzman's pictures had lain on the table, gathering dust. Occasionally as Leo sat studying, or enjoying a cup of tea, his eyes fell on the manila envelope, but he never opened it.

The days went by and no social life to speak of developed with a member of the opposite sex—it was difficult, given the circumstances of his situation. One morning Leo toiled up the stairs to his room and stared out the window at the city. Although the day was bright his view of it was dark. For some time he watched the people in the street below hurrying along and then turned with a heavy heart to his little room. On the table was the packet. With a sudden relentless gesture he tore it open. For a half-hour he stood by the table in a state of excitement, examining the photographs of the ladies Salzman had included. Finally, with a deep sigh he put them down. There were six, of varying degree of attractiveness, but look at them long enough and they all became Lily Hirschorn: all past their prime, all starved behind bright smiles, not a true personality in the lot. Life, despite their frantic yoohooings, had passed them by; they were pictures in a brief case that stank of fish. After a while, however, as Leo attempted to return the photographs into the envelope, he found in it another, a snapshot of the type taken by a machine for a quarter. He gazed at it a moment and let out a cry.

Her face deeply moved him. Why, he could at first not say. It gave him the impression of youth—spring flowers, yet age—a sense of having been used to the bone[14], wasted; this came from the eyes which were hauntingly[15] familiar, yet absolutely strange. He had a vivid impression that he had seen her before, but try as he might he could not place her although he could almost recall her name, as if he had read it in her own handwriting. No, this couldn't be; he would have remembered her. It was not, he affirmed, that she had an extraordinary beauty—no, though her face was attractive enough; it was that something about her moved him. Feature for feature, even some of the ladies of the photographs could do better; but she leaped forth to his heart—had lived or wanted to—more than just wanted, perhaps regretted how she had lived—had somehow deeply suffered. It could be seen in the depths of those reluctant eyes, and from the way the light enclosed and shone from her, and within her, opening realms of possibility: this was her own. Her he desired. His head ached and eyes narrowed with the intensity of his gazing, then as if an obscure fog had blown up in the mind, he experienced fear of her and was aware that he had received an impression, somehow, of evil. He shuddered saying softly, it is thus with us all. Leo brewed some tea in a small pot and sat sipping it without sugar, to calm himself. But before he had finished drinking, again with excitement he examined the face and found it good: good for Leo Finkle. Only such a one could understand him and help him seek whatever he was seeking. She might perhap, love him. How she had happened to be among the discards in Salzman's barrel he could never guess, but he knew he must urgently go find her.

Leo rushed downstairs, grabbed up the Bronx[16] telephone book, and searched for Salzman's home address. He was not listed, nor was his office. Neither was he in the Manhattan book. But Leo remembered having written down the address on a slip of paper after he had read Salzman's advertisement in the "personal" column of the Forward. He ran up to his room and tore through his papers, without luck. It was exasperating[17]. Just when he needed the matchmaker he was nowhere to be found. Fortunately Leo remembered to look in his wallet. There on a card he found his name written and a Bronx address. No phone number was listed, the reason—Leo now recalled—he had originally communicated with Salzman by letter. He got on his coat, put a hat on over his skullcap and hurried to the subway station. All the way to the far end of the Bronx he sat on the edge of his seat. He was more than once tempted to take out the picture and see if the girl's face was as he remembered it, but he refrained, allowing the snapshot to remain in his inside coat pocket, content to have her so close. When the train pulled into the station he was waiting at the door and bolted out. He quickly located the street Salzman had advertised.

The building he sought was less than a block from the subway, but it was not an office building, nor even a loft, nor a store in which one could rent office space. It was a very old tenement house. Leo found Salzman's name in pencil on a soiled tag under the bell and climbed three dark flights to his apartment. When he knocked, the door was opened by a thin, asthmatic, gray-haired woman, in felt slippers.

"Yes?" she said, expecting nothing. She listened without listening. He could have sworn he had seen her, too, before but knew it was an illusion.

"Salzman—does he live here? Pinye Salzman," he said, "the matchmaker?"

She stared at him a long minute. "Of course."

He felt embarrassed. "Is he in?"

"No." Her mouth, though left open, offered nothing more.

"The matter is urgent. Can you tell me where his office is?"

"In the air." She pointed upward.

"You mean he has no office?" Leo asked.

"In his socks."

He peered into the apartment. It was sunless and dingy, one large room divided by a half-open curtain, beyond which he could see a sagging metal bed. The near side of a room was crowded with rickety chairs, old bureaus, a three-legged table, racks of cooking utensils, and all the apparatus of a kitchen. But there was no sign of Salzman or his magic barrel, probably also a figment of the imagination. An odor of frying fish made Leo weak to the knees.

"Where is he?" he insisted. "I've got to see your husband."

At length she answered, "So who knows where he is? Every time he thinks a new thought he runs to a different place. Go home, he will find you."

"Tell him Leo Finkle."

She gave no sign she had heard.

He walked downstairs, depressed.

But Salzman, breathless, stood waiting at his door.

Leo was astounded and overjoyed. "How did you get here before me?"

"I rushed."

"Come inside."

They entered. Leo fixed tea, and a sardine sandwich for Salzman. As they were drinking he reached behind him for the packet of pictures and handed them to the marriage broker.

Salzman put down his glass and said expectantly, "You found somebody you like?"

"Not among these."

The marriage broker turned away.

"Here is the one I want." Leo held forth the snapshot.

Salzman slipped on his glasses and took the picture into his trembling hand. He turned ghastly and let out a groan.

"What's the matter?" cried Leo.

"Excuse me. Was an accident this picture. She isn't for you."

Salzman frantically shoved the manila[18] packet into his portfolio[19]. He thrust[20] the snapshot into his pocket and fled down the stairs.

Leo, after momentary paralysis, gave chase and cornered the marriage broker in the vestibule[21]. The landlady made hysterical outcries but neither of them listened.

"Give me back the picture, Salzman."

"No." The pain in his eyes was terrible.

"Tell me who she is then."

"This I can't tell you. Excuse me."

He made to depart, but Leo, forgetting himself, seized the matchmaker by his tight coat and shook him frenziedly.

"Please," sighed Salzman. "Please."

Leo ashamedly let him go. "Tell me who she is," he begged. "It's very important for me to know."

"She is not for you. She is a wild one—wild, without shame. This is not a bride for a rabbi."

"What do you mean wild?"

"Like an animal. Like a dog. For her to be poor was a sin. This is why to me she is dead now."

"In God's name, what do you mean?"

"Her I can't introduce to you," Salzman cried.

"Why are you so excited?"

"Why, he asks," Salzman said, bursting into tears. "This is my baby, my Stella, she should burn in hell."

Leo hurried up to bed and hid under the covers. Under the covers he thought his life through. Although he soon fell asleep he could not sleep her out of his mind. He woke, beating his breast. Though he prayed to be rid of her, his prayers went unanswered. Through days of torment he endlessly struggled not to love her; fearing success, he escaped it. He then concluded to convert her to goodness, himself to God. The idea alternately nauseated[22] and exalted him.

He perhaps did not know that he had come to a final decision until he encountered Salzman in a Broadway caferia. He was sitting alone at a rear table, sucking the bony remains of a fish. The marriage broker appeared haggard[23], and transparent to the point of vanishing.

Salzman looked up at first without recognizing him. Leo had grown a pointed beard and his eyes were weighted with wisdom.

"Salzman," he said, "love has at last come to my heart."

"Who can love from a picture?" mocked the marriage broker.

"It is not impossible."

"If you can love her, then you can love anybody. Let me show you some new clients that they just sent me their photographs. One is a little doll."

"Just her I want," Leo murmured.

"Don't be a fool, doctor. Don't bother with her.

"Put me in touch with her, Salzman," Leo said humbly. "Perhaps I can be of service."

Salzman had stopped eating and Leo understood with emotion that it was now arranged.

Leaving the cafeteria, he was, however, afflicted by a tormenting suspicion that Salzman had planned it all to happen this way. Leo was informed by letter that she would meet him on a certain corner, and she was there one spring night, waiting under a street lamp. He appeared, carrying a small bouquet of violets and rosebuds. Stella stood by the lamppost, smoking. She wore white with red shoes, which fitted his expectations, although in a troubled moment he had imagined the dress red, and only the shoes white. She waited uneasily and shyly. From afar he saw that her eyes—clearly her father's—were filled with desperate innocence. He pictured, in her, his own redemption. Violins and lit candles revolved in the sky. Leo ran forward with flowers outthrust[24].

Around the corner, Salzman, leaning against a wall, chanted prayers for the dead.

1958

Notes:

1. rabbinical: pertaining to rabbis, pertaining to Jewish laws and teachings
2. Yeshivah: religious learning institution (Judaism)
3. congregation: the members of a church or synogogue
4. menagerie: zoo, collection of strange or exotic animals, animal exhibit; diverse combination of things
5. clientele: customer base, group of customers
6. protestations: objection; opposition; formal declaration, solemn assertion
7. straps: thin strip of flexible material, band, strip
8. crumbs: exclamation of surprise or astonishment
9. entangled: embroiled, involved; enmeshed, ensnared
10. fedora: type of hat
11. au courant: (French) "in the current"
12. wilted: wither, become limp, lose freshness; lose spirit; weaken; become weak
13. mea culpa: official acknowledgment of fault or error (Latin for "my fault", "my mistake")
14. used to the bone: used up, tired and weaked
15. hauntingly: repeatedly; difficult to ignore or forget

16. Bronx: a borough in the north-east of New York City

17. exasperating: infuriating, annoying, irritating

18. manila: a kind of material from manila hemp

19. portfolio: a portable case for holding material, such as loose papers, photographs, or drawings

20. thrust: push (something or someone) suddenly or violently in the specified direction

21. vestibule: an antechamber, hall, or lobby next to the outer door of a building

22 nauseated: feeling nausea; feeling about to vomit

23. haggard: tired, worn, gaunt

24. outthrust: to extend or cause to extend outward

Questions for Study and Discussion:

1. Why would Salzman introduce such kind of girls like widow, handicapped or high aged to Leo?

2. If Salzman did not lie to Leo and Lily, could they have the opportunity to meet?

3. What made Leo an unloved and loveless man, and why could he regain his desire to love after a week's depression?

4. Do you consider love to be a by-product of living and worship or a thing having its own end? Give your explanation.

5. Do you think the introduction of Stella to Leo Finkle is a setup of Salzman? Explain the reasons.

6. Why would Leo so attracted by the photo? Do you think this situation would occur in common people?

7. What did Stella do in the past which made her a demon in her father's eyes?

8. What was Salzman chanting prayer for at the end of the story?

9. How do you think the prospect of the love affair between Leo and Stella?

Saul Bellow (1915—2005)

Life and Major Works

Saul Bellow was brought up in a Jewish household and fluent in Yiddish—which influenced his energetic English style—he was representative of the Jewish American writers whose works became central to American literature after World War II.

Bellow's parents emigrated in 1913 from Russia to Montreal. When he was nine they moved to Chicago. He attended the University of Chicago and Northwestern University (B.S., 1937) and afterward combined writing with a teaching career at various universities, including the University of Minnesota, Princeton University, New York University, Bard College, the University of Chicago, and Boston University.

Saul Bellow

Bellow won a reputation among a small group of readers with his first two novels, *Dangling Man* (1944), a story in diary form of a man waiting to be inducted into the army, and *The Victim* (1947), a subtle study of the relationship between a Jew and a Gentile, each of whom becomes the other's victim. *The Adventures of Augie March* (1953) brought wider acclaim and won the National Book Award (1954). It is a picaresque story of a poor Jewish youth from Chicago, his progress—sometimes highly comic—through the world of the 20th century, and his attempts to make sense of it. In this novel Bellow employed for the first time a loose, breezy style in conscious revolt against the preoccupation of writers of that time with perfection of form.

Henderson the Rain King (1959) continued the picaresque approach in its tale of an eccentric American millionaire on a quest in Africa. *Seize the Day* (1956), a novella, is a unique treatment of a failure in a society where the only success is success. He also wrote a volume of short stories, *Mosby's Memoirs* (1968), and *To Jerusalem and Back* (1976) about a trip to Israel.

In his later novels and novellas—*Herzog* (1964; National Book Award, 1965), *Mr. Sammler's Planet* (1970; National Book Award, 1971), *Humboldt's Gift* (1975; Pulizer Prize, 1976), *The Dean's December* (1982), *More Die of Heartbreak* (1987), *A Theft* (1989), *The Bellarosa Connection* (1989), and *The Actual* (1997)—Bellow arrived at his most characteristic vein. The heroes of these works are often Jewish intellectuals whose interior monologues range from the sublime to the absurd. At the same time, their surrounding world, peopled by energetic and incorrigible realists, acts as a corrective to their intellectual speculations. It is this combination of cultural sophistication and the wisdom of the streets that constitutes Bellow's greatest originality.

Brief Introduction and Appreciation

One way of honoring Bellow while continuing to tangle with him critically might be to point readers to his Nobel Prize Acceptance Speech, from 1976.

Amongst the various "noble" sentiments he offers in the lecture, Bellow makes a pretty specific point about the function of character in contemporary writing. He tangles with Alain Robbe-Grillet's claim that the novel of bourgeois individualism is "obsolete" because in the latter half of the 20th century individuals are less important than ideas, systems, processes. Here is his quote from Robbe-Grillet's essay On Several "Obsolete Notions":

"Fifty years of disease, the death notice signed many times over by the serious essayists," says Robbe-Grillet, "yet nothing has managed to knock it ["character"] off the pedestal on which the 19th century had placed it. It is a mummy now, but one still enthroned with the same phony majesty, among the values revered by traditional criticism."

Bellow's lecture defends complex human character as the subject of literature, whose death is rather prematurely announced by Robbe-Grillet and others, beginning in the 1960s.

"And art and literature—what of them? Well, there is a violent uproar but we are not absolutely dominated by it. We are still able to think, to discriminate, and to feel. The purer, subtler, higher activities have not succumbed to fury or to nonsense. Not yet. Books continue to be written and read. It may be more difficult to reach the whirling mind of a modern reader but it is possible to cut through the noise and reach the quiet zone. In the quiet zone we may find that he is devoutly waiting for us. When complications increase, the desire for essentials increases too. The unending cycle of crises that began with the First World War has formed a kind of person, one who has lived through terrible, strange things, and in whom there is an observable shrinkage of prejudices, a casting off of disappointing ideologies, an ability to live with many kinds of madness, an immense desire for certain durable human goods—truth, for instance, or freedom, or wisdom. I don't think I am exaggerating; there is plenty of evidence for this."

Take away the damage done by war and the noise of ideology, and the reader is still there.

But why do many contemporary writers fail to hold the place of importance they once did for readers? Bellow feels that literature has become in some sense marginal to the center of human activity, and goes to Hegel:

"But for a long time art has not been connected, as it was in the past, with the main enterprise. The historian Edgar Wind tells us in Art and Anarchy that Hegel long ago observed that art no longer engaged the central energies of man. These energies were now engaged by science—a 'relentless spirit of rational inquiry.' Art had moved to the margins. There it formed 'a wide and splendidly varied horizon.' In an age of science people still painted and wrote poetry but, said Hegel, however splendid the gods looked in modern works of art and whatever dignity and perfection we might find 'in the images of God the Father and the Virgin Mary' it was of no use: we no longer bent our knees. It is a long time since the knees were bent in piety. Ingenuity, daring exploration, freshness of invention replaced the art of 'direct relevance.' The most significant achievement of this pure art, in Hegel's view, was that, freed from its former responsibilities, it was no longer 'serious.' Instead it raised the soul through the 'serenity of form above any painful involvement in the limitations of reality.' I don't know who would make such a claim today for an art that raises the soul above painful involvements with reality. Nor am I sure that at this moment, it is the spirit of rational inquiry in pure science that engages the central energies of man. The center seems (temporarily perhaps) to be filled up with the crises I have been describing."

So Bellow isn't sure if "science" rules the roost after all. The prospect of centrality is still available to writers if they are inspired enough to enter it. As he says at the end of the essay, "If writers do not come again into the center it will not be because the center is pre-empted. It is not. They are free to enter. If they so wish."

In his resistance to Robbe-Grillet, Bellow sounds an awful lot like people today who (like Terry Eagleton, say) complain about the drift of both contemporary literature and the criticism that is associated with it. It's not just an old debate, it's a very old debate.

In this business about centers and margins, and the purpose of art, for Bellow, the time when art inspired the bending of knees was also the time when it had a ritualistic function when it was the image of Jesus and the Virgin Mary that inspired one, not the precision of the craftsmanship or the verisimilitude of the image. Arguably, in a secular culture art and literature can never be quite as powerful as in the kind of pre-modern society Bellow is thinking of, where the thing that "high" art represents is never in fact merely physically present. Perhaps Bellow's idea of the "center" is just a euphemism for writing really, really well. Or maybe it's more serious: but what might it mean to make a work of art that accesses the central nerves of human development at the present moment? More concretely, if it were a novel, what kind of novel would it be? Would it look like Saul Bellow's own work?

Selected Reading

Nobel Prize Acceptance Speech

Every year we see scores of books and articles which tell the Americans what a state they are in—which make intelligent or simpleminded or extravagant or lurid or demented statements. All reflect the crises we are in while telling us what we must do about them; these analysts are produced by the very disorder and confusion they prescribe for. It is as a writer that I am considering their extreme moral sensitivity, their desire for perfection, their intolerance of the defects of society, the touching, the comical boundlessness of their demands, their anxiety, their irritability, their sensitivity, their tendermindedness, their goodness, their convulsiveness[1], the recklessness with which they experiment with drugs and touch-therapies and bombs. The ex-Jesuit Malachi Martin in his book on the Church compares the modern American to Michelangelo's sculpture, *The Captive*. He sees "an unfinished struggle to emerge whole" from a block of matter. The American "captive" is beset in his struggle by "interpretations, admonitions, forewarnings and descriptions of himself by the self-appointed prophets, priests, judges and prefabricators of his travail[2]," says Martin.

Let me take a little time to look more closely at this travail. In private life, disorder or near-panic. In families—for husbands, wives, parents, children—confusion; in civic behavior, in personal loyalities, in sexual practices (I will not recite the whole list; we are tired of hearing it) —further confusion. And with this private disorder goes public bewilderment. In the papers we read what used to amuse us in science fiction—*The New Tork Times* speaks of death rays and of Russian and American satellites at war in space. In *The November Encounter* so sober and responsible an economist as my colleague, Milton Friedman, declares that Great Britain by its public spending will soon go the way of poor countries like Chile. He is appalled by his own forecast. What—the source of that noble tradition of freedom and democratic rights that began with Magna Carta ending in dictatorship? "It is almost impossible for anyone brought up in that tradition to utter the word that Britain is in danger of losing freedom and democracy; and yet it is a fact!"

It is with these facts that knock us to the ground that we try to live. If I were debating with Professor Friedman I might ask him to take into account the resistance of institutions, the cultural differences between Great Britain and Chile, differences in national character and traditions, but my purpose is not to get into debates I can't win but to direct your attention to the terrible predictions we have to live with, the background of disorder, the visions of ruin.

You would think that one such article would be enough for a single number of a magazine but on another page of *Encounter* Professor Hugh Seton-Watson discusses George Kennan's recent survey of American degeneracy and its dire[3] meaning for the world. Describing America's failure, Kennan speaks of crime, urban decay, drug-addiction, pornography, frivolity, deteriorated educational standards and concludes that our immense power counts for nothing. We cannot lead the world and, undermined by sinfulness, we may not be able to defend ourselves. Professor Seton-Watson writes, "Nothing can defend a society if its upper 100,000 men and women, both the decision-makers and those who help to mould the thinking of the decision-makers, are resolved to capitulate[4]."

So much for the capitalist superpower. Now what about its ideological adversaries? I turn the pages of *Encounter* to a short study by Mr. George Watson, Lecturer in English at Cambridge, on the racialism of the Left. He tells us that Hyndman, the founder of the Social Democratic Federation, called the South African war the Jews' war; that the Webbs at times expressed racialist views (as did Ruskin, Carlyle and T. H. Huxley before them); he relates that Engels denounced the smaller Slav peoples of Eastern Europe as counter-revolutionary ethnic trash; and Mr. Watson in conclusion cites a public statement by Ulrike Meinhof of the West German "Red Army Faction" made at a judicial hearing in 1972 approving of "revolutionary extermination". For her, German anti-semitism[5] of the Hitler period was essentially anticapitalist. "Auschwitz," she is quoted as saying, "meant that six million Jews were killed and thrown on the waste heap of Europe for what they were: money Jews (Geldjuden)."

I mention these racialists of the Left to show that for us there is no simple choice between the children of light and the children of darkness. Good and evil are not symmetrically distributed along political lines. But I have made my point; we stand open to all anxieties. The decline and fall of everything is our daily dread, we are agitated in private life and tormented by public questions.

And art and literature—what of them? Well, there is a violent uproar but we are not absolutely dominated by it. We are still able to think, to discriminate, and to feel. The purer, subtler, higher activities have not succumbed[6] to fury or to nonsense. Not yet. Books continue to be written and read. It may be more difficult to reach the whirling mind of a modern reader but it is possible to cut through the noise and reach the quiet zone. In the quiet zone we may find that he is devoutly waiting for us. When complications increase, the desire for essentials increases too. The unending cycle of crises that began with the First World War has formed a kind of person, one who has lived through terrible, strange things, and in whom there is an observable shrinkage of prejudices, a casting off of disappointing ideologies, an ability to live with many kinds of madness, an immense desire for certain durable human goods—truth, for instance, or freedom, or wisdom. I don't think I am exaggerating; there is plenty of evidence for this. Disintegration? Well, yes. Much is disintegrating but we are experiencing also an odd kind of refining process. And this has been going on for a long time. Looking into Proust's *Time Regained* I find that he was clearly aware of it. His novel, describing French society during the Great War, tests the strength of his art. Without art, he insists, shirking[7] no personal or collective horrors, we do not know ourselves or anyone else. Only art penetrates what pride, passion, intelligence and habit erect on all sides—the seeming realities of this world. There is another reality, the genuine one, which we lose sight of. This other reality is always sending us hints, which, without art, we can't receive. Proust calls these hints our "true impressions." The true impressions, our persistent intuitions, will, without art, be hidden from us and we will be left with nothing but a "terminology for practical ends which we falsely call life." Tolstoy put the matter in much the same way. A book like his *Ivan Ilyitch* also describes these same "practical ends" which conceal both life and death from us. In his final sufferings *Ivan Ilyitch* becomes an individual, a "character", by tearing down the concealments, by seeing through the "practical ends."

Proust was still able to keep a balance between art and destruction, insisting that art was a necessity of life, a great independent reality, a magical power. But for a long time art has not been connected, as it was in the past, with the main enterprise. The historian Edgar Wind tells us in *Art and Anarchy* that Hegel long ago observed that art no longer engaged the central energies of man. These energies were now engaged by science—a "relentless spirit of rational inquiry." Art had moved to the margins. There it formed "a wide and splendidly varied horizon." In an age of science people still painted and wrote poetry but, said Hegel, however splendid the gods looked in modern works of art and whatever dignity and perfection we might find "in the images of God the Father and the Virgin Mary" it was of no use: we no longer bent our knees. It is a long time since the knees were bent in piety. Ingenuity, daring exploration, freshness of invention replaced the art of "direct relevance." The most significant achievement of this pure art, in Hegel's view, was that, freed from its former responsibilities, it was no longer "serious." Instead it raised the soul through the "serenity of form above any painful involvement in the limitations of reality." I don't know who would make such a claim today for an art that raises the soul above painful involvements with reality. Nor am I sure that at this moment, it is the spirit of rational inquiry in pure science that engages the central energies of man. The center seems (temporarily perhaps) to be filled up with the crises I have been describing.

There were European writers in the 19th Century who would not give up the connection of literature with the main human enterprise. The very suggestion would have shocked Tolstoy and Dostoevski. But in the West a separation between great artists and the general public took place. They developed a marked contempt for the average reader and the bourgeois mass. The best of them saw clearly enough what sort of civilization Europe had produced, brilliant but unstable, vulnerable, fated to be overtaken by catastrophe, the historian Erich Auerbach tells us. Some of these writers, he says, produced "strange and vaguely terrifying works, or shocked the public by paradoxical and extreme opinions. Many of them took no trouble to facilitate the understanding of what they wrote—whether out of contempt for the public, the cult of their own inspiration, or a certain tragic weakness which prevented them from being at once simple and true."

In the 20th Century, theirs is still the main influence, for despite a show of radicalism and innovation our contemporaries are really very conservative. They follow their 19th-Century leaders and hold to the old standard, interpreting history and society much as they were interpreted in the last century. What would writers do today if it would occur to them that literature might once again engage those "central energies", if they were to recognize that an immense desire had arisen for a return from the periphery, for what was simple and true?

Of course we can't come back to the center simply because we want to; but the fact that we are wanted might matter to us and the force of the crisis is so great that it may summon us back to such a center. But prescriptions are futile. One can't tell writers what to do. The imagination must find its own path. But one can fervently wish that they—that we—would come back from the periphery. We do not, we writers, represent mankind adequately. What account do Americans give of themselves, what accounts of them are given by psychologists, sociologists, historians, journalists, and writers? In a kind of contractual daylight they see themselves in the ways with which we are so desperately familiar. These images of contractual daylight, so boring to Robbe-Grillet and to me, originate in the contemporary world view: We put into our books the consumer, civil servant, football fan, lover, television viewer. And in the contractual daylight version their life is a kind of death. There is another life coming from an insistent sense of what we are which denies these daylight formulations and the false life—the death in life—they make for us. For it is false, and we know it, and our secret and incoherent resistance to it cannot stop, for that resistance arises from persistent intuitions. Perhaps humankind cannot bear too much reality, but neither can it bear too much unreality, too much abuse of the truth.

We do not think well of ourselves; we do not think amply about what we are. Our collective achievements have so greatly "exceeded" us that we "justify" ourselves by pointing to them. It is the jet plane in which we commonplace human beings have crossed the Atlantic in four hours that embodies such value as we can claim. Then we hear that this is closing time in the gardens of the West, that the end of our capitalist civilization is at hand. Some years ago Cyril Connolly wrote that we were about to undergo "a complete mutation, not merely to be defined as the collapse of the capitalist system, but such a sea-change in the nature of reality as could not have been envisaged by Karl Marx or Sigmund Freud." This means that we are not yet sufficiently shrunken; we must prepare to be smaller still. I am not sure whether this should be called intellectual analysis or analysis by an intellectual. The disasters are disasters. It would be worse than stupid to call them victories as some statesmen have tried to do. But I am drawing attention to the fact that there is in the intellectual community a sizeable inventory of attitudes that have become respectable—notions about society, human nature, class, politics, sex, about mind, about the physical universe, the evolution of life. Few writers, even among the best, have taken the trouble to re-examine these attitudes or orthodoxies. Such attitudes only glow more powerfully in Joyce or D.H. Lawrence than in the books of lesser men; they are everywhere and no one challenges them seriously. Since the Twenties, how many novelists have taken a second look at D.H. Lawrence, or argued a different view of sexual potency or the effects of industrial civilization on the instincts? Literature has for nearly a century used the same stock of ideas, myths, strategies. "The most serious essayists of the last fifty years," says Robbe-Grillet. Yes, indeed. Essay after essay, book after book, confirm the most serious thoughts—Baudelairian, Nietzschean, Marxian, Psychoanalytic, etcetera[8], etcetera—of these most serious essayists. What Robbe-Grillet says about character can be said also about these ideas, maintaining all the usual things about mass society, dehumanization and the rest. How weary we are of them. How poorly they represent us. The pictures they offer no more resemble us than we resemble the reconstructed reptiles and other monsters in a museum of paleontology. We are much more limber, versatile, better articulated, there is much more to us, we all feel it.

What is at the center now? At the moment, neither art nor science but mankind determining, in confusion and obscurity, whether it will endure or go under. The whole species—everybody—has gotten into the act. At such a time it is essential to lighten ourselves, to dump encumbrances[9], including the encumbrances of education and all organized platitudes[10], to make judgments of our own, to perform acts of our own. Conrad was right to appeal to that part of our being which is a gift. We must hunt for that under the wreckage of many systems. The failure of those systems may bring a blessed and necessary release from formulations, from an over-defined and misleading consciousness. With increasing frequency I dismiss as merely respectable opinions I have long held—or thought I held—and try to discern what I have really lived by, and what others live by. As for Hegel's art freed from "seriousness" and glowing on the margins, raising the soul above painful involvement in the limitations of reality through the serenity of form, that can exist nowhere now, during this struggle for survival. However, it is not as though the people who engaged in this struggle had only a rudimentary humanity, without culture, and knew nothing of art. Our very vices, our mutilations, show how rich we are in thought and culture. How much we know. How much we even feel. The struggle that convulses us makes us want to simplify, to reconsider, to eliminate the tragic weakness which prevented writers—and readers—from being at once simple and true.

Writers are greatly respected. The intelligent public is wonderfully patient with them, continues to read them and endures disappointment after disappointment, waiting to hear from art what it does not hear from theology, philosophy, social theory, and what it cannot hear from pure science. Out of the struggle at the center has come an immense, painful longing for a broader, more flexible, fuller, more coherent, more comprehensive account of what we human beings are, who we are, and what this life is for. At the center humankind struggles with collective powers for its freedom, the individual struggles with dehumanization for the possession of his soul. If writers do not come again into the center it will not be because the center is pre-empted[11]. It is not. They are free to enter. If they so wish.

The essence of our real condition, the complexity, the confusion, the pain of it is shown to us in glimpses, in what Proust and Tolstoy thought of as "true impressions". This essence reveals, and then conceals itself. When it goes away it leaves us again in doubt. But we never seem to lose our connection with the depths from which these glimpses come. The sense of our real powers, powers we seem to derive from the universe itself, also comes and goes. We are reluctant to talk about this because there is nothing we can prove, because our language is inadequate and because few people are willing to risk talking about it. They would have to say, "There is a spirit" and that is taboo. So almost everyone keeps quiet about it, although almost everyone is aware of it.

The value of literature lies in these intermittent[12] "true impressions". A novel moves back and forth between the world of objects, of actions, of appearances, and that other world from which these "true impressions" come and which moves us to believe that the good we hang onto so tenaciously[13]—in the face of evil, so obstinately—is no illusion.

No one who has spent years in the writing of novels can be unaware of this. The novel can't be compared to the epic, or to the monuments of poetic drama. But it is the best we can do just now. It is a sort of latter-day lean-to, a hovel in which the spirit takes shelter. A novel is balanced between a few true impressions and the multitude of false ones that make up most of what we call life. It tells us that for every human being there is a diversity of existences, that the single existence is itself an illusion in part, that these many existences signify something, tend to something, fulfill something; it promises us meaning, harmony and even justice. What Conrad said was true, art attempts to find in the universe, in matter as well as in the facts of life, what is fundamental, enduring, essential.

(From Nobel Prize Acceptance Speech, Literature 1968-1980, Editor-in-Charge Tore Fr ngsmyr, Editor Sture All n, World Scientific Publishing Co., Singapore, 1993)

Notes:

1. convulsiveness: the state of being violent shaking
2. travail: (French) work
3. dire: extremely serious or urgent
4. capitulate: cease to resist an opponent or an unwelcome demand; surrender
5. anti-semitism: hostility to or prejudice against Jews
6. succumbed: give in, surrender, yield, submit; die
7. shirking: evade one's duty, avoid fulfilling a responsibility
8. etcetera: and so on
9. encumbrances: burden, hindrance, impediment; one who is dependent on another for support (especially a child)
10. platitudes: superficiality, state of being commonplace, banality; trite saying, cliche, dull remark
11. pre-empted: If you pre-empt an action, you prevent it from happening by doing something which makes it unnecessary or impossible.
12. intermittent: not continuous, sporadic, fitful, alternately stopping and starting
13. tenaciously: persistently, resolutely, stubbornly

Questions for Study and Discussion:
1. Do you think that Great Britain is going to lose its democracy? Why?
2. Do you think that the art is no longer the center concern of the human energy? Give your idea.
3. What does "Perhaps humankind cannot bear too much reality, but neither can it bear too much unreality, too much abuse of the truth" mean? What is your opinion about the reality and unreality that you can bear?
4. Explain the importance of being simple and true both in writing and daily life.
5. What is your opinion on the function of novels in your everyday life?

Joseph Heller (1923—1999)

Life and Major Works

Joseph Heller was born on May 1, 1923, in the Coney Island district of Brooklyn, New York, the son of Isaac and Lena Heller. His parents were Jewish immigrants from Russia. Isaac, who arrived in America in 1913, was agnostic, interested in socialist politics, and a delivery truck driver for a wholesale baker. Joseph had a half-sister, Sylvia, seven years older than he, and a half-brother, Lee (originally Eli), fourteen years older and born in Russia; their mother had died.

Joseph Heller

Joseph's father died following an operation in 1929, as Joseph began his formal education at Coney Island's Public School No. 188. After graduating from Abraham Lincoln High School in 1941, Joseph immediately went to work as a file clerk for an insurance agency. When the United States entered World War II in December of that year, he took a job as a blacksmith's assistant in the Norfolk Navy Yard. World War II would become the key formative event in Heller's life, providing him with rich experiences in the military and, eventually, a formal education.

In 1942, as the war progressed, Heller joined the Army and worked as a file clerk. In October, he switched to the Army Air Forces, as the aviation branch was known prior to the establishment of the United States Air Force in 1947. Joseph initially intended to be a gunner on a bomber; when he was told, erroneously, that the average life span of a gunner in combat was three days, he quickly enrolled in cadet school to become an officer and bombardier.

After graduating from cadet school as a first lieutenant early in 1944, Heller was assigned to the 488th Squadron of the Twelfth Air Force in Corsica. Heller later said that, as a twenty-one-year-old officer, he initially had no serious complaints about his life in a combat unit. He enjoyed the camaraderie of his fellow airmen on the base and the pleasures of visits to the group's officer apartments in Rome, following the city's liberation in June. The bombing runs went well enough.

All that changed on Heller's thirty-seventh mission, a raid on Avignon, on the Rhone River in southeast France, the basis of a fictionalized account that is central to *Catch-22*. During the bombing run, a co-pilot panicked and set the B-25 into a dive, causing Heller to be pressed against the top of the bombardier's compartment. After the plane was again under control, the co-pilot called over the intercom, "Help him! Help him!" Heller replied, "Help who?" "Help the bombardier!" was the co-pilot's response. "I'm the bombardier; I'm all right," Heller answered. When he then checked the rear of the plane, however, Heller found that one of the gunners was, in fact, wounded, and Heller realized that death lay near on these flights. The young lieutenant's war was not the same after that. He did complete sixty missions in the Mediterranean and received an Air Medal as well as a Presidential Unit Citation with his honorable discharge.

Because of the GI Bill, a federal program that helped tens of thousands of veterans to pursue higher education following the war, Heller was able to enroll at the University of Southern California in 1945. He published his first short story in the prestigious *Story* magazine that year and was married to Shirley Held, with whom he eventually had two children, Erica Jill and Theodore Michael. The next year, he transferred to New York University.

At NYU, under the tutelage of Professor Maurice Baudin, Heller came to believe that he could be a professional writer. He received his Bachelor of Arts degree in 1948, with the distinction of being named to the academic honor society Phi Beta Kappa. That year he also published two short stories in *The Atlantic Monthly* and two more in *Esquire*. Heller earned his Master of Arts degree in American Literature from Columbia University the next year as well as a Fulbright Scholarship to study for a year at Oxford University in England.

Following a short teaching stint at Pennsylvania State University, Heller joined the corporate world as advertising manager at *Time* magazine. In 1953, he began working on a novel tentatively titled *Catch-18*. He later changed the title to avoid confusion with Leon Uris's novel, *Mila-18*. Heller accepted a managerial advertising job at *Look* magazine in 1956 and moved to *McCall's* in 1958, still spending two hours a night on his novel. He later said that he once became discouraged, leaving the manuscript for a week to seek diversions, including watching television, but he was so bored that he hurried back to the book. He wondered how in the world people lived without a novel to write.

Catch-22 was published in 1961. Although he taught creative writing courses at Yale and the University of Pennsylvania, Heller became a full-time writer for most of the next decade, returning to teaching at City College of New York from

1971 to 1975.

Heller's personal life took traumatic turns in 1981 as he separated from his wife, Shirley, from whom he was divorced in 1984. In December 1981, Heller discovered that he had Guillain-Barr syndrome, a rare paralytic disease. His struggle with and slow recovery from the disease is recorded in *No Laughing Matter* (1986) written with his friend Speed Vogel. During his rehabilitation, Heller met a nurse, Valerie Humphries, whom he married in 1987.

In addition to his fiction and memoirs, Heller wrote for the theater, television, and motion pictures. He continued his writing and teaching career until his death, of a heart attack, at his home in East Hampton, New York, on December 12, 1999.

Brief Introduction and Appreciation

Catch-22 is like no other novel. It is one of the funniest books ever written, a keystone work in American literature, and even added a new term to the dictionary.

When Yossarian reports to Colonel Cathcart and Colonel Korn back at the base, they have a surprise for him: "We're sending you home." The catch is that Yossarian must agree to cooperate with his commanding officers and speak well of them to other members of the squadron as well as the press and others back in the States. Colonel Korn, who usurps Cathcart's authority in this scene, affably offers the deal. They will promote Yossarian to major, give him another medal, and send him home a hero. All that Yossarian needs to do, Korn says, is behave like a team player, promote their best interests, and indicate affection for his commanders: "Like us. Join us. Be our pal. Say nice things about us...Become one of the boys."

If anyone asks why he refused to fly, Yossarian is to say that he had been told in confidence that he would soon return home; he didn't want to take any unnecessary risks. That's all. If Yossarian rejects the offer, however, he will be court-martialed. Yossarian makes his decision. While leaving the office, he is met with a further surprise.

Yossarian is faced with an offer that is difficult to refuse. Colonel Korn, who is stronger, sharper, and more sinister than Cathcart, concedes that Yossarian has presented the commanding officers with a serious problem. On the one hand, they cannot simply send him home if it looks like a reward for not flying more missions—that would destroy morale. On the other hand, Korn and Cathcart are concerned about their own careers if Yossarian remains with the squadron, refuses to fly, and has other men following his example. For once, the tables have turned.

Yossarian seems to have the system in a Catch-22. The commanding officers ask Yossarian, one more time, to recant and rejoin the war effort. He refuses. Cathcart, who spends most of the scene grousing around the perimeters, moans that he never should have promoted Yossarian to captain or honored him for the raid on Ferrara; he should have court-martialed him instead. Now, Yossarian refuses to obey orders but is difficult to deal with because he is supposed to be a hero. To Korn, Cathcart repeats a standard clich of the time: "Doesn't he know there's a war going on?" Colonel Korn sardonically responds, "I'm quite sure he does. That's probably why he refuses to fly…"

Still, Colonel Korn's offer to Yossarian is tempting. The Captain can go home a hero and never fly another mission. Yossarian wavers. Korn explains that he must accept or be court-martialed immediately for going AWOL to Rome. It is an open-and-shut case. The practical response for Yossarian is simple: Take the deal. But he is faced with a moral dilemma, the kind of conflict of conscience that Yossarian likes to laugh at publicly but privately takes seriously. He reflects that the agreement would be a "scummy trick" to play on the other men. Colonel Korn, with evil intent, quietly agrees that it is "odious." But Yossarian caves. He accepts the deal. Others will simply have to look out for themselves.

The three suddenly are pals. Colonel Korn insists that Yossarian use the colonels' nicknames: Korn is "Blackie; Cathcart is good old "Chuck." Yossarian cheerfully points out that *his* friends call him "Yo-Yo." The three plan to have dinner together soon. Yossarian exits "almost bursting into song." He starts for the staircase "with a jaunty and exhilarated air." He is free at last. A private in green fatigues salutes him. The private looks vaguely familiar. As Yossarian returns the salute, the private in green fatigues turns into Nately's whore and lunges at him with a bone-handled kitchen knife. Yossarian is already unconscious when Cathcart and Korn rush out of the office, frightening the assailant away.

Selected Reading

Catch-22

Chapter 40

There was, of course, a catch[1].

"Catch-22?" inquired Yossarian.

"Of course," Colonel Korn answered pleasantly, after he had chased the mighty guard of massive M.P. sout with an insouciant flick of his hand and a slightly contemptuous nod—most relaxed, as always,when he could be more cynical. His rimless square eye-glasses glinted with sly amusement as he gazed at Yossarian. "After all, we can't simply send you home for refusing to fly more missions and keep the rest of the men here, can't we? That would hardly be fair to them."

"You're goddam right!" Colonel Cathcart Blurted out, lumbering back and forth gracelessly like a winded bull[2], puffing and pouting angrily. "I'd like to tie him up hand and foot and throw him aboard a plane on every mission, That's what I'd like to do." Colonel Korn motioned Colonel Cathcart to be silent and smiled at Yossarian. "You know, your eally have been making things terribly difficult for Colinel Cathcart," he observed with flip good humor, as though the fact did not displease him at all. "The men are unhappy and morale is beginning to deteriorate. And it's all your fault."

"It's your fault," Yossarian argued, "for raising the number of missions[3]"

"No, it's your fault for refusing to fly them," Colonel Korn retorted. "The men were perfectly content to fly as many missions as we asked as long as they thought they had no alternative. Now you've given them hope, and they're unhappy. So the blame is all yours."

"Doesn't he know there's a war going on?" Colonel Cathcart, still stamping back and forth, demanded morosely without looking at Yossarian.

"I'm quite sure he does." Colonel Korn answered. "That's probably why he refuses to fly them."

"Doesn't it make any difference to him?"

"Will the knowledge that there's a war going on weaker your decision to refuse to participate in it?" Colonel Korn inquired with sarcastic seriousness, mocking Colonel Cathcart.

"No, sir," Yossarian replied, almost returning Colonel Korn's smile.

"I was afraid of that," Colonel Korn remarked with an elaborate sigh, locking his fingers together comfortably on top of his smooth, bald, broad, shiny brown head. "You know, in all fairness, we really haven't treated you too badly, have we? We've fed you and paid you on time. We gave you a medal and even made you a captain."

"I never should have made him a captain," Colonel Cathcart exclaimed bitterly.

"I should have given him a courtmartial after he loused up[4] that Ferrara mission and went around twice."

"I told you not to promote him," said Colonel Korn, "but you wouldn't listen to me."

"No you didn'd. You told me to promote him, didn't you?"

"I told you not to promote him. But you just wouldn't listen."

"I should have listened."

"You never listen to me," Colonel Korn persisted with relish. "That's the reason we're in this spot[5]."

"All right, gee whiz. Stop rubbing it in[6], will you?" Colonel Cathcart burrowed his fists down deep inside his pockets and turned away in slouch. "Instead of picking on me[7], why don't you figure out what we're going to do about him?"

"We're going to send him home, I'm afraid." Colonel Korn was chuckling triumphantly when he turned away from Colonel Cathcart to face Yossarian. "Yossarian, the war is over for you.We're going to send you home. You really don't deserve it, you know, which is one if one of the reasons I don't mind doing it. Since there's nothing else we can risk doing to you at this time, we've decided to return you to the States. We've worked out this little deal to—"

"What kind of dead?" Yossarian demanded with defiant mistrust.

Colonel Korn tossed his head back and laughed. "Oh, a thoroughly despicable deal, make no mistake about that. It's absolutely revolting. But you'll accept it quickly enough."

"Don't be too sure."

"I haven't the slightest doubt you will, even though it stinks to high heaven. Oh, by the way. You haven't told any of the men you've refused to fly more missions, have you?"

"No, sir." Yossarian answered promptly.

Colonel Korn nodded approvingly. "That's good. I like the way you lie. You'll go far in this world if you ever acquire some decent ambition."

"Doesn't he know there a war going on?" Colonel Cathcart yelled out suddenly, and blew with vigorous disbelief into the open end of his cigarette holder.

"I'm quite sure he does," Colonel Korn replied acidly, "since you brought that identical point to his attention just a moment ago." Colonel Korn frowned wearily for Yossarian's benefit, his eyes twinkling swarthily with sly and daring scorn. Gripping the edge of Colonel Cathcart's desk with both hands, he lifted his flaccid haunches far back on the corner to sit with both short legs dangling freely. His shoes kicked lightly against the yellow oak wood, his sludgebrown socks, garterless, collapsed in sagging circles below ankles that were surprising small and white. "You know, Yossarian," he mused affably in a manner of casual reflection that seemed both derisive and sincere, "I really do admire you a bit. You're an intelligent person of great moral character who has taken a very courageous stand. I'm an intelligent person with no moral character at all, so I'm in an ideal position to appreciate it."

"These are very critical times," Colonel Cathcart asserted petulantly from a far corner of the office, paying no attention to Colonel Korn.

"Very critical times indeed," Colonel Korn agreed with a placid nod. "We've just had a change of command above, and we can't afford a situation that might put us in a bad light with either General Scheisskopf of General Peckem. Isn't that what you mean, Colonel?"

"Hasn't he got any Patriotism?"

"Won't you fight for your country?" Colonel Korn demanded, emulating Colonel Cathcart's harsh, self-righteous tone. "Won't you give up your life for Colonel Cathcart and me?"

Yossarian tensed with alert astonishment when he heard Colonel Korn's concluding words. "What's that?" he exclaimed "What have you and Colonel Cathcart got to do with my country? You're not the same."

"How can you separate us?" Colonel Korn inquired with ironical tranquillity.

"That's right," Colonel Cathcart cried emphatically. "You're either for us or against us. There's no two ways about it."

"I'm afraid he's got you," added Colonel Korn. "You're either for us or against your country. It's as simple as that."

"Oh, no, Colonel. I don't buy that."

Colonel Korn was unruffled. "Neither do I, frankly, but everyone else will. So there you are."

"You're a disgrace to your uniform!" Colonel Cathcart declared with blustering wrath, whirling to confront Yossarian for the first time. "I'd like to know you ever got to be a captain, anyway."

"You promoted him," Colonel Korn reminded sweetly, stifling a snicker.

"Don't you remember?"

"Well, I never should have done it."

"I told you not to do it," Colonel Korn said. "But you just wouldn't listen to me."

"Gee whiz, will you stop rubbing it in?" Colonel Cathcart cried. He furrowed his brow and glowered at Colonel Korn through eyes narrow with suspicion, his fists clenched on his hips. "Say, whose side are you on,anyway?"

"Your side, Colonel. What other side could I be on?"

"Then stop picking on me, will you? Get off my back, will you?"

"I'm on your side, Colonel. I'm just loaded with patriotism ."

"Well, just make sure you don't forget that." Colonel Cathcart turned away grudgingly after another moment, incompletely reassured, and began striding the floor again, his hands kneading his long cigarette holder. He jerked a thumb toward Yossarian. "Let's settle with him. I know what I'd like to do with him. I'd like to take him outside and shoot him. That's what I'd like to do with him. That's what General Dreedle would do with him."

"But General Dreedle isn't with us any more," said Colonel Korn, "so we can't take him outside and shoot him." Now that his moment of tension with Colonel Cathcart had passed, Colonel Korn relaxed again and resumed kicking softly against Colonel Cathcart's desk.He returned to Yossarian. "So we're going to send you home instead. It took a bit of thinking, but we finally woeked out this horrible little plan for sending you home without causing too much dissatisfaction among the friends you'll leave behind. Doesn't that make you happy?"

"What kind of plan? I'm not sure I'm going to like it."

"I know you're not going to like it," Colonel Korn laughed, locking his hands contentedly on top of his head again. "You're going to loathe it. It really is odious and certainly will offend your conscience. But you'll agree to it quickly enough. You'll agree to it because it will send you home safe and sound in two weeks, and because you have no choice. It's that or a court-martial. That it or leave it."

Yossarian snorted. "Stop bluffing, Colonel. You can't court-martial me for desertion in the face of the enemy. It would make you look bad and you probably couldn't get a conviction."

"But we can court-martial you now for desertion from duty, since you went to Rome without a pass. And we could make it stick[8]. If you think about it, a minute, you'll see that you'd leave us no alternative. We can't simply let you keep walking around in open insubordination without punishing you. All the other men would stop flying missions, too. No, you have my word for it. We will court-martial you if you turn our deal down, even though it would raise a lot of questions and be a terrible black eye[9] for Colonel Cathcart." Colonel Cathcart winced at the words "black eye" and, without any apparent premeditation, hurled his slender onyx-and-ivory cigarette holder down viciously on the wooden surface on his desk. "Jesus Christ!" he shouted unexpectedly. "I hate this goddam cigarette holder!" The cigarette holder bounced off the desk to the wall, ricocheted across the window still to the floor and came to a stop almost, where he was standing. Colonel Cathcart stared down at it with an irascible scowl. "I wonder if it's really doing me any good."

"It's a feather in your cap[10] with General Peckem, but a black eye for you with General Scheisskopf," Colonel Korn informed him with a mischievous look of innocence.

"Well, which one am I supposed to please?"

"Both."

"How can I please them both? They hate each other.How am I ever going to get a feather in my cap from General Scheisskopf without getting a black eye from General Peckem?"

"March."

"Yeah, march. That's the only way to please him. March. March." Colonel Cathcart grimaced sullenly. "Some generals! They're a disgrace to their uniforms. If people like those two can make general, I don't see how I can miss."

"You're going to go far," Colonel Korn assured him with a flat lack of conviction, and turned back chuckling to Yossarian, his disdainful merriment increasing at the sight of Yossarian's unyielding expression of antagonism and distrust. "And there you have the crux of the situation. Colonel Cathcart wants to be a general and I want to be a colonel, and that's why we have to send you home."

"Why does he want to be a general?"

"Why? For the same reason that I want to be a colonel. What else have we got to do? Everyone teaches us to aspire to higher things. A general is higher than a colonel, and a colonel is higher than a lieutenant colonel. So we're both aspiring. And you know, Yossarian,it's a lucky thing for you that we are.Your timing on this is absolutely perfect, but I suppose you took that factor into account in your calculations."

"I haven't been doing any calculating," Yossarian retorted.

"Yes, I really do enjoy the way you lie," Colonel Korn answered. "Won't it make you proud to have your commanding officer promoted to general—to know you served in an outfit that averaged more combat missions and more oak leaf clusters[11] for your Air Medal? Where's your sprit de corps[12] ? Don't you want to contribute further to this great record by flying more combat missions? It's your last chance to answer yes."

"No."

"In that case, you have us over a barrel[13]" said Colonel Korn without rancor.

"He ought to be ashamed of himself!"

"and we have to send you home. Just do a few little things for us, and…"

"What sort of things?" Yossarian interrupted with belligerent misgiving.

"Oh, thing, insignificant things. Really, this is a very generous deal we're making with you. We will issue orders returning you to the States—really, we will—and all you have to do in return is…"

"What? What must I do?" Colonel Korn laughed curtly. "Like us."

Yossarian blinked ."Like you?"

"Like us."

"Like you?"

"That's right," said Colonel Korn, nodding, gratified immeasurably by Yossarian's guileless surprise and bewilderment." Like us. Join us. Be our pal. Say nice things about us here and back in the States. Become one of the boys[14]. Now, that isn't asking too much, is it?"

"You just want me to like you? Is that all?"

"That's all."

"That's all?"

"Just find it in your heart to like us." Yossarian wanted to laugh confidently when he saw with amazement that Colonel Korn was telling the truth. "That isn't going to be too easy ,"he sneered.

"Oh, it will be a lot easier than you think," Colonel Korn taunted in return, undismayed by Yossarian's barb." You'll be surprised at how easy you'll find it to like us once you begin." Colonel Korn hitched up the waist of his loose, voluminous trousers. The deep black grooves isolating his square chin from his jowls were bent again in a kind of jeering and reprehensible mirth. "You see, Yossarian, we're going to put you on easy street[15]. We're going to promote you to major and even give you another medal. Captain Flume is already working on glowing press releases describing your valor over Ferrata, your deep and abiding loyalty to your outfit and your consummate dedication to duty. Those phrases are

355

all actual quotations, by the way. We're going to glorify you and send you home a hero, recalled by the Pentagon for morale and public-relations purposes. You'll live like a millionaire. Everyone will lionize you. You'll have parades in your honor and make speeches to raise money for war bonds. A whole new world of luxury awaits you once you become our pal. Isn't it lovely?" Yossarian found himself listening intently to the fascinating elucidation of details. "I'm not sure I want to make speeches."

"Then we'll forget the speeches. The important thing is what you say to people here." Colonel Korn leaned forward earnestly, no longer smiling. "We don't want any of the men in the group to know that we're sending you home as a result of your refusal to fly more missions. And we don't want General Peckem or General Scheisskopf to get wind of[16] any friction between us, either. That's why we're going to become such good pals."

"What will I say to the men who asked me why I refused to fly more missions?"

"Tell them you had been informed in confidence that you were being returned to the States and that you were unwilling to risk your life for another mission or two. Just a minor disagreement between pals, that's all."

"Will they believe it, once they see what great friends we've become and when they see the press releases and read the flattering things you have to say about me and Colonel Cathcart. Don't worry about the men. They'll be easy enough to discipline and control when you've gone. It's only while you're still here that they may prove troublesome. You know, one good apple can spoil the rest[17]," Colonel Korn concluded with conscious irony. "You know—this would really be wonderful—you might even serve as an inspiration to them to fly more missions."

"Suppose I denounce you when I get back to the States?"

"After you've accepted our medal and promotion and all the fanfare? No one would believe you, the Army wouldn't let you, and why in the world should you want to? You're going to be one of the boys, remember? You'll enjoy a rich, rewarding, luxurious, privileged existence. You'd have to be a fool to throw it all away just for a moral principle, and you're not a fool. Is it a deal?"

"I don't know."

"It's that or a court-martial."

"That's a pretty scummy trick I'd playing on the men in the squadron, isn't it?"

"Odious," Colonel Korn agreed amiably, and waited, watching Yossarian patiently with a glimmer of private delight.

"But what the hell!" Yossarian exclaimed. "If they don't want to fly more missions, let them stand up and do something about it the way I did. Right?"

"Of course," said Colonel Korn.

"There's no reason I have to risk my life for them, is there?"

"Of course not."

Yossarian arrived at his decision with a swift grin. "It's a deal!" he announced jubilantly.

"Great," said Colonel Korn with somewhat less cordiality than Yossarian had expected, and he slid himself off Colonel Cathcart's desk to stand on the floor. He tugged the folds of cloth of his pants and undershorts free from his crotch and gave Yossarian a limp hand to shake. "Welcome aboard[18]."

"Thanks, Colonel.I…"

"Call me Blackie, Joh .We're pals now."

"Sure, Blackie. My friends call me Yo-Yo. Blackie, I…"

"His friends call him Yo-Yo," Colonel Korn sang out to Colonel Cathcart." Why don't you congratulate Yo-Yo on what a sensible move he's making?"

"That's a real sensible move you're making, Yo-Yo," Colonel Cathcart said, pumping Yossarian's hand with clumsy zeal.

"Thank you, Colonel, I…"

"Call him Chuck," said Colonel Korn.

"Sure, call me Chuck," said Colonel Cathcart with a laugh that was hearty and awkward." We're all pals now."

"Sure, Chuck."

"Exit smiling," said Colonel Korn, his hands on both their shoulders as the three of them moved to the door.

"Come on over for dinner with us some night, Yo-Yo," Colonel Cathcart invited hospitably." How about tonight? In the group dining room."

"I'd love to, sir."

"Chuck," Colonel Korn corrected reprovingly.

"I'm sorry, Blackie. Chuck. I can't get used to it."

"That's all right, pal."

"Sure, pal."

"Thanks pal."

"Don't mention it, pal."

"So long, pal." Yossarian waved goodbye fondly to his new pals and sauntered out onto the balcony corridor, almost bursting into song the instant he was alone.

He was home free: he had pulled it off[19]; his act of rebellion had succeeded; he was safe, and he had nothing to be ashamed of to anyone. He started toward the staircase with a jaunty and exhilarated air. A private in green fatigues saluted him, Yossarian returned the salute happily, staring at the private with curiosity. He looked strangely familiar. When Yossarian returned the salute, the private in green fatigues turned suddenly into Nately's whore and lunged at him murderously with a bone-handled kitchen knife that caught him in the side below his upraised arm.Yossarian sank to the floor with a shriek, shutting his eyes in overwhelming terror as he saw the girl lift the knife to strike him again. He was already uncouscious when Colonel Korn and Colonel Cathcart dashed out of the office and saved his life by frightening her away.

Notes:

1. catch: a rule that disciplined the pilots and places them in an awkward condition
2. a winded bull: a bull that breathes with difficulty
3. the number of missions: originally the quota of combat missions a flier must fly in Catch-22 is 25, but Colonel Cathcart and Korn keep raising the number of missions for the purpose of possible promotion to the rank of general.
4. loused up: spoiled
5. in this spot: in such an awkward situation, implying that they lost a chance of promotion
6. rubbing it in: keeping reminding him of it
7. picking on me: blaming me
8. make it stick: make the charge(for desertion from duty) valid
9. black eye: shame, disgrace
10. feather in your cap: achievement to be proud of
11. oak leaf clusters: symbol of honor or award
12. spirit de corps: (French) group spirit; an attitude of enthusiasm and devotion among members of a group for each other, the group, and its cause
13. over a barrel: in a helpless position
14. Become one of the boys: be like us; join us
15. put you on easy street: make things easy
16. get wind of: hear about

17. one good apple can spoil the rest: the original saying is "one bad apple can spoil the barrel."
18. Welcome aboard: you are welcome to join us
19. pull it off: succeed in achieving his goal

Questions for Study and Discussion:
1. What does "Catch-22" mean?
2. Why was Yossarian allowed to return home?
3. What was Yossarian asked to do in return?
4. What was the deal made between Yossarian and Colonel Korn?
5. Can you make a brief comment on the literary techniques of black humor just from the conversation between Yossarian, Colonel Korn and Colonel Cathcart?

N. Scott Momaday (1934—)

Life and Major Works

Born in Oklahoma, Momaday claims Kiowa heritage on his father's side, and both Cherokee and French heritage on his mother's side. His parents worked as teachers, so Momaday gained a strong interest in language and literature from the English-language stories read to him by his mother and from the Kiowa tales recounted by his grandmother and his father. His youth was spent on Navaho reservations in the Southwest, where he experienced the Native American traditions of oral stories and religious rituals. In 1946, the family settled

N.Scott Momaday

at Jemez Pueblo, New Mexico, which became his most memorable childhood home. He attended the University of New Mexico, left for a year of law school, but returned to complete his bachelor's degree in political science in 1958. Then, he began teaching on the Jicarilla Apache Reservation. In 1959, he won a prestigious Wallace Stegner Creative Writing Fellowship at Stanford University and began studying with not only Stegner, but also poet Yvor Winters, who was to prove a tremendous influence on the budding writer.

An aspiring academic, Momaday earned a master's degree in 1960 and a Ph.D. in 1963 writing a dissertation under the influence of Edmund Wilson. He went on to teach English and comparative literature—including courses in the Native American oral tradition—at the University of California at Santa Barbara and Berkeley, as well as Stanford and the University of Arizona. During his research to prepare for teaching American Indian studies, he gathered together a book of Kiowa tales that he privately printed as *The Journey to Tai-Mei* (1967), which he later incorporated into *The Way to Rainy Mountain* (1969). Just as important was his opportunity to view the sacred Sun Dance doll of Tai-me, which the Kiowa tribe had stored away since 1888. For Momaday, this was an intensely religious experience which gave him an intimate connection to the past and culture of his tribe.

His first writing was poetry, which has influenced the rhythm and imagery of his fictional prose, but he has also written autobiography and essays. After achieving fame with his fiction, he became a prolific lecturer and an accomplished painter, like his father. Drawing from his Native American heritage and identity, Momaday has developed three related themes throughout his work: Indian's relationship with the earth, imaginatively experienced; the power of language; and self-knowledge. His first novel, *House Made of Dawn* (1968), tells of a recovery of Native American identity in the anti-hero Able, a Navaho World War II veteran who feels alienated not only from white society, but also from the Pueblo reservation where he returns to try to find himself. The specific discussion of the novel will be in the next part.

His second book, *The way to Rainy Mountain,* is a tribal history structured by the Kiowas' journey from their ancestral lands in the northern Rockies to the plains of Oklahoma. On this slow migration that becomes a dramatic cultural transformation, the tribe adopts the Sun Dance religion from the Crows and the horse from the whites, thereby choosing a warrior lifestyle of hunting, thievery, and fighting. One importance of this work is Momaday's preservation and celebration of the traditional Kiowa narratives that impart the tribe's essential myths. In *The Names* (1977), Momady writes a childhood memoir that examines the relationship between language and human significance, and the nature of ethnic Indian identity. After this book, he published nothing for over a decade, working more on painting than writing. This experience provided ample background for *The Ancient Child* (1989), a novel about an unfulfilled but internationally successful painter who must discover his Kiowa roots in order to overcome a nervous breakdown and to satisfy his religious longings. The novel

360

ends with his transformation into a bear through a ritual ceremony. Unlike modernist novelists who might use mythology as "symbolism or allegory, he is writing about a different plane of reality". In effect, the author is recreating a mythic present infused by aspects of the past and the supernatural."

In many ways, Momaday has successfully combined two very different literary traditions: a postmodern sensibility toward nonsequential narrative, fragmented characters, and open-ended interpretation with a richly textured oral style that finds meaning through tribal community and a mystical experience of nature. From this perspective, "nature integrates sense perception and memory, fusing the visible with collective and personal wisdom about the universe". For instance, just as Canyon de Chelly became a sacred place for the Southwest Indians, the personal experience of places where we feel at home is made sacred by treasuring and preserving them in imagination; as these places are shared through story and a mythologizing process, they become a community resource. This "imaginative involvement in the natural world...relies, in native cultures, on the racial experience that is perpetuated through the oral tradition". What Momaday has achieved—through fiction, poetry, and memoir—is a literary re-creation of that tradition.

Brief Introduction and Appreciation

His first novel, *House Made of Dawn* (1968), tells of a recovery of Native American identity in the anti-hero Able, a Navaho World War II veteran who feels alienated not only from white society, but also from the Pueblo reservation where he returns to try to find himself. Momaday makes clear that Abel's "personal and cultural alienation correlates with his emotional and geographical distance from his ancestral land". But before he can find himself in this sacred space, Able must first wander in the spiritually arid urban landscape of Los Angeles, where he meets the Reverend Tosamah, the major figure in the excerpt bellow. The Reverend is a mouthpiece for Momaday's own views about the power of language, even though this character is truly no friend to the protagonist. In fact, he "detests Able for being a 'longhair'—an unassimilated Indian who is looked down upon by whites and is therefore a discredit to his race". However, Able transcends this and the necessity of actively determining the self within the mix of Southwestern cultures: Hispanic Catholic, Pueblo Indian, Anglo-American, and Navaho. *House Made of*

Dawn, which won the Pulitzer Prize in 1969, ushered in a veritable renaissance of Native American writers.

The text for the excerpt from *House Made of Dawn* is from the reprint edition (New York: Perennial, 1989), pages 89-98.

Selected Reading

House Made of Dawn
THE PRIEST OF THE SUN

The Priest of the Sun lived with his disciple Cruz on the first floor of a two-story red-brick building in Los Angeles. The upstairs was maintained as a storage facility by the A. A. Kaul Office supply Company. The basement was a kind of church. There was a signboard[1] on the wall above the basement steps, encased in glass. In neat, movable white block letters on a black field it read:

LOS ANGELES

HOLINESS PAN-INDIAN[2] RESCUE MISSION

Rev. J. B. B. Tosamah, Pastor & Priest of the Sun

Saturday 8:30 P.M.

"The Gospel According to John"

Sunday 8:30 P.M.

"The Way to Rainy Mountain"

Be kind to a white man today

The basement was cold and dreary, dimly illuminated by two 40-wattbulbs which were screwed into the side walls above the dais[3]. This platform was made out of rough planks of various woods and dimensions, thrown together without so much as[4] a hammer and nails; it stood seven or eight inches above the floor, and it supported the tin firebox[5] and the crescent altar. Off to one side was a kind of lectern, decorated with red and yellow symbols of the sun and moon. In back of the dais there was a screen of purple drapery[6], threadbare and badly faded. On either side of the aisle which led to the altar there were chairs and crates[7], fashioned into pews[8]. The walls were bare and gray and streaked with water. The only windows were small, rectangular openings near the ceiling, at ground level; the panes[9] were covered over with a thick film of coal oil and dust, and spider webs clung to the frames or floated out like smoke across the room. The air was heavy and stale; odors of old smoke and incense lingered all around. The people had filed into the pews and were waiting silently.

Cruz, a squat[10], oily man with blue-black hair that stood out like spines from his head, stepped forward on the platform on the platform and raised his hands as if to ask for the quiet that already was.

Everyone watched him for a moment; in the dull light his skin shone yellow with sweat. Turning slightly and extending his arm behind him, he said, "The Right Reverend John Big Bluff Tosamah."

There was a ripple in the dark screen; the drapes parted and the Priest of the Sun appeared, moving shadow-like to the lectern[11]. He was shaggy and awful-looking in the thin, naked light: big, lithe as a cat, narrow-eyed, suggesting in the whole of his look and manner both arrogance and agony. He wore black like a cleric; he had the voice of a great dog:

"'*In principio erat Verbum.*'[12] Think of Genesis. Think of how it was before the world was made. There was nothing, the Bible says. 'And the earth was without form, and void; and darkness was upon the face of the deep.' It was dark, and there was nothing. There were no mountains, no trees, no rocks, no rivers. There was nothing. But there was darkness all around, and in the darkness something happened. *Something happened!* There was a single sound. Far away in the darkness there was a single sound. Nothing made it, but it was there; and there was no one to hear it, but it was there, it was there, and there was nothing else. It rose up in the darkness, little and still, almost nothing in itself—like a single soft breath, like the wind arising; yes, like the whisper of the wind rising slowly and going out into the early morning. But there was no wind. There was only the sound, little and soft. It was almost nothing in itself, the smallest seed of sound—but it took hold of the darkness and there was light; it took hold of the stillness and there was motion forever, it took told of the silence and there was sound. It was almost nothing in itself, a single sound, a word—a word broken off at the darkest center of the night and let go in the awful void, forever and forever. And it was almost nothing in itself. It scarcely was; but it was, and everything began."

Just then a remarkable thing happened. The Priest of the Sun seemed stricken; he let go of his audience and withdrew into himself, into some strange potential of himself. His voice, which had been low and resonant, suddenly became harsh and flat; his shoulders sagged and his stomach protruded[13], as if he had held his breath to the limit of endurance; for a moment there was a look of amazement, then utter carelessness in his face. Conviction, caricature[14], callousness[15]: the remainder of his sermon was a going back and forth among these.

"Thank you so much, Brother Cruz. Good evening, blood brothers and sisters, and welcome, welcome. Gracious me, I see lots of new faces out there tonight Gracious me! May the Great Spirit—can we knock off that talking in the back there?—be with you always."

"'In the beginning was the Word.' I have taken as my text this evening the almighty Word itself. Now get this: 'There was a man sent from god, whose name was John. The same came for a witness, to bear witness of the Light, that all men through him might believe.' Amen, brothers and sisters, Amen. And the riddle of the Word, 'In the beginning was the Word....' Now what do you suppose old John *meant* by that? That cat was a preacher, and, well, you know how it is with preachers; he had something big on his mind. Oh my, it was big it was the *Truth*, and it was heavy, and old John hurried to set it down. And in his hurry he said too much. 'In the beginning was the Word, and the Word was with God, and the Word was God.' It was the Truth, all right, but it was more than the Truth. The Truth was overgrown with fat, and the fat was God. The fat was *John's* God, and God stood between John and the Truth. Old John, see he got up one morning and caught sight of the truth. It must have been like a bolt of lightning, and the sight of it made him blind. And for a moment the vision burned on in back of his eyes, and he knew what it was. In that instant he saw something he had never seen before and would never see again. That was the instant of revelation, inspiration, Truth. And old John, he must have fallen down on his knees. Man, he must have been shaking and laughing and crying and yelling and praying—all at the same time—and he must have been drunk and delirious[16] with the Truth. Yu see, he had lived all his life waiting for that one moment, and it came, and it took him by surprise, and it was gone. And he said, 'In the beginning was the Word....' And, man, right then and there he should have stopped. There was nothing more to say, but he went on. He had said all there was to say, everything, but he went on. 'In the beginning was the Word....' Brothers and sisters, *that* was the Truth, the whole of it, that essential and eternal Truth, the bone and blood and muscle of the Truth. But he went on, old John, because he was a preacher. The perfect vision faded from his mind, and he went on. The instant passed, and then he had nothing but memory. He was desperate and confused, and in his confusion he stumble and went on. 'In the beginning was the Word, and the Word was with god, and the Word was God.' He went on to talk about Jews and Jerusalem, Levites[17] and Pharisees[18], Moses and Philip and Andrew and Peter. Don't you see? Old John *had* to go on. That cat had a whole lot at stake. He couldn't let the truth alone. He couldn't see that he had come to the end of the Truth, and he went on. He tried to make it bigger and better than it was, but instead he only demeaned[19] and encumbered it. He made it soft and big with fat. He was a preacher, and he made a complex sentence of the Truth, two sentences, three, a paragraph. He made a sermon and theology of the Truth. He imposed his idea of God upon the everlasting Truth. 'In the beginning was the Word....'" And that is all there was, and it was enough.

"Now, brothers and sisters, old John was a white man, and the white man has his ways. Oh gracious me, he has his ways. He adds and divides and multiplies the Word. And in all of this he subtracts the Truth. And, brothers and sisters, you have come here to live in the white man's world. Now the white man deals in words, and he deals easily, with grace and sleight of hand. And in his presence, hire on his own ground, you are as children, mere babes in the woods. You must not mind, for in this you have a certain advantage. A child can listen and learn. The word is sacred to a child."

"My grandmother was a storyteller; she knew her way around words. She never learned to read and write, but somehow she knew the good of reading and writing; she had learned how to listen and delight. She had learned that in words and in language, and there only, she could have whole and consummate being. She told me stories, and she taught me how to listen. I was a child and I listened. She told me stories, and she taught me how to listen. I was a child and I listened. She could neither read nor write, you see, but she taught me how to live among her words, how to listen and delight. 'Storytelling; to utter and to hear....' And the simple act of listening is crucial to the concept of language, more crucial even than reading and writing, and language in turn is crucial to human society. There is proof of that, I think, in all the histories and prehistories of human experience. When that old Kiowa woman told me stories, I listened with only one ear. I was a child, and I took the words for granted. I did not know what all of them meant, but somehow I held on to them; I remembered them, and I remember them now. The stories were old and dear; they meant, a great deal to my grandmother. It was not until she died that I knew how *much* they meant to her. I began to think about it, and then I knew. When she told me those old stories, something strange and good and powerful was going on. I was a child, and that old woman was asking me to come directly into the presence of her mind and spirit; she was taking hold of my imagination, giving me to share in the great fortune of her wonder and delight. She was asking me to go with her to the confrontation of something that was sacred and eternal. It was a timeless, *timeless* thing; nothing of her old age or of my childhood came between us."

"Children have a greater sense of the power and beauty of words than have the rest of us in general. And if that is so, it is because there occurs—or reoccurs—in the mind of every child something like a reflection of all human experience. I have heard that the human fetus[20] corresponds in its development, stage by stage, to the scale of evolution. Surely it is no less reasonable to suppose that the waking mind of a child corresponds in the same way to the whole evolution of human thought and perception."

"In the white man's world, language, too—and the way in which the white man thinks of it—has undergone a process of change. The white man takes such things as words and literatures for granted, as indeed he must, for nothing in his world is so commonplace. On every side of him there are words by the millions, and unending succession of pamphlets and papers letters and books, bills and bulletins, commentaries and conversations. He has diluted and multiplied the Word, and words have begun to close in upon him. He is sated and insensitive; his regard for language—for the Word itself—as an instrument of creation has diminished nearly to the point of no return. It may be that he will perish by the Word."

"But it was not always so with him, and it is not so with you. Consider for a moment that old Kiowa[21] woman, my grandmother, whose use of language was confined to speech. And be assured that her regard for words was always keen in proportion as she depended upon them. You see, for her words were medicine; they were magic and invisible. They came from nothing into sound and meaning. They were beyond price; they could neither be bought nor sold. And she never threw words away."

My grandmother used to tell me the story of Tai-me[22], of how Tai-me came to the Kiowas. The Kiowas were a sun dance culture, and Tai-me was their sun dance doll, their most sacred fetish; no medicine was ever more powerful. There is a story about the coming of Tai-me. This is what my grandmother told me:

Long ago there were bad times. The Kiowas were hungry and there was no food. There was a man who heard his children cry from hunger, and he began to search for food. He walked four days and became very weak. On the fourth day he came to a great canyon. Suddenly there was thunder and lightning. A Voice spoke to him and said, "Why are you following me? What do you want? The man was afraid. The thing standing before him had the feet of a deer, and its body was covered with feathers. The man answered that the Kiowas were hungry. "Take me with you," the Voice said, "and I will give you whatever you want." From that day Tai-me has belonged to the Kiowas.

"Do you see? There, far off in the darkness, something happened. Do you see? Far, far away in the nothingness something happened. There was a voice, a sound a word—and everything began. The story of the coming of Tai-me has existed for hundreds of years by word of mouth. It represents the oldest and best idea that man has of himself. It represents a very rich literature, which, because it was never written down, was always but one generation form extinction. But for the same reason it was cherished and revered. I could see that reverence in my grandmother's eyes, and I could hear it in her voice. It was that, I think, that old saint John had in mind when he said, 'In the beginning was the Word....' But he went on. He went on to lay a scheme about the Word. He could find no satisfaction in the simple fact that the Word was; he had to account for it, not in terms of that sudden and profound insight, which must have devastated him at once, but in terms of the moment afterward, which was irrelevant and remote; not in terms of his imagination, but only in terms of his prejudice.

"Say this: 'In the beginning was the Word....' There was nothing. There was *nothing!* Darkness. There was darkness, and there was no end to it. You look up sometimes in the night and there are stars; you can see all the way to the stars. And you begin to know the universe, how awful and great it is. The stars lie out against the sky and do not fill it. A single star, flickering out in the universe, is enough to fill the mind, but it is nothing in the night sky. The darkness looms[23] around it. The darkness flows among the stars, and beyond them forever. In the beginning flat is how it was, but there were no stars. There was only the dark infinity in which nothing was. And something happened. At the distance of a star something happened, and everything began. The Word did not come into being, but *it was*. It did not break upon the silence, but *it was older than the silence and the silence and the silence was made of it.*

"Old John caught sight of something terrible. The thing standing before him said, 'Why are you following me? What do you want?' and from that day the Word has belonged to us, who have heard it for what it is, who have lived in fear and awe of it. In the Word was the beginning; '*In the beginning was the Word...*'"

The Priest of the Sun appeared to have spent himself. He stepped back from the lectern and hung his head, smiling. In his mind the earth was spinning and the stars rattled around in the heavens. The sun shone, and the moon. Smiling in a kind of transport, the Priest of the Sun stood silent for a time while the congregation waited to be dismissed.

"Good night," he said, "and get yours"....

Notes:

1. signboard: a board carrying a sign or notice, usually used for advertising of products, events, houses for sale or let, etc.
2. PAN-INDIAN: throughout much of recent U.S. history American Indians have sometimes organized themselves into more complex political and social units that crossed tribal lines, often described by non-Indians as "pan-Indian movements".
3. dais: a raised platform, as in a lecture hall, for speakers or honored guests
4. so much as: used as an intensive to indicate something unexpected
5. firebox: a chamber, such as the furnace of a steam locomotive, in which fuel is burned
6. drapery: a piece or pieces of heavy fabric hanging straight in loose folds, used as a curtain
7. crate: a container, such as a slatted wooden case, used for storing or shipping
8. pew: a pew is a long bench used for seating of a church congregation
9. pane: window glass
10. squat: short and thickset, pudgy, stocky
11. lectern: reading stand, stand with a slanted top on which a speaker or lecturer puts his books or papers (in a church, etc.)
12. "*in principio erat verbum*": (Latin) in the beginning was the word
13. protrude: to push or thrust outward
14. caricature: drawing that exaggerates certain physical characteristics; something absurd
15. callousness: hardness; heartlessness, lack of sympathy
16. delirious: overly excited
17. Levite: Levite, member of the tribe of Levi (one of the 12 tribes of Israel); Leviticus, third book of the Old Testament (contains the Levitical laws and

rituals)

18. Pharisee: a member of an ancient Jewish sect that emphasized strict interpretation and observance of the Mosaic law in both its oral and written form.

19. demean: to conduct or behave (oneself) in a particular manner

20. fetus: young of a human or animal while in the womb or egg

21. Kiowa: the Kiowa are a nation of Native Americans who lived mostly in the plains of west Texas, Oklahoma and eastern New Mexico at the time of the arrival of Europeans. Today the Kiowa Tribe is federally recognized, with about 12,000 members living in southwestern Oklahoma.

22. Tai-me: the Tai-me was a sacred image of a human figure. The Kiowa kept a feathered effigy called the Tai-Me. The keeper of the Tai-Me made a smoke offering before the image is exposed in the Sun Dance ceremony

23. loom: appear as a large and indistinct form; appear as larger than life

Questions for Study and Discussion:

1. Explain reverend Tosamah's description of white people's relationship to language. By contrast, how does Tosamah characterize Indians' relationship to language?

2. Explain the connection Tosamah makes between the Gospel of John and Kiowa mythology. Why is it important that this character connect "white" Christianity with Indian religion for his audience at the Pan Indian Rescue Mission? Speculate about Momaday's message in developing the character of this preacher.

3. Explain the reason for the change of manner and speech content between Tosamah's first part of sermon and the following part? What do you think happened to him?

4. What is Tosamah's opinion concerning the relationship of words, existence and nothingness?

5. How do you understand "It was the truth, all right, but it was more than the Truth, the Truth was overgrown with fat, and the fat was God. The fat was John's God, and God stood between john and the truth."? What does Tosamah mean by "fat"? What do you think is the relationship of truth, fat and God?

Leslie Marmon Silko (1948—)

Life and Major Works

Leslie Marmon Silko was born on March 5, 1948, in Albuquerque, New Mexico. Raised on the Laguna Pueblo Reservation in northern New Mexico, Silko's cultural and ethnic heritage was a mix of Laguna Pueblo, Plains Indian, Mexican, and Anglo-American. She attended schools run by the Bureau of Indian Affairs (BIA) and Catholic schools in Albuquerque. Also central to her education were several generations of women in her family, such as her grandmother

Leslie Marmon Silko

and aunt, from whom she learned much about her cultural traditions.

In 1969 Silko received her B.A. from the University of New Mexico, where she graduated summa cum laude. Her short story "The Man to Send Rain Clouds" was first published while she was still in college, and has since been reprinted in several anthologies. She briefly attended law school, but left in order to pursue a career in writing. Silko has taught at Navajo Community College in Tsaile, Arizona; the University of New Mexico; and the department of English at the University of Arizona, Tucson. She spent two years living in Alaska, where she wrote her first novel, *Ceremony* (1977).As the first Native American woman ever to publish a novel. Silko is widely recognized as one of the most important Native American writers of her generation. The publication of *Ceremony* brought her widespread critical attention and acclaim. The novel is set primarily in the years following World War II and revolves around Tayo, a veteran of mixed white and Laguna heritage who returns to the reservation shattered by his war experiences. He ultimately finds healing, however, with the help of Betonie, an elderly man who, like Tayo, is an outcast from Laguna society due to his white heritage, and T'seh Montano, a medicine woman who embodies the feminine, life-giving aspects of the earth. Through them, Tayo learns that his community's ancient ceremonies are not merely rituals, but a means of achieving one's proper place within the universe. To underscore this concept, Silko incorporates Laguna myths and historical incidents, reflecting the Pueblo's abiding connection to the natural world which counteracts the despair and alienation engendered by white society.

Silko's collection *Storyteller,* published in 1981, includes some of her earlier poems from *Laguna Woman,* as well as autobiographical reminiscences, short stories, songs, and newer poems, as well as photographs of her family and ancestors taken by her father, who is a professional photographer. In this interweaving of various literary forms, Silko attempted to capture the storytelling forms of the oral tradition in Native American culture. In 1983, Silko received the distinguished Mac Arthur Foundation award of $176,000. This allowed her to devote herself full time to her next novel, *Almanac of the Dead,* which took almost ten years to write and was published in 1991. It is of epic proportions, and includes a wide range of characters. It covers five centuries of conflict between Native American and European cultures, focusing on a mixed – race family. *Almanac of the Dead* has received a mixed response from critics. While some have rated the novel highly for its mythical elements, others have criticized it for its sprawling structure and underdeveloped characterization. In 1996, Silko published a collection of her own essays entitled *Yellow Woman and a Beauty of the Spirit: Essays on Native American Life Today,* which includes discussion of Native American tradition, philosophy, and politics. Her novel *Gardens in the Dunes* was published in 1999. It focuses on the character of Indigo, a Native American woman who runs away from a white government school and ends up traveling throughout Europe, England and Brazil.

Brief Introduction and Appreciation

The short story "Lullaby" is one of the most noted of the *Storyteller* collection, and has been anthologized in *The Best American Short Stories of 1985,* as well as the *Norton Anthology of Women's Literature.*

The story begins with Ayah, an old Native American woman, leaning against a tree near a stream, reminiscing about some of the most tragic events of her life, as well as about the role of her grandmother in some of the most happy events of her life: "She was an old woman now, and her life had become memories." She recalls watching her mother weaving outside on a big loom, while her grandmother spun wool into yarn. She remembers her mother and the old woman who helped her give birth to her first child, Jimmie. Yet she also recalls the time the white man came to her door to announce that Jimmie had died in a helicopter crash in the war. Because Ayah could not speak English, her husband, Chato, had to translate the tragic news to her. As Ayah reminisces about her life, including the loss of her children, the eventual rift between her husband and herself, and other tragic losses, the narrative slowly catches up to the present. In recent years, Ayah and Chato have begun receiving federal assistance checks in order to survive—Chato would immediately cash the check and go to spend it at the bar. In the present tense of the story, Ayah goes there to look for him. When she does not find him there, she goes out in the snow to search for him, and comes upon him walking toward home. When they stop to rest, he lies down in the snow, and she realizes that he is dying. She tucks a blanket around him and begins to sing a lullaby her grandmother had sung when she was little: "And she sang the only song she knew how to sing for babies. She could not remember if she had ever sung it to her children, but she knew that her grandmother had sung it and her mother had sung it." The lullaby she sings to her husband at the end of the story, as he lies dying in the snow, brings the oral tradition full circle, as she recalls this song that her grandmother sang to her as a child.Thus, Silko draws upon religious and philosophic ideas from her Native American oral and cultural storytelling traditions to create poignant artistic creations.

Silko's body of work has been noted for the ways in which her characters incorporate Native American tradition and ritual into a context of experiences in contemporary Native American life. She has been particularly interested in the role of the storyteller in Native American culture, and the transformative power of the act of storytelling itself. Her writing style has attempted to represent the Native American literary tradition in a written English form by interweaving memoirs, songs, poems, and photography into non-linear narrative. Of mixed Anglo and Native American heritage herself, Silko's characters are often of mixed race, and must struggle to reconcile their dual cultural heritage. Having learned much about her Laguna Pueblo cultural heritage from her grandmother and other female relatives, Silko often focuses on themes of the ways in which native culture is passed on through the matrilinear generations. She has explained that Pueblo Indian culture is in many ways matriarchal, and that women and men do not suffer the kinds of gender inequalities present in Anglo culture.

Selected Reading

Lullaby

The sun had gone down but the snow in the wind gave off its own light. It came in thick tufts like new wool—washed before the weaver spins it. Ayah[1] reached out for it like her own babies had, and she smiled when she remembered how she had laughed at them. She was an old woman now, and her life had become memories. She sat down with her back against the wide cottonwood tree, feeling the rough bark on her back bones; she faced east and listened to the wind and snow sing a high-pitched Yeibechei[2] song. Out of the wind she felt warmer, and she could watch the wide fluffy snow fill in her tracks, steadily, until the direction she had come from was gone. By the light of the snow she could see the dark outline of the big arroyo a few feet away. She was sitting on the edge of Cebolleta[3] Creek, where in the springtime the thin cows would graze on grass already chewed flat to the ground. In the wide deep creek bed where only a trickle of water flowed in the summer, the skinny cows would wander, looking for new grass along winding paths splashed with manure.

Ayah pulled the old Army blanket over her head like a shawl. Jimmie's blanket—the one he had sent to her. That was a long time ago and the green wool was faded, and it was unraveling on the edges. She did not want to think about Jimmie. So she thought about the weaving and the way her mother had done it. On the tall wooden loom set into the sand under a tamarack[4] tree for shade. She could see it clearly. She had been only a little girl when her grandma gave her the wooden combs to pull the twigs and burrs from the raw, freshly washed wool. And while she combed the wool, her grandma sat beside her, spinning a silvery strand of yarn around the smooth cedar spindle. Her mother worked at the loom with yarns dyed bright yellow and red and gold. She watched them dye the yarn in boiling black pots full of beeweed petals, juniper berries, and sage. The blankets her mother made were soft and woven so tight that rain rolled off them like birds' feathers. Ayah remembered sleeping warm on cold windy nights, wrapped in her mother's blandest on the hogan's[5] sandy floor.

The snow drifted now, with the north-west wind hurling it in gusts. It drifted up around her black overshoes—old ones with little metal buckles. She smiled at the snow which was trying to cover her little by little. She could remember when they had no black rubber overshoes; only the high buck-skin leggings that they wrapped over their elkhide moccasins. If the snow was dry or frozen, a person could walk all day and not get wet; and in the evenings the beams of the ceiling would hang with lengths of pale buckskin leggings, drying out slowly.

She felt peaceful remembering. She didn't feel cold any more. Jimmie's blanket seemed warmer than it had ever been. And she could remember the morning he was born. She could remember whispering to her mother, who was sleeping on the other side of the hogan, to tell her it was time now. She did not want to wake the others. The second time she called to her, her mother stood up and pulled on her shoes; she knew. They walked to the old stone hogan together, Ayah walking a step behind her mother. She waited alone, learning the rhythms of the pains while her mother went to call the old woman to help them. The morning was already warm even before dawn and Ayah smelled the bee flowers blooming and the young willow growing at the springs. She could remember that so clearly, but his birth merged into the births of the other children and to her it became all the same birth. They named him for the summer morning and in English they called him Jimmie.

It wasn't like Jimmie died. He just never came back, and one day a dark blue sedan with white writing on its doors pulled up in front of the boxcar shack where the rancher let the Indians live. A man in a khaki uniform trimmed in gold gave them a yellow piece of paper and told them that Jimmie was dead. He said the Army would try to get the body back and then it would be shipped to them; but it wasn't likely because the helicopter had burned after it crashed. All of this was told to Chato[6] because he could understand English. She stood inside the doorway holding the baby while Chato listened. Chato spoke English like a white man and he spoke Spanish too. He was taller than the white man and he stood straighter too. Chato didn't explain why; he just told the military man they could keep the body if they found it. The white man looked bewildered; he nodded his head and he left. Then Chato looked at her and shook his head, and then he told her, "Jimmie isn't coming home anymore," and when he spoke, he used the words to speak of the dead. She didn't cry then, but she hurt inside with anger. And she mourned him as the years passed, when a horse fell with Chato and broke his leg, and the white rancher told them he wouldn't pay Chato until he could work again. She mourned Jimmie because he would have worked for his father then; he would have saddled the big bay[7] horse and ridden the fence lines each day, with wire cutters and heavy gloves, fixing the break in the barbed wire and putting the stray cattle back inside again.

She mourned him after the white doctors came to take Danny and Ella away. She was at the shack alone that day they came. It was back in the days before they hired Navajo women to go with them as interpreters. She recognized one of the doctors. She had seen him at the children's clinic at Canoncito[8] about a month ago.

They were wearing khaki uniforms and they waved papers at her and a black ball-point pen, trying to make her under- stand their English words. She was frightened by the way they looked at the children, like the lizard watches the fly. Danny was swinging on the tire swing on the elm tree behind the rancher's house, and Ella was toddling around the front door, dragging the broomstick horse Chato made for her. Ayah could see they wanted her to sign the papers, and Chato had taught her to sign her name. It was something she was proud of. She only wanted them to go and to take their eyes away from her children.

She took the pen from the man without looking at his face and she signed the papers in three different places he pointed to. She stared at the ground by their feet and waited for them to leave. But they stood there and began to point and gesture at the children. Danny stopped swinging. Ayah could see his fear. She moved suddenly and grabbed Ella into her arms; the child squirmed, trying to get back to her toys. Ayah ran with the baby toward Danny; she screamed for him to run and then she grabbed him around his chest and carried him too. She ran south into the foothills of juniper trees and black lava rock. Behind her she heard the doctors running, but they had been taken by surprise, and as the hills became steeper and the cholla cactus were thicker, they stopped. When she reached the top of the hill, she stopped to listen in case they were circling around her. But in a few minutes she heard a car engine start and they drove away. The children had been too surprised to cry while she ran with them. Danny was shaking and Ella's little fingers were gripping Ayah's blouse.

She stayed up in the hills for the rest of the day, sitting on a black lave boulder in the sunshine where she could see for miles all around her. The sky was light blue and cloud-less, and it was warm for late April. The sun warmth relaxed her and took the fear and anger away. She lay back on the rock and watched the sky. It seemed to her that she could walk into the sky, stepping through clouds endlessly. Danny played with little pabbles and stones, pretending they were birds'eggs and then little rabbits. Ella sat at her feet and dropped fistfuls of dirt into the breeze, watching the dust and particles of sand intently. Ayah watched a hawk soar high above them, dark wings gliding; hunting or only watching, she did not know. The hawk was patient and he circled all afternoon before he disappeared around the high volcanic peak the Mexicans called Guadalupe.

Late in the afternoon, Ayah looked down at the gray boxcar shack with the paint all peeled from the wood; the stove pipe on the roof was rusted and crooked.

The fire she had built that morning in the oil drum stove had burned out. Ella was asleep in her lap now and Danny sat close to her, complaining that he was hungry; he asked when they would go to the house. "We will stay up here until your father comes," she told him, "because those white men were chasing us." The boy remembered then and he nodded at her silently.

If Jimmie had been there he could have read those papers and explained to her what they said. Ayah would have known then, never to sign them. The doctors came back the next day and they brought a BIA[9] policeman with them. They told Chato they had her signature and that was all they needed. Except for the kids. She listened to Chato sullenly; she hated him when he told her it was the old woman who died in the winter, spitting blood; it was her old grandma who had given the children this disease. "They don't spit blood," she said coldly. "The whites lie." She held Ella and Danny close to her, ready to run to the hills again. "I want a medicine man first," she said to Chato, not looking at him. He shook his head. "It's too late now. The policeman is with them. You signed the paper." His voice was gentle.

It was worse than if they had died: to lose the children and to know that somewhere, in a place called Colorado, in a place full of sick and dying strangers, her children were without her. There had been babies that died soon after they were born, and one that died before he could walk. She had carried them herself, up to the boulders and great pieces of the cliff that long ago crashed down from Long Mesa; she laid them in the crevices of sandstone and buried them in fine brown sand with round quartz pebbles that washed down the hills in the rain. She had endured it because they had been with her. But she could not bear this pain. She did not sleep for a long time after they took her children. She stayed on the hill where they had fled the first time, and she slept rolled up in the blanket Jimmie had sent her. She carried the pain in her belly and it was fed by everything she saw: the blue sky of their last day together and the dust and pebbles they played with; the swing in the elm tree and broomstick horse choked life from her. The pain filled her stomach and there was no room for food or for her lungs to fill with air. The air and the food would have been theirs.

She hated Chato, not because he let the policeman and doctors put the screaming children in the government car, but because he had caught her to sign her name. Because it was like the old ones always told her about learning their language or any of their ways: it endangered you. She slept alone on the hill until the middle of November when the first snows came. Then she made a bed for herself where the children had slept. She did not lie down beside Chato again until many years later, when he was sick and shivering and only her body could keep him warm. The illness came after the white rancher told Chato he was too old to work for him anymore, and Chato and his old woman should be out of the shack by the next afternoon because the rancher had hired new people to work there. That had satisfied her. To see how the white man repaid Chato's years of loyalty and work. All of Chato's fine-sounding English talk didn't change things.

It snowed steadily and the luminous light from the snow gradually diminished into the darkness. Somewhere in Cebolleta a dog barded and other village dogs joined with it. Ayah looked in the direction she had come, from the bar where Chato was buying the wine. Sometimes he told her to go on ahead and wait; and then he never came. And when she finally went back looking for him, she would find him passed out at the bottom of the wooden steps to Azzie's Bar. All the wine would be gone and most of the money too, from the pale blue check that came to them once a month in a government envelope. It was then that she would look at his face and his hands, scarred by ropes and the barbed wire of all those years, and she would think, this man is a stranger; for forty years she had smiled at him and cooked his food, but he remained a stranger. She stood up again, with the snow almost to her knees, and she walked back to find Chato.

It was hard to walk in the deep snow and she felt the air burn in her lungs. She stopped a short distance from the bar to rest and readjust the blanket. But this time he wasn't waiting for her on the bottom step with his old Stetson hat pulled down and his shoulders hunched up in his long wool overcoat.

She was careful not to slip on the wooden steps. When she pushed the door open, warm air and cigarette smoke hit her face. She looked around slowly and deliberately, in every corner, in every dark place that the old man might find to sleep. The bar owner didn't like Indians in there, especially Navajos, but he let Chato come in because he could talk Spanish like he was one of them. The men at the bar stared at her, and the bartender saw that she left the door open wide. Snowflakes were flying inside like moths and melting into a puddle on the oiled wood floor. He motioned to her to close the door, but she did not see him. She held herself straight and walked across the room slowly, searching the room with every step. The snow in her hair melted and she could feel it on her forehead. At the far corner of the room, she saw red flames at the mica window of the old stove door;

she looked behind the stove just to make sure. The bar got quiet except for the Spanish polka music playing on the jukebox. She stood by the stove and shook the snow from her blanket and held it near the stove to dry. The wet wool smell reminded her of new-born goats in early March, brought inside to warm near the fire. She felt clam.

In past years they would have told her to get out. But her hair was white now and her face was wrinkled. They looked at her like she was a spider crawling slowly across the room. They were afraid; she could feel the fear. She looked at their faces steadily. They reminded her of the first time the white people brought her children back to her that winter. Danny had een shy and hid behind the thin white woman who brought them. And the baby had not known her until Ayah took her into her arms, and then Ella had nuzzled close to her as she had when she was nursing. The blonde woman was nervous and kept looking at a dainty gold watch on her wrist. She sat on the bench near the small window and watched the dark snow clouds gather around the mountains; she was worrying about the unpaved road. She was frightened by what she saw inside too: the strips of venison drying on a rope across the ceiling and the children jabbering excitedly in a language she did not know. So they stayed for only a few hours. Ayah watched the government car disappear down the road and she knew they were already being weaned from these lava hills and from this sky. The last time they came was in early June, and Ella stared at her the way the men in the bar were now staring. Ayah did not try to pick her up; she smiled at her instead and spoke cheerfully to Danny. When he tried to answer her, he could not seem to remember and he spoke English words with the Navajo. But he gave her a scrap of paper that he had found somewhere and carried in his pocked; it was folded in half, and he shyly looked up at her and said it was a bird. She asked Chato if they were home for good this time. He spoke to the white woman and she shook her head. "How much longer?" he asked, and she said she didn't know; but Chato saw how she stared at the boxcar shack. Ayah turned away then. She did not say good-bye.

She felt satisfied that the men in the bar feared her. Maybe it was her face and the way she held her mouth with teeth clenched tight, like there was nothing anyone could do to her now. she walked north down the road, searching for the old man. She did this because she had the blanket, and there would be no place for him except with her and the blanket in the old adobe barn near the arroyo. They always slept there when they came to Cebolleta. If the money and the wine were gone, she would be relieved because then they could go home again: back to the old hogan with a dirt roof and rock walls where she herself had been born. And the next day the old man could go back to the few sheep they still had, to follow along behind them, guiding them, into dry sandy arroyos where sparse grass grew. She knew he did not like walking behind old ewes when for so many years he rode big quarter horses and worked with cattle. But she wasn't sorry for him; he should have known all along what would happen.

There had not been enough rain for their garden in five years; and that was when Chato finally hitched a ride into the town and brought back brown boxes of rice and sugar and big tin cans of welfare [10] peaches. After that, at the first of the month they went to Cebolleta to ask the postmaster for the check; and then Chato would go to the bar and cash it. They did this as they planted the garden every May, not because anything would survive the summer dust, but because it was time to do this. The journey passed the days that smelled silent and dry like the caves above the canyon with yellow painted buffaloes on their walls.

He was walking along the pavement when she found him. He did not stop or turn around when he heard her behind him. She walked beside him and she noticed how slowly he moved now. He smelled strong of woodsmoke and urine. Lately he had been forgetting. Sometimes he called her by his sister's name and she had been gone for a long time. Once she had found him wandering on the road to the white man's ranch, and she asked him why he was going that way; he laughed at her and said, "You know they can't run that ranch without me," and he walked on determined, limping on the leg that had been crushed many years before. Now he looked at her curiously, as if for the first time, but he kept shuffling along, moving slowly along the side of the highway. His gray hair had grown long and spread out on the shoulders of the long overcoat. He wore the old felt hat pulled down over his ears. His boots were worn out at the toes ad he had stuffed pieces of an old red shirt in the holes. The rags made his feet look like little animals up to their ears in snow. She laughed at his feet; the snow muffled the sound of her laugh. He stopped and looked at her again. The wind had quit blowing and the snow was falling straight down; the southeast sky was beginning to clear and Ayah could see a star.

"Let's rest awhile," she said to him. They walked away from the road and up the slope to the giant boulders that had tumbled down from the red sandrock mesa throughout the centuries of rainstorms and earth tremors. In a place where the boulders shut out the wind, they sat down with their backs against the rock. She offered half of the blanket to him and they sat wrapped together.

The storm passed swiftly. The clouds moved east. They were massive and full, crowding together across the sky. She watched them with the feeling of horses—steely blue-gray horses startled across the sky. The powerful haunches pushed into the distances and the tail hairs streamed white mist behind them. The sky cleared. Ayah saw that there was nothing between her and the stars. The light was crystalline. [11] There was no shimmer, no distortion through earth haze. She breathed the clarity of the night sky; she smelled the purity of the half moon and the stars. He was lying on his side with his knees pulled up near his belly for warmth. His eyes were closed now, and in the light from the stars and the moon, he looked young again.

She could see it descend out of the night sky: an icy stillness from the edge of the thin moon. She recognized the freezing. It came gradually, sinking snowflake by snowflake until the crust was heavy and deep. It had the strength of the stars in Orion, and its journey was endless. Ayah knew that with the wine he would sleep. He would not feel it. She tucked the blanket around him, remembering how it was when Ella had been with her; and she felt the rush so big inside her heart for the babies. And she sang the only song she knew to sing for babies. She could not remember if she had ever sung it to her children, but she knew that her grandmother had sung it and her mother had sung it:

> The earth is your mother,
> she holds you.
> The sky is your father,
> he protects you.
> Sleep,
> sleep.
> Rainbow is your sister,
> she loves you.
> The winds are your brothers,
> they sing to you.
> Sleep,
> sleep.
> We are together always

> We are together always
>
> There never was a time
>
> when this
>
> was not so.

Notes:

1. Ayah refers to an old Native American woman in the story.
2. The Yeibechei are masked Navajo dancers who sing in high-pitched voices.
3. Cebolleta is also the name of a town in the story.
4. tamarack: another name for the larch, a tree in the pine family.
5. Traditionally, a hogan is a Navajo dwelling made of wood and covered with earth.
6. Chato refers to Ayah's husband in the story.
7. Here, bay is the horse's color—a reddish brown.
8. Canoncito is the name of the Navajo reservation located in west central New Mexico.
9. The Bureau of Indian Affairs, or BIA, is the federal agency in charge of administering government policies toward Native Americans.
10. The canned peaches came from a government welfare program to help needy people.
11. Here, crystalline means "clear and pure as a crystal."

Questions for Study and Discussion:

1. past? What are those events?
2. What happened to Jimmie, to Danny and Ella, and to Ayah's other children?
3. Describe the type of life Ayah and Chato are living at the present time. Why have they come to Cebolleta?
4. How does Chato look and act when Ayah finally finds him?
5. Describe Ayah's thoughts and actions after she and Chato find shelter among the boulders.
6. Why might Ayah's thoughts turn so often to the past?
7. How did Ayah react to what happened to Jimmie? To Danny and Ella? To her other children? Explain why you think Ayah reacted the way she did. Use details from the story to support your answers. In the first three paragraphs of the story, what things around Ayah remind her of events in the
8. In your opinion, how does Ayah feel about her husband? Use evidence from the story to support your ideas.

9. What is the mood at the end of the story,when Ayah and Chato are resting? What details help to create that mood?

10. In your opinion,is "Lullaby"an appropriate title for the story? Explain.

Louise Erdrich (1954—　)

Life and Major Works

Born in Minnesota, near the Turtle Mountain Chippewa reservation in North Dakota, on July 6, 1954, Louise Erdrich was the eldest of seven children. A strong influence was her severe Catholic upbringing in Wahpeton, North Dakota, but she was also exposed to the storytelling

Louise Erdrich

of her German-American father and of her maternal grandparents whom she visited on the reservation. Her parents, both teachers for the Bureau of Indian Affairs, encouraged her childhood story-writing efforts, though she never spoke a tribal language and was little aware of her Native American heritage. That ignorance changed at Dartmouth; where she enrolled in 1972, when the college first accepted female students and initiated an innovative Native-American Studies program with anthropologist Michael Dorris as chair. In his classes, Erdrich began to explore her own Chippewa heritage, which has stimulated her writing ever since.

As a young adult, Erdrich worked in a variety of jobs, including beet-weeder, lifeguard, waitress, poetry teacher to prison inmates, hospital psychiatric aide, and construction flagger. After completing her B. A. at Dartmouth, she did graduate work at Johns Hopkins, where she also taught writing for a year, earning an M.A. in 1979. She returned to Dartmouth as a visiting fellow and writer-in-residence. At a reading that Erdrich gave, Dorris was impressed with her poetry and became interested in collaborating with her, so they began trading drafts of stories and poems they were working on. The following year, she served as editor for *The Circle*, the newspaper of the Boston Indian Council. This experience with urban, mixed-blood Indians further validated her own confusion about her ethnic identity and stimulated her interest in writing about her Native American roots.

When Dorris returned to New Hampshire from a research trip, Erdrich moved back too, and the couple began writing short stories together. In fact, the collaboration was so successful that one story, "The World's Greatest Fisherman," won a $5,000 prize, and Erdrich decided to expand this work into her first novel, *Love Medicine* (1984). As they worked together, their relationship grew more personal, and they were married in 1981. Their collaboration technique was meticulous, if not exhausting. Typically, the originating author of an idea would create a first draft and then receive editing suggestions from the other. This process might be repeated through five drafts, until both would read the manuscript aloud and edit every word together. This process has helped to create rich narratives, dense with incident and idiosyncratic characterizations. *Love Medicine*, a complex Faulkneresque story told by seven narratives voices, won the 1985 National Book Critics Circle Award for best fiction.

In subsequent novels— *The Beet Queen* (1986) and *Tracks* (1988)—Erdrich has developed many of the same characters and settings as in the first book, and these works have also become national best-sellers. In the series, the author explores universal family life-cycles while also communicating a sense of the changes and loss involved in the twentieth-century Native American experience. Erdrich's major theme in these works is the breakdown of families and the sustaining continuity of reservation culture even amid the traumatic dislocation and marginalization of Indian life. Among many families in these novels, mothers abandon their children, while fathers are either abusive or absent, emotionally and physically. However, Erdrich is most concerned with the tribal members who share the mothering role toward the cast-off children. According to Hentha D. Wong, "mothering is not merely an activity but an orientation to the world—a recognition of a responsibility to the interrelatedness of all beings". But this sustaining relationship is available only on the reservation, to those who leave both children and parents—suffer alienation from their immediate family and their tribal community. Thus, a related theme in Erdrich's work is that of homecoming, which is especially acute among the mixed-bloods, whose ethnicity and personal identity are often in doubt.

Brief Introduction and Appreciation

Love Medicine, a novel by Louise Erdrich, was first published in 1984 and republished in an expanded version in 1993. Among the first works by a Native American woman to portray modern Indian life, *Love Medicine* depicts several generations of three families whose members search for an identity that fuses their

Native and European American roots. Erdrich, whose ancestry includes both Ojibwa and German Americans, is a member of the Turtle Mountain community of the Chippewa Nation. She drew on memories of childhood visits to North Dakota reservations for the book. The novel interlaces the narratives of the families, who live on a fictionalized reservation, offering multiple authentic "Indian" points of view through sharply individual characters.

Each chapter is narrated by a different character. These narratives are very conversational, as if the narrators were telling a story, often from the first-person perspective. There are, however, five chapters that are told from a limited third-person perspective. The narratives follow a loose chronology aside from the first chapter (set in 1981). The tone of the novel is very conversational and indicative of the storytelling tradition in Native American culture. It draws from Ojibwa myths, story-telling technique and culture. However, it also incorporates the Euro-Indian experience especially through the younger generations who have been forced by government policy to accept, if not possess, Euro-American culture.

Academic critics have praised *Love Medicine* for its lyrical prose, complex nonlinear narrative, Native and European tropes, and themes including both opposing heritages and cultural hybridity. Some Native American writers, however, have asserted that Erdrich's novels have become the dominant representation of Native life, rather than one facet of a diverse culture. Some Turtle Mountain readers have objected to Erdrich's stylistic flourishes and impoverished, despairing characters. Nonetheless, *Love Medicine* has been a groundbreaking text, generating wider appreciation for works representing Natives as contemporary Americans rather than romanticized noble savages.

In "Saint Marie", the main character, fourteen-year-old Marie Lazarre, narrates the tale of her near transformation to Catholicism and sainthood fifty years after the event. Resisting her Native-American ancestry, Marie considers her skin "white" and seeks to escape her seemingly ill-fated life on the reservation through inclusion in the Sacred Heart Convent. In classes taught *Old Testament* style by Sister Leopolda, who later sponsors Marie at the convent, the nun recognizes Marie's desire for acceptance. She names her propensity for daydreaming as the work of the "Dark One," thus inspiring Marie to accept her (and Christ's) teachings. In an effort to fight off the devil and tame Marie's proud spirit, Sister Leopolda pours scalding hot water on the girl's back and pierces her hand with a fork. Marie passes out from the pain of this last wound and wakes to find the nuns all kneeling before her, awaiting her blessing, as Leopolda has told them that it is a holy wound which magically appeared on the girl's hand. In "Saint Marie," Erdrich explores such themes as racism and prejudice. For instance, she examines the various ways Sister Leopolda discriminates against Native Americans, while pushing her audience to understand why it is important to question such behavior. Faced with an ambitious Marie who seeks sainthood and to "inherit [her] keys," Sister Leopolda senses implicit animosity from forces outside her order, both literal and metaphorical. Leopolda's behavior indicates how racism can stem from fear of displacement. Though "Saint Marie" is a story told largely in chronological order, it is simultaneously told through a flashback. An older Marie Kaspaw outlines the events that took place during her fourteenth year as Marie Lazarre, a young girl wishing to enter a local convent. As narrator, Marie provides subtle clues that the event is a disastrous one yet withholds enough information to keep readers interested in plot development. Through use of realism and evocative visual imagery, Erdrich captures the contemporary audience.

Selected Reading:

Love Medicine
Chapter Two
Saint Marie
(1934)
Marie Lazarre

So when I went there, I knew the dark fish must rise. Plumes of radiance had soldered on me. No reservation girl had ever prayed so hard. There was no use in trying to ignore me any longer. I was going up there on the hill with the black robe women. They were not any lighter than me. I was going up there to pray as good as they could. Because I don't have that much Indian blood. And they never thought they'd have a girl from this reservation as a saint they'd have to kneel to. But they'd have me. And I'd be carved in pure gold. With ruby lips. And my toenails would be little pink ocean shells, which they would have to stoop down off their high horse to kiss.

I was ignorant. I was near age fourteen. The length of sky is just about the size of my ignorance. Pure and wide. And it was just that—the pure and wideness of my ignorance —that got me up the hill to Sacred Heart Convent and brought me back down alive. For maybe Jesus did not take my bait, but them Sisters tried to cram me right down whole.

You ever see a walleye strike so bad the lure is practically out its back end before you reel it in? That is what they done with me. I don't like to make that low comparison, but I have seen a walleye do that once. And it's the same attempt as Sister Leopolda made to get me in her clutch.

I had the mail-order Catholic soul you get in a girl raised out in the bush, whose only thought is getting into town. For Sunday Mass is the only time my father brought his children in except for school, when we were harnessed. Our soul went cheap. We were so anxious to get there we would have walked in on our hands and knees. We just craved going to the store, slinging bottle caps in the dust, making fool eyes at each other. And of course we went to church.

Where they have the convent is on top of the highest hill, so that from its windows the Sisters can be looking into the marrow of the town. Recently a windbreak was planted before the bar "for the purposes of tornado insurance." Don't tell me that. That poplar stand was put up to hide the drinkers as they get the transformation. As they are served into the beast of their burden. While they're drinking, that body comes upon them, and then they stagger or crawl out the bar door, pulling a weight they can't move past the poplars. They don't want no holy witness to their fall.

Anyway, I climbed. That was a long-ago day. There was a road then for wagons that wound in ruts to the top of the hill where they had their buildings of painted brick. Gleaming white. So white the sun glanced off in dazzling display to set forms whirling behind your eyelids. The face of God you could hardly look at. But that day it drizzled[1], so I could look all I wanted. I saw the homelier side. The cracked whitewash and swallows nesting in the busted ends of eaves. I saw the boards sawed the size of broken windowpanes and the fruit trees, stripped. Only the tough wild rhubarb flourished. Goldenrod rubbed up their walls. It was a poor convent. I didn't see that then but I know that now. Compared to others it was humble, ragtag, out in the middle of no place. It was the end of the world to some. Where the maps stopped. Where God had only half a hand in the creation. Where the Dark One had put in thick bush, liquor, wild dogs, and Indians.

I heard later that the Sacred Heart Convent was a catchall place for nuns that don't get along elsewhere. Nuns that complain too much or lose their mind. I'll always wonder now, after hearing that, where they picked up Sister Leopolda. Perhaps she had scarred someone else, the way she left a mark on me. Perhaps she was just sent around to test her Sisters' faith, here and there, like the spot-checker in a factory. For she was the definite most-hard trial to anyone's endurance, even when they started out with veils of wretched love upon their eyes.

I was that girl who thought the black hem of her garment would help me rise. Veils of love which was only hate petrified by longing—that was me. I was like those bush Indians who stole the holy black hat of a Jesuit and swallowed little scraps of it to cure their fevers. But the hat itself carried smallpox and was killing them with belief. Veils of faith! I had this confidence in Leopolda. She was different. The other Sisters had long ago gone blank and given up on Satan. He slept for them. They never noticed his comings and goings. But Leopolda kept track of him knew his habits, minds he burrowed in, deep spaces where he hid. She knew as much about him as my grandma, who called him by other names and was not afraid.

In her class, Sister Leopolda carried a long oak pole for opening high windows. It had a hook made of iron on one end that could jerk a patch of your hair out or throttle you by the collar—all from a distance. She used this deadly hook-pole for catching Satan by surprise. He could have entered without your knowing it—through your lips or your nose or any one of your seven openings—and gained your mind. But she would see him. That pole would brain you from behind. And he would gasp, dazzled, and take the first things she offered, which was pain.

She had a stringer of children who could only breathe if she said the word. I was the worst of them. She always said the Dark One wanted me most of all, and I believed this. I stood out. Evil was a common thing I trusted. Before sleep sometimes he came and whispered conversation in the old language of the bush. I listened. He told me things he never told anyone but Indians. I was privy to both worlds of his knowledge. I listened to him, but I had confidence in Leopolda. She was the only one of the bunch he even noticed.

There came a day, though, when Leopolda turned the tide with her hook-pole.

It was a quiet day with everyone working at their desks, when I heard him. He had sneaked into the closets in the back of the room. He was scratching around, tasting crumbs in our pockets, stealing buttons, squirting his dark juice in the linings and the boots. I was the only one who heard him, and I got bold. I smiled. I glanced back and smiled and looked up at her sly to see if she had noticed. My heart jumped. For she was looking straight at me. And she sniffed. She had a big stark bony nose stuck to the front of her face for smelling out brimstone and evil thoughts. She had smelled him on me. She stood up. Tall, pale, a blackness leading into the deeper blackness of the slate wall behind her. Her oak pole had flown into her grip. She had seen me glance at the closet. Oh, she knew. She knew just where he was. I watched her watch him in her mind's eye. The whole class was watching now. She was staring, sizing, following his scuffle. And all of a sudden she tensed down, posed on her bent kneesprings, cocked her arm back. She threw the oak pole singing over my head, through my braincloud. It cracked through the thin wood door of the back closet, and the heavy pointed hook drove through his heart. I turned. She'd speared her own black rubber overboot where he'd taken refuge in the tip of her darkest toe.

Something howled in my mind. Loss and darkness. I understood. I was to suffer for my smile.

He rose up hard in my heart. I didn't blink when the pole cracked. My skull was tough. I didn't flinch when she shrieked in my ear. I only shrugged at the flowers of hell. He wanted me. More than anything he craved me. But then she did the worst. She did what broke my mind to her. She grabbed me by the collar and dragged me, feet flying, through the room and threw me in the closet with her dead black overboot. And I was there. The only light was a crack beneath the door. I asked the Dark One to enter into me and boost my mind. I asked him to restrain my tears, for they was pushing behind my eyes. But he was afraid to come back there. He was afraid of her sharp pole. And I was afraid of Leopolda's pole for the first time, too. I felt the cold hook in my heart. How it could crack through the door at any minute and drag me out, like a dead fish on a gaff, drop me on the floor like a gutshot squirrel.

I was nothing. I edged back to the wall as far as I could. I breathed the chalk dust. The hem of her full black cloak cut against my cheek. He had left me. Her spear could find me any time. Her keen ears would aim the hook into the beat of my heart.

What was that sound?

It filled the closet, filled it up until it spilled over, but I did not recognize the crying waling voice as mine until the door cracked open, brightness, and she hoisted me to her camphor-smelling lips.

"He *wants* you," she said. "That's the difference. I give you love."

Love. The black hook. The spear singing through the mind. I saw that she had tracked the Dark One to my heart and flushed him out into the open. So now my heart was an empty nest where she could lurk.

Well, I was weak. I was weak when I let her in, but she got a foothold there. Hard to dislodge as the year passed. Sometimes I felt him—the brush of dim wings—but only rarely did his voice compel. It was between Marie and Leopolda now, and the struggle changed. I began to realize I had been on the wrong track with the fruits of hell. The real way to overcome Leopolda was this: I'd get to heaven first. And then, when I saw her coming, I'd shut the gate. She'd be out! That is why, besides the bowing and the scraping I'd be dealt, I wanted to sit on the altar as a saint.

To this end, I went up on the hill. Sister Leopolda was the consecrated nun who had sponsored me to come there.

"You're not vain," she said. "You're too honest, looking into the mirror, for that. You're not smart. You don't have the ambition to get clear. You have two choices. One, you can marry a no-good Indian, bear his brats, die like a dog. Or two, you can give yourself to God."

"I'll come up there," I said, "but not because of what you think."

I could have had any damn man on the reservation at the time. And I could have made him treat me like his own life. I looked good. And I looked white. But I wanted Sister Leopolda's heart. And here was the thing: sometimes I wanted her heart in love and admiration. Sometimes. And sometimes I wanted her heart to roast on a black stick.

She answered the back door where they had instructed me to call. I stood there with my bundle. She looked me up and down.

"All right," she said finally. "Come in."

She took my hand. Her fingers were like a bundle of broom straws, so thin and dry, but the strength of them was unnatural. I couldn't have tugged loose if she was leading me into rooms of white-hot coal. Her strength was a kind of perverse miracle, for she got it from fasting herself thin. Because of this hunger practice her lips were a wounded brown and her skin deadly pale. Her eye sockets were two deep lashless hollows in a taut skull. I told you about the nose already. It stuck out far and made the place her eyes moved even deeper, as if she stared out the wrong end of a gun barrel. She book the bundle from my hands and threw it in the corner.

"You'll be sleeping behind the stove, child."

It was immense, like a great furnace. There was a small cot close behind it.

"Looks like it could get warm there," I said.

"Hot. It does."

"Do I get a habit?"

I wanted something like the thing she wore. Flowing black cotton. Her face was strapped in white bandages, and a sharp crest of starched white cardboard hung over her forehead like a glaring beak. If possible, I wanted a bigger, longer, whiter beak than hers.

"No," she said, grinning her great skull grin. "You don't get one yet. Who knows, you might not like us. Or we might not like you."

But she had loved me, or offered me love. And she had tried to hunt the Dark One down. So I had this confidence.

"I'll inherit your keys from you," I said.

She looked at me sharply, and her grin turned strange. She hissed, taking in her breath. Then she turned to the door and took a key from her belt. It was a giant key, and it unlocked the larder where the food was stored.

Inside there was all kinds of good stuff. Things I'd tasted only once or twice in my life. I saw sticks of dried fruit, jars of orange peel, spice like cinnamon. I saw tins of crackers with ships painted on the side. I saw pickles. Jars of herring[2] and the rind of pigs. There was cheese, a big brown block of it from the thick milk of goats. And besides that there was the everyday stuff, in great quantities, the flour and the coffee.

It was the cheese that got to me. When I saw it my stomach hollowed. My tongue dripped. I loved that goat-milk cheese better than anything I'd ever ate. I stared at it. The rich curve in the buttery cloth.

"When you inherit my keys," she said sourly, slamming the door in my face, "you can eat all you want of the priest's cheese."

Then she seemed to consider what she'd done. She looked at me. She took the key from her belt and went back, sliced a hunk off, and put it in my hand.

"If you're good you'll taste this cheese again. When I'm dead and gone," she said.

Then she dragged out the big sack of flour. When I finished that heaven stuff she told me to roll my sleeves up and begin doing God's labor. For a while we worked in silence, mixing up the dough and pounding it out on stone slabs.

"God's word," I said after a while. "If this is God's work, then I've done it all my life."

"Well, you've done it with the Devil in your heart then," she said. "Not God."

"How do you know?" I asked. But I knew she did. And I wished I had not brought up the subject.

"I see right into you like a clear glass," she said. "I always did."

"You don't know it," she continued after a while, "but he's come around here sulking. He's come around here brooding. You brought him in. He knows the smell of me, and he's going to make a last ditch try to get you back. Don't let him." She glared over at me. Her eyes were cold and lighted. "Don't let him touch you. We'll be a long time getting rid of him."

So I was careful. I was careful not to give him an inch. I said a rosary, two rosaries, three, underneath my breath. I said the Creed[3]. I said every scrap of Latin I knew while we punched the dough with our fists. And still, I dropped the cup. It rolled under that monstrous iron stove, which was getting fired up for baking.

And she was on me. She saw he'd entered my distraction.

"Our good cup," she said. "Get it out of there, Marie."

I reached for the poker to snag it out from beneath the stove. But I had a sinking feel in my stomach as I did this. Sure enough, her long arm darted past me like a whip. The poker lighted in her hand.

"Reach," she said. "Reach with your arm for that cup. And when your flesh is hot, remember that the flames you feel are only one fraction of the heat you will feel in his hellish embrace."

She always did things this way, to teach you lessons. So I wasn't surprised. It was playacting, anyway, because a stove isn't very hot underneath right along the floor. They aren't made that way. Otherwise a wood floor would burn. So I said yes and got down on my stomach and reached under. I meant to grab it quick and jump up again, before she could think up another lesson, but here it happened. Although I groped for the cup, my hand closed on nothing. That cup was nowhere to be found. I heard her step toward me, a slow step. I heard the creak of thick shoe leather, the little *plat* as the folds of her heavy skirts met, a trickle of fine sand sifting, somewhere, perhaps in the bowels of her, and I was afraid. I tried to scramble up, but her foot came down lightly behind my ear, and I was lowered. The foot came down more firmly at the base of my neck, and I was held.

"You're like I was," she said. "He wants you very much."

"He doesn't want me no more," I said. "He had his fill. I got the cup!"

I heard the valve opening, the hissed intake of breath, and knew that I should not have spoke.

"You lie," she said. "You're cold. There is a wicked ice forming in your blood. You don't have a shred of devotion for God. Only wild cold dark lust. I know it. I know how you feel. I see the beast...the beast watches me out of your eyes sometimes. Cold."

The urgent scrape of metal. It took a moment to know from where. Top of the stove. Kettle. Lessons. She was steadying herself with the iron poker. I could feel it like pure certainty, driving into the wood floor. I would not remind her of pokers. I heard the water as it came, tipped from the spout, cooling as it fell but still scalding as it struck. I must have twitched beneath her foot, because she steadied me, and then the poker nudged up beside my arm as if to guide. "To warm your cold ash heart," she said. I felt how patient she would be. The water came. My mind went dead blank. Again. I could only think the kettle would be cooling slowly in her hand. I could not stand it. I bit my lip so as not to satisfy her with a sound. She gave me more reason to keep still.

"I will boil him from your mind if you make a peep," she said, "by filling up your ear."

Any sensible fool would have run back down the hill the minute[4] Leopolda let them up from under her heel. But I was snared in her black intelligence by then. I could not think straight. I had prayed so hard I think I broke a cog in my mind. I prayed while her foot squeezed my throat. While my skin burst. I prayed even when I heard the wind come through, shrieking in the busted bird nests. I didn't stop when pure light fell, turning slowly behind my eyelids. God's face. Even that did not disrupt my continued praise. Words came. Words came from nowhere and flooded my mind.

Now I could pray much better than any one of them. Than all of them full force. This was proved. I turned to her in a daze when she let me up. My thoughts were gone, and yet I remember how surprised I was. Tears glittered in her eyes, deep down, like the sinking reflection in a well.

"It was so hard, Marie," she gasped. Her hands were shaking. The kettle clattered against the stove. "But I have used all the water up now. I think he is gone."

"I prayed," I said foolishly. "I prayed very hard."

"Yes," she said. "My dear one, I know."

We sat together quietly because we had no more words. We let the dough rise and punched it down once. She gave me a bowl of mush, unlocked the sausage from a special cupboard, and took that in to the Sisters. They sat down the hall, chewing their sausage, and I could hear them. I could hear their teeth bite through their bread and meat. I couldn't move. My shirt was dry but the cloth stuck to my back, and I couldn't think straight. I was losing the sense to understand how her mind worked. She'd gotten past me with her poker and I would never be a saint. I despaired. I felt I had no inside voice, nothing to direct me, no darkness, no Marie. I was about to throw that cornmeal mush out to the birds and make a run for it, when the vision rose up blazing in my mind.

I was rippling gold. My breasts were bare and my nipples flashed and winked. Diamonds tipped them. I could walk through panes of glass. I could walk through windows. She was at my feet, swallowing the glass after each step I took. I broke through another and another. The glass she swallowed ground and cut until her starved insides were only a subtle dust. She coughed. She coughed a cloud of dust. And then she was only a black rag that flapped off, snagged in bob wire, bung there for an age, and finally rotted into the breeze.

I saw this, mouth hanging open, gazing off into the flagged boughs of trees.

"Get up!" she cried. "Stop dreaming. It is time to bake."

Two other Sisters had come in with her, wide women with hands like paddles. They were evening and smoothing out the firebox beneath the great jaws of the oven.

"Who is this one?" they asked Leopolda. "Is she yours?"

"She is mine," said Leopolda. "A very good girl."

"What is your name?" one asked me.

"Marie."

"Marie. Star of the Sea."

"She will shine," said Leopolda, "when we have burned off the dark corrosion."

The others laughed, but uncertainly. They were mild and sturdy French, who did not understand Leopolda's twisted jokes, although they muttered respectfully at things she said. I knew they wouldn't believe what she had done with the kettle. There was no question. So I kept quiet.

"*Elle est docile*,"[5] they said approvingly as they left to starch the linens.

"Does it pain?" Leopolda asked me as soon as they were out the door.

I did not answer. I felt sick with the hurt.

"Come along," she said.

The building was wholly quiet now. I followed her up the narrow staircase into a ball of little rooms, many doors. Her cell was the quietest, at the very end. Inside, their smelled stale, as if the door had not been opened for years. There was a crude straw mattress, a tiny bookcase with a picture of Saint Francis hanging over it, a ragged palm, a stool for sitting on, a crucifix[6]. She told me to remove my blouse and sit on the stool. I did so. She took a pot of salve from the bookcase and began to smooth it upon my burns. Her hands made slow, wide circles, stopping the pain. I closed my eyes. I expected to see blackness. Peace. But instead the vision reared up again. My chest was still tipped with diamonds. I was walking through windows. She was chewing up the broken litter I left behind.

"I am going," I said. "Let me go."

But she held me down.

"Don't go," she said quickly. "Don't. We have just begun."

I was weakening. My thoughts were whirling pitifully. The pain had kept me strong, and as it left me I began to forget it; I couldn't hold on. I began to wonder if she'd really scalded me with the kettle. I could not remember. To remember this seemed the most important thing in the world. But I was losing the memory. The scalding. The pouring. It began to vanish. I felt like my mind was coming off its hinge, flapping in the breeze, hanging by the hair of my own pain. I wrenched out of her grip.

"He was always in you," I said. "Even more than in me. He wanted you even more. And now he's got you. Get thee behind me!"

I shouted that, grabbed my shirt, and ran through the door throwing it on my body. I got down the stairs and into the kitchen, even, but no matter what I told myself, I couldn't get out the door. It wasn't finished. And she knew I would not leave. Her quiet step was immediately behind me.

"We must take the bread from the oven now," she said.

She was pretending nothing happened. But for the first time I had gotten through some chink she'd left in her darkness. Touched some doubt. Her voice was so low and brittle it cracked off at the end of her sentence.

"Help me, Marie," she said slowly.

But I was not going to help her, even though she had calmly buttoned the back of my shirt up and put the bit cloth mittens in my hands for taking out the loaves. I could have bolted for it then. But I didn't. I knew that something was nearing completion. Something was about to happen. My back was a wall of singing flame. I was turning. I watched her take the long fork in one hand, to tap the loaves. In the other hand she gripped the black poker to hook the pans.

"Help me," she said again, and I thought, Yes, this is part of it. I put the mittens on my hands and swung the door open on its hinges. The oven gaped. She stood back a moment, letting the first blast of heat rush by. I moved behind her. I could feel the heat at my front and at my back. Before, behind. My skin was turning to beaten gold. It was coming quicker than I thought. The over was like the gate of a personal hell. Just big enough and hot enough for one person, and that was her. One kick and Leopolda would fly in headfirst. And that would be one-millionth of the heat she would feel when she finally collapsed in his hellish embrace.

Saints know these numbers.

She bent forward with her fork held out. I kicked her with all my might. She flew in. But the outstretched poker hit the back wall first, so she rebounded. The oven was not so deep as I had thought.

There was a moment when I felt a sort of thin, hot disappointment, as when a fish slips off the line. Only I was the one going to be lost. She was fearfully silent. She whirled. Her veil had cutting edges. She had the poker in one hand. In the other she held that long sharp fork she used to tap the delicate crusts of loaves. Her face turned upside down on her shoulders. Her face turned blue. But saints are used to miracles. I felt no trace of fear.

If I was going to be lost, let the diamonds cut! Let her eat ground glass!

"Bitch of Jesus Christ!" I shouted. "Kneel and beg! Lick the floor!"

That was when she stabbed me through the hand with the fork, then took the poker up alongside my head, and knocked me out.

It must have been a half an hour later when I came around. Things were so strange. So strange I can hardly tell it for delight at the remembrance. For when I came around this was actually taking place. I was being worshiped. I had somehow gained the altar of a saint.

I was laying back on the stiff couch in the Mother Superior's office. I looked around me. It was as though my deepest dream had come to life. The sisters of the convent were kneeling to me. Sister Bonaventure. Sister Dympan. Sister Cecilia Saint-Claire. The two French with hands like paddles. They were down on their knees. Black capes were slung over some of their heads. My name was buzzing up and down the room, like a fat autumn fly lighting on the tips of their tongues between Latin, bumming up the heavy blood-dark curtains, circling their little cosseted heads. Marie! Marie! A girl thrown in a closet. Who was afraid of a rubber overboot. Who was half overcome. A girl who came in the back door where they threw their garbage. Marie! Who never found the cup. Who had to eat their cold mush. Marie ! Leopolda had her face burried in her knuckles. Saint Marie of the Holy Slops! Saint Marie of the Bread Fork! Saint Marie of the Burnt Back and Scalded Butt!

I broke out and laughed.

They looked up. All holy hell burst loose when they saw I'd woke. I still did not understand what was happening. They were watching, talking, but not to me.

"The marks…"

"She has her hand closed."

"Je ne peux pas voir." [7]

I was not stupid enough to ask what they were talking about. I couldn't tell why I was laying in white sheets. I couldn't tell why they were praying to me. But I'll tell you this: it seemed entirely natural. It was me. I lifted up my hand as in my dream. It was completely limp with sacredness.

"Peace be with you."

My arm was dried blood from the wrist down to the elbow. And it hurt. Their faces turned like flat flowers of adoration to follow that hand's movements. I let it swing through the air, imparting a saint's blessing. I had practiced. I knew exactly how to act.

They murmured. I heaved a sigh, and a golden beam of light suddenly broke through the clouded window and flooded down directly on my face. A stroke of perfect luck! They had to be convinced.

Leopolda still knelt in the back of the room. Her knuckles were crammed halfway down her throat. Let me tell you, a saint has senses honed keen as a wolf. I knew that she was over my barrel now. How it happened did not matter. The last thing I remembered was how she flew from the oven and stabbed me. That one thing was most certainly true.

"Come forward, Sister Leopolda." I gestured with my heavenly wound. Oh, it hurt. It bled when I reopened the slight heal. "Kneel beside me," I said.

She kneeled, but her voice box evidently did not work, for her mouth opened, shut, opened, but no sound came out. My throat clenched in noble delight I had read of as befitting a saint. She could not speak. But she was beaten. It was in her eyes. She stared at me now with all the deep hate of the wheel of devilish dust that rolled wild within her emptiness.

"What is it you want to tell me?" I asked. And at last she spoke.

"I have told my sisters of your passion," she managed to choke out. "How the stigmata[8]...the marks of the nails...appeared in your palm and you swooned at the holy vision...."

"Yes," I said curiously.

And then, after a moment, I understood.

Leopolda had saved herself with her quick brain. She had witnessed a miracle. She had hid the fork and told this to the others. And of course they believed her, because they never knew how Satan came and went or where he took refuge.

"I saw it from the first," said the large one who put the bread in the oven. "Humility of the spirit. So rare in these girls."

"I saw it too," said the other one with great satisfaction. She sighed quietly. "If only it was me."

Leopolda was kneeling bolt upright, face blazing and twitching, a barely held fountain of blasting poison.

"Christ has marked me," I agreed.

I smiled the saint's smirk into her face. And then I looked at her. That was my mistake.

For I saw her kneeling there. Leopolda with her soul like a rubber overboot. With her face of a starved rat. With the desperate eyes drowning in the deep wells of her wrongness. There would be no one else after me. And I would leave. I saw Leopoolda kneeling within the shambles of her love.

My heart had been about to surge from my chest with the blackness of my joyous heat. Now it dropped. I pitied her. I pitied her. Pity twisted in my stomach like that hook-pole was driven through me. I was caught. It was a feeling more terrible than any amount of boiling water and worse than being forked. Still, still, I could not help what I did. I had already smiled in a saint's mealy forgiveness. I heard myself speaking gently.

"Receive the dispensation of my sacred blood," I whispered.

But there was no heart in it. No joy when she bent to touch the floor. No dark leaping. I fell back into the white pillows. Blank dust was whirling through the light shafts. My skin was dust. Dust my lips. Dust the dirty spoons on the ends of my feet.

Rise up! I thought. Rise up and walk! There is no limit to this dust!

Notes:

1. drizzled: (of rain) to fall in very small drops
2. herring: a gregarious, edible fish found in the colder areas of North Atlantic
3. the Creed: the formal summaries of Christian beliefs used liturgically
4. the minute: as soon as; the moment
5. "*Elle est docile*,": (French) " She is amenable."
6. crucifix: a cross with a figure of Christ on it.
7. "*Je ne peux pas voir*.": (French) "I can't see."
8. stigmata: the plural form of stigma

Questions for Study and Appreciation:

1. What seems to be Sister Leopolda's obsession?
2. Marie is doing something she says no other girl on the reservation has dared to do; why does she dare to ask for admission to the convent?
3. Marie undergoes Leopolda's "treatment" for the "ice forming in [her] blood"; what does the nun seem to be talking about?
4. What is Marie's vision?
5. What does Marie attempt to do to Leopolda?
6. What is happening to Marie when she wakes up after Leopolda knocked her unconscious with the poker? what does she do in response? Marie speaks of Leopolda's love; can you see "love" in her actions?
7. Identify Marie's understanding of sainthood. Is it indicative of her age or cultural upbringing? In what ways does her understanding of sainthood shift in the story?
8. Discuss the fish and/or fishing imagery used in the story. In what ways does Erdrich capitalize upon its connection to Catholicism and to the Native American community?
9. Discuss the use of lightness and darkness in the story. How do color differences suggest division in this community?

Philip Milton Roth (1933—)

Life and Major Works

Philip Milton Roth was born in Newark, New Jersey, in 1933, the son of

American-born parents and the grandson of European Jews who were part of the nineteenth-century wave of immigration to the United States. He grew up in the city's lower-middle-class section of Weequahic. This place became the scene for some of his novels. He later attended Bucknell University, where he received his B. A., and the University of Chicago, where he completed his M. A. and taught English. Afterwards, at both Iowa and Princeton, he has ever taught creative writing, and for many years he taught comparative literature at the

Philip Roth

University of Pennsylvania. He retired from teaching in 1992. In fact from 1958 onward he has supported himself mainly as a writer.

Goodbye, Columbus (1959) and some other short fictions published between 1959 and 1968 belong to the earliest phase of Roth's writing career. The content of the novels of this phase is firmly grounded in the models, tenets, and restraints of traditional realism with a moral emphasis. In *Portnoy's Complaint* (1969), and *The Great American Novel* (1973), Roth employed wilder comic techniques which echo the raucous and ribald qualities of nineteenth century native American humor. In *The Breast* (1972), and *The Professor of Desire* (1977), he has attempted to synthesize the techniques of the earlier phases in Kafkaesque tales which vividly convey the confluence of the real and the fantastic in the quotidian. Philip Roth has never been satisfied merely to repeat himself. His work has changed from early realistic fiction influenced by Henry James and Gustave Flaubert, through purely comic work reminiscent of the American frontier humor and embodying Kafkaesque excursions into surrealism, to more recent explorations of the boundaries between art and reality, and between the creator and his creation.

Starting from *My Life As a Man* (1974), Roth introduces his most developed protagonist, Nathan Zuckerman for the first time. Following with it he published his significant Zuckerman trilogy: *The Ghost Writer* (1979), *Zuckerman Unbound* (1981), and *The Anatomy Lesson* (1983). These novels trace the development of Roth's alter ego, Nathan Zuckerman, from an aspiring young writer to a socially compromised, and psychologically besieged literary celebrity. At this time his fiction becomes highly self-reflexive. The year 1986 is a critical moment in Roth's career. This year he published *The Counterlife* (1986), which is Roth's most ambitious and meticulously structured novel. Roth not only starts to use a lot of evident postmodernistic techniques, but also engages in a sustained examination of the relationship between American and Israeli Jews. Roth has been into the mature phase of his life. *The Counterlife* (1986), *Sabbath Theatre* (1995), *American Pastoral* (1997), *The Human Stain* (2000) , *The Dying Animal* (2001), *The Plot Against America* (2004), and *Exit Ghost* (2007) represent an extraordinary run of novels that readers enjoy reading and any other writer would envy. Postmodern techniques, such as metafiction and black humor, can be traced in these novels. In his novels, Roth engages energetically with themes like the ethnic identity, the Holocaust, sexuality, American history, and the human psyche itself.

Brief Introduction and Appreciation

Roth has demonstrated a unique ability not only to sustain his literary output, but even surpass the scope and talent inherent in his previous writings. *American Pastoral, I Married a Communist* and *The Human Stain* are designated a trilogy because they highlight three historical occurrences that fundamentally damaged American society after the Second World War: the Vietnam War and the rebellions of the '60s and '70s, McCarthyism in the '50s, and the Political Correctness of the '80s and '90s. *American Pastoral* was published in 1997. Because of it, Philip Roth won the Pulitzer Prize the following year. They think that never before Roth has written with such clear conviction and has assembled so many fully formed characters.

American Pastoral depicts a story of tragic loss. Nathan Zuckerman, Philip Roth's alter-ego for nearly four decades now, is settling uncomfortably into old age. Now a literary recluse, Zuckerman has survived prostate cancer. As the novel begins, he has returned once more to his school days in Newark, New Jersey. The device here is a class reunion, a gathering of former athletes, beauties, and outsiders, transformed by time into uncanny snapshots of their own immigrant grandparents. The real protagonist of this novel is this Seymour "Swede" Levov who was the hero in Zuckerman high school. Seymour comes of age just after World War II, in a thriving and triumphant America. As a legendary high school athlete, the diligent and successful inheritor of his father's glove factory, the proprietor of an eighteenth-century stone house in the heart of WASP country, the devoted husband of a beautiful and intelligent wife, and the father of a charming daughter, Seymour seems to have realized his American dream and have fulfilled the ambitions of generations of his struggling forebears. But his carefully constructed life begins to collapse as he and America face the challenges of the turbulent 1960s. He sees that his adored daughter, Merry, grows up first as a rebellious adolescent and then a revolutionary terrorist, and at last a messy Jain. Swede Levov watches in bewilderment that everything he treasures, everything so industriously created by his family over the course of three generations, are totally blown up by his angry daughter's bomb. Seymour's pastoral American Dream is shattered. The narrator Zuckerman see Seymour as being more like Sisyphus, living in an absurd universe where life made no sense.

In the novel, the pastoral vision with its conventions of innocent shepherds and meadows is set into juxtaposition with the twentieth-century American society engaged in the controversial Vietnam War, a society which lacks morality and is interested only in material gains. Roth uses the metafictional form and combines laughter and pain, farce and deadly seriousness, as he lampoons the sentimental yearning for the American Dream and People's incapacity to face its collapse. Roth imbeds the great grief in parody and slapstick. The apparent discrepancies between what we surmise the narrator can know and what he tells us in his narration develop into a postmodern game of following clues. In fact, no causal information is found in the novel. Roth's readers try to follow clues about what Jerry could have told Zuckerman, what Zuckerman could have learned himself as a youth, what must be only based on Zuckerman's imagination, and what biographical information about Newark experiences could possibly relate to Zuckerman's author Philip Roth. When readers try to find answers, they can only find ambiguity. Readers are looking for facts and there are no "facts" in this literary work.

American Pastoral is divided into three main parts. "Paradise Remembered", "The Fall" and "Paradise Lost". The selective reading is chosen from Chapter 5 which belongs to the second part "The Fall". This chapter is the climax of the novel. It describes in detail the American dreams and disillusionments of the heroes and heroines. It also analyzes the roots of the beautiful American pastoral dreams and how protagonists are drawn unwillingly yet uncontrollably into the ugly and shocking reality in the contemporary American society.

Selected Reading

American Pastoral

Sept.1, 1973

Dear Mr. Levov,

Merry is working in the old dog and cat hospital on New Jersey Railroad Avenue in the Ironbound Section of Newark, 115 NJ. Railroad Avenue, five minutes from Penn Station. She is there every day. If you wait outside you can catch her leaving work and heading home just after four p.m. She doesn't know I'm writing this letter to you. I am at the breaking point and can't go on. I want to go away but I can leave her to no one. You have to take over. Though I warn you that if you tell her that it was from me that you discovered her whereabouts, you will be doing her serious harm. She is an incredible spirit. She has changed everything for me. I got into this over my head because I couldn't ever resist her power. That is too much to get into here. You must believe me when I tell you that I never said anything or did anything other than what Merry demanded me to say and to do. She is an overwhelming force. You and I were in the same boat. I lied to her only once. That was about what happened at the hotel. If I had told her that you refused to make love with me she would have refused to take the money. She would have been back begging on the streets. I would never have made you suffer so if I hadn't the strength of my love for Merry to help me. To you that will sound crazy, I am telling you it is so. Your daughter is divine. You cannot be in the presence of such suffering without succumbing to its holy power. You don't know what a nobody I was before I met Merry. I was headed for oblivion. But I can't take anymore. YOU MUST NOT MENTION ME TO MERRY EXCEPT AS SOMEONE WHO TORMENTED YOU EXACTLY AS I DID. DO NOT MENTION THIS LETTER IF YOU CARE ABOUT MERRY'S SURVIVAL. You must take every precaution[1] before getting to the hospital. She could not survive the FBI. Her name is Mary Stoltz. She must be allowed to fulfill her destiny. We can only stand as witnesses to the anguish that sanctifies her.

The Disciple Who Calls Herself "Rita Cohen"

He could never root out the unexpected thing. The unexpected thing would be waiting there unseen, for the rest of his life ripening, ready to explode, just a millimeter behind everything else. The unexpected thing was the other side of everything else. He had already parted with everything, then remade everything, and now, when everything appeared to be back under his control, he was being incited to part with everything again. And if that should happen, the unexpected thing becoming the only thing...

Thing, thing, thing, thing——but what other word was tolerable? They could not be forever in bondage to this fucking thing! For five years he had been waiting for just such a letter——it had to come. Every night in bed he begged God to deliver it the following morning. And then, in this amazing transitional year, 1973, the year of Dawn's miracle, during these months when Dawn was giving herself over to designing the new house, he had begun to dread what he might find in the morning's mail or hear each time he picked up the phone. How could he allow the unexpected thing back into their lives now that Dawn had ruled out of their lives forever the improbability of what had happened? Leading his wife back to herself had been like flying them through a five-year storm. He had fulfilled every demand. To disentangle her from her horror, there wasn't anything he had omitted to do. Life had returned to some thing like its recognizable proportions. Now tear the letter up and throw it away. Pretend it never arrived.

Because Dawn had twice been hospitalized in a clinic near Princeton for suicidal depression, he had come to accept that the damage was permanent and that she would be able to function only under the care of psychiatrists and by taking sedatives and an antidepressant medication——that she would be in and out of psychiatric hospitals and that he would be visiting her in those places for the rest of their lives. He imagined that once or twice a year he would find himself sitting at the side of her bed in a room where there were no locks on the door. There would be flowers he'd sent her in a vase on the writing desk; on a windowsill, the ivy plants he'd brought from her study, thinking it might help her to care for something; on the bedside table framed photographs of himself and Merry and Dawn's parents and brother. At the side of the bed he himself would be holding her hand while she sat propped up against the pillows in her Levi's and a big turtleneck sweater and wept." I'm frightened, Seymour. I'm frightened all the time." He would sit patiently there beside her whenever she began to tremble and he would tell her to just breathe, slowly breathe in and out and think of the most pleasant place on earth that she knew of, imagine herself in the most wonderfully calming place in the entire world, a tropical beach, a beautiful mountain, a holiday landscape from her childhood... and he would do this even when the trembling was brought on by a tirade aimed at him. Sitting up on the bed, with her arms crossed in front of her as though to warm herself, she would hide the whole of her body inside the sweater——turn the sweater into a tent by extending the turtleneck up over her chin, stretching the back under her buttocks, and drawing the front across her bent knees, down over her legs, and beneath her feet. Often she sat tented like that all the time he was there. "You know when I was in Princeton last? I do! I was invited by the governor. To his mansion. Here, to Princeton, to his mansion. I had dinner at the governor's mansion. I was twenty-two——in an evening gown and scared to death. His chauffeur drove me from Elizabeth and I danced in my crown with the governor of New Jersey——so how did this happen? How have I wound up here? You, that's how! You wouldn't leave me alone! Had to have me! Had to marry me! I just wanted to become a teacher! That's what I wanted. I had the job. I had it waiting. To teach kids music in the Elizabeth system, and to be left alone by boys, and that was it. I never wanted to be Miss America! I never wanted to marry anyone! But you wouldn't let me breathe——you wouldn't let me out of your sight. All I ever wanted was my college education and that job. I should never have left Elizabeth! Never! Do you know what Miss New Jersey did for my life? It ruined it. I only went after the damn scholarship so Danny could go to college and my father wouldn't have to pay. Do you think if my father didn't have the heart attack I would have entered for Miss Union County? No! I just wanted to win the money so Danny could go to college without the burden on my dad! I didn't do it for boys to go traipsing after me everywhere——I was trying to help out at home! But then you arrived. You! Those hands! Those shoulders! Towering over me with your jaw! This huge animal I couldn't get rid of! You wouldn't leave me be! Every time I looked up, there was my boyfriend, gaga because I was a ridiculous beauty queen! You were like some kid! You had to make me into a princess. Well, look where I have wound up! In a madhouse! Your princess is in a madhouse!"

For years to come she would be wondering how what happened to her could have happened to her and blaming him for it, and he would be bringing her food she liked, fruit and candy and cookies, in the hope that she might eat something aside from bread and water, and bringing her magazines in the hope that she might be able to concentrate on reading for even just half an hour a day, and bringing clothes that she could wear around the hospital grounds to accommodate to the weather when the seasons changed. At nine o'clock every evening, he would put away in her dresser whatever he'd brought for her, and he would hold her and kiss her goodbye, hold her and tell her he'd be seeing her the next night after work, and then he would drive the hour in the dark back to Old Rimrock remembering the terror in her face when, fifteen minutes before visiting hours were to end, the nurse put her head in the door to kindly tell Mr. Levov that it was almost time for him to go.

The next night she'd be angry all over again. He had swayed her from her real ambitions. He and the Miss America Pageant[2] had put her off her program. On she went and he couldn't stop her. Didn't try. What did any of what she said have to do with why she was suffering? Everybody knew that what had broken her was quite enough in itself and that what she said had no bearing on anything. That first time she was in the hospital, he simply listened and nodded, and strange as it was to hear her going angrily on about an adventure that at the time he was certain she couldn't have enjoyed more, he sometimes wondered if it wasn't better for her to identify what had happened to her in 1949, not what had happened to her in 1968, as the problem at hand." All through high school people were telling me, "You should be Miss America." I thought it was ridiculous. Based on what should I be Miss America? I was a clerk in a dry-goods store after school and in the summer, and people would come up to my cash register and say, "You should be Miss America." I couldn't stand it. I couldn't stand when people said I should do things because of the way that I looked. But when I got a call from the Union County pageant to come to that tea, what could I do? I was a baby. I thought this was a way for me to kick in a little money so my father wouldn't have to work so hard. So I filled out the application and I went, and after all the other girls left, that woman put her arm around me and she told all her neighbors, I want you to know that you've just spent the afternoon with the next Miss America." I thought, "This is all so silly. Why do people keep saying these things to me? I don't want to be doing this." And when I won Miss Union County, people were already saying to me, "We'll see you in Atlantic City'——people who know what they're talking about saying I'm going to win this thing, so how could I back out? I couldn't. The whole front page of the Elizabeth Journal was about me winning Miss Union County. I was mortified. I was. I thought somehow I could keep it all a secret and just win the money. I was a baby! I was sure at least I wasn't going to win Miss New Jersey, I was positive. I looked around and there was this sea of good-looking girls and they all knew what to do, and I didn't know anything. They knew how to use hair rollers and put false eyelashes on, and I couldn't roll my hair right until I was halfway through my Miss New Jersey year. I thought, "Oh, my God, look at their makeup," and they had beautiful wardrobes and I had a prom dress and borrowed clothes, and so I was convinced there was no way I could ever win. I was so introverted. I was so unpolished. But I won again. And then they were coaching me on how to sit and how to stand, even how to listen——they sent me to a model agency to learn how to walk. They didn't like the way I walked. I didn't care how I walked——I walked! I walked well enough to become Miss New Jersey, didn't I? If I don't walk well enough to become Miss America, the hell with it! But you have to glide. No! I will walk the way I walk! Don't swing your arms too much, but don't hold them stiffly at your side. All these little tricks of the trade to make me so self-conscious I could barely move! To land not on your heels but on the balls of your feet——this is the kind of thing I went through. If I can just drop out of this thing! How can I back out of this thing? Leave me alone! All of you leave me alone! I never wanted this in the first place! Do you see why I married you? Now do you understand? One reason only! I wanted something that seemed normal! So desperately after that year, I wanted something normal! How I wish it had never happened! None of it! They put you up on a pedestal, which I didn't ask for, and then they rip you off it so damn fast it can blind you! And I did not ask for any of it! I had nothing in common with those other girls. I hated them and they hated me. Those tall girls with their big feet! None of them gifted. All of them so chummy! I was a serious music student! All I wanted was to be left alone and not to have that goddamn crown sparkling like crazy up on top of my head! I never wanted any of it! Never!"

It was a great help to him, driving home after one of those visits, to remember her as the girl she had really been back then, who, as he recalled it, was nothing like the girl she portrayed as herself in those tirades. During the week in September of 1949 leading up to the Miss America Pageant, when she called Newark every night from the Dennis Hotel to tell him about what happened to her that day as a Miss America contestant, what radiated from her voice was sheer delight in being herself. He'd never heard her like that before—it was almost frightening, this undisguised exulting in being where she was and who she was and what she was. Suddenly life existed rapturously and for Dawn Dwyer alone. The surprise of this new and uncharacteristic immoderation even made him wonder if, when the week was over, she could ever again be content with Seymour Levov. And suppose she should win. What chance would he have against all the men who set their sights on marrying Miss America? Actors would be after her.

Millionaires would be after her. They'd flock to her—the new life opening up to her could attract a host of powerful new suitors and wind up excluding him. Nonetheless, as the current suitor, he was spellbound by the prospect of Dawn's winning; the more real a possibility it was, the more reasons he had to flush and perspire.

They would talk long distance for as long as an hour at a time—she was too excited to sleep, even though she had been on the go since breakfast, which she'd eaten in the dining room with her chaperone[3], just the two of them at the table, the chaperone a large local woman in a small hat, Dawn wearing her Miss New Jersey sash pinned to her suit and, on her hands, white kid gloves, tremendously expensive gloves, a present to her from Newark Maid, where the Swede was beginning his training to take over the business. All the girls wore the same style of white kid glove, four-button in length, up over the wrist. Dawn alone had got hers for nothing, along with a second pair of gloves—opera length, in black, Newark Maid's formal, sixteen-button kid glove (a small fortune at Saks), the table-cut workmanship as expert as anything from Italy or France—and, in addition, a third pair of gloves, above the elbow, custom made to match her evening gown. The Swede had asked Dawn for a yard of fabric the same as her gown, and a friend of the family's who did fabric gloves made them for Dawn as a courtesy of Newark Maid. Three times a day, seated across from the chaperone in the small hats, the girls, with their beautiful, nicely combed hair, and neat, nice dresses and four-button gloves, attempted to have a meal, something of each course, at least, between giving autographs to all the people in the dining room who came over to gawk and to say where they were from. Because Dawn was Miss New Jersey and the hotel guests were in New Jersey, she was the most popular girl by far, and so she had to say a kind word to everyone and smile and sign autographs and still try to get something to eat. "This is what you have to do," she told him on the phone, "this is why they give you the free room."

When she arrived at the train station, they'd put her in a little convertible, a Nash Rambler, that had her name and her state on it, and her chaperone was in the convertible too. Dawn's chaperone was the wife of a local real-estate dealer, and everywhere Dawn went the chaperone was sure to go—in the car with her when she got in, and out of the car with her when she got out. "She does not leave my side, Seymour. You don't see a man the whole time except the judges. You can't even talk to one. A few boyfriends are here. Some are even fianc s. But what's the sense? The girls aren't allowed to see them. There's a book of rules so long I can hardly read through it. 'Members of the male sex are not permitted to talk to contestants except in the presence of their hostesses. At no time is a contestant permitted to enter a cocktail lounge or partake of an intoxicating beverage. Other rules include no padding—'" The Swede laughed. "Uh-oh." "Let me finish, Seymour—it just goes on and on." 'No one is permitted an interview with a contestant without her hostess present to protect her interests...'"

Not just Dawn but all the girls got the little Nash Rambler convertibles—though not to keep. You got to keep it only if you became Miss America. Then it would be the car from which you waved to the capacity crowd when you were driven around the edge of the field at the most famous of college football games. The pageant was pushing the Rambler because American Motors was one of the sponsors. There had been a box of Fralinger's Original saltwater taffy in the room when she arrived, and a bouquet of roses; everybody got both, compliments of the hotel, but Dawn's roses never opened, and the rooms the girls got—at least the girls put up at Dawn's hotel—were small, ugly, and at the back. But the hotel itself, as Dawn excitedly described it, at Boardwalk and Michigan Avenue, was one of the swanky ones where every afternoon they had a proper tea with little sandwiches and croquet was played on the lawn by the paying guests, who rightly enough got the big, beautiful rooms and the ocean views. Every night she'd come back exhausted to the ugly back room with the faded wallpaper, check to see if the roses had opened, and then phone to answer his questions about her chances.

She was one of four or five girls whose photographs kept appearing in the papers, and everybody said that one of these girls had to win——the New Jersey pageant people were sure they had a winner, especially when the photographs of her popped up every morning. "I hate to let them down," she told him. "You're not going to. You're going to win," he told her. "No, this girl from Texas is going to win. I know it. She's so pretty. She has a round face. She has a dimple. Not a beauty but very, very cute. And a great figure. I'm scared to death of her. She's from some tacky little town in Texas and she tap-dances and she's the one." "Is she in the papers with you?" "Always. She's one of the four or five always. I'm there because it's Atlantic City and I'm Miss New Jersey and the people on the boardwalk see me in my sash and they go nuts, but that happens to Miss New Jersey every year. And she never wins. But Miss Texas is there in those papers, Seymour, because she's going to win."

Earl Wilson, the famous syndicated newspaper columnist, was one of the ten judges, and when he heard that Dawn was from Elizabeth he was reported to have said to someone at the float parade, in which Dawn had ridden along the boardwalk with two other girls on the float of her hotel, that Elizabeth's longtime mayor Joe Brophy, was one of his friends. Earl Wilson told someone who told someone who then told Dawn's chaperone. Earl Wilson and Joe Brophy were old friends——that was all Earl Wilson said, or was able to say in public, but Dawn's chaperone was sure he'd said it because after he'd seen Dawn in her evening gown on the float she'd become his candidate. "Okay," said the Swede, "one down, nine to go. You're on your way, Miss America."

All she talked about with her chaperone was who they thought her closest competition was; apparently this was all any of the girls talked about with their chaperones and all they wound up talking about when they called home, even if, among themselves, they pretended to love one another. The southern girls in particular, Dawn told him, could really lay it on: "Oh, you're just so wonderful, your hair's so wonderful..." The veneration of hair took some getting used to for a girl as down-to-earth as Dawn; you might almost think, from listening to the conversation among the other girls, that life's possibilities resided in hair——not in the hands of your destiny but in the hands of your hair.

Together with the chaperones, they visited the Steel Pier and had a fish dinner at Captain Starn's famous seafood restaurant and yacht bar, and a steak dinner at Jack Guischard's Steak House, and the third morning they had their picture taken together in front of Convention Hall, where a pageant official told them the picture was one they would treasure for the rest of their lives, that the friendships they were making would last the rest of their lives, that they would keep up with one another for the rest of their lives, that when the time arrived they would name their children after one another——and meanwhile, when the papers came out in the morning, the girls said to their chaperones, "Oh God, I'm not in this. Oh God, this one looks like she's going to win."

Every day there were rehearsals[4] and every night for a week they gave a show. Year after year people visited Atlantic City just for the Miss America contest and bought tickets for the nightly show and came all dressed up to see the girls on the stage individually exhibiting their talent and performing as an ensemble in costumed musical numbers. The one other girl who played piano played "Clair de Lune" for her solo performance and so Dawn had to herself the much flashier number, the currently popular hit "Till the End of Time," a danceable arrangement of a Chopin polonaise. "I'm in show business. I don't stop all day. You don't have a moment. Because New Jersey's host state there's all this focus on me, and I don't want to let everybody down, I really don't, I couldn't bear it—" "You won't, Dawnie. Earl Wilson's in your pocket, and he's the most famous of all the judges. I feel it. I know it. You're going to win."

But he was wrong. Miss Arizona won. Dawn didn't make it even into the top ten. In those days the girls waited backstage while the winners were announced. There was row after row of mirrors and tables lined up alphabetically by state, and Dawn was right in the middle of everyone when the announcement was made, so she had to start smiling to beat the band and clapping like crazy because she had lost and then, to make matters worse, had to rush back onstage and march around with the other losers, singing along with ME Bob Russell the Miss America song of that era: "Every flower, every rose, stands up on her tippy toes... when Miss America marches by!" while a girl just as short and slight and dark as she was—little Jacque Mercer from Arizona, who won the swimsuit competition but who Dawn never figured would win it all—took the crowd at Convention Hall by storm. Afterward, at the farewell ball, though it was for Dawn a terrific letdown, she wasn't nearly as depressed as most of the others. The same thing she had been told by the New Jersey pageant people they'd been told by their state pageant people: "You're going to make it. You're going to be Miss America." So the ball, she told him, was the saddest sight she'd ever seen. "You have to go and smile and it's awful" she said. "They have these people from the Coast Guard or wherever they're from—Annapolis. They have fancy white uniforms and braid and ribbons. I guess they're considered safe enough for us to dance with. So they dance with you with their chin tucked in, and the evenings over, and you go home."

Still, for months afterward the super stimulating adventure refused to die; even while she was being Miss New Jersey and going around snipping ribbons and waving at people and opening department stores and auto showrooms, she wondered aloud if anything so wonderfully unforeseen as that week in Atlantic City would ever happen to her again. She kept beside her bed the 1949 Official Yearbook of the Miss America Pageant, a booklet prepared by the pageant that was sold all week at Atlantic City: individual photos of the girls, four to a page, each with a tiny outline drawing of her state and a capsule biography. Where Miss New Jersey's photo portrait appeared—smiling demurely, Dawn in her evening gown with the matching twelve-button fabric gloves—the corner of the page had been neatly turned back. "Mary Dawn Dwyer, 22 year old Elizabeth, NJ. Brunette, carries New Jersey's hopes in this year's Pageant. A graduate of Upsala College, East Orange, NJ., where she majored in music education, Mary Dawn has the ambition of becoming a high school music teacher. She is 5′ 2 and a half and blue-eyed, and her hobbies are swimming, square dancing, and cooking. (Left above)" Reluctant to give up excitement such as she'd never known before, she talked on and on about the fairy tale it had been for a kid from Hillside Road, a plumber's daughter from Hillside Road, to have been up in front of all those people, competing for the title of Miss America. She almost couldn't believe the courage she'd shown. "Oh, that ramp, Seymour. That's a long ramp, a long runway, it's a long way to go just smiling..."

In 1969, when the invitation arrived in Old Rimrock for the twentieth reunion of the Miss America contestants of her year, Dawn was back in the hospital for the second time since Merry's disappearance. It was May. The psychiatrists were as nice as they were the first time, and the room was as pleasant, and the rolling landscape as pretty, and the walks were even prettier, with tulips around the bungalows where the patients lived, the huge fields green this time around, beautiful, beautiful views—and because this was the second time in two years, and because the place was beautiful, and because when he arrived directly from Newark in the early evening, after they had just cut the grass, there was a smell in the air as fresh and sharp as the smell of chives, it was all a thousand times worse. And so he did not show Dawn the invitation for the 1949 reunion. Things were bad enough—the things she was saying to him were bizarre enough; the relentless crying about her shame, her mortification, the futility of her life was all quite sad enough—without any more of the Miss New Jersey business.

And then the change occurred. Something made her decide to want to be free of the unexpected, improbable thing. She was not going to be deprived of her life.

The heroic renewal began with the face-lift at the Geneva clinic she'd read about in Vogue. Before going to bed he'd see her at her bathroom mirror drawing the crest of her cheekbones back between her index fingers while simultaneously drawing the skin at her jawline back and upward with her thumbs, firmly tugging the loose flesh until she had eradicated even the natural creases of her face, until she was staring at a face that looked like the polished kernel of a face. And though it was clear to her husband that she had indeed begun to age like a woman in her mid-fifties at only forty-five, the remedy suggested in Vogue in no way addressed anything that mattered; so remote was it from the disaster that had befallen them he saw no reason to argue with her, thinking she knew the truth better than anyone, however much she might prefer to imagine herself another prematurely aging reader of Vogue rather than the mother of the Rimrock Bomber. But because she had run out of psychiatrists to see and medications to try and because she was terrified at the prospect of electric shock therapy should she have to be hospitalized a third time, the day came when he took her to Geneva. They were met at the airport by the liveried chauffeur and the limousine, and she booked herself into Dr. LaPlante's clinic.

In their suite of rooms the Swede slept in the bed beside hers. The night after the operation, when she could not stop vomiting, he was there to clean her up and to comfort her. During the next several days, when she wept from the pain, he sat at her bedside and, as he had night after night at the psychiatric clinic, held her hand, certain that this grotesque surgery, this meaningless, futile ordeal, was ushering in the final stage of her downfall as a recognizable human being: far from assisting at his wife's recovery, he understood himself to be acting as the unwitting accomplice[5] to her mutilation. He looked at her head buried in bandages and felt he might as well be witnessing the preparation for burial of her corpse.

He was totally wrong. As it was to turn out, only a few days before the letter from Rita Cohen reached his office, he happened to pass Dawn's desk and to see there a brief handwritten letter beside an envelope addressed to the plastic surgeon in Geneva: "Dear Dr. LaPlante: A year has passed since you did my face. I do not feel that when I last saw you I understood what you have given me. That you would spend five hours of your time for my beauty fills me with awe. How can I thank you enough? I feel it's taken me these full twelve months to recover from the surgery. I believe, as you said, that my system was more beaten down than I had realized. Now it is as if I have been given a new life. Both from within and from the outside. When I meet old friends I have not seen for a while, they are puzzled as to what happened to me. I don't tell them. It is quite wonderful, dear doctor, and without you it would never have been possible. Much love and thank you, Dawn Levov."

Almost immediately after the reconstitution of her face to its former pert, heart-shaped pre-explosion perfection, she decided to build a small contemporary house on a ten-acre lot the other side of Rimrock ridge and to sell the big old house, the outbuildings, and their hundred-odd acres. (Dawn's beef cattle and the farm machinery had been sold off in '69, the year after Merry became a fugitive from justice; by then it was clear that the business was too demanding for Dawn to continue to run on her own, and so he took an ad in one of the monthly cattle magazines and within only weeks had got rid of the baler, the kicker, the rake, the livestock—everything, the works.) When he overheard her telling the architect, their neighbor Bill Orcutt, that she had always hated their house, the Swede was as stunned as if she were telling Orcutt she had always hated her husband. He went for a long walk, needed to walk almost the five miles down into the village to keep reminding himself that it was the house she said she'd always hated. But even her meaning no more than that left him so miserable it took all his considerable powers of suppression to turn himself around and head home for lunch, where Dawn and Orcutt were to review with him Orcutt's first set of sketches.

Hated their old stone house, the beloved first and only house? How could she? He had been dreaming about that house since he was sixteen years old and, riding with the baseball team to a game against Whippany—sitting there on the school bus in his uniform, idly rubbing his fingers around the deep pocket of his mitt as they drove along the narrow roads curving westward through the rural jersey hills—he saw a large stone house with black shutters set on a rise back of some trees. A little girl was on a swing suspended from a low branch of one of those big trees, swinging herself high into the air, just as happy, he imagined, as a kid can be. It was the first house built of stone he'd ever seen, and to a city boy it was an architectural marvel. The random design of the stones said "House" to him as not even the brick house on Keer Avenue did, despite the finished basement where he'd taught Jerry Ping-Pong and checkers; despite the screened-in back porch where he'd lie in the dark on the old sofa and listen on hot nights to the Giant games; despite the garage where as a boy he would use a roll of black tape to affix a ball to the end of a rope hanging from a cross beam, where, all winter long, assuming his tall, erect, no-nonsense stance, he would duteously spend half an hour swinging at it with his bat after he came home from basketball practice, so as not to lose his timing; despite the bedroom under the eaves, with the two dormer windows, where the year before high school he'd put himself to sleep reading and rereading The Kid from Tomkinsville—A. gray-haired man in a dingy shirt and a blue baseball cap well down over his eyes shoved an armful of clothes at the Kid and indicated his locker. "Fifty-six. In the back row, there." The lockers were plain wooden stalls about six feet high with a shelf one or two feet from the top. The front of his locker was open and along the edge at the top was pasted: 'tucker. no. 56. "There was his uniform with the word 'dodgers' in blue across the front and the number 56 on the back of the shirt..."

The stone house was not only engagingly ingenious-looking to his eyes—all that irregularity regularized, a jigsaw puzzle fitted patiently together into this square, solid thing to make a beautiful shelter—but it looked indestructible, an impregnable house that could never burn to the ground and that had probably been standing there since the country began. Primitive stones, rudimentary[6] stones of the sort that you would see scattered about among the trees if you took a walk along the paths in Weequahic Park, and out there they were a house. He couldn't get over it.

At school he'd find himself thinking about which girl in each of his classes to marry and take to live with him in that house. After the ride with the team to Whippany, he had only to hear someone saying "stone"—even saying "west"—and he would imagine himself going home after work to that house back of the trees and seeing his daughter there, his little daughter high up in the air on the swing he'd built for her. Though he was only a high school sophomore, he could imagine a daughter of his own running to kiss him, see her flinging herself at him, see himself carrying her on his shoulders into that house and straight on through to the kitchen, where standing by the stove in her apron, preparing their dinner, would be the child's adoring mother, who would be whichever Weequahic girl had shimmied down in the seat in front of him at the Roosevelt movie theater just the Friday before, her hair hanging over the back of her chair, within stroking distance, had he dared. All of his life he had this ability to imagine himself completely. Everything always added up to something whole. How could it not when he felt himself to add up, add up exactly to one? Then he saw Dawn at Upsala. She'd be crossing the common to Old Main where the day students hung out between classes; she'd be standing under the eucalyptus trees talking with a couple of the girls who lived in Kenbrook Hall. Once he followed her down Prospect Street toward the Brick Church bus station when suddenly she stopped in front of the window at Best 8c Co. After she went inside the store, he went up to the window to look at the mannequin in a long "New Look" skirt and imagined Dawn Dwyer in a fitting room trying the skirt on over her slip. She was so lovely that it made him extraordinarily shy even to glance her way, as though glancing were itself touching or clinging, as though if she knew (and how could she not?) that he was uncontrollably looking her way, she'd do what any sensible, self-possessed girl would do, disdain him as a beast of prey. He'd been a U.S. Marine, he'd been engaged to a girl in South Carolina, at his family's request had broken off the engagement, and it was years since he'd thought about that stone house with the black shutters and the swing out front. Sensationally handsome as he was, fresh from the service and a glamorous campus athletic star however determinedly he worked at containing conceit and resisting the role, it took him a full semester to approach Dawn for a date, not only because nakedly confronting her beauty gave him a bad conscience and made him feel shamefully voyeuristic but because once he approached her there'd be no way to prevent her from looking right through him and into his mind and seeing for herself how he pictured her: there at the stove of the stone house's kitchen when he came trundling in with their daughter, Merry, on his back—"Merry" because of the joy she took in the swing he'd built her. At night he played continuously on his phonograph a song popular that year called "Peg o' My Heart." A line in the song went, "It's your Irish heart I'm after," and every time he saw Dawn Dwyer on the paths at Upsala, tiny and exquisite, he went around the rest of the day unaware that he was whistling that damn song nonstop. He would find himself whistling it even during a ballgame, while swinging a couple of bats in the on-deck circle, waiting his turn at the plate. He lived under two skies then—the Dawn Dwyer sky and the natural sky overhead. But still he didn't immediately approach her, for fear that she'd see what he was thinking and laugh at his intoxication with her, this ex-marine's presumptuous innocence about the Upsala Spring Queen. She would think that his imagining, before they were even introduced, that she was especially intended to satisfy Seymour Levov's yearnings meant that he was still a child, vain and spoiled, when in fact what it meant to the Swede was that he was fully charged up with purpose long, long before anyone else he knew, with a grown man's aims and ambitions, someone who excitedly foresaw, in perfect detail, the outcome of his story. He had come home from the service at twenty in a rage to be "mature." If he was a child, it was only insofar as he found himself looking ahead into responsible manhood with the longing of a kid gazing into a candy-store window.

Understanding all too well why she wanted to sell the old house, he acceded to her wish without even trying to make her understand that the reason she wanted to go—because Merry was still there, in every room, Merry at age one, five, ten—was the reason he wanted to stay, a reason no less important than hers. But as she might not survive their staying—and he, it still seemed, could endure anything, however brutally it flew in the face of his own inclinations—he agreed to abandon the house he loved, not least for the memories it held of his fugitive child. He agreed to move into a brand-new house, open everywhere to the sun, full of light, just big enough for the two of them, with only a small extra room for guests out over the garage. A modern dream house—"luxuriously austere[7]" was how Orcutt described it back to Dawn after sounding her out on what she had in mind—with electric baseboard heating (instead of the insufferable forced hot air that gave her sinusitis) and built-in Shaker-like furniture (instead of those dreary period pieces) and recessed ceiling lighting (instead of the million standing lamps beneath the gloomy oak beams) and large, clear casement windows throughout (instead of those mullioned old sashes that were always sticking), and with a basement as technologically up-to-date as a nuclear submarine (instead of that dank, cavernous cellar where her husband took guests to see the wine he had "laid down" for drinking in his old age, reminding them as they shuffled between the mildewed stone walls to be on guard against the low slung cast-iron drainage pipes: "Your head, be careful, watch it there..."). He understood everything, all of it, understood just how awful it was for her, and so what could he do but accede? "Property is a responsibility," she said. "With no machinery and no cattle, you grow up a lot of grass. You're going to keep this mowed two or three times a year to keep it down. You have to have it bush-hogged—you can't just let things grow up into woods. You've got to keep them mowed and it's just ridiculously expensive and it's crazy for you to keep laying that money out year after year. There's keeping the barns from falling down—there's a responsibility you have with land. You just can't let it go. The best thing to do, the only thing to do," she told him, "is to move"

Okay. They'd move. But why did she have to tell Orcutt she'd hated that house "from the day we found it"? That she was there only because her husband had "dragged" her there when she was too young to have any idea what it would be like trying to run a huge, antiquated[8], dark barn of a place in which something was always leaking or rotting or in need of repair? The reason she first went into cattle, she told him, was to get out of that terrible house.

And if that was true? To find this out so late in the game! It was like discovering an infidelity[9]—all these years she had been unfaithful to the house.

How could he have gone around dopily believing he was making her happy when there was no justification for his feelings, when they were absurd, when, year in, year out, she was seething with hatred for their house? How he had loved the providing. Had he only been given the opportunity to provide for more than the three of them. If only there had been more children in that big house, if only Merry had been raised among brothers and sisters whom she loved and who loved her, this thing might never have happened to them. But Dawn wanted from life something other than to be the slavish mom to half a dozen kids and the nursemaid to a two-hundred-year-old house—she wanted to raise beef cattle. Because of her being introduced, no matter where they went, as "a former Miss New Jersey," she was sure that even though she had a bachelor's degree people were always dismissing her as a bathing beauty, a mindless china doll, capable of doing nothing more productive for society than standing around looking pretty. It did not matter how many times she patiently explained to them, when they brought up her title, that she had entered at the local Union County level only because her father had the heart attack, and money was tight, and her brother Danny was graduating from St. Mary's, and she thought that if she won—and she believed she had a chance not because of having been Upsala Spring Queen but because she was a music-education major who played classical piano—she could use the scholarship money that went with the title for Danny's college tuition, thereby unburdening...

But it didn't matter what she said or how much she said or how often she mentioned the piano: nobody believed her. Nobody really believed that she never wanted to look better than everybody else. They only thought that there are lots of other ways to get a scholarship than to go walking around Atlantic City in high heels and a bathing suit. She was always telling people her serious reasons for becoming Miss New Jersey and nobody even listened. They smiled. To them she couldn't have serious reasons. They didn't want her to have serious reasons. All she could have for them was that face. Then they could go away saying, "Oh her, she's nothing but a face," and pretend they weren't jealous or intimidated by her looks. "Thank God," Dawn would mutter to him, "I didn't win Miss Congeniality. If they think Miss New Jersey has to be dumb, imagine if I'd won the booby prize. Though," she'd then add wistfully[10], "it would have been nice to bring home the thousand dollars."

After Merry was born, when they first began going to Deal in the summer, people used to stare at Dawn in her bathing suit. Of course she never wore the white Catalina one-piece suit that she'd worn on the runway in Atlantic City, with the logo, just below the hip, of the traditional swim girl in her bathing cap. He loved that bathing suit, it fit her so marvelously, but after Atlantic City she never put it on again. They stared at her no matter what style or color suit she wore, and sometimes they would come up and snap her picture and ask for an autograph. More disturbing, however, than the staring and the photographs was their suspiciousness of her. "For some strange reason," she said, "the women always think that because I'm a former whatever I want their husbands." And probably, the Swede thought, what made it so frightening for them is that they believed Dawn could get their husbands—they'd noticed how men looked at her and how attentive they were to her wherever she went. He'd noticed it himself but never worried, not about a wife as proper as Dawn who'd been brought up as strictly as she was. But all of this so rankled Dawn that first she gave up going to the beach club in a bathing suit, any bathing suit; then, much as she loved the surf, she gave up going to the beach club at all and whenever she wanted to swim drove the four miles down to Avon, where, as a child, she used to vacation with her family for a week in the summertime. On the beach at Avon she was just a simple, petite Irish girl with her hair pulled back about whom nobody cared one way or another.

She went to Avon to get away from her beauty, but Dawn couldn't get away from it any more than she could openly flaunt it. You have to enjoy power, have a certain ruthlessness, to accept the beauty and not mourn the fact that it overshadows everything else. As with any exaggerated trait that sets you apart and makes you exceptional—and enviable, and hate able—to accept your beauty, to accept its effect on others, to play with it, to make the best of it, you're well advised to develop a sense of humor. Dawn was not a stick, she had spirit and she had spunk, and she could be cutting in a very humorous way, but that wasn't quite the inward humor it took to do the job and make her free. Only after she was married and no longer a virgin did she discover the place where it was okay for her to be as beautiful as she was, and that place, to the profit of both husband and wife, was with the Swede, in bed.

They used to call Avon the Irish Riviera. The Jews without much money went to Bradley Beach, and the Irish without much money went next door to Avon, a seaside town all of ten blocks long. The swell Irish—who had the money, the judges, the builders, the fancy surgeons—went to Spring Lake, beyond the imposing manorial gates just south of Belmar (another resort town, which was more or less a mixture of everybody). Dawn used to get taken to stay in Spring Lake by her mother's sister Peg, who'd married Ned Ma honey, a lawyer from Jersey City. If you were an Irish lawyer in that town, her father told her, and you played ball with City Hall, Mayor "I-am-the-law" Hague took care of you. Since Uncle Ned, a smooth talker, a golfer, and good-looking, had been on the Hudson County gravy train from the day he graduated John Marshall and signed on across the street with a powerful firm right there in Journal Square, and since he seemed to love pretty Mary Dawn best of all his nieces and nephews, every summer after the child had spent her week in the Avon rooming house with her mother and father and Danny, she went on by herself to spend the next week with Ned and Peg and all the Mahoney kids at the huge old Essex and Sussex Hotel right on the oceanfront at Spring Lake, where every morning in the airy dining room overlooking the sea she ate French toast with Vermont maple syrup. The starched white napkin that covered her lap was big enough to wrap around her waist like a sarong, and the sparkling silverware weighed a ton. On Sunday, they all went together to St. Catherine's, the most gorgeous church the little girl had ever seen. You got there by crossing a bridge—the loveliest bridge she had ever seen, narrow and humpbacked and made of wood—that spanned the lake back of the hotel. Sometimes when she was unhappy at the swim club she'd drive beyond Avon into Spring Lake and remember how Spring Lake used to materialize out of nowhere every summer, magically full blown, Mary Dawn's Brigadoon. She remembered how she dreamed of getting married in St. Catherine's, of being a bride there in a white dress, marrying a rich lawyer like her Uncle Ned and living in one of those grand summer houses whose big verandas overlooked the lake and the bridges and the dome of the church while only minutes from the booming Atlantic. She could have done it, too, could have had it just by snapping her fingers. But her choice was to fall in love with and marry Seymour Levov of Newark instead of any one of those dozens and dozens of smitten Catholic boys she'd met through her Mahoney cousins, the smart, rowdy boys from Holy Cross and Boston College, and so her life was not in Spring Lake but down in Deal and up in Old Rimrock with Mr. Levov. "Well, that's the way it happened," her mother would say sadly to whoever would listen, "Could have had a wonderful life there just like Peg's. Better than Peg's. St. Catherine's and St. Margaret's are there. St. Catherine's is right by the lake there. Beautiful building. Just beautiful. But Mary Dawn's the rebel in the family—always was. Always did just what she wanted, and from the time she marched off to be in that contest, fitting in like everybody else is apparently not something she wanted."

Dawn went to Avon strictly to swim. She still hated lying on the beach to take the sun, still resented having been made to expose her fair skin to the sun every day by the New Jersey pageant people—on the runway, they told her, her white swimsuit would look striking against a deep tan. As a young mother she tried to get as far as she could from everything that marked her as "a former whatever" and that aroused insane contempt in other women and made her feel unhappy and like a freak. She even gave away to charity all the clothes the pageant director (who had his own idea of what kind of girl should be presented by New Jersey to the Miss America judges) had picked out for her at the designers' showrooms in New York during Dawn's daylong buying trip for Atlantic City. The Swede thought she'd looked great in those gowns and he hated to see them go, but at least, at his urging, she kept the state crown so that someday she could show it to their grandchildren.

And then, after Merry started at nursery school, Dawn set out to prove to the world of women, for neither the first time nor the last, that she was impressive for something more than what she looked like. She decided to raise cattle. That idea, too, went back to her childhood—way back to her grandfather, her mother's father, who as a twenty-year-old from County Kerry came to the port in the 1880s, married, settled in south Elizabeth close to St. Mary's, and proceeded to father eleven children. His living he earned at first as a hand on the docks, but he bought a couple of cows to provide milk for the family, wound up selling the surplus to the big shots on West Jersey Street—the Moores from Moore Paint, Admiral "Bull" Halsey's family, Nicholas Murray Butler the Nobel Prize winner and soon became one of the first independent milkmen in Elizabeth. He had about thirty cows on Murray Street, and though he didn't own much property, it didn't matter—in those days you could let them graze anywhere. All his sons went into the business and stayed in it until after the war, when the big supermarkets came along and knocked out the little man. Dawn's father, Jim Dwyer, had worked for her mother's family, and that was how Dawn's parents had met. When he was still only a kid, before refrigeration, Jim Dwyer used to go out on the milk truck at twelve o'clock at night and stay out till morning delivering milk off the back of the truck. But he hated it. Too tough a life. The heck with that, he finally said, and took up plumbing. Dawn, as a small child, loved to visit the cows, and when she was about six or seven, she was taught by one of her cousins how to milk them, and that thrill—squirting the milk out of those udders, the animals just standing there eating hay and letting her tug to her heart's content—she never forgot. With beef cattle, however, she wouldn't need the manpower to milk and she could run the operation almost entirely by herself. The Simmental, which made a lot of milk but was a beef animal as well, still weren't a registered breed in the United States at that time, so she could get in on the ground floor. Crossbreeding—Simmental to polled Hereford—was what interested her, the genetic vigor, the hybrid vigor, the sheer growth that results from crossbreeding. She studied the books, took the magazines, the catalogs started coming in the mail, and at night she would call him over to where she was paging through a catalog and say, "Isn't that a good looking heifer? Have to go out and take a look at her." Pretty soon they were traveling together to shows and sales. She loved the auctions. "This reminds me just a little too much" she whispered to the Swede, "of Atlantic City. It's the Miss America Pageant for cows." She wore a tag identifying herself—"Dawn Levov, Arcady Breeders," which was the name of her company, taken from their Old Rimrock address, Box 62, Arcady Hill Road—and found it very hard to resist buying a nice cow.

A cow or a bull would be led into the ring and paraded around and the show sponsors would give the background of the animal, the sire and the dam and what they did, what the potential was, and then the people would bid, and though Dawn bought carefully, her pleasure just in raising her hand and topping the previous bid was serious pleasure. Much as he wanted more children, not more cows, he had to admit that she was never so fascinating to him, not even when he first saw her at Upsala, as in those moments at the auctions when her beauty came enticingly[11] cloaked in the excitement of bidding and buying. Before Count arrived—the champion bull she bought at birth for ten thousand dollars, which her husband, who was a hundred percent behind her, still had to tell her was an awful lot of money—his accountant would look at her figures for Arcady Breeders at the end of each year and tell the Swede, "This is ridiculous, you can't go on this way." But they really couldn't take a beating as long as it was mostly her own time she put into it, and so he told the accountant, "Don't worry, she'll make some money." He wouldn't have dreamed of stopping her, even if eventually she didn't make a cent, because, as he said to himself when he watched her and the dog out with the herd, "These are her friends."

She worked like hell, all by herself, keeping track of the calving, getting the calves drinking out of a plastic bottle with a nipple if they didn't get the idea of sucking, tending to the mothers' feeding before she put them back in the herd. For the fencing she had to hire a man, but she was out there with him baling hay, the eighteen hundred, two thousand bales that saw them through the winter, and when Count was on in years and got lost one winter day she was heroic in hunting him down, for three days combed the woods for him before she found him where he had got himself onto a little island out in the swamp. Getting him back to the barn was ghastly. Dawn weighed a hundred and three pounds and was five feet two inches tall, and Count weighed about twenty-five hundred pounds, a very long, very beautiful animal with big brown spots around either eye, sire of the most sought-after calves. Dawn kept all the bull calves, breeding for other cattle owners, who would keep these bulls in their herds; the heifers she didn't sell often, but when she did, people wanted them. Count's progeny won year after year at the national shows and the investment returned itself many times over. But then Count got stranded out in the swamp because he had thrown his stifle out; it was icy and he must have got his foot caught in a hole, between roots, and when he saw that to get off this little island he had to get through wet mud, he just quit, and it was three days before Dawn could find him anywhere. Then, with the dog and Merry, she went out with a halter and tried to get him out but he hurt too much and didn't want to get up. So they came back later with some pills, loaded him up with cortisone and different things and sat there with him for another few hours in the rain, and then they tried again to move him. They had to get him through roots and stones and deep muck, and he'd walk a bit and stop, walk a bit and stop, and the dog got behind him and she'd bark and so he'd walk another couple of steps, and that was the way it went for hours. They had him on a rope and he'd take his head, this great big head, all curly with those beautiful eyes, and he'd pull the rope and just swing the two of them, Dawn and Merry together—boom! So then they'd get themselves up and start all over again. They had some grain and he'd eat a little and then he'd come a little farther, but all together it took four hours to get him out of the woods. Ordinarily he led very well, but he hurt so that they had to get him home almost piece by piece. Seeing his petite wife—a woman who could, if she'd wanted to, have been just a pretty face—and his small daughter drenched and covered with mud when they emerged with the bull on the rain-soaked field back of the barn was something the Swede never forgot. "This is right," he thought.

"She is happy. We have Merry and that's enough." He was not a religious man but at that moment he offered up thanks, saying aloud, "Something is shining down on me."

To get the bull to the barn took Dawn and Merry nearly another hour, and there he just lay down in the hay for four days. They got the vet, and the vet said, "You're not going to get him any better. I can make him more comfortable, that's all I can do for you." Dawn brought him water to drink in buckets and food to eat, and one day (as Merry used to tell the story to whoever came to the house) he decided, "Hey, I'm all right" and he got up and he wandered out and he took it easy and that's when he fell in love with the old mare and they became inseparable. The day they had to ship Count—send him to the butcher—Dawn was in tears and kept saying, "I can't do this," and he kept saying, "You've got to do this," and so they did it. Magically (Merry's word) the night before Count left he bred a perfect little heifer, his parting shot. She got the brown spots around the eyes—"He th-th-th-threw brown eyes all around him"—but after that, though the bulls were well bred, never again was there an animal to compare with the Count.

So did it matter finally that she told people she hated the house? He was now far and away the stronger partner, she was now far and away the weaker; he was the fortunate, doubtlessly undeserving recipient of so much—what the hell, to whatever demand she made on him, he acceded. If he could bear something and Dawn couldn't, he didn't understand how he could do anything but accede. That was the only way the Swede knew for a man to go about being a man, especially one as lucky as himself. From the very beginning it had been a far greater strain for him to bear her disappointments than to bear his own; her disappointments seemed to dangerously rob him of himself—once he had absorbed her disappointments it became impossible for him to do nothing about them. Half measures wouldn't suffice. His effort to arrive at what she wanted always had to be wholehearted; never was he free of his quiet wholeheartedness. Not even when everything was on top of him, even when giving everyone what they needed from him at the factory and everyone what they needed from him at home—dealing promptly with the suppliers' screw-ups, with the union's exactions, with the buyers' complaints; contending with an uncertain marketplace and all the overseas headaches; attending, on demand, to the importuning of a stuttering child, an independent-minded wife, a putatively[12] retired, easily riled-up father—did it occur to him that this relentlessly impersonal use of himself might one day wear him down. He did not think like that any more than the ground under his feet thought like that. He seemed never to understand or, even in a moment of fatigue, to admit that his limitations were not entirely loathsome and that he was not himself a one-hundred-and-seventy-year-old stone house, its weight borne imperturbably by beams carved of oak—that he was something more transitory and mysterious.

It wasn't this house she hated anyway; what she hated were memories she couldn't shake loose from, all of them associated with the house, memories that of course he shared. Merry as a grade school kid lying on the floor of the study next to Dawn's desk, drawing pictures of Count while Dawn did the accounts for the farm. Merry emulating her mother's concentration, enjoying working with the same discipline, silently delighting to feel an equal in a common pursuit, and in some preliminary way offering them a glimpse of herself as the adult—yes, of the adult friend to them that she would someday be. Memories particularly of when they weren't being what parents are nine-tenths of the time—the taskmasters, the examples, the moral authorities, the nags of pick that-up and you're-going-to-be-late, keepers of the diary of her duties and routines—memories, rather, of when they found one another afresh, beyond the tensions between parental mastery and inept[13] childish uncertainty, of those moments of respite in a family's life when they could reach one another in calm.

The early mornings in the bathroom shaving while Dawn went to wake Merry up—he could not imagine a better start to the morning than catching a glimpse of that ritual. There was never an alarm clock in Merry's life—Dawn was her alarm clock. Before six o'clock Dawn was already out in the barn, but at promptly six thirty she stopped tending the herd, came back in the house, and went up to the child's room, where, as she sat at the edge of the bed, daybreak's comforting observance began. Without a word it began—Dawn simply stroking Merry's sleeping head, a pantomime that could go on for two full minutes. Next, almost singing the whispered words, Dawn lightly inquired, "A sign of life?" Merry responded not by opening her eyes but by moving a little finger. "Another sign, please?" On the game went—Merry playing along by wrinkling her nose, by moistening her lips, by sighing just audibly—till eventually she was up out of bed ready to go. It was a game embodying a loss, for Merry the state of being completely protected, for Dawn the project of completely protecting what once had seemed completely protect able Waking The Baby: it continued until the baby was nearly twelve, the one rite of infancy that Dawn could not resist indulging, that neither one of them ever appeared eager to outgrow.

How he loved to sight them doing together what mothers and daughters do. To a father's eye, one seemed to amplify the other. In bathing suits rushing out of the surf together and racing each other to the towels—the wife now a little past her robust moment and the daughter edging up to the beginning of hers. A delineation[14] of life's cyclical nature that left him feeling afterward as though he had a spacious understanding of the whole female sex. Merry, with her growing curiosity about the trappings of womanhood, putting on Dawn's jewelry while, beside her at the mirror, Dawn helped her preen. Merry confiding in Dawn about her fears of ostracism—of other kids ignoring her, of her girlfriends ganging up on her. In those quiet moments from which he was excluded (daughter relying on mother, Dawn and Merry emotionally one inside the other like those Russian dolls), Merry appeared more poignantly than ever not a small replica of his wife, or of himself, but an independent little being—something similar, a version of them, yet distinctive and new—for which he had the most passionate affinity.

It wasn't the house Dawn hated—what she hated, he knew, was that the motive for having the house (for making the beds, for setting the table, for laundering the curtains, for organizing the holidays, for apportioning her energies and differentiating her duties by the day of the week) had been destroyed right along with Hamlin's store; the tangible daily fullness, the smooth regularity that was once the underpinning of all of their lives survived in her only as an illusion, as a mockingly inaccessible, bigger-than life-size fantasy, real for every last Old Rimrock family but hers. He knew this not just because of the million memories but also because in the top drawer of his office desk he still kept handy a ten-year-old copy of a local weekly, the Denville-Randolph Courier, featuring on the first page the article about Dawn and her cattle business. She had consented to be interviewed only if the journalist promised not to mention her having been Miss New Jersey of 1949. The journalist agreed and the piece was titled "Old Rimrock Woman Feels Lucky to Love What She's Doing," and concluded with a paragraph that, simple as it was, made him proud of her whenever he went back to read it: "'People are lucky if they get to do what they love and are good at it,' Mrs. Levov declared."

The Courier story testified just how much she had loved the house, as well as everything else about their lives. Beneath a photograph of her standing before the pewter plates lined up on the fireplace mantel—in her white turtleneck shirt and cream-colored blazer, with her hair styled in a pageboy and her two delicate hands in front of her, the fingers decorously intertwined, looking sweet though a bit plain—the caption read, "Mrs. Levov, the former Miss New Jersey of 1949, loves living in a 170-year-old home, an environment which she says reflects the values of her family." When Dawn called the paper in a fury about mentioning Miss New Jersey, the journalist answered that he had kept to his promise not to mention it in the article; it was the editor who had put it in the caption.

No, she had not hated the house, of course she hadn't—and that didn't matter anyway. All that mattered now was the restoration of her well-being; the foolish remarks she might make to this one or that one were of no consequence beside the recovery taking hold. Maybe what was agitating him was that the self-adjustments on which she was building a recovery were not regenerative for him or entirely admirable to him, were even something of an affront to him. He could not tell people—certainly couldn't convince himself—that he hated the things he'd loved...

He was back to it. But he couldn't help it, not when he remembered how at seven Merry would eat herself sick with the raw batter while baking two dozen tollhouse cookies, and a week later they'd still be finding batter all over the place, even up on top of the refrigerator. So how could he hate the refrigerator? How could he let his emotions be reshaped, imagine himself being rescued, as Dawn did, by their leaving it behind for an all-but-silent new Ice Temp the Rolls-Royce of refrigerators? He for one could not say he hated the kitchen in which Merry used to bake her cookies and melt her cheese sandwiches and make her baked ziti, even if the cupboards weren't stainless steel or the counters Italian marble. He could not say he hated the cellar where she used to go to play hide-and-seek with her screaming friends, even if sometimes it spooked even him a little to be down there in the wintertime with those scuttling mice. He could not say he hated the massive fireplace adorned with the antique iron kettle that was all at once insufferably corny in Dawn's estimation, not when he remembered how, early every January, he would chop up the Christmas tree and set it afire there, the whole thing in one go, so that the explosive blaze of the bone-dry branches, the great whoosh and the loud crackling and the dancing shadows, cavorting devils climbing to the ceiling from the four walls, would transport Merry into a delirium of terrified delight. He could not say he hated the ball and claw-foot bathtub where he used to give her baths, just because decades of indelible mineral stains from the well water streaked the enamel and encircled the drain. He could not even hate the toilet whose handle required all that jiggling[15] to get the thing to stop gushing, not when he remembered her kneeling beside it and throwing up while he knelt next to her, holding her sick little forehead.

Nor could he say he hated his daughter for what she had done—if he could! If only, instead of living chaotically in the world where she wasn't and in the world where she once was and in the world where she might now be, he could come to hate her enough not to care anything about her world, then or now. If only he could be back thinking like everybody else, once again the totally natural man instead of this riven charlatan of sincerity, an artless outer Swede and a tormented inner Swede, a visible stable Swede and a concealed beleaguered Swede, an easygoing, smiling sham Swede enshrouding the Swede buried alive. If only he could even faintly reconstitute the undivided oneness of existence that had made for his straightforward physical confidence and freedom before he became the father of an alleged murderer. If only he could be as unknowing as some people perceived him to be—if only he could be as perfectly simple as the legend of Swede Levov concocted by the hero-worshiping kids of his day. If only he could say, "I hate this house!" and be Weequahic's Swede Levov again. If he could say, "I hate that child! I never want to see her again!" and then go ahead, disown her, forever more despise and reject her and the vision for which she was willing, if not to kill, then to cruelly abandon her own family, a vision having nothing whatsoever to do with "ideals" but with dishonesty, criminality, megalomania, and insanity. Blind antagonism and an infantile desire to menace—those were her ideals. In search always of something to hate. Yes, it went way, way beyond her stuttering. That violent hatred of America was a disease unto itself. And he loved America. Loved being an American. But back then he hadn't dared begin to explain to her why he did, for fear of unleashing the demon, insult. They lived in dread of Merry's stuttering tongue. And by then he had no influence anyway. Dawn had no influence. His parents had no influence. In what way was she "his" any longer if she hadn't even been his then, certainly not his if to drive her into her frightening blitzkrieg mentality it required no more than for her own father to begin to explain why his affections happened to be for the country where he'd been born and raised. Stuttering, sputtering little bitch! Who the fuck did she think she was?

Imagine the vileness with which she would have assaulted him for revealing to her that just reciting the names of the forty-eight states used to thrill him back when he was a little kid. The truth of it was that even the road maps used to give him a kick when they gave them away free at the gas station. So did the offhand[16] way he had got his nickname. The first day of high school, down in the gym for their first class, and him just jerking around with the basketball while the other kids were still all over the place getting into their sneakers. From fifteen feet out he dropped in two hook shots—swish! swish!—just to get started. And then that easygoing way that Henry "Doc" Ward, the popular young phys ed teacher and wrestling coach fresh from Montclair State, laughingly called from his office doorway—called out to this lanky blond fourteen year-old with the brilliant blue gaze and the easy, effortless style whom he'd never seen in his gym before—"Where'd you learn that, Swede?" Because the name differentiated Seymour Levov from Seymour Munzer and Seymour Wishnow, who were also on the class roll, it stuck all through gym his freshman year; then other teachers and coaches took it up, then kids in the school, and afterward, as long as Weequahic remained the old Jewish Weequahic and people there still cared about the past, Doc Ward was known as the guy who'd christened Swede Levov. It just stuck. Simple as that, an old American nickname, proclaimed by a gym teacher, bequeathed in a gym, a name that made him mythic in a way that Seymour would never have done, mythic not only during his school years but to his schoolmates, in memory, for the rest of their days. He carried it with him like an invisible passport, all the while wandering deeper and deeper into an American's life, forthrightly evolving into a large, smooth, optimistic American such as his conspicuously raw forebears—including the obstinate father whose American claim was not inconsiderable—couldn't have dreamed of as one of their own.

The way his father talked to people, that got him too, the American way his father said to the guy at the pump, "Filler up, Mac. Check the front end, will ya, Chief?" The excitement of their trips in the DeSoto. The tiny, musty tourist cabins they stopped at overnight while meandering up through the scenic back roads of New York State to see Niagara Falls. The trip to Washington when Jerry was a brat all the way. His first liberty home from the marines, the pilgrimage to Hyde Park with the folks and Jerry to stand together as a family looking at FDR's grave. Fresh from boot camp and there at Roosevelt's grave, he felt that something meaningful was happening; hardened and richly tanned from training through the hottest months on a parade ground where the temperature rose some days to a hundred twenty degrees, he stood silent, proudly wearing his new summer uniform, the shirt starched, the khaki pants sleekly pocket less over the rear and perfectly pressed, the tie pulled taut, cap centered on his close-shaven head, black leather dress shoes spit-shined, agleam, and the belt—the belt that made him feel most like a marine, that tightly woven khaki fabric belt with the metal buckle—girding a waist that had seen him through some ten thousand sit-ups as a raw Parris Island recruit. Who was she to sneer at all this, to reject all this, to hate all this and set out to destroy it? The war, winning the war—did she hate that too? The neighbors, out in the street, crying and hugging on V-J Day, blowing car horns and marching up and down front lawns loudly banging kitchen pots. He was still at Parris Island then, but his mother had described it to him in a three-page letter. The celebration party at the playground back of the school that night, everyone they knew, family friends, school friends, the neighborhood butcher, the grocer, the pharmacist, the tailor, even the bookie from the candy store, all in ecstasy, long lines of staid middle-aged people madly mimicking Carmen Miranda and dancing the conga, one two-three kick, one-two-three kick, until after two a.m. The war. Winning that war. Victory, victory, victory had come! No more death and war!

His last months of high school, he'd read the paper every night, following the marines across the Pacific. He saw the photographs in life—photographs that haunted his sleep—of the crumpled bodies of dead marines killed on Peleliu, an island in a chain called the Palaus. At a place called Bloody Nose Ridge, Japs ferreted in old phosphate mines, who were themselves to be burned to a crisp by the flamethrowers, had cut down hundreds and hundreds of young marines, eighteen-year-olds, nineteen-year-olds, boys barely older than he was. He had a map up in his room with pins sticking out of it, pins he had inserted to mark where the marines, closing in on Japan, had assaulted from the sea a tiny atoll or an island chain where the Japs, dug into coral fortresses, poured forth ferocious[17] mortar and rifle fire. Okinawa was invaded on April 1, 1945, Easter Sunday of his senior year and just two days after he'd hit a double and a home run in a losing game against West Side. The Sixth Marine Division overran Yontan, one of the two island air bases, within three hours of wading ashore. Took the Motobu Peninsula in thirteen days. Just off the Okinawa beach, two kamikaze pilots attacked the flagship carrier Bunker Hill on May 14—the day after the Swede went four for four against Irvington High, a single, a triple, and two doubles—plunging their planes, packed with bombs, into the flight deck jammed with American planes all gassed up to take off and laden with ammunition. The blaze climbed a thousand feet into the sky, and in the explosive firestorm that raged for eight hours, four hundred sailors and aviators died. Marines of the Sixth Division captured Sugar Loaf Hill, May 14, 1945—three more doubles for the Swede in a winning game against East Side—maybe the worst, most savage single day of fighting in marine history. Maybe the worst in human history. The caves and tunnels that honeycombed Sugar Loaf Hill at the southern end of the island, where the Japs had fortified and hidden their army, were blasted with flamethrowers and then sealed with grenades and demolition charges. Hand-to-hand fighting went on day and night.

Jap riflemen and machine gunners, chained to their positions and unable to retreat, fought until they died. The day the Swede graduated from Weequahic High, June 22—having racked up the record number of doubles in a single season by a Newark City League player—the Sixth Marine Division raised the American flag over Okinawa's second air base, Kadena, and the final staging area for the invasion of Japan was secured. From April 1, 1945, to June 21, 1945—coinciding, give or take a few days, with the Swede's last and best season as a high school first baseman—an island some fifty miles long and about ten miles wide had been occupied by American forces at the cost of 15,000 American lives. The Japanese dead, military and civilian, numbered 141,000. To conquer the Japanese homeland to the north and end the war meant the number of dead on each side could run ten, twenty, thirty times as great. And still the Swede went out and, to be a part of the final assault on Japan, joined the U.S. Marines, who on Okinawa, as on Tarawa, Iwo Jima, Guam, and Guadalcanal, had absorbed casualties that were stupefying[18].

The marines. Being a marine. Boot camp. Knocked us around every which way, called us all kinds of names, physically and mentally murdered us for three months, and it was the best experience I ever had in my life. Took it on as a challenge and I did it. My name became "Ee-oh." That's the way the southern drill instructors pronounced Levov, dropping the L and the two v's—all consonants overboard—and lengthening out the two vowels. "Ee-oh!" Like a donkey braying. "Ee-oh!" "Yes, sir!" Major Dunleavy, the athletic director, big guy, Purdue football coach, stops the platoon one day and the hefty sergeant we called Sea Bag shouts for Private Ee-oh and out I run with my helmet on, and my heart was pounding because I thought my mother had died. I was just a week away from being assigned to Camp

Lejeune, up in North Carolina, for advanced weaponry training, but Major Dunleavy pulled the plug on that and so I never got to fire a bar. And that was why I'd joined the marines—wanted more than anything to fire the bar from flat on my belly with the barrel elevated on a mount. Eighteen years old and that was the Marine Corps to me, the rapid-firing, air-cooled caliber machine gun. What a patriotic kid that innocent kid was. Wanted to fire the tank killer, the hand-held bazooka rocket, wanted to prove to myself I wasn't scared and could do that stuff. Grenades, flamethrowers, crawling under barbed wire, blowing up bunkers, attacking caves. Wanted to hit the beach in a duck. Wanted to help win the war. But Major Dunleavy had got a letter from his friend in Newark, what an athlete this Levov was, glowing letter about how wonderful I was, and so they reassigned me and made me a drill instructor to keep me on the island to play ball—by then they'd dropped the atomic bomb and the war was over anyway. "You're in my unit, Swede. Glad to have you" A great break, really. Once my hair grew in, I was a human being again. Instead of being called "shithead" all the time or "shithead move your-ass," suddenly I was a DI the recruits called Sir. What the Dl called the recruits was You People! Hit the deck, You People! On your feet, You People! Double time, You People, double time hup." Great, great experience for a kid from Keer Avenue. Guys I would never have met in my life. Accents from all over the place. The Midwest. New England. Some farm boys from Texas and the Deep South I couldn't even understand. But got to know them. Got to like them. Hard boys, poor boys, lots of high school athletes. Used to live with the boxers. Lived with the recreation gang. Another Jewish guy, Manny Rabinowitz from Altoona. Toughest Jewish guy I ever met in my life. What a fighter. A great friend. Didn't even finish high school. Never had a friend like that before or since. Never laughed so hard in my life as I did with Manny. Manny was money in the bank for me. Nobody ever gave us any Jewboy shit. A little back in boot camp, but that was it. When Manny fought, the guys would bet their cigarettes on him. Buddy Falcone and Manny Rabinowitz were always the two winners for us whenever we fought another base. After the fight with Manny the other guy would say that nobody had ever hit him as hard in his life. Manny ran the entertainment with me, the boxing smokers. The duo—the Jewish leathernecks. Manny got the wise guy recruit who made all the trouble and weighed a hundred and forty-five pounds to fight somebody a hundred and sixty pounds who he could be sure would beat the shit out of him. "Always pick a redhead, Ee-oh," Manny said, "he'll give you the best fight in the world, Redhead'll never quit." Manny the scientist. Manny going up to Norfolk to fight a sailor, a middleweight contender before the war, and whipping him. Exercising the battalion[19] before breakfast. Marching the recruits down to the pool every night to teach them to swim. We practically threw them in—the old-fashioned way of teaching swimming, but you had to swim to be a marine. Always had to be ready to do ten more push-ups than any of the recruits. They'd challenge me, but I was in shape. Getting on the bus going to play ball. The long distances we flew. Bob Collins on the team, the big St. John's guy. My teammate. Terrific athlete. Boozer. With Bob C. got drunk for the first time in my life, talked for two hours nonstop about playing ball for Weequahic and then threw up all over the deck. Irish guys, Italian guys, Slovaks, Poles, tough little bastards from Pennsylvania, kids who'd run away from fathers who worked in the mines and beat them with belt buckles and with their fists—these were the guys I lived with and ate with and slept alongside. Even an Indian guy, a Cherokee, a third baseman. Called him Piss Cutter, the same as the name for our caps. Don't ask me why. Not all of them decent people but on the whole all right. Good guys. Lots of organized grab ass Played against Fort Benning. Cherry Point, North Carolina, the marine air base. Beat them. Beat Charleston Navy Yard. We had a couple of boys who could throw that ball. One pitcher went on to the Tigers. Went down to Rome, Georgia, to play ball, over to Waycross, Georgia, to an army base. Called the army guys doggies. Beat them. Beat everybody. Saw the South. Saw things I never saw. Saw the life the Negroes live. Met every kind of Gentile you can think of. Met beautiful southern girls. Met common whores. Used a condom. Skinned 'er back and squeezed 'er down. Saw Savannah. Saw New Orleans. Sat in a rundown slop chute in Mobile, Alabama, where I was damn glad the shore patrol was just outside the door. Playing basketball and baseball with the Twenty-second Regiment. Got to be a United States Marine. Got to wear the emblem with the anchor and the globe. "No pitcher in there, Ee-oh, poke it outta here, Ee-oh—" Got to be Ee-oh to guys from Maine, New Hampshire, Louisiana, Virginia, Mississippi, Ohio—guys without an education from all over America calling me Ee-oh and nothing more. Just plain Ee-oh to them. Loved that. Discharged June 2, 1947. Got to marry a beautiful girl named Dwyer. Got to run a business my father built, a man whose own father couldn't speak English. Got to live in the prettiest spot in the world. Hate America? Why, he lived in America the way he lived inside his own skin. All the pleasures of his younger years were American pleasures, all that success and happiness had been American, and he need no longer keep his mouth shut about it just to defuse her ignorant hatred. The loneliness he would feel as a man without all his American feelings. The longing he would feel if he had to live in another country. Yes, everything that gave meaning to his accomplishments had been American. Everything he loved was here.

For her, being an American was loathing America, but loving America was something he could not let go of any more than he could have let go of loving his father and his mother, any more than he could have let go of his decency. How could she "hate" this country when she had no conception of this country? How could a child of his be so blind as to revile the "rotten system" that had given her own family every opportunity to succeed? To revile her "capitalist" parents as though their wealth were the product of anything other than the un stinting industry of three generations. The men of three generations, including even himself, slogging through the slime and stink of a tannery. The family that started out in a tannery, at one with, side by side with, the lowest of the low——now to her "capitalist dogs." There wasn't much difference, and she knew it, between hating America and hating them. He loved the America she hated and blamed for everything that was imperfect in life and wanted violently to overturn, he loved the "bourgeois values" she hated and ridiculed and wanted to subvert, he loved the mother she hated and had all but murdered by doing what she did. Ignorant little fucking bitch! The price they had paid! Why shouldn't he tear up this Rita Cohen letter? Rita Cohen! They were back! The sadistic mischief-makers with their bottomless talent for antagonism who had extorted the money from him, who, for the fun of it, had extracted from him the Audrey Hepburn scrapbook, the stuttering diary, and the ballet shoes, these delinquent young brutes calling themselves "revolutionaries" who had so viciously played with his hopes five years back had decided the time had again rolled around to laugh at Swede Levov.

We can only stand as witnesses to the anguish that sanctifies[20] her. The Disciple Who Calls Herself "Rita Cohen" They were laughing at him. They had to be laughing. Because the only thing worse than its all being a wicked joke was its not being a wicked joke. Your daughter is divine. My daughter is anything and everything but. She is all too frail and misguided and wounded—she's hopeless! Why did you tell her that you slept with me? And tell me that it was she who wanted you to. You say these things because you hate us. And you hate us because we don't do such things. You hate us not because we're reckless but because we're prudent and sane and industrious and agree to abide by the law. You hate us because we haven't failed. Because we've worked hard and honestly to become the best in the business and because of that we have prospered, so you envy us and you hate us and want to destroy us. And so you used her. A sixteen-year-old kid with a stutter. No, nothing small about you people. Made her into a "revolutionary" full of great thoughts and high-minded ideals. Sons of bitches. You enjoy the spectacle of our devastation. Cowardly bastards. It isn't cliches that enslaved her, it's you who enslaved her in the loftiest of the shallow cliches—and that resentful kid, with her stutterer's hatred of injustice, had no protection at all. You got her to believe she was at one with the downtrodden people—and made her into your patsy, your stooge. And Dr. Fred Comon, as a result, is dead. That was who you killed to stop the war: the chief of staff up at the hospital in Dover, the guy who in a small community hospital established a coronary care unit of eight beds. That was his crime.

Instead of exploding in the middle of the night when the village was empty, the bomb, either as planned or by mistake, went off at five a.m.—an hour before Hamlin's store opened for the day and the moment that Fred Comon turned away from having dropped into the mailbox envelopes containing checks for household bills that he'd paid at his desk the evening before. He was on his way to the hospital. A chunk of metal flying out of the store struck him at the back of the skull.

Dawn was under sedation and couldn't see anyone, but the Swede had gone to Russ and Mary Hamlin's house and expressed his sympathy about the store, told the Hamlins how much the store had meant to Dawn and him, how it was no less a part of their lives than it was of everyone else's in the community; then he went to the wake—in the coffin Comon looked fine, fit, just as affable as ever—and the following week, with their doctor already arranging for Dawn's hospitalization, the Swede went alone to visit Comon's widow. How he managed to get to that woman's house for tea is another story—another book—but he did it, he did it, and heroically she served him tea while he extended his family's condolences in the words that he had revised in his mind five hundred times but that, when spoken, were still no good, even more hollow than those he'd uttered to Russ and Mary Hamlin: "deep and sincere regrets... the agony of your family... my wife would like you to know..." After listening to everything he had to say, Mrs. Comon quietly replied, displaying an outlook so calm and kind and compassionate that the

Swede wanted to disappear, to hide like a child, while at the same time the urge was nearly overpowering to throw himself at her feet and to remain there forever, begging for her forgiveness. "You are good parents and you raised your daughter the way you thought best" she said to him. "It was not your fault and I don't hold anything against you. You didn't go out and buy the dynamite. You didn't make the bomb. You didn't plant the bomb. You had nothing to do with the bomb. If, as it appears, your daughter turns out to be the one who is responsible, I will hold no one responsible but her. I feel badly for you and your family, Mr. Levov. I have lost a husband, my children have lost a father. But you have lost something even greater. You are parents who have lost a child. There is not a day that goes by that you won't be in my thoughts and in my prayers." The Swede had known Fred Comon only slightly, from cocktail parties and charity events where they found themselves equally bored. Mainly he knew him by reputation, a man who cared about his family and the hospital with the same devotion——a hard worker, a good guy. Under him, the hospital had begun to plan a building program, the first since its construction, and in addition to the new coronary care unit, during his stewardship there had been a long-overdue modernization of emergency room facilities. But who gives a shit about the emergency room of a community hospital out in the sticks? Who gives a shit about a rural general store whose owner has been running it since 1921? We're talking about humanity! When has there ever been progress for humanity without a few small mishaps and mistakes? The people are angry and they have spoken! Violence will be met by violence, regardless of consequences, until the people are liberated! Fascist America down one post office, facility completely destroyed.

Except, as it happened, Hamlin's was not an official U.S. post office nor were the Hamlins U.S. postal employees—theirs was merely a postal station contracted, for x number of dollars, to handle a little postal business on the side. Hamlin's was no more a government installation than the office where your accountant makes out your tax forms. But that is a mere technicality to world revolutionaries.

Facility destroyed! Eleven hundred Old Rimrock residents forced, for a full year and a half, to drive five miles to buy their stamps and to get packages weighed and to send anything registered or special delivery. That'll show Lyndon Johnson who's boss.

They were laughing at him. Life was laughing at him.

Mrs. Comon had said, "You are as much the victims of this tragedy as we are.

The difference is that for us, though recovery will take time, we will survive as a family. We will survive as a loving family. We will survive with our memories intact and with our memories to sustain us. It will not be any easier for us than it will be for you to make sense of something so senseless. But we are the same family we were when Fred was here, and we will survive." The clarity and force with which she implied that the Swede and his family would not survive made him wonder, in the weeks that followed, if her kindness and her compassion were so all-encompassing as he had wanted at first to believe.

He never went to see her again.

(This passage is Chapter 5 taken from Philip Roth: *American Pastoral* , New York: Vintage Books, 1997, p.175-271)

Notes:

1. precaution: an action taken in advance to protect against possible danger or failure
2. pageant: an elaborate public dramatic presentation that usually depicts a historical or traditional event; a spectacular procession or celebration
3. chaperone: older person, usually a woman, who on social occasions, took care of a young woman who was not married.
4. rehearsals: the act of practicing in preparation for a public performance
5. accomplice: one who aids or abets a lawbreaker in a criminal act, either as a principal or an accessory
6. rudimentary: being in the earliest stages of development; incipient
7. austere: plain and without decoration, comforts, or anything extra
8. antiquated: old-fashioned or unsuitable for modern society
9. infidelity: the act of having sex with someone who is not your husband or wife
10. wistfully: sadly and thinking about something that is impossible or past
11. enticing: something that is enticing attracts or interests you a lot.
12. putative: believed or accepted by most people
13. inept: not skilled or effective
14. delineate: to describe or draw something carefully so that people can understand it
15. jiggle: to make something move from side to side or up and down with short quick movements
16. offhand: not very friendly toward someone when you are talking to them
17 ferocious: violent, dangerous and frightening

18. stupefying: making you feel extremely surprised, tired, or bored
19. battalion: a large group of soldiers consisting of several companies.
20. sanctify: to make something seem morally right or acceptable or to give something official approval

Questions for Study and Discussion:

1. Seymour saw "a large stone house with black shutters set on a rise back of some trees. A little girl was on a swing suspended from a low branch of one of those big trees, swinging herself high into the air, just happy, he imagined, as a kid can be." This is an important image in the novel. What does the happy image symbolize?
2. Does Dawn, in reinventing herself after Merry's disappearance, seem ruthless to you, or do you sympathize with her struggle for survival?
3. When Dawn tells Bill Orcutt that she always hates the Old Rimrock house, does she tell the truth?
4. Why does Dawn hate the house which Levov has tried hard to build?
5. In this chapter, all of the three protagonists appear—the husband Levov, the wife Dawn and the daughter Merry. What are the differences of their attitudes towards their family, their country and their life?
6. What do you think has caused their differences?

John Simmons Barth (1930—   )

Life and Major Works

John Simmons Barth was born on May, 27, 1930, to John Jacob and Georgia Barth in Cambridge, Maryland. After graduating from public high school in 1947, he enrolled in the prestigious Julliard School of music with dreams of becoming an arranger, or orchestrator. He soon shifted his interest, however, and enrolled in Johns Hopkins University in Baltimore and began his lifelong involvement with literature and writing. By the time he had received his B.A. from

John Barth

Johns Hopkins in 1951, he was married and the father of a daughter. Barth continued at Johns Hopkins and received his M.A. in creative writing in 1952.

After the birth of his second child, he was forced for financial reasons to discontinue his doctoral work and accept a teaching position at Pennsylvania State University.

Barth's eight long fictions can be divided into four couplets. His first two novels, which one is *The Floating Opera,* was published in 1956, was nominated for the National Book Award, he was promoted to the rank of assistant professor, the other is *The End of the Road* (1958). They are largely realistic and more traditional than his later works, and reveal his nihilist philosophy, but they follow the literary conventions in the diction and technique. The former is about a nihilist who, contemplating suicide, decides not to kill himself after all. The novel is informed by the sense of the absurd which has colored all his work. It is appealing for its playful, colloquial speech and for his ability to spin marvelously funny yarns fringed with metaphysical speculation. The latter is "realistically" filled with narrative games. In it the author practices an inventive and amusing questioning of moral and philosophical values in an extremely funny manner.

In his next couplet, Barth turns away from the contemporary scene, abandoning the realistic novel: while *The Sot-Weed Factor* (1960) is set in the 17th century, *Giles Goat-Boy* (1966) takes place in the future. Both works, however, continues Barth's concern with cosmopsis. The protagonists of these novels lack consistent identities until they practice a form of mythotherapy. There novels also display Barth's return to the self-conscious play with narrative form that characterized *Floating Opera.* In *Sot-Weed* the reader encounters the parodic reworking of 18th–century fictional themes and techniques, the incorporation of digressions and non-existent historical documents, and an excessiveness in action and dialogue that suggests that they are included in the novel more for their own sake than for what they reveal about the main character. Likewise, in *Ciles*, Barth presents a farcical reworking of mythic elements and a series of frames for his narrative that continually point to its artificiality. Before published the *Giles Goat-Boy,* he moved to Buffalo to become professor of English at the State University of New York in 1965.

His next couplet, *Lost in the Funhouse* (1968) and *Chimera* (1974), reveals Barth's deepening exploration of narrative form and language. *Funhouse* is a series of 14 short fictions that include a three-dimensional, Moebius-strip story, a story is embedded in which the story is the narrator, a fiction about writing fictions, and a story embedded in a story embedded in a story embedded in a story.

Chimera, a National Book Award winner, consists of three novellas in which narrators discourse on the nature and function of fiction while acting within their own fictions. In both collections, Barth also reveals his continuing concern with mythology. To understand and revivify narrative, he returns to its Greco-Roman roots.

Letters (1979) and *Sabbatical* (1982) both signal Barth's return to the novel after more than a decade. They also signal his attempt to bring together the various themes of his previous fiction. His examination of self, his experiments with form, his involvement with the contemporary scene, and myth—all come together in these two novels. It is as if he himself is the heroes of *Letters* and *Sabbatical* looking back on his accomplishments at mid-career before setting of in a new direction. Reviewing Barth's career to this point, we can assume that this direction will be as innovative, interesting, and intellectually challenging as his earlier turnings. In the eyes of many readers, John Barth is the central spokesperson for postmodernism. The title of two of his essays, "The Literature of Exhaustion" (1967) and "The Literature of Replenishment" (1980), sum up his attitudes toward fiction and reality. In these essays and his fiction he suggests that they have lost whatever power and value they may have had. Barth's role, as he sees it, is to replenish, re-energize, these concepts by examining them and positing alternatives to them. The fictions that result from this program are highly experimental, intellectually ambitious, and wildly comic.

In 1990 he retired with the rank of Professor Emeritus, but has remained an active and productive writer. His latest novel, *The Tidewater Tales,* was published in 1997.

Three aspects of Barth's life have shaped and colored his remarkable literary career. The first is his early and sustained interest in music. Although he discontinued his formal study at Julliard, Barth has remained fascinated with playing the role of the arranger in his fiction. The second aspect of his life reflected in his work is the landscape and history of his native Maryland where he has lived for nearly all of his life and where much of his fiction is set. Finally, Barth's work is also informed by his long career in academia, where he was immersed in the influence of literary criticism and theory.

Brief Introduction and Appreciation

Lost in the Funhouse has given another generation of readers and scholars the opportunity to work out their theories of language and storytelling. On the surface, *Lost in the Funhouse* is the story of a thirteen-year-old boy's trip to the beach with his family on the fourth of July during World War II. With Ambrose are his older brother Peter, their mother and father, their Uncle Karl, and a fourteen-year-old neighbor girl, Magda, to whom both Ambrose and Peter are attracted. Having learned that the beach is covered in oil and tar from the fleet off-shore, the group decides to go through the funhouse instead. Both boys fantasize about going through the maze with Magda, but it suddenly becomes clear to Ambrose that he has misunderstood the meaning of the funhouse, has failed to see "that to get through expeditiously was not the point." He realizes that he is too young to understand or engage in the sexual play associated with the funhouse's dark corners. More profoundly, however, he also realizes that he is constitutionally different from his bother and Magda: he is not the type of person for whom funhouses are fun. Confused and separated from the others, Ambrose takes a wrong turn and loses his way. During the process of finding his way out of the dark corridors and back hallways, he comes to some realizations about himself and about funhouses. Specifically, he understands that his crippling self-consciousness also comes with a gift, an extraordinary imagination. Recognizing that the artistic life brings alienation as well as satisfaction he resolves to "construct funhouses for others and be their secret operator — though he would rather be among the lovers for whom funhouses are constructed." The first two paragraphs in *Lost in the Funhouse* are typical of the representation of exposure of narrative artifice. The former part of the paragraph is a conventional beginning; its latter part abruptly turns into the specific explanation of the function of italic. The artificial elements involved in the storytelling are purposefully made discernible, which the traditional novelists attempt to conceal. The two tightly held processes disturb the readerly involvement in the story of actual experience and bring fictionality of novel to the fore. The last two italicized words "italic mine" emphatically foregrounds the voice of author. Traditionally, "the voice of author has been to ensure the credibility of the fictive story and to shorten the distance of the fictive world". However the function of the author in the novel seems to be on the contrary. Its frequent emergence in the narration of the first clue and the expository discussion of the second remind the reader that what they are reading is nothing but fictive that is under the control of the author. In other parts of the story, the author's presence is constantly intruded. "There is no point in going further".

The voice of the author is heard when he feels frustrated with his writing. "Is it likely, does it violate the principle of verisimilitude that a thirteen-year-old boy could make such a sophisticated observation?" "Is there really such a person as Ambrose, or is he a figment of the author's imagination? Was it Assawomen Bay or Sinepuxend? Are there other errors of fact in this fiction?" The author raises such questions concerned with authenticity of narration to his reader after providing some descriptions of Ambrose's adventure in the funhouse. Sometimes the author criticizes and comments his own writing in the process of the storytelling. The second paragraph is dealt with the same manner. Its former parts switches back to the story of Ambrose, in which the basic information of major character is introduced.

Again, the quite familiar pattern of introductory description is interrupted by the explanation of and the comment on the function of blank and initial in realistic writing. Thereby the purpose of the techniques is disclosed: they are the means of reinforcing the illusion. In the following parts of the story, the employment of the realistic techniques is laid bare in the same way. When the vivid description of the appearance of the other characters are made, the narrator comments:

The teaching of a bit of such literary knowledge is inserted in the process of storytelling about Ambrose. "The more closely an author identifies with the narrator, literary or metaphorically, the less advisable it is, as a rule, to use the first person narrative viewpoint." "Narrative ordinarily consists of alternating dramatization and summarization". "The inverted tag in dialogue writing is still considered permissible with proper names or epithets, but sounds old-fashioned with personal pronouns."

Beside the employment and disclosure of the realistic techniques, the conventional patterns of arrangement are also brought under his comments. For instance, followed the beginning part of the story is the discussion about the function of the beginning in the novel writing.

When the story proceeds to the middle part, the author summarizes and comments on the general pattern of plot.

From the illustration made above, it's noticeable that the author does not intend to tell the readers a story with a stale theme. The intention of providing the story of Ambrose is to set up a frame against which the conventions of realist writing can be laid bare. Frames are set up only to be continually broken. Contexts are constructed only to be subsequently deconstructed, just as Patricia Waugh comments "In John Barth's story *Lost in the Funhouse* almost every statement is undermined and exposed as fictional."

The major theme of the story is Sex, Consciousness, and Storytelling. Just as the funhouse poses mirrors in front of mirrors, tempting the viewer to mistake image for substance, *Lost in the Funhouse* seduces readers into believing the familiar literary truism that sex is a metaphor for language. What Ambrose learns in his journey through the three dimensional funhouse in Ocean City and the narrative funhouse of the story is that the opposite is true: language is just a metaphor for sex. Sex, in fact, is the "whole point...Of the entire funhouse!" Everywhere Ambrose hears the sound of sex, "The shluppish whisper, continuous as seawash round the globe, tidelike falls and rises with the circuit of dawn and dusk." He imagines if he had "X-ray eyes" he would see that "all that normally *showed,* like restaurants and dance halls and clothing and test-your strength machines was merely preparation and intermission." Ambrose's fascination with and fear of sex derives not just from his age, but also from his special temperament. He knows that the funhouse is fun for lovers and that he's not one of the lovers. Recalling the time when Magda initiated him into the world of sex during a childhood game, he remembers most poignantly not the passion or the physical pleasure, but the cognitive dimensions of the experience. Unable to "forget the least detail of his life," Ambrose remembers "standing beside himself with awed impersonality," cataloging the details of the scene in the woodshed, like the design of the label of a cigar box. Later he describes his "odd detachment" at that moment: "Strive as he might to be transported, he heard his mind take notes upon the scene: *This is what they call* passion. *I am experiencing it.*" One of the key elements in any funhouse is the hall of mirrors where visitors see images of images of themselves in strange and unfamiliar shapes. Of course, this awareness of self, or consciousness, is one of the distinguishing and most problematic features of humanness. Ambrose and his narrator alter ego are both marked by their exceptionally keen awareness of self. This is why they are drawn to the hidden levers of funhouses and are resigned to take pleasure in manipulating them rather than enjoying them.

Selected Reading

Lost in the Funhouse

For whom is the funhouse fun? Perhaps for lovers. For Ambrose *it is a place of fear and confusion.* He has come to the seashore with his family for the holiday, *the occasion of their visit is Independence Day, the more important secular holiday of the United States of America.* A single straight underline is the manuscript mark for italic type, which in turn is the printed equivalent to oral emphasis of words and phrases as well as the customary type for titles of complete works, not to mention. Italics are also employed, in fiction stories especially, for "outside," intrusive, or artificial voices, such as radio announcements, the texts of telegrams and newspaper articles, et cetera. They should be used *sparingly.* If passages originally in roman type are italicized by someone repeating them, it's customary to acknowledge the fact, *Italics* mine.

Ambose was "at that awkward age." His voice came out high-pitched as a child's if he let himself get carried away: to be on the safe side, therefore, he moved and spoke with *deliberate calm* and *adult gravity.* Talking soberly of unimportant or irrelevant matters and listening consciously to the sound of your own voice are useful habits for maintaining control in this difficult interval. *En route* to Ocean City he sat in the back seat of the family car with his brother Peter, age fifteen, and Mahda G—, age fourteen, a pretty girl an exquisite young lady, who lived not far from them on B—Street in the town of D—, Maryland. Initials, blanks, or both were often substituted for proper names in nineteen-century fiction to enhance the *illusion* of reality. It is as if the author felt it necessary to delete the names for reasons of tact or legal liability. Interestingly, as with other aspects of realism, it is an *illusion* that be enhanced, by purely artificial means. Is it likely, does it violate the principle of verisimilitude, that a thirteen is *the psychological coeval* of a boy of fifteen or sixteen; a thirteen-year-old boy, therefore, even one precocious in some other respects, might be three years *her emotional junior.*

Thrice a year—on Memorial, Independence, and Labor Days—the family visits Ocean City for the afternoon and evening. When Ambrose and Peter's father was their age, the excursion was made by train, as mentioned in the novel The 42nd *Parallel* by John Dos Passos. Many families from the same neighborhood used to travel together, with dependent relatives and often with Negro servants; schoolfuls of children swarmed through the railway cars; everyone shared everyone else's

Maryland fried chicken, Virginia ham, deviled eggs, potato salad, beaten biscuits, iced tea. Nowadays (this is, in 19—, the years of ours story) the journey is made by automobile—more comfortably and quickly though without the extra fun though without the *camaraderie of* a general excursion. It's all part of the deterioration of American life, their father declares; Uncle Karl supposes that when the boys take *their* families to Ocean City for the holidays they'll fly in Autogiros. Their mother, sitting in the middle of the front seat like Magda in the second, only with her arms on the seat-back behind the men's shoulders, wouldn't want the good old days back again, the steaming trains and stuffy long dress; on the other hand she can do without Autogiros, too, if she has to become a grandmother to fly in them.

Description of physical appearance and mannerisms is one of standard methods of characterization used by writers of fiction. It is also important to "keep the senses operating"; when a detail from one of the five senses, say visual, is "crossed" with a detail from another, say auditory, the reader's imagination is oriented to the scene, perhaps unconsciously. This procedure may be compared to the way surveyors and navigators determine their positions by two or more compass bearings, a process known as triangulation[1]. The brown hair on Ambrose's mother's forearms gleamed in the sun like. Though right-handed, she took her left arm from the seat-back to press the dashboard cigar lighter for Uncle Karl. When the glass bead in its handle glowed red, the lighter was ready for use. The smell of Uncle Karl's cigar smoke reminded one of. The fragrance of the ocean came strong to the picnic ground where they always stopped for lunch, two miles inland from Ocean City. Having to pause for a full hour almost within sound of the breakers was difficult for Peter and Ambrose when they were younger; even at their present age it was not easy to keep their anticipation, *stimulated by the briny spume*, from turning into short temper. The Irish author James Joyce, in his unusual novel entitled *Ulysses,* now available in this country, uses the adjectives *snotgreen* and *scrotum-tightening* to describe the sea. Visual, auditory, tactile, olfactory, gustatory. Peter and Ambrose's father, while steering their black 1936 LaSalle sedan with one hand, could with the other remove the first cigarette from a while pack of Lucky Strikes and, more remarkably, light it with a match forefingered from its book and thumbed against the flint paper without being detached. The match book cover merely advertised U. S. War Bonds and Stamps. A fine metaphor, simile, or other figure of speech, in addition to its obvious "first order" relevance to the thing it describes, will be seen upon reflection to have a second order of significance: it may be drawn from the *milieu* of the action, for example, or be particularly appropriate to the sensibility of the narrator, even hinting to the reader upon the thing it describes, sometimes ironically qualifying the more evident sense of the comparison.

To say that Ambrose's and Peter's mother was *pretty* is to accomplish nothing: The reader may acknowledge the proposition, but his imagination is not engaged. Besides, Magda was also pretty, yet in an altogether different way. Although she lived on B—Street she had very good manners and did better than average in school. Her figure was very well developed for her age. Her right hand lay casually on the plush upholstery of the seat, very near Ambrose's left leg, on which his own hand rested. The space between their legs, between her right and his left leg, was out of the line of sight of anyone sitting on other side of Magda's left hand was probably in a similar position on her left side. The boy's father is difficult to describe; no particular feature of his appearance or manner stood out. He wore glasses and was principal of a T—County grade school. Uncle Karl was a masonry contractor.

Although Peter must have known as well as Ambrose that the latter, because of his position in the car, would be the first to see the electrical towers of the power plant at V—, the halfway point of their trip, he leaned forward and slightly toward the center of the car and pretended to be looking for them through the flat pinewoods and tuckahoe creeks along the highway. For as long as the boys could remember, "looking for the Towers" had been a feature of the first half of their excursion to Ocean City, "looking for the standpipe" of the second. Though the game was childish, their mother preserved the tradition of rewarding the first to see the Towers with a candy-bar or piece of fruit. She insisted now that Magda play the game; the prize, she said, was "something hard to get nowadays." Ambrose decided not to join in; he sat far back in his seat. Magda, like Peter, leaned forward. Two sets of straps were discernible through the shoulders of her sun dress; the inside right one, a brassiere-strap, was fastened or shorted with a small safety pin. The right armpit of her dress, presumably the left as well, was damp with perspiration. The simple strategy for being first to espy the Towers, which Ambrose had understood by the age of four, was to sit on the right-hand side of the car. Whoever sat there, however, had also to put up with the worst of the sun, and so Ambrose, without mentioning the matter, chose sometimes the one and sometimes the other. Not impossibly Peter had never caught on to the trick, or thought that his brother hadn't simply because Ambrose on occasion preferred shade to a Baby Ruth or tangerine.

The shade-sun situation didn't apply to the front seat, owing to the windshield; if anything the driver got more sun, since the person on the passenger side not only was shaded below by the door and dashboard but might swing down his sunvisor all the way too.

"*Is that them?*" Magda asked. Ambrose's mother teased the boys for letting Magda win, insinuating that "somebody [had] a girlfriend." Peter and Ambrose's father reached a long thin arm across their mother to butt his cigarette in the dashboard ashtray, under the lighter. The prize this time for seeing the Towers first was a banana. Their mother bestowed it after chiding their father for wasting a half-smoked cigarette when everything was so scarce. Magda, to take the prize, moved her hand from so near Ambrose's that he could have touched it as though accidentally. She offered to share the prize, things like that were so hard to find; but everyone insisted it was hers alone. Ambrose's mother sang an iambic trimeter couplet from a popular song, femininely rhymed:

> "*What's good is in the Army.*
> *What's left will never harm me.*"

Uncle Karl tapped his cigar ash out the ventilator window; some particles were sucked by the slipstream back into the car through the rear window on the passenger side. Magda demonstrated her ability to hold a banana in one hand and peel it with her teeth. She still sat forward; Ambrose pushed his glasses rack onto the bridge of his nose with his left hand, which he then negligently let fall to the seat cushion immediately behind her. He even permitted the single hair, gold, on the second joint of his thumb to brush the fabric of her skirt. Should she have sat back at that instant, his hand would have been caught under her.

Plush upholstery prickles uncomfortably through gabardine slacks in the July Sun. The function of the *beginning* of a story is to introduce the principal characters, establish their initial relationships, set the scene for the main action, expose the background of the situation if necessary, plant motifs and foreshadowings where appropriate, and initiate the first complication or whatever of the "rising action." Actually if one imagines a story called "The Funhouse," or

"Lost in the Funhouse," the details of the drive to Ocean City don't seem especially relevant. The *beginning* should recount the events between Ambrose's first sight of the funhouse early in the afternoon and his entering it with Magda and Peter in the evening. The *middle* would narrate all relevant events from the time he goes in to the time he loses his way; middles have the double and contradictory function of delaying the climax while at the same time preparing the reader for it and fetching[2] him to it. Then the *ending* would tell what Ambrose does while he's lost, how he finally finds his way out, and what everybody makes of the experience. So far there's been no real dialogue, very little sensory detail, and nothing in the way of *a theme*. And a long line has gone by already without anything happening; it makes a person wonder. We haven't even reached Ocean City yet; we will never get out of the funhouse.

The more closely an author identifies with file narrator, literally metaphorically, the less advisable it is, as a rule, to use the first-person narrative viewpoint Once three years previously the young people *aforementioned* played Niggers and Masters in the backyard; when it was Ambrose's turn to be Master and theirs to be Niggers Peter had to go serve his evening papers; Ambrose was afraid to punish Magda alone, but she led him to the whitewashed Torture Chamber between the woodshed and the privy in the Slaves Quarters; there she knelt sweating among bamboo rakes and dusty Mason jars, pleadingly embraced his knees, and while bees droned in the lattice as if on an ordinary summer afternoon, purchased clemency at a surprise price set by herself. *Doubtless she remembered noting of this event*; Ambrose on the other hand seemed unable to forget the least detail of his life. He even recalled how, standing beside himself with awed impersonality in the reeky heat, he'd stared the while at an empty cigar box in which Uncle Karl kept stone-cutting chisels; beneath the words *El Producto*, a laureled, loose-toga'd lady regarded the sea from a marble bench; beside or not yet turned to, was a five-stringed lyre. Her shin reposed on the back of her right hand; her left depended negligently from the bencharm. The lower half of scene and lady was peeled away; the words EXAMINED BY—were inked there into the wood. Nowadays cigar boxes are made of pasteboard. Ambrose wondered what Magda would have done. Ambrose wondered what Magda would do when she sat back on his hand as he resolved she should. Be angry. Make a teasing joke of it. Give on sign at all. For a long time she learned forward, playing cowpoker with Peter against Uncle Karl and Mother and watching for the first sign of Ocean City. AT

Nearly the same instant, picnic ground and Ocean City standpipe[3] have into view; an Amoco filling station on their side of the road cost Mother and Uncle Karl fifty cows and the game; Magda bounced back, clapping her right hand on Mother's right arm; Ambrose moved clear "in the nick of time."

At this rate our hero, at this rate our protagonist will remain in the funhouse forever. Narrative ordinarily consists of alternating dramatization and summarization. One symptom of nervous tension, paradoxically, is repeated and violent yawning; neither Peter not Magda nor Uncle Karl nor Mother reacted in this manner. Although they were no longer small children, Peter and Ambrose were each given a dollar to spend on boardwalk amusements in addition to what money of their own they'd brought along. Ambrose too, though she protested she had ample spending money the boys' mother made a little scene out of distributing the bills; she prentended that her sons and Magda were small children and cautioned them not to spend the sum too quickly or in one place. Magda promised with a merry laugh and, having both hands free, took the bill with her left. Peter laughed also and pledged in a falsetto[4] to be a good boy. His imitation of a child was not clever. The boys' father was tall and thin, balding, fair-complexioned. Assertion of that sort are not effective; the reader may acknowledge the proposition, but. We should be much father along than we are; something has gone wrong; not much of this preliminary rambling seems relevant. Yet everyone begins in the same place; how is it that most go along without difficulty but a few lose their way?

"Stay out from under the boardwalk," Uncle Karl growled from the side of his mouth. The boys' mother pushed his shoulder *in mock annoyance.* They were all standing before Fat May the Laughing Lady who advertised the funhouse. Larger than life, Fat May mechanically shook, rocked on her heels, slapped her thighs while recorded laughter—up-roarious, female—came amplified from a hidden loudspeaker. It chuckled, wheezed, wept; tried in vain to catch its breath; tittered, groaned, exploded raucous and anew. You couldn't hear it without laughing yourself, no matter how you felt. Father came back from talking to a Coast Guardsman on duty and reported that the surf was spoiled with crude oil from tankers recently torpedoed offshore. Lumps of it, difficult to remove, made tarry tidelines on the beach and stuck on swimmers. Many bathed in the surf nevertheless and came out speckled; others paid to use a municipal pool and only sunbathed on the beach. We would do the latter. We would do the latter. We would do the latter.

Under the boardwalk, matchbook covers, grainy other things. What is the story's theme? Ambrose is ill. He perspires in the dark passages; candied apples-on-a-stick, delicious-looking, disappointing to eat. Funhouses need men's and ladies' room at intervals. Others perhaps have also vomited in corners and corridors; may even have had bowel movements liable to be stepped in the dark. The word *fuck* suggests suction and/or and/or flatulence[5]. Mother and Father; grandmothers and grandfathers on both sides; great-grandmothers and great-grandfather son four sides, et cetera. Count a generation as thirty years; in approximately the year when Lord Baltimore was granted charter to the province of Maryland by Charles I, five hundred twelve women—English, Welsh, Bavarian, Swiss—of every class and character; received into themselves the penises the intromittent[6]organs of: five hundred twelve men, ditto[7], in every circumstance and posture, to conceive the five hundred twelve ancestors of the two hundred fifty-six ancestors of the et cetera et cetera et cetera et cetera et cetera et cetera et cetera et cetera of the author, of the narrator, of this story, *Lost in the Funhouse.* In alleyways, ditches, canopy beds, pinewoods, bridal suites, ship's cabins, coach-and-fours, coaches-and-four, sultry toolsheds; on the cold sand under boardwalks, littered with *El Pro-ducto* cigar butts treasured with Lucky Strike cigarette stubs, Coca-Cola caps gritty turds, cardboard lollipop sticks, matchbook covers warning that A Slip of the Lip Can Sink a Ship. The shluppish whisper, continuous as seawash round the globe, tidelike falls and rises with the circuit of dawn and dusk.

Magda's teeth. She *was* left-handed. Perspiration. They've gone all the way, through, Magda and Peter, they've been waiting for hours with Mother and Uncle Karl while Father searches for his lost son; they draw french-fried potatoes from a paper cup and shake their heads. They've named the children they'll one day have and bring to Ocean City on holidays. Can spermatozoa[8] properly be thought of as male animalcules when there are no female spermatozoa? They grope through hot, dark windings, past Love's Tunnel's fearsome obstacles. Some perhaps lose their way.

Peter suggested then and there that they do the funhouse; he had been through it before, so had Magda, Ambrose hadn't and suggested, this voice cracking on account of Fat May's laughter, that they swim first. All were chuckling, couldn't help it; Ambrose's father, Ambrose's and Peter's father came up grinning like a lunatic with two boxes of syrup-coated popcorn, one for Mother, one for Magda;

the men were to help themselves. Ambrose walked on Magda's right; being by nature left-hand, she carried the box in her left hand. Up front the situation was reversed.

"What are you limping for?" Magda inquired of Ambrose. He supposed in a husky tone that his foot had gone to sleep in the car. Her teeth flash. "Pins and needles?" It was the honeysuckle on the lattice of the former privy that drew the bees. Imagine being stung there. How long is this going to take?

The adults decided to forgot the pool; but Uncle Karl insisted they change into swimsuits and do the beach. "He wants to watch the pretty girls," Peters teased, and ducked behind Magda from Uncle Karl's pretended wrath. "You've got all the pretty girls you need right here," Magda declared, and Mother said; "Now that's the gospel[9] truth." Magda scolded Peter, who reached over her shoulder to sneak some popcorn. "Your brother and father aren't getting any." Uncle Karl wondered if they were going to have fireworks that night, what with the shortages. It wasn't the shortages, Mr. M-replied; Ocean City had fireworks from prewar. But it was too risky on account of the enemy submarines, some people thought.

"Don't seem like Fourth of July without fireworks," said Uncle Karl. The inverted tag in dialogue writing is still considered permissible with proper names or epithets, but sounds old-fashioned with personal pronouns. "We'll have'em again soon enough," predicted the boys' father. Their mother declared she could do without fireworks: they reminded her too much of the real thing. Their father said all the more reason to shoot off a few now and again. Uncle Karl asked *rhetorically* who needed reminding, just look at people's hair skin.

"The oil, yes," said Mrs. M—

Ambrose had a pain in his stomach and so didn't swim but enjoyed watching the others. He and his father burned red easily. Magda's figure was exceedingly well developed for her age. She too declined to swim, and got mad, and became angry when Peter attempted to drag her into the pool. She always swam, he insisted; what did she mean not swim? Why did a person come to Ocean City?

"Maybe I want lay here with Ambrose," Magda teased.

Nobody likes a pedant.

"Aha," said Mother. Peter grabbed Magda by one ankle and ordered Ambrose to grab the other. She squealed and rolled over on the beach blanket. Ambrose pretended to help hold her back. Her tan was darker than even Mother's and Peter's. "Help out, Uncle Karl!" Peter cried. Uncle Karl went to seize the other ankle inside the top of her swimsuit, however, you could see the line where the sunburn ended and, when she hunched her shoulders and squealed again, one nipple's auburn[10] edge. Mother made them behave themselves. "You should certainly know," she said to Uncle Karl. Archly. "That when a lady says she doesn't feel like swimming, a gentleman doesn't ask questions." Uncle Karl said excuse *him*; Mother winked at Magda; Ambrose blushed; stupid Peter kept saying "Phooey on *feel like!*" And tugging at Magda's ankle; then even he got the point, and cannonballed with a holler into the pool.

"I swear," Magda said, in mock in *feigned* exasperation.

The diving would make a suitable literary symbol. To go off the high board you had to wait in a line along the poolside and up the ladder. Fellows tickled girls and goosed one another and shouted to the ones at the top to hurry up, or razzed them for bellyfloppers. Once on the springboard some took a great while posing or clowning or deciding on a dive or getting up their nerve; others ran right off. Especially among the younger fellows the idea was to strike the funniest pose or do the craziest stunt as you tell, a thing that got harder to do as you kept on and kept. But whether you hollered *Geronimo! or Sieg heil!*, held your nose or rode a bicycle, pretended to be shot or did a perfect jacknife or changed your mind half-way down and ended up with nothing, it was over in two seconds, after all that wait Spring, pose, splash. Spring, neat-o, splash. Spring, aw fooey, splash.

The grown-ups had gone on; Ambrose wanted to converse with Magda; she was remarkably well developed for her age; it was said that that came from rubbing with a turkish towel, and there were other theories. Ambrose could think of nothing to say except how good a diver Peter was, who was showing off for her benefit. You could pretty well tell by looking at their bathing suits and arm muscles how far along the different fellows were. Ambrose was glad he hadn't gone in swimming, the cold water shrank you up so. Magda pretended to be uninterested in the diving; she probably weighed as much as he did. If you knew your way around in the funhouse like your own bedroom, you could wait until a girl came along and then slip away without ever getting caught, even if her boyfriend was right with her. She'd think *he* did it! It would be better to be the boyfriend, and act-outraged, and tear the funhouse apart.

Not act; *be*.

"He's a master diver," Ambrose said. In feigned admiration. "You really have to slave away at it to get that good." What would it matter anyhow if he asked her right out whether she remembered, even teased her with it as Peter would have?

There's no point in going farther; this isn't getting anybody anywhere; they haven't even come to the funhouse yet. Ambrose is off the track, in some new or old part of the place that's not supposed to be used; he strayed into it by someone-in-a-million chance, like the time the roller-coaster car left the tracks in the nineteen-teens against all the laws of physics and sailed over the boardwalk in the dark. And they can't locate him because they don't know where to look. Even the designer and operator have forgotten this other part. That winds around on itself like a whelk [11] shell. That winds around the right part like the snakes on Mercury's caduceus. Some people, perhaps, don't "hit their stride" until their twenties, when the growing-up business is over and women appreciate other things besides wisecracks and teasing and strutting. Peter didn't have one-tenth the imagination he had, not one-tenth. Peter did this naming-their-children thing as a .joke, making up names like Aloysius and Murgatroyd, but Ambrose knew *exactly* how it would feel to be married and have children of your own, and be a loving husband and father, and go comfortable to work in the morning and to bed with your wife at night, and wake up with her there. With a breeze coming through the sash and birds and mockingbirds singing in the Chinese-cigar trees. His eyes watered, there aren't enough ways to say that. He would be quite famous in his line of work. Whether Magda was his wife or not, one evening when he was wise-lined and gray at the temples he'd smile gravely, at a fashionable dinner party, and remind her of his youthful passion. The time they went with his family to Ocean City; *the erotic fantasies* he used to have about her. How long ago it seemed and childish! Yet tender, too, *n'est-ce pas?* Would she have imagined that the world-famous whatever remembered how many strings were on the lyre on the bench beside the girl on the label of cigar box he'd stared at in the toolshed at age ten while she, age eleven. Even then he had felt *wise beyond his years*; he'd stroked her hair and said in his deepest voice and correctest English as to a dear child: "I shall never forget this moment."

But though he had breathed heavily groaned as if ecstatic, what he'd really felt throughout was an odd detachment as though someone else were Master. Strive as he might to be transported, he heard his mind take notes upon the scene: *This is what they call* passion. *I am experience it.* Many of the digger machines were out of order in the penny arcades and could not be repaired or replaced for the duration. Moreover the prizes made now in USA were less interesting than formerly, pasteboard items for the most part, and some of the machines wouldn't work on white pennies. The gypsy fortune-teller machine might have provided a foreshadowing of the climax of this story if Ambrose had operated it. It was even dilapidateder than most: the silver coating was worn off the brown metal handles, the glass windows around the dummy were cracked and taped, her kerchiefs and silks long-faded If a man lived by himself he could take a department-store mannequin with flexible joints and modify her in certain ways. *However*: by the time he was that old he'd have a real woman. There was a machine that stamped your name around a white-metal coin with a star in the middle: A— His son would be the second and when the lad reached thirteen or so he would put a strong arm around his shoulder and tell him calmly: "It is perfectly normal. We have all been though it. It will not last forever." Nobody knew how to be what they were right. He'd smoke a pipe, each his son how to fish and softcrab, assure him he needn't worry about himself. Magda would certainly give, Magda would certainly yield a great deal of milk although guilty of occasional solecisms. It will not taste so bad. Suppose the light cane on now!

The day wore on. You think you're yourself, but there are other persons in you. Ambrose gets hard when Ambrose doesn't want to, *and obversely*. Ambrose watch them disagree; Ambrose watches him watch In the funhouse mirror-room you can't see yourself go on forever, because no matter how you stand, your head get in the way. Even if you had a glass periscope[12], the image of your eye would cover up tile thing you really wanted to see. The police will come; there'll be a story in the papers. That must be where it happened, unless he can find a surprise exit, an unofficial backdoor or escape hatch opening on an alley, say, and then stroll up to the family in front of the funhouse and ask where everybody's been; *he's* been out of the place for ages. That's just where it happened, in that last lighted room: Peter and Magda found the right exit; he found one that you weren't supposed to find and strayed off into the works somewhere. In a perfect funhouse you'd be able to go only one way, like the divers off the high board; getting lost would be impossible; the doors and halls would work like minnow traps or the valves in veins.

On account of German U-boats, Ocean City was "browned out" streetlights were shaded on the seaward side; shop-windows and boardwalk amusement places were kept dim, not to silhouette tankers and Liberty-ships for torpedoing. In a short story about Ocean City, Maryland, during World Wart II, the author could make use of the image of sailors on leave in the penny arcades and shooting galleries, sighting through the crosshairs of toy machine guns at swastika'd[13] subs, while out in the black Atlantic a U-boat skipper squints through his periscope at real ships outlined by the glow of penny arcades. After dinner the family strolled back to the amusement end of the boardwalk. The boys' father had burnt red as always and was masked with Noxzema, a minstrel in reverse. The grownups stood at the end of the boardwalk where the Hunricane of '33 had cut an inlet from the ocean to Assawoman Bay.

"Pronounced with a long *o*," Uncle Karl reminded Magda with a wink. His shirt sleeves were rolled up; Mother punched his brown biceps with the arrowedheart on it and said his mind *was* naughty. Fat May's laugh came suddenly from the funhouse, as if she'd just got the joke; the family laughed too at the coincidence. Ambrose went under the boardwalk to search for out-of-town matchbook covers with the aid of his pocket flashlight; he looked out from the edge of the North American continent and wondered how far their laughter carried over the water. Spies in rubber rafts; survivors in lifeboats. If the joke had been beyond his understanding, he could have said: *"The laughter was over his head."* And let the reader see the serious wordplay on second reading.

He turned the flashlight on and then off at once even before the woman whooped . He sprang away, heart athud, dropping the light. What had the man grunted? Perspiration drenched and chilled him by the time he scrambled up to the family. "See anything?" his father asked. His voice wouldn't come; he shrugged and violently brushed sand from his pants legs.

"Let's ride the old flying horses!" Magda cried. I'll never be an author. It's been forever already, everybody's gone home, Ocean City's deserted, the ghostcrabs[14] are tickling across the beach and down the littered cold streets. A tidal wave the empty halls of clabboard[15] hotels and abandoned funhouses. A tidal wave; an enemy air raid; a monster-crab swelling like an island from the sea. *The inhabitants fled in terror.* Magda clung to his trouser leg; he alone knew the maze's secret. "He gave his life that we might live said Uncle Karl with a scowl of pain, as he. The fellow's hands had been tattooed; the woman's legs, the woman's fat white legs had. An *astonishing coincidence.* He yearned to tell Peter. He wanted to throw up for excitement. They hadn't even chased him. He wished he were dead.

One possible ending would be to have Ambrose come across another lost person in the dark. They'd match their wits together against the funhouse, struggle like Ulysses past obstacle after obstacle, help and encourage each other. Or a girl. By the time they found the exit they'd be closest friends, sweethearts if it were a girl; they'd know each other's inmost souls, be bound together *by the cement of shared adventure*; then they'd emerge into the light and it would turn out that his friend was a Negro. A blind girl. President Roosevelt's son. Ambrose s former archenemy.

Shortly after the mirror room he'd groped along a musty corridor, his heart already misgiving him at the absence of phosphorescent arrows and other signs. He'd found a crack of light—not a door, it turned out, but a seam between the plyboard was panels — and squinting up to it, espied a small old man, *in appearance not unlike* the photographs at home of Ambrose's late grandfather, nodding upon a stool beneath a bare, speckled bulb. A crude panel of toggle-and knife-switches hung beside the open fuse box near his head; elsewhere in the little room were wooden levers and ropes belayed to boat cleats. At the time, Ambrose wasn't lost enough to rap or call; later he couldn't find that crack. Now it seemed to him that he'd possibly dozed off for a few minutes somewhere along the way; certainly he was exhausted from the afternoon's sunshine and the evening's problems; he couldn't be sure he hadn't dreamed part or all of the sight. Had an old black wall fan droned like bees and shimmied two flypaper streamers? Had the funhouse operator—gentle, somewhat sad and tired-appearing, in expression not unlike the photographs at home of Ambrose's late Uncle Konrad—murmured in his sleep? Is there really such a person as Ambrose, or is he a figment of the author's imagination? Was it Assawoman Bay or Sinepuxent? Are there other errors of fact in this fiction? Was there another sound besides the little slap of thigh on ham, like water sucking at the chine-boards of a skiff?

When you're lost, the smartest thing to do is stay put till you're found, hollering if necessary. But to holler guarantees humiliation as well as rescue; keeping silent permits some saving of face—you can act surprised at the fuss when your rescuers find you and swear you weren't lost, if they do. What's more you might found you own way yet *however belatedly*.

"Don't tell me your foot's still asleep!" Magda exclaimed as the three young people walked from the inlet to the area set aside for ferris wheels, carrousels, and other carnival rides, they having decided in favor of the vast and ancient merry-go-round instead of the funhouse. What a sentence, everything was wrong from the outset. People don't know what to make of him, he doesn't know what to make of himself, he's only thirteen, *athletically and socially* inept, not astonishingly bright, but there are antennae; he has ... some sort of receivers in his head; things speak to him, he understands more than he should, the world winks at him through its objects, grabs grinning at his coat. Everybody else is in on some secret he doesn't know; they've forgotten to tell him. Through simple *procrastination* his mother put off his baptism until this year. Everyone else had it done as a baby; he'd assumed the same of himself, as had his mother, so she claimed, until it was time for him to join Grace Mehodist-protestant and the oversight came out. He was mortified, but pitched sleepless through his private catechizing[16], intimidated by the ancient mysteries, a thirteen years old would never say that, resolved to experience conversion like St. Augustine. When the water touched his brow and Adam's sin left him, he contrived by a strain like defecation to bring tears into his eyes—but felt nothing. There was some simple, radical difference about him; he hoped it was genius, feared it was madness, devoted himself to amiability and inconspicuousness. Alone on the seawall near his house he was seized by the terrifying transports he'd thought to find in tootshed, in Communion-cup. The grass was alive! The town, the river, himself, were not imaginary; time roared in his ears like wind; the world was *going on!* This part ought to be dramatized. The Irish author James Joyce once wrote. Ambrose M——-is going to scream.

There is no *texture of rendered sensory detail*, for one thing. The faded distorting mirrors beside Fat May; the impossibility of choosing a mount when one had but a single ride on the great carrousel; the *vertigo attendant on his recognition* that Ocean City was worn out, the place of fathers and grandfathers, straw-boatered men and parasoled[17] ladies survived by their amusements. Money spent, the three paused at Peter's insistence beside fat May to watch the girls get their skirts blown up. The object was to tease Magda, who said: "I swear, Peter M—, you've got a one-track mind! Amby and me aren't *interested* in such things." "In the tumbling-barred, too, just inside the Devil's-mouth entrance to the funhouse, the girls were upended and their boyfriends and others could see up their dresses if they cared to. Which was the whole point, Ambrose realized. Of the entire funhouse! If you looked around, you noticed that almost all the people on the boardwalk were paired off into couples except the small children; in a way, that was tile whole point of Ocean City! If you had X-ray eyes and could see everything going on at that instant under the boardwalk and in all the hotel rooms and cars and alleyways, you'd realize that all that normally *showed*, like restaurants and dance halls and clothing and test-your-machines, was merely preparation and intermission. Fat May screamed.

Because he watched the goings-on from the corner of his eye, it was Ambrose who spied the half-dollar on the boardwalk near the tumbling-barrel. Losers weepers. The first lime he'd heard some people moving through a corridor not far away, just after he'd lost sight of the crack of light, he'd decided not to call to them, for fear they'd guess he was scared and poke fun; it sounded like roughneck; he'd hoped they'd come by and he could follow in the dark without their knowing. Another time he'd heard just one person, unless he imagined it, bumping along as if on the other side of the plywood; perhaps peter coming back for him, or Father, or Magda lost too. Or the owner and operator of funhouse. He'd called out once, as though merrily: "Anybody know where the heck we are?" but the query was too stiff, his voice cracked, when the sounds stopped he was terrified: maybe it was a queer who waited for fellows to get lost, or a long haired filthy monster that lived in some cranny of the funhouse. He stood rigid for hours it seemed like, scarely respiring. His future was shockingly clear, in outline. He tired holding his breath to the point of unconsciousness. There ought to be a button you could push to end your life absolutely without pain; disappear in a flick, like turning out a light. He would push it instantly! He despised Uncle Karl. But he despised his father too, for not being what he was supposed to be. Perhaps his father hated *his* father, and so on, and his son would hate him, and so on. Instantly!

Naturally he didn't have nerve enough to ask Magda to go through the funhouse with him. With incredible nerve and to everyone's surprise he invited Magda, quietly and politely, to go through the funhouse with him. "I warn you, I've never been through it before," he added, *laughing easily*; "but I reckon we can manage somehow. The important thing to remember after all is that it's meant to be a funhouse: that is a place of amusement. If' people really got lost or injured or too badly frightened in it, the owner'd go out of business. There'd even be law-suits. No character in a work of fiction can make a speech this long without interruption or acknowledgment from the other characters."

Mother teased Uncle Karl: "There's a crowd I always heard." But actually Ambrose was relieved that Peter now had a quarter too. Nothing was what it looked like. Every instant, under tile surface of the Atlantic Ocean, millions of living animals devoured one another. Pilots were falling in flames over Europe;

women were being forcibly raped in tile South Pacific. His father should have taken him aside and said: "There is a simple secret to getting through the funhouse simple as being first to see the Towers. Here it is. Peter does not know it; neither does your Uncle Karl. You and I are different. Not surprisingly you've often him you weren't. Don't think I haven't noticed how unhappy your child hood has been! But you'll understand when I tell you, why it had to be kept secret until now. And you won't regret not being like your brother and your uncle. *"On the contrary!"* If you knew all the stories behind all the people on the boardwalk you'd see that nothing was what it looked like. Husbands and wives often hate each other; parents didn't necessarily love their children; et cetera. A child took things for granted because he had nothing to compare his life to and everybody as if things were as they should be. Therefore each saw himself as the hero of story, when the truth might turn out to be that he's the villain, or the coward. And there wasn't one thing you could do about it!

Hunchbacks, fat ladies, fools — that no one chose what I was unbearable. In the movies he'd meet a beautiful young girl in the funhouse; they'd have hairs-breadth escapes from real dangers ;he'd do and say the right things; she also; in the end they'd be lovers; their dialogue lines would match up; he'd be perfectly at ease; she'd not only like him well enough, she'd think he was *marvelous*; she'd lie awake thinking about *him*, instead of vice versa—he way *his face* looked in different lights and how he stood and exactly what he'd said — and yet that would be only one small episode in his wonderful life, among many others. Not a *turning point* at all. What had happened in the toolshed was nothing. He hated, he loathed his parents! One reason for not writing a lost in-the-funhouse story is that either everybody's felt what Ambrose feels, in which case it goes without saying, or else no normal person feels such things, in which case Ambrose is a freak. "Is anything more tiresome, in fiction, than the problems of sensitive adolescents?" And it's all too long and rambling, as if the author. For all a person knows the first time through, the end could be just around any corner; perhaps, *not impossibly* it's been within reach any number of times. On the other hand he may be scarcely past the start, with everything yet to get through, an intolerable idea.

Fill in: His father's rinsed eyebrows when he announced his decision to do the funhouse with Magda. Ambrose understands now, but didn't then, that his father was wondering whether he knew what the funhouse was for—especially since he didn't object, as he should have, when Peter decided to come along too. The ticket-woman, witchlike, mortifying him when inadvertently he gave her his name-coin instead of the half-dollar, then unkindly calling Magda's attention to the birthmark on his temple: "Watch out for him, girlie, he's a marked man!" She wasn't even cruel, he understood, only vulgar and insensitive. Somewhere in the world there was a young woman with such splendid understanding that she'd see him entire, like a poem or story, and find his words so valuable after all that when he confessed his apprehensions she would explain why they were in fact the very things that made him precious to her ... and to Western Civilization! There was no such girl, the simple truth being. Violent yawns as they approached the mouth. Whispered advice from an old-timer on a bench near the barrel: "Go crabwise and ye'll get an eyeful without upsetting!" Composure vanished at the first pitch: Peter hollered joyously, Magda tumbled, shrieked, clutched her skirt; Ambrose scrambled crabwise, tight-lipped with terror, was soon out, watched his dropped name-coin slide among the couples. Shame-faced he saw that to get through expeditiously was not the point; Peter feigned assistance in order to trip Magda up, shouted "I see Christmas!" when her legs went flying. The old man, his latest betrayer, cackled approval. A dim hall then of black-thread cobwebs and recorded gibber: he took Magda's elbow to steady her against revolving discs set in the slanted floor to throw your feet out from under, and explained to her in a calm, deep voice his theory that each phase of the funhouse was triggered either automatically, by a series of photoelectric devices, or else manually by operator stationed at peepholes. But lost his voice thrice as the discs unbalanced him; Magda was anyhow squealing but at one point she clutched him about the waist to keep from falling, and her right cheek pressed for a moment against his belt-buckle. Heroically he drew her up, it was his chance to clutch her close as if tot support and say: "I love you." He even put an arm lightly about the small of her back before a sailor-and-girl pitched into them from behind, sorely treading his left big toe and knocking Magda asprawl with them. The sailor's girl was a string-haired hussy[18] with a loud laugh and light blue drawers; Ambrose realized that he wouldn't have said "I love you" anyhow, and was smitten with self-contempt. How much better it would be to be that common sailor! A wiry little Seaman 3rd, the fellow squeezed a girl to each side and stumbled hilarious into the mirror room, closer to Magda in thirty seconds than Ambrose had got in thirteen years. She giggled at something the fellow said to Peter; she drew her hair from her eyes with a movement so womanly it struck Ambrose's heart; Peter's smacking her backside then seemed particularly coarse. But Magda made a pleased indignant face and cried, "All right for you, mister!" and pursued Peter into the maze without a backward glance. The sailor followed after, leisurely, drawing his girl against his hip; Ambrose understood not only that they were all so relieved to be rid of his burdensome company that they didn't even notice his absence, but that he himself shared their relief. Stepping from the treacherous passage at last into the mirror-maze he saw once again more clearly than ever, how readily he deceived himself into supposing he was a person. He even foresaw, wincing at his dreadful self-knowledge, that he would repeat the deception at ever-rarer intervals, all his wretched life, so fearful were the alternatives. Fame, madness suicide; perhaps all three. It's not believable that so young a boy could articulate that reflection and in fiction the merely true must always yield to the plausible. Moreover, the symbolism is in places heavy-footed. Yet Ambrose M— understood, as few adults do, that the famous loneliness of the great was no popular myth but a general truth—further more, that it was as much cause as effect.

All the preceding except the last few sentences is exposition that should've been done earlier or interspersed with the present action instead of lumped together. No reader would put up with so much with such *prolixity*. It's interesting that Ambrose's father, though presumably an intelligent man (as indicated by as role as grade-school principal) neither encouraged nor discoursed his sons at all in any way as if he either didn't care about them or cared all right but didn't know how to act. If this fact should contribute to one of them's becoming a celebrated but wretchedly unhappy scientist was it a good thing or not? He too might someday face the question; it would be useful to know whether it had tortured his father for years, for example, or, ever once crossed his mind.

In the maze two important things happened. First, our hero found a name-coin someone else had lost or discarded: AMBROSE, suggestive of the famous lightship and of his late grandfather's favorite dessert, which his mother used to prepare on special occasions out of coconut, oranges, grapes, and what else. Second, as he wondered at the endless replication of his image in the mirrors, second, as he *lost himself in the reflection* that the necessity for an observer makes perfect observation impossible, better make him eighteen at least, yet that would render other things unlikely, he heard Peter and Mgada chuckling somewhere together in the maze. "Here!" " No, here!" they shouted to each other; Peter said,

"Where's Am by?" Magda murmured. "Amb?" Peter called. In a pleased, friendly voice. He didn't reply. Tile truth was, his brother was a *happy-go-lucky youngster* who'd've been better off with a regular brother of his own, but who seldom complained of his lot and was generally cordial. Ambrose's throat ached; there aren't enough different ways to say that. He stood quietly while the two young people giggled and thumped through the glittering maze, hurrah'd their discovery of its exit, cried out in joyful alarm at what next beset them. Then he set his mouth and followed after, as he supposed, took a wrong turn, strayed into the pass *wherein he lingers yet.*

The action of conventional dramatic narrative may be represented by a diagram called Freitag's Triangle:

$$\begin{array}{c} B \\ \diagup \diagdown \\ A \qquad C \end{array}$$

or more accurately, by a variant of that diagram :

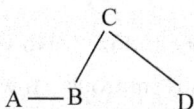

$$\begin{array}{c} C \\ \diagup \diagdown \\ A - B \qquad D \end{array}$$

in which *AB* represents the exposition, *B* the introduction of conflict, *BC* the "rising action," complication, or development of the conflict, *C* the climax, or turn of the action, *CD* the denouement, or resolution of the conflict. While there is no reason to regard this pattern as an absolute necessity, like many other conventions it became conventional because great numbers of people over many years learned by trial and error that it was effective; one ought not to forsake it, therefore, unless one wishes to forsake as well the effect of drama or has clear cause to feel that deliberate violation of the "normal" pattern can better can better effect that effect. This can't go on much longer; it can go on forever, he died telling stories to himself in the dark; years later when that vast unsuspected area of the funhouse came to light, the first expedition found his skeleton in one of its labyrinthine corridors and mistook it for part of the entertainment. He died of starvation telling himself stories in the dark; but unbeknownst unbeknownst to him, an assistant operator of the funhouse, happening to overhear him, crouched just behind the plyboard partition and wrote down his every word. The operator's daughter, an exquisite young woman with a figure unusually well developed for her age, crouched just behind the partition and transcribed his every word. Though she had never laid eyes on him, she recognized that here was one of Western Culture's truly great imaginations, the eloquence of whose suffering would be an inspiration to unnumbered. And her heart was torn between her love for the misfortunate young man (yes, she loved him, though she had never laid though she knew him only —but how well! —though his words, and the deep, calm voice in which he spoke them) between her love et cetera and her womanly intuition that only in suffering and isolation could he give voice et cetera. Lone dark dying. Quietly she kissed the rough plyboard, and a tear fell upon the page. Where *she had written in shorthand* Where she had written in shorthand Where she had written in shorthand *Where she et cetera.* A long time ago we should have passed the apex of Freitag's Triangle and made brief work of the *denouement*; the plot doesn't rise by meaningful steps but winds upon itself, digresses, retreats, hesitates, sighs, collapses, expires. The climax of the story must be its protagonist's discovery of a way to get through the funhouse. But he has found none, may have ceased to search.

What relevance does the war have to the story? Should there be fireworks outside or not?

Ambrose wandered, languished, dozed. Now and then he fell into his habit of rehearsing to himself the unadventurous stow of his life, narrated from the third-person point of view, from his earliest memory parenthesis of maple leaves stirring in the summer breath of tidewater Maryland end of parenthesis to the present moment. Its principal events, on this telling, would appear to have been *A, B, C,* and *D*.

He imagined himself years hence, successful, married, at ease in the world, the trials of his adolescence far behind him. He has come to the seashore with his family or the holiday: how Ocean City has changed! But at one seldom at one ill-frequented end of the boardwalk a few derelict amusements survive from times gone by: the great carrousel from the turn of the century, with its monstrous griffins and mechanical concert band; the roller coaster rumored since 1916 to have been condemned; the mechanical shooting in which only the image of our enemies changed. His own son laughs with Fat May and wants to know what a funhouse is; Ambrose hugs the sturdy lad close and similes around his pipestem at his wife.

The family's going home. Mother sits between Father and Uncle Karl, who teases him good-naturedly who chuckles over the fact that the comrade with whom he'd fought his way shoulder to shoulder though the funhouse had turned out to be a blind Negro girl — to their mutual discomfort, as they'd opened their souls. But such are the walls of custom, which even. Whose arm is where? How must it feel. He dreams of a funhouse vaster by far titan any yet constructed; but by then they may be out of fashion, like steamboats and excursion trains. Already quaint and seedy: the draperied ladies on the frieze of the carrousel are his father's father's mooncheeked dreams; if he thinks of it more he will vomit his apple-on-a-stick.

He wonders: will he become a regular person? Something has gone wrong; his vaccination didn't take; at the Boy-Scout initiation campfire he only pretended to be deeply moved, as he pretends to this hour that it is not so bad after all in the funhouse, and that he has a little limp. How long will it last? He envisions a truly astonishing funhouse, incredibly complex yet utterly controlled from a great central switchboard like the console of a pipe organ. Nobody had enough imagination. He could design such a place himself, wiring and all, and he's only thirteen years old. Be its would be its operator: panel lights would show what was up in every cranny of its cunning of its multifarious vastness; a switch-flick would ease this fellow's way, complicate that's, to balance things out; if anyone seemed lost or frightened, all the operator had to do was.

He wishes he had never entered the funhouse. But he has. Then he wishes he were dead. But he's not. Therefore he will construct funhouses for others and be their secret operator—though he would rather be among the lovers for whom funhouses are designed.

Notes:

1. triangulation: a method of surveying in which an area is divided into triangles, one side (the base line) and all angles of which are measured and the lengths of the other lines calculated by trigonometry
2. fetching: (of a person or a piece of clothing) attractive in appearance
3. standpipe: a large vertical pipe into which water is pumped in order to produce a desired pressure
4. falsetto: 1) A male voice in an upper register beyond its normal range; 2) One who sings or talks in this register
5. flatulence: the condition of having too much gas in your stomach
6. intromittent: (adj) to cause or permit to enter; introduce or admit
7. ditto: a mark (...) meaning the same as the word above
8. spermatozoa: the mature fertilizing gamete of a male organism, usually consisting

of a round or cylindrical nucleated cell, a short neck, and a thin motile tail. Also called *sperm cell, zoosperm.*

9. gospel: the four books in the Bible about the life and teachings of Christ

10. auburn: reddish-brown (used especially of hair)

11. whelk: a sea animal which lives in a shell, and is sometimes used as food

12. periscope: a long tube with mirrors fitted in it so that people in a Submarine can see what is above them

13. swastika: a cross with each arm bent back at a bright angle, which was used as a sign by Nazis in Germany

14. ghostcrab: any of several light-colored burrowing crabs of the genus *Ocypoda* frequenting the tide line along sandy shores from the northeast United States to Brazil

15. clapboard: long narrow board with one edge thicker than the other, overlapped horizontally to cover the outer walls of frame structures.

16. catechize: to teach the principles of Christian dogma, discipline, and ethics by means of questions and answers

17. parasol: light, usually small umbrella carried as protection from the sun

18. hussy: old fascia young woman who behaves in a sexually improper way

Questions for Study and Discussion:

1. What are the indications in the story that Barth has taught creative writing courses? Is this story good pedagogy, or a parody thereof?

2. What kind of narrator do we have here? Whose story is he telling?

3. In what sense is it a story of Ambrose becoming a writer?

4. Why doesn't the narrator complete many of his sentences? How does this fit with Barth's interest in the literature of exhaustion? How does Barth attempt here to replenish the exhausted story of sensitive adolescents?

5. In what way is the narrative mode different from that of a traditional story?

6. What is the metafictional writing in the story?

Toni Morrison (1931—   )

Life and Major Works

As the only African American female to receive the
Nobel Prize for literature, Toni Morrison stands as a
monument, whose writing is acclaimed to be in Hurstonian
tradition, characterized by "racial health: a sense of black
people as complete, complex, undiminished human
beings, a sense that is lacking in so much black writing
and literature."

Toni Morrison (Chloe Anthony Wofford)—was born
on February 18, 1931, in Lorain, Ohio, to George
Wofford, and Ramah (Willis) Wofford as the second of

Toni Morrison

their four children. She grew up in a lively household and was surrounded by
songs, fairy tales, ghost stories, myths, music, and the language of their
African-American heritage, as common practice in her family was storytelling,
which contributed to Morrison's profound love of reading. Morrison's parents
encouraged her passion for learning, and culture, as well as confidence in her own
abilities and attributes as woman. Growing up during a time marked by overt
racism and open hostility toward blacks, Morrison learned early on that in order to
survive, she had to develop a strong character and create her own life. She also
learned the value of being part of a loving, supportive family and community, the
futility and self-destructiveness of hatred, and the healing power of music.

After graduating from Lorain High School with honors, Morrison moved to
Washington, D.C., to attend Howard University, where she began writing short
stories with the changed name Toni, and resolved to write books that focused on
"black people...talking to black people." In 1955, Morrison received a master's
degree in English at Cornell University. Two years later, she returned to teach
English at Howard University, and married Harold Morrison, a Jamaican architect
the next year. She joined a small writer's group as a temporary escape from an
unhappy marriage: "I had nothing left but my imagination. I had no will, no
judgment, no perspective, no power, no authority, no self—just this brutal sense of
irony, melancholy, and a trembling respect for words." After a later divorce, she

465

started her first novel, *The Bluest Eye*, published in 1970. Also that year, Morrison began work on *Sula*, her second novel with which Morrison established a theme that would pervade each of her subsequent works: the secret, mystical world of the black woman living in a pariah community. During this time, Morrison took a job as an editor at Random House, where she worked with some of the prominent Black authors of the 1970s. The third novel, *Song of Solomon*, came out in 1977. This was followed by *Tar Baby* in 1981, an allegorical fable about colonialism, commitment, and black identity, based on white folklorist Joel Chandler Harris' "Uncle Remus" story. In 1983, after working at Random House for almost twenty years, Morrison left and was named the Albert Schweitzer Professor of the Humanities at the State University of New York in Albany in 1984. The book considered her masterpiece, *Beloved,* got published in 1987. Based on the life of Margaret Garner, an escaped Kentucky slave, *Beloved* tells the harrowing story of a mother who kills her infant daughter rather than see her enslaved; she is forced to come to terms with her desperate act when, twenty years later, the dead daughter's ghost returns to haunt her and demands an explanation for her murder. Her sixth novel, *Jazz* that explores the relationship between Joe and Violet Trace, a middle-aged couple who find their way back to each other after the husband has a tragic affair with an eighteen-year-old girl, was published in 1992. In 1999 to complete the trilogy that includes *Beloved* and *Jazz*, she published *Paradise*, a story taking place in an all-black town called Ruby, and describing a violent attack that a group of men make on a small, all-female community at the edge of town. In 2003 she published *Love*, describing life and love during the 1940's and 1950's on a black seaside resort.

In recent years, Morrison has broken away from her traditional work as a novelist and turned out several works of nonfiction, writing *Playing in the Dark: Whiteness and the Literary Imagination* and publishing essays on the Clarence Thomas/Anita Hill hearings, the O. J. Simpson case, and other current events.

Academically, Morrison has held teaching posts at Yale, Bard College, and Rutgers, among others. She held the Albert Schweitzer Chair in the Humanities at the State University of New York for six years. Since 1988, Morrison has held the Robert F. Goheen Professorship of the Humanities at Princeton University and became the first black woman writer to hold a named chair at an Ivy League University. In 1990, she delivered the Clark Lectures at Trinity College, Cambridge, and the Massey Lectures at Harvard, receiving honorary degrees from many prestigious institutions, including Harvard, Yale, Dartmouth, Sarah Lawrence, and Brown.

In 1993, Toni Morrison became the first African-American writer to win the Nobel Prize for literature. The prestigious honor, which marks the crowning achievement of Morrison's literary career, was one of numerous awards in her distinguished career: In 1978, with her third novel, *Song of Solomon*, Morrison won 1978 National Critic's Circle Award and was named Distinguished Writer of 1978 by the American Academy of Arts and Letters; In 1980 President Jimmy Carter appointed her to the National Council on the Arts and in 1981 she was elected to the American Academy and Institute of Arts and Letters, the Writer's Guild, and the Author's League. With the publication of her *Tar Baby* in 1981 she became the first African-American woman who appeared on the cover of *Newsweek*. Her international fame was established when *Beloved* (1987) won the 1988 Pulitzer Prize. In 1989, she won the Modern Language Association of America's Commonwealth Award in Literature. That same year, she accepted the Robert F. Goheen Professor in the Humanities Council at Princeton University. In 1993, she was awarded the Nobel Prize for she "in novels characterized by visionary force and poetic import, gives life to essential aspects of American reality".

Renowned for her detailed imagery and visual language, her powerful metaphors, her "righting" of black history, and her inimitable gift of fusing fantasy and reality, In her multiple roles as writer, editor, educator, scholar, parent, and activist, Morrison has consistently demonstrated her commitment to black literature and culture. Speaking of her concern for black people, who provide the catalyst for her art and activism, she has said, "If anything I do, in the way of writing novels or whatever I write, isn't about the village or the community or about you, then it isn't about anything. I am not interested in indulging myself in some private exercise of my imagination."

Brief Introduction and Appreciation

Song of Solomon, Toni Morrison's third novel quickly became a bestseller when first published in 1977, and over half a million copies are in print now, with translation rights having been sold in more than ten countries. It is this book, as Nellie Y. Mckay puts it, that has "changed Morrison's public reputation from aspiring novelist to outstanding American writer", or as Carol Iannone wrote in

Commentary, "[i]n *Song of Solomon* Miss Morrison at last permits herself to work her material through." It won fiction awards from the National Book Critics' Circle and the American Academy and Institute of Letters, and National Book Award for best novel and made the front page of the *New York Times Book Review*.

Drawn on the African-American folktale about black slaves who escape slavery by flying back to their native land, Africa, the novel tells the story of a black young man Milkman Dead, who once alienated himself from his family, community, and cultural roots, embarks on a physical search for gold, which later transforms into a spiritual quest to decode the meaning of a song about his family history. The story ends when Milkman recognizes that: "a genuine bluesman does not really fly solo since he is connected musically to the other musicians, to their shared pasts: only as each bluesman adds his personal history to that shared past may he be said to launch into a solo flight", which signals true understanding and acceptance of the intertwined love, hatred, hope, and despair that define the existence of himself and his people in a mainstream white society. Embracing the contradictions of humanity allows one to live and die in joyful freedom. It may be said that flight is an act that symbolizes movement from the material world toward a better, more spiritual and free existence.

The narration comprises two distinct sections within a time span of more than 30 years. Part I (Chapters 1-9) is set in a town in Michigan, covering Milkman's life from birth to age 32 where readers are presented with his spiritually aimless life caught between his father Macon's materialistic lifestyle and his aunt Pilate's traditional values. These chapters are interspersed with various characters' flashbacks to their pasts. This section ends with Milkman's decision to leave Michigan in search of Pilate's illusory gold—Milkman's "inheritance"—which Macon is sure his sister hid. Part II (Chapters 10-15) begins with Milkman's arrival in Danville, where his paternal grandfather had built the near-mythological Lincoln's Heaven. Unable to find Pilate's gold in Danville and prompted by the mysterious stories surrounding his ancestors, Milkman traces his ancestry to the town of Shalimar, Virginia, where he meets his father's "people" and discovers the true spiritual meaning of his inheritance. The novel's ambiguous ending centers on Milkman's "flight" across Solomon's Leap.

To a great extent, the novel reflects archetypal Bildungsroman, or a coming-of-age story patterns found throughout western literature: by following a quest, first for gold, then for knowledge about his ancestors, Milkman develops morally and psychologically, and moves from a selfish and juvenile immaturity to a complex knowledge of adult. Though 32 years old, Milkman resists the sense of connection and commitment to others that are required of adults. As he seeks the lost gold, he discovers instead his family's history: the legacy of his great-grandfather, who flies back to Africa by himself, the murder of his grandfather and the childhood of his father. He then begins to define himself as the descendant of a man who could fly, but also to recognize the costs of his great-grandfather's transcendence. In so doing, he learns his duty to his family and community. In his search for self, Milkman matures gradually from a middle-class brat unaware of his race, his family history and the true meaning of life to a man ready to assume the responsibility and accept the cultural heritage and historical bequest of African culture.

Also, according to Morrison, "It's about the ways in which we discover, all of us, who and what we are. And how important and truly exciting that journey is." Though investigating how Black men in America survive and how they position themselves in relation to themselves, as well as to their own families and communities, *Song of Solomon* stands as a wakeup call for young black males struggling to survive in white America. Often, the struggle for the identity of a black has led to one of two opposite approaches: mainstream assimilation or radical separatism. Two characters in the novel illustrate these warring factions: Macon Dead, Milkman's father who keeps distance from his own fellows and yearns to get accommodated in the white society, and Guitar Bains, Milkman's friend who takes the fight strategy to its logical extreme. Milkman on the other hand, adopts a viable strategy of struggling in a racist society. While he honors both the "fight" and "flight" strategies of his ancestors, the most effective strategy he figures is to fly without leaving the ground as Pilate does. Taking advantages of both fight and flight may be the best way to survival for the colored in the white-dominating social and political structures.

Moreover, *Song of Solomon* demonstrates Morrison's commitment to black culture. "I simply wanted to write literature that was irrevocably, indisputably Black," she once claimed. Through this story, there are three cultural issues deliberately worked on: folklore tradition, family roots, and blues. As Morrison herself explains: "Let me give you an example: the flying myth in *Song of Solomon*. If it means Icarus to some readers, fine; I want to take credit for that. But my meaning is specific: it is about black people who could fly. That was always part of the folklore of my life; flying was one of our gifts. I don't care how silly it may seem." In addition, Morrison emphasizes that roots are essential for an enlightened existence. She suggests that "living with unexamined roots as much as living with no roots…creates a stunted and deformed tree" (Schultz 143) and she has clearly taken this lesson to heart in the creation of her own storytelling style. Through the lives of the characters Milkman and Guitar, their tragedies and frustrations, Morrison drives home the importance of knowing and connecting with one's ancestors. Finally, this novel reaffirms the place of the blues as an integral part of African-American art and culture. Slave spirituals were among the earliest forms of artistic self-expression available to African Americans; This spiritual tradition provided the birthing ground for what Levine calls "the most highly personalized" genre of African American music: the blues that emerged as a dynamic and powerful addition to the music of black America: "In the spirituals, black Americans first started to sing of their feelings of homelessness; in the blues, they continued to sing it" (Schultz 127). The deep despair that fills so many blues songs provides a communal outlet for emotions that would otherwise choke the singer; the blues may provide a way of recognizing and sharing human pain in order to overcome it.

Morrison's blend of fantasy and reality and her use of myths and folktales to portray Black life in *Song of Solomon* have won the book both acclaim from scholars and popularity among readers. Regarded as the best black novel since *Native Son* by Richard Right and *Invisible Man* by Ralph Ellison, its positive critical reputation has grown even stronger, with topics varied from coming of age, folklore and mystery, traditional culture, significance of naming, revolt to logocentric orders, and quest for identification, and theories ranging from structurism, feminism, to many post-modernist ones, testifying the book's inclusive charm.

The excerpted part here is the first chapter of *Song of Solomon*, which sets the stage for the development of the major themes: the myth of flight; the complex interplay of class, race, and gender; and the significance of names. The story begins when an insurance agent Robert Smith announces in a note that he will "fly away on my own wings" (Morrison 3) from the roof of the local hospital. On the appointed afternoon, a crowd gathers to watch as Mr. Smith spreads his blue silk wings and launches himself into empty air and plunges to his death, which makes the hospital admit a colored woman Ruth to give birth inside its wards. The son, Macon Dead III, when discovering that only birds and airplanes can fly at age four, loses all interest in himself, and becomes a "peculiar" and "deep" guy.

One element is the white dominance and the black resistance. Readers see racial inequality the moment they are introduced to where the story begins: somewhere called the Not doctor's Street. Originally, it was nicknamed Doctor's Street before by her black residents when the first doctor moved in there. The fact that a whole street has only one black doctor points sharply to at least two realities: white doctors do not live among blacks, while black doctors are rare. Later, "Some of the city legislators", whites of course, decide the name not "appropriate" since it confuses the "landmarks" (between blacks and whites) therefore should be denied "any official capacity". The exact spot of this flight, the "Mercy Hospital", supply another clue to racial discrimination where no "expectant mother was allowed to give birth inside its wards and not on its steps", and the Negro doctor "had never been granted hospital privileges"; the only two ever admitted are both white. The hospital people, when they find what happens, "swiftly got down to business, giving orders. Their shouts and bustling caused great confusion." One nurse asks for help by hauntingly giving orders: "you," she said, moving toward the stout woman. "Listen!" "Move!"

Meanwhile, the blacks have their own way of resistance, as they always do. When notified the name of their residence is Main Avenue, not Doctor's Street, they begin to call it Not Doctor's Street. In this way, they "keep their memories alive" and mock the authorities as well. Complying with the letter rather than the spirit of the law, the community effectively resists the city's racist power structure without confronting it directly. Similarly, they call the charity hospital No Mercy Hospital, accusing its refusal to accept colored patients. When the nurse bosses around, a stout woman (later we know she is Pilate, the woman who represents the author's ideal image of African American females) avoids her by lowering her brows and veiling her eyes. The nurse wants Pilate to send for a boy to ask the guard to come: "That boy there can go. That one.", but Pilate cunningly defies her by pretending not to understand what she means and tell her the name of the boy instead. The boy, Guitar, "had just begun to learn he could speak up to white people" when he told the nurse about her wrong spelling of missing an "s" in "admission". His Granny plainly shows her disgust against the arrogance and ignorance of the nurse when mentioning that she misses not only a letter but also a "thanks".

Another recurring theme is the myth of flight rooted in the African folklore.

According to Morrison, the novel is about a man (Milkman) who "learns to fly and all that that means." The birth of Milkman coincides with the failed and suicidal flight of Mr. Smith: "the little insurance agent's conviction that he could fly...certainly contributed to...time", and he is forever affected by the circumstances of his birth, for "when the little boy discovered, at four...that only birds and airplanes could fly—he lost all interest in himself". And he spends his life searching for the wings that will finally give him the power of flight. Pilate refers to Milkman as "a little bird", who "will be here in the morning," So already in this very first chapter, Morrison situates Milkman as someone who is eager, and has the potential, although deeply buried, to fly, to depart from this material world into spiritual freedom.

Blues, as "the most highly personalized" genre of African American music, may provide a communal outlet for emotions that would otherwise choke the singer. According to one blues musician Sidney Bechet, "Me, I want to explain myself so bad. I want to have myself understood. And the music, it can do that. The music, it's my whole story". The most distinguishing feature of the blues is, according to Morrison, that it's not "crying": "but for me it's a question of not whining. The blues is about some loss, some pain, and some other things, and it's not triumphant in that sense. But it doesn't whine, it doesn't, even when it's begging to be understood in the lyrics, the music contradicts that feeling of being a complete victim and completely taken over...I don't see it as a crying music." In this first chapter, readers can clearly see the strength of blues in the archetypical folk singer, Pilate, who is initially introduced as the "woman who suddenly burst into song". Her voice disrupts the gaze of the crowd at the spectacle of Mr. Smith, whose story in the song prompts the crowd to listen "as though it were the helpful and defining piano music in a silent movie": O Sugarman done fly away/Sugarman done gone/Sugarman cut across the sky/Sugarman gone home... The words of the song seem to indicate a connection between the anticipated "flight" of the insurance man and the legendary flight of an African ancestor. In addition, the blues she sings accompanies Mr. Smith to his death and he, at least, "had seen the rose petals, heard the music", which can be interpreted as his last comfort.

Selected Reading

Song of Solomon

Chapter 1

The North Carolina Mutual Life Insurance agent promised to fly from Mercy to the other side of Lake Superior at three o'clock. Two days before the event was to take place he tacked a note on the door of his little yellow house:

At 3:00 p.m. on Wednesday the 18th of February, 1931, I will take off from Mercy and fly away on my own wings. Please forgive me. I loved you all.

(signed) Robert Smith,

Ins. Agent

Mr. Smith didn't draw as big a crowd as Lindbergh had four years earlier—not more than forty or fifty people showed up—because it was already eleven o'clock in the morning, on the very Wednesday he had chosen for his flight, before anybody read the note. At that time of day, during the middle of the week, word-of-mouth news just lumbered along. Children were in school; men were at work; and most of the women were fastening their corsets and getting ready to go see what tails or entrails the butcher might be giving away. Only the unemployed, the self-employed, and the very young were available—deliberately available because they'd heard about it, or accidentally available because they happened to be walking at that exact moment in the shore end of Not Doctor Street, a name the post office did not recognize. Town maps registered the street as Mains Avenue, but the only colored doctor in the city had lived and died on that street, and when he moved there in 1896 his patients took to calling the street, which none of them lived in or near, Doctor Street. Later, when other Negroes moved there, and when the postal service became a popular means of transferring messages among them, envelopes from Louisiana, Virginia, Alabama, and Georgia began to arrive addressed to people at house numbers on Doctor Street. The post office workers returned these envelopes or passed them on to the Dead Letter Office. Then in 1918, when colored men were being drafted, a few gave their address at the recruitment office as Doctor Street. In that way, the name acquired a quasi-official status. But not for long. Some of the city legislators, whose concern for appropriate names and the maintenance of the city's landmarks was the principal part of their political life, saw to it that "Doctor Street" was never used in any official capacity. And since they knew that only Southside residents kept it up, they had notices posted in the stores, barbershops, and restaurants in that part of the city saying that the avenue running northerly and southerly from Shore Road fronting the lake to the junction of routes 6 and 2 leading to Pennsylvania, and also running parallel to and between Rutherford Avenue and Broadway, had always been and would always be known as Mains Avenue and not Doctor Street.

It was a genuinely clarifying public notice because it gave Southside residents a way to keep their memories alive and please the city legislators as well. They called it Not Doctor Street, and were inclined to call the charity hospital at its northern end No Mercy Hospital since it was 1931, on the day following Mr. Smith's leap from its cupola[1], before the first colored expectant mother was allowed to give birth inside its wards and not on its steps. The reason for the hospital's generosity to that particular woman was not the fact that she was the only child of this Negro doctor, for during his entire professional life he had never been granted hospital privileges and only two of his patients were ever admitted to Mercy, both white. Besides, the doctor had been dead a long time by 1931. It must have been Mr. Smith's leap from the roof over their heads that made them admit her. In any case, whether or not the little insurance agent's conviction that he could fly contributed to the place of her delivery, it certainly contributed to its time.

When the dead doctor's daughter saw Mr. Smith emerge as promptly as he had promised from behind the cupola, his wide blue silk wings curved forward around his chest, she dropped her covered peck basket, spilling red velvet rose petals. The wind blew them about, up, down, and into small mounds of snow. Her half-grown daughters scrambled about trying to catch them, while their mother moaned and held the underside of her stomach. The rose-petal scramble got a lot of attention, but the pregnant lady's moans did not. Everyone knew the girls had spent hour after hour tracing, cutting, and stitching the costly velvet, and that Gerhardt's Department Store would be quick to reject any that were soiled.

It was nice and gay there for a while. The men joined in trying to collect the scraps before the snow soaked through them—snatching them from a gust of wind or plucking them delicately from the snow. And the very young children couldn't make up their minds whether to watch the man circled in blue on the roof or the bits of red flashing around on the ground. Their dilemma was solved when a woman suddenly burst into song. The singer, standing at the back of the crowd, was as poorly dressed as the doctor's daughter was well dressed. The latter had on a neat gray coat with the traditional pregnant-woman bow at her navel, a black cloche[2], and a pair of four-button ladies' galoshes[3]. The singing woman wore a knitted navy cap pulled far down over her forehead. She had wrapped herself up in an old quilt instead of a winter coat. Her head cocked to one side, her eyes fixed on Mr. Robert Smith, she sang in a powerful contralto[4]:

> *O Sugarman done fly away*
> *Sugarman done gone*
> *Sugarman cut across the sky*
> *Sugarman gone home...*

A few of the half a hundred or so people gathered there nudged each other and sniggered. Others listened as though it were the helpful and defining piano music in a silent movie. They stood this way for some time, none of them crying out to Mr. Smith, all of them preoccupied with one or the other of the minor events about them, until the hospital people came.

They had been watching from the windows—at first with mild curiosity, then, as the crowd seemed to swell to the very walls of the hospital, they watched with apprehension. They wondered if one of those things that racial-uplift groups were always organizing was taking place. But when they saw neither placards nor speakers, they ventured outside into the cold: white-coated surgeons, dark-jacketed business and personnel clerks, and three nurses in starched jumpers.

The sight of Mr. Smith and his wide blue wings transfixed them for a few seconds, as did the woman's singing and the roses strewn about. Some of them thought briefly that this was probably some form of worship. Philadelphia, where Father Divine reigned, wasn't all that far away. Perhaps the young girls holding baskets of flowers were two of his virgins. But the laughter of a gold-toothed man brought them back to their senses. They stopped daydreaming and swiftly got down to business, giving orders. Their shouts and bustling caused great confusion where before there had been only a few men and some girls playing with pieces of velvet and a woman singing.

One of the nurses, hoping to bring some efficiency into the disorder, searched the faces around her until she saw a stout woman who looked as though she might move the earth if she wanted to.

"You," she said, moving toward the stout woman. "Are these your children?"

The stout woman turned her head slowly, her eyebrows lifted at the carelessness of the address. Then, seeing where the voice came from, she lowered her brows and veiled her eyes.

"Ma'am?"

"Send one around back to the emergency office. Tell him to tell the guard to get over here quick. That boy there can go. That one." She pointed to a cat-eyed boy about five or six years old.

The stout woman slid her eyes down the nurse's finger and looked at the child she was pointing to.

"Guitar, ma'am."

"What?"

"Guitar."

The nurse gazed at the stout woman as though she had spoken Welsh. Then she closed her mouth, looked again at the cat-eyed boy, and lacing her fingers, spoke her next words very slowly to him.

"Listen. Go around to the back of the hospital to the guard's office. It will say 'Emergency Admissions' on the door. A-D-M-I-S-I-O-N-S. But the guard will be there. Tell him to get over here— on the double. Move now. Move!" She unlaced her fingers and made scooping motions with her hands, the palms pushing against the wintry air.

A man in a brown suit came toward her, puffing little white clouds of breath.

"Fire truck's on its way. Get back inside. You'll freeze to death."

The nurse nodded.

"You left out a s, ma'am," the boy said. The North was new to him and he had just begun to learn he could speak up to white people. But she'd already gone, rubbing her arms against the cold.

"Granny, she left out a s."

"And a 'please.'"

"You reckon he'll jump?"

"A nutwagon do anything."

"Who is he?"

"Collects insurance. A nutwagon."

"Who is that lady singing?"

"That, baby, is the very last thing in pea-time[5]." But she smiled when she looked at the singing woman, so the cat-eyed boy listened to the musical performance with at least as much interest as he devoted to the man flapping his wings on top of the hospital.

The crowd was beginning to be a little nervous now that the law was being called in. They each knew Mr. Smith. He came to their houses twice a month to collect one dollar and sixty-eight cents and write down on a little yellow card both the date and their eighty-four cents a week payment. They were always half a month or so behind, and talked endlessly to him about paying ahead—after they had a preliminary discussion about what he was doing back so soon anyway.

"You back in here already? Look like I just got rid of you."

"I'm tired of seeing your face. Really tired."

"I knew it. Soon's[6] I get two dimes back to back, here you come. More regular than the reaper. Do Hoover know about you?"

They kidded him, abused him, told their children to tell him they were out or sick or gone to Pittsburgh. But they held on to those little yellow cards as though they meant something—laid them gently in the shoe box along with the rent receipts, marriage licenses, and expired factory identification badges. Mr. Smith smiled through it all, managing to keep his eyes focused almost the whole time on his customers' feet. He wore a business suit for his work, but his house was no better than theirs. He never had a woman that any of them knew about and said nothing in church but an occasional "Amen." He never beat anybody up and he wasn't seen after dark, so they thought he was probably a nice man. But he was heavily associated with illness and death, neither of which was distinguishable from the brown picture of the North Carolina Mutual Life Building on the back of their yellow cards. Jumping from the roof of Mercy was the most interesting thing he had done. None of them had suspected he had it in him. Just goes to show, they murmured to each other, you never really do know about people.

The singing woman quieted down and, humming the tune, walked through the crowd toward the rose-petal lady, who was still cradling her stomach.

"You should make yourself warm," she whispered to her, touching her lightly on the elbow. "A little bird'll be here with the morning."

"Oh?" said the rose-petal lady. "Tomorrow morning?"

"That's the only morning coming."

"It can't be," the rose-petal lady said. "It's too soon."

"No it ain't. Right on time."

The women were looking deep into each other's eyes when a loud roar went up from the crowd—a kind of wavy oo sound. Mr. Smith had lost his balance for a second, and was trying gallantly to hold on to a triangle of wood that jutted from the cupola. Immediately the singing woman began again:

> *O Sugarman done fly*
> *O Sugarman done gone...*

Downtown the firemen pulled on their greatcoats, but when they arrived at Mercy, Mr. Smith had seen the rose petals, heard the music, and leaped on into the air.

The next day a colored baby was born inside Mercy for the first time. Mr. Smith's blue silk wings must have left their mark, because when the little boy discovered, at four, the same thing Mr. Smith had learned earlier—that only birds and airplanes could fly—he lost all interest in himself. To have to live without that single gift saddened him and left his imagination so bereft that he appeared dull even to the women who did not hate his mother. The ones who did, who accepted her invitations to tea and envied the doctor's big dark house of twelve rooms and the green sedan, called him "peculiar." The others, who knew that the house was more prison than palace, and that the Dodge sedan was for Sunday drives only, felt sorry for Ruth Foster and her dry daughters, and called her son "deep." Even mysterious.

"Did he come with a caul[7]?"

"You should have dried it and made him some tea from it to drink. If you don't he'll see ghosts."

"You believe that?"

"I don't, but that's what the old people say."

"Well, he's a deep one anyway. Look at his eyes."

And they pried pieces of baked-too-fast sunshine cake from the roofs of their mouths and looked once more into the boy's eyes. He met their gaze as best he could until, after a pleading glance toward his mother, he was allowed to leave the room.

It took some planning to walk out of the parlor, his back washed with the hum of their voices, open the heavy double doors leading to the dining room, slip up the stairs past all those bedrooms, and not arouse the attention of Lena and

Corinthians sitting like big baby dolls before a table heaped with scraps of red velvet. His sisters made roses in the afternoon. Bright, lifeless roses that lay in peck baskets for months until the specialty buyer at Gerhardt's sent Freddie the janitor over to tell the girls that they could use another gross. If he did manage to slip by his sisters and avoid their casual malice, he knelt in his room at the windowsill and wondered again and again why he had to stay level on the ground. The quiet that suffused the doctor's house then, broken only by the murmur of the women eating sunshine cake, was only that: quiet. It was not peaceful, for it was preceded by and would soon be terminated by the presence of Macon Dead.

Solid, rumbling, likely to erupt without prior notice, Macon kept each member of his family awkward with fear. His hatred of his wife glittered and sparked in every word he spoke to her. The disappointment he felt in his daughters sifted down on them like ash, dulling their buttery complexions and choking the lilt out of what should have been girlish voices. Under the frozen heat of his glance they tripped over doorsills and dropped the salt cellar into the yolks of their poached eggs. The way he mangled their grace, wit, and self-esteem was the single excitement of their days. Without the tension and drama he ignited, they might not have known what to do with themselves. In his absence his daughters bent their necks over blood-red squares of velvet and waited eagerly for any hint of him, and his wife, Ruth, began her days stunned into stillness by her husband's contempt and ended them wholly animated by it.

When she closed the door behind her afternoon guests, and let the quiet smile die from her lips, she began the preparation of food her husband found impossible to eat. She did not try to make her meals nauseating; she simply didn't know how not to. She would notice that the sunshine cake was too haggled to put before him and decide on a rennet dessert. But the grinding of the veal and beef for a meat loaf took so long she not only forgot the pork, settling for bacon drippings poured over the meat, she had no time to make a dessert at all. Hurriedly, then, she began to set the table. As she unfolded the white linen and let it billow over the fine mahogany table, she would look once more at the large water mark. She never set the table or passed through the dining room without looking at it. Like a lighthouse keeper drawn to his window to gaze once again at the sea, or a prisoner automatically searching out the sun as he steps into the yard for his hour of exercise, Ruth looked for the water mark several times during the day. She knew it was there, would always be there, but she needed to confirm its presence. Like the keeper of the lighthouse and the prisoner, she regarded it as a mooring, a checkpoint, some stable visual object that assured her that the world was still there; that this was life and not a dream. That she was alive somewhere, inside, which she acknowledged to be true only because a thing she knew intimately was out there, outside herself.

Even in the cave of sleep, without dreaming of it or thinking of it at all, she felt its presence. Oh, she talked endlessly to her daughters and her guests about how to get rid of it—what might hide this single flaw on the splendid wood: Vaseline, tobacco juice, iodine, a sanding followed by linseed oil. She had tried them all. But her glance was nutritious; the spot became, if anything, more pronounced as the years passed.

The cloudy gray circle identified the place where the bowl filled every day during the doctor's life with fresh flowers had stood. Every day. And when there were no flowers, it held a leaf arrangement, a gathering of twigs and berries, pussy willow, Scotch pine ... But always something to grace the dinner table in the evening.

It was for her father a touch that distinguished his own family from the people among whom they lived. For Ruth it was the summation of the affectionate elegance with which she believed her childhood had been surrounded. When Macon married her and moved into Doctor's house, she kept up the centerpiece-arranging. Then came the time she walked down to the shore through the roughest part of the city to get some driftwood. She had seen an arrangement of driftwood and dried seaweed in the home makers section of the newspaper. It was a damp November day, and Doctor was paralyzed even then and taking liquid food in his bedroom. The wind had lifted her skirt from around her ankles and cut through her laced shoes. She'd had to rub her feet down with warm olive oil when she got back. At dinner, where just the two of them sat, she turned toward her husband and asked him how he liked the centerpiece. "Most people overlook things like that. They see it, but they don't see anything beautiful in it. They don't see that nature has already made it as perfect as it can be. Look at it from the side. It is pretty, isn't it?"

Her husband looked at the driftwood with its lacy beige seaweed, and without moving his head, said, "Your chicken is red at the bone[8]. And there is probably a potato dish that is supposed to have lumps in it. Mashed ain't the dish."

Ruth let the seaweed disintegrate, and later, when its veins and stems dropped and curled into brown scabs on the table, she removed the bowl and brushed away the scabs. But the water mark, hidden by the bowl all these years, was exposed. And once exposed, it behaved as though it were itself a plant and flourished into a huge suede-gray flower that throbbed like fever, and sighed like the shift of sand dunes. But it could also be still. Patient, restful, and still.

But there was nothing you could do with a mooring except acknowledge it, use it for the verification of some idea you wanted to keep alive. Something else is needed to get from sunup to sundown: a balm, a gentle touch or nuzzling[9] of some sort. So Ruth rose up and out of her guileless inefficiency to claim her bit of balm right after the preparation of dinner and just before the return of her husband from his office. It was one of her two secret indulgences—the one that involved her son—and part of the pleasure it gave her came from the room in which she did it. A damp greenness lived there, made by the evergreen that pressed against the window and filtered the light. It was just a little room that Doctor had called a study, and aside from a sewing machine that stood in the corner along with a dress form, there was only a rocker and tiny footstool. She sat in this room holding her son on her lap, staring at his closed eyelids and listening to the sound of his sucking. Staring not so much from maternal joy as from a wish to avoid seeing his legs dangling almost to the floor.

In late afternoon, before her husband closed his office and came home, she called her son to her. When he came into the little room she unbuttoned her blouse and smiled. He was too young to be dazzled by her nipples, but he was old enough to be bored by the flat taste of mother's milk, so he came reluctantly, as to a chore, and lay as he had at least once each day of his life in his mother's arms, and tried to pull the thin, faintly sweet milk from her flesh without hurting her with his teeth.

She felt him. His restraint, his courtesy, his indifference, all of which pushed her into fantasy. She had the distinct impression that his lips were pulling from her a thread of light. It was as though she were a cauldron[10] issuing spinning gold. Like the miller's daughter—the one who sat at night in a straw-filled room, thrilled with the secret power stilt skin had given her: to see golden thread stream from her very own shuttle. And that was the other part of her pleasure, a pleasure she hated to give up. So when Freddie the janitor, who liked to pretend he was a friend of the family and not just their flunky as well as their tenant, brought his rent to the doctor's house late one day and looked in the window past the evergreen, the terror that sprang to Ruth's eyes came from the quick realization that she was to lose fully half of what made her daily life bearable. Freddie, however, interpreted her look as simple shame, but that didn't stop him from grinning.

"Have mercy. I be damn."

He fought the evergreen for a better look, hampered more by his laughter than by the branches. Ruth jumped up as quickly as she could and covered her breast, dropping her son on the floor and confirming for him what he had begun to suspect—that these were strange and wrong.

Before either mother or son could speak, rearrange themselves properly, or even exchange looks, Freddie had run around the house, climbed the porch steps, and was calling them between gulps of laughter.

"Miss Rufie. Miss Rufie. Where you? Where you all at?" He opened the door to the green room as though it were his now.

"I be damn, Miss Rufie. When the last time I seen that? I don't even know the last time I seen that. I mean, ain't nothing wrong with it[11]. I mean, old folks swear by it. It's just, you know, you don't see it up here much..." But his eyes were on the boy. Appreciative eyes that communicated some complicity she was excluded from. Freddie looked the boy up and down, taking in the steady but secretive eyes and the startling contrast between Ruth's lemony skin and the boy's black skin. "Used to be a lot of womenfolk nurse they kids a long time down South. Lot of 'em. But you don't see it much no more. I knew a family—the mother wasn't too quick, though—nursed hers till the boy, I reckon, was near 'bout thirteen. But that's a bit much, ain't it?" All the time he chattered, he rubbed his chin and looked at the boy. Finally he stopped, and gave a long low chuckle. He'd found the phrase he'd been searching for. "A milkman. That's what you got here, Miss Rufie. A natural milkman if ever I seen one. Look out, women. Here he come. Huh!"

Freddie carried his discovery not only into the homes in Ruth's neighborhood, but to Southside, where he lived and where Macon Dead owned rent houses. So Ruth kept close to home and had no afternoon guests for the better part of two months, to keep from hearing that her son had been re-christened with a name he was never able to shake and that did nothing to improve either one's relationship with his father.

Macon Dead never knew how it came about—how his only son acquired the nickname that stuck in spite of his own refusal to use it or acknowledge it. It was a matter that concerned him a good deal, for the giving of names in his family was always surrounded by what he believed to be monumental foolishness. No one mentioned to him the incident out of which the nickname grew because he was a difficult man to approach—a hard man, with a manner so cool it discouraged casual or spontaneous conversation. Only Freddie the janitor took liberties with Macon Dead, liberties he purchased with the services he rendered, and Freddie was the last person on earth to tell him. So Macon Dead neither heard of nor visualized Ruth's sudden terror, her awkward jump from the rocking chair, the boy's fall broken by the tiny footstool, or Freddie's amused, admiring summation of the situation.

Without knowing any of the details, however, he guessed, with the accuracy of a mind sharpened by hatred, that the name he heard schoolchildren call his son, the name he overheard the ragman use when he paid the boy three cents for a bundle of old clothes—he guessed that this name was not clean. Milkman. It certainly didn't sound like the honest job of a dairyman, or bring to his mind cold bright cans standing (in the back porch, glittering like captains on guard. It sounded dirty, intimate, and hot. He knew that wherever the name came from, it had something to do with his wife and was, like the emotion he always felt when thinking of her, coated with disgust.

This disgust and the uneasiness with which he regarded his son affected everything he did in that city. If he could have felt sad, simply sad, it would have relieved him. Fifteen years of regret at not having a son had become the bitterness of finally having one in the most revolting circumstances.

There had been a time when he had a head full of hair and when Ruth wore lovely complicated underwear that he deliberately took a long time to undo. When all of his fore play was untying, unclasping, unbuckling the snaps and strings of what must have been the most beautiful, the most delicate, the whitest and softest underwear on earth. Each eye of her corset he toyed with (and there were forty—twenty on each side); each grosgrain ribbon that threaded its pale-blue way through the snowy top of her bodice he unlaced. He not only undid the blue bow; he pulled it all the way out of the hem, so she had to rethread it afterward with a safety pin. The elastic bands that connected her perspiration shields to her slip he unsnapped and snapped again, teasing her and himself with the sound of the snaps and the thrill of his fingertips on her shoulders. They never spoke during these undressings. But they giggled occasionally, and as when children "doctor," undressing of course was the best part play.

When Ruth was naked and lying there as moist and crumbly as unbleached sugar, he bent to unlace her shoes. That was the final delight, for once he had undressed her feet, had peeled her stockings down over her ankles and toes, he entered her and ejaculated quickly. She liked it that way. So did he. And in almost twenty years during which he had not laid eyes on her naked feet, he missed only the underwear.

Once he believed that the sight of her mouth on the dead man's fingers would be the thing he would remember always. He was wrong. Little by little he remembered fewer and fewer of the details, until finally he had to imagine them, even fabricate them, guess what they must have been. The image left him, but the odiousness[12] never did. For the nourishment of his outrage he depended on the memory of her underwear; those round, innocent corset eyes now lost to him forever.

So if the people were calling his son Milkman, and if she was lowering her eyelids and dabbing at the sweat on her top lip when she heard it, there was definitely some filthy connection and it did not matter at all to Macon Dead whether anyone gave him the details or not.

And they didn't. Nobody both dared enough and cared enough to tell him. The ones who cared enough, Lena and Corinthians, the living proof of those years of undressing his wife, did not dare. And the one person who dared to but didn't care to was the one person in the world he hated more than his wife in spite of the fact that she was his sister. He had not crossed the tracks to see her since his son was born and he had no intention of renewing their relationship now.

Macon Dead dug' in his pocket tor his keys, and curled his lingers around them, letting their bunchy solidity calm him. They were the keys to all the doors of his houses (only four true houses; the rest were really shacks), and he fondled them from time to time as he walked down Not Doctor Street to his office. At least he thought of it as his office, had even painted the word OFFICE on the door. But the plate-glass window contradicted him. In peeling gold letters arranged in a semicircle, his business establishment was declared to be Sonny's Shop. Scraping the previous owner's name off was hardly worth the trouble since he couldn't scrape it from anybody's mind. His storefront office was never called anything but Sonny's Shop, although nobody now could remember thirty years back, when, presumably, Sonny did something or other there.

He walked there now—strutted is the better word, for he had a high behind and an athlete's stride—thinking of names. Surely, he thought, he and his sister had some ancestor, some lithe young man with onyx skin and legs as straight as cane stalks, who had a name that was real. A name given to him at birth with love and seriousness. A name that was not a joke, nor a disguise, nor a brand name. But who this lithe young man was, and where his cane-stalk legs carried him from or to, could never be known. No. Nor his name. His own parents, in some mood of perverseness or resignation, had agreed to abide by a naming done to them by somebody who couldn't have cared less. Agreed to take and pass on to all their issue this heavy name scrawled in perfect thoughtlessness by a drunken Yankee in the Union Army. A literal slip of the pen handed to his father on a piece of paper and which he handed on to his only son, and his son likewise handed on to his; Macon Dead who begat a second Macon Dead who married Ruth Foster (Dead) and begat Magdalene called Lena Dead and First Corinthians Dead and (when he least expected it) another Macon Dead, now known to the part of the world that mattered as Milkman Dead. And as if that were not enough, a sister named Pilate Dead, who would never mention to her brother the circumstances or the details of this foolish misnaming of his son because the whole thing would have delighted her. She would savor it, maybe fold it too in a brass box and hang it from her other ear.

He had cooperated as a young father with the blind selection of names from the Bible for every child other than the first male. And abided by whatever the finger pointed to, for he knew every configuration of the naming of his sister. How his father, confused and melancholy over his wife's death in childbirth, had thumbed through the Bible, and since he could not read a word, chose a group of letters that seemed to him strong and handsome; saw in them a large figure that looked like a tree hanging in some princely but protective way over a row of smaller trees. How he had copied the group of letters out on a piece of brown paper; copied, as illiterate people do, every curlicue, arch, and bend in the letters, and presented it to the midwife.

"That's the baby's name."

"You want this for the baby's name?"

"I want that for the baby's name. Say it."

"You can't name the baby this."

"Say it."

"It's a man's name."

"Say it."

"Pilate."

"What?"

"Pilate. You wrote down Pilate."

"Like a river boat pilot?"

"No. Not like no river boat pilot. Like a Christ-killing Pilate. You can't get much worse than that for a name. And a baby girl at that."

"That's where my finger went down at."

"Well, your brain ain't got to follow it[13]. You don't want to give this motherless child the name of the man that killed Jesus, do you?"

"I asked Jesus to save me my wife."

"Careful, Macon."

"I asked him all night long."

"He give you your baby."

"Yes. He did. Baby name Pilate."

"Jesus, have mercy."

"Where you going with that piece of paper?"

"It's going back where it came from. Right in the Devil's flames."

"Give it here. It come from the Bible. It stays in the Bible."

And it did stay there, until the baby girl turned twelve and took it out, folded it up into a tiny knot and put it in a little brass box, and strung the entire contraption through her left ear-lobe. Fluky about her own name at twelve, how much more fluky she'd become since then Macon could only guess. But he knew for certain that she would treat the naming of the third Macon Dead with the same respect and awe she had treated the boy's birth.

Macon Dead remembered when his son was born, how she seemed to be more interested in this first nephew of hers than she was in her own daughter, and even that daughter's daughter. Long after Ruth was up and about, as capable as she ever would be—and that wasn't much—of running the house again, Pilate continued to visit, her shoelaces undone, a knitted cap pulled down over her forehead, bringing her foolish earring and sickening smell into the kitchen. He had not seen her since he was sixteen years old, until a year before the birth of his son, when she appeared in his city. Now she was acting like an in-law, like an aunt, dabbling at helping Ruth and the girls, but having no interest in or knowledge of decent housekeeping, she got in the way. Finally she just sat in a chair near the crib, singing to the baby. That wasn't so bad, but what Macon Dead remembered most was the expression on her face. Surprise, it looked like, and eagerness. But so intense it made him uneasy. Or perhaps it was more than that. Perhaps it was seeing her all those years after they had separated outside that cave, and remembering his anger and her betrayal. How far down she had slid since then. She had cut the last thread of propriety. At one time she had been the dearest thing in the world to him. Now she was odd, murky, and worst of all, unkempt. A regular source of embarrassment, if he would allow it. But he would not allow it.

Finally he had told her not to come again until she could show some respect for herself. Could get a real job instead of running a wine house.

"Why can't you dress like a woman?" He was standing by the stove. "What's that sailor's cap doing on your head? Don't you have stockings? What are you trying to make me look like in this town?" He trembled with the thought of the white men in the bank—the men who helped him buy and mortgage houses— discovering that this raggedy bootlegger was his sister. That the propertied Negro who handled his business so well and who lived in the big house on Not Doctor Street had a sister who had a daughter but no husband, and that daughter had a daughter but no husband. A collection of lunatics who made wine and sang in the streets "like common street women! Just like common street women!"

Pilate had sat there listening to him, her wondering eyes resting on his face. Then she said, "I been worried sick about you too, Macon.[14]"

Exasperated, he had gone to the kitchen door. "Go 'head, Pilate. Go on now. I'm on the thin side of evil[15] and trying not to break through."

Pilate stood up, wrapped her quilt around her, and with a last fond look at the baby, left through the kitchen door. She never came back.

When Macon Dead got to the front door of his office he saw a stout woman and two young boys standing a few feet away. Macon unlocked his door, walked over to his desk, and settled himself behind it. As he was thumbing through his accounts book, the stout woman entered, alone.

"Afternoon Mr. Dead, sir. I'm Mrs. Bains. Live over at number three on Fifteenth Street."

Macon Dead remembered—not the woman, but the circumstances at number three. His tenant's grandmother or aunt or something had moved in there and the rent was long overdue.

"Yes, Mrs. Bains. You got something for me?"

"Well, that's what I come to talk to you about. You know Cency left all them babies with me. And my relief check ain't no more'n it take to keep a well-grown yard dog alive[15]—half alive, I should say."

"Your rent is four dollars a month, Airs. Bains. You two months behind already."

"I do know that, Mr. Dead, sir, but babies can't make it with nothing to put in they stomach."

Their voices were low, polite, without any hint of conflict.

"Can they make it in the street, Mrs. Bains? That's where they gonna be if you don't figure out some way to get me my money."

"No, sir. They can't make it in the street. We need both, I reckon. Same as yours does."

"Then you better rustle it up[16], Mrs. Bains. You got till"—he swiveled around to consult the calendar on the wall—"till Saturday coming. Saturday, Mrs. Bains. Not Sunday. Not Monday. Saturday."

If she had been younger and had more juice, the glitter in her eyes would have washed down onto her cheeks. New, at her time of life, it simply gleamed. She pressed the flat of her hand on Macon Dead's desk and, holding the gleam steady in her eyes, pushed herself up from the chair. She turned her head a little to look out the plate-glass window, and then back at him.

"What's it gonna profit you, Mr. Dead, sir, to put me and them children out?"

"Saturday, Mrs. Bains."

Lowering her head, Mrs. Bains whispered something and walked slowly and heavily from the office. As she closed the door to Sonny's Shop, her grandchildren moved out of the sunlight into the shadow where she stood.

"What he say, Granny?"

Mrs. Bains put a hand on the taller boy's hair and fingered it lightly, absently searching with her nails for tatter spots. "He must've told her no," said the other boy.

"Do we got to move?" The tall boy tossed his head free of her fingers and looked at her sideways. His cat eyes were gashes of gold.

Mrs. Bains let her hand fall to her side. "A nigger in business is a terrible thing to see. A terrible, terrible thing to see."

The boys looked at each other and back at their grandmother. Their lips were parted as though they had heard something important.

When Mrs. Bains closed the door, Macon Dead went back to the pages of his accounts book, running his fingertips over the figures and thinking with the unoccupied part of his mind about the first time he called on Ruth Foster's father. He had only two keys in his pocket then, and if he had let people like the woman who just left have their way, he wouldn't have had any keys at all. It was because of those keys that he could dare to walk over to that part of Not Doctor Street (it was still Doctor Street then) and approach the most important Negro in the city. To lift the lion's paw knocker[17], to entertain thoughts of marrying the doctor's daughter was possible because each key represented a house which he owned at the time. Without those keys he would have floated away at the doctor's first word: "Yes?" Or he would have melted like new wax under the heat of that pale eye. Instead he was able to say that he had been introduced to his daughter, Miss Ruth Foster, and would appreciate having the doctor's permission to keep her company now and then. That his intentions were honorable and that he himself was certainly worthy of the doctor's consideration as a gentleman friend for Miss Foster since, at twenty-five, he was already a colored man of property.

"I don't know anything about you," the doctor said, "other than your name, which I don't like, but I will abide by my daughter's preference."

In fact the doctor knew a good deal about him and was more grateful to this tall young man than he ever allowed himself to show. Fond as he was of his only child, useful as she was in his house since his wife had died, lately he had begun to chafe under her devotion. Her steady beam of love was unsettling, and she had never dropped those expressions of affection that had been so lovable in her childhood. The good-night kiss was itself a masterpiece of slow-wittedness on her part and discomfort on his. At sixteen, she still insisted on having him come to her at night, sit on her bed, exchange a few pleasantries, and plant a kiss on her lips. Perhaps it was the loud silence of his dead wife, perhaps it was Ruth's disturbing resemblance to her mother. More probably it was the ecstasy that always seemed to be shining in Ruth's face when he bent to kiss her—an ecstasy he felt inappropriate to the occasion.

None of that, of course, did he describe to the young man who came to call. Which is why Macon Dead still believed the magic had lain in the two keys.

In the middle of his reverie, Macon was interrupted by rapid tapping on the window. He looked up, saw Freddie peeping through the gold lettering, and nodded for him to enter. A gold-toothed bantamweight, Freddie was as much of a town crier[18] as South side had. It was this same rapid tapping on the window-pane, the same flash-of-gold smile that had preceded his now-famous scream to Macon: "Mr. Smith went splat!" It was obvious to Macon that Freddie now had news of another calamity.

"Porter gone crazy drunk again! Got his shotgun!"

"Who's he out for?" Macon began closing books and opening desk drawers. Porter was a tenant and tomorrow was collection day.

"Ain't out for nobody in particular[19]. Just perched himself up in the attic window and commenced to waving a shotgun. Say he gotta kill him somebody before morning."

"He go to work today?"

"Yep. Caught the eagle too."

"Drunk it all up?"

"Not all of it. He only got one bottle, and he still got a fist fulla money."

"Who's crazy enough to sell him any liquor?"

Freddie showed a few gold teeth but said nothing, so Macon knew it was Pilate. He locked all his drawers save one—the one he unlocked and took a small.32[20] from.

"Police warn every bootlegger in the county, and he still gets it somehow." Macon went on with the charade, pretending he didn't know his sister was the one Porter and anybody else—adult, child, or beast—could buy wine from. He thought for the hundredth time that she needed to be in jail and that he would be willing to put her there if he could be sure she wouldn't loud-mouth him and make him seem trashy in the eyes of the law—and the banks.

"You know how to use that thing, Mr. Dead, sir?"

"I know how."

"Porter's crazy when he drunk."

"I know what he is."

"How you aiming to get him down?"

"I ain't aiming to get him down. I'm aiming to get my money down. He can go on and die up there if he wants to. But if he don't toss me my rent, I'm going to blow him out of that window."

Freddie's giggle was soft, but his teeth strengthened its impact. A born flunky, he loved gossip and the telling of it. He was the ear that heard even' murmur of complaint, every name-calling; and his was the eye that saw everything: the secret loving glances, the fights, the new dresses.

Macon knew Freddie as a fool and a liar, but a reliable liar. He was always right about his facts and always wrong about the motives that produced the facts. Just as now he was right about Porter having a shotgun, being in the attic window, and being drunk. But Porter was not waiting to kill somebody, meaning anybody, before morning. In fact he was very specific about whom he wanted to kill—himself. However, he did have a precondition which he shouted down, loud and clear, from the attic. "I want to fuck! Send me up somebody to fuck! Hear me? Send me up somebody, I tell ya, or I'ma blow my brains out!"

As Macon and Freddie approached the yard, the women from the rooming house were hollering answers to Porter's plea.

"What kinda bargain is that?"

"Kill yourself first and then we'll send you somebody."

"Do it have to be a woman?"

"Do it got to be human?"

"Do it got to be alive?"

"Can it be a piece of liver?"

"Put that thing down and throw me my goddam money!" Macon's voice cut through the women's fun. "Float those dollars down here, nigger, then blow yourself up!"

Porter turned and aimed his shotgun at Macon.

"If you pull that trigger," shouted Macon, "you better not miss. If you take a shot you better make sure I'm dead, cause if you don't I'm gonna shoot your balls up in your throat!" He pulled out his own weapon. "Now get the hell outta that window!"

Porter hesitated for only a second, before turning the barrel of the shotgun toward himself—or trying to. Its length made it difficult; his drunkenness made it impossible. Struggling to get the right angle, he was suddenly distracted. He leaned his shotgun on the windowsill, pulled out his penis and in a high arc, peed over the heads of the women, making them scream and run in a panic that the shotgun had not been able to create. Macon rubbed the back of his head while Freddie bent double with laughter.

For more than an hour Porter held them at bay: cowering, screaming, threatening, urinating, and interspersing all of it with pleas for a woman.

He would cry great shoulder-heaving sobs, followed by more screams.

"I love ya! I love ya all. Don't act like that. You women. Stop it. Don't act like that. Don't you see I love ya? I'd die for ya, kill for ya. I'm saying I love ya. I'm telling ya. Oh, God have mercy. What I'm gonna do? What in this fuckin world am I gonna dooooo?"

Tears streamed down his face and he cradled the barrel of the shotgun in his arms as though it were the woman he had been begging for, searching for, all his life. "Gimme hate, Lord," he whimpered. "I'll take hate any day. But don't give me love. I can't take no more love, Lord. I can't carry it. Just like Mr. Smith. He couldn't carry it. It's too heavy. Jesus, you know. You know all about it. Ain't it heavy? Jesus? Ain't love heavy? Don't you see, Lord? You own son couldn't carry it. If it killed Him, what You think it's gonna do to me? Huh? Huh?" He was getting angry again.

"Come down outta there, nigger!" Macon's voice was still loud, but it was getting weary.

"And you, you baby-dicked baboon"—he tried to point at Macon—"you the worst. You need killin, you really need killin. You know why? Well, I'm gonna tell you why. I know why. Everybody..."

Porter slumped down in the window, muttering, "Everybody knows why," and fell fast asleep. As he sank deeper into it, the shotgun slipped from his hand, rattled down the roof, and hit the ground with a loud explosion. The shot zipped past a by stander's shoe and blew a hole in the tire of a stripped Dodge parked in the road.

"Go get my money," Macon said.

"Me?" Freddie asked. "Suppose he ..."

"Go get me my money."

Porter was snoring. Through the blast of the gun and the picking of his pocket he slept like a baby.

When Macon walked out of the yard, the sun had disappeared behind the bread company. Tired, irritable; he walked down Fifteenth Street, glancing up as he passed one of his other houses, its silhouette melting in the light that trembled between dusk and twilight. Scattered here and there, his houses stretched up beyond him like squat ghosts with hooded eyes. He didn't like to look at them in this light. During the day they were reassuring to see; now they did not seem to belong to him at all—in fact he felt as though the houses were in league with one another to make him feel like the outsider, the propertyless, landless wanderer. It was this feeling of loneliness that made him decide to take a shortcut back to Not

Doctor Street, even though to do so would lead him past his sister's house. In the gathering darkness, he was sure his passing would be unnoticed by her. He crossed a yard and followed a fence that led into Darling Street where Pilate lived in a narrow single-story house whose basement seemed to be rising from rather than settling into the ground. She had no electricity because she would not pay for the service. Nor for gas. At night she and her daughter lit the house with candles and kerosene lamps; they warmed themselves and cooked with wood and coal, pumped kitchen water into a dry sink through a pipeline from a well and lived pretty much as though progress was a word that meant walking a little farther on down the road.

Her house sat eighty feet from the sidewalk and was backed by four huge pine trees, from which she got the needles she stuck into her mattress. Seeing the pine trees started him thinking about her mouth; how she loved, as a girl, to chew pine needles and as a result smelled even then like a forest. For a dozen years she had been like his own child. After their mother died, she had come struggling out of the womb without help from throbbing muscles or the pressure of swift womb water. As a result, for all the years he knew her, her stomach was as smooth and sturdy as her back, at no place interrupted by a navel. It was the absence of a navel that convinced people that she had not come into this world through normal channels; had never lain, floated, or grown in some warm and liquid place connected by a tissue-thin tube to a reliable source of human nourishment. Macon knew otherwise, because he was there and had seen the eyes of the midwife as his mother's legs collapsed. And heard as well her shouts when the baby, who they had believed was dead also, inched its way headfirst out of a still, silent, and indifferent cave of flesh, dragging her own cord and her own afterbirth behind her. But the rest was true. Once the new baby's lifeline was cut, the cord stump shriveled, fell off, and left no trace of having ever existed, which, as a young boy taking care of his baby sister, he thought no more strange than a bald head. He was seventeen years old, irreparably separated from her and already pressing forward in his drive for wealth, when he learned that there was probably not another stomach like hers on earth.

Now, nearing her yard, he trusted that the dark would keep anyone in her house from seeing him. He did not even look to his left as he walked by it. But then he heard the music. They were singing. All of them. Pilate, Reba, and Reba's daughter, Hagar. There was no one on the street that he could see; people were at supper, licking their fingers, blowing into saucers of coffee, and no doubt chattering about Porter's escapade and Macon's fearless confrontation of the wild man in the attic. There were no street lights in this part of town; only the moon directed the way of a pedestrian. Macon walked on, resisting as best he could the sound of the voices that followed him. He was rapidly approaching a part of the road where the music could not follow, when he saw, like a scene on the back of a postcard, a picture of where he was headed—his own home; his wife's narrow unyielding back; his daughters, boiled dry from years of yearning; his son, to whom he could speak only if his words held some command or criticism. "Hello, Daddy." "Hello, son, tuck your shirt in." "I found a dead bird, Daddy." "Don't bring that mess in this house." There was no music there, and tonight he wanted just a bit of music—from the person who had been his first caring for.

He turned back and walked slowly toward Pilate's house. They were singing some melody that Pilate was leading. A phrase that the other two were taking up and building on. Her powerful contralto, Reba's piercing soprano[21] in counterpoint, and the soft voice of the girl, Hagar, who must be about ten or eleven now, pulled him like a carpet tack under the influence of a magnet.

Surrendering to the sound, Macon moved closer. He wanted no conversation, no witness, only to listen and perhaps to see the three of them, the source of that music that made him think of fields and wild turkey and calico. Treading as lightly as he could, he crept up to the side window where the candlelight flickered lowest, and peeped in. Reba was cutting her toenails with a kitchen knife or a switchblade, her long neck bent almost to her knees. The girl, Hagar, was braiding her hair, while Pilate, whose face he could not see because her back was to the window, was stirring something in a pot. Wine pulp, perhaps. Macon knew it was not food she was stirring, for she and her daughters ate like children. Whatever they had a taste for. No meal was ever planned or balanced or served. Nor was there any gathering at the table. Pilate might bake hot bread and each one of them would eat it with butter whenever she felt like it. Or there might be grapes, left over from the wine making, or peaches for days on end. If one of them bought a gallon of milk they drank it until it was gone. If another got a half bushel of tomatoes or a dozen ears of corn, they ate them until they were gone too. They ate what they had or came across or had a craving for. Profits from their wine-selling evaporated like sea water in a hot wind—going for junk jewelry for Hagar, Reba's gifts to men, and he didn't know what all.

Near the window, hidden by the dark, he felt the irritability of the day drain from him and relished the effortless beauty of the women singing in the candlelight. Reba's soft profile, Hagar's hands moving, moving in her heavy hair, and Pilate. He knew her face better than he knew his own. Singing now, her face would be a mask; all emotion and passion would have left her features and entered her voice. But he knew that when she was neither singing nor talking, her face was animated by her constantly moving lips. She chewed things. As a baby, as a very young girl, she kept things in her mouth—straw from brooms, gristle, buttons, seeds, leaves, string, and her favorite, when he could find some for her, rubber bands and India rubber erasers. Her lips were alive with small movements. If you were close to her, you wondered if she was about to smile or was she merely shifting a straw from the baseline of her gums to her tongue. Perhaps she was dislodging a curl of rubber band from inside her cheek, or was she really smiling? From a distance she appeared to be whispering to herself, when she was only nibbling or splitting tiny seeds with her.

Notes:

1. cupola: a small ornamental structure rising from a roof
2. cloche: a woman's close-fitting hat with a deep, bell-shaped crown and often a narrow, turned-down brim
3. galosh: waterproof overshoe, esp. a high one
4. contralto: the lowest female voice or voice part, intermediate between soprano and tenor
5. pea-time: wonderful thing
6. Soon's: as soon as
7. caul: a part of the amnion sometimes covering the head of a child at birth
8. red at the bone: the dish of the chicken still has got the blood, not boiled enough for eating
9. nuzzle: to burrow or root with the nose, snout, etc., as an animal does
10. cauldron: a large kettle or boiler
11. ain't nothing wrong with it: there is nothing wrong with it
12. odiousness: highly offensive; repugnant; disgusting
13. your brain ain't got follow it: your reason doesn't have to follow this ridiculous procedure of naming by the random coming across the word in the Bible
14. I benn worried sick about you too, macon: I am worrying a lot about you so

much so that I feel sick

15. my relief...yard dog alive: my relief check is no more than to keep a dog alive

16. rustle it up: to find, gather, or assemble by effort or search

17. lions paw knocker: an item of door furniture that allows people outside a house to alert those inside to their presence

18. crier: a person employed by a town to make public announcements or proclamations, usually by shouting in the streets. *Informal* A gossip

19. Ain't out for nobody in particular: He does not have someone as his target in particular

20. 32: 0.32 caliber handgun

21. soprano: The highest range of the female singing voice

Questions for Study and Discussion:

1. Comment on the following: Robert Smith's attempt to fly; Not Doctor Street; Song: "O Sugarman done fly away"; Milkman; born with a caul; Water mark on the Dead's dining room table; Porter, the drunk, his actions.

2. Why does Ruth Dead continue to breast, feed Milkman?

3. How are names chosen for die Dead family?

4. Why is Dr. Foster relieved to have a suitor for Ruth?

5. Why does Macon enjoy hearing Pilate and her family sing as he listens outside?

Maxine Hong Kingston (1940—   )

Life and Major Works

Maxine Hong Kingston (1940—   ) was born to Chinese immigrant parents, Tom Hong and Chew Ying Lan, in Stockton, California, on 27th, October 1940. Her American name, Maxine, was after a blonde who was always lucky in gambling. Ting Ting, her Chinese name, comes from a Chinese poem about self-reliance.

She is the eldest of the six American-born Hong children. She had a terrible time talking in the early part of her school education which she called her "silent

Maxine Hong Kingston

years". She flunked kindergarten, but once she could talk well, she became a straight-A student and won a scholarship to the University of California, Berkeley. In 1962 she got her bachelor's degree in English and married Earll Kingston, a

Berkeley graduate and an actor. She returned to the university in 1964, earned a teaching certificate in 1965, and taught English and mathematics from 1965 to 1967 in Hayward, California. During their time at Berkeley, the Kingstons were involved in the antiwar movement on campus. In 1967 they decided to leave the country because the movement was getting more and more violent, and their friends were too involved in drugs.

On their way to Japan the Kingstons stopped in Hawaii and stayed there for seventeen years. At first Kingston taught language arts and English as a second language in a private school. In 1977 she became a visiting professor at the University of Hawaii at Honolulu. A few days after she finished the final revisions of *China Men* (1980), a Honolulu Buddhist sect claimed Kingston as a "Living Treasure of Hawaii." Kingston herself, however, was still looking homeward, having always felt like a stranger in the islands. She and her husband moved back to California. In 1992 Kingston became a member of the Academy of Arts and Sciences.

Maxine Hong Kingston is one of the first Asian American writers in the United States to achieve great acclaim for both her nonfiction and fiction. With her vivid portrayals of the magic of her Chinese ancestry and the struggle of Chinese immigrants to the United States, she makes the Asian American experience come alive for her readers. With prose that both unsettles Chinese American sexism and American racism, Kingston is a "word warrior" who battles social and racial injustice. On September 29, 1997, President Bill Clinton awarded Maxine Hong Kingston a National Humanities Medal for her work as a writer and a supporter of both the California and Hawaii Councils for the Humanities.

Kingston's writing relies heavily on memory and imagination, and the major sources of memory and imagination are her mother's stories and her father's silence. As a youngster, Kingston was profoundly influenced by her parents' struggle to deal with the difficulties of assimilation and their need to remind their children and themselves of their rich cultural heritage. She recalls listening intently to her mother's "talk-stories" about her ancestors and also delighted in hearing her recount mystical Chinese folk tales. She ever said that she was a born storyteller, because she very much wanted to write down everything her mother told her. While she was intrigued by the myth and magic of China, she was deeply disturbed by the family secrets revealed in her mother's stories. Learning about the adversity that so many of her relatives had known in their lives also troubled her. Writing thus became her way of understanding their pain and working toward some sort of resolution. In particular, Kingston was drawn to the narratives about women who had been considered especially privileged or damned. These women haunted her as she later sought to give voice not only to their experiences but also her own.

Her first book *The Woman Warrior* appeared in 1976, more than three decades ago. In 1980, she published a second memoir, *China Men*; in 1987, a collection of essays on Hawai'i, *Hawai'i One Summer*; in 1989, a novel, *Tripmaster Monkey: His Fake Book*; in 2002, a book of and about poetry, *To Be the Poet*; in 2003, a mixed-genre volume, *The Fifth Book of Peace*. In 2006, she edited a volume of writings by war veterans, *Veterans of War*, and *Veterans of Peace*.

Kingston's works covers a range of genres coming out of a powerful literary imagination. All her writing is different from all her other writing. According to her, her first book *The Woman Warrior* is an I-book which is very self-centered. It explores the lives of women who have had the strongest impact on her throughout her life—women whose voices have never been heard. *Time* magazine named *The Woman Warrior* one of the top ten nonfiction works of literature of the 1970s.

Kingston was also interested in giving voice to the male side of her family. Her second book *China Men,* another blend of fact and fantasy, won the 1981 American Book Award for nonfiction and was runner-up for the Pulitzer Prize. Based on the experiences of her father and several generations of other male relatives, the book explores the lives of Chinese men who left their homeland to settle in the United States. It contains stories of loneliness and discrimination as well as determination and strength, enhanced and embellished by Kingston's own formidable imagination.

Kingston's third book, *Tripmaster Monkey: His Fake Book*, earned the 1989 PEN West Award in fiction. In this book, Kingston examines the life of a young, fifth-generation Chinese American named Wittman Ah Sing (a tribute to poet Walt Whitman). Somewhat of a hippie who believes in doing what he likes no matter what the consequences are, Wittman majors in English in college during the 1960s and then sets out to find his place in the world. He ends up in Berkeley, California, where he struggles to make a go of it as a playwright. Many readers and critics have found Wittman especially annoying, and Kingston admits that Wittman was meant to be offensive, because she believes that it is his way of making himself his own man. That American people do not like Wittman means that they do not like the personalities of a lot of actual Asian American men. But she thinks that minority people in America all know how to be charming, because there are very charming stereotypes out there. She was dismayed by the racial discrimination there.

Kingston also published numerous poems, short stories, and articles in her career. *Hawaii One Summer*, a book of 12 prose essays, was published in a limited edition in 1987. In 1991, she co-authored *Learning True Love: How I Learned and Practiced Social Change in Vietnam*, essentially a compilation of talks given by a Vietnamese Buddhist nun who has spent her life in service to the poor of her country. That same year, fire raged through Kingston's home in Oakland, California, and destroyed the manuscript of *The Fourth Book of Peace*, a project she had been working on that was inspired by the Chinese legend of the three lost books of peace. She has since completed *The Fifth Book of Peace*, which attempts to imagine in realistic rather than utopian terms what a world of peace might be like.

Brief Introduction and Appreciation

The Woman Warrior: Memoirs of a Girlhood Among Ghosts is a nonfictional memoir by Kingston, published by Vintage Books in 1976. It is semi-autobiographical, incorporating many elements of fiction. Through the book, Kingston explores ethnicity and gender roles, especially in the context of her experience as a Chinese-American woman. She creates stories by filling in the blanks of her mother's talk-story. She entitled the book *The Woman Warrior: Memoirs of a Girlhood Among Ghosts* to show the pain, the plight (ghosts) a girl like her who was torn between two vastly different cultures had to suffer in the process of growth, and her courage to fight against those "ghosts".

The Woman Warrior has been reported by the Modern Language Association as the most commonly taught text in modern university education, used in disciplines that include American literature, anthropology, Asian studies, composition, education, psychology, sociology, and women's studies. Though widely praised by critics, the book has been criticized by fellow Chinese American author Frank Chin as perpetuating racist stereotypes.

The Woman Warrior is an example of how Kingston likes to experiment with various genres, as she weaves together myth, fiction, nonfiction, autobiography, and history in what is sometimes both true and imagined. Thirty years later, *The*

Woman Warrior still remains one of the most widely taught books on college campuses. In addition, it has also won the National Book Critics Circle Award and has been named one of *Time* Magazine's top nonfiction books of the 1970s. *The Woman Warrior* is currently considered "the most widely taught book by a living writer in US colleges and universities."

The book is divided into five interconnected stories. In the first story, "No Name Woman," Kingston the narrator describes the suicide of her aunt, as told by her mother, after she gave birth to an illegitimate child. The narrator is warned to never again speak of her un-named aunt, but she still creates a history for her in her memoir. In the second story, "White Tigers", the narrator creates a fantastic allegory to describe her childhood. She imagines herself as a version of the legendary Chinese woman warrior, Fa Mulan, who, having learned the warrior's arts from an elderly couple who are hundreds of years old, raises an army and overthrows the corrupt government. After her battles, she takes up the traditional woman's roles of mother and wife. In "Shaman", the third story, the narrator describes her mother's experience in Chinese medical school. Mixing fantasy and autobiography, she details her mother's physical and mental battles with spirits and ghosts. In the fourth chapter, "At the Western Palace", she describes her aunt Moon Orchid's mental breakdown after she emigrates to the United States from China in order to find her estranged husband. In the final story, "A Song for a Barbarian Reed Pipe", she describes her childhood experiences in the California public school system, and her parents' attitudes toward her. She closes the book with a reinterpretation of the story of early third century Chinese poet Ts'ai Yen, who, like the narrator, had to learn to sing in a foreign tongue.

In *Woman Warrior*, Kingston touches several themes, including silence (both gendered and racially constituted), necessity for speech, the discovery of voice, the construction of identity and the search for self-realization, the mother-daughter relationship and the conflicts that it engenders, memory, acculturation and biculturalism, and cultural alienation. Kingston well handled a theme that pervades the literature of diaspora and immigrant communities, i.e. the theme of cross-cultural conflict. She captures the pain of an American-born child who inevitably reject the expectations and authority of her family in favor of the values of the new land. It is a personal narrative that represents Kingston's effort to reconcile American and Chinese female identities. It is remarkable in its insights into the plight of individuals pulled between two cultures.

The excerpt below is the beginning part of the fourth story "At the Western Palace". It is about how a wrinkled old Chinese lady, Moon Orchid, Brave Orchid's sister, under the latter's encouragement, flies all the long way to reclaim her Americanized husband who left her several decades ago, but failed, turned insane, and finally died in a mental asylum. Her husband has got remarried to a beautiful young lady and become a successful neuron-surgeon in America, and the only bond between them is the money he mails back regularly.

The story is structured by the Chinese tale that an emperor had four wives, with the first wife living in the Eastern Palace, the second wife in the Western Palace, and the one who failed in the battle for their man would be sent to the Northern Palace. The one living in the West would connive for power and imprison the emperor in her palace, while the one living in the East was good, kind and full of light. Her mission was to break the spell of the second wife cast on the emperor and restore his love for her. Brave Orchid tries hard to convince Moon Orchid that she is the empress living in the East, who has lost her husband's favor and should restore her position as the first wife by reducing the little wife who lives in the Western Palace to the second wife. This shows that in China, a man can have more than one wife. However, Moon Orchid does not have the courage at all either to ask the husband for the compensation, or to challenge the little wife for her justified position. She dares not see the husband because she is not invited. When she at last sees him, there are no moving scenes of long-parted husband and wife getting reunited. Instead, she is wildly scolded by the husband and ordered to stay away from his family, otherwise, he would cut off her financial support. Although she has suffered loneliness and sadness from the absence of the husband for so many years, she still abides by the responsibilities an obedient wife is supposed to abide by in ancient China, and stands back silently and shamefully. She stays with her sister's family for some time, but she is capable of doing nothing for survival, and what is worse, she gets hopelessly insane due to the shame of being deserted by the husband. She is haunted by disillusions and becomes insane completely. Even with all the efforts of Brave Orchid to help her recover, her condition deteriorates. She finally dies in a mental asylum. Her husband never inquires after her, let alone see her again since that meeting of them.

The selected part is about what happens at the San Francisco International Airport when Brave Orchid takes a day off to wait for Moon Orchid. It dramatizes how old Moon Orchid is and how long she has been living alone without her husband, thus paving the way for how much she should be compensated and how tragic she would be when she is bitterly criticized and cruelly rejected by the ghostly husband. Brave Orchid's own age (sixty-eight years old), her eagerness to see Moon Orchid (*took a day off, not seen her for thirty years, begun this waiting at home, getting up a half-hour before Moon Orchid's plane took off, already been waiting for nine hours, was wakeful, ...*), her mistaking a girl even younger than her sister's daughter for her sister, their exclamations about how old the other one is when they meet, etc., all accumulate to bring home to the readers how much time has gone by, why the lady hasn't come earlier, and how miserable a life she must have led during the long years, and how justifiable she should be compensated by the husband. All these lay the foundation for the further development of the story and help deepen the tragic sense of the story.

The author bitterly criticizes the patriarchal order of the old China under which women must be faithful to their miserable marriage and cold husbands, while husbands enjoyed the freedom to marry other women. And in the new land of paradise, the husbands who had wives back in China had legitimate excuses to desert their former wives. Moon Orchid's life-long waiting for her husband seems extremely ridiculous. With this story, Kingston utters very loudly her feminist idea that the women should not be the passive, weak, dependent and obedient party in marriage. The story renders very vividly the cultural gap between China and America, implying a solution for women like Moon Orchid who are torn apart between two cultures about how to cope with their life and marriage.

Selected Reading

The Woman Warrior
Chapter IV
At the Western Palace

When she was about sixty-eight years old, Brave Orchid took a day off to wait at San Francisco International Airport for the plane that was bringing her sister to the United States. She had not seen Moon Orchid for thirty years. She had begun this waiting at home, getting up a half-hour before Moon Orchid's plane took off in Hong Kong.

Brave Orchid would add her will power to the forces that keep an airplane up. Her head hurt with the concentration. The plane had to be light, so no matter how tired she felt, she dared not rest her spirit on a wing but continuously and gently pushed up on the plane's belly. She had already been waiting at the airport for nine hours. She was wakeful.

Next to Brave Orchid sat Moon Orchid's only daughter, who was helping her aunt wait. Brave Orchid had made two of her own children come too because they could drive, but they had been lured away by the magazine racks and the gift shops and coffee shops. Her American children could not sit for very long. They did not understand sitting; they had wandering feet. She hoped they would get back from the pay T.V.'s or the pay toilets or wherever they were spending their money before the plane arrived. If they did not come back soon, she would go look for them. If her son thought he could hide in the men's room, he was wrong.

"Are you all right, Aunt?" asked her niece.

"No, this chair hurts me. Help me pull some chairs together so I can put my feet up."

She unbundled a blanket and spread it out to make a bed for herself. On the floor she had two shopping bags full of canned peaches, real peaches, beans wrapped in taro[1] leaves, cookies, Thermos bottles, enough food for everybody, though only her niece would eat with her. Her bad boy and bad girl were probably sneaking hamburgers, wasting their money. She would scold them.

Many soldiers and sailors sat about, oddly calm, like little boys in cowboy uniforms. (She thought "cowboy" was what you would call a Boy Scout.) They should have been crying hysterically on their way to Vietnam. "If I see one that looks Chinese," she thought, "I'll go over and give him some advice." She sat up suddenly, she had forgotten about her own son, who was even now in Vietnam. Carefully she split her attention, beaming half of it to the ocean, into the water to keep him afloat. He was on a ship. He was in Vietnamese waters. She was sure of it. He and the other children were lying to her. They had said he was in Japan, and then they said he was in the Philippines. But when she sent him her help, she could feel that he was on a ship in Da Nang[2]. Also she had seen the children hide the envelopes that his letters came in.

"Do you think my son is in Vietnam?" she asked her niece, who was dutifully eating.

"No. Didn't your children say he was in the Philippines?"

"Have you ever seen any of his letters with Philippine stamps on them?"

"Oh, yes. Your children showed me one."

"I wouldn't put it past them to send the letters to some Filipino they know. He puts Manila[3] postmarks on them to fool me."

"Yes, I can imagine them doing that. But don't worry. Your son can take care of himself. All your children can take care of themselves."

"Not him. He's not like other people. Not normal at all. He sticks erasers in his ears, and the erasers are still attached to the pencil stubs. The captain will say, 'Abandon ship,' or 'Watch out for bombs,' and he won't hear. He doesn't listen to orders. I told him to flee to Canada, but he wouldn't go.'

She closed her eyes. After a short while, plane and ship under control, she looked again at the children in uniforms. Some of the blond ones looked like baby chicks, their crew cuts like the downy yellow on baby chicks. You had to feel sorry for them even though they were Army and Navy Ghosts.

Suddenly her son and daughter came running. "Come, Mother. The plane's landed early. She's here already." They hurried, folding up their mother's encampment. She was glad her children were not useless. They must have known what this trip to San Francisco was about then. "It's a good thing I made you come early," she said.

Brave Orchid pushed to the front of the crowd. She had to be in front. The passengers were separated from the people waiting for them by glass doors and walls. Immigration Ghosts were stamping papers. The travelers crowded along some conveyor belts to have their luggage searched. Brave Orchid did not see her sister anywhere. She stood watching for four hours. Her children left and came back. "Why don't you sit down?" they asked.

"The chairs are too far away,' she said.

"Why don't you sit on the floor then?"

No, she would stand, as her sister was probably standing in a line she could not see from here. Her American children had no feelings and no memory.

To while away time, she and her niece talked about the Chinese passengers. These new immigrants had it easy. On Ellis Island the people were thin after forty days at sea and had no fancy luggage.

"That one looks like her," Brave Orchid would say.

"No, that's not her."

Ellis Island[4] had been made out of wood and iron. Here everything was new plastic, a ghost trick to lure immigrants into feeling safe and spilling their secrets. Then the Alien Office could send them right back. Otherwise, why did they lock her out, not letting her help her sister answer questions and spell her name? At Ellis Island when the ghost asked Brave Orchid what year her husband had cut off his pigtail, a Chinese who was crouching on the floor motioned her not to talk. "I don't know," she had said. If it weren't for that Chinese man, she might not be here today, or her husband either. She hoped some Chinese, a janitor or a clerk, would look out for Moon Orchid. Luggage conveyors fooled immigrants into thinking the Gold Mountain[5] was going to be easy.

Brave Orchid felt her heart jump—Moon Orchid. "There she is," she shouted. But her niece saw it was not her mother at all. And it shocked her to discover the woman her aunt was pointing out. This was a young woman, younger than herself, no older than Moon Orchid the day the sisters parted. "Moon Orchid will have changed a little, of course," Brave Orchid was saying. "She will have learned to wear western clothes." The woman wore a navy blue suit with a bunch of dark cherries at the shoulder.

"No, Aunt," said the niece. "That's not my mother."

"Perhaps not. It's been so many years. Yes, it is your mother. It must be. Let her come closer, and we can tell. Do you think she's too far away for me to tell, or is it my eyes getting bad?"

"It's too many years gone by," said the niece.

Brave Orchid turned suddenly—another Moon Orchid, this one a neat little woman with a bun. She was laughing at something the person ahead of her in line said. Moon Orchid was just like that, laughing at nothing. "I would be able to tell the difference if one of them would only come closer," Brave Orchid said with tears, which she did not wipe. Two children met the woman with the cherries, and she shook their hands. The other woman was met by a young man. They looked at each other gladly, then walked away side by side.

Up close neither one of those women looked like Moon Orchid at all. "Don't worry, Aunt," said the niece. "I'll know her."

"I'll know her too. I knew her before you did."

The niece said nothing, although she had seen her mother only five years ago. Her aunt liked having the last word.

Finally Brave Orchid's children quit wandering and drooped on a railing. Who knew what they were thinking? At last the niece called out, "I see her! I see her! Mother! Mother!" whenever the doors parted, she shouted, probably embarrassing the American cousins, but she didn't care. She called out, "Mama! Mama!" until the crack in the sliding doors became too small to let in her voice. "Mama!" What a strange word in an adult voice. Many people turned to see what adult was calling, "Mama!" like a child. Brave Orchid saw an old, old woman jerk her head up, her little eyes blinking confusedly, a woman whose nerves leapt toward the sound anytime she heard "Mama!" Then she relaxed to her own business again. She was a tiny, tiny lady, very thin, with little fluttering hands, and her hair was in a gray knot. She was dressed in a gray wool suit; she wore pearls around her neck and in her earlobes. Moon Orchid *would* travel with her jewels showing. Brave Orchid momentarily saw, like a larger, younger outline around this old woman, the sister she had been waiting for. The familiar dim halo faded, leaving the woman so old, so gray. So old. Brave Orchid pressed against the glass. *That* old lady? Yes, that old lady facing the ghost who stamped papers without noticing her family, Moon Orchid walked smiling over to the Suitcase Inspector Ghost, who took her boxes apart, pulling out puffs of tissue. From where she was, Brave Orchid could not see what her sister had chosen to carry across the ocean. She wished her sister would look her way. Brave Orchid thought that if *she* were entering a new country, she would be at the windows. Instead, Moon Orchid hovered over the unwrapping, surprised at each reappearance as if she were opening presents after a birthday party.

"Mama!" Moon Orchid's daughter kept calling. Brave Orchid said to her children, "Why don't you call your aunt too? Maybe she'll hear us if all of you call out together." But her children slunk away. Maybe that shame-face they so often wore was American politeness.

"Mama!" Moon Orchid's daughter again, and this time her mother looked right at her. She left her bundles in a heap and came running. "Hey!" the Customs Ghost yelled at her. She went back to clear up her mess, talking inaudibly to her daughter all the while. Her daughter pointed toward Brave Orchid. And at last Moon Orchid looked at her—two old women with faces like mirrors.

Their hands reached out as if to touch the other's face, then returned to their own, the fingers checking the grooves in the forehead and along the side of the mouth. Moon Orchid, who never understood the gravity of things, started smiling and laughing, pointing at Brave Orchid. Finally Moon Orchid gathered up her stuff, strings hanging and papers loose, and met her sister at the door, where they shook hands, oblivious to blocking the way.

"You're an old woman," said Brave Orchid.

"Aiaa. You're an old woman."

"But you are really old. Surely, you can't say that about me. I'm not old the way you're old."

"But you really are old. You're one year older than I am."

"Your hair is white and your face all wrinkled."

"You're so skinny."

"You're so fat."

"Fat women are more beautiful than skinny women."

The children pulled them out of the doorway. One of Brave Orchid's children brought the car from the parking lot, and the other heaved the luggage into the trunk. They put the two old ladies and the niece in the back seat. All the way home—across the Bay Bridge, over the Diablo hills, across the San Joaquin River to the valley, the valley moon so white at dusk—all the way home, the two sisters exclaimed every time they turned to look at each other, "Aiaa! How old!"

Brave Orchid forgot that she got sick in cars, that all vehicles but palanquins made her dizzy. "You're so old," she kept saying. "How did you get so old!"

Brave Orchid had tears in her eyes. But Moon Orchid said, "You look older than I. You are older than I," and again she'd laugh. "You're wearing an old mask to tease me." It surprised Brave Orchid that after thirty years she could still get annoyed at her sister's silliness.

Notes:

1. taro (t r´ō): a tropical Asian plant with broad leaves. It is customary in Chinese cooking to wrap rice, vegetables, or fish in the leaves for steaming
2. Da Nang: a port city in South Vietnam, was the site of a major U.S. military base during the Vietnam War
3. Manila: the capital of the Philippines and its largest city
4. Ellis Island: from 1892 to 1943, Ellis Island, in upper New York Bay, was the chief U.S. immigration station.
5. Gold Mountain: referring to America which was regarded as the land of opportunities for all, esp. for immigrants

Questions for Study and Discussion:

1. How do the names of Brave Orchid and Moon Orchid relate to their personalities?
2. What is the function of "She had not seen Moon Orchid for thirty years" in the whole story?
3. Try to summarize the personality of Brave Orchid.
4. How are the word "ghost" different when used in different places?
5. How does the little wife help convey the theme of the story?
6. What does the title "At the Western Place" imply?
7. Please find out the cultural gap between China and America in the story.

References

[1] Acknowledgment must be made to the following works and websites, from which we have benefited a great deal in the course of editing *A Course Book of American Literature*. The list is arranged in alphabetical order:

[2] Abramson, Edward A., *Bernard Malamud Revisited*. Boston:Wayne Publishers, 1993

[3] Adler, Joyce. *War in Melville's Imagination*. New York: New York University Press, 1981.

[4] Alexander, Doris. *The Tempering of Eugene O'Neill*. New York: Harcourt, Brace & World, 1962.

[5] Alkana, Joseph. *The Social Self: Hawthorne, Howells, William James, and Nineteenth-Century Psychology*. Lexington: Kentucky University Press, 1997.

[6] Allen, Gay Wilson. *Waldo Emerson: A Biography*. New York: Viking P, 1981.

[7] Andrew, Turnbull., ed. *The Letters of F. Scott Fitzgerald*. New York: Charles Scribner's Sons, 1963.

[8] Bailyn, Bernard. *The Ideological Origins of the American Revolution*. Cambridge: The Belknap Press of Harvard University Press, 1992.

[9] Baker, Carlos. *Ernest Hemingway: A Life Story*. New York: Scribner's, 1969.

[10] Barbour, Philip L. *The Three Worlds of Captain John Smith*. Boston: Houghton Mifflin Co., 1964.

[11] Basch, Norma. *In the Eyes of the Law: Women, Marriage, and Property in 19th Century New York*. Ithaca: Cornell University Press, 1982.

[12] Baym, Nina., et al., eds. *The Norton Anthology of American Literature*. 7th edition. New York : Norton, 1999.

[13] Booch,V.Jack. et al., eds.American Literature.Mission Hills:Macmillan,1987

[14] Boorstin, Daniel J. *The Lost World of Thomas Jefferson*. Chicago: Chicago

University Press, 1993.

[15] Bowden, Mary Weatherspoon. *Philip Freneau.* Boston: Twayne Pubs., 1976.

[16] Bowden, Mary Weatherspoon. *Washington Irving.* Boston: Twayne Pubs., 1981.

[17] Brooks, Cleanth and Robert Penn Warren, *Understanding Poetry.* 4th edition. Beijing: Foreign Language Teaching and Research Press, 2004.

[18] Brooks, Cleanth and Robert Penn Warren, *Understanding Fiction.* 3rd edition. Beijing: Foreign Language Teaching and Research Press, 2004.

[19] Brooks, Cleanth.et al., eds. *American Literature: The Makers and the Making* (Volumes 1& 2). New York: st. Martin's Press, 1973.

[20] Bruccoli, Matthew J. *Some Sort of Epic Grandeur: The Life of F. Scott Fitzgerald.* New York: Harcourt Brace Jovanovich, Inc., 1980.

[21] Bufithis, Philip H. *Norman Mailer.* New York: Frederick Ungar, 1978

[22] Bunge, Nancy. *Nathaniel Hawthorne: A Study of the Short Fiction.* New York: Twayne, 1993.

[23] Burt,Daniel S., The Chronology of American Literature,Boston:Houghton Mifflin Company,2004

[24]Buxbaum, Melvin H., ed. *Critical essays on Benjamin Franklin.* Boston: G.K. Hall, 1987.

[25] Callow, Philip. *From Noon to Starry Night: A Life of Walt Whitman.* Chicago: I.R. Dee, 1992.

[26] Cargill, Oscar. *Intellectual America: Ideas on the March.* New York: Cooper Square Publishers, 1968

[27] Cargill, Oscar. *The Novels of Henry James.* New York: Hafner Pub. Co., 1971

[28] Chin, BeverlyAnn. et al., eds. American Literature. New York: McGraw-Hill,2002

[29] Cowley, Malcolm. *Fitzgerald and The Jazz Age.* New York: Charles Scribner's Sons, 1951.

[30] Cunliffe, Marcus. *The Literature of the United State*s. Baltimore: Penguin Books, 1967

[31] Darnel, Donald. *James Fenimore Cooper: Novelist of Manners.* Newark: University of Delaware Press, 1993.

[32] Davis, David B. *The Problem of Slavery in the Age of Revolution, 1770-1823.* Ithaca: Cornell University Press, 1975.

[33] Donaldson, Scott., ed. *The Cambridge Companion to Ernest Hemingway.*

Shanghai: Shanghai Foreign Language Education Press, 2000.

[34] Douglas, Emily Taft. *Remember the Ladies: The Story of Great Women Who Helped Shape America.* New York: Putnam, 1966.

[35] Dunham, Montrew. *Anne Bradstreet: Young Puritan Poet.* Indianapolis: Bobbs-Merrill, 1969.

[36] Dutton, Robert R. *Saul Bellow.* New York: Twayne, 1971

[37] Edel, Leon. *The Modern Psychological Novel.* New York: Grosset and Dunlap, 1964.

[38] Elkins, Stanley M. Slavery; *A Problem in American Institutional and Intellectual Life.* Chicago: Chicago University Press, 1968.

[39] Elliott, Emory. et al., eds.American Literature:A Prentice Hall Anthology. Englewood Cliffs: Prentice Hall,1991

[40] Elliott, Emory., ed, *Columbia Literary History of the United States.* New York: Columbia University Press, 1988.

[41] Emerson, Everett H. *Captain John Smith.* New York: Twayne Publishers, Inc., 1971.

[42] Field, Leslie A.,*Bernard Malamud:A Collection of Critical Essays.* Prentice-Hall, 1975.

[43] French, Warren. *John Steinbeck.* Boston: Twayne Publishers, 1975.

[44] Gerteis, Louis S. *Morality and Utility in American Antislavery Reform.* Chapel Hill: U of North Carolina Press, 1987.

[45] Guerin, Wilfred L., *A Handbook of Critical Approaches to Literature.* Beijing: Foreign Language Teaching and Research Press, 2004.

[46] Hart, James D. *The Oxford Companion to American Literature.* 5th edition. Oxford: Oxford University Press, 1983.

[47] Hedrick, Joan D. *Harriet Beecher Stowe: A Life.* New York: Oxford University Press, 1994.

[48] Herbert, T. Walter. *Dearest Beloved: The Hawthornes and the Making of the Middle-Class Family.* Berkeley: U of California P, 1993.

[49] Hoffman Andrew. *Inventing Mark Twain: The Lives of Samuel Langhorne Clemens.* New York: William Morrow and Company, 1997.

[50] Hollis, C. Carroll. *Language and Style in Leaves of Grass.* Baton Rouge: Louisiana State University Press, 1983.

［51］ Horton, Rod W and Edwards, Herbert W., *Backgrounds of American literary Thought.* 2nd edition. New York: Appleton Century Crofts, 1967.

［52］ Huddleston, Eugene L. *Thomas Jefferson: A Reference Guide.* Boston: Hall, 1982.

［53］ Kaplan, Justin. *Walt Whitman, A Life.* New York: Simon and Schuster, 1980.

［54］ Kennedy, J. Gerald. *Poe, Death, and the Life of Writing.* New Haven: Yale UP, 1987.

［55］ King, Bruce., et al. eds. *New National and Post-colonial Literatures: An Introduction.* Oxford: Clarendon Press, 1998.

［56］ Kim, Elaine H. *Asian American Literature: An Introduction to the Writings and Their Social Context.* Beijing: Foreign Language Teaching and Research Press, 2004.

［57］ Kimball, Gayle. *The religious ideas of Harriet Beecher Stowe: her gospel of womanhood.* NY: Mellen P, 1982.

［58］ Kirby, David. *Herman Melville.* New York: Continuum, 1993.

［59］ Lauter, Paul., ed. *The Heath Anthology of American Literature.* 3rd edition. New York: Houghton Mifflin, 1998.

［60］Lawrence, D. H. *Studies in Classic American Literature.* New York: Penguin USA, 1991.

［61］ Lemay, J.A. Leo. *Did Pocahontas Save Captain John Smith?* Georgia: The University of Georgia Press, 1992.

［62］ Lemay, Ja. A. Leo. *The American Dream of Captain John Smith.* Charlottesville: University Press of Virginia, 1991.

［63］ Long, Robert Emmet. *James Fenimore Cooper.* New York: Continuum Publishing Company, 1990.

［64］ Lyons,Greg. Literature of the American West. New York:Longman.2003

［65］ Malamud, Bernard. *Magic Barrel.* New York:Farrar, Straus and Giroux, 2003

［66］Manheim, Michael., ed. *The Cambridge Companion to Eugene O'Neill.* Shanghai: Shanghai Foreign Language Education Press, 2000.

［67］ Martin, Terence. *Nathaniel Hawthorne.* Boston: Twayne Publishers, 1983.

［68］ Matthiessen, F.O. *American Renaissance: Art and Expression in the Age of Emerson and Whitman.* London: Oxford University Press, 1968.

［69］ May, Charles E. *Edgar A. Poe: A Study of the Short Fiction.* Boston: Twayne, 1991.

〔70〕 Michaels, W.B. and Pease, Donald E. *The American Renaissance Reconsidered.* Baltimore: Johns Hopkins University Press, 1985.

〔71〕 Miller, John C. *Origins of the American Revolution.* Stanford: Stanford University Press, 1979.

〔72〕Mossiker, Frances. *Pocahontas: The Life and Legend.* New York: Alfred A. Knopf, 1976.

〔73〕 Piercy, Josephine K. *Anne Bradstreet..* New York: Twayne Publishers, Inc., 1965.

〔74〕Rakove, Jack N. *The Beginnings of National Politics.* New York: Alfred A. Knopf, Inc., 1979.

〔75〕 Ringe, Donald A. *James Fenimore Cooper.* Boston: Twayne, 1988.

〔76〕 Robertson-Lorant, Laurie. *Melville: a biography.* New York: Clarkson Potter Publishers, 1996.

〔77〕 Rubin-Dorsky, Jeffrey. *Adrift in the Old World: The Psychological Pilgrimage of Washington Irving.* Univ. of Chicago Press, 1988.

〔78〕 Schneider, Herbert W. *The Puritan Mind.* Ann Arbor: University of Michigan Press, 1958.

〔79〕 Smith, Bradford. *Captain John Smith: His Life and Legend.* Philadelphia: J. B. Lippincott Company, 1953.

〔80〕 Smith, Page. *Jefferson: A Revealing Biography.* New York: American Heritage Publishing Co., 1976.

〔81〕 Spiller, Robert E., et al. eds. *Literary History of the United States: History.* 4th edition. New York: Macmillan, 1974.

〔82〕 Stanford, Ann. *Anne Bradstreet, The Worldly Puritan: An Introduction to Her Poetry.* New York: B. Franklin, 1975.

〔83〕 Toming. *A History of American Literature.* Nanjing: Yilin Press, 2002.

〔84〕 Trilling, Lionel. *The Experience of Literature.* New York: Doubleday & Company, Inc. 1967.

〔85〕 Vaughan, Alden T. *American Genesis: Captain John Smith and the Founding of Virginia.* Boston: Little, Brown & Co., 1975.

〔86〕 Velie,Alan R.,American Indian Literature:An Anthology. Norman:University of Oklahoma Press,1991

〔87〕Wagenknecht, Edward. *The Novels of Henry James.* New York: F. Ungar Pub. Co., 1983.

[88] Wagenknecht, Edward. *Henry Wadsworth Longfellow, His Poetry and Prose.* New York: F. Ungar Pub. Co., 1986.

[89] Walker, I. M., ed. *Edgar A. Poe: The Critical Heritage.* New York: Routledge & K. Paul, 1986.

[90] Weinstein, P. M., ed. *The Cambridge Companion to William Faulkner.* Shanghai: Shanghai Foreign Language Education Press, 2000.

[91] Wills, Gary. *Inventing America: Jefferson's Declaration of Independence.* New York: Doubleday & Company, Inc., 1978.

[92] Zall, Paul M. *Franklin's Autobiography: A Model Life.* Boston: Twayne, 1989.

[93] 鲍秀文，王卫新主编.美国文学名著故事梗概及作品导读.天津：天津人民出版社, 2008.

[94] 曹曼主编.美国文学教程.武汉：武汉大学出版社，2007.

[95] 常耀信.美国文学简史.天津：南开大学出版社，1990.

[96] 常耀信.美国文学批评.天津：南开大学出版社,2007.

[97] 程爱民主编.美国文学阅读教程.南京：南京师范大学出版社，1998.

[98] 查尔斯·米尔斯·盖雷著.英美文学和艺术中的古典神话.上海：上海人民出版社, 2005.

[99] 陈晓辉.当代美国华人文学中的"她"写作.北京：中国华侨出版社，2007.

[100] 董衡巽等编著.美国文学简史.北京：人民文学出版社,1978.

[101] 郭继德主编.美国文学研究(第二辑).济南：山东大学出版社,2004.

[102] 亨利　詹姆斯.小说的艺术.朱雯、朱乃长等译,上海：上海译出版社,2001.

[103] 胡艳主编,美国文学精要,北京：冶金工业出版社,2008.

[104] 胡全生等.20 世纪英美文学选读——后现代主义卷.上海：上海交通大学出版社，2003.

[105] 胡全生.20 世纪英美文学选读 现代主义卷.上海：上海交通大学出版社,2003.

[106] 黄家修主编.美国文学阅读与欣赏.武汉：武汉大学出版社，2007.

[107] 蹇昌槐.西方小说与文化帝国.武汉：武汉大学出版社，2004.

[108] 李公昭主编.新编美国文学选读.西安：西安交通大学出版社,2000.

[109] 李维屏.英美现代主义文学概观.上海：上海外语教育出版社,1998.

［110］刘海平,王守仁主编.新编美国文学史.1--4 卷.上海：上海外语教育出版社,2001.

［111］刘世沐等.英美文学欣赏.北京：北京出版社,1982.

［112］刘守兰.英美名诗解读.上海：上海外语教育出版社，2003.

［113］刘晓鹏,田野,廖国强,孟宏党主编.应用英语教程.汕头:汕头大学出版社,2002.

［114］楼光庆,屠蓓编.美国文学名著简介.北京：外语教学与研究出版社,1986.

［115］毛信德.美国小说发展史.杭州：浙江大学出版社，2004.

［116］钱青主编.美国文学名著精选.北京：商务印书馆,1994.

［117］宋元康编著.美国文学导读.昆明：云南大学出版社,2007.

［118］陶洁.灯下西窗：美国文学和美国文化.北京–北京大学出版社,2004.

［119］陶洁.美国文学选读.北京：高等教育出版社,2000.

［120］田野,蒋璐,高传香,邓云华.新编英美概况.汕头：汕头大学出版社，2002.

［121］王蕾，刘著妍主编.美国文学选读.天津：天津大学出版社,2007.

［122］王逢振.美国文学大花园.武汉：湖北教育出版社, 2007.

［123］汪义群.奥尼尔研究.上海：上海外语教育出版社,2006.

［124］吴建国.菲茨杰拉德研究.上海：上海外语教育出版社,2002.

［125］吴伟仁.美国文学史及选读.北京：外语教学与研究出版社,1990.

［126］杨任敬.20 世纪美国文学史.青岛：青岛出版社,2000.

［127］杨仁敬,杨凌雁著.美国文学简史.上海：上海外语教育出版社,2008.

［128］虞建华主编.美国文学辞典.上海：复旦大学出版社,2005.

［129］张冲，张琼，王爱萍编.美国文学选读.上海：复旦大学出版社,2008.

［130］张强.美国文学选读.重庆：重庆大学出版社,2008.

［131］张颖主编.美国文学.长春：北师范大学出版社,2007.

［132］张耘.现代西方戏剧名家名著选评.北京：外语教学与研究出版社,1999.

［133］郑克鲁.外国文学史.北京：高等教育出版社,2006.

［134］http://andromeda.rutgers.edu/

［135］http://www.bartleby.com/198/

［136］http://www.bibliomania.com/

［137］http://www.biography.com/

［138］http://www.bookrags.com/

［139］http://www.britannia.com/

［140］http://www.classicreader.com/author/

［141］http://www.cliffsnotes.com/

［142］http://www.csustan.edu/english/

［143］http://dictionary.reference.com/

［144］http://en.allexperts.com/

［145］http://encarta.msn.com/

［146］http://www.encyclopedia.com/

［147］http://en.wikipedia.org/

［148］http://www.gradesaver.com/

［149］http://www.historylearningsite.co.uk/

［150］http://www.iep.utm.edu/

［151］http://www.infoplease.com/

［152］http://itech.fgcu.edu/&/issues/

［153］http://library.thinkquest.org/

［154］http://www.literatureclassics.com/

［155］http://www.mapability.com/travel/p2i/book.html

［156］http://www.novelguide.com/

［157］http://www.online-literature.com/

［158］http://www.poets.org/

［159］http://www.poetseers.org/

［160］http://www.sparknotes.com/

［161］http://www.spartacus.schoolnet.co.uk/

［162］http://www.thefreedictionary.com/

［163］http://www.victorianweb.org/authors/index.html/

后 记

　　教材是教学之本，它规范着某一门课程的基本内容，保证教学内容的规范化和科学化，以实现教学目的。因此，教材建设是实现教学计划和达到教学目的的基本建设工程。根据杭州电子科技大学和浙江省教育厅有关"精品课程"立项建设的要求，我们组织编写了《精编美国文学教程》，作为校级与省级"精品课程"《英美文学导论》建设的重要组成部分。具体分工如下：

陈许，陈庆生（主编）： Historical Background and Literary Review of Part One, Part
　　　　　Two, Part Three, Part Four and Part Five

陈许：Bret Harte, Henry James, Hamlin Garland, Leslie Marmon Silko, Louise Erdrich

王祖友（副主编）：Philip Roth, John Barth

周小娉（副主编）：Robert Frost, Eugene O'Neill, Ernest Hemingway, William Faulkner

陈怡：Mark Twain, Joseph Heller

许焕荣：F.Scott Fitzgerald, Maxine Hong Kingston

敬南菲：Nathaniel Hawthorne, Emily Dickinson, Walt Whitman, Toni Morrison

钟京霞：John Smith, Anne Bradstreet, Benjamin Franklin, Thomas Jefferson

陈圣：William Bryant, Edgar Allen Poe, Ralph Waldo Emerson

张婷婷：Washington Irving, James Fenimore Cooper

田智文：Bernard Malamud, Saul Bellow, N. Scott Momaday

　　在本书的编写过程中，我们吸收了许多专家学者的研究成果，参阅了大量的书籍和资料，在此，我们谨向有关著作者和出版单位表示衷心的感谢！

陈庆生　陈　许

2009 年 9 月于杭州电子科技大学

图书在版编目 (CIP) 数据

精编美国文学教程 / 陈许,陈庆生主编. —杭州:浙江
大学出版社,2009.11(2018.1 重印)

ISBN 978-7-308-07144-4

Ⅰ.精… Ⅱ.①陈…②陈… Ⅲ.文学史－美国－高等学
校－教材 Ⅳ.I712.09

中国版本图书馆 CIP 数据核字 (2009) 第 190566 号

精编美国文学教程

陈　许　陈庆生　主编

责任编辑	葛　娟	
封面设计	刘依群	
出版发行	浙江大学出版社	
	（杭州天目山路 148 号　邮政编码 310028）	
	（网址：http://www.zjupress.com）	
排　版	杭州中大图文设计有限公司	
印　刷	虎彩印艺股份有限公司	
开　本	710mm×1000mm　1/16	
印　张	33.25	
字　数	685 千	
版 印 次	2009 年 11 月第 1 版　2018 年 1 月第 2 次印刷	
书　号	ISBN 978-7-308-07144-4	
定　价	50.00 元	